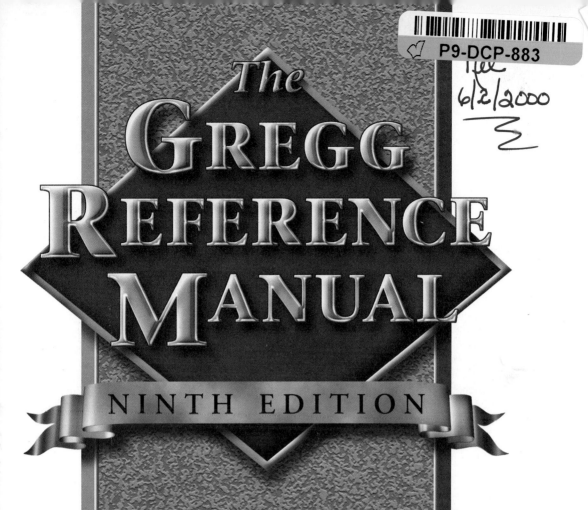

The GREGG REFERENCE MANUAL

NINTH EDITION

William A. Sabin

Glencoe McGraw-Hill

New York, New York   Columbus, Ohio   Woodland Hills, California   Peoria, Illinois

DEDICATION

The ninth edition of The Gregg Reference Manual is dedicated to my dear friend, Helen Green, a teacher and an
author who has touched the lives of many people.

Library of Congress Cataloging-in-Publication Data

Sabin, William A.
    The Gregg reference manual / William A. Sabin.—9th ed.
        p.   cm.
    Includes index.
    ISBN 0-02-804046-5. -- ISBN 0-02-804048-1
    1. English language--Business English Handbooks, manuals, etc.
2. English language--Grammar Handbooks, manuals, etc.   3. English
language--Transcription Handbooks, manuals, etc.   4. Business
writing Handbooks, manuals, etc.   I. Title.
PE1479.B87S23   1999
808' .042--dc21   99-23789
                                                                CIP

Glencoe/McGraw-Hill

A Division of The McGraw·Hill Companies

Send all inquiries to:
Glencoe/McGraw-Hill
936 Eastwind Drive
Westerville, Ohio 43081

ISBN 0-02-804047-3 (spiral-with-flap edition)
ISBN 0-02-804046-5 (spiral-bound text edition)
ISBN 0-02-804048-1 (hardcover text edition)
ISBN 0-02-804049-X (basic worksheets)
ISBN 0-02-804050-3 (comprehensive worksheets)
ISBN 0-02-804052-X (instructor's resource manual)

1 2 3 4 5 6 7 8 9 0   003   04 03 02 01 00 99

CONTENTS

PART 1
Grammar, Usage, and Style

PART 2
Techniques and Formats

PART 3
References

The Gregg Reference Manual is intended for anyone who writes, edits, or prepares material for distribution or publication. It addresses the concerns of experienced professionals, especially those who no longer enjoy the help of trained assistants to ensure the quality of the documents that these professionals must produce. Moreover, the manual serves the needs of students who are preparing to become experienced professionals in their chosen field of work.

To accommodate this wide range of readers, *The Gregg Reference Manual* presents the *basic rules* that apply in virtually every piece of writing, as well as the *fine points* that occur less often but cause no less trouble when they do. This manual offers an abundance of examples and computer-generated illustrations so that you can quickly find models on which to pattern a solution to the various problems you encounter in your communications—from e-mail messages to formal reports. It also provides the rationale underlying specific rules so that you can manipulate the principles of style with intelligence and taste.

Features of the New Edition. The ninth edition of *The Gregg Reference Manual* has been revised and enhanced in many ways to span the stylistic demands of business and academic writing.

1. The most significant changes in the ninth edition reflect the enormous impact that *computer technology* has had on the way written communications are created and produced.

   - The easy access to *word processing templates* has greatly simplified the way in which letters, memos, reports, and other documents can be prepared. Yet the formats provided by these templates may, for a variety of reasons, not be suitable for your purposes. To help you cope with this situation, Section 13 (dealing with letters and memos) and Section 14 (dealing with reports) illustrate sample templates provided by Microsoft Word for Windows and then provide guidelines showing you how to modify these templates or create your own for more effective results.
   - The ninth edition discusses the *special features of word processing software* that make it easier for you to create and format various elements in business documents—for example, footnotes, endnotes, and tables (including a table of contents for a formal report). The manual also discusses the problems that may be created by these time-saving features. Thus Section 16 (on tables) provides an all-new 8-page sequence of illustrations that shows how a table created with the table feature of Microsoft Word for Windows can be progressively modified to achieve more readable and more attractive results. Similarly, Section 15 (on notes) shows how you can enhance the formats created by the footnote and endnote features of Microsoft Word for Windows.
   - Paragraphs ¶¶1532–1546 provide completely new coverage on dealing with *online source material.* These paragraphs will not only show you how to construct footnotes, endnotes, and bibliographic entries based on online sources; they will suggest sensible precautions to observe when you are citing electronic material, which—as we all know—can rapidly change, move to a new location, or completely disappear.
   - For those new to the Internet, ¶¶1532–1533 will show how to decode *Web site addresses* (URLs) and *e-mail addresses.* Moreover, ¶¶1538–1539 will show how to divide these addresses (if necessary) at the end of a line.
   - Anyone looking for a job these days needs to be aware of the impact of computer technology on the way job applicants are now being screened. Paragraphs ¶¶1714–1717 provide all-new format guidelines for preparing a *scannable résumé* (scannable by an optical character reader) that will help you survive the initial winnowing process.

Preface

- The *glossary of computer terms* in Appendix B has been expanded to 20 pages to accommodate the rapidly evolving vocabulary of this new technology. If you are puzzled by terms like *bandwidth, cybrarian, dot, firewall, intranet, mouse potato, spider,* and *userid,* turn to pages 562–581.
- Is it *e-mail, E-mail,* or *email?* Is it *Web site, Website,* or *website?* Consult ¶847 for help in resolving the confusion caused by the various ways in which computer terms are being spelled and styled.
- As the *standards of desktop publishing* increasingly supplant the older standards reflected in typewritten documents, new stylistic issues have to be addressed. Thus ¶102 confronts the surprisingly vigorous debate over 1 versus 2 spaces following punctuation at the end of a sentence. Section 2 deals with different styles of dashes (¶¶216–217), different styles of quotation marks (page 59), and different guidelines for the use of italics and underlining (¶290).

2. Questions and suggestions from readers of the previous edition have also had a major impact on what has been added to the ninth edition.[*] For example:

   - How do you pronounce words like *affluent, chaise longue,* and *forte?* And how about place names like *Cairo* (in Illinois), *Mackinac* (in Michigan), and *Natchitoches* (in Louisiana)? See pages 582–591 for an all-new, 10-page appendix that will offer some reassuring guidance on pronunciation problems like these.
   - How do you refer to a resident of Arkansas? For that matter, what do you call the residents of the other 49 states? See ¶336.
   - What is the proper way to refer to the class of 2000 and the first decade of the twenty-first century? See ¶¶412c, 439b.
   - What does a plus sign mean when it precedes a phone number? See ¶454f.
   - Why do dictionaries treat similar compound words differently (for example, *payoff/play-off, skydiving/skin diving*)? Is there some sensible way to resolve these inconsistencies in style? See ¶801b-c.
   - Do you use *a* or *an* before a phrase like *NBC poll? NATO strategy?* See pages 281–282.
   - How do you format a news release? See ¶1707 and page 512.
   - How do you format a one-page résumé if you're just out of school and don't have much work experience to cite? See ¶1713 and pages 526–527.
   - For once and for all, is it okay to end a sentence with a preposition? See ¶1080.

3. The text and illustrations have been changed throughout the ninth edition to reflect the new words, phrases, acronyms, and initialisms that are continually entering the language. If you don't know the meaning of *PONA, WOMBAT,* or *PEBCAK,* turn at once to ¶522a. If you are unfamiliar with *Parkinson's Law of Data* or a proverb called *Hanlon's Razor,* consult ¶346c.

4. The use of a larger page size and a new design gives the ninth edition a more open look and makes the text and the illustrations easier to read. Also note that certain rule numbers in Sections 1–11 appear in white within a blue panel. This graphic device serves to call attention to the *basic rules* of grammar, usage, and style—those dealing with problems

---

[*]Because of the immense value that readers' comments have in ensuring that each new edition is truly responsive to users' needs, I invite you to submit your questions and suggestions to me through the publisher's office in Westerville, Ohio. Please see the copyright page for the address.

Preface

that will frequently arise in your work. If you want to reduce the number of things you need to look up, these highlighted rules are the ones you need to master.

An Overview of the Organization of the Ninth Edition. This edition of *The Gregg Reference Manual* consists of 18 sections and 3 appendixes, organized in three parts:

Part 1 (Sections 1–11) deals with grammar, usage, and the chief aspects of style—punctuation, capitalization, numbers, abbreviations, plurals and possessives, spelling, compound words, and word division.

Part 2 (Sections 12–18) deals with the techniques and procedures for creating and formatting all kinds of written communications—letters, memos, reports, manuscripts, tables, agendas, minutes, itineraries, fax cover sheets, news releases, e-mail, outlines, and résumés and other employment communications. It also provides detailed guidelines on forms of address.

Part 3 (Appendixes A, B, and C) provides a glossary of grammatical terms, a glossary of computer terms, and a new appendix dealing with troublesome pronunciation problems.

Other Components of the Ninth Edition. Accompanying the ninth edition of *The Gregg Reference Manual* are the following components:

Basic Worksheets on Grammar, Usage, and Style. This set of worksheets focuses on the basic rules presented in Sections 1–11. These worksheets have been designed to build three critical skills. First, they will familiarize you with the potential problems that frequently occur in any material that you create or produce. Second, these worksheets will direct you to the appropriate rules in Sections 1–11 so that later on, when you encounter similar problems in your own work, you will know where to look. Third, they will sharpen your ability to apply the rules correctly under many different circumstances.

This set of worksheets begins with a diagnostic survey of your editing skills at the outset. Then, after you complete a series of 21 worksheets, you will encounter a parallel survey at the end that will show you how much your editing skills have improved. In most of the intervening worksheets, rule numbers are provided alongside the answer blanks so that you can quickly locate the answer you need to solve the problem at hand. At the end of each of these worksheets is an editing exercise that requires you to identify and correct the implanted errors on your own, without the help of rule numbers alongside. Interspersed within this sequence of worksheets are three editing surveys that will help you integrate all the things you have been learning in the preceding worksheets.

Comprehensive Worksheets. This set of worksheets has been designed to build the same three skills as the worksheets described above. However, this comprehensive set draws on material from the entire manual and not simply from Sections 1–11. Moreover, these worksheets deal with problems of formatting letters, memos, and other business documents. This program begins with a diagnostic survey and then, after a series of 31 worksheets, concludes with a parallel survey that allows you to demonstrate how much your editing skills have increased. Interspersed within this sequence of worksheets are four editing surveys that will help you integrate all the things you have been learning up to that point.

Instructor's Resource Manual. The *Instructor's Resource Manual* provides strategies showing how to make the best use of the two sets of worksheets. This guide also provides full-size

Preface

keys to the *Basic Worksheets* and the *Comprehensive Worksheets*. Packaged with the *Instructor's Resource Manual* is a CD-ROM containing a comprehensive set of the grammar, usage, and style rules found in Sections 1–11 of *The Gregg Reference Manual*. The rules are formatted as PowerPoint slides for instructors to use during classroom presentations and discussions. This CD-ROM replaces the print version of the transparency masters, which was available in previous editions.

As you make your own survey of the ninth edition of *The Gregg Reference Manual*, you will want to give special attention to the basic rules that deserve further study; these are the rules that you will encounter in everyday situations, the rules you need to have at your command. You will also want to develop a passing acquaintance with the fine points of style. It is sufficient simply to know that such rules exist. Then, when you need them, you will know where to find them. Finally, you will want to take note of special word lists, sentence patterns, and illustrations that could be useful to you later on. If you find out now what the manual provides, you will know what kind of help you can count on in the future. And what is more important, you will be able to find what you are looking for faster.

Acknowledgments

A book of this type cannot be put together without the help and support of many people. To my colleagues in Glencoe/McGraw-Hill, to my many good friends in business and office education, and to the teachers and professional business training consultants who allowed me to observe their classes and their training programs, I want to express a deep feeling of gratitude. I also need to thank the countless teachers, administrators, students, and professionals who all helped me—by their questions and suggestions—to see how things could be made better in this new edition.

There is not enough space to acknowledge all of these people individually. However, I must single out a few people by name in order to offer special thanks:

To Olive Collen, my gifted editor, for her masterful work on the manuscript and for her constant commitment to the highest standards of publishing.

To Barbara Oakley, my close friend and colleague for many years, for her indispensable help in revising Sections 12–17.

To Price Voiles, another dear friend and colleague, for his close reading of the ninth edition and his invaluable comments and suggestions.

To Eva and Russell Lewis, my sharp-eyed readers and long-time friends, who have helped to make this manual as free of errors and inconsistencies as is humanly possible.

To those instructors and professional consultants who provided many helpful suggestions:

Murlene Asadi, Scott Community College, Davenport, Iowa

Lenette Baker, Bessemer State Technical College, Bessemer, Alabama

Belinda K. Belisle, Belisle & Associates, West Garden Grove, California

Melanie Booth, Heald Colleges, San Francisco, California

Janet I. Boring Seggern, Lehigh Carbon Community College, Schnecksville, Pennsylvania

Patricia Boyle-Steed, Boyle-Steed Writing Services, Salem, New Hampshire

Shirley Breeze, Meramec Community College, St. Louis, Missouri

Wendy Brog, Bridgerland Applied Technology Center, Logan, Utah

Connie Jo Clark, Lane Community College, Eugene, Oregon

Martha J. Coleman, El Paso Community College, El Paso, Texas

Linda Comerford, Comerford Consulting, Indianapolis, Indiana

Dr. Judy H. Diffley, Washburn University, Topeka, Kansas

Dr. Allan Doerr, Montgomery County Community College, Blue Bell, Pennsylvania

Barbara B. Foti, Washington Business School, Vienna, Virginia

Louis Fucilo, Chase Education, a division of The Chase Manhattan Bank, New York, New York

Cynthia L. Govreau, Kentucky College of Business, Florence, Kentucky

Raenelle Hanes, Pikes Peak Community College, Colorado Springs, Colorado

Cynthia Hanna, Empire College, Santa Rosa, California

Carole Inglish, Salt Lake Community College, Salt Lake City, Utah

Lee Clark Johns, Professional Writing Consultants, Tulsa, Oklahoma

Ron Kapper, College of DuPage, Glen Ellyn, Illinois

Dr. Rebecca Limback, Central Missouri State University, Warrensburg, Missouri

Patricia L. Malone, Chemeketa Community College, Salem, Oregon

Barbara McGovern, WD Communications, Red Bank, New Jersey

Carolyn Mehl, State Farm Insurance, Bloomington, Illinois

Virginia Melvin, CPS, State Tech at Memphis, Memphis, Tennessee

Carol Y. Mull, Asheville-Buncombe Technical Community College, Asheville, North Carolina

Carol O'Grady, Tampa Technical Institute, Tampa, Florida

Glenna Oakley, Francis Tuttle Tech, Oklahoma City, Oklahoma

Wilma J. Payne, Education America–Fort Worth, Fort Worth, Texas

Ronald C. Pellerin, Stone Academy, Hamden, Connecticut

Mark Rau, Lincoln Training Center, Sacramento, California

Ann Rosenblatt, Metro Community College, Omaha, Nebraska

Barbara Wascher, Elgin Community College, Elgin, Illinois

To those professional colleagues who have been especially generous with their help and support on the ninth edition—and in many cases on earlier editions as well.

Kathleen Abromeit, editorial consultant, Oberlin, Ohio

Anne Block, senior editor, Tivoli Systems, Indianapolis, Indiana

Marie Longyear Dunphy, McGraw-Hill author and former director of communications, McGraw-Hill, Woodstock, New York

Geraldine Fahey, editorial consultant, New York, New York

Preface

Don K. Ferguson, editorial consultant, Knoxville, Tennessee

Beverley Funk, Glencoe author and former instructor, Everett Community College, Everett, Washington

Dr. Helen Green, Glencoe author and emerita professor of business education, Michigan State University, East Lansing, Michigan

Dr. Karen Larsen, editorial consultant, Portland, Oregon

Mary Madden, former supervisor of business and distributive education, New Orleans Public Schools, New Orleans, Louisiana

Dr. Gloria Vacca Mahoney, business training consultant, GLOEDCO, Inc., Hollywood, Florida

Ann Miller, business training consultant, WD Communications, Newark, Delaware

Gail Modlin, former editorial director, Glencoe/McGraw-Hill, Tampa, Florida

Sibyl Parker, former publisher, technical, reference, and new media, McGraw-Hill, New York, New York

Dr. Robert Poland, emeritus professor of business and marketing education, Michigan State University, East Lansing, Michigan

Barry Richman, executive vice president for business development, DATAFUSION, Inc., San Francisco, California

Margaret Sabin, editorial consultant, Montclair, New Jersey

Barbara Sacker, business training consultant, Pro-Action, Inc., Brooklyn, New York

Dr. Jeffrey Stewart, Glencoe author and emeritus professor of education, Virginia Polytechnic Institute and State University, Blacksburg, Virginia

Cherie Tucker, GrammarWorks, Seattle, Washington

Nina Watson Wells, editorial director, FSCreations, Inc., Cincinnati, Ohio

Carol Ann Wilson, vice president for information, National Law Library, Inc., Houston, Texas

Merle Wood, Glencoe author and former supervisor of business education, Oakland Unified School District, Lafayette, California

Mark Yannone, CEO, Perfect Data, Peoria, Arizona

And to my family—to my mother, who gave me my first sense of what language could accomplish (and a good deal more); to Margaret, John, Kate, Chris, and Jim, from whom I have gained much wisdom; and ultimately to my wife Marie, who has made the journey worth the struggle—my thanks and my love.

William A. Sabin

Suppose you were writing to someone in another department:

> I understand you are doing a confidential study of the Bronson matter. May I please get an advance copy of your report [At this point you hesitate. Should this sentence end with a period or a question mark?]

This is the kind of problem that continually comes up in any type of written communication. How do you find a fast answer to such questions? In this manual there are several ways to proceed.

Use the Index. The surest approach, perhaps, is to check the detailed index at the back of the manual (19 pages, with over 2500 entries). For example, any of the following entries will lead you to the right punctuation for the problem sentence above:

Periods, **101–109**	Question marks, **110–118**	Request, punctuation
. . .	. . .	of, **103**
at end of requests, **103**	at end of requests, **103, 113**	

In each entry a **boldface number** refers to the proper rule, **¶103.** (If you look up ¶103, you will find that a question mark is the right punctuation for the sentence in question.)

In almost all the index entries, references are made to specific rule numbers so that you can find what you are looking for fast. In a few cases, where a page reference will provide a more precise location (for example, when a rule runs on for several pages), a page number is given in lightface type. Suppose you were confronted with this problem:

> If you compare the performance records of Catano, Harris, and Williams, you won't find much difference *(between/among)* them.

The index will show the following entries:

> *among* (see *between,* 287)   **OR**   *between–among,* 287

The entry on page 287 indicates that *between* is correct in this situation.

Use a Fast-Skim Approach. Many users of reference manuals have little patience with detailed indexes. They would rather open the book and skim through the pages until they find what they are looking for. If you prefer this approach, you will find several features of this manual especially helpful.

- The brief topical index on the inside front cover indicates the key paragraphs for each major topic.
- At the start of each section except the appendixes, you will find a detailed list of all the topics covered in that section. This list will help you quickly focus on the rule or rules that pertain to your problem. Suppose the following problem came up:

> The only point still at issue is whether or not new *Federal* [or is it *federal*?] legislation is required.

The index on the inside front cover indicates that ¶¶301–366 deal with the topic of capitalization. A fast skim of the outline preceding ¶301 (on page 86) will turn up the entry *Names of Government Bodies (¶¶325–330).* If you turn to that set of rules, you will find in ¶328 that *federal* is the proper form.

- Extensive cross-references have also been provided throughout the manual so that you can quickly locate related rules that could prove helpful. Some cross-references take this form: *See ¶324;* others may read *See also ¶324.* The form *See ¶324* indicates that ¶324 contains significant information that adds to or qualifies the rule you are currently reading; the word *See* suggests that you really ought to pursue the cross-reference before making a decision. The form *See also* *¶324* carries a good deal less urgency. It indicates that you will find some additional examples in ¶324 and perhaps a restatement of the rule you are currently reading but nothing altogether new. In effect, *See also* suggests that you don't have to pursue the cross-reference if you don't want to— but it couldn't hurt.

Play the Numbers. There is still a third way to find the answer to a specific problem— and this is an approach that will grow in appeal as you become familiar with the organization and the content of the manual. From a fast inspection of the rule numbers, you will observe that they all carry a section number as a prefix. Thus Section 3 (on capitalization) has a "300" series of rules—from 301 to 366; Section 4 (on number style) has a "400" series—from 401 to 470; and so on. Once you become familiar with the section numbers and the section titles, you can find your way around fairly quickly, without reference to either index, by using the section number tabs. For example, you are about to write the following sentence:

> 43 percent of the questionnaires have now been returned. [Or should it be "*Forty-three* percent of the questionnaires . . . "?]

If you know that matters of number style are treated in Section 4, you can quickly turn to the pages tabbed for Section 4, where a fast skim of the outline of topics at the start of the section will lead you to the answer in ¶421. (*Forty-three percent* is the right answer in this instance.)

A familiarity with the section numbers and section titles can also save you time when you are using the index. If your index entry lists several different paragraph numbers, you can often anticipate what the paragraphs will deal with. For example, if you want to know whether to write *5 lb* or *5 lbs* on a purchase order, you might encounter the following entry in the index:

> Weights, **429–431, 535–538, 620**

If you know that Section 6 deals with plurals, you will try ¶620 first.

Look Up Specific Words. Many of the problems that arise deal with specific words. For this reason the index provides as many entries for such words as space will permit. For example, in the following sentence, should *therefore* be set off by commas or not?

> It is(,) *therefore*(,) essential that operations be curtailed.

A check of the index will show the following entry:

> *therefore,* **122, 138–142, 178**

A reading of the rules in ¶141 will indicate that no commas should be used in this sentence. If you ask the same question about another specific word and do not find it listed as a separate entry in the index, your best approach will be to check the index under "Comma" and investigate the most promising references or make a direct scan of the comma rules in Section 1 until you find the answer you are looking for.

If you are having difficulty with words that look alike and sound alike—*gibe* and *jibe* or *affect* and *effect*—turn directly to ¶719. For other troublesome words, consult Section 11.

The six brief essays which follow deal with a number of points of style that cause great difficulty for those who work with words. Out of this consideration of specific problems, these essays attempt to draw broader conclusions about the nature of style and the art of tailoring one's use of language to fit the needs of each situation.

Mastering Number Style: One (or 1?) Approach

A number of years ago, while making a presentation on the subject of style, I asked the audience to select the preferable form in each of the following pairs of examples:

$87,525	**OR**	eighty-seven thousand five hundred and twenty-five dollars
$5.6 trillion	**OR**	$5,600,000,000,000
4:30 p.m., January 19	**OR**	half after four o'clock, on the nineteenth of January

No one could see any use for the forms in the second column. Those in the first column were far easier to read and simpler to write and were clearly to be preferred in business writing. However, after some discussion, we tended to agree that Tiffany's had had the right idea in a recent ad, where beneath a picture of an elegant diamond necklace was the legend "Eighty-seven thousand five hundred and twenty-five dollars." Somehow, we felt, if they were going to charge that elegant a price, the least they could do was spell it out. Moreover, we tended to agree that a liberal in fiscal matters might dismiss the federal debt as "only $5.6 trillion," whereas a fiscal conservative who wanted to emphasize the enormity of the amount might well have written "The federal debt now stands at $5,600,000,000,000" and thereby have forced upon us a sense of the magnitude of the amount by making us calculate it for ourselves. Finally, we agreed that we would much rather be married at "half after four o'clock, on the nineteenth of January" than at "4:30 p.m., January 19."*

These, admittedly, are extreme examples of occasions on which an unusual number style could be justified, but they tend to throw light on the more customary style for expressing numbers and on the notion of style in general. At the very least, these examples suggest that style should not be thought of as a rigid set of rules but rather as a set of principles for adjusting one's means of expression to fit a particular set of circumstances. We express our style in clothes through a varied wardrobe that suits the needs not only of everyday situations but of formal and informal occasions as well. It is the impoverished person who meets every situation with the same set of clothes. By the same token, it is an impoverished writer who meets all situations with a rigid set of rules. The writer of the Tiffany ad, who chose words instead of figures to express an amount of money, in this instance had some true sense of how to vary style for best effect.

---

*One dissenter indicated that she simply wanted to get married and didn't much care how the invitations read.

Essays

Manipulating principles of style for specific effect ought not to be a random, hit-or-miss exercise but should proceed from some coherent notion about style itself. In the case of numbers, an intelligent control of number style proceeds from an awareness of the difference in effect that results from using figures or words to express numbers.

Figures are big (like capital letters); when used in a sentence, they stand out clearly from the surrounding tissue of words. As a result, they are easier to grasp on first reading, and they are easier to locate for subsequent reference. Thus whenever quick comprehension and fast reference are important (and this is true of most business writing), figures are to be preferred to words.

But the very characteristics of figures that make them preferable to words can be disadvantageous in certain circumstances. Figures stand out so sharply against a background of words that they achieve a special prominence and obtain a special emphasis. Not all numbers warrant that kind of emphasis, however, and in such cases words are preferable to figures. Keep in mind, too, that figures have the conciseness and the informality of an abbreviation. Thus the more formal the occasion, the more likely one is to spell numbers out (as in the wedding announcement cited on page xiii).

Given these basic differences between using figures and using words, it is quite clear why figures are preferred in ordinary business letters. These are typically straightforward communications that pass between business firms and their suppliers or their customers, containing frequent references to price quotations, quantities, shipping dates, credit terms, and the like. Frequently, these numbers represent data that has to be extracted from the letter and processed in some way; they may have to be checked against other numbers or included in some computation or simply transferred to another document. The advantage of figures over words in these ordinary cases is so clear that the point does not need to be argued.

But there is another kind of business writing in which the writer is not dealing with the workaday transactions of the business. It may be a special promotion campaign with an air of elegance and formality; it may be a carefully constructed letter with special stylistic objectives in mind; or it may be a special report which involves community relations and will have a wider distribution than the normal technical business report. This kind of writing tends to occur more often at the executive level, and it tends to occur in the more creative departments of a business (such as sales promotion, advertising, public relations, and customer relations). In this kind of writing, numbers don't occur very frequently; when they do, they are usually expressed in words.

As a response to the different needs posed by these two kinds of writing, there are two basic number styles in use today. Both use figures and words but in different proportions. The *figure style* uses figures for all numbers above 10, whether exact or approximate; the *word style* spells out all numbers up through 100 and all numbers above 100 that can be expressed in one or two words (such as *twenty-five hundred*).

As a practical matter, your immediate job may require you to use only the figure style. However, your next job may call for the use of the word style. And if you are working and going to school at the same time (as more and more people are these days), you will probably find yourself following one style for office work and another for your academic work.

Under these circumstances, if you grasp the basic difference between using words and figures to express numbers, you will be better able to decide how to proceed in specific situations without having to consult a style manual each time. In any case, keep the following ideas in mind:

1. There are no absolute rights and wrongs in number style—only varying sets of stylistic conventions that people follow in one set of circumstances or another. There are, however, effective differences in using words or figures, and you should take these differences into account.

2. Before deciding on which number style to follow for a given piece of writing, first determine the basic objective of the material. If the material is intended to communicate information as simply and as briefly as possible, use the *figure style*. If the material is of a formal nature or aspires to a certain level of literary elegance, use the *word style*.

3. Having decided on a basic style, *be consistent in context*. When related numbers occur together in the same context and according to the rules some should go in figures and some should go in words, treat these related numbers all the same way.

4. Treat an approximate number exactly the same way you would treat an exact number. If you would write *50 orders*, then you should also write *about 50 orders*. (If the figure 50 looks too emphatic to you when used in an approximation, the chances are that you should be using the word style—and not just for approximate numbers but throughout.)

5. In areas where the style could go either way (for example, *the 4th of June* vs. *the fourth of June* or *9 o'clock* vs. *nine o'clock*), decide in accordance with your basic style. Thus if you are following the figure style, you will automatically choose the *4th of June* and *9 o'clock*.

6. In expressions involving ages, periods of time, and measurements, use figures whenever these numbers have technical significance or serve as measurements or deserve special emphasis; otherwise, use words. (For example, *you receive these benefits at 65, the note will be due in 3 months, the parcel weighs over 2 pounds*; but *my father will be sixty-five next week, that happened three months ago, I hope to lose another two pounds this week.*)

7. Use figures in dates *(June 6)* and in expressions of money *($6)*, except for reasons of formality or special effect (as in the wedding announcement or the Tiffany ad). Also use figures with abbreviations and symbols and in percentages, proportions, ratios, and scores.

8. Use words for numbers at the beginning of a sentence, for most ordinals *(the third time, the twentieth anniversary)*, and for fractions standing alone *(one-third of our sales)*.

All manuals of style (including this one) include many more than eight rules. They give exceptions and fine points beyond those just summarized. Yet for all practical purposes these eight rules—and the philosophy that underlies them—will cover almost every common situation. Just remember that the conventions of number style were meant to be applied, not as an absolute set of dogmas, but as a flexible set of principles that help to fit the form to the occasion. When manipulated with intelligence and taste, these principles of style can enhance and support your broader purposes in writing.

➤ *For a further discussion of number style, see Section 4, pages 110–131.*

A Fresh Look at Capitalization

The rules on capitalization give most people fits. First of all, there are a seemingly endless number of rules to master; second, the authorities themselves don't agree on the rules; and third, the actual practices of writers often don't agree with any of the contradictory recommendations of the authorities.

A frequent solution is to pretend that disagreements on capitalization style don't exist; instead, people are given one fixed set of rules to be applied under all circumstances. Yet all too many people never do remember the full complement of rules, and those they do remember they apply mechanically without comprehension. As a result, they never get to see that capitalization can be a powerful instrument of style if it is shrewdly and knowingly used.

To understand the basic function of capitalization, you should know that capitalization gives importance, emphasis, and distinction to everything it touches. That's why we capitalize the first word of every sentence—to signify emphatically that a new sentence has begun.* That's why we capitalize proper nouns like *Marianne* and *California* and *April*—to indicate distinctively that these are the official names of particular people, places, or things. Moreover, when we take a word that normally occurs as a common noun and capitalize it, we are loading into that word the special significance that a proper noun possesses. The *fourth of July,* for example, is just another day in the year; when it signifies a national holiday, it becomes the *Fourth of July.* In exactly the same way, the *white house* that stands at 1600 Pennsylvania Avenue becomes the *White House* when we think of it, not as one of many white houses, but as the residence of the *President,* who is himself something special compared to the *president* of a business organization.

This process of giving special significance to a common noun and transforming it into a proper noun explains why we capitalize names coined from common nouns—for example, the *Windy City,* the *First Lady,* the *Sunflower State,* the *Stars and Stripes, Mother's Day,* and the *Industrial Revolution.* And it also explains why manufacturers who coin trade names try to register them whenever possible. As long as they can get legal protection for these names, they are entitled to capitalize them. The owners of such trade names as *Coke, Kleenex, Frisbee, Dacron, Levi's,* and *Xerox* are likely to take legal action against anyone who uses such words generically. They are determined to protect their rights zealously because they don't want to lose the distinctive forcefulness that a capitalized noun possesses. In this respect they demonstrate an understanding of the function of capitalization that few of us can compete with.

Once it becomes clear that capitalization is a process of loading special significance into words, it's easier to understand why capitalization practices vary so widely. Individual writers will assign importance to words from their own vantage points. The closer they are to the term in question, the more inclined they will be to capitalize it. Thus it is quite possible that what is important to me (and therefore worthy of capitalization) may not be important to you and thus will not be capitalized.

---

*Several years ago a group of students at Williams College objected to capitalizing the first letter of the first word of a sentence on the grounds that it "unfairly prioritizes that letter at the expense of the other underprivileged letters that follow."

One could cite any number of examples to prove the point. A retail merchant will take out full-page ads so that he can exclaim in print about his *Year-End Clearance Sale*. The rest of us can respect his right to capitalize the phrase, but we are under no obligation to share his enthusiasm for what is, after all, just another *year-end clearance sale*. In legal agreements, as another example, it's customary to load such terms as *buyer* and *seller* with the significance of proper nouns and thus write, "The *Buyer* agrees to pay the *Seller* . . ."; in all other contexts, however, this kind of emphasis would not be warranted.

When it is understood that it is appropriate to capitalize a given term in some contexts but not necessarily in all contexts, a lot of the agony about capitalization disappears. Instead of trying to decide whether *Federal Government* or *federal government* is correct, you should recognize that both forms are valid and that depending on the context and the importance you want to attach to the term, one form will be more appropriate to your purpose than another. If you are a federal employee, you are very likely to write *Federal Government* under all circumstances, out of respect for the organization that employs you. If you are not a government employee, you are more likely to write *federal government* under ordinary circumstances. If, however, you are writing to someone connected with the federal government or you are writing a report or document in which the federal government is strongly personified, you will probably choose the capitalized form.

By the same token, you need not agonize over the proper way to treat terms like *advertising department, finance committee,* and *board of directors.* These are well-established generic terms as well as the official names of actual units within an organization. Thus you are likely to capitalize these terms if they refer to units within your own organization, because you would be expected to assign a good deal of importance to such things. But you wouldn't have to capitalize these terms when referring to someone else's organization unless for reasons of courtesy or flattery you wanted to indicate that you considered that organization important. (For example, "I would like to apply for a job as copywriter in your Advertising Department.") Moreover, when writing to outsiders, you should keep in mind whether or not they would assign the same importance you do to units within your organization. In an interoffice memo you would no doubt write, "David Walsh has been appointed to the Board of Directors"; in a news release intended for a general audience, you would more likely write, "David Walsh has been appointed to the board of directors of the Wilmington Corporation."

This switch in form from one context to another will appear surprising only to those who assume that one form is intrinsically right and the other intrinsically wrong. Actually, there are many more familiar instances of this kind of flexibility. We normally write the names of seasons in lowercase (for example, *spring*), but when the season is meant to be personified, we switch to uppercase *(Spring)*. The words *earth, sun,* and *moon* are normally expressed in lowercase, but when these terms are used in the same context with proper names like *Mars* and *Venus,* they also become capitalized. Or we write that we are taking courses in *history* and *art,* but once these terms become part of the official names of college courses, we write *History 101* and *Art 5C.*

Once you come to view capitalization as a flexible instrument of style, you should be able to cope more easily with ambiguous or conflicting rules. For example, one of the most troublesome rules concerns whether or not to capitalize titles when they follow a person's name or are used in place of the name. According to a number of authorities, only the titles of

Essays

"high-ranking" officials and dignitaries should be capitalized when they follow or replace a person's name. But how high is high? Where does one draw the line? You can easily become confused at this point because the authorities as well as individual writers have drawn the line at various places. So it helps to understand that the answer to how high is high will depend on where you stand in relation to the person named. At the international level, a lot of us would be willing to bestow initial caps on the *Queen of England,* the *Pope,* the *Secretary General of the United Nations,* and people of similar eminence. At the national level in this country, many of us would agree on honoring with caps the *President,* the *Vice President,* Cabinet members (such as the *Attorney General* and the *Secretary of Defense*), the heads of federal agencies and bureaus (such as the *Director* or the *Commissioner*), but probably not lower-ranking officials in the national government. (However, if you worked in Washington and were closer to those lower-ranking people, you might very well draw the line so as to include at least some of them.) At the state level, we would probably all agree to honor the *Governor* and even the *Lieutenant Governor,* but most of us would probably refer to the *attorney general* of the state in lowercase (unless, of course, we worked for the state government or had dealings with the official in question, in which case we would write the *Attorney General*). Because most people who write style manuals are removed from the local levels of government, they rarely sanction the use of caps for the titles of local officials; but anyone who works for the local government or on the local newspaper or has direct dealings with these officials will assign to the titles of these officials a good deal more importance than the writers of style manuals typically do. Indeed, if I were writing to the mayor of my town or to someone in the mayor's office, I would refer to the *Mayor.* But if I discuss this official with you in writing, I would refer to the *mayor;* in this context it would be bestowing excessive importance on this person to capitalize the title.

What about titles of high-ranking officials in your own organization? They certainly are important to you, even if not to the outside world. Such titles are usually capped in formal minutes of a meeting or in formal documents (such as a company charter or a set of bylaws). In ordinary written communications, however, these titles are not—as a matter of taste— usually capitalized, for capitalization would confer an excessive importance on a person who is neither a public official nor a prominent dignitary. But those who insist on paying this gesture of respect and honor to their top executives have the right to do it if they want to. (And in some companies this gesture is demanded.)

In the final analysis, the important thing is for you to establish an appropriate capitalization style for a given context—and having established that style, to follow it consistently within that context, even though you might well adopt a different style in another context. Though others may disagree with your specific applications of the rules, no one can fault you if you have brought both sense and sensitivity to your use of capitalization.

➤ *For a further discussion of capitalization style, see Section 3, pages 86–109.*

The Comma Trauma

Consider the poor comma, a plodding workhorse in the fields of prose—exceedingly useful but like most workhorses overworked. Because it can do so many things, a number of writers dispense the comma to cure their ailing prose the way doctors dispense aspirin: according to this prescription, you take two at frequent intervals and hope the problem will go away. Other writers, having written, stand back to admire their handiwork as if it were a well-risen cake—and for the final touch they sprinkle commas down upon it like so much confectioners' sugar. And one writer I know, when pushed to desperation, will type several rows of commas at the bottom of her letter and urge you to insert them in the copy above wherever you think it appropriate.

It's too bad that commas induce a trauma in so many writers. Despite the seemingly endless set of rules that describe their varied powers, commas have only two basic functions: they either separate or set off. Separating requires only one comma; setting off requires two.

The separating functions of the comma, for the most part, are easy to spot and not hard to master. A separating comma is used:

1. To separate the two main clauses in a compound sentence when they are joined by *and, but, or,* or *nor.*

2. To separate three or more items in a series *(Tom, Dick, and Harry)*—unless all the items are joined by *and* or *or (Bob and Carol and Ted and Alice).*

3. To signify the omission of *and* between adjectives of equal rank (as in a *quiet, unassuming personality*).

4. To separate the digits of numbers into groups of thousands *(30,000).*

Writers get into trouble here mostly as a result of separating things that should not be separated—for example, a subject and a verb *(Bob, Carol, Ted, and Alice, decided to see a movie)* or an adjective and a noun *(a quiet, unassuming, personality).* Yet this is not where the comma trauma begins to set in.

The real crunch comes with the commas that set off. These are the commas that set off words, phrases, or clauses that (1) provide additional but nonessential information or (2) are out of their normal order in the sentence or (3) manage, in one way or another, to disrupt the flow of the sentence from subject to verb to object or complement. What makes it so difficult for people to use these commas correctly is that they have a hard time analyzing the difference between an expression used as an essential element in one context and as a nonessential element in another.

Consider the following example. I would venture that most people have been taught to punctuate the sentence exactly as it is given here:

> It is, therefore, essential that we audit all accounts at once.

To be specific, they have probably been taught that *therefore* is always nonessential when it occurs within a sentence and that it must therefore always be set off by commas. What they probably have not been taught is that commas that set off (unlike commas that separate) usually signal the way a sentence should sound when spoken aloud. For example, if I were to

Essays

read the foregoing sentence aloud the way it has been punctuated, I would pause slightly at the sign of the first comma and then let my voice drop on the word *therefore:*

IT IS, therefore, ESSENTIAL . . .

Now if this is the reading that is desired, then the use of commas around *therefore* is quite correct. Yet I would venture that most people would read the sentence this way:

It is THEREFORE essential . . .

letting the voice rise on *therefore* to give it the special emphasis it demands. If this is the desired reading, then commas would be altogether wrong in this sentence, for they would induce a "nonessential" inflection in the voice where none is wanted.

If people have been mechanically inserting commas around *therefore* and similar words where commas do not belong, it is because they have not been encouraged to listen to the way the sentences are supposed to sound. Certainly once you become aware of the differences in inflection and phrasing that accompany essential and nonessential elements, it becomes a lot easier for you to distinguish between them and to insert or omit commas accordingly. Given this kind of approach, sentences like the following pair are simple to cope with.

Please let me know *if I have remembered everything correctly.*
He said he would meet us at three, *if I remember correctly.*

Although it would be possible, by means of a structural analysis, to establish why the first *if* clause is essential and why the second is not, you would do well to be guided by the inflection implied in each sentence. In the first instance, the voice arcs as it bridges the gap between *Please let me know* and *if I have remembered everything correctly.* In the second instance, the inflectional arc embraces only the first part of the sentence, *He said he would meet us at three;* then comes a slight pause followed by the *if* clause, which is uttered in a much lower register, almost as if it were an afterthought.

As you gain confidence in your ability to detect the inflectional patterns characteristic of essential and nonessential expressions, you should have no difficulty in picking your way through a variety of constructions like these:

I must report, *nevertheless,* that his work is unsatisfactory.
I must *nevertheless* report that his work is unsatisfactory.

The location, *I must admit,* is quite attractive.
The location is one *I must admit* I find attractive.

There are, *of course,* other possible answers to the problem.
It is *of course* your prerogative to change your mind.

This awareness of inflectional patterns is especially helpful when it comes to coping with appositives, a frustrating area in which the use or omission of commas often seems illogical. When the appositive expression is truly nonessential, as in:

Ed Brown, *the president of Apex,* would like to meet you.

the customary pause and the characteristic drop in voice are there. And when the appositive expression is essential, as in phrases like *the year 2001* and *the term "recommend,"* you can hear the single inflectional arc that embraces each group of words in one closely knit unit. You can also hear the same continuous arc in the phrase *my wife Marie.* By all that is logical, the name

Marie should be set off by commas because it is not needed to establish which of my wives I'm speaking about; I have only one wife. Yet according to today's standards, *my wife Marie* is considered good form. Although not essential to the meaning, the name *Marie* is treated as if it were essential because of what style manuals call "a very close relationship with the preceding words." Although it is difficult, if not impossible, to state in concrete terms what constitutes "a very close relationship," you can tell by the sound when it exists. There is a very subtle but very real difference in the phrases *my sister Florence* and *my sister, Florence Stern.* When the full name is given, there tends to be a slight pause after *sister* and the voice tends to drop while uttering the full name. Yet it is not safe to conclude that adding the second name accounts for the difference in the inflection, for when one speaks of *the composer John Cage* or *the author Toni Morrison,* one hears the same inflectional pattern as in *my wife Marie* or *the year 2003.* So in the case of appositives, it is wise to be wary of simple generalizations and to listen attentively in each case to the way the expression ought to sound.

In stressing, as I have, the significance of inflection and phrasing as a guide to the use of commas, I do not mean to suggest that one can punctuate by sound alone and can safely ignore structure and meaning. What I am suggesting is that in a number of cases, such as those I have cited, an awareness of the sound of sentences can help you grasp relationships that might otherwise be obscure.

There are many other problems involving the comma that should be discussed here, but someone else (Ogdcn Nash, perhaps) will have to take over . . .

> And now if you'll excuse me comma
> I must lie down and have my trauma . . . ,,,,,,,,,,,,,,,,,,,,,,,,,,,,,,,

➤ *For a further discussion of the rules governing the use of commas, see ¶¶122–175.*

The Plight of the Compound Adjective—Or, Where Have All the Hyphens Gone?

The hyphen, it grieves me to report, is in trouble. Indeed, unless concerted action is taken at once, the hyphen is likely to become as extinct as the apostrophe in *ladies aid.* The problem can be traced to two dangerous attitudes that are afoot these days. One is revolutionary in tone; its motto: "Compound adjectives, unite! You have nothing to lose but your hyphens." The other attitude reflects the view of the silent majority. These are the people who don't pretend to know how to cope with the "hyphen" mess; they just earnestly wish the whole problem would quickly disappear. It may now be too late to reverse the long-range trend. For the present, however, the hyphen exists—and anyone who expects to work with words at an acceptable level of proficiency needs to come to terms with the noble beast. Here, then, is a last-ditch effort to make sense out of an ever-changing and possibly fast-disappearing (but not-soon-to-be-forgotten) aspect of style.

Essays

As a general rule, the English language depends largely on word order to make the relationships between words clear. When word order alone is not sufficient to establish these relationships, we typically resort to punctuation. It is in this context that the hyphen has a real service to offer. The function of the hyphen is to help the reader grasp clusters of words—or even parts of words—as a unit. When a word has to be divided at the end of a line, the hyphen signifies the connection between parts. Whenever two or more words function as a unit but cannot (for one reason or another) be written either as a solid word or as separate words, the hyphen clearly links these words and prevents a lapse in comprehension.

If hyphens are typically required in compound adjectives, it is because there is something "abnormal" about the word order of such expressions. Other kinds of modifiers, by contrast, do not require hyphens. For example, if I write about "a *long, hard* winter," I am actually referring to a winter *that will be long and hard;* so I need a comma—not a hyphen—to establish the fact that *long* and *hard* modify *winter* independently. If I write about "a *long opening* paragraph," the word order makes it clear that *opening* modifies *paragraph* and that *long* modifies the two words together; so no punctuation is needed to establish the fact that I'm speaking about "*an opening paragraph that is long.*"

However, if I write about "a *long-term* loan," an entirely different relationship is established between the elements in the modifier. I am not speaking of a *loan* that is *long* and *term,* nor am I referring to a *term loan* that is *long.* I am speaking about a loan "that is to run for a *long term* of years." The words *long-term* (unlike *long, hard* or *long opening*) have an internal relationship all their own; it is only as an integral unit that these two words can modify a noun. Thus a hyphen is inserted to establish this fact clearly.

For a better understanding of the internal relationship that exists between the elements in a compound adjective, one has to go back to its origins. A compound adjective is actually a compressed version of an adjective phrase or clause. For example, if I describe a product as carrying "a *money-back* guarantee," I am actually talking about "a guarantee *to give you your money back if you are not satisfied with the product.*" Or if I refer to "a *take-charge* kind of guy," I am really speaking of "the kind of guy *who always takes charge of any situation he finds himself in.*" One can easily see from these examples why compound adjectives are so popular, for these expressions are usually a good deal crisper and livelier than the phrases or clauses they represent. These examples give further evidence of why a hyphen is needed. In each case we have zeroed in on a couple of words, we have wrenched them out of context and out of their normal order in a descriptive phrase or clause, and we have inserted them before a noun as if they were an ordinary adjective—a role these two words were never originally designed to play. Deprived of all the other words that would clearly establish the relationship between them, these elements require a hyphen to hold them together.

The two factors of compression and dislocation are all the justification one needs to hyphenate a compound adjective. However, there are often additional clues to the need for a hyphen. In the process of becoming a compound adjective, the individual words frequently undergo a change in form: "a contract for *two years*" becomes "a *two-year* contract"; "a blonde with *blue eyes*" becomes "a *blue-eyed* blonde." Sometimes the words are put in inverted order: "lands *owned* by the *government*" becomes "*government-owned* lands." Sometimes the elements undergo a change both in form *and* in word order: "an employee *who works hard*" becomes "a *hardworking* employee"; "bonds *exempt from taxation*" becomes "*tax-exempt* bonds." The change in form or the inversion in word order is an additional signal that you are in the presence of a compound adjective and ought to hyphenate it.

If the compound adjective is so simple to understand in theory, why is it so difficult to handle in practice? A good deal of the problem can be traced to that neat but now-discredited rule, "Hyphenate compound adjectives when they precede the noun but not when they follow the noun." It was indeed a very neat rule but not a very precise one. Let's take it apart and see why.

It is quite true that compound adjectives should be hyphenated when they occur *before* a noun—for the most part. There's the catch—"for the most part." The exceptions seem to occur in such a random, hit-and-miss, now-and-then, flip-a-coin, make-it-up-as-you-go-along fashion that one begins to lose respect for the rule. Yet there is a very definite pattern to the exceptions. Keep in mind that the hyphen serves to hold a cluster of words together as a unit. If, through some other means, these words make themselves clearly recognizable as a unit, the hyphen is superfluous and can be omitted. There are at least three such situations where a hyphen is unnecessary: when the compound modifier is a proper name, when it is a well-recognized foreign expression, and when it is a well-established compound noun serving as a compound adjective. Let's look at some samples.

If I speak of "a *Madison Avenue* agency," the capital *M* and *A* virtually guarantee that the expression will be quickly grasped as a unit. And if I talk about "a *bona fide* contract," the reader will recognize this Latin expression as a unit without the help of a hyphen. By the same token, terms like *social security, life insurance,* and *high school* are so well established as compound nouns that when they are used as adjectives, we immediately grasp such expressions as a unit, without the support of any punctuation.

If no hyphen is needed in "*social security* benefits," one may well ask why a hyphen is required in "*short-term* benefits." After all, words like *short term* and *long range* are adjective-noun combinations that closely resemble *social security, life insurance,* and *high school.* Why hyphenate some and not others? The reason is this: Words like *short term, long range,* and *high level* don't have any standing as compound nouns in their own right; they do not represent a concept or an institution (as terms like *social security* and *life insurance* do). Therefore, these words require a hyphen to hold them together when they occur before a noun.

Once you grasp the difference between *social security* and *short-term* as compound adjectives, you can use these two expressions as touchstones in deciding how to handle other adjective-noun combinations. With a principle like this in hand, you don't have to engage in profound analysis to resolve the "hyphen problem." Consider a random list of examples such as these:

> a *red letter* day
> a *civil service* test
> *income tax* refund
> *long distance* calls
> a *white collar* worker
> a *real estate* agent
> *word processing* software
> *high level* decisions

The expressions *civil service, income tax, real estate,* and *word processing* all resemble *social security,* since they stand for well-known concepts or institutions; therefore, as compound adjectives they can all be written without hyphens. However, *red-letter, long-distance, white-collar,* and *high-level* are much more like *short-term* and should have a hyphen.

Essays

So much for compound adjectives before the noun. When they occur *after* the noun, according to the traditional rule, they should not be hyphenated. Yet this traditional formulation is somewhat misleading. If we aren't supposed to hyphenate a "compound adjective" when it follows a noun, it's for the simple reason that the words in question no longer function as a compound adjective—they are playing a normal role in a normal order. It's one thing to use hyphens in the expression "an *up-to-date* report," for a prepositional phrase doesn't normally belong before a noun. However, if I said "This report is *up to date*," there would be no more justification for hyphenating here than there would be if I said "This report is *in good shape*." Both expressions—*in good shape* and *up to date*—are prepositional phrases playing a normal role in the predicate.

However, if the expression still exhibits an abnormal form or inverted word order in the predicate, it is still a compound adjective—and it must still be hyphenated. For example, whether I speak of "*tax-exempt* items" or say "these items are *tax-exempt*," the hyphen must be inserted because regardless of where it appears—*before* or *after* the noun—the expression is a compressed version of the phrase "exempt from taxation."

There are at least four kinds of compound adjectives that must always be hyphenated *after* as well as *before* the noun (because of inverted word order or change of form). These compound adjectives consist of the following patterns:

noun + adjective *(duty-free)*
noun + participle *(interest-bearing)*
adjective + participle *(soft-spoken)*
adjective + noun + *ed (old-fashioned)*

Once you learn to recognize these four patterns, you can safely assume that any compound adjective that fits one of these patterns must always be hyphenated, no matter where it falls in a sentence.*

It does no good to pretend that compound adjectives are an easy thing to master. They aren't. And for that very reason people who have to cope with these expressions need more guidance than they get from a simple "hyphenate before but not after" kind of rule. In the final analysis, what becomes of the hyphen over the long run is of little consequence. What does matter is that we express ourselves with precision, verve, and grace. If the hyphen can help us toward that end, why not make use of it?

➢ *For a further discussion of the treatment of compound adjectives, see ¶¶813–832.*

---

*There is only one worm in this rosy apple: some of the words that fit these patterns are now acceptably spelled as one word. For example:

Normal Pattern	Exception
water-repellent	waterproof
time-consuming	timesaving
half-baked	halfhearted
clear-sighted	clearheaded

The Semicolon; and Other Myths

In certain circles that I move in, the fastest way I know to start a quarrel is to attack the semicolon. If I knocked my friends' politics or sneered at their religious beliefs, they would simply smile. But attack their views on the semicolon and they reach for a bread knife. Why this particular mark of punctuation should excite such intense passion escapes me. The semicolon has always been a neurotic creature, continually undergoing an identity crisis. After all, it is half comma and half period, and from its name you would think it is half a colon. It is hardly any wonder, then, that a lot of people are half crazy trying to determine who the semicolon really is and what its mission in life is supposed to be.

In the course of this brief essay, I am going to explore three myths that have grown up over the years about the semicolon and about some other marks of punctuation.

Myth No. 1: If either clause in a compound sentence contains an internal comma, use a semicolon (not a comma) before the coordinating conjunction that connects the clauses. According to this line of reasoning, it is all right to use a comma in a compound sentence like this:

> The meeting in Salem has been canceled, but all other meetings will go on as scheduled.

However, if I use commas for a lesser purpose within either clause (for example, by inserting *Oregon* after *Salem* and setting if off with commas), then the comma before the conjunction must be upgraded to a semicolon.

> The meeting in Salem, Oregon, has been canceled; but all other meetings will go on as scheduled.

It is harsh, I concede, to dismiss this rule as a myth when it has been taught for years in various classes and various texts. But the unhappy fact is that outside those classes and those texts, almost no one punctuates that way anymore. The trouble with using a semicolon in such sentences is that it creates a break that is too strong for the occasion. It closes down the action of the sentence at a point where the writer would like it to keep on going. So contemporary writers see nothing wrong with using commas simultaneously to separate clauses and to perform lesser functions within the clauses—unless, of course, total confusion or misreading is likely to result. But in most cases it doesn't. In the following sentence, commas are used both *within* clauses and *between* clauses without any loss of clarity and also without any loss of verbal momentum.

> On March 14, 2000, I wrote to your credit manager, Mr. Lopez, but I have not yet heard from him.

This simultaneous use of commas within and between clauses may look offensive to anyone accustomed to the traditional rule. The fact remains that we have been using commas for both purposes in *complex* sentences all along, and it has never occasioned any comment.

> Although I wrote to your credit manager, Mr. Lopez, on March 14, 2000, I have not yet heard from him.

It should be clearly understood that the use of a semicolon before the conjunction in a compound sentence is not wrong. If you want a strong break at that point, the semicolon can and should be used. But you ought to know that the reason for using it is the special effect it creates—and not the presence of internal commas. For example:

> I have tried again and again to explain to George why the transaction had to be kept secret from him; but he won't believe me.

➤ *For a further discussion of the use of a semicolon in a compound sentence, see ¶176–177.*

Essays

Myth No. 2: Always use a semicolon before an enumeration or an explanation introduced by *for example, namely,* or *that is.* In many cases this rule is quite true, but in other cases either a colon or a comma is better suited to the occasion. Let's look at some examples.

> There are several things you could do to save your business (?) namely, try to get a loan from the bank, find yourself a partner with good business judgment, or pray that your competitor goes out of business before you do.

If you put a semicolon before *namely,* you will close the action down just when the sentence is starting to get somewhere. Because the first part of the sentence creates an air of anticipation, because it implicitly promises to reveal several ways of saving the business, you need not a mark that closes the action down but one that supports the air of anticipation. Enter the colon.

The colon is one of the underrated stars in the firmament of punctuation. It would be more widely used, perhaps, if its sound effects were better understood. The colon is the mark of anticipation. It is a blare of trumpets before the grand entrance; it is the roll of drums before the dive off the 100-foot tower. It marks the end of the buildup and gets you ready for "the real thing." Thus:

> There are several things you can do to save your business: namely, try to get a loan . . .

Consider this example, however:

> Always express numbers in figures when they are accompanied by abbreviations; for example, *4 p.m., 8 ft.*

The first part of this sample sentence expresses a self-contained thought. If the sentence ended right there, the reader would not be left up in the air. The examples that follow are unexpected, unanticipated, added on almost as an afterthought. We're glad to have them, but they aren't anything we were counting on. The semicolon here is quite appropriate; it momentarily closes down the action of the sentence after the main point is expressed.

In other situations a comma may be the best mark to use before *namely, for example,* or *that is.* Consider this sentence as an example:

> Do not use quotation marks to enclose an *indirect quotation,* that is, a restatement of a person's exact words.

In this case, a semicolon would be inappropriate before *that is* because it would close off the action just as we were about to get a definition of a term within the main clause. Moreover, a colon would be inappropriate because it would imply that the sentence up to that point was a buildup for what follows—and that is not true in this case. Here all that is needed is a simple comma to preserve the close relationship between the term *indirect quotation* and the explanatory expression that follows it.

> ➤ *For a further discussion of the use of a semicolon with* for example, namely, *or* that is, *see* ¶¶181–183.

Myth No. 3: When a polite request is phrased as a question, end it with a period. This is another statement that does not, unfortunately, always hold true. In fact, once a period is used at the end of some requests, they no longer sound very polite. I once posted the following note in my home: "Will you please close the door." My children knew that this was not really a polite request but a firm parental command. When they chose to ignore it, I amended the sign to read, "Will you please close the door!" (I was relying on the exclamation point to carry the full force of my exasperation.) That approach failed too, so I tried a new tack in diplomacy, amending the sign once again: "Will you please close the door?" My children now knew they had broken my spirit. They now sensed in the sign a pleading note, a petitioning tone, the begging of a favor. They also knew that now I was asking them a real yes-or-no question (or at least I was creating the illusion of asking). Then, in the paradoxical way that children have, once they knew they had the chance to say no, they began to answer my question with tacit affirmations, tugging the door after them on the way out or kicking it shut behind them on the way in.

My problems with my kids are, of course, my own, but learning how to express and punctuate polite requests tends to be a problem for all of us. Consider, for a moment, the wording of those three signs, alike in all respects except for the final mark of punctuation. The version that ends with a period is really a quiet but nonetheless firm demand. There is no element of a question in it at all. The voice rises in an arc and then flattens out at the end on a note of resolution. In the version that ends with an exclamation point, the voice rises in a higher arc and resounds with greater intensity and force of feeling, but it, too, comes down at the end—this time with something of a bang. In the final version, the one with the question mark, the voice starts on an upward curve and then trails off, still on an upward note. Three different readings of the same words, each with a different impact on the reader—all evoked by three different punctuation marks at the end.

Once you become sensitive to the effects produced by these marks of punctuation, handling polite requests becomes quite simple. All you have to do is say the sentence aloud and listen to the sound of your own voice. If you end the sentence with your voice on an upward note, you know that a question mark is the right punctuation to use. If your voice comes down at the end, you know that you need a period. (And if you really feel forceful about it, you probably want an exclamation point.)

If there is any potential danger in so simple a rule, it is this: we sometimes express our requests orally as flat assertions ("Will you please do this for me.") when, as a matter of good taste and good manners, we ought to be asking a question ("Will you please do this for me?").

Now it is true that in the normal course of events we all make demands on one another, and though we tack on a "Will you please" for the sake of politeness, these are still demands, not questions. As long as your reader is not likely to consider them presumptuous, it is appropriate to punctuate these demands with periods:

> Will you please sign both copies of the contract and return the original to me.
> May I suggest that you confirm the departure time for your flight before you leave for the airport.
> Will you please give my best regards to your family.

As opposed to these routine demands, there is the kind of polite request that asks the reader for a special favor. Here, if you really want to be polite, you will punctuate your request as a question so as to give your reader the chance to say no.

> May I please see you sometime next week?
> May I please get an advance copy of the confidential report you are doing?
> Will you please acknowledge all my correspondence for me while I'm away?

In these cases you are asking for things that the reader may be unable or unwilling to grant; therefore, you ought to pose these requests as questions. (If you try reading them as

Essays

statements, you will observe how quickly they change into peremptory demands.) Suppose, however, that these requests were addressed to your subordinates. Under those conditions you would have the right to expect your reader to make the time to see you, to supply you with an advance copy of the confidential report, and to handle your mail for you; therefore, you would be justified in ending these sentences with periods. But even when you have this authority over your reader, you ought to consider the alternative of asking. The inspired public official who replaced the "Keep Off the Grass" signs with a simple "PLEASE?" understood people and how they like to be talked to. If a question mark will get faster results or establish a nicer tone, why not use it?

➢ *For a further discussion of polite requests, see ¶103.*

There are other myths that one could discuss, but these three are sufficient to permit me to make one central point. Mastery over the rules of punctuation depends to a considerable extent on cultivating a sensitivity to the way a sentence moves and the way it sounds.

Punctuating by ear has come to be frowned on—and with much justification—for it has come to mean punctuating solely by feeling, by instinct, by intuition, without much regard for (or knowledge of) the structure of the language and the function of punctuation. Yet the solution, it seems to me, is not to abandon the technique of punctuating by ear but to cultivate it, to develop in yourself a disciplined sense of the relationship between the sound and the structure and the mechanics of language. Many authorities on language, if pressed, have to concede that they often consider first whether a thing sounds right or looks right: only then do they utter a pronouncement as to why it is right. If they rely on their ears for this kind of assurance, then why don't you cultivate the same skill?

Re: Abbrevs.

Sensitive environmentalists will tell you that emissions from smokestacks and automobile exhaust pipes are not the only forms of pollution that are potentially deadly to human beings. All about us are forces of depersonalization that continually menace the human touches that have previously graced our lives. Most of us have become reconciled to being numerical entities on computer printouts. Those of us who remember those elegant telephone exchanges *(PLaza 9, ASpinwall 7)* have had to reconcile ourselves to their numerical replacements *(759, 277)*.

But new forms of pollutants continually appear on the atmospheric scene. We are beginning to choke—some of us—on the fog of initials and abbreviations and "memorable" acronyms that are intended to identify worthwhile examples of human endeavor. One gem is *HURRAH* (*H*elp *U*s *R*each & *R*ehabilitate *A*merica's *H*andicapped), an instance where a dignified cause is demeaned by a fatuous label, a hollow cheer, an irrelevant salute. Perhaps in self-defense I ought to found a group called *HELP* (*H*elp *E*liminate *L*inguistic *P*ollution).

To put matters in perspective, it may help to think of abbreviations as belonging to the same class of objects as instant coffee, powdered eggs, and TV dinners. They don't take up much space and they're great when you're in a hurry, but they never have the taste of the real thing. Abbreviations are always appropriate in highly expedient documents (such as invoices, purchase orders, low-level interoffice memos, and routine correspondence), where the emphasis is on precise communication of data in the briefest possible space without concern for style or elegance of expression. But in other kinds of writing, where some attention is given to the *effect* to be made on the reader, a more formal style prevails—and under these circumstances only certain kinds of abbreviations are acceptable.

Some that are always acceptable, even in the most formal contexts, are those that precede or follow personal names *(Mr., Mrs., Ms., Jr., Sr., Ph.D., Esq.)*, those that are part of an organization's legal name *(Inc., Ltd., Co.)*, those used in expressions of time *(a.m., p.m., PST, EDT)*, and a few miscellaneous expressions (such as *B.C.* and *A.D.*).

Those venerable Latin abbreviations *etc., i.e., e.g.,* and the like are usually acceptable, but in writing that aspires to a certain elegance or formality they ought to be replaced, not by the full Latin expressions, but rather by the English expressions *and so forth* (or *and the like*), *that is, for example,* or appropriate equivalents.

Organizations with long names are now commonly identified by their initials in all but the most formal writing—*AFL-CIO, UNICEF, FBI, PBS.* Even the initials *U.S.* are now acceptable in all but the most formal writing when used in the names of federal agencies (such as the *U.S. Department of Labor*); however, using the initials by themselves (as in *throughout the U.S.*) is bad form.

Abbreviations of days of the week, of names of months, of geographic names, and of units of measure are appropriate only in business forms, in correspondence that is clearly expedient, and in tables where space is tight.

Although it may seem troublesome knowing *when* to abbreviate, it is often more troublesome knowing *how* to abbreviate. There are so many variations in style (involving the use of caps or small letters, the use or omission of periods, and the use or omission of internal space) that it is often difficult to find an authoritative source to follow. (The tenth edition of *Merriam-Webster's New Collegiate Dictionary*, for example, omits virtually all periods from its list of abbreviations, as if this were now the commonly accepted practice. Merriam-Webster, of course, uses periods with many of the abbreviations that appear in the main text. See ¶503, note.)

Here are a few safe guidelines:

1. An all-capital abbreviation made up of the initials of several words is normally written without periods and without internal space (for example, *IBM, UAW, CEO, CD-ROM, SEC, IQ*). The only major exceptions are geographic names (such as *U.S.A.*), academic degrees (such as *B.A., M.D.*), and a few odd expressions (such as *A.D., B.C.,* and *P.O.*).

2. A small-letter abbreviation that consists of the initials of several words is normally written *with* a period after each initial but *without* space after internal periods (for example, *a.m., e.g.*).

Essays

3. When an abbreviation can be styled in all caps *(COD, FOB)* or in small letters *(c.o.d., f.o.b.),* reserve the use of all caps for business forms and similar documents where the blatant look of the capitals will not matter.

4. When an abbreviation stands for several words and consists of more than initials, insert a period and a space after each element in the abbreviation (for example, *Lt. Col., op. cit.*). Academic degrees, however, are an exception: write them *with* the periods but *without* internal space (for example, *Ph.D., Ed.D., LL.B.*).

5. A person's initials are now usually written without periods and space (as in *JFK*) unless they are part of the full name (as in *J. F. Kennedy*).

So much, in brief, for abbreviations. Useful devices on many occasions, but—except for an *R.S.V.P.* delicately scripted in the lower left corner of a formal invitation—not very elegant.

➢ *For a further discussion of the treatment of abbreviations, see Section 5, pages 132–155.*

PART 1

Grammar, Usage, and Style

SECTION **1**

Punctuation: Major Marks

The Period (¶¶101–109)
At the End of a Statement or Command (¶¶101–102)
At the End of a Polite Request or Command (¶103)
At the End of an Indirect Question (¶104)
With Decimals (¶105)
In Outlines and Displayed Lists (¶¶106–107)
With Headings (¶108)
A Few Don'ts (¶109)

The Question Mark (¶¶110–118)
To Indicate Direct Questions (¶¶110–113)
To Indicate Questions Within Sentences (¶¶114–117)
To Express Doubt (¶118)

The Exclamation Point (¶¶119–121)
To Express Strong Feeling (¶¶119–120)
With *Oh* and *O* (¶121)

The Comma (¶¶122–175)
Basic Rules for Commas That Set Off (¶122)
Basic Rules for Commas That Separate (¶¶123–125)
With Clauses in Compound Sentences (¶¶126–129)
With Clauses in Complex Sentences (¶¶130–132)
      Introductory Dependent Clauses (¶130)
      Dependent Clauses Elsewhere in the Sentence (¶¶131–132)
With Clauses in Compound-Complex Sentences (¶¶133–134)
With Participial, Infinitive, and Prepositional Phrases (¶¶135–137)
      Introductory Phrases (¶135)
      Phrases at the Beginning of a Clause (¶136)
      Phrases Elsewhere in the Sentence (¶137)
With Transitional Expressions and Independent Comments (¶¶138–143)
      At the Beginning of a Sentence (¶139)
      At the End of a Sentence (¶140)
      Within the Sentence (¶141)
      At the Beginning of a Clause (¶142)
      With the Adverb *Too* (¶143)

The Semicolon (¶¶176–186)

The Colon (¶¶187–199)

➤ *For definitions of grammatical terms, see the appropriate entries in the Glossary of Grammatical Terms (Appendix A).*

¶101

Punctuation marks are the mechanical means for making the meaning of a sentence easily understood. They indicate the proper relationships between words, phrases, and clauses when word order alone is not sufficient to make these relationships clear.

One important caution about punctuation: If you find it particularly hard to determine the appropriate punctuation for a sentence you have written, the chances are that the sentence is improperly constructed. To be on the safe side, recast your thought in a form you can handle with confidence. In any event, do not try to save a badly constructed sentence by means of punctuation.

Section 1 deals with the three marks of terminal punctuation (the period, the question mark, and the exclamation point) plus the three major marks of internal punctuation (the comma, the semicolon, and the colon). All other marks of punctuation are covered in Section 2.

The Period
At the End of a Statement or Command

101 **a.** Use a period to mark the end of a sentence that makes a statement or expresses a command.

> A nanosecond is one-billionth of a second.
>
> An ohnosecond is an equally brief moment in which you realize that you goofed in a big way.
>
> John W. Hirsch, president of Seglin Controls Inc., has announced the company's plan to acquire Parker Associates before the end of this year.
>
> I question the need to cut advertising and promotion expenses at this time.
>
> All monthly expense reports must be in by the 10th of the following month.
>
> Make sure that Kate gets to the airport by 10 a.m. (The period that marks the end of the abbreviation also serves to mark the end of the sentence.)

b. Use a period to mark the end of an *elliptical* (condensed) expression that represents a complete statement or command. Elliptical expressions often occur as answers to questions or as transitional phrases.

> Yes.   No.   Of course.   Indeed.   Been there. Done that.
>
> Enough on that subject.   Now, to proceed to your next point.

c. Do not confuse elliptical expressions with sentence fragments. An elliptical expression represents a complete sentence. A sentence fragment is a word, phrase, or clause that is incorrectly treated as a separate sentence when it ought to be incorporated with adjacent words to make up a complete sentence.

> Great news! The laser printer arrived yesterday. After we had waited for six weeks. (*Great news* is an elliptical expression; it represents a complete sentence, *I have great news.* The clause *After we had waited for six weeks* is a sentence fragment, incorrectly treated as a sentence in its own right; this dependent clause should be linked with the main clause that precedes it.)
>
> **REVISED:** Great news! The laser printer arrived yesterday, after we had waited for six weeks.

102 The following guidelines will help you decide whether to use one or two spaces following a period at the end of a sentence.

> **NOTE:** These spacing guidelines also apply to any other element that comes at the end of a sentence—for example, a question mark, an exclamation point, a dash, a closing parenthesis, a closing quotation mark, or a superscript (a raised figure or symbol) keyed to a footnote.

a. As a general rule, use one space after the period at the end of a sentence, but switch to two spaces whenever you feel a stronger visual break between sentences is needed. In all cases, the deciding factor should be the appearance of the breaks between sentences in a given document.

b. When monospace fonts (in which all the characters have exactly the same width) were in wide use, it was traditional to leave two spaces between the period and the start of the next sentence.

```
This example is set in 10-point Courier, a
monospace font.  Note the use of two spaces
after the period at the end of the previous
sentence.
```

Now that the standards of desktop publishing predominate, the use of only one space after the period is quite acceptable with monospace fonts.

```
This example is also set in 10-point Courier, a
monospace font. Note the use of only one space
after the period at the end of the previous
sentence.
```

c. Proportional fonts (in which the width of the characters varies) are now much more commonly used. The standard here has always been the same: use only one space between the period and the start of the next sentence.

d. With some proportional fonts—such as 10-point Times New Roman (the default font for Microsoft Word)—the use of only one space after the period may not always provide a clear visual break between sentences. Consider these examples:

> This example is set in 10-point Times New Roman with proportional spacing. Note that the use of only *one* space does not create much of a visual break between sentences.
>
> This example is also set in 10-point Times New Roman, but it uses *two* spaces after the period. Note the improvement in the visual break.

e. When an abbreviation ends one sentence and begins the next, the use of one space after the period that ends the sentence may also be inadequate. (The following examples are set in 10-point Garamond.)

> Let's plan to meet at 10 a.m. Mr. F. J. Calabrese will serve as the moderator. (Only *one* space follows *a.m.* at the end of the first sentence.)
>
> Let's plan to meet at 10 a.m. Mr. F. J. Calabrese will serve as the moderator. (Note the improvement in the visual break when *two* spaces follow the period at the end of the first sentence.)

Continued on page 6

¶103

Punctuation: Major Marks

1

f. If you prepare a document with a justified right margin (so that every line ends at the same point), the width of a single space between sentences can vary from line to line. (The following examples are set in 10-point Arial.)

> We need to start lining up speakers right away. Please consider Patricia Cunningham for the keynote address. Frederick Haley could be approached if she is not available. (The single space after the first sentence is less than the single space after the second sentence.)

> We need to start lining up speakers right away. Please consider Patricia Cunningham for the keynote address. Frederick Haley could be approached if she is not available. (Although *two* spaces have been inserted at the end of each sentence, the break after the second sentence looks excessive.)

➤ *For a summary of guidelines for spacing with punctuation marks, see ¶299.*

At the End of a Polite Request or Command

103 **a.** Requests, suggestions, and commands are often phrased as questions out of politeness. Use a period to end this kind of sentence if you expect your reader to respond by *acting* rather than by giving you a yes-or-no answer.

> Will you please call us at once if we can be of further help.
> Would you please send all bills to my bank for payment while I'm out of the country.
> May I suggest that you refer to computer criminals who break into other people's computers as crackers, not hackers. (Hackers are actually dedicated computer programmers.)
> If you can't attend the meeting, could you please send someone else in your place.

NOTE: Use a period only when you are sure that your reader is not likely to consider your request presumptuous.

b. If you are asking a favor or making a request that your reader may be unable or unwilling to grant, use a question mark at the end of the sentence. The question mark offers your reader a chance to say no to your request and helps to preserve the politeness of the situation.

> May I ask a favor of you? Could you spare fifteen minutes to tell my son about career opportunities in your company?
> Will you be able to have someone in your department help me on the Woonsocket project?
> Will you please handle the production reports for me while I'm away?

c. If you are not sure whether to use a question mark or a period, reword the sentence so that it is clearly a question or a statement; then punctuate accordingly. For example, the sentence directly above could be revised as follows:

> Would you be willing to handle the production reports for me while I'm away?
> I would appreciate your handling the production reports for me while I'm away.

d. When you are addressing a request to someone who reports to you, you expect that person to comply. Therefore, a period can properly be used to punctuate such requests. However, since most people prefer to be *asked* to do something rather than be *told* to do it, a question mark establishes a nicer tone and often gets better results. Consider using a question mark when your request to a subordinate involves something beyond the routine aspects of the job.

> Will you please let me know what your vacation plans are for the month of August. (Routine request to a subordinate.)
>
> May I ask that you avoid scheduling any vacation time during August this year? I will need your help in preparing next year's forecasts and budgets. (Special request to a subordinate. The question mark suggests that the writer is sensitive to the problems this request could cause.)

NOTE: If you are unwilling to give your subordinate the impression that your request allows for a yes-or-no answer, simply drop the attempt at politeness and issue a straightforward command.

> I must ask that you not schedule any vacation time during August this year. I will need your help in preparing next year's forecasts and budgets.

At the End of an Indirect Question

104 Use a period to mark the end of an indirect question. (See also ¶¶115–116.)

> Frank Wilcox has asked whether an exception can be made to our leave-of-absence policy.
> The only question she asked was when the report had to be on your desk.
> Why Janet Murray left the company so quickly has never been explained.
> We know what needs to be done; the question is how to pay for it.

With Decimals

105 Use a period (without space before or after it) to separate a whole number from a decimal fraction; for example, *$5.50, 33.33 percent.*

In Outlines and Displayed Lists

106 Use periods after numbers or letters that enumerate items in an outline or a displayed list—unless the numbers or letters are enclosed in parentheses. Set a tab one or two spaces after these periods in order to achieve an adequate visual break between the numbers or letters and the items that follow on the same line. If you use the automatic numbering feature in Microsoft Word, the program will position the numbers or letters at the left margin and start the text of each item and any turnover lines 0.25 inch from the left margin. (See ¶¶107, 199c, 222, 223, 1357d, 1424f, 1724–1726; for illustrations, see pages 539 and 541.)

NOTE: Do not use periods after bullets that introduce items in a displayed list. (See ¶¶1357e, 1424g.)

107 **a.** Use periods after independent clauses, dependent clauses, or long phrases that are displayed on separate lines in a list. Also use periods after short phrases that are essential to the grammatical completeness of the statement introducing the list. (In the following example the three listed items are all objects of the preposition *on* in the introductory statement.)

> Please get me year-end figures *on:*   **OR**   Please get me year-end figures *on:*
>   a. Domestic sales revenues.   • Domestic sales revenues.
>   b. Total operating costs.   • Total operating costs.
>   c. Net operating income.   • Net operating income.

Continued on page 8

¶108

NOTE: Avoid the following treatment of displayed lists:

You'll profit from inquiries through:	Please get me year-end figures on:
1. Your 800 number;	• Domestic sales revenues;
2. A reader service card; and	• Total operating costs; and
3. A fax-on-demand service.	• Net operating income.

b. No periods are needed after short phrases in a list if the introductory statement is grammatically complete (as in the first example below) or if the listed items are like those on an inventory sheet or a shopping list.

The notebook computers in this price range offer the following features:

• 366-MHz Pentium II processor
• 14.1" active-matrix color display
• 128 MB of RAM

When you next order office supplies, please include these items:

Copier toner
Fax paper
File folder labels for laser printers

With Headings

108   **a.** Use a period after a *run-in* heading (one that begins a paragraph and is immediately followed by text matter on the same line) unless some other mark of punctuation, such as a question mark, is required.

> **Insuring Your Car.** Automobile insurance is actually a package of six different types of coverage. . . .

> **How Much Will It Cost?** How much automobile insurance will cost you depends on your driving record, your age, and how much shopping . . .

b. Omit the period if the heading is *freestanding* (displayed on a line by itself). However, retain a question mark or an exclamation point with a freestanding head if the wording requires it.

TAX-SAVING TECHNIQUES

Create Nontaxable Income

One of the easiest ways to reduce your tax bill is to invest in municipal bonds. Since the interest payable on these bonds is nontaxable, investing in municipals has become one of the most popular ways to avoid . . .

Is It Legal?

Investing your money so as to avoid taxes is perfectly legal. It is quite different from tax evasion, which is a deliberate attempt to . . .

NOTE: A period follows a run-in expression like *Table 6*, even though the heading as a whole is freestanding.

Table 6. SALARY RANGES   Figure 2-4. Departmental Staff Needs

c. When using a period or some other mark of punctuation after a run-in heading or a run-in expression (like those illustrated in *a* and *b* above), leave one or two spaces after the punctuation mark as needed to achieve an adequate visual break at that point. (See ¶102.)

➢ *For the treatment of headings in reports and manuscripts, see ¶1425; for the treatment of headings in tables, see ¶¶1617–1620.*

A Few Don'ts

109 Don't use a period:

a. After letters used to designate persons or things (for example, *Client A*, *Class B*, *Grade C*, *Brand X*). **EXCEPTION:** Use a period when the letter is the initial of a person's last name (for example, *Mr. A.* for *Mr. Adams*).

b. After contractions (for example, *cont'd;* see ¶505).

c. After ordinals expressed in figures *(1st, 2d, 3d, 4th).*

d. After roman numerals (for example, *Volume I, David Weild III*).

   EXCEPTION: Periods follow roman numerals in an outline. (See ¶¶223, 1725–1726.)

➤ *Periods with abbreviations: see ¶¶506–513, 515.*
Periods with brackets: see ¶296.
Periods with dashes: see ¶¶213, 214a, 215a.
Periods with parentheses: see ¶¶224c, 225a, 225c, 226c.
Periods with quotation marks: see ¶¶247, 252, 253a, 257, 258, 259.
Three spaced periods (ellipsis marks): see ¶¶274–280, 291, 299.
Spacing with periods: see ¶¶299, 1433e.

The Question Mark

To Indicate Direct Questions

110 **a.** Use a question mark at the end of a direct question. Leave one or two spaces between the question mark and the start of the next sentence. (See ¶102. For a summary of guidelines on spacing, see ¶299.)

   Will you be able to meet with us after 5 p.m.?
   Either way, how can we lose?

   NOTE: Be sure to place the question mark at the *end* of the question.

   How do you account for this entry: "Paid to E. M. Johnson, $300"?
   (**NOT:** How do you account for this entry? "Paid to E. M. Johnson, $300.")

➤ *For the punctuation of indirect questions, see ¶¶104, 115–116.*

b. Use a question mark (or, for special emphasis, an exclamation point) after a *rhetorical question*, a question to which no reply is expected.

   Who came up with the idea of replacing the term *e-mail* with *e-pistle?*
   Who wouldn't snap up an opportunity like that? (See also ¶119b.)
   Wouldn't you rather be stuck in the sands of Florida this winter than in the snowdrifts of New England?
   Isn't it incredible that people could fall for a scheme like that?
   OR: Isn't it incredible that people could fall for a scheme like that!

   NOTE: If the first clause of a compound sentence is a rhetorical question and the second clause is a statement, use a period to end the sentence.

   Why don't you look at the attached list of tasks, and then let's discuss which ones you would like to take on.

111   **a.** Use a question mark at the end of an *elliptical* (condensed) *question*, that is, a word or phrase that represents a complete question.

> Marion tells me that you are coming to the Bay Area. When? (The complete question is, "When are you coming?")

NOTE: When a single word like *how*, *when*, or *why* is woven into the flow of a sentence, capitalization and special punctuation are not usually required.

> The questions we need to address at our next board meeting are not *why* or *whether* but *how* and *when*.

  b. Punctuate complete and elliptical questions separately, according to your meaning.

> When will the job be finished? In a week or two?
> (**NOT:** When will the job be finished in a week or two?)
> Where shall we meet? At the airport? (With this punctuation, the writer allows for the possibility of meeting elsewhere.)
> Where shall we meet at the airport? (With this punctuation, the writer simply wants to pinpoint a more precise location within the airport.)

112   Use a question mark at the end of a sentence that is phrased like a statement but spoken with the rising intonation of a question.

> You expect me to believe this story?   He still intends to proceed?
> I'm correct in assuming you'll finish the job on schedule, aren't I? (The idiomatic expression *aren't I*—which uses a third person plural verb, *are,* with a first person singular pronoun, *I*—is acceptable in informal writing and speech. In formal situations use *am I not.*)

113   A request, suggestion, or command phrased as a question out of politeness may not require a question mark. (See ¶103.)

To Indicate Questions Within Sentences

114   When a short direct question falls *within a sentence*, set the question off with commas and put a question mark at the end of the sentence. However, when a short direct question falls *at the end of a sentence*, use a comma before it and a question mark after.

> I can alter the terms of my will, *can't I,* whenever I wish?
> We aren't obligated to attend the meeting, *are we?*

NOTE: Short questions falling within a sentence may also be set off with dashes or parentheses in place of commas. (See ¶¶214b, 224d.)

115   When a longer direct question comes *at the end of a sentence*, it starts with a capital letter and is preceded by a comma or a colon. The question mark that ends the question also serves to mark the end of the sentence.

NOTE: In the following examples and in ¶116, notice how a simple shift in word order converts a direct question to an indirect question. When the verb precedes the subject *(shall we, can we),* the question is *direct.* When the verb follows the subject *(we shall, we can),* the question is *indirect.*

> The key question is, Whom *shall we* nominate for next year's election?
> This is the key question: Whom *shall we* nominate for next year's election? (Use a colon if the introductory material is an independent clause.)
> **BUT:** We now come to the key question of whom *we shall* nominate for next year's election. (An indirect question requires no special punctuation or capitalization.)
> **OR:** We now come to the key question of whom to nominate for next year's election.

116 When a longer direct question comes *at the beginning of a sentence*, it is followed by a question mark (for emphasis) or simply a comma.

> How *can we* achieve these goals? is the next question. (Leave one space after a question mark within a sentence.)
>
> **OR:** How *can we* achieve these goals, is the next question.
>
> **BUT:** How *we can* achieve these goals is the next question. (Indirect question; no special punctuation is needed. See ¶115, note.)

117 **a.** A series of brief questions at the end of a sentence may be separated by commas or (for emphasis) by question marks. Do not capitalize the individual questions.

> Who will be responsible for drafting the proposal, obtaining comments from all the interested parties, preparing the final version, and coordinating the distribution of copies? (As punctuated, this sentence implies that one person may be asked to perform all these tasks.)
>
> **OR:** Who will be responsible for drafting the proposal? obtaining comments from all the interested parties? preparing the final version? coordinating the distribution of copies? (As punctuated, this sentence implies that different people may be asked to perform each of these tasks.)

NOTE: Leave one space after a question mark within a sentence and one or two spaces after a question mark at the end of a sentence. (See ¶102. For complete guidelines on spacing, see ¶299.)

b. The brief questions in *a* above are all related to the same subject and predicate *(Who will be responsible for)*. Do not confuse this type of sentence pattern with a series of independent questions. Each independent question starts with a capital letter and ends with a question mark.

> Before you accept the job offer, think about the following: Will this job give you experience relevant to your real career goal? Will it permit you to keep abreast of the latest technology? Will it pay what you need?

NOTE: Leave one or two spaces after a question mark that marks the end of an independent question. (See ¶102. For complete guidelines on spacing, see ¶299.)

c. Independent questions in a series are often elliptical expressions. (See ¶111.)

> Has Walter's loan been approved? *When? By whom? For what amount?* (In other words: *When* was the loan approved? *By whom* was the loan approved? *For what amount* was the loan approved?)
>
> (**NOT:** Has Walter's loan been approved, when, by whom, and for what amount?)

To Express Doubt

118 A question mark enclosed in parentheses may be used to express doubt or uncertainty about a word or phrase within a sentence. Do not insert any space before the opening parenthesis; leave one space after the closing parenthesis unless another mark of punctuation is required at that point.

> He joined the firm after his graduation from Columbia Law School in 1999(?).

NOTE: When dates are already enclosed within parentheses, question marks may be inserted as necessary to indicate doubt.

> the explorer Verrazano (1485?-1528?)

➤ *Question marks with dashes: see ¶¶214b, 215a.*
Question marks with parentheses: see ¶¶224d, 225a, 225d, 226c.
Question marks with quotation marks: see ¶¶249, 252, 254, 257–259, 261.
Spacing with question marks: see ¶¶299, 1433e.

¶119

The Exclamation Point

The exclamation point is an emotional mark of punctuation that is most often found in sales and advertising copy. Like the word *very*, it loses its force when overused, so avoid using it wherever possible.

To Express Strong Feeling

119 **a.** Use an exclamation point at the end of a sentence (or an elliptical expression that stands for a sentence) to indicate enthusiasm, surprise, disbelief, urgency, or strong feeling. Leave one or two spaces between the exclamation point and the start of the next sentence. (See ¶102. For complete guidelines on spacing, see ¶299.)

> Yes! We're selling our entire inventory below cost! Doors open at 9 a.m.!
> No! I don't believe it!   Hang in there!   Incredible!   Yesss!

b. An exclamation point may be used in place of a question mark to express strong feeling. (See also ¶110b.)

> How could you do it! What made you think I'd welcome a call at 2:30 a.m.!

c. The exclamation point may be enclosed in parentheses and placed directly after a word that the writer wants to emphasize. Do not insert any space before the opening parenthesis, and leave one space after the closing parenthesis unless another mark of punctuation is required at that point.

> We won exclusive(!) distribution rights in the Western Hemisphere.

120 **a.** A single word may be followed by an exclamation point to express intense feeling. The sentence that follows it is punctuated as usual.

> Congratulations! Your summation at the trial was superb.

b. When a word is repeated for emphasis, an exclamation point should follow each repetition.

> Going! Going! Our bargains are almost gone!

c. When exclamations are mild, a comma or a period is sufficient.

> Well, well, things could be worse.
> No. I won't accept those conditions.

With *Oh* and *O*

121 The exclamation *oh* may be followed by either an exclamation point or a comma, depending on the emphasis desired. It is capitalized only when it starts a sentence. The capital *O*, the sign of direct address, is not usually followed by any punctuation.

> Oh! I didn't expect that!
> Oh, what's the use?
> O Lord, help me!
> O America, where are you headed?

> ➤ *Exclamation point with dashes: see ¶¶214b, 215a.*
> *Exclamation point with parentheses: see ¶¶224d, 225a, 225d, 226c.*
> *Exclamation point with quotation marks: see ¶¶249, 252, 254, 257–259, 261.*
> *Spacing with exclamation points: see ¶¶299, 1433e.*

The Comma

The comma has two primary functions: it *sets off* nonessential expressions that interrupt the flow of thought from subject to verb to object or complement, and it *separates* elements within a sentence to clarify their relationship to one another. Two commas are typically needed to set off, but only a single comma is needed to separate.

The following paragraphs (¶¶122–125) present an overview of the rules governing the use of the comma. For a more detailed treatment of the specific rules, see ¶¶126–175.

Basic Rules for Commas That Set Off

122 Use commas to set off *nonessential expressions*—words, phrases, and clauses that are not necessary for the meaning or the structural completeness of the sentence.

> **IMPORTANT NOTE:** In many sentences you can tell whether an expression is nonessential or essential by trying to omit the expression. If you can leave it out without affecting the meaning or the structural completeness of the sentence, the expression is nonessential and should be set off by commas.
>
> > **NONESSENTIAL:** Let's get the advice of Harry Stern, *who has in-depth experience with all types of personal computers.* (When a specific person is named, the *who* clause provides welcome but nonessential information.)
> >
> > **ESSENTIAL:** Let's get the advice of someone *who has in-depth experience with all types of personal computers.* (Without the *who* clause, the meaning of the sentence would be incomplete.)
> >
> > **NONESSENTIAL:** There is, *no doubt,* a reasonable explanation for his behavior at the board meeting.
> >
> > **ESSENTIAL:** There is *no doubt* about her honesty. (Without *no doubt,* the structure of the sentence would be incomplete.)
>
> However, in other sentences the only way you can tell whether an expression is nonessential or essential is by the way you would say it aloud. If your voice tends to *drop* as you utter the expression, it is nonessential; if your voice tends to *rise*, the expression is essential.
>
> > **NONESSENTIAL:** Finch and Helwig would prefer, *therefore,* to limit the term of the agreement to two years.
> >
> > **ESSENTIAL:** Finch and Helwig would *therefore* prefer to limit the term of the agreement to two years.
>
> ➤ *For additional examples, see ¶141, note.*
>
> **a. Interrupting Elements.** Use commas to set off words, phrases, and clauses when they break the flow of a sentence from subject to verb to object or complement. (See also ¶¶144–147.)
>
> > We can deliver the car on the day of your husband's birthday or, *if you wish,* on the Saturday before then. (When this sentence is read aloud, notice how the voice drops on the nonessential expression *if you wish.*)
> >
> > They have sufficient assets, *don't they,* to cover these losses?
> >
> > Let's take advantage of the special price and order, *say,* 200 reams this quarter instead of our usual quantity of 75.
> >
> > Mary Cabrera, *rather than George Spengler,* has been appointed head of the New Albany office.
> >
> > **BUT:** Mary Cabrera has been appointed head of the New Albany office *rather than George Spengler.* (The phrase is not set off when it does not interrupt.)

Continued on page 14

¶123

b. Afterthoughts. Use commas to set off words, phrases, or clauses loosely added onto the end of a sentence. (See also ¶144.)

> Send us your check as soon as you can, *please*.
> Grant promised to share expenses with us, *if I remember correctly*.
> It is not too late to place an order, *is it?*

c. Transitional Expressions and Independent Comments. Use commas to set off transitional expressions (like *however*, *therefore*, *on the other hand*) and independent comments (like *obviously*, *in my opinion*, *of course*) when they interrupt the flow of the sentence. Do not set these elements off, however, when they are used to emphasize the meaning; the voice goes up in such cases. In the examples that follow, consider how the voice drops when the expression is nonessential and how it rises when the expression is essential. (See also ¶¶138–143.)

> **NONESSENTIAL:** We are determined, *nevertheless,* to finish on schedule.
> **ESSENTIAL:** We are *nevertheless* determined to finish on schedule.
>
> **NONESSENTIAL:** It is, *of course,* your prerogative to change your mind. (Here the voice rises on *is* and drops on *of course*.)
> **ESSENTIAL:** It is *of course* your prerogative to change your mind. (Here the voice rises on *of course*.)

d. Descriptive Expressions. When descriptive expressions *follow* the words they refer to and provide additional but nonessential information, use commas to set them off. (See also ¶¶148–153.)

> **NONESSENTIAL:** His most recent article, *"How to Make a Profit With High-Tech Investments,"* appeared in the June 1 issue of *Forbes*. (*His most recent* indicates which article is meant; the title gives additional but nonessential information.)
> **ESSENTIAL:** The article *"How to Make a Profit With High-Tech Investments"* appeared in the June 1 issue of *Forbes*. (Here the title is needed to indicate which article is meant.)
>
> **NONESSENTIAL:** Thank you for your letter of April 12, *in which you questioned our discount terms*. (The date indicates which letter; the *in which* clause gives additional information. See also ¶152.)
> **ESSENTIAL:** Thank you for your letter *in which you questioned our discount terms*. (Here the *in which* clause is needed to indicate which letter is meant.)

e. Dates. Use commas to set off the year in complete dates (for example, Sunday, June 1, *2003*, . . .). (See also ¶¶154–155.)

f. Names. Use commas to set off abbreviations that follow a person's name (Julie Merkin, *Ph.D.*, announces the opening . . .) and to set off names of states or countries following city names (Rye, *New York*, will host . . .). In personal names and company names, the trend is not to set off elements like *Jr., Sr., III, Inc.,* or *Ltd.* (for example, *Guy Tracy Jr.* and *Redd Inc.*); however, individual preferences should be respected when known. (See also ¶¶156–160.)

Basic Rules for Commas That Separate

123 Use a single comma:

a. To separate the two main clauses in a compound sentence when they are joined by *and, but, or,* or *nor.* (See also ¶¶126–129.)

> We can't accept the marketing restrictions you proposed, *but* we think there is some basis for a mutually acceptable understanding.

b. To separate three or more items in a series—unless all the items are joined by *and* or *or*. (See also ¶¶162–167.)

> It takes time, effort, *and* a good deal of money.
> **BUT:** It takes time *and* effort *and* a good deal of money.

c. To separate two or more adjectives that modify the same noun. (See also ¶¶168–171.)

> We need to mount an *exciting, hard-hitting* ad campaign.

d. To separate the digits of numbers into groups of thousands.

> Sales projections for the Southern Region next year range between $900,000 and $1,000,000.

NOTE: The comma is now commonly omitted in four-digit whole numbers (*1000* through *9999*) except in columns with larger numbers that require commas. (See also ¶461.)

e. To indicate the omission of key words or to clarify meaning when the word order is unusual. (See also ¶¶172–175.)

> Half the purchase price is due on delivery of the goods; the balance, in three months. (The comma here signifies the omission of *is due.*)
> What will happen, we don't know. (The comma here helps the reader cope with the unusual word order; it separates the object, *What will happen,* from the subject, *we,* which follows.)

124 Use a single comma after *introductory elements*—items that begin a sentence and come before the subject and verb of the main clause.

> *Yes,* we can. *Well,* that depends. (Introductory words.)
> *Taking all the arguments into consideration,* we have decided to modernize these facilities rather than close them down. (Introductory participial phrase.)
> *To determine the proper mix of ingredients for a particular situation,* see the table on page 141. (Introductory infinitive phrase.)
> *Before we can make a final decision,* we will need to run another cost-profit analysis. (Introductory dependent clause.)

a. Use a comma after an *introductory request* or *command*.

> *Look,* we've been through tougher situations before.
> *You see,* the previous campaigns never did pan out.
> *Please remember,* all expense reports must be on my desk by Friday.
> **BUT:** *Please remember that* all . . . (When *that* is added, *please remember* becomes the main verb and is no longer an introductory element.)

b. Commas are not needed after *ordinary introductory adverbs* or *short introductory phrases* that answer such questions as:

WHEN:	tomorrow, yesterday, recently, early next week, in the morning, soon, in five years, in 2004
HOW OFTEN:	occasionally, often, frequently, once in a while
WHERE:	here, in this case, at the meeting
WHY:	for that reason, because of this situation

However, commas are used after introductory adverbs and phrases:

(1) When they function as *transitional expressions* (such as *well, therefore, however, for example, in the first place*), which provide a transition in meaning from the previous sentence.

Continued on page 16

¶125

(2) When they function as *independent comments* (such as *in my opinion*, *by all means*, *obviously*, *of course*), which express the writer's attitude toward the meaning of the sentence. (See also ¶¶138–143.)

In the morning things may look better. (Short prepositional phrase telling *when;* no comma needed.)

In the first place, they don't have sufficient capital. (Transitional expression; followed by comma.)

In my opinion, we ought to look for another candidate. (Independent comment; followed by comma.)

Recently we had a request for school enrollment trends. (Introductory adverb telling *when;* no comma needed.)

Consequently, we will have to cancel the agreement. (Transitional expression; followed by comma.)

Obviously, the request will have to be denied. (Independent comment; followed by comma.)

NOTE: Many writers use commas after *all* introductory elements to avoid having to analyze each situation.

125 Separating commas are often improperly used in sentences. In the following examples the diagonal marks indicate points at which single commas *should not* be used.

a. Do not separate a subject and its verb.

The person she plans to hire for the job/ is Peter Crotty.

BUT: The person she plans to hire for the job, *I believe,* is Peter Crotty. (Use *two* commas to set off an interrupting expression.)

Whether profits can be improved this year/ depends on several key variables. (Noun clause as subject.)

BUT: *Anyone who contributes, contributes* to a most worthy cause. (In special cases like this, a comma may be required for clarity. See also ¶175b.)

b. Do not separate a verb and its object or complement.

The test mailing *has not produced/ the results* we were hoping for. (Verb and object.)

Mrs. Paterra *will be/ the company's new director of marketing.* (Verb and complement.)

The equipment *is/ easy to operate, inexpensive to maintain, and built to give reliable service for many years.* (Verb and complement.)

Rebecca Hingham *said/ that the research data would be on your desk by Monday morning.* (Noun clause as object.)

BUT: Rebecca Hingham *said,* "The research data will be on your desk by Monday morning." (A comma ordinarily follows a verb when the object is a direct quotation. See also ¶256.)

The question we really need to address is, *Do we have a better solution to propose?* (A comma also follows a verb when the object or complement is a direct question. See also ¶115.)

c. Do not separate an adjective from a noun that follows it.

The project requires a highly motivated, research-oriented, *cost-conscious/ manager.*

d. Do not separate a noun and a prepositional phrase that follows.

The board of directors/ of the Fastex Corporation will announce its decision this Friday.

BUT: The board of directors, *of necessity,* must turn down the merger at this time. (Use *two* commas to set off an interrupting expression.)

e. Do not separate a coordinating conjunction *(and, but, or,* or *nor)* and the following word.

You can read the draft of the division's medium-range plan now *or/ when* you get home tonight.

BUT: You can read the draft of the division's medium-range plan now or, *if you prefer,* when you get home tonight. (Use *two* commas to set off an interrupting expression.)

¶**127**

f. Do not separate *two* words or phrases that are joined by a coordinating conjunction.

> *These letters/* and *those from Mr. Day* should be shown to Ann Poe. (Two subjects.)
>
> I *have read Ms. Berkowitz's proposal/* and *find it well done.* (Two predicates. See also ¶127.)
>
> We hope *that you will visit our store soon/* and *that you will find the styles you like.* (Two noun clauses serving as objects of the verb *hope.*)
>
> The CEO plans *to visit the Western Region/* and *call personally on the large accounts that have stopped doing business with us.* (Two infinitive phrases serving as objects of the verb *plans.*)
>
> He may go on to graduate school at *Stanford/* or *Harvard.* (Two objects of the preposition *at.*)
>
> **BUT:** *Frank Albano will handle the tickets,* and *Edna Hoehn will be responsible for publicity.* (A comma separates two independent clauses joined by a coordinating conjunction. See ¶126.)

The following rules (¶¶126–137) deal with the punctuation of clauses and phrases in sentences.

With Clauses in Compound Sentences

126 **a.** When a compound sentence consists of *two* independent clauses joined by a coordinating conjunction *(and, but, or, or nor),* place a separating comma before the conjunction. (See ¶129.)

> Mrs. Fenster noticed a small discrepancy in the figures, *and* on that basis she decided to re-analyze the data.
>
> **BUT:** Mrs. Fenster noticed a small discrepancy in the figures *and* on that basis decided to re-analyze the data. (See ¶127a–b.)
>
> Show this proposal to Mr. Florio, *and* ask him for his reaction. (See ¶127c.)
>
> Either we step up our promotion efforts, *or* we must be content with our share of the market.
>
> Not only were we the developers of this process, *but* we were the first to apply it successfully.

b. For special effect, the comma before the coordinating conjunction can be replaced by a period, a question mark, or an exclamation point. The coordinating conjunction is then capitalized, and the second independent clause is treated as a separate sentence. However, this treatment, if overused, can lose its effectiveness very quickly. (See page 284 for a usage note on *and.*)

> Is it self-confidence that makes you successful? Or is it success that makes you self-confident?
>
> I told Callahan that we would not reorder unless he cut his prices by 20 percent. And he did.

NOTE: Do not insert a comma directly after the coordinating conjunction unless a parenthetical element begins at that point.

> I told Callahan that we would not reorder unless he cut his prices by 20 percent. And, to my total amazement, he did.

c. When a compound sentence consists of *three* or more independent clauses, punctuate this series like any other series. (See also ¶162.)

> Bob can deal with the caterer, Nora can handle publicity, and I can take care of the rest.

127 Do not confuse a *compound sentence* with a simple sentence containing a *compound predicate.*

a. A *compound sentence* contains at least two independent clauses, and each clause contains a subject and a predicate.

> *Barbara just got her master's,* and *she is now looking for a job in sales.*

b. A sentence may contain one subject with a *compound predicate,* that is, two predicates connected by a coordinating conjunction. In such sentences no comma separates the two predicates.

Continued on page 18

¶128

Barbara *just got her master's* and *is now looking for a job in sales.* (When *she* is omitted from the previous example, the sentence becomes a simple sentence with a compound predicate.)

Ogleby not only *wants a higher discount* but also *demands faster turnarounds on his orders.* (Compound predicate; no comma before *but.*)

BUT: *Ogleby not only wants a higher discount,* but *he also demands faster turnarounds on his orders.* (Compound sentence; comma before *but.*)

c. When one or both verbs are in the imperative and the subject is not expressed, treat the sentence as a compound sentence and use a comma between the clauses.

Please look at the brochure I have enclosed, and then *get* back to me if you have additional questions.

You may not be able to get away right now, but *do plan* to stay with us whenever you find the time.

Call Ellen Chen sometime next week, and *ask* her whether she will speak at our conference next fall.

BUT: *Call* Ellen Chen and *ask* her whether she will speak at our conference next fall. (Omit the comma if either clause is short. See ¶129.)

d. When nonessential elements precede the second part of a *compound predicate*, they are treated as interrupting expressions and are set off by two commas. When these same expressions precede the second clause of a *compound sentence*, they are treated as introductory expressions and are followed by one comma.

We can bill you on our customary terms or, *if you prefer,* can offer you our new deferred payment plan. (Interrupting expression requires two commas.)

We can bill you on our customary terms, or *if you prefer,* we can offer you our new deferred payment plan. (Introductory expression requires one comma.)

Frank Bruchman went into the boardroom and, *without consulting his notes,* proceeded to give the directors precise details about our financial situation. (Interrupting expression.)

Frank Bruchman went into the boardroom, and *without consulting his notes,* he proceeded to give the directors precise details about our financial situation. (Introductory expression.)

➤ *See also ¶¶131c, 136a, 142.*

128 Do not use a comma between two independent clauses that are not joined by a coordinating conjunction *(and, but, or, or nor).* This error of punctuation is known as a *comma splice* and produces a *run-on sentence.* Use a semicolon, a colon, or a dash (whichever is appropriate), or start a new sentence. (See ¶¶176, 187, 204–205.)

WRONG: Please review these spreadsheets quickly, I need them back tomorrow.

RIGHT: Please review these spreadsheets quickly; I need them back tomorrow.

OR: Please review these spreadsheets quickly. I need them back tomorrow.

129 If either clause of a compound sentence is short, the comma may be omitted before the conjunction.

Their prices are low and their service is efficient.

Please initial these forms and return them by Monday.

Consider leasing and see whether it costs less in the long run than buying.

Consider whether leasing costs more than buying and then decide.

NOTE: Make sure that the omission of a comma does not lead to confusion.

CLEAR: Please don't litter, and recycle whenever possible.

CONFUSING: Please don't litter and recycle whenever possible. (Without a comma after *litter,* the sentence could seem to be saying, " . . . and please don't recycle whenever possible.")

¶**130**

With Clauses in Complex Sentences

A complex sentence contains one independent clause and one or more dependent clauses. *After*, *although*, *as*, *because*, *before*, *if*, *since*, *unless*, *when*, and *while* are among the words most frequently used to introduce dependent clauses. (See ¶132 for a longer list.)

130 **Introductory Dependent Clauses**

a. When a dependent clause precedes the independent clause, separate the clauses with a comma.

> *Before we can make a decision,* we must have all the facts.
>
> *When you read the Weissberg study,* look at Appendix 2 first.
>
> *If they had invested more carefully,* they could have avoided bankruptcy.
>
> *After we have studied all aspects of the complaint,* we will make a recommendation.
>
> **BUT:** *Only after we have studied all aspects of the complaint* will we make a recommendation. (No comma follows the introductory clause when the word order in the main clause is abnormal. Compare the abnormal *will we make* here with the normal *we will make* in the preceding example.)

b. Be sure you can recognize an introductory dependent clause, even if some of the essential words are omitted from the clause. (Such constructions are known as *elliptical clauses.*)

> *Whenever possible,* he leaves his office by six. (Whenever *it is* possible, . . .)
>
> *If so,* I will call you tomorrow. (If *that is* so, . . .)
>
> *Should you be late,* just call to let me know. (*If* you should be late, . . .)

c. Do not use a comma after an introductory clause when it serves as the *subject* of a sentence.

> *Whomever you nominate* will have my support. (Introductory clause as subject.)
>
> **BUT:** *Whomever you nominate,* I will support. (Introductory clause as object.)
>
> *That the department must be reorganized* is no longer questioned. (Introductory clause as subject.)
>
> **BUT:** *That the department must be reorganized,* I no longer question. (Introductory clause as object.)
>
> *Whatever Helen decides to do* is no concern of mine. (Introductory clause as subject.)
>
> **BUT:** *Whatever Helen decides to do,* she needs some professional advice. (Introductory clause as adverb.)

d. Sentences like those shown in *a–c* are often introduced by an expression such as *he said that*, *she believes that*, or *they know that*. In such cases use the same punctuation as prescribed in *a–c*.

> Liz believes that *before we can make a decision,* we must have all the facts. (A separating comma follows the dependent clause, just as if the sentence began with the word *Before*. No comma precedes the dependent clause because it is considered introductory, not interrupting.)
>
> I think that *when you read the Weissberg study,* you will gain a new perspective on the situation.
>
> Harry says that *whenever possible,* he leaves his office by six.
>
> Everyone knows that *whomever you nominate* will have my support in the next election.
>
> **BUT:** He said that, *as you may already know,* he was planning to take early retirement. (Two commas are needed to set off an interrupting dependent clause. See also ¶131c.)

¶131

131 **Dependent Clauses Elsewhere in the Sentence**

When a dependent clause *follows* the main clause or *falls within* the main clause, commas are used or omitted depending on whether the dependent clause is essential (restrictive) or nonessential (nonrestrictive).

a. An *essential* clause is necessary to the meaning of the sentence. Because it *cannot be omitted*, it should not be set off by commas.

> The person *who used to be Englund's operations manager* is now doing the same job for Jenniman Brothers. (Tells which person.)
>
> The Pennington bid arrived *after we had made our decision.* (Tells when.)
>
> Damato's suggestion *that we submit the issue to arbitration* may be the only sensible alternative. (Tells which of Damato's suggestions is meant.)
>
> Mrs. Foy said *that she would send us an advance program.* (Tells what was said.)

Compare these examples with those in *b* below.

b. A *nonessential* clause provides additional descriptive or explanatory detail. Because it *can be omitted* without changing the meaning of the sentence, it should be set off by commas.

> George Pedersen, *who used to be Englund's operations manager,* is now doing the same job for Jenniman Brothers. (The name indicates which person; the *who* clause simply gives additional information.)
>
> The Pennington bid arrived on Tuesday, *after we had made our decision.* (*Tuesday* tells when; the *after* clause simply adds information.)
>
> Damato's latest suggestion, *that we submit the issue to arbitration,* may be the only sensible alternative. (*Latest* tells which suggestion is meant; the *that* clause is not essential.)

c. A dependent clause occurring within a sentence must always be set off by commas when it *interrupts* the flow of the sentence.

> We can review the wording of the announcement over lunch or, *if your time is short,* over the phone.
>
> Please tell us when you plan to be in town and, *if possible,* where you will be staying. (The complete dependent clause is *if it is possible.*)
>
> Senator Hemphill, *when offered the chance to refute his opponent's charges,* said he would respond at a time of his own choosing.
>
> Ann Kourakis is the type of person who, *when you need help badly,* will be the first to volunteer.
>
> If, *when you have weighed the alternatives,* you choose one of the models that cost over $500, we can arrange special credit terms for you.
>
> **BUT:** He said that *if we choose one of the models that cost over $500,* his firm can arrange special credit terms for us. (See ¶130d for dependent clauses following *he said that, she knows that,* and similar expressions.)

132 The following list presents the words and phrases most commonly used to introduce dependent clauses. For most of these expressions two sentences are given: one containing an essential clause and one a nonessential clause. In a few cases only one type of clause is possible. If you cannot decide whether a clause is essential or nonessential (and therefore whether commas are required or not), compare it with the related sentences that follow.

> **After.** **ESSENTIAL:** His faxed response came *after you left last evening.* (Tells when.)
>
> **NONESSENTIAL:** His faxed response came this morning, *after the decision had been made.* (The phrase *this morning* clearly tells when; the *after* clause provides additional but nonessential information.)

All of which. ALWAYS NONESSENTIAL: The rumors, *all of which were unfounded,* brought about his defeat in the last election.

Although, even though, and **though. ALWAYS NONESSENTIAL:** She has typed her letter of resignation, *although I do not believe she will submit it.*

As. ESSENTIAL: The results of the mailing are *as you predicted they would be.*

> **NONESSENTIAL:** The results of the mailing are disappointing, *as you predicted they would be.* (See page 285 for a usage note on *as.*)

As . . . as. ALWAYS ESSENTIAL: He talked *as* persuasively at the meeting *as* he did over the telephone. (See page 285 for a usage note on *as . . . as.*)

As if and **as though. ESSENTIAL:** She drove *as if* (or *as though*) *the road were a minefield.* (The *as if* clause tells how she drove.)

> **NONESSENTIAL:** She drove cautiously, *as if* (or *as though*) *the road were a minefield.* (The adverb *cautiously* tells how she drove; the *as if* clause provides additional but nonessential information.)

As soon as. ESSENTIAL: We will fill your order *as soon as we receive new stock.*

> **NONESSENTIAL:** We will fill your order next week, *as soon as we receive new stock.*

At, by, for, in, and **to which. ESSENTIAL:** I went to the floor *to which I had been directed.*

> **NONESSENTIAL:** I went to the tenth floor, *to which I had been directed.*

Because. *Essential or nonessential,* depending on closeness of relation.

> **ESSENTIAL:** She left *because she had another appointment.* (Here the reason expressed by the *because* clause is essential to complete the meaning.)

> **NONESSENTIAL:** I need to have two copies of the final report by 5:30 tomorrow, *because I am leaving for Chicago on a 7:30 flight.* (Here the meaning of the main clause is complete; the reason expressed in the *because* clause offers additional but nonessential information.)

> **NOTE:** See how the use or omission of a comma in the following sentences affects the meaning: I'm not taking that course of action, *because I distrust Harry's recommendations.* **BUT:** I'm not taking that course of action *because I distrust Harry's recommendations.* (I based my decision on another reason altogether.)

Before. ESSENTIAL: The shipment was sent *before your letter was received.*

> **NONESSENTIAL:** The shipment was sent on Tuesday, *before your letter was received.* (*Tuesday* tells when the shipment was sent; the *before* clause provides additional but nonessential information.)

Even though. See *Although.*

For. ALWAYS NONESSENTIAL: Jim needs to raise money quickly, *for his tuition bill has to be paid by next Friday.* (A comma should always precede *for* as a conjunction to prevent misreading *for* as a preposition.)

If. ESSENTIAL: Let us hear from you *if you are interested.*

> **NONESSENTIAL:** She promised to write from Toronto, *if I remember correctly.* (Clause added loosely.)

In order that. *Essential or nonessential,* depending on closeness of relation.

> **ESSENTIAL:** Please notify your instructor *in order that a makeup examination may be scheduled.*

> **NONESSENTIAL:** Please notify your instructor if you will be unable to attend the examination on Friday, *in order that a makeup examination may be scheduled.*

No matter what (why, how, etc.). ALWAYS NONESSENTIAL: The order cannot be ready by Monday, *no matter what the store manager says.*

Continued on page 22

¶132

None of which. ALWAYS NONESSENTIAL: We received five boxes of samples, *none of which are in good condition.*

None of whom. ALWAYS NONESSENTIAL: We have interviewed ten applicants, *none of whom were satisfactory.*

Not so . . . as. ALWAYS ESSENTIAL: The second copy was *not so* clear *as* the first one. (See page 285 for a usage note on *as . . . as—not so . . . as.*)

Since. ESSENTIAL: We have taken no applications *since we received your memo.*

NONESSENTIAL: We are taking no more applications, *since our lists are now closed.* (Clause of reason.)

So that. *Essential or nonessential,* depending on closeness of relation.

ESSENTIAL: Examine all shipments *so that any damage may be detected promptly.*

NONESSENTIAL: Examine all shipments as soon as they arrive, *so that any damage may be detected promptly.*

So . . . that. ALWAYS ESSENTIAL: The costs ran *so* high *that we could not make a profit.*

Some of whom. ALWAYS NONESSENTIAL: The agency has sent us five applicants, *some of whom seem promising.*

Than. ALWAYS ESSENTIAL: The employees seem to be more disturbed by the rumor *than they care to admit.*

That. When used as a relative pronoun, *that* refers to things; it also refers to persons when a class or type is meant.

ALWAYS ESSENTIAL: Here is a picture of the plane *that I own.* She is the candidate *that I prefer.* (See also ¶1062.)

When used as a subordinating conjunction, *that* links the dependent clause it introduces with the main clause.

ALWAYS ESSENTIAL: We know *that we will have to make cuts in the budget.* (See page 306 for a usage note on *that.*)

Though. See *Although.*

Unless. ESSENTIAL: This product line will be discontinued *unless customers begin to show an interest in it.*

NONESSENTIAL: I plan to work on the Aspen proposal all through the weekend, *unless Cindy comes into town.* (Clause added loosely as an afterthought.)

Until. ALWAYS ESSENTIAL: I will continue to work *until my children are out of school.*

When. ESSENTIAL: The changeover will be made *when Mr. Ruiz returns from his vacation.*

NONESSENTIAL: The changeover will be made next Monday, *when Mr. Ruiz returns from his vacation.* (*Monday* tells when; the *when* clause provides additional but nonessential information.)

Where. ESSENTIAL: I plan to visit the town *where I used to live.*

NONESSENTIAL: I plan to stop off in Detroit, *where I used to live.*

Whereas. ALWAYS NONESSENTIAL: The figures for last year cover urban areas only, *whereas those for this year include rural areas as well.* (Clause of contrast.)

Which. Use *which* (rather than *who*) when referring to animals, things, and ideas. Always use *which* (instead of *that*) to introduce nonessential clauses.

The revised report, *which was done by Mark,* is very impressive.

NOTE: *Which* may also be used to introduce essential clauses. (See ¶1062b, note.)

While. **ESSENTIAL:** The union has decided not to strike *while negotiations are still going on.* (Here *while* means "during the time that.")

> **NONESSENTIAL:** The workers at the Apex Company have struck, *while those at the Powers Company are still at work.* (Here *while* means "whereas.")

Who. **ESSENTIAL:** All students *who are members of the Backpackers Club* will be leaving for Maine on Friday.

> **NONESSENTIAL:** John Behnke, *who is a member of the Backpackers Club,* will be leading a group on a weekend trip to Maine.

Whom. **ESSENTIAL:** This package is for the friend *whom I am visiting.*

> **NONESSENTIAL:** This package is for my cousin Amy, *whom I am visiting.*

Whose. **ESSENTIAL:** The prize was awarded to the employee *whose suggestion yielded the greatest cost savings.*

> **NONESSENTIAL:** The prize was awarded to Joyce Bruno, *whose suggestion yielded the greatest cost savings.*

With Clauses in Compound-Complex Sentences

133 A compound-complex sentence typically consists of two independent clauses (joined by *and, but, or,* or *nor*) and one or more dependent clauses. To punctuate a sentence of this kind, first place a separating comma before the conjunction that joins the two main parts. Then consider each half of the sentence alone and provide additional punctuation as necessary.

> The computer terminals were not delivered until June 12, five weeks after the promised delivery date, and *when I wrote to complain to your sales manager,* it took another three weeks simply for him to acknowledge my letter. (No comma precedes *when* because the *when* clause is considered an introductory expression, not an interrupting expression. See ¶127d.)
>
> Jeff Adler, the CEO of Marshfield & Duxbury, is eager to discuss a joint venture with my boss, *who is off on a six-week trip to the Far East,* but the earliest date I see open for such a meeting is Wednesday, October 20.

NOTE: If a misreading is likely or a stronger break is desired, use a semicolon rather than a comma to separate the two main clauses. (See ¶177.)

134 When a sentence starts with a dependent clause that applies to both independent clauses that follow, do not use a comma to separate the independent clauses. (A comma would make the introductory dependent clause seem to apply only to the first independent clause.)

> Before you start to look for venture capital, you need to prepare an analysis of the market *and* you must make a detailed set of financial projections. (The *before* clause applies equally to the two independent clauses that follow; hence no comma before *and.*)
>
> **BUT:** Before you start to look for venture capital, you need to prepare an analysis of the market, *but* don't think that's all there is to it. (The *before* clause applies only to the first independent clause; hence a comma is used before *but.*)

With Participial, Infinitive, and Prepositional Phrases

135 Introductory Phrases

a. Use a comma after an *introductory participial phrase.*

> *Seizing the opportunity,* I presented an overview of our medium-range plans.
> *Established in 1905,* our company takes great pride in its reputation for high-quality products.
> *Having checked the statements myself,* I feel confident that they are accurate.

Continued on page 24

¶135

NOTE: Watch out for phrases that look like introductory participial phrases but actually serve as the subject of the sentence or part of the predicate. Do not put a comma after these elements.

Looking for examples of good acknowledgment letters in our files has taken me longer than I had hoped. (Gerund phrase as subject.)

BUT: *Looking for examples of good acknowledgment letters in our files,* I found four that you can use. (Participial phrase used as an introductory element; the subject is *I.*)

Following Mrs. Fahnstock's speech was a presentation by Ms. Paley. (With normal word order, the sentence would read, "A presentation by Ms. Paley was *following Mrs. Fahnstock's speech.*" The introductory phrase is part of the predicate; the subject is *a presentation by Ms. Paley.*)

BUT: *Following Mrs. Fahnstock's speech,* Ms. Paley made her presentation. (Participial phrase used as an introductory element; the subject is *Ms. Paley.*)

b. Use a comma after an *introductory infinitive phrase* unless the phrase is the subject of the sentence. (Infinitive phrases are introduced by *to*.)

To get the best results from your dishwasher, follow the printed directions. (The subject *you* is understood.)

To have displayed the goods more effectively, he should have consulted a lighting specialist. (The subject is *he.*)

BUT: *To have displayed the goods more effectively* would have required a lighting specialist. (Infinitive phrase used as subject.)

c. As a general rule, use a comma after all *introductory prepositional phrases*. A comma may be omitted after a short prepositional phrase if (1) the phrase does not contain a verb form, (2) the phrase is not a transitional expression or an independent comment, or (3) there is no sacrifice in clarity or desired emphasis. (Many writers use a comma after all introductory prepositional phrases to avoid analyzing each situation.)

In response to the many requests of our customers, we are opening a branch in Kenmore Square. (Comma required after a long phrase.)

In 1999 our entire inventory was destroyed by fire. (No comma required after a short phrase.)

BUT: *In 1999,* 384 cases of pneumonia were reported. (Comma required to separate two numbers. See ¶456.)

In preparing your report, be sure to include last year's figures. (Comma required after a short phrase containing a verb form.)

In addition, a 6 percent city sales tax must be imposed. (Comma required after a short phrase used as a transitional expression. See ¶¶138a, 139.)

In my opinion, your ads are misleading as they now appear. (Comma required after a short phrase used as an independent comment. See ¶¶138b, 139.)

In legal documents, amounts of money are often expressed both in words and in figures. (Comma used to give desired emphasis to the introductory phrase.)

CONFUSING: After all you have gone through a great deal.

CLEAR: *After all,* you have gone through a great deal. (Comma required after a short phrase to prevent misreading.)

NOTE: Omit the comma after an introductory prepositional phrase if the word order in the rest of the sentence is inverted.

Out of an initial investment of $5000 came a stake that is currently worth over $2,500,000. (Normal word order: A stake that is currently worth over $2,500,000 came out of an initial investment of $5000.)

In an article I read in Time was an account of his trip. (Omit the comma after the introductory phrase when the verb in the main clause immediately follows.)

BUT: *In an article I read in Time,* there was an account . . .

*Punctuation:
Major Marks*

1

d. When a compound sentence starts with a phrase that applies to both independent clauses, do not use a comma to separate the two clauses if doing so would make the introductory phrase seem to apply only to the first clause. (See also ¶134.)

> *In response to the many requests of our customers,* we are opening a branch in Kenmore Square and we are extending our evening hours in all our stores.

136 Phrases at the Beginning of a Clause

a. When a participial, infinitive, or prepositional phrase occurs *at the beginning of a clause within the sentence*, insert or omit the comma following, just as if the phrase were an introductory element at the beginning of the sentence. (See ¶135.)

> I was invited to attend the monthly planning meeting last week, and *seizing the opportunity,* I presented an overview of our medium-range plans. (A separating comma follows the participial phrase just as if the sentence began with the word *Seizing.* No comma precedes the phrase because the phrase is considered introductory, not interrupting. See ¶127d.)

> The salesclerk explained that *to get the best results from your dishwasher,* you should follow the printed directions.

> We would like to announce that *in response to the many requests of our customers,* we are opening a branch in Kenmore Square.

> Last year we had a number of thefts, and *in 1999* our entire inventory was destroyed by fire. (No comma is needed after a short introductory prepositional phrase.)

b. If the phrase interrupts the flow of the sentence, set it off with two commas.

> Pamela is the type of person who, *in the midst of disaster,* always finds something to laugh about.

> If, *in the attempt to push matters to a resolution,* you offer that gang new terms, they will simply dig in their heels and refuse to bargain.

137 Phrases Elsewhere in the Sentence

When a participial, infinitive, or prepositional phrase occurs *at some point other than the beginning of a sentence* (see ¶135) *or the beginning of a clause* (see ¶136), commas are omitted or used depending on whether the phrase is essential or nonessential.

a. An *essential* participial, infinitive, or prepositional phrase is necessary to the meaning of the sentence and cannot be omitted. Do not use commas to set it off.

> The catalog *scheduled for release in November* will have to be delayed until January. (Participial.)
> The decision *to expand our export activities* has led to a significant increase in profits. (Infinitive.)
> The search *for a new general manager* is still going on. (Prepositional.)

b. A *nonessential* participial, infinitive, or prepositional phrase provides additional information but is not needed to complete the meaning of the sentence. Set off such phrases with commas.

> This new collection of essays, *written in the last two years before his death,* represents his most distinguished work. (Participial.)
> I'd rather not attend her reception, *to be frank about it.* (Infinitive.)
> Morale appears to be much better, *on the whole.* (Prepositional.)

c. A phrase occurring within a sentence must always be set off by commas when it *interrupts* the flow of the sentence.

> The commission, *after hearing arguments on the proposed new tax rate structure,* will consider amendments to the tax law.

> The company, *in its attempt to place more women in high-level management positions,* is undertaking a special recruitment program.

¶138

The following rules (¶¶138–161) deal with the various uses of commas to set off nonessential expressions. See also ¶¶201–202 and ¶¶218–219 for the use of dashes and parentheses to set off these expressions.

With Transitional Expressions and Independent Comments

138   **a.** Use commas to set off *transitional expressions*. These nonessential words and phrases are called *transitional* because they help the reader mentally relate the preceding thought to the idea now being introduced. They express such notions as:

ADDITION:	additionally (see page 282), also, besides, furthermore, in addition, moreover, too (see ¶143), what is more
CONSEQUENCE:	accordingly, as a result, consequently, hence (see ¶139b), otherwise, so (see ¶179), then (see ¶139b), therefore, thus (see ¶139b)
SUMMARIZING:	after all, all in all, all things considered, briefly, by and large, in any case, in any event, in brief, in conclusion, in short, in summary, in the final analysis, in the long run, on balance, on the whole, to sum up
GENERALIZING:	as a rule, as usual, for the most part, generally, generally speaking, in general, ordinarily, usually
RESTATEMENT:	in essence, in other words, namely, that is, that is to say
CONTRAST AND COMPARISON:	by contrast, by the same token, conversely, instead, likewise, on one hand, on the contrary, on the other hand, rather, similarly, yet (see ¶¶139b, 179)
CONCESSION:	anyway, at any rate, be that as it may, even so, however, in any case, in any event, nevertheless, still, this fact notwithstanding
SEQUENCE:	afterward, at first, at the same time, finally, first, first of all, for now, for the time being, in conclusion, in the first place, in time, in turn, later on, meanwhile, next, respectively, second, then (see ¶139b), to begin with
DIVERSION:	by the by, by the way, incidentally
ILLUSTRATION:	for example, for instance, for one thing

NOTE: The coordinating conjunctions *and, but, or,* and *nor* are sometimes used as transitional expressions at the beginning of a sentence. (See ¶126b.)

➤ *For the punctuation of transitional expressions depending on where they occur in a sentence, see ¶¶139–142.*

b. Use commas to set off *independent comments*, nonessential words or phrases that express the writer's attitude toward the meaning of the sentence. By means of these independent comments, writers indicate that what they are about to say carries their wholehearted endorsement *(indeed, by all means)* or deserves only their lukewarm support *(apparently, presumably)* or hardly requires saying *(as you already know, clearly, obviously)* or represents only their personal views *(in my opinion, personally)* or arouses some emotion in them *(unfortunately, happily)* or presents their honest position *(frankly, actually, to tell the truth)*. Such terms modify the meaning of the sentence as a whole rather than a particular word within the sentence.

¶**140**

AFFIRMATION:	by all means, indeed, of course, yes
DENIAL:	no
REGRET:	alas, unfortunately, regrettably
PLEASURE:	fortunately, happily
QUALIFICATION:	ideally, if necessary, if possible, literally, strictly speaking, theoretically, hopefully (see page 295)
PERSONAL VIEWPOINT:	according to her, as I see it, in my opinion, personally
ASSERTION OF CANDOR:	actually, frankly, in reality, to be honest, to say the least, to tell the truth
ASSERTION OF FACT:	as a matter of fact, as it happens, as you know, believe it or not, certainly, clearly, doubtless, in fact, naturally, needless to say, obviously, without doubt
WEAK ASSERTION:	apparently, perhaps, presumably, well

➤ *For the punctuation of independent comments depending on where they occur in a sentence, see ¶¶139–142.*

139 **At the Beginning of a Sentence**

a. When the words and phrases listed in ¶138a–b appear at the beginning of a sentence, they should be followed by a comma unless they are used as essential elements.

> **NONESSENTIAL:** *After all,* you have done more for him than he had any right to expect.
> **ESSENTIAL:** *After all* you have done for him, he has no right to expect more.
>
> **NONESSENTIAL:** *However,* you look at the letter yourself to see whether you interpret it as I do.
> **ESSENTIAL:** *However* you look at the letter, there is only one interpretation.
>
> **NONESSENTIAL:** *Obviously,* the guest of honor was quite moved by the welcome she received. (Here *obviously* modifies the meaning of the sentence as a whole.)
> **ESSENTIAL:** *Obviously* moved by the welcome she received, the guest of honor spoke with an emotion-choked voice. (Here *obviously* modifies *moved.*)

b. When *hence, then, thus, so,* or *yet* occurs at the beginning of a sentence, the comma following is omitted unless the connective requires special emphasis or a nonessential element occurs at that point.

> *Thus* they thought it wise to get an outside consultant's opinion.
> *Then* they decided to go back to their original plan.
> **BUT:** *Then,* after they rejected the consultant's recommendation, they decided to go back to their original plan.

➤ *See also ¶142a, note.*

c. When an introductory transitional expression or independent comment is incorporated into the flow of the sentence without any intervening pause, the comma may be omitted.

> *Of course* I can handle it.   *Perhaps* she was joking.
> *No doubt* he meant well.   *Indeed* she was not.

140 **At the End of a Sentence**

Use one comma to set off a transitional expression or an independent comment at the end of a sentence. However, be sure to distinguish between nonessential and essential elements.

Continued on page 28

¶141

Punctuation: Major Marks

1

NONESSENTIAL: Philip goes to every employee reception, *of course.*

ESSENTIAL: Philip goes to every employee reception as a matter *of course.*

NONESSENTIAL: The deal is going to fall through, *in my opinion.*

ESSENTIAL: She doesn't rank very high *in my opinion.*

141 Within the Sentence

Use two commas to set off a transitional expression or an independent comment when it occurs as a nonessential element within the sentence.

I, *too,* was not expecting a six-month convalescence.

The doctors tell me, *however,* that I will regain full use of my left leg.

If, however, the expression is used as an essential element, leave the commas out.

NONESSENTIAL: Let me say, *to begin with,* that I think very highly of him.

ESSENTIAL: If you want to improve your English, you ought *to begin with* a good review of grammar.

NOTE: In many sentences the only way you can tell whether an expression is nonessential or essential is by the way you say it. If your voice tends to *drop* as you utter the expression, it is nonessential and should be set off by commas.

We concluded, *nevertheless,* that their offer was not serious.

Millie understands, *certainly,* that the reassignment is only temporary.

It is critical, *therefore,* that we rework all these cost estimates.

If your voice tends to *rise* as you utter the expression, it is essential and should not be set off by commas.

We *nevertheless* concluded that their offer was not serious.

Millie *certainly* understands that the reassignment is only temporary.

It is *therefore* critical that we rework all these cost estimates.

If commas are inserted in the previous example, the entire reading of the sentence will be changed. The voice will rise on the word *is* and drop on *therefore.* (If this is the way you want the sentence to be read, then commas around *therefore* are correct.)

It is, *therefore,* critical that we rework all these cost estimates.

142 At the Beginning of a Clause

a. When a transitional expression or independent comment occurs *at the beginning of the second independent clause* in a compound sentence and is *preceded by a semicolon,* use one comma following the expression.

I would love to work in a side trip to Vail; *however,* I don't think I can pull it off.

My boss just approved the purchase; *therefore,* let's confirm a delivery date.

In sentences like the two above, a period may be used in place of a semicolon. The words *however* and *therefore* would then be capitalized to mark the start of a new sentence, and they would be followed by a comma.

NOTE: When *hence, then, thus,* or *so* appears at the beginning of an independent clause, the comma following is omitted unless the connective requires special emphasis or a nonessential element occurs at that point. (See also ¶139b.)

Melt the butter over high heat; *then* add the egg.

BUT: Melt the butter over high heat; *then,* when the foam begins to subside, add the egg.

➤ *For the use of a semicolon before a transitional expression, see ¶¶178–180.*

¶144

b. When the expression occurs *at the beginning of the second independent clause* in a compound sentence and is *preceded by a comma and a coordinating conjunction*, use one comma following the expression. (See also ¶127d.)

> The location of the plant was not easy to reach, and *to be honest about it,* I wasn't very taken with the people who interviewed me.
>
> The job seemed to have no future, and *to tell the truth,* the salary was pretty low.
>
> *In the first place,* I think the budget for the project is unrealistic, and *in the second place,* the deadlines are almost impossible to meet.

NOTE: If the expression is a simple adverb like *therefore*, the comma following the expression is usually omitted. (See also ¶180.)

> The matter must be resolved by Friday, and *therefore* our preliminary conference must be held no later than Thursday.
>
> All the general managers have been summoned to a three-day meeting at the home office, and *consequently* I have had to reschedule all my meetings.

c. If the expression occurs *at the beginning of a dependent clause*, either treat the expression as nonessential (and set it off with two commas) or treat it as essential (and omit the commas).

> If, *moreover,* they do not meet the deadline, we have the right to cancel the contract.
>
> If *indeed* they want to settle the dispute, why don't we suggest that they submit to arbitration?
>
> He is a man who, *in my opinion,* will make a fine marketing director.
>
> She is a woman who *no doubt* knows how to run a department smoothly and effectively.
>
> The situation is so serious that, *strictly speaking,* bankruptcy is the only solution.
>
> The situation is so serious that *perhaps* bankruptcy may be the only solution.

143 **With the Adverb** *Too*

a. When the adverb *too* (in the sense of "also") occurs at the end of a clause or a sentence, the comma preceding is omitted.

> If you feel that way *too,* why don't we just drop all further negotiation?
>
> They are after a bigger share of the market *too.*

b. When *too* (in the sense of "also") occurs elsewhere in the sentence, particularly between subject and verb, set it off with two commas.

> You, *too,* could be in the Caribbean right now.
>
> Then, *too,* there are the additional taxes to be considered.

c. When *too* is used as an adverb meaning "excessively," it is never set off with commas.

> The news is almost *too* good to be believed.

With Interruptions and Afterthoughts

144 Use commas to set off words, phrases, or clauses that interrupt the flow of a sentence or that are loosely added at the end as an afterthought.

> Pam is being pursued, *so I've been told,* by three headhunters.
>
> Bob spoke on state-of-the-art financial software, *if I remember correctly.*
>
> Our order processing service, *you must admit,* leaves much to be desired.
>
> His research work has been outstanding, *particularly in the field of ergonomics.*

➤ *See also ¶¶131c, 136b, 137c.*

Continued on page 30

Punctuation: Major Marks

1

¶145

CAUTION: When enclosing an interrupting expression with two commas, be sure the commas are inserted accurately.

WRONG: That is the best, *though not the cheapest way,* to proceed.
RIGHT: That is the best, *though not the cheapest,* way to proceed.

WRONG: This book is better written, *though less exciting than,* her last book.
RIGHT: This book is better written, *though less exciting,* than her last book.

WRONG: Glen has a deep interest in, *as well as a great fondness,* for jazz.
RIGHT: Glen has a deep interest in, *as well as a great fondness for,* jazz.

WRONG: Her work is as good, *if not better than,* that of the man she replaced.
RIGHT: Her work is as good as, *if not better than,* that of the man she replaced. (Note that the second *as* is needed to preserve the meaning of the basic sentence.)

With Direct Address

145   Names and titles used in direct address must be set off by commas.

No, *sir,* that is privileged information.   I count on your support, *Bob.*
We agree, *Mrs. Connolly,* that your order was badly handled.

With Additional Considerations

146 **a.** When a phrase introduced by *as well as, in addition to, besides, along with, including, accompanied by, together with, plus,* or a similar expression falls between the subject and the verb, it is ordinarily set off by commas. Commas may be omitted, however, if the phrase fits smoothly into the flow of the sentence or is essential to the meaning.

Everyone, *including the top corporate managers,* will be required to attend the in-house seminars on the ethical dimensions of business.

The business plan *including strategies for the new market segments we hope to enter* is better than the other plans I have reviewed. (The *including* phrase is needed to distinguish this plan from the others; hence no commas.)

One *plus one* doesn't always equal two, as we have seen in the Parker-Jackel merger. (The *plus* phrase is essential to the meaning; hence no commas.)

Jo *as well as Nina* should be invited to participate. (The *as well as* phrase fits smoothly in this sentence.)

➢ *For the effect these phrases have on the choice of a singular or a plural verb, see ¶1007; for a usage note on* as well as, *see page 286.*

b. When the phrase occurs elsewhere in the sentence, commas may be omitted if the phrase is closely related to the preceding words.

The refinancing terms have been approved by the trustees *as well as the creditors.*

BUT: I attended the international monetary conference in Bermuda, *together with five associates from our Washington office.*

With Contrasting Expressions

147   Use commas to set off contrasting expressions. (Such expressions often begin with *but*, *not*, or *rather than*.)

The Sanchezes are willing to sell, *but only on their terms.*
He had changed his methods, *not his objectives,* we noticed.
Paula, *rather than Al,* has been chosen for the job.

NOTE: When such phrases fit smoothly into the flow of the sentence, no commas are required.

> It was a busy *but enjoyable* trip.   They have chosen Paula *rather than Al.*
> The unit managers *and not the CEO* have to make those decisions. (See ¶1006b.)

➤ *For the punctuation of balancing expressions, see ¶172d.*

The following rules (¶¶148–153) deal with descriptive expressions that immediately follow the words to which they refer. When nonessential, these expressions are set off by commas.

With Identifying, Appositive, or Explanatory Expressions

148 Use commas to set off expressions that provide additional but *nonessential* information about a noun or pronoun immediately preceding. Such expressions serve to further identify or explain the word they refer to.

> Harriet McManus, *an independent real estate broker for the past ten years,* will be joining our agency on Tuesday, *October 1.* (Phrases such as those following *Harriet McManus* and *Tuesday* are appositives.)
> Acrophobia, *that is, the fear of great heights,* can now be successfully treated. (See also ¶¶181–183 for other punctuation with *that is, namely,* and *for example.*)
> His first book, *written while he was still in graduate school,* launched a successful writing career.
> Our first thought, *to run to the nearest exit,* would have resulted in panic.
> Ms. Ballantine, *who has been a copywriter for six years,* will be our new copy chief.
> Everyone in our family likes outdoor sports, *such as tennis and swimming.* (See ¶149, note.)

NOTE: In some cases other punctuation may be preferable in place of commas.

> **CONFUSING:** Mr. Newcombe, *my boss,* and I will discuss this problem next week. (Does *my boss* refer to Mr. Newcombe, or are there three people involved?)
> **CLEAR:** Mr. Newcombe (my boss) and I will be discussing this problem next week. (Use parentheses or dashes instead of commas when an appositive expression could be misread as a separate item in a series.)
> There are two factors to be considered, *sales and collections.* (A colon or a dash could be used in place of the comma. See ¶¶189, 201.)
> **BUT:** There are three factors to be considered: sales, collections, and inventories. (When the explanatory expression consists of a series of *three* or more items and comes at the end of the sentence, use a colon or dash. See ¶¶189, 201.)
> **OR:** These three factors—sales, collections, and inventories—should be considered. (When the explanatory series comes within the sentence, set it off with dashes or parentheses. See ¶¶183, 202, 219.)

149 When the expression is *essential* to the completeness of the sentence, do not set it off. (In the following examples the expression is needed to identify which particular item is meant. If the expression were omitted, the sentence would be incomplete.)

> The year *2003* marks the one hundredth anniversary of our company.
> The word *liaison* is often misspelled.
> The novelist *Anne Tyler* gave a reading last week from a work in progress.
> The statement *"I don't remember"* was frequently heard in court yesterday.
> The impulse *to get away from it all* is very common.
> The notes *in green ink* were made by Mrs. Long.
> The person *who takes over as general manager* will need everyone's support.

Continued on page 32

¶150

NOTE: Compare the following sets of examples:

> Her article *"Color and Design"* was published in June. (The title is essential; it identifies *which* article.)
>
> Her latest article, *"Color and Design,"* was published in June. (Nonessential; the word *latest* already indicates which article.)
>
> Her latest article *on color and design* was published in June. (Without commas, this means she had earlier articles on the same subject.)
>
> Her latest article, *on color and design,* was published in June. (With commas, this means her earlier articles were on other subjects.)
>
> Everyone in our family likes such outdoor sports *as tennis and swimming.* (The phrase *as tennis and swimming* is essential; without it, the reader would not know which outdoor sports were meant.)
>
> Everyone in our family likes outdoor sports, *such as tennis and swimming.* (The main clause, *Everyone in our family likes outdoor sports,* expresses a complete thought; the phrase *such as tennis and swimming* gives additional but nonessential information. Hence a comma is needed before *such as.*)
>
> Words *such as peak, peek, and pique* can be readily confused. (The *such as* phrase is essential; it indicates which words are meant.)
>
> A number of Fortune 500 companies, *such as GE, TRW, and DuPont,* have introduced new programs to motivate their middle managers. (The *such as* phrase provides additional but nonessential information.)

150 A number of expressions are treated as essential simply because of a very close relationship with the preceding words. (If read aloud, the combined phrase sounds like one unit, without any intervening pause.)

> After a while Gladys *herself* became disenchanted with the Washington scene.
>
> We *legislators* must provide funds for retraining displaced workers.
>
> *My wife Eve* has begun her own consulting business. (Strictly speaking, *Eve* should be set off by commas, since the name is not needed to indicate *which* wife. However, commas are omitted in expressions like these because they are read as a unit.)
>
> **BUT:** Eve, *my wife,* has begun her own consulting business. (When the word order is changed, the phrase *Eve, my wife* is no longer read as a unit. Hence commas are needed to set off *my wife.*)
>
> *My brother Paul* may join us as well.
>
> **BUT:** My brother, *Paul Engstrom,* may join us.
>
> The composer *Stephen Sondheim* has many Broadway hits to his credit.
>
> **BUT:** My favorite composer, *Stephen Sondheim,* has many Broadway hits . . .
>
> If you want some solid advice, *101 Ways to Power Up Your Job Search* by J. Thomas Buck, William R. Matthews, and Robert N. Leech could be just the book for you. (Unless there is another book with the same title, the *by* phrase identifying the authors is not essential and, strictly speaking, should be set off by commas. However, since a book title and a *by* phrase are typically read as a unit, commas are usually omitted.)

151 When *or* introduces a word or a phrase that identifies or explains the preceding word, set off the explanatory expression with commas.

> Determine whether the clauses are coordinate, *or of equal rank.* (The nonessential *or* phrase may also be set off by parentheses.)

If *or* introduces an alternative thought, the expression is essential and should not be set off by commas.

> Determine whether the clauses are coordinate *or noncoordinate.*

152 When a business letter or some other document is referred to by date, any related phrases or clauses that follow are usually nonessential.

> Thank you for your letter of February 27, *in which you questioned the balance on your account.* (The date is sufficient to identify which letter is meant; the *in which* clause simply provides additional but nonessential information. Of course, if one received more than one letter with the same date from the same person, the *in which* clause would be essential and the comma would be omitted.)

No comma is needed after the date if the following phrase is short and closely related.

> Thank you for your letter of February 27 *about the balance on your account.*

NOTE: Under certain circumstances—for example, around the end of the year—it is better to provide the full date rather than the month and day alone.

> Thank you for your letter of *December 27, 2000,* in which . . .

➤ *For a full discussion of this issue, see ¶409.*

With Residence and Business Connections

153 Use commas to set off a *long phrase* that denotes a person's residence or business connections.

> Gary Kendall, *of the Van Houten Corporation in Provo, Utah,* will be visiting us next week.
>
> Gary Kendall *of Provo, Utah,* will be visiting us next week. (Omit the comma before *of* to avoid too many breaks in a short phrase. The state name must always be set off by commas when it follows a city name. See also ¶160.)
>
> Gary Kendall *of the Van Houten Corporation* will be visiting us next week. (Short phrase; no commas.)
>
> Gary Kendall *of Provo* will be visiting us next week. (Short phrase; no commas.)

The following rules (¶¶154–161) deal with the "nonessential" treatment of certain elements in dates, personal names, company names, and addresses. These elements cannot truly be called nonessential, but the traditional style is to set them off with commas.

In Dates

154 **a.** Use two commas to set off the year when it follows the month and day.

> On October 31, *2002,* I plan to retire and open a bookshop in Maine.
>
> The July 5, *1999,* issue of *Business Week* predicted that e-commerce, the source of $301 billion in revenues the previous year, would continue to produce fundamental changes in the U.S. economy and generate much of its future growth.

b. When the month, day, and year are used as a nonessential expression, be sure to set the entire phrase off with commas.

> The conference scheduled to begin on Monday, *November 26, 2001,* has now been rescheduled to start on *February 6, 2002.*
>
> Payment of estimated income taxes for the fourth quarter of 2002 will be due no later than Wednesday, *January 15, 2003.*

155 Omit the commas when only the month and year are given.

> In *August 2000* Glen and I dissolved our partnership and went our independent ways.
>
> Isn't it about time for *Consumer Reports* to update the evaluation of printers that appeared in the *March 1999* issue?

➤ *For additional examples involving dates, see ¶410.*

Punctuation: Major Marks

1

¶156

With *Jr., Sr.,* Etc.

156 Do not use commas to set off *Jr., Sr.,* or roman or arabic numerals following a person's name unless you know that the person in question prefers to do so.

> Kelsey R. Patterson Jr.
> Christopher M. Gorman Sr.
> Benjamin Hart 2d
> Anthony Jung III
> John Bond Jr.'s resignation will be announced tomorrow.

NOTE: When a person prefers to use commas in his name, observe the following style:

> Peter Passaro, Jr. (Use one comma when the name is displayed on a line by itself.)
> Peter Passaro, Jr., director of . . . (Use two commas when other copy follows.)
> Peter Passaro, Jr.'s promotion . . . (Drop the second comma when a possessive ending is attached.)

157 Abbreviations like *Esq.* and those that stand for academic degrees or religious orders are set off by two commas when they follow a person's name.

> Address the letter to Helen E. Parsekian, *Esq.,* in New York.
> Roger Farrier, *LL.D.,* will address the Elizabethan Club on Wednesday.
> The Reverend James Hanley, *S.J.,* will serve as moderator of the panel.

158 When a personal name is given in inverted order, set off the inverted portion with commas.

> McCaughan, James W., Jr.

With *Inc.* and *Ltd.*

159 Do not use commas to set off *Inc., Ltd.,* and similar expressions in a company name unless you know that a particular company prefers to do so. (See also ¶¶1328–1329.)

> Time Inc.   Field Hats, Ltd.
> Time *Inc.* has expanded its operations beyond magazine publishing.
> Field Hats, *Ltd.,* should be notified about this mistake.

NOTE: When commas are to be used in a company name, follow this style:

> Alwyn & Hyde, Inc. (Use one comma when the name is displayed on a line by itself.)
> Alwyn & Hyde, Inc., announces the publication of . . . (Use two commas when other copy follows.)
> Alwyn & Hyde, Inc.'s annual statement . . . (Drop the second comma when a possessive ending is attached.)

➤ *For the use of commas with other parts of a company name, see ¶163.*

In Geographic References and Addresses

160 Use two commas to set off the name of a state, a country, or the equivalent when it directly follows the name of a city or a county.

> Four years ago I was transferred from Bartlesville, *Oklahoma,* to Bern, *Switzerland.*
> The MIT Press is located in Cambridge, *Massachusetts,* not Cambridge, *England.*
> Could Pickaway County, *Ohio,* become a haven for retired editors?
> Our Pierre, *South Dakota,* office is the one nearest to you.
> **OR:** Our Pierre (South Dakota) office is the one nearest to you. (Parentheses are clearer than commas when a city-state expression serves as an adjective.)
> Washington, *D.C.'s* transportation system has improved greatly since I was last there. (Omit the second comma after a possessive ending.)

NOTE: In sentences that mention one or more cities, omit the state or country names if the cities are well known and are clearly linked with only one state or country.

> We'll be holding meetings in Atlanta, Baltimore, and Chicago.
>
> My agent has arranged for me to address groups of business executives in Oslo, Stockholm, and Copenhagen later this year.

161   When expressing complete addresses, follow this style:

> **IN SENTENCES:** During the month of September you can send all documents directly to me at 402 Woodbury Road, Pasadena, CA 91104, or you can ask my assistant to forward it. (Note that a comma does not precede the Zip Code but follows it in this sentence to indicate the end of the first independent clause.)
>
> **IN DISPLAYED BLOCKS:**   402 Woodbury Road
> Pasadena, CA 91104

The following rules (¶¶162–175) deal with various uses of separating commas: to separate items in a series, to separate adjectives that precede a noun, and to clarify meaning in sentences with unusual word order or omitted words.

In a Series

162 **a.** When three or more items are listed in a series and the last item is preceded by *and*, *or*, or *nor*, place a comma before the conjunction as well as between the other items. (See also ¶126c.)

> Study the rules for the use of the comma, the semicolon, *and* the colon.
>
> The consensus is that your report is well written, that your facts are accurate, *and* that your conclusions are sound.
>
> The show will appeal equally to women and men, adults and children, *and* sophisticates and innocents. (See page 284 for a usage note on *and*.)
>
> Only this software lets you fax, transfer files, exchange e-mail, access the Internet, *and* manage phone calls—all from one window on your computer.

NOTE: Some writers prefer to omit the comma before *and*, *or*, or *nor* in a series, but the customary practice in business is to retain the comma before the conjunction.

b. If a nonessential element follows the conjunction *(and, or,* or *nor)* in a series, omit the comma before the conjunction to avoid excessive punctuation.

> We invited Ben's business associates, his friends and, of course, his parents.
>
> (**RATHER THAN:** . . . his friends, and, of course, his parents.)

163 For a series in an organization's name, always follow the style preferred by that organization.

> Merrill Lynch, Pierce, Fenner & Smith Inc.
>
> Morgan Stanley Dean Witter & Co.
>
> Legg Mason Wood Walker, Inc.

If you do not have the organization's letterhead or some other reliable resource at hand, follow the standard rule on commas in a series (see ¶162).

> Our primary supplier is *Ames, Koslow, Milke, and Company*.

NOTE: Do not use a comma before an ampersand (&) in an organization's name unless you know that a particular organization prefers to do so.

> Aspinwall, Bromley, Carruthers & Dalgleish

¶164

164 When an expression such as *and so on* or *etc.* closes a series, use a comma before and after the expression (except at the end of a sentence).

> Our sale of suits, coats, hats, *and so on,* starts tomorrow.
>
> Tomorrow morning we will start our sale of suits, coats, hats, *etc.*

➢ *For a usage note on* etc., *see page 291.*

165 Do not insert a comma after the last item in a series unless the sentence structure demands a comma at that point.

> May 8, June 11, and July 14 are the dates for the next three hearings.
>
> May 8, June 11, and July 14, 2003, are the dates for the next three hearings. (The comma after *2003* is one of the pair that sets off the year. See ¶154.)

166 When *and*, *or*, or *nor* is used to connect all the items in a series, do not separate the items by commas. (See also ¶123b.)

> Send copies to our employees *and* stockholders *and* major customers.

167 If a series consists of only two items, do not separate the items with a comma. (See also ¶125f.)

> We can send the samples to you *by regular mail* or *by one of the express services.*

NOTE: Use a comma, however, to separate two independent clauses joined by *and, but, or,* or *nor.* (See ¶126a.)

➢ *For the use of semicolons in a series, see ¶¶184–185.*

With Adjectives

168 When two consecutive adjectives modify the same noun, separate the adjectives with a comma.

> Jean is a *generous, outgoing* person. (A person who is *generous and outgoing.*)

NOTE: Do *not* use a comma between the adjectives if they are connected by *and, or,* or *nor.*

> Jean is a *generous* and *outgoing* person.

169 When two adjectives precede a noun, the first adjective may modify the combined idea of the second adjective plus the noun. In such cases do not separate the adjectives by a comma.

> The estate is surrounded by an *old stone* wall. (A *stone* wall that is *old.*)
>
> Here is the *annual financial* statement. (A *financial* statement that is *annual.*)

TEST: To decide whether consecutive adjectives should be separated by a comma or not, try using them in a relative clause *after* the noun, with *and* inserted between them. If they read smoothly and sensibly in that position, they should be separated by a comma in their actual position.

> We need an *intelligent, enterprising* person for the job. (One can speak of "a person who is *intelligent* and *enterprising*," so a comma is correct.)
>
> Throw out your *old down* coat. (One cannot speak of "a coat that is *old* and *down*," so no comma should be used in the actual sentence.)
>
> You can purchase any of these printers with a *low down* payment. (In this case the adjective *low* modifies a compound noun, *down payment.*)
>
> To put it gently but plainly, I think Jason is a *low-down* scoundrel. (In this case *low-down* is a compound adjective and requires a hyphen to connect *low* and *down*. See ¶¶813–832 for a discussion of compound adjectives.)

170 When more than two adjectives precede a noun, insert a comma only between those adjectives where *and* could have been used.

> a relaxed, unruffled, confident manner (a relaxed *and* unruffled *and* confident manner)
>
> an experienced, efficient legal assistant (an experienced *and* efficient legal assistant)
>
> the established American political system (*and* cannot be inserted between these three adjectives)

171 Do not use a comma between the final adjective in a series and the following noun.

> I put in a long, hard, *demanding day* on Monday.
>
> (**NOT:** I put in a long, hard, *demanding, day* on Monday.)

To Indicate Omitted Words

172 **a. Omission of Repetitive Wording.** Use a comma to indicate the omission of repetitive wording in a compound sentence. (This use of the comma usually occurs when clauses are separated by semicolons.)

> Employees aged 55 and over are eligible for a complete physical examination every year; those between 50 and 54, every two years; and those under 50, every three years.

NOTE: If the omitted words are clearly understood from the context, simpler punctuation may be used.

> Employees aged 55 and over are eligible for a complete physical examination every year, those between 50 and 54 every two years, and those under 50 every three years.

b. Omission of *That*. In some sentences the omission of the conjunction *that* creates a definite break in the flow of the sentence. In such cases insert a comma to mark the break.

> Remember, this offer is good only through May 31.
>
> The problem is, not all of these assumptions may be correct.
>
> The fact is, things are not working out as we had hoped.
>
> Chances are, the deal will never come off.

NOTE: In sentences that are introduced by expressions such as *he said, she thinks, we feel,* or *they know,* the conjunction *that* is often omitted following the introductory expression. In such cases no comma is necessary because there is no break in the flow of the sentence.

> We know you can do it.
>
> They think our price is too high.
>
> She said she would handle everything.
>
> We believe we offer the best service.

c. Omission of Some Other Connective. In some sentences the omission of a preposition or some other connective creates a break in the flow of the sentence. In such cases insert a comma to mark the break.

> **NOT:** Our store is open from 9:30 a.m. to 6 p.m. Monday through Friday. (The omission of a connective before *Monday* creates a break.)
>
> **BUT:** Our store is open from 9:30 a.m. to 6 p.m., Monday through Friday.

As an alternative, reword the sentence to eliminate the break and the need for a comma.

> Our store is open Monday through Friday from 9:30 a.m. to 6 p.m.
>
> Our store is open between 9:30 a.m. and 6 p.m. from Monday through Friday.

Continued on page 38

¶173

d. Balancing Expressions. Use a comma to separate the two parts of a balancing expression from which many words have been omitted.

> First come, first served.
> First in, last out.
> Here today, gone tomorrow.
> The more we give, the more they take.
> GIGO: garbage in, garbage out.
> The less I see of him, the better I like it.

NOTE: The phrase *the sooner the better* usually appears without a separating comma.

To Indicate Unusual Word Order

173   In some colloquial sentences, clauses or phrases occur out of normal order and connective words may be omitted. Use a comma to mark the resulting break in the flow of the sentence.

> You must not miss the play, it was that good.
> (**NORMAL ORDER:** The play was so good that you must not miss it.)
> Why he took the money, I'll never understand.
> That the shipment would be late, we were prepared to accept; that you would ship the wrong goods, we did not expect.

NOTE: In formal writing, these sentences should be recast in normal word order.

➢ *See also ¶135c, note.*

For Special Emphasis

174   Individual words may be set off by commas for special emphasis.

> I have tried, *sincerely,* to understand your problems.
> They contend, *unrealistically,* that we can cut back on staff and still generate the same amount of output.

NOTE: The use of commas in the examples above forces the reader to dwell momentarily on the word that has been set off in each case. Without this treatment *sincerely* and *unrealistically* would not receive this emphasis.

For Clarity

175 **a.** Use a comma to prevent misreading.

> As you know, nothing came of the meeting.
> (**NOT:** As you know nothing came of the meeting.)
> To a liberal like Bill, Buckley seems hard to take.
> Soon after, the committee disbanded without accomplishing its goal.
> At our outdoor party last Saturday night, I watched my brother as he stepped backward into our swimming pool, and burst out laughing. (Believe me, it wasn't my brother who was laughing.)

b. Sometimes, for clarity, it is necessary to separate two verbs.

> All any insurance policy is, is a contract for services.
> **BUT:** I can prove that that conversation never took place.

c. Use a comma to separate repeated words.

> It was a *long, long* time ago.   *Well, well,* we'll find a way.
> That was a *very, very* old argument.   *Now, now,* you don't expect me to believe that!

¶**177**

➤ *Commas with dashes: see ¶¶213, 215b.*
Commas in numbers: see ¶¶461–463.
Commas with questions within sentences: see ¶¶114–117.
Commas with parentheses: see ¶224a.
Commas inside closing quotation marks: see ¶247.
Commas at the end of quotations: see ¶¶253–255.
Commas preceding quotations: see ¶256.
Commas with quotations within a sentence: see ¶¶259–262.
Commas to set off interruptions in quoted material: see ¶262.
Spacing with commas: see ¶299.

The Semicolon

Between Independent Clauses—*And, But, Or,* or *Nor* Omitted

176 **a.** When a coordinating conjunction *(and, but, or,* or *nor)* is omitted between two independent clauses, use a semicolon—not a comma—to separate the clauses. (See ¶187.) If you prefer, you can treat the second clause as a separate sentence.

> Most of the stockholders favored the sale; the management did not.
>
> **OR:** Most of the stockholders favored the sale. The management did not.
>
> (**NOT:** Most of the stockholders favored the sale, the management did not.)
>
> Bob is going for his M.B.A.; Janet already has hers.
>
> Subnotebooks aren't just smaller; they're cheaper.
>
> (**NOT:** Subnotebooks aren't just smaller, they're cheaper.)

b. If the clauses are not closely related, treat them as separate sentences.

> **WEAK:** Thank you for your letter of September 8; your question has already been passed on to the manager of mail-order sales, and you should be hearing from Mrs. Livonia within three days.
>
> **BETTER:** Thank you for your letter of September 8. Your question has already been passed on to the manager of mail-order sales, and you should be . . .

c. The omission of *but* between two independent clauses requires, strictly speaking, the use of a semicolon between the two clauses. However, when the clauses are short, a comma is commonly used to preserve the flow of the sentence.

> Not only was the food bad, the portions were minuscule.

NOTE: As a general rule, a semicolon is used only to separate independent clauses. For one exception, see ¶182a.

Between Independent Clauses—*And, But, Or,* or *Nor* Included

177 A comma is normally used to separate two independent clauses joined by a coordinating conjunction. However, under certain circumstances a semicolon may be used.

a. Use a semicolon in order to achieve a stronger break between clauses than a comma provides.

> **NORMAL BREAK:** Many people are convinced that they could personally solve the problem if given the authority to do so, but no one will come forward with a clear-cut plan that we can evaluate in advance.
>
> **STRONG BREAK:** Many people are convinced that they could personally solve the problem if given the authority to do so; but no one will come forward with a clear-cut plan that we can evaluate in advance.

Continued on page 40

¶178

b. Use a semicolon when one or both clauses have internal commas and a misreading might occur if a comma also separated the clauses.

> **CONFUSING:** I sent you an order for copier paper, computer paper, and No. 10 envelopes, and shipping tags, cardboard cartons, stapler wire, and binding tape were sent to me instead.
>
> **CLEAR:** I sent you an order for copier paper, computer paper, and No. 10 envelopes; and shipping tags, cardboard cartons, stapler wire, and binding tape were sent to me instead.

NOTE: To prevent misreading, you will usually find it better to reword the sentence than rely on stronger punctuation.

> **BETTER:** I sent you an order for copier paper, computer paper, and No. 10 envelopes, and you sent me shipping tags, cardboard cartons, stapler wire, and binding tape instead. (The shift in the verb from passive to active eliminates any confusion and produces a stronger sentence as well.)

c. If no misreading is likely, a comma is sufficient to separate the clauses, even though commas are also used within the clauses.

> On June 8, 2001, I discussed this problem with your customer service manager, Betty Dugan, but your company has taken no further action.
>
> All in all, we're satisfied with the job Bergquist Associates did, and in view of the tight deadlines they had to meet, we're pleased that they came through as well as they did.

➤ *For additional examples, see ¶133.*

NOTE: Some writers still insist on using a semicolon in sentences like those in *c* above simply because of the presence of internal commas in the clauses, even though no misreading is possible. Yet no one appears to be troubled by the use of a comma to separate clauses in a complex sentence when commas also appear within the clauses.

> Although I discussed this problem with your customer service manager, Fay Dugan, on June 8, 2001, your company has taken no further action.

In summary, do not use a semicolon in sentences like those in *c* above except to prevent misreading or to deliberately create a stronger break between clauses.

With Transitional Expressions

178 When independent clauses are linked by transitional expressions (see a partial list below), use a semicolon between the clauses. (You can also treat the second independent clause as a separate sentence.)

accordingly	however	so (see ¶179)
besides	moreover	that is (see ¶181)
consequently	namely (see ¶181)	then
for example (see ¶181)	nevertheless	therefore
furthermore	on the contrary	thus
hence	otherwise	yet (see ¶179)

> They have given us an oral okay to proceed; *however,* we're still waiting for written confirmation. (**OR:** . . . okay to proceed. *However,* we're still . . .)
>
> Our costs have started to level off; our sales, *moreover,* have continued to grow.
>
> Let's give them another month; *then* we can pin them down on their progress.

NOTE: Use a comma after the transitional expression when it occurs at the start of the second clause. (See the first example above.) However, no comma is needed after *hence*, *then*, *thus*, *so*, and *yet* unless a pause is wanted at that point. (See the third example at the bottom of page 40.)

➤ *For the use of commas with transitional expressions, see ¶¶138–143.*

179   An independent clause introduced by *so* (in the sense of "therefore") or *yet* may be preceded by a comma or a semicolon. Use a comma if the two clauses are closely related and there is a smooth flow from the first clause to the second. Use a semicolon or a period if the clauses are long and complicated or if the transition between clauses calls for a long pause or a strong break.

> Sales have been good, *yet* profits are low.
>
> This report explains why production has slowed down; *yet* it does not indicate how to avoid future glitches.
>
> These sale-priced attaché cases are going fast, *so* don't delay if you want one.
>
> We have been getting an excessive number of complaints during the last few months about our service; *so* I would like each of you to review the operations in your department and indicate what corrective measures you think ought to be taken. (**OR:** . . . about our service. *So* I would like . . .)

180   If both a coordinating conjunction and a transitional expression occur at the start of the second clause, use a comma before the conjunction.

> The site has a number of disadvantages, *and furthermore* the asking price is quite high. (See ¶142b and note.)

REMEMBER: A semicolon is needed to separate independent clauses, not so much because a transitional expression is present but because a coordinating conjunction is absent.

With *For Example, Namely, That Is,* Etc.

181   Before an Independent Clause

a. In general, when two independent clauses are linked by a transitional expression such as *for example (e.g.), namely,* or *that is (i.e.),* use a semicolon before the expression and a comma afterward.

> She is highly qualified for the job; *for example,* she has had ten years' experience as a research chemist.

NOTE: You can also replace the semicolon with a period and treat the second clause as a separate sentence.

> She is highly qualified for the job. *For example,* she has had . . .

b. If the first clause serves to anticipate the second clause and the full emphasis is to fall on the second clause, use a colon before the transitional expression.

> Your proposal covers all but one point: *namely,* who is going to foot the bill?

c. For a stronger but less formal break between clauses, the semicolon or the colon may be replaced by a dash.

> Hampton says he will help–*that is,* he will help if you ask him to.

NOTE: Use the abbreviated forms *e.g.* and *i.e.* only in informal, technical, or "expedient" documents (such as business forms, catalogs, and routine memos and letters between business offices).

Punctuation: Major Marks

1

¶182

182 **At the End of a Sentence**

When *for example*, *namely*, or *that is* introduces words, phrases, or a series of clauses *at the end of a sentence*, the punctuation preceding the expression may vary as follows:

a. If the first part of the sentence expresses the complete thought and the explanation that follows seems to be added as an afterthought, use a semicolon before the transitional expression.

> Always use figures with abbreviations; *for example*, 6 m, 9 sq in, 4 p.m. (Here the earlier part of the sentence carries the main thought; the examples are a welcome but nonessential addition.)

NOTE: The use of a semicolon before *for example* with a series of phrases is an exception to the general rule that a semicolon is always followed by an independent clause.

b. If the first part of the sentence suggests that an important explanation or illustration will follow, use a colon before the transitional expression to throw emphasis on what *follows*.

> My assistant has three important duties: *namely,* attending all meetings, writing the minutes, and sending out notices. (The word *three* anticipates the enumeration following *namely*. The colon suggests that what follows is the main thought of the sentence.)

NOTE: Use a comma before the transitional expression to throw emphasis on what *precedes*.

> I checked these figures with three people, *namely,* Alma, Andy, and Jim. (This punctuation emphasizes *three people* rather than the specific names.)

c. If *for example*, *namely*, or *that is* introduces an appositive that explains a word or phrase immediately preceding, a comma should precede the transitional expression.

> Do not use quotation marks to enclose an indirect quotation, *that is, a restatement of a person's exact words*. (Here again, a comma is used because what precedes the transitional expression is more important than what follows.)

d. The semicolon, the colon, and the comma in the examples in ¶182a–c may be replaced by a dash or by parentheses. The dash provides a stronger but less formal break; the parentheses serve to subordinate the explanatory element. (See also ¶¶201–205, 219.)

183 **Within a Sentence**

When *for example*, *namely*, or *that is* introduces words, phrases, or clauses *within a sentence*, treat the entire construction as nonessential and set it off with commas, dashes, or parentheses. Dashes will give emphasis to the interrupting construction; parentheses will make the construction appear less important than the rest of the words in the sentence.

> Many of the components, *for example, the motor,* are manufactured by outside suppliers.
> Many of the components—*for example, the motor*—are manufactured by outside suppliers.
> Many of the components *(for example, the motor)* are manufactured by outside suppliers.

NOTE: Commas can be used to set off the nonessential element so long as it contains no internal punctuation (other than the comma after the introductory expression). If the nonessential element is internally punctuated with several commas, set it off with either dashes or parentheses.

Many of the components—*for example, the motor, the batteries, and the cooling unit*—are manufactured . . . (Use dashes for emphasis. See ¶201.)

OR: Many of the components *(for example, the motor, the batteries, and the cooling unit)* are manufactured . . . (Use parentheses for subordination. See ¶219b.)

In a Series

184 Use a semicolon to separate items in a series if any of the items already contain commas.

The company will be represented on the Longwood Environmental Council by Martha Janowski, director of public affairs; Harris Mendel, vice president of manufacturing; and Daniel Santoya, director of environmental systems.

NOTE: As an alternative use parentheses to enclose the title following each name. Then use commas to separate the items in the series.

The company will be represented on the Longwood Environmental Council by Martha Janowski (director of public affairs), Harris Mendel (vice president of manufacturing), and Daniel Santoya (director of environmental systems).

185 Avoid starting a sentence with a series punctuated with semicolons. Try to recast the sentence so that the series comes at the end.

AWKWARD: New offices in Framingham, Massachusetts; Rochester, Minnesota; Metairie, Louisiana; and Bath, Maine, will be opened next year.

IMPROVED: Next year we will open new offices in Framingham, Massachusetts; Rochester, Minnesota; Metairie, Louisiana; and Bath, Maine.

NOTE: In sentences that mention one or more cities, omit the state names if the cities are well known and are clearly linked with only one state. (See also ¶160, note.)

Next year we will open new offices in St. Louis, Denver, and Fort Worth.

With Dependent Clauses

186 Use semicolons to separate a series of parallel dependent clauses if they are long or contain internal commas.

If you have tried special clearance sales but have not been able to raise the necessary cash; if you have tried to borrow the money and have not been able to find a lender; if you have offered to sell part of the business but have not been able to find a partner, then it seems to me that your only course of action is to go out of business. (See ¶185.)

They promised that they would review the existing specifications, costs, and sales estimates for the project; that they would analyze Merkle's alternative figures; and that they would prepare a comparison of the two proposals and submit their recommendations.

NOTE: A simple series of dependent clauses requires only commas, just like any other kind of series. (See also ¶162.)

Mrs. Bienstock said that all the budgets had to be redone by Monday, that she could not provide us with any extra help, and that we'd better cancel any weekend plans.

➤ *Semicolons with dashes: see ¶¶213, 215c.*
Semicolons with parentheses: see ¶224a.
Semicolons with quotation marks: see ¶248.
Spacing with semicolons: see ¶299.

¶187

The Colon

Between Independent Clauses

187 **a.** Use a colon between two independent clauses when the second clause explains or illustrates the first clause and there is no coordinating conjunction or transitional expression linking the two clauses.

> I have a special fondness for the Maine coast: it reminds me of the many happy summers we spent there before our children went off to college.
>
> I have two major hurdles to clear before I get my Ph.D.: I need to pass the oral exam and write a dissertation.

The second clause that explains or illustrates the first clause may itself consist of more than one independent clause.

> It has been said that a successful project goes through three stages: it won't work, it costs too much, and I always knew it was a good idea.

NOTE: It has been traditional to leave two spaces after a colon. Now that the standards of desktop publishing predominate, the use of only one space is appropriate. Unlike the spacing *between* sentences, where two spaces may be needed to improve the visual break, the use of only one space after a colon *within* a sentence normally provides an adequate visual break (just as it does for a semicolon or a comma).

b. Compare the use of the colon and the semicolon in the following sentences.

> The job you have described sounds very attractive: the salary, the benefits, and the opportunities for training and advancement seem excellent. (Use a colon when the second clause explains the first.)
>
> The job you have described sounds very attractive; it is the kind of job I have been looking for. (Use a semicolon when the second clause does not explain the first clause.)
>
> The job you have described sounds very attractive; for example, the salary and the benefits are good, and the opportunities for advancement seem excellent. (Ordinarily, use a semicolon when a transitional expression links the clauses. However, see ¶188.)

c. If you aren't sure whether to use a semicolon or a colon between two independent clauses, you can treat each clause as a separate sentence and use a period at the end of each.

> The job you have described sounds very attractive. For example, the salary and the benefits are good, and the opportunities for advancement seem excellent.

Before Lists and Enumerations

188 Place a colon before such expressions as *for example*, *namely*, and *that is* when they introduce words, phrases, or a series of clauses anticipated earlier in the sentence. (See ¶¶181–182.)

> The company provides a number of benefits not commonly offered in this area: for example, free dental insurance, low-cost term insurance, and personal financial counseling services.

➤ *For spacing after a colon when it is used with a list or an enumeration within a sentence, see ¶187a, note.*

189 When a clause contains an anticipatory expression (such as *the following*, *as follows*, *thus*, and *these*) and directs attention to a series of explanatory words, phrases, or clauses, use a colon between the clause and the series.

These are some of the new features in this year's models: a fuel economy indicator, a new rear suspension, and a three-year limited warranty.

The following staff members have been selected to attend the national sales conference in Honolulu:

    Frances Berkowitz
    Thomas Gomez
    Thomas Miscina

NOTE: Use *as follows* (not *as follow*), even though this phrase refers to a plural noun.

The *restrictions* on the use of this property are *as follows:* . . .

190   Use a colon even if the anticipatory expression is only implied and not stated.

The house has attractive features: cross ventilation in every room, a two-story living room, and two terraces.

Scientists have devised a most appropriate name for a physical property opposed to gravity: levity. (The colon may be used even when what follows is only a single word. See also ¶210.)

191   Do not use a colon in the following cases:

a. If the anticipatory expression occurs near the beginning of a long sentence.

We have set *the following* restrictions on the return of merchandise, so please be aware of this new policy when dealing with customers. Goods cannot be returned after five days, and price tags must not be removed.

BUT: We have set *the following* restrictions on the return of merchandise: goods cannot be returned . . .

b. If the sentence that contains the anticipatory expression is followed by another sentence.

Campers will find that *the following* items will add much to their enjoyment. These articles may be purchased from a store near the camp.

    Lightweight backpack
    Unbreakable vacuum bottle
    Insulated sleeping bag
    Polarized sunglasses

c. If an explanatory series follows an introductory clause that does not express a complete thought. (In such cases the introductory element often ends with a verb or a preposition.)

WRONG: Some of the questions that this book answers are: How can you reduce your insurance expenses without sacrificing protection? How can you avoid being over- or underinsured? How can you file a claim correctly the first time around? (Here the introductory clause is incomplete. It has a subject, *Some,* and a verb, *are,* but it lacks a complement.)

RIGHT: Some of the questions that this book answers are these: How can you . . . ? (Here the introductory clause is complete; hence a colon is acceptable.)

RIGHT: Here are some of the questions that this book answers: How can you . . . ? (Here again the introductory clause is complete; hence a colon is acceptable.)

WRONG: The panel consists of: Ms. Seidel, Mrs. Kitay, and Mr. Haddad.

RIGHT: The panel consists of Ms. Seidel, Mrs. Kitay, and Mr. Haddad.

RIGHT: The panel consists of the following people: Ms. Seidel, Mrs. Kitay, and Mr. Haddad.

WRONG: This set of china includes: 12 dinner plates, 12 salad plates, and 12 cups and saucers.

RIGHT: This set of china includes 12 dinner plates, 12 salad plates, and 12 cups and saucers.

RIGHT: This set of china includes the following pieces: 12 dinner plates, 12 salad plates, and 12 cups and saucers.

Continued on page 46

¶192

NOTE: A colon may be used after an incomplete introductory clause if the items in the series are listed on separate lines.

This set of china includes:	The panel consists of:
12 dinner plates	Ms. Seidel
12 salad plates	Mrs. Kitay
12 cups and saucers	Mr. Haddad

In Expressions of Time and Proportions

192   When hours and minutes are expressed in figures, separate them with a colon, as in the expression *8:25*. (No space precedes or follows this colon. See also ¶299.)

193   A colon is used to represent the word *to* in proportions, as in the ratio *2:1*. (No space precedes or follows this colon. See also ¶299.)

In Business Documents

194   **a.** In business letters, use a colon after the salutation (see also ¶1346). In social-business letters, use a comma (see also ¶1395b).

b. In business letters, a colon is often used with elements displayed on separate lines. (In some cases another type of punctuation is also acceptable.)

REFERENCE NOTATIONS:	When replying, refer to: Policy 356 627 894 (see ¶1316)
ATTENTION LINE:	Attention: Ms. Jane Palmer (see ¶1344)
SUBJECT LINE:	Subject: Amendments to Berkowitz Contract (see ¶1353)
REFERENCE INITIALS:	DMD:SBC **OR** dmd/sbs **OR** sbc (see ¶1370c)
ENCLOSURE NOTATION:	Enclosures: **OR** Under separate cover: (see ¶¶1373–1374)
COPY NOTATION:	cc: P. Malone **OR** c: P. Malone **OR** Copies to: P. Malone (see ¶1376d–f)
POSTSCRIPT:	PS: Please call on Monday **OR** PS. Please call . . . (see ¶1381)

NOTE: Leave one or two spaces after the colon as needed to achieve an adequate visual break. You may also use the first preset tab after the colon to establish the starting point for what follows. (A colon used in reference initials should not be followed or preceded by any space.)

c. In memos and other business documents, use a colon after displayed guide words.

TO: FROM: DATE: SHIP TO: BILL TO: *Distribution:*

NOTE: Leave a minimum of two spaces after displayed guide words like these. If a number of displayed guide words are arranged in a column (as in the heading of a memo), set a tab a minimum of two spaces after the longest guide word in the column so that the entries following the guide words will all align at the same point. You may be able to use a preset tab instead of setting a new tab. (See ¶1393f.)

In References to Books or Publications

195   **a.** Use a colon (followed by one space) to separate the title and the subtitle of a book.

Be sure to read *The New Positioning: The Latest on the World's No. 1 Business Strategy.*

b. A colon may be used to separate volume number and page number in footnotes and similar references. (Leave no space before or after this colon. See also ¶299.)

8:763-766 (meaning *Volume 8, pages 763-766;* see also ¶1512, note)

NOTE: A reference to chapter and verse in the Bible is handled the same way:

Is. 55:10 (meaning *Chapter 55, verse 10* in the Book of Isaiah)

Capitalizing After a Colon

196 Do not capitalize after a colon if the material that follows cannot stand alone as a sentence.

All cash advances must be countersigned by me, with one exception: when the amount is less than $50. (Dependent clause following a colon.)

Two courses are required: algebra and English. (Words following a colon.)

EXCEPTION: Capitalize the first word after the colon if it is a proper noun, a proper adjective, or the pronoun *I*.

Two courses are required: English and algebra.

197 Do not capitalize the first word of an independent clause after a colon if the clause explains, illustrates, or amplifies the thought expressed in the first part of the sentence. (See ¶196, exception.)

Essential and nonessential elements require altogether different punctuation: the latter should be set off by commas; the former should not.

198 Capitalize the first word of an independent clause after a colon only if it requires special emphasis or is presented as a formal rule. (In such cases the independent clause expresses the main thought; the first part of the sentence usually functions only as an introduction.)

Let me say this: If the company is to recover from its present difficulties, we must immediately devise an entirely new marketing strategy.

Here is the key principle: Nonessential elements must be set off by commas; essential elements should not.

Although index investing derives from the theory that the markets operate efficiently, its intellectual foundation is based on a simple truth: It is impossible for all stock investors *together* to outperform the overall stock market.

NOTE: Some writers like to capitalize *every* independent clause that follows a colon, even though they would not be tempted to capitalize independent clauses that follow a semicolon or a dash. The best policy is *not* to capitalize independent clauses after a colon except as specifically noted in ¶¶197–199.

199 Also capitalize the first word after a colon under these circumstances:

a. When the material following the colon consists of two or more sentences.

There are several drawbacks to this proposal: First, it will tie up a good deal of capital for the next five years. Second, the likelihood of a significant return on the investment has not been shown.

b. When the material following the colon is a quoted sentence.

Frederick Fontina responded in this way: "We expect to win our case once all the facts are brought out in the trial." (See ¶256 for the use of a colon before a quoted sentence.)

Continued on page 48

¶199

c. When the material following the colon starts on a new line (for example, the body of a letter following the salutation or the individual items displayed on separate lines in a list).

Dear John:

I have read your latest draft, and I find it much improved. However, on page 4 I wish you would redo . . .

Capitalize the first word of:

a. Every sentence.
b. Direct quotations.
c. Salutations in letters.

d. When the material *preceding* the colon is a short introductory word such as *Note, Caution, Remember,* or *Wanted.*

Note: All expense reports must be submitted no later than Friday.

Remember: All equipment must be turned off before you leave.

e. When the material *preceding* the colon is the name of a speaker in the transcription of court testimony or in a script for a play. (See also ¶270.)

SPELLMAN: According to Mrs. Genovese's testimony, you called Mr. Mellon "a person of hidden depths."

RISKIN: What I actually said was that I found Mr. Mellon to be a person of hidden shallows.

➤ *Colons with dashes: see ¶¶213, 215c.*
Colons with parentheses: see ¶224a.
Colons with quotation marks: see ¶¶248, 256.
Spacing with colons: see ¶187a, note, and ¶¶299, 1433e.

SECTION **2**
Punctuation: Other Marks

The Dash (¶¶201–217)

Parentheses (¶¶218–226)

Quotation Marks (¶¶227–284)

Italics and Underlining (¶¶285–290)

Other Marks of Punctuation (¶¶291–298)

Spacing With Punctuation Marks (¶299)

➢ *For definitions of grammatical terms, see the appropriate entries in the Glossary of Grammatical Terms (Appendix A).*

The Dash

Although the dash has a few specific functions of its own, it most often serves in place of the comma, the semicolon, the colon, or parentheses. When used as an alternative to these other marks, it creates a much more emphatic separation of words within a sentence. Because of its versatility, some writers are tempted to use a dash to punctuate almost any break within a sentence. Indeed, some writers mistakenly think it is fashionable to use dashes in place of periods at the end of sentences. However, this indiscriminate use of dashes destroys the special forcefulness that a dash can convey. So please use the dash sparingly—and then only for deliberate effect.

IMPORTANT NOTE: Dashes come in different lengths—one em, two ems, three ems, and one en. (An em has the same width as a capital M; an en is one-half the width of an em.)

The term *dash*—as used in ¶¶201–215—refers in all cases to a one-em dash; ¶¶216–217 deal in part with the use of two-em, three-em, and en dashes. (In the preceding sentence the

¶207

dash used in the phrase *¶¶201–215* is an illustration of an *en dash*. The dashes used to set off the phrase *as used in ¶¶201–215* as a whole are illustrations of an *em dash,* the simpler way of referring to a one-em dash.)

In Place of Commas

201 Use dashes in place of commas to set off a nonessential element that requires special emphasis.

> At this year's annual banquet, the speakers—and the food—were superb.
>
> Of all the color samples you sent me, there was only one I liked—taupe.

202 If a nonessential element already contains internal commas, use dashes in place of commas to set the element off. (If dashes provide too emphatic a break, use parentheses instead. See ¶¶183, 219.)

> Our entire inventory of Oriental rugs—including a fine selection of Sarouks, Kashans, and Bokharas—will be offered for sale at a 40 percent discount.

203 To give special emphasis to the second independent clause in a compound sentence, use a dash rather than a comma before the coordinating conjunction.

> The information I sent you is true—and you know it!

In Place of a Semicolon

204 For a stronger but less formal break, use a dash in place of a semicolon between closely related independent clauses. (See ¶¶176, 178.)

> I do the work—he gets the credit!
>
> The job needs to be done—moreover, it needs to be done well.
>
> Wilson is totally unqualified for a promotion—for example, he still does not grasp the basic principles of good management.

In Place of a Colon

205 For a stronger but less formal break, use a dash in place of a colon to introduce explanatory words, phrases, or clauses. (See ¶¶187–189.)

> I need only a few items for my meeting with Kaster—namely, a copy of his letter of May 18, a copy of the contract under dispute, and a bottle of aspirin.
>
> My arrangement with Gina is simple—she handles sales and I take care of promotion.

In Place of Parentheses

206 Use dashes instead of parentheses when you want to give the nonessential element strong emphasis. (See ¶¶183, 219.)

> Call Mike Habib—he's with Jax Electronics—and get his opinion.

To Indicate an Abrupt Break or an Afterthought

207 Use a dash to show an abrupt break in thought or to separate an afterthought from the main part of a sentence. When a sentence breaks off after a dash, leave one or two spaces before the next sentence. (See ¶102.)

> I wish you would— Is there any point in telling you what I wish for you?
>
> We offer the best service in town—and the fastest!
>
> According to Bertrand Russell, "Many people would sooner die than think—and usually do."

¶208

208 If a *question* or an *exclamation* breaks off abruptly before it has been completed, use a dash followed by a question mark or an exclamation point as appropriate. If the sentence is a *statement,* however, use a dash alone. Leave one or two spaces before the next sentence. (See ¶102.)

> Do you want to tell him or–? Suppose I wait to hear from you.
>
> If only– Yet there's no point in talking about what might have been.
>
> (**NOT:** If only–. Yet there's no point in talking about what might have been.)

➢ *For the use of ellipsis marks to indicate a break in thought, see ¶291b.*

To Show Hesitation

209 Use a dash to indicate hesitation, faltering speech, or stammering.

> The work on the Patterson project was begun–oh, I should say–well, about May 1–certainly no later than May 15.

To Emphasize Single Words

210 Use dashes to set off single words that require special emphasis.

> Jogging–that's what he lives for.
>
> There is, of course, a secret ingredient in my pasta sauce–fennel.

With Repetitions, Restatements, and Summarizing Words

211 **a.** Use dashes to set off and emphasize words that repeat or restate a previous thought.

> Next week–on Thursday at 10 a.m.–we will be making an important announcement at a press conference.
>
> Don't miss this opportunity–the opportunity of a lifetime!

b. Use a dash before such words as *these, they,* and *all* when these words stand as subjects summarizing a preceding list of details.

> Network television, magazines, and newspapers–*these* will be the big losers in advertising revenues next year.
>
> India, Korea, and Australia–*all* are important new markets for us.
>
> **BUT:** India, Korea, and Australia are all important new markets for us. (No dash is used when the summarizing word is not the subject.)

Before Attributions

212 When providing an attribution for a displayed quotation—that is, when identifying the author or the source of the quotation—use a dash before the name of the author or the title of the work.

> Never put off till tomorrow that which you can do today.
> —Benjamin Franklin
>
> Never do today what you can put off till tomorrow.
> —Aaron Burr
>
> Never put off until tomorrow what you can do the day after tomorrow.
> —Mark Twain

NOTE: The attribution typically appears on a separate line, aligned at the right with the longest line in the displayed quotation above. For additional examples, see ¶284b.

Punctuation Preceding an Opening Dash

213   Do not use a comma, a semicolon, or a colon before an opening dash. Moreover, do not use a period before an opening dash (except a period following an abbreviation).

> Quality circles boost productivity–and they pay off in higher profits too.
> (**NOT:** Quality circles boost productivity,–and they pay off in higher profits too.)
> The catalog proofs arrived before 11 a.m.–just as you promised.

Punctuation Preceding a Closing Dash

214   **a.** When a *statement* or a *command* is set off by dashes within a sentence, do not use a period before the closing dash (except a period following an abbreviation).

> Ernie Krauthoff–he used to have his own consulting firm–has gone back to his old job at Marker's.
> (**NOT:** Ernie Krauthoff–He used to have his own consulting firm.–has gone back to his old job at Marker's.)
> Your proposal was not delivered until 6:15 p.m.–more than two hours after the deadline.

b. When a *question* or an *exclamation* is set off by dashes within a sentence, use a question mark or an exclamation point before the closing dash.

> The representative of the Hitchcock Company–do you know her?–has called again for an appointment.
> The new sketches–I can't wait to show them to you!–should be ready by Monday or Tuesday at the latest.

NOTE: When a complete sentence is set off by dashes, do not capitalize the first word unless it is a proper noun, a proper adjective, the pronoun *I,* or the first word of a quoted sentence.

Punctuation Following a Closing Dash

215   When the sentence construction requires some mark of punctuation following a closing dash, either retain the dash or use the sentence punctuation—but do not use both marks together.

a. When a closing dash falls at the end of a sentence, it should be replaced by the punctuation needed to end the sentence—a period, a question mark, or an exclamation point. (See ¶208 for exceptions.)

> Wheeler's Transport delivers the goods–on time!
> (**NOT:** Wheeler's Transport delivers the goods–on time–!)

b. When a closing dash occurs at a point where the sentence requires a comma, retain the closing dash and omit the comma.

> The situation has become critical–indeed dangerous–but no one seems to care. (Here the closing dash is retained, and the comma before the coordinating conjunction is omitted.)
> If you feel you are qualified for the job–and you may very well be–you ought to take the employment test and go for an interview. (Here the closing dash is retained, and the comma that separates a dependent clause from an independent clause is omitted.)
> Brophy said–and you can check with him yourself–"This office must be vacated by Friday." (Here the closing dash is retained, and the comma before the quotation is omitted.)

NOTE: Do not put a phrase in dashes if the closing dash occurs at a point where a comma is needed after an item in a series. Put the phrase in parentheses instead.

Continued on page 54

CONFUSING: I plan to ask Spalding, Crawford–Betty, not Harold–Higgins, and Martin to investigate why sales have fallen off so sharply.

CLEAR: I plan to ask Spalding, Crawford (Betty, not Harold), Higgins, and Martin to investigate why sales have fallen off so sharply.

c. If a closing dash occurs at a point where the sentence requires a semicolon, a colon, or a closing parenthesis, drop the closing dash and use the required sentence punctuation.

Please try to get your sales projections to us by Wednesday–certainly by Friday at the latest; otherwise, they will be of no use to us in planning next year's budget.

Here is what Marsha had to say–or at least the gist of it: look for new opportunities in niche marketing, and move quickly to capitalize on them.

You need a volunteer (for example, someone like Louis Morales–he's always cooperative) to play the part of the customer.

Typing Dashes

216 **a.** If you are using word processing software, you will very likely have access to a special character called an *em dash*—so called because it is as wide as a capital M. (This is the dash that appears in all the examples in ¶¶201–215.) If you do not have access to this special character, you can construct a dash by striking the hyphen key *twice* with no space between the hyphens. Whether you use an em dash or two hyphens, leave no space before or after the dash.

Don't believe him–ever!   (**NOT:** Don't believe him – ever!)

OR: Don't believe him--ever!   (**NOT:** Don't believe him -- ever!)

BUT: If only I had realized– But now it's too late. (When a statement breaks off abruptly, leave one or two spaces between the dash and the start of the next sentence. See ¶208 and an important spacing guideline in ¶102.)

b. Never use a single hyphen to represent a dash.

There's only one person who can do this job--you!
(**NOT:** There's only one person who can do this job-you! **OR:** . . . this job – you!)

c. A two-em dash is used to indicate that letters are missing from a word. If you do not have access to a two-em dash, type four consecutive hyphens (with no space between). If the letters are missing from *within* a word, leave no space before or after the two-em dash. If the letters are missing *at the end* of a word, leave no space before; leave one space after unless a mark of punctuation is required at that point.

Mr. T—n was the one who tipped off the police.   **OR:**   Mr. T----n was the one . . .

Mrs. J— asked not to be identified.   **OR:**   Mrs. J---- asked not to be identified.

d. A three-em dash is used to indicate that an entire word has been left out or needs to be provided. If you do not have access to a three-em dash, type six consecutive hyphens (with no space between hyphens). Since the three-em dash represents a complete word, leave one space before and after the three-em dash unless a mark of punctuation is required after the missing word.

We expect our sales will reach —— by the end of the year.   **OR:**   . . . reach ------ by the . . .

NOTE: A three-em dash is also used in bibliographies to represent an author's name in subsequent entries, after the first entry in which the author's name is given in full. See ¶1550 and the illustration on page 465.

e. Type a dash at the end of a line (rather than at the start of a new line).

He lives in Hawaii–   **NOT:** He lives in Hawaii
on Maui, I believe.   –on Maui, I believe.

217 **a.** Use an *en* dash—half the length of an em dash but longer than a hyphen—to connect numbers in a range. The en dash means "up to and including" in expressions like these:

open 10 a.m.–6 p.m., Monday–Friday	see Chapters 2-3, pages 86-124
planned for the week of March 2-8	a loan of $50,000-$60,000 for 10-15 years
during the years 1999-2003	retirement plans for employees aged 55-62
a seminar scheduled for May–June 2002	new offices located on Floors 16-17

➤ *For the use of an en dash in certain compound adjectives, see ¶819b, note, and ¶821b, note. For other examples showing the use of an en dash, see ¶¶459–460.*

b. If the equipment you are using does not offer access to an en dash, use a hyphen in expressions like those in *a* above.

c. In manuscript being prepared for publication, it is often necessary to use special proofreaders' marks to distinguish en dashes from em dashes and hyphens, especially when hyphens have been used throughout the manuscript to represent dashes of varying length.

The proper way to code the length of dashes is as follows:

$$\frac{1}{N} \qquad \frac{1}{M} \qquad \frac{2}{M} \qquad \frac{3}{M}$$

The proper way to indicate which hyphens are to be treated as hyphens is to double the hyphen to look like an equal sign. For example:

first-rate   first=rate

A two-day conference will take place early this spring—sometime during the week of

April 4-10, I believe. The registration fee of $250-$300 will be reduced for those who

sign up for the first=day program.

Parentheses

Parentheses and dashes serve many of the same functions, but they differ in one significant respect: parentheses can set off only nonessential elements, whereas dashes can set off essential and nonessential elements. **REMEMBER:** In setting off elements, dashes emphasize; parentheses de-emphasize.

With Explanatory Material

218 Use parentheses to enclose explanatory material that is independent of the main thought of the sentence. The material within parentheses may be a single word, a phrase, an entire sentence, a number, or an abbreviation.

We called him Mr. B. for so long that when I ran into him last week, I couldn't remember his last name (Bertolucci). (A single word.)

Continued on page 56

¶219

By Friday (and sooner if possible) I will have an answer for you. (A phrase.)

Our competitors (we consistently underprice them) can't understand how we are able to do it. (A sentence.)

This note for Five Thousand Dollars ($5000) is payable within ninety (90) days. (Numbers. See ¶¶420, 436, note.)

Many corporations have created a new top-level job: chief information officer (CIO). (Abbreviation. See ¶504, note.)

NOTE: Be sure the parentheses enclose only what is truly parenthetical.

WRONG: I merely said I was averse (not violently opposed *to*) your suggestion.

RIGHT: I merely said I was averse (not violently opposed) *to* your suggestion.

219 Use parentheses to set off a nonessential element when dashes would be too emphatic and commas might create confusion.

a. Parentheses are clearer than commas when a city-state expression occurs as an adjective.

Sales are down in our Middletown (Connecticut) office.

BETTER THAN: Sales are down in our Middletown, Connecticut, office.

b. Parentheses are clearer than commas when the nonessential element already contains commas. (See ¶¶183, 202.)

In three of our factories (Gary, Detroit, and Milwaukee) output is up.

With References

220 Use parentheses to set off references and directions.

When I last wrote to you (see my letter of July 8 attached), I enclosed photocopies of checks that you had endorsed and deposited.

When a reference falls *at the end of a sentence*, it may be treated as part of the sentence or as a separate sentence. (See also ¶225, note.)

This point is discussed at greater length in Chapter 7 (see pages 90–101).

OR: This point is discussed at greater length in Chapter 7. (See pages 90–101.)

➤ *For the use of parentheses in footnotes, endnotes, and textnotes, see Section 15.*

With Dates

221 Use parentheses to enclose dates that accompany a person's name, a publication, or an event.

He claims that he can trace his family back to Charlemagne (742–814).

The "Sin On" Bible (1716) got its name from an extraordinary typographical error: instead of counseling readers to "sin no more," it urged them to "sin on more."

With Enumerated Items

222 a. Within a Sentence.   Use parentheses to enclose numbers or letters that accompany enumerated items within a sentence.

We need the following information to complete our record of Ms. Pavlick's experience: (1) the number of years she worked for your company, (2) a description of her duties, and (3) the number of promotions she received.

NOT: . . . our record of Ms. Pavlick's experience: 1) the number of years she worked for your company, 2) a description of her duties, and 3) the number of promotions she received. (The only acceptable use of a single closing parenthesis is in an outline. See ¶223.)

NOTE: Use letters to enumerate items within a sentence when the sentence itself is part of a *numbered* sequence.

> 3. Please include these items on your expense report: (a) the cost of your hotel room, (b) the cost of meals, and (c) the amount spent on travel.

b. In a Displayed List.   If the enumerated items appear on separate lines, the letters or numbers are usually followed only by periods. (See ¶107.)

223 Subdivisions in outlines are often enclosed in parentheses. It is sometimes necessary to use a single closing parenthesis to provide another level of subdivision.

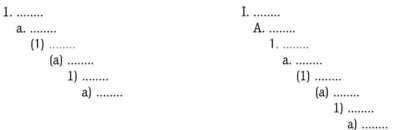

NOTE: At every level of an outline there should be at least two items. If an item is labeled *A,* there must be at least one more item (labeled *B*) at the same level.

➤ *For guidelines on formatting outlines, see ¶¶1722–1727.*

Parenthetical Items Within Sentences

224 If the item in parentheses falls *within a sentence:*

a. Make sure that any punctuation that comes after the item (such as a comma, a semicolon, a colon, or a dash) falls *outside* the closing parenthesis.

> Unless I hear from you within five working days (by May 3), I will turn this matter over to my attorney.
>
> I tried to reach you last Monday (I called just before noon); however, no one in your office knew where you were.
>
> For Jane there is only one goal right now (and you know it): getting that M.B.A.
>
> I saw your picture in a magazine last week (in *People,* I think)—and how I laughed when I saw who was standing next to you!

NOTE: Do not insert a comma, a semicolon, a colon, or a dash *before* an opening parenthesis.

b. Do not capitalize the first word of the item in parentheses, even if the item is a complete sentence. **EXCEPTIONS:** Proper nouns, proper adjectives, the pronoun *I,* and the first word of a quoted sentence. (See examples in *c* and *d.*)

c. Do not use a period before the closing parenthesis except with an abbreviation.

> Plan to stay with us (we're only fifteen minutes from the airport) whenever you come to New Orleans.
>
> **NOT:** Plan to stay with us (We're only fifteen minutes from the airport.) whenever you come to New Orleans.
>
> Paul Melnick (he's Boyd's new sales manager) wants to take you to lunch.
>
> At last week's hearing (I had to leave at 4 p.m.), was the relocation proposal presented?

Continued on page 58

¶225

d. Do not use a question mark or an exclamation point before the closing parenthesis unless it applies solely to the parenthetical item *and* the sentence ends with a different mark of punctuation.

> At the coming meeting (will you be able to make it on the 19th?), let's plan to discuss next year's budget. (A question mark is used in parentheses because the sentence ends with a period.)
>
> May I still get tickets to the show (and may I bring a friend), or is it too late? (A question mark is omitted in parentheses because the sentence ends with a question mark.)
>
> **NOT:** May I still get tickets to the show (and may I bring a friend?), or is it too late?

Parenthetical Items at the End of Sentences

225 If the item in parentheses is to be incorporated *at the end of a sentence:*

a. Place the punctuation needed to end the sentence *outside* the closing parenthesis.

> Please return the payroll review sheets by Monday (October 8).
>
> Is it true that there is a special term for gossip spread by e-mail (word of mouse)?
>
> What a prima donna I work with (you know the one I mean)!

b. Do not capitalize the first word of the item in parentheses, even if the item is a complete sentence. **EXCEPTIONS:** Proper nouns, proper adjectives, the pronoun *I,* and the first word of a quoted sentence. (See examples in *c* and *d* below.)

c. Do not use a period before the closing parenthesis except with an abbreviation.

> Our office is open late on Thursdays (until 9 p.m.).
>
> Our office is open late on Thursdays (we're here until nine).
>
> **NOT:** Our office is open late on Thursdays (We're here until nine.).

d. Do not use a question mark or an exclamation point before the closing parenthesis unless it applies solely to the parenthetical element *and* the sentence ends with a different mark of punctuation.

> My new assistant is Bill Romero (didn't you meet him once before?).
>
> Be sure to send the letter to Portland, Oregon (not Portland, Maine!).
>
> Then he walked out and slammed the door (can you believe it?)!
>
> Do you know Ellen Smyth (or is it Smythe)?
>
> **NOT:** Do you know Ellen Smyth (or is it Smythe?)?
>
> I'm through with the job (and I mean it)!
>
> **NOT:** I'm through with the job (and I mean it!)!

NOTE: When a complete sentence occurs within parentheses at the end of another sentence, it may be incorporated into the sentence (as in the examples above) so long as it is fairly short and closely related. If the sentence in parentheses is long or requires special emphasis, it should be treated as a separate sentence (see ¶226).

Parenthetical Items as Separate Sentences

226 If the item in parentheses is to be treated as a *separate sentence:*

a. The preceding sentence should close with a punctuation mark of its own.

b. The item in parentheses should begin with a capital letter.

c. A period, a question mark, or an exclamation point (whichever is appropriate) should be placed *before* the closing parenthesis.

d. No other punctuation mark should follow the closing parenthesis. Leave one or two spaces before the start of the next sentence. (See ¶102.)

¶226

Then Steven Pelletier made a motion to replace the board of directors. (He does this at every stockholders' meeting.) However, this year . . .

I was most impressed with the speech given by Helena Verdi. (Didn't you used to work with her?) She knew her subject and she knew her audience.

➢ *Parentheses around question marks: see ¶118.*
Parentheses around exclamation points: see ¶119c.
Parentheses around confirming figures: see ¶420a.
Parentheses around area codes in telephone numbers: see ¶454c.
Parenthetical elements within parenthetical elements: see ¶297.
Plural endings in parentheses: see ¶626.

Quotation Marks

Quotation marks have three main functions: to indicate the use of someone else's exact words (see ¶¶227–234), to set off words and phrases for special emphasis (see ¶¶235–241), and to display the titles of certain literary and artistic works (see ¶¶242–244).

IMPORTANT NOTE: There are three styles of quotation marks: *curly* (" "), *slanted* (` ´), and *straight* ("). (Curly quotation marks are often referred to as *smart quotes*.)

In the following examples, note that curly and slanted quotation marks require a different symbol to mark the opening and closing of the quoted material; straight quotation marks are the same, whether they open or close the quoted material. (Note also that the style of the apostrophe in *won't* matches the style of the quotation marks.)

> **CURLY:** Paul simply said, "It won't work."
> **SLANTED:** Paul simply said, ´It won't work.´
> **STRAIGHT:** Paul simply said, "It won't work."

The font you select will determine the style of quotation marks to be used. If you wish, you can switch from the default style to an alternative style by accessing an extended character set.

Quotation marks usually appear as a doubled set of symbols, but in certain circumstances single quotation marks are called for. (See ¶¶245–246, 247b, 248b, 249d, 250b, 265b, 298a.)

For guidance on how to position punctuation marks in relation to the closing quotation mark—*inside* or *outside*—see ¶¶247–251.

For more specific guidance on when to use punctuation with quoted material and which punctuation to use, refer to the following paragraphs:

➢ *Quotations standing alone: see ¶252.*
Quotations at the beginning of a sentence: see ¶¶253–255.
Quotations at the end of a sentence: see ¶¶256–258.
Quotations within a sentence: see ¶¶259–261.
Quotations with interrupting expressions: see ¶¶262–263.
Quotations within quotations: see ¶¶245–246.
Long quotations: see ¶¶264–265.
Quoted letters: see ¶266.
Quoted poetry: see ¶¶267–268.
Quoted dialogues and conversations: see ¶¶269–270.
Quotation marks as a symbol for inches: see ¶432.

¶227

With Direct Quotations

227 Use quotation marks to enclose a *direct quotation*, that is, the exact words of a speaker or a writer.

> According to F. P. Jones, "Experience is that marvelous thing that enables you to recognize a mistake when you make it again."
>
> I overheard a senior economist on our staff say this to a young colleague: "Your idea may be fine in practice, but it will never work in theory."
>
> Casey Stengel once said, "The secret of managing is to keep the guys who hate you from the guys who are undecided."
>
> When I asked Diana whether she liked the new format of the magazine, all she said was "No." (See ¶¶233, 256a, note.)

228 **a.** Do not use quotation marks for an *indirect quotation*, that is, a restatement or a rearrangement of a person's exact words. (An indirect quotation is often introduced by *that* or *whether* and usually differs from a direct quotation in person, verb tense, or word order.)

> **DIRECT QUOTATION:** Mrs. Knudsen asked her supervisor, "<u>Am I</u> still being considered for the transfer?"
>
> **INDIRECT QUOTATION:** Mrs. Knudsen asked her supervisor <u>whether she was</u> still being considered for the transfer.
>
> **DIRECT QUOTATION:** Her supervisor said, "<u>You're</u> still in the running, but <u>don't</u> expect a quick decision."
>
> **INDIRECT QUOTATION:** Her supervisor said <u>that she was</u> still in the running but <u>should not</u> expect a quick decision.

NOTE: Sometimes *direct* quotations are introduced by *that*. See ¶¶256f and 272, note.

b. In some cases a person's exact words may be treated as either a direct or an indirect quotation, depending on the kind of emphasis desired.

> The chairman himself said, "The staff should be told at once that the rumors about a new building have no foundation." (The use of quotation marks emphasizes that these are the chairman's exact words.)
>
> The chairman himself said the staff should be told at once that the rumors about a new building have no foundation. (Without quotation marks, the emphasis falls on the message itself. The fact that the chairman used these exact words is not important.)

229 Do not use quotation marks to set off a *direct question* at the end of a sentence unless it is also a *direct quotation* (one that uses someone's exact words.)

> **DIRECT QUESTION:** The question is, Who will pay for restoring the landmark?
>
> **DIRECT QUOTATION:** Mrs. Burchall then asked, "Who will pay for restoring the landmark?"
>
> **DIRECT QUOTATION:** Mrs. Burchall then replied, "The question is, Who will pay for restoring the landmark?" (See also ¶115.)

230 Quotation marks are not needed to set off interior thoughts or imagined dialogue. Treat this kind of material like a *direct question* (as shown in ¶229 above).

> After I left Joe's office, I thought, He has no business telling me what to do.
>
> I should have said, I can handle this situation—thank you very much!—without any of your help.

NOTE: In special cases quotation marks may help to preserve clarity or maintain stylistic consistency (for example, when imaginary dialogue is interspersed with actual dialogue).

231   a. When only a word or phrase is quoted from another source, be sure to place the quotation marks only around the words extracted from the original source and not around any rearrangement of those words.

> Tanya said she would need "more help" in order to finish your report by this Friday. (Tanya's exact words were, "How can he expect me to finish his report by this Friday without more help?")

b. When a quoted word or phrase comes at the end of a statement, the period goes *inside* the closing quotation mark.

> G. K. Chesterton explained that angels can fly "because they take themselves lightly."

NOTE: When a quoted word or phrase comes at the end of a question or an exclamation, the placement of punctuation with respect to the quotation marks will vary. (See ¶258 for guidelines. See also ¶247a, particularly examples 2–4.)

c. Be particularly sure not to include such words as *a* and *the* at the beginning of the quotation or *etc.* at the end unless these words were actually part of the original material.

> Ben thought you did a "super" job on the packaging design. (Ben's exact words were, "Tell Bonnie I thought the job she did on the packaging design was super.")

> Explain the decision any way you want, but tell George I said, "I'm truly sorry about the way things turned out," etc., etc.

232   When quoting a series of words or phrases in the exact sequence in which they originally appeared, use quotation marks before and after the complete series. However, if the series of quoted words or phrases did not appear in this sequence in the original, use quotation marks around each word or phrase.

> According to Selma, the latest issue of the magazine looked "fresh, crisp, and appealing." (Selma's actual words were, "I think the new issue looks especially fresh, crisp, and appealing.")
>
> **BUT:** Selma thinks the magazine looks "fresh" and "crisp."
> (**NOT:** Selma thinks the magazine looks "fresh and crisp.")

233   Do not quote the words *yes* and *no* unless you wish to emphasize that these were (or will be) the exact words spoken.

> Please answer the question yes or no.
> Don't say no until you have heard all the terms of the proposal.
> You need to start saying no to cookies and yes to laps around the block.
> When asked if he would accept a reassignment, Nick thought for a moment; then, without any trace of emotion, he said "Yes." (The quotation marks imply that Nick said precisely this much and no more. See ¶256a, note, for the use or omission of a comma after *he said.*)

NOTE: When quoting the words *yes* and *no,* capitalize them if they represent a complete sentence.

> All she said was "No."
> I would have to answer that question by saying "Yes and no."
> **BUT:** That question requires something more than a yes-or-no answer.

234   Do not use quotation marks with well-known proverbs and sayings. They are not direct quotations.

> When I was young, I was taught that the person who laughs last laughs best.
> When I was older, I learned that the person who laughs last thinks slowest.
> Now that I'm old, I know that people who laugh last.

¶235

Punctuation: Other Marks

2

For Special Emphasis

235   When using technical terms, business jargon, or coined words or phrases not likely to be familiar to your reader, enclose them in quotation marks when they are first used.

> One computer support center reports that some software users become confused when they are directed to press any key. They call to complain that they cannot find the "any" key.
>
> It takes Joe a long time to get himself "booted up" in the morning. (The quoted phrase refers to the technique whereby a computer gets itself up and running. The quotation marks are unnecessary if you are writing to someone familiar with computer terms.)

236   **a.** Words used humorously or ironically may be enclosed in quotation marks. However, unless you are convinced your reader will otherwise miss the humor or the irony, omit the quotation marks.

> I was totally underwhelmed by Joe's proposal to centralize all purchasing.
> (**RATHER THAN:** I was totally "underwhelmed" by Joe's proposal . . .)
>
> HDL cholesterol is the good kind; it's LDL that's the bad kind.
> (**RATHER THAN:** . . . the "good" kind . . . the "bad" kind . . .)
>
> Nothing would please me more than looking at the slides of Mike's tour of Egypt. (One might reasonably conclude that the writer takes unalloyed pleasure at the prospect.)
>
> **BUT:** "Nothing" would please me more than looking at the slides of Mike's tour of Egypt. (When *Nothing* is enclosed in quotation marks, the writer makes it clear that doing nothing would be preferable to looking at Mike's slides.)

b. A slang expression, the use of poor grammar, or a deliberate misspelling is enclosed in quotation marks to indicate that such usage is not part of the writer's normal way of speaking or writing.

> Now that his kids have run off to Europe with the college tuition money, Bob has stopped boasting about his close-knit "nucular" family. (The writer is mimicking Bob's habitual mispronunciation of *nuclear.*)
>
> As far as I'm concerned, Polly Harrington's version of what happened "ain't necessarily so."

c. Quotation marks are not needed for colloquial expressions.

> She cares less about the salary than she does about the perks—you know, chauffeured limousine, stock options, and all the rest of it. (*Perks* is short for *perquisites,* meaning "special privileges.")
>
> Pam is planning to temp until she's sure about staying in Los Angeles. (*To temp* means "to do temporary work.")

237   **a.** Use quotation marks to enclose words and phrases that have been made to play an abnormal role in a sentence—for example, verb phrases made to function as adjectives.

> We were all impressed by her "can do" attitude. (*Can do* is a verb phrase used here as an adjective modifying *attitude.*)
>
> **OR:** We were all impressed by her can-do attitude. (A hyphen may also be used to hold together a phrase used as an adjective before a noun. See ¶828.)
>
> **BUT NOT:** We were all impressed by her "can-do" attitude. (Do not use both quotation marks and a hyphen for the same purpose.)
>
> I'm selling my car on an "as is" (**OR** as-is) basis.
>
> "Backspace and overstrike" is a hacker's way of saying that you ought to take back something you just said or undo something you just did.

NOTE: When a verb like *must* or a preposition-adverb like *in* becomes established as a noun or an adjective (as indicated in the dictionary), use quotation marks only in those constructions where confusion could otherwise result.

¶242

You have to read that book; it's a must.

BUT: You have to get that book; it's "must" reading.

Frank must have an in with their purchasing department.

BUT: I guess she thinks it's still the "in" thing to do.

This has been an off year for real estate sales and housing starts.

b. Do not use quotation marks to enclose phrases taken from other parts of speech and now well established as nouns; for example, *haves and have-nots, pros and cons, ins and outs.* (See also ¶625.)

a helpful list of dos and don'ts

all the whys and wherefores

a lot of ifs, ands, or buts (see also ¶285a)

238 When a word or an expression is formally defined, the word to be defined is usually italicized or underlined and the definition is usually quoted so that the two elements may be easily distinguished. (See ¶286.)

➢ *For guidelines on italics and underlining, see ¶290.*

239 A word referred to as a word may be enclosed in quotation marks but is now more commonly italicized or underlined. (See ¶285a.)

240 **a.** Words and phrases introduced by such expressions as *marked, labeled, signed, entitled,* or *titled* are enclosed in quotation marks.

The carton was marked "Fragile."

He received a message signed "A Friend."

The article entitled "Write Your Senator" was in that issue. (See ¶260.)

NOTE: Titles of complete published works following the expression *entitled* or *titled* require italics or underlining rather than quotation marks. (See ¶289 for titles to be italicized or underlined; ¶¶242–244 for titles to be quoted.)

➢ *For a usage note on* entitled *and* titled, *see Section 11, page 291.*

b. Words and phrases introduced by *so-called* do not require quotation marks, italics, or underlining. The expression *so-called* is sufficient to give special emphasis to the term that follows.

The so-called orientation session struck me as an exercise in brainwashing.

241 The translation of a foreign expression is enclosed in quotation marks; the foreign word itself is italicized or underlined. (See ¶287.)

With Titles of Literary and Artistic Works

242 Use quotation marks around the titles that represent only *part* of a complete published work—for example, the titles of chapters, lessons, topics, sections, and parts within a book; the titles of articles and feature columns in newspapers and magazines; and the titles of essays, short poems, lectures, sermons, and conference themes. (Italicize or underline titles of *complete* published works. See ¶289.)

The heart of her argument can be found in Chapter 3, "The Failure of Traditional Therapy." You'll especially want to read the section entitled "Does Father Know Best?"

An exciting article—"Can Cancer Now Be Cured?"—appears in the magazine I'm enclosing. (See ¶¶260–261 for the use of commas, dashes, and parentheses with quoted titles.)

Continued on page 64

Punctuation:
Other Marks

2

¶243

> The theme of next month's workshop is "Imperatives for the New Millennium—From the Ragged Edge to the Cutting Edge."
>
> The title of my speech for next month's luncheon will be "Reforming Our Local Tax Policy."
>
> **BUT:** At next month's luncheon I will be talking about reforming our local tax policy. (Do not enclose the words with quotation marks when they describe the topic rather than signify the exact title.)

NOTE: The titles *Preface, Contents, Appendix*, and *Index* are not quoted, even though they represent parts within a book. They are often capitalized, however, for special emphasis.

> All the supporting data is given in the Appendix. (Often capitalized when referring to another section within the same work.)
>
> **BUT:** You'll find that the most interesting part of his book is contained in the appendix. (Capitalization is not required when reference is made to a section within another work.)

243 Use quotation marks around the titles of *complete but unpublished* works, such as manuscripts, dissertations, and reports.

> I would like to get a copy of Sandor's study, "Criteria for Evaluating Staff Efficiency."
>
> Thank you for giving us the chance to review "Working out of Your Home." I have given your manuscript to an editor with a good deal of personal experience in this field.

244 Use quotation marks around the titles of songs and other short musical compositions and around the titles of individual segments or programs that are part of a larger television or radio series. (Series titles are italicized or underlined. See ¶289.)

> Just once I would like to get through a company party without having to hear Reggie sing "Danny Boy,"
>
> I understand that our company was briefly mentioned on the *Frontline* program entitled "Pentagon, Inc.," which was shown last Tuesday night.

Quotations Within Quotations

245 A quotation within another quotation is enclosed in single quotation marks.

NOTE: If you do not have access to single quotation marks, you may use the apostrophe under certain circumstances. (See ¶298a.)

> Dorothy Parker once said, "The most beautiful words in the English language are 'Check enclosed.'"
>
> According to an unnamed twelve-year-old (quoted in a BellSouth ad), "The most dreaded words in the English language are 'Some assembly required.'"

246 If a quotation appears within the single-quoted material, revert to double quotation marks for the inner portion.

> Mrs. DeVries then remarked, "I thought it a bit strange when Mr. Fowler said, 'Put these checks in an envelope marked "Personal Funds," and set them aside for me.'" (When single and double quotation marks occur together, insert extra space between the two marks to keep them distinct.)

NOTE: For the positioning of punctuation in relation to a single quotation mark, see the following paragraphs:

➢ *For placement of periods and commas, see ¶247b.*
  For placement of semicolons and colons, see ¶248b.
  For placement of question marks and exclamation points, see ¶249d.
  For placement of dashes, see ¶250b.

¶**248**

The following rules (¶¶247–251) indicate how to position punctuation marks in relation to the closing quotation mark—inside *or* outside.

With Periods and Commas

247 **a.** Periods and commas always go *inside* the closing quotation mark. This is the preferred American style. (Some writers in the United States follow the British style: Place the period *outside* when it punctuates the whole sentence, *inside* when it punctuates only the quoted material. Place the comma *outside,* since it always punctuates the sentence, not the quoted material.)

> Pablo Picasso is the person who said, "Computers are useless. They can only give you answers."
>
> He wants to change "on or about May 1" to read "no later than May 1."
>
> When your mind suddenly goes blank, it's not the start of Alzheimer's; you may simply be having a "senior moment."
>
> The price tag on the leather sofa was clearly marked "Sold."
>
> Sign your name wherever you see an "X."
>
> "Let's go over the details again," she said.
>
> "The date stamp indicates that my copy arrived at 10:50 a.m.," he said.
>
> Their latest article, "Scanning the Future of E-Commerce," will appear in next month's issue of *Inc.* magazine.
>
> "Witty," "clever," "amusing," and "hilarious" are only a few of the adjectives that are being applied to her new book.
>
> The package was labeled "Fragile," but that meant nothing to your delivery crew.

b. Periods and commas also go *inside* the single closing quotation mark.

> Mr. Poston said, "Please let me see all the orders marked 'Rush.'"
>
> "All he would say was 'I don't remember,'" answered the witness.

NOTE: Do not confuse a single quotation mark with an apostrophe used to show possession. When a sentence requires the use of a comma or a period at the same point as an apostrophe showing possession, the comma or period follows the apostrophe.

> I recently took over the management of the Murrays', the Boyarskys', and the Cabots' investment portfolios.

With Semicolons and Colons

248 **a.** Semicolons and colons always go *outside* the closing quotation mark.

> Last Tuesday you said, "I will mail a check today"; it has not yet arrived.
>
> When the announcement of the changeover was made, my reaction was "Why?"; John's only reaction was "When?"
>
> The memo I sent you yesterday said that the new workstations would cost "a nominal egg"; it should have said "an arm and a leg."
>
> Please send me the following items from the file labeled "In Process": the latest draft of the Berryman agreement and FASB Statement 33.

b. Semicolons and colons also go *outside* the single closing quotation mark.

> Alice Arroyo called in from Dallas to say, "Please send me the following items from the file labeled 'In Process': the latest draft of the Berryman agreement, the comments provided by our lawyer, and FASB Statement 33."

¶249

With Question Marks and Exclamation Points

249 **a.** At the end of a sentence, a question mark or an exclamation point goes *inside* the closing quotation mark when it applies only to the quoted material.

> His first question was, "How long have you worked here?" (Quoted question at the end of a statement.)
>
> Garland still ends every sales meeting by shouting, "Go get 'em!" (Quoted exclamation at the end of a statement.)

b. At the end of a sentence, a question mark or an exclamation point goes *outside* the closing quotation mark when it applies to the entire sentence.

> When will she say, for a change, "You did a nice job on that"? (Quoted statement at the end of a question.)
>
> Stop saying "Don't worry"! (Quoted statement at the end of an exclamation.)

c. If a sentence ends with quoted material and both the sentence and the quoted material require the same mark of punctuation, use only one mark—the one that comes first. (See also ¶¶257–258.)

> Have you seen the advertisement that starts, "Why pay more?" (Quoted question at the end of a question.)
>
> Let's not panic and yell "Fire!" (Quoted exclamation at the end of an exclamation.)

d. These same principles govern the placement of a question mark or an exclamation point in relation to a single quotation mark.

> What prompted her to say, "Be careful in handling documents marked 'Confidential'"? (Quoted phrase within a quoted statement within a question.)
>
> Dr. Marks asked, "Was the check marked 'Insufficient Funds'?" (Quoted phrase within a quoted question within a statement.)
>
> Miss Parsons then said, "How did you answer him when he asked you, 'How do you know?'" (Quoted question within a quoted question within a statement.)

With Dashes

250 **a.** A dash goes *inside* the closing quotation mark to indicate that the speaker's or writer's words have broken off abruptly.

> It was tragic to hear Tom say, "If he had only listened–"

b. A dash goes *outside* the closing quotation mark when the sentence breaks off abruptly *after* the quotation.

> If I hear one more word about "boosting productivity"–
>
> **BUT:** Mrs. Halliday said, "If I hear one more word from the general manager about 'boosting productivity'–"

c. A closing dash goes *outside* the closing quotation mark when the quotation itself is part of a nonessential element being set off by a pair of dashes.

> Get the latest draft–it's the one with the notation "Let's go with this"–and take it to Gladys.

With Parentheses

251 **a.** The closing parenthesis goes *inside* the closing quotation mark when the parenthetical element is part of the quotation.

> Fox agreed to settle his account "by Friday (July 28)" when he last wrote us.

b. The closing parenthesis goes *outside* the closing quotation mark when the quotation is part of the parenthetical element.

> Joe Elliott (the one everyone calls "Harper's gofer") will probably get the job.

¶256

The following rules (¶¶252–270) indicate what punctuation to use with various kinds of quoted material.

Punctuating Quotations That Stand Alone

252 When a quoted sentence stands alone, put the appropriate mark of terminal punctuation—a period, a question mark, or an exclamation point—*inside* the closing quotation mark.

> "I think we should switch suppliers at once."
> "Can you send us your comments within two weeks?"
> "I won't accept that kind of response!"

Punctuating Quotations That Begin a Sentence

253 **a.** When a quoted *statement* occurs at the beginning of a sentence, omit the period before the closing quotation mark and use a comma instead.

> "I think we should switch suppliers at once," he said.
> (**NOT:** . . . at once.," he said.)

EXCEPTION: Retain the period if it accompanies an abbreviation.

> "I'm still planning to go on for an LL.B.," she said.

b. Omit the comma after a quoted statement if it is smoothly woven into the flow of the sentence.

> "I haven't a clue" is all Bert says when you ask what he plans to do next.
> (**NOT:** "I haven't a clue," is all Bert says . . .)

254 When a quoted *question* or *exclamation* occurs at the beginning of a sentence, retain the question mark or the exclamation point before the closing quotation mark and do *not* insert a comma.

> "Can you send us your comments within two weeks?" she asked.
> (**NOT:** . . . within two weeks?," she asked.)
> "I won't accept that kind of response!" I told him.
> (**NOT:** . . . that kind of response!," I told him.)

255 When a quoted *word* or *phrase* occurs at the beginning of a sentence, no punctuation should accompany the closing quotation mark unless required by the overall construction of the sentence.

> "An utter bore" was the general reaction to yesterday's speaker.
> "Managing Your Portfolio," the second chapter in the Klingenstein book, sets forth some guidelines I have never seen anywhere else. (The comma that follows the chapter title is the first of a pair needed to set off a nonessential expression.)

Punctuating Quotations That End a Sentence

256 **a.** When a quoted *statement, question,* or *exclamation* comes at the end of a sentence and is introduced by an expression such as *he said* or *she said,* a comma usually precedes the opening quotation mark.

> Mr. Kelley said, "We'll close early on Friday."
> In her letter Diana said, "I plan to arrive on Thursday at 6 p.m."
> Ulysses S. Grant explained his military success by saying, "The fact is, I think I am a verb instead of a personal pronoun."

Continued on page 68

Punctuation:
Other Marks

2

¶257

NOTE: If the quotation is quite short or is woven into the flow of the sentence, omit the comma.

> All she said was "No." **OR:** All she said was, "No." (The comma creates a slight pause and throws greater emphasis on the quotation.)
>
> Why does he keep saying "It won't work"?

b. Use a colon in place of a comma if the introductory expression is an independent clause.

> The artist Willem de Kooning had this to say about poverty: "The trouble with being poor is that it takes up all your time."
>
> Miss Manners, as usual, makes her point simply but well: "If you can't be kind, at least be vague."
>
> When you can't make up your mind, remember Yogi Berra's sage advice: "If you come to a fork in the road, take it."

c. Use a colon in place of a comma if the quotation contains more than one sentence.

> Professor Robert Silensky then said: "We've all heard how 1,000,000 monkeys pounding on 1,000,000 typewriters will eventually reproduce Shakespeare's entire works. Well, now thanks to the Internet, we know that's not true."

d. Use a colon in place of a comma if the quotation is set off on separate lines as an extract. (See also ¶265.)

> Sheila's letter said in part:
>
> > I have greatly valued your assistance. You have always acted as if you were actually part of our staff, with our best interests in mind.

e. Do not use either a comma or a colon before an indirect quotation.

> Sheila said that she had always valued Bob's assistance on various projects.

f. Do not use either a comma or a colon when a direct quotation is introduced by *that* or is otherwise woven into the flow of the sentence.

> In a previous letter to you, I noted that "you have always acted as if you were actually part of our staff, with our best interests in mind."

NOTE: The first word of the quotation is not capitalized in this case, even though it was capitalized in the original. Compare *you* here with *You* in the example in *d* above. (See ¶272 for the rule on capitalizing the first word of a quoted sentence.)

257 When a quoted *sentence* (a statement, a question, or an exclamation) falls at the end of a larger sentence, do not use double punctuation—that is, one mark to end the quotation and another to end the sentence. Choose the stronger mark. (**REMEMBER:** *A question mark is stronger than a period; an exclamation point is stronger than a period or a question mark.*) If the same mark of punctuation is required for both the quotation and the sentence as a whole, use the one within quotation marks.

> **Quoted Sentences at the End of a Statement**
> Bob said, "I can't wait to get back to work." (**NOT** .".)
> Mrs. Fahey asked, "How long have you been away?" (**NOT** ?".)
> Mr. Auden shouted, "We can't operate a business this way!" (**NOT** !".)
>
> **Quoted Sentences at the End of a Question**
> Did you say, "I'll help out"? (**NOT** ."?)
> Why did Mary ask, "Will Joe be there?" (**NOT** ?"?)
> Who yelled "Watch out!" (**NOT** !"?)

¶**259**

Quoted Sentences at the End of an Exclamation

How could you forget to follow up when you were specifically told, "Give this order special attention"! (**NOT** ."!)

Stop saying "How should I know"! (**NOT** ?"!)

How I'd like to walk into his office and say, "I quit!" (**NOT** !"!)

NOTE: When a quoted sentence ends with an abbreviation, retain the abbreviation period, even though a question mark or an exclamation point follows as the terminal mark of punctuation.

The reporter asked, "When did you first hear about the board's decision to sell the company to Modem Inc.?"

Didn't Larry tell Meg, "I'll help you with the tuition for your M.D."?

However, if a period is required as the terminal mark of punctuation, use only one period to mark the end of the abbreviation and the end of the sentence.

Gloria said, "You can call as early as 6:30 a.m." (**NOT** ".)

➤ *For the placement of periods, see ¶247; for the placement of question marks and exclamation points, see ¶249.*

258 When a quoted *word* or *phrase* occurs at the end of a sentence, punctuate according to the appropriate pattern in the following examples. (**NOTE:** If the quoted word or phrase represents a complete sentence, follow the patterns shown in ¶257.)

Quoted Words and Phrases at the End of a Statement

He says he is willing to meet "at your convenience." (**NOT** ".)

I thought her letter said she would arrive "at 10 p.m." (**NOT** .".)

I've been meaning to read "Who Pays the Bill?" (**NOT** ?".)

Critics have praised his latest article, "Freedom Now!" (**NOT** !".)

Quoted Words and Phrases at the End of a Question

Why is he so concerned about my "convenience"?

Didn't she clearly state she would arrive "at 10 p.m."?

Have you had a chance to read "Who Pays the Bill?" (**NOT** ?"?)

What did you think of the article "Freedom Now!"?

Quoted Words and Phrases at the End of an Exclamation

He couldn't care less about my "convenience"!

You're quite mistaken she clearly said "at 10 a.m."!

Don't waste your time reading "Who Pays the Bill?"!

What a reaction he got with his article "Freedom Now!" (**NOT** !"!)

Punctuating Quotations Within a Sentence

259 Do not use a comma before or after a quotation when it is woven into the flow of the sentence.

Don't say "I can't do it" without trying.

No considerate person would say "Why should I care?" under such desperate circumstances.

The audience shouted "Bravo!" and "Encore!" at the end of Emanuel Ax's recital last night.

NOTE: In such cases do not use a period at the end of a quoted statement, but retain the question mark or the exclamation point at the end of a quoted question or exclamation (as illustrated in the examples above).

¶260

260 Do not use commas to set off a quotation that occurs within a sentence as an *essential* expression. (See ¶149.)

> The luxurious practice of booking passage between England and India on the basis of "Port Outward, Starboard Homeward" (so as to get a cabin on the cooler side of the ship) is said to be the origin of the word *posh.*

> The chapter entitled "Locating Sources of Venture Capital" will give you specific leads.

261 **a.** When a quotation occurs within a sentence as a *nonessential* expression, use a comma before the opening quotation mark and before the closing quotation mark.

> His parting words, "I hardly know how to thank you," were sufficient.

> The next chapter, "The Role of Government," further clarifies the answer.

b. If the *nonessential* quoted matter requires a question mark or an exclamation point before the closing quotation mark, use a pair of dashes or parentheses (rather than commas) to set off the quoted matter.

> Your last question—"How can we improve communications between departments?"—can best be answered by you.

> **RATHER THAN:** Your last question, "How can we improve communications between departments?," can best be answered by you.

NOTE: When some or all of the quoted items in a series end with a question mark or an exclamation point, display them in a list to avoid the awkwardness of inserting commas before the quotation marks.

> Next month's issue will feature the following articles:
> "Will the Internet Replace Long-Distance Telephone Service?"
> "Tax Law Changes—Again!"
> "Are Business Cycles Obsolete?"
> "Whither Wall Street?"

> **RATHER THAN:** Next month's issue will feature the following articles: "Will the Internet Replace Long-Distance Telephone Service?," "Tax Law Changes—Again!," "Are Business Cycles Obsolete?," and "Whither Wall Street?"

c. If *essential* quoted material ends with a question mark or an exclamation point and occurs within a sentence where a comma would ordinarily follow (for example, at the end of an introductory clause or phrase), omit the comma.

> Although we were all asked last week to read an article entitled "Can U.S. Manufacturers Prosper in Today's World Markets?" the topic was totally ignored in this week's seminar.

> **RATHER THAN:** . . . an article entitled "Can U.S. Manufacturers Prosper in Today's World Markets?," the topic was . . .

NOTE: If the omission of a comma at this point could lead to confusion, reword the sentence to avoid the problem.

> We were all asked last week to read an article entitled "Can U.S. Manufacturers Prosper in Today's World Markets?" Yet the topic was . . .

> **OR:** We were all asked last week to read an article entitled "Can U.S. Manufacturers Prosper in Today's World Markets?"; yet the topic was . . .

Punctuating Quoted Sentences With Interrupting Expressions

262 When a quoted sentence is interrupted by an expression such as *he asked* or *she said,* use a comma and a closing quotation mark before the interrupting expression and another comma after it. Then resume the quotation with an opening quotation mark,

¶**265**

but do not capitalize the first word unless it is a proper noun, a proper adjective, or the pronoun *I*.

> "During the past month," the memo said in part, "we have received some welcome news from our overseas branches."

263 If the interrupting expression ends the sentence and the quotation continues in a new sentence, put a period after the interrupting expression and start the new sentence with an opening quotation mark and a capital letter.

> "We should decline the invitation," he said. "It would be better not to go than to arrive late."

Punctuating Long Quotations

264 If a quotation consists of more than one sentence without any interrupting elements, use quotation marks only at the beginning and at the end of the quotation. Do not put quotation marks around each sentence within the quotation.

> Here is the full text of the release he gave to the media: "I have decided to withdraw from the upcoming election. I wish to thank my supporters for their enormous help."

265 A long quotation that will make four or more lines may be handled in one of the following ways:

a. The preferred style for displaying the quoted material is to treat it as a single-spaced extract. Indent the extract a half inch from each side margin, and leave a blank line above and below the extract. Do not enclose the quoted material in quotation marks; the indention replaces the quotation marks. If any quoted material appears within the extract, retain the quotation marks around this material. If the extract consists of more than one paragraph, leave a blank line between paragraphs. (See page 349 for an illustration of an extract in the body of a letter.)

NOTE: Ordinarily, start the quoted material flush left on the shorter line length; however, if a paragraph indention was called for in the original, indent the first line a half inch. Indent the first line of any additional paragraphs a half inch also, but do not leave a blank line between indented paragraphs.

b. Use the same line length and spacing for the quoted material as for other text material on the page.

(1) If the quoted material consists of one paragraph only, place quotation marks at the beginning and end of the paragraph. Use the normal paragraph indention of a half inch.

(2) If the quoted material consists of two or more paragraphs, place a quotation mark at the start of each paragraph but at the end of only one paragraph—the last one.

(3) Change double quotation marks within the quoted material to single quotation marks, and vice versa. (See ¶¶245–246.)

> "When you are writing a letter that grants a request, you can follow this pattern:
> "First, express appreciation for the writer's interest in the company's product or service.
> "Next, give the exact information requested and, if possible, additional information that may be of interest.
> "Finally, express willingness to 'be of further help.'"

¶266

Quoting Letters

266   Letters and other business documents that are to be quoted word for word may be handled in one of the following ways:

a. Make a printout, a photocopy, or a scanner copy of the material. In this case no quotation marks are used.

b. If no equipment is available, type the material on a separate sheet of paper headed *COPY.* In this case no quotation marks are used.

c. The material, if short, may be treated like a long quotation (see ¶265). If you use a shorter line length, omit the quotation marks. If you use the same line length as you do for other material on the page, then place the opening quotation mark before the first word and the closing quotation mark after the last word.

Quoting Poetry

267   When quoting a complete poem (or an extended portion of one) in a letter or a report, type it line for line, single-spaced (except for stanza breaks). If the line length is shorter than that of the normal text above and below the poem, no quotation marks are needed; the poem will stand out sufficiently as an extract. If, however, quotation marks are needed to indicate the special nature of the material, place a quotation mark at the beginning of each stanza and at the end of only the last stanza. (See also ¶284b.)

NOTE: As a rule, follow the poet's layout of the poem. If the poet uses an irregular pattern of indention (instead of the customary practice of aligning all lines at the left), try to reproduce this layout.

268   A short extract from a poem is sometimes woven right into a sentence or a paragraph. In such cases use quotation marks at the beginning and end of the extract, and use a diagonal line (with one space before and after) to indicate where each line breaks in the actual poem.

> In a poem about the death of an American poet, Richard Wilbur refers scathingly to the more prominent notices given to a "cut-rate druggist, a lover of Giving, / A lender, and various brokers: gone from this rotten / Taxable world to a higher standard of living."

Quoting Dialogues and Conversations

269   When quoting dialogues and conversations, start the remarks of each speaker as a new paragraph, no matter how brief.

> "Waiter, what was in that glass?"
> "Arsenic, sir."
> "*Arsenic.* I asked you to bring me absinthe."
> "I thought you said arsenic. I beg your pardon, sir."
> "Do you realize what you've done, you clumsy fool? I'm dying."
> "I am extremely sorry, sir."
> "I DISTINCTLY SAID ABSINTHE."
> "I realize that I owe you an apology, sir. I am extremely sorry."
>
> —Myles na Gopaleen

270   In plays, court testimony, and transcripts of conversations where the name of the speaker is indicated, quotation marks are not needed. (The following example is taken from a transcript of an actual radio conversation released by the U.S. chief of naval operations.)

> **STATION 1:** Please divert your course 15 degrees to the north to avoid a collision.
>
> **STATION 2:** Recommend you divert YOUR course 15 degrees to the south to avoid a collision.
>
> **STATION 1:** This is the captain of a U.S. Navy ship. I say again, divert YOUR course.
>
> **STATION 2:** No, I say again, you divert YOUR course.
>
> **STATION 1:** THIS IS THE AIRCRAFT CARRIER ENTERPRISE. WE ARE A LARGE WARSHIP OF THE U.S. NAVY. DIVERT YOUR COURSE NOW!
>
> **STATION 2:** This is the Puget Sound lighthouse. It's your call.

The following rules (¶¶271–284) cover a number of stylistic matters, such as how to style quoted material (¶271), how to capitalize in quoted material (¶¶272–273), how to handle omissions in quoted material (¶¶274–280), how to handle insertions in quoted material (¶¶281–283), and how to align quotation marks (¶284).

Style in Quoted Material

271   In copying quoted material, follow the style of the extract exactly in punctuation, spelling, hyphenation, and number style. (See ¶283 for the use of [*sic*] to indicate errors in the original.)

Capitalization in Quoted Material

272   Ordinarily, capitalize the first word of every complete sentence in quotation marks.

> I overheard Ellis mutter, "Only a fool would make such a claim."
>
> Here is the key sentence in her memo: "Despite the understaffing in the department, everyone is expected to meet the goals established for the coming year."

NOTE: If the quoted sentence is preceded by *that* or is otherwise incorporated into the flow of a larger sentence, do not capitalize the first word (unless it is a proper noun, a proper adjective, or the pronoun *I*).

> I overheard Ellis mutter that "only a fool would make such a claim."
>
> In essence, she says that "despite the understaffing in the department, everyone is expected to meet the goals established for the coming year."

273   When quoting a word or phrase, do not capitalize the first word unless it meets *one* of these conditions:

a. The first word is a proper noun, a proper adjective, or the pronoun *I*.

> No one is terribly impressed by what Jim calls his "Irish temper."

b. The first word was capitalized in its original use.

> I watched her scrawl "Approved" and sign her name at the bottom of the proposal.

c. The quoted word or phrase occurs at the beginning of a sentence.

> "Outrageous" was the publisher's reaction to Maxon's attempt to duck the questions of the reporters. (Even if the expression was not capitalized in the original material, it is capitalized here to mark the start of the sentence.)

d. The first word represents a complete sentence.

> The Crawleys said "Perhaps"; the Calnans said "No way."

➢ *See ¶¶277–278 on capitalizing the first word of a quoted sentence fragment.*

¶274

Omissions in Quoted Material

274   If one or more words are omitted *within a quoted sentence*, use ellipsis marks (three spaced periods, with one space before and after each period) to indicate the omission.

> "During the past fifty years . . . we have been witnessing a change in buying habits, particularly with respect to food."

NOTE: Omit any marks of internal punctuation (a comma, a semicolon, a colon, or a dash) on either side of the ellipsis marks unless they are required for the sake of clarity.

> **ORIGINAL VERSION:** "The objectives of the proposed bill are admirable, I will cheerfully concede; the tactics being used to gain support for the bill are not."
>
> **CONDENSED VERSION:** "The objectives of the proposed bill are admirable . . . ; the tactics being used to gain support for the bill are not." (The comma preceding the omitted phrase is not needed; however, the semicolon following the omitted phrase must be retained for clarity.)

275   If one or more words are omitted *at the end of a quoted sentence*, use three spaced periods followed by the necessary terminal punctuation for the sentence as a whole.

> "Can anyone explain why . . . ?" (The original question read, "Can anyone explain why this was so?")
>
> "During the past fifty years, starting in the late 1950s, we have been witnessing a change in buying habits . . . . Consumers have become more concerned with what's in the package rather than with the package itself." (The first three periods represent the omitted words "particularly with respect to food"; the fourth period marks the end of the sentence. One or two spaces follow before the next sentence; see ¶102.)

NOTE: If the quotation is intended to trail off, use only three spaced periods at the end of the sentence. (See also ¶291b.)

> His reaction was, "If I had only known . . ."

276   If one or more sentences are omitted *between other sentences* within a long quotation, use three spaced periods *after* the terminal punctuation of the preceding sentence.

> "During the past fifty years, starting in the late 1950s, we have been witnessing a change in buying habits, particularly with respect to food. . . . How far this pattern of change will extend cannot be estimated."

NOTE: There is no space between *food* and the first period because that period marks the end of a sentence. The remaining three periods signify the omission of one or more complete sentences. One or two spaces follow before the next sentence. (See ¶102.)

277   If only a fragment of a sentence is quoted within another sentence, it is not necessary to use ellipsis marks to signify that words before or after the fragment have been omitted.

> According to Robertson's report, there has been "a change in buying habits" during the past fifty years.

Moreover, if the fragment as given can be read as a complete sentence, capitalize the first word in the quoted fragment, even though this word was not capitalized in the original. (Compare *We* in the following example with *we* in the example in ¶276.)

> According to Robertson's report, "We have been witnessing a change in buying habits, particularly with respect to food."

278   If a displayed quotation starts in the middle of a sentence, use three spaced periods at the beginning of the quotation.

> According to Robertson's report, there has been
>
> > . . . a change in buying habits, particularly with respect to food. . . . How far this pattern of change will extend cannot be estimated.

If the fragment, however, can be read as a complete sentence, capitalize the first word of the fragment and omit the ellipsis marks. (Compare *Starting* in the following example with *starting* in the example in ¶276.)

> According to Robertson's report:
>
> > Starting in the late 1950s, we have been witnessing a change in buying habits, particularly with respect to food.

279 When a long quotation starts with a complete sentence and ends with a complete sentence, do not use three spaced periods at the beginning or the end of the quotation unless you need to emphasize that the quotation has been extracted from a larger body of material.

280 If one or more paragraphs are omitted within a long quotation, indicate the omission by adding three spaced periods *after* the terminal punctuation that concludes the preceding paragraph.

Insertions in Quoted Material

281 For clarity, it is sometimes necessary to insert explanatory words or phrases within quoted material. Enclose such insertions in brackets. (See also ¶¶296–297.)

> Miss Rawlings added, "At the time of the first lawsuit [1999], there was clear-cut evidence of an intent to defraud."

282 For special emphasis, you may wish to italicize words that were not so treated in the original. In such cases insert a phrase like *emphasis added* in brackets immediately after the italicized words or in parentheses immediately after the quotation.

> In the course of testifying, she stated, "I never met Mr. Norman in my life, *to the best of my recollection.*" (Emphasis added.)
>
> **OR:** . . . met Mr. Norman in my life, *to the best of my recollection* [emphasis added]."

NOTE: If the equipment you are using does not provide *italic* type, underline the words to be emphasized. (See ¶290 for guidelines on italics and underlining.)

283 When the original wording contains a misspelling, a grammatical error, or a confusing expression of thought, insert the term *sic* (meaning "so" or "this is the way it was") in brackets to indicate that the error existed in the original material.

> As he wrote in his letter, "I would sooner go to jail then [*sic*] have to pay your bill."

NOTE: Italicize the word *sic* when it is used in this way. If you do not have access to an italic font, do not underline *sic*.

➢ *For simple interruptions such as* he said *or* she said, *see ¶¶262–263.*

Aligning Quotation Marks

284 **a.** In a list, any opening quotation mark should align with the first letter of the other items.

> I urge you to read the following materials (which I am sending to you under separate cover):
>
> > *The PC Is Not a Typewriter* by Robin Williams
> >
> > "How Do I Make Type More Readable?" by Daniel Will-Harris

Continued on page 76

¶285

b. In a poem, the opening quotation mark at the beginning of each stanza should clear the left margin so that the first letter of each line will align. (See ¶267.)

> "So here I am, in the middle way, having had twenty years—
> Twenty years largely wasted, the years of *l'entre deux guerres*—
> Trying to learn to use words, and every attempt
> Is a wholly new start, and a different kind of failure
> Because one has only learnt to get the better of words
> For the thing one no longer has to say, or the way in which
> One is no longer disposed to say it. And so each venture
> Is a new beginning, a raid on the inarticulate
> With shabby equipment always deteriorating
> In the general mess of imprecision of feeling . . ."
>
> —T. S. Eliot

NOTE: When a quoted extract is displayed beneath the title of a chapter or some other work, quotation marks are not necessary.

> For all that has been, thanks.
> For all that is yet to come, yes!
> —Dag Hammarskjöld

➤ *For other examples of displayed quotations, see ¶212.*

Italics and Underlining

IMPORTANT NOTE: *Italic type* (the counterpart of underlining or underscoring) is now provided in word processing and desktop publishing software, and it is the preferred means of giving special emphasis to words and phrases and to the titles of literary and artistic works.

For Special Emphasis

285 a. A word referred to as a word is usually italicized or underlined. (Some writers prefer to enclose the word in quotation marks instead.) A word referred to as a word is often introduced by the expression *the term* or *the word*.

> The term *muffin-choker* refers to a bizarre item in the morning newspaper that you read as you eat your breakfast.
>
> A number of years ago a newspaper editor expressed his feelings about a certain word as follows: "If I see *upcoming* in the paper again, I will be downcoming and the person responsible will be outgoing."
>
> If you used fewer compound sentences, you wouldn't have so many *and*s (**OR** ands) in your writing. (Only the root word is italicized or underlined, not the *s* that forms the plural.)
>
> **BUT:** She refused to sign the contract because she said it had too many ifs, ands, or buts. (Neither italics nor underlining is required for the phrase *ifs, ands, or buts* because the writer is not referring literally to these words as words. The phrase means "too many conditions and qualifications.")

b. Letters referred to as letters are usually italicized or underlined if they are not capitalized. In such cases underlining may be preferable since a single italic letter may not look sufficiently different to stand out.

> dotting your i's (**OR** *i*'s)   the three Rs
> minding your p's and q's (**OR** *p*'s and *q*'s)   three Bs and one C
> solving for x when y = 3 (**OR** for *x* when *y*)   **BUT:** to the nth degree

➤ *For the plurals of letters such as i's and Rs, see ¶¶622–623.*

c. As a rule, do not use all-capital letters to give a word or phrase special emphasis. The use of all-caps for that purpose is typically overpowering. Indeed, the use of all-caps in e-mail messages is considered "shouting." In special circumstances, however, the use of all-caps may be justified.

It IS as bad as you think, and they ARE out to get you. (For other examples, see ¶¶269–270.)

286 In a formal definition, the word to be defined is usually italicized or underlined and the definition quoted. In this way the two elements may be easily distinguished.

The verb *prevaricate* (a polite way of saying "to lie") comes from the Latin word *praevaricari,* which means "to go zigzag, to walk crookedly."

NOTE: An informal definition does not require any special punctuation.

Fishing has been defined as a jerk at the end of one line waiting for a jerk on the other.

Thomas Hobson was an English stablekeeper who insisted that every customer take the horse nearest the door. Hence the term *Hobson's choice* means that you really have no choice at all. (Because the definition is informal, it does not have to be set off in quotation marks. However, *Hobson's choice* is italicized or underlined, as indicated in ¶285a, because the words are referred to as words.)

The word *blamestorming* refers to the process by which a group of people discuss why something went wrong and who's responsible.

287 Italicize or underline foreign expressions that are not considered part of the English language. (Use quotation marks to set off translations of foreign expressions.)

It's true, *n'est-ce pas?* (Meaning "isn't that so?")

NOTE: Once a foreign expression has become established as part of the English language, italics or underlining is no longer necessary. (Most dictionaries offer guidance on this point.) Here are some frequently used expressions that do not need italics or any other special display:

à la carte	de jure	magnum opus	pro tem
à la mode	double entendre	maven	quid pro quo
a priori	en masse	modus operandi	raison d'être
ad hoc	en route	modus vivendi	rendezvous
ad infinitum	esprit de corps	non sequitur	repertoire
ad nauseam	et al.	ombudsman	résumé
alfresco	etc.	op. cit.	savoir faire
alma mater	ex officio	per annum	sic (see ¶283)
alter ego	fait accompli	per capita	sine qua non
bona fide	habeas corpus	per diem	status quo
carte blanche	ibid. (see ¶1530)	per se	summa cum laude
caveat emptor	in absentia	prima facie	tête-à-tête
chutzpah	in toto	prix fixe	tour de force
cul-de-sac	joie de vivre	pro forma	vice versa
de facto	laissez-faire	pro rata	vis-à-vis

➤ *For the use of accents and other diacritical marks with foreign words, see ¶718.*

288 The names of *individual* ships, trains, airplanes, and spacecraft may be italicized or underlined for special display or written simply with initial caps.

The S.S. *Parlin* will sail on Thursday.   **OR:** The S.S. Parlin . . .

BUT: I flew to Paris on a Concorde and came back on a DC-10. (No special display is needed for the names *Concorde* and *DC-10* because they identify classes of aircraft but are not the names of individual planes.)

Punctuation: Other Marks

2

¶289

With Titles of Literary and Artistic Works

289 **a.** Italicize or underline titles of *complete* works that are published as separate items—for example, books, pamphlets, long poems, magazines, and newspapers. Also italicize or underline titles of movies, plays, musicals, operas, individual videocassettes, television and radio series, long musical pieces, paintings, and works of sculpture.

> Our ads in *The Wall Street Journal* have produced excellent results.
>
> **OR:** Our ads in <u>The Wall Street Journal</u> have produced excellent results.
>
> Her letter appears in the latest issue of *Sports Illustrated.*
>
> You will particularly enjoy a cookbook entitled *The Supper of the Lamb.*
>
> Next Friday we will hear *Der Rosenkavalier.*
>
> The painting that is popularly referred to as *Whistler's Mother* is actually entitled *Arrangement in Gray and Black No. 1.* (For a usage note on *entitled* and *titled,* see Section 11, page 291.)

NOTE: Do not italicize, underline, or quote the titles of musical pieces that are identified by form (for example, *symphony, concerto, sonata*) or by key (for example, *A major, B flat minor*). However, if a descriptive phrase accompanies this type of title, italicize or underline this phrase if the work is long; quote this phrase if the work is short.

> Beethoven's Sonata No. 18 in E flat minor, Op. 31, No. 3
>
> Tchaikovsky's Symphony No. 6 in B flat minor (the *Pathétique*)
>
> Chopin's Étude No. 12 (the "Revolutionary" Étude)

b. Titles of complete works may be typed in all-capital letters as an alternative to italics or underlining.

> Every executive will find RIGHT ON TIME! a valuable guide.

NOTE: The use of all-capital letters is acceptable when titles occur frequently (as in the correspondence of a publishing house) or when the use of all-capital letters is intended to have an eye-catching effect. In other circumstances use italics or underlining.

c. In material that is being prepared for publication, titles of complete works must be italicized or underlined. This special display indicates that the title must appear in italics in the final version.

> Every executive will find *Right on Time!* a valuable guide.

d. In titles of magazines, do not italicize, underline, or capitalize the word *magazine* unless it is part of the actual title.

> *Time* magazine   **BUT:** *Harper's Magazine*

e. In some cases the name of the publishing company is the same as the name of the publication. Italicize or underline the name when it refers to the *publication* but not when it refers to the *company*.

> I saw her column in *Business Week.*   I wrote to Business Week about a job.
>
> Joe used to be *Fortune's* management editor; now he works as a management consultant to half a dozen Fortune 500 companies.

f. Italicize or underline a subtitle (but not an edition number) that accompanies the main title of a book.

> I think you'll find some good tips in *Outsmarting Wall Street: A Profit-Proven System for Picking Stocks and Timing the Market,* Third Edition.

¶290

g. Italicize or underline the titles of books, newspapers, and magazines that are published in electronic form.

> *Britannica Online* (the electronic version of the *Encyclopaedia Britannica*)
> *@times* (the electronic version of *The New York Times*)
> *Boston.com* (the electronic version of *The Boston Globe*)
> *Wired Online* (an electronic magazine based on *Wired,* a print magazine)
> *Slate, Word, Salon,* and *Feed* (electronic magazines, also referred to as *e-zines* or *Web zines*)

➤ *For the use of quotation marks with titles of literary and artistic works, see ¶¶242–244; for the treatment of titles of sacred works, see ¶350.*

Guidelines for Italics and Underlining

290 Italicize or underline as a unit whatever should be grasped as a unit—individual words, titles, phrases, or even whole sentences. For reasons of appearance or ease of execution, the guidelines for italicizing differ slightly from those of underlining.

a. When you want to give special emphasis to a unit consisting of two or more words, be sure to italicize or underline the entire unit, including the space between words.

> I would not use the phrase *in a nutshell* in the sentence where you sum up your feelings about the place where you work.
>
> **OR:** I would not use the phrase <u>in a nutshell</u> in the sentence . . .

b. When using *italics* to give special emphasis to words or phrases in a series, it is customary—for reasons of appearance—to italicize any accompanying marks of punctuation (such as colons, semicolons, question marks, and exclamation points) so that they slant the same way that the italic letters do. For simplicity of execution, it is also appropriate to italicize commas, periods, and other internal marks of punctuation.

> *Ipso facto, sine qua non,* and *pro forma:* these are the kinds of expressions you must be able to define if you work for Mr. Lynch. (**NOT:** and *pro forma:*)
>
> Have you ever read *Moby Dick* or *War and Peace?* (**NOT:** *War and Peace*?)

➤ *For the use of italics with parentheses and brackets, see ¶290f and g.*

c. When using *underlining* to give special emphasis to words or phrases in a series, underline only the terms themselves and not any punctuation that intervenes or follows.

> <u>Ipso facto</u>, <u>sine qua non</u>, and <u>pro forma</u>: these are the kinds of expressions . . .
> Have you ever read <u>Moby Dick</u> or <u>War and Peace</u>?
>
> **EXCEPTION:** This week the Summertime Playhouse is presenting <u>Oklahoma!</u>, next week <u>Where's Charley?</u>, and the following week <u>My Fair Lady</u>. (The exclamation point and the question mark are underlined in this sentence because they are an integral part of the material to be emphasized; however, the commas and the sentence-ending period are not.)

d. Do not italicize or underline a possessive or plural ending that is added on to a word being emphasized.

> the *Times-Picayune* 's editorial   too many *whereas*es
> **OR** the <u>Times-Picayune</u>'s editorial   **OR** too many <u>whereas</u>es

Continued on page 80

¶291

e. When giving special emphasis to an element that has to be divided at the end of a line, italicize or underline the dividing hyphen as well.

> For a Wall Street exposé with "the suspense of a first-rate thriller," read *Bar-barians at the Gate.*

> **OR:** For a Wall Street exposé with "the suspense of a first-rate thriller," read <u>Bar-barians at the Gate</u>.

f. Parentheses are italicized when the words they enclose begin and end with italicized words. Do not italicize the parentheses, however, if the italicized words appear only at the beginning or the end of the parenthetical expression.

> Use a comma to separate independent clauses joined by a coordinating conjunction *(and, but, or,* or *nor)*.

> Use commas to set off transitional expressions (like *however* and *therefore*).

> (*What we need* is the subject of that sentence.)

g. Brackets are not usually italicized, even when they enclosed italicized words; for example, [*sic*]. (See ¶¶271, 283.)

Other Marks of Punctuation

Ellipsis Marks (. . .)

291   Ellipsis marks are three spaced periods, with one space before and after each period.

a. As a general rule, do not use ellipsis marks in place of a period at the end of a sentence. However, ellipsis marks may be used to indicate that a sentence trails off before the end. The three spaced periods create an effect of uncertainty or suggest an abrupt suspension of thought. (No terminal punctuation is used with ellipsis marks in this kind of construction.)

> He could easily have saved the situation by . . . But why talk about it?

➤ *For the use of ellipsis marks to indicate omissions in quoted material, see ¶¶274–280.*

b. Ellipsis marks are often used in advertising to display individual items or to connect a series of loosely related phrases.

> Where can you match these services?
> . . . Free ticket delivery
> . . . Flight insurance
> . . . On-time departures

> The Inn at the End of the Road . . . where you may enjoy the epicure's choicest offerings . . . by reservation only . . . closed Tuesdays.

The Asterisk (*)

292   The asterisk may be used to refer the reader to a footnote placed at the bottom of a page or a table. (See ¶¶1502f, 1636c.)

a. When the asterisk and some other mark of punctuation occur together within a sentence, the asterisk *follows* the punctuation mark, with no intervening space. (See also ¶1502b.)

b. In the footnote itself, leave no space after the asterisk.

293   Asterisks are used to replace words that are considered unprintable.

> If the TV cameras had been present when Finney called Schultz a ***** (and about 50 other names as well), tonight's newscast would have contained the longest bleep in television history.

The Diagonal (/)

294   The diagonal occurs (without space before or after) in certain abbreviations and expressions of time.

> B/S   bill of sale   w/   with
>
> c/o   care of   n/30   net amount due in 30 days
>
> The copy deadline for the fall '01/winter '02 catalog is April 15.
>
> Please check the figures for fiscal year 2002/03.
>
> I'm concerned about their P/E ratio. (Referring to the price/earnings ratio of a company's stock.)

295   **a.** The diagonal is used to express alternatives.

> read/write files   an AM/FM tuner
>
> an on/off switch   an either/or proposition
>
> a go/no-go decision   meet on Monday and/or Tuesday
>
> input/output systems   (see a usage note for *and/or* on page 284)

b. The diagonal may be used to indicate that a person has two functions or a thing has two components.

> the owner/manager   zoned for commercial/industrial activities
>
> our secretary/treasurer   planning to hold a dinner/dance
>
> a Time/CNN poll   a client/server network

NOTE: A hyphen may also be used in such expressions. (See ¶806, 818b, 819b.)

c. The diagonal is also used in writing fractions (for example, 4/5) and in some code and serial numbers (for example, 2S/394756).

> ➤ *For the use of the diagonal when quoting poetry, see ¶268; for the use of the diagonal in telephone numbers, see ¶454c.*

Brackets ([ ])

296   A correction or an insertion in a quoted extract should be enclosed in brackets. (See also ¶¶281–283.)

> His final request was this: "Please keep me appraised [*sic*] of any new developments." (See ¶283, note.)
>
> The transcript of his testimony contains this incredible statement: "I did not approach Commissioner Zajac *at any time* [emphasis added] while my petition was being considered."
>
> "If we all pull together, we can bring a new level of political leadership to this state. [Extended applause.] Please give me your support in this campaign." (Note the capitalization of *Extended* and the use of a period before the closing bracket when the bracketed element is treated as a separate sentence. See also ¶¶226, 282.)

297   When a parenthetical element falls within another parenthetical element, enclose the smaller element in brackets and enclose the larger element in parentheses.

> Scalzo said on television yesterday that prices would begin to fall sharply. (However, in an article published in the *Times* [May 15, 2002], he was quoted as saying that prices would remain steady for the foreseeable future.)

¶298

The Apostrophe (')

298   The apostrophe is a versatile mark of punctuation that comes in three styles: *curly* ('), *slanted* ('), and *straight* ('). The font you select will determine the style of apostrophe to be used. If you wish, you can switch from the default style to an alternative style by accessing an extended character set. (See the important note that precedes ¶227.)

The apostrophe may be used:

a. As a single *closing* quotation mark. (See ¶¶245–246, 247b, 248b, 249d, 250b, 265b.)

> **NOTE:** The straight apostrophe (') may also be used as a single *opening* quotation mark. The curly and slanted styles use different symbols for a single opening quotation mark (' and ').

b. To indicate the omission of figures in dates. (See ¶¶412, 624.)

c. As a symbol for feet. (See ¶¶432, 543.) Use either the slanted or straight apostrophe for this function (but not the curly style).

d. To form contractions. (See ¶505.)

e. To form the plurals of figures, letters, and words in a few special cases. (See ¶¶622–625.)

f. To form possessives. (See ¶¶247b, note; 627–652.)

g. To form expressions derived from all-capital abbreviations. (See ¶522d.)

Punctuation: Other Marks

2

Spacing With Punctuation Marks

299   The following guidelines provide a handy summary of the number of spaces to be left before and after marks of punctuation.

> **IMPORTANT NOTE:** When you are offered a choice of one or two spaces following a mark of punctuation at the end of a sentence, choose one space as a rule unless two spaces are needed to create an adequate visual break between sentences. For a fuller discussion of this issue as well as a number of helpful illustrations, see ¶102.

Period (.)

No space *before*.

One or two spaces *after* the end of a sentence. (See ¶¶102, 1433e.)

One or two spaces *after* a period when it follows a number or letter that indicates an enumeration. (See ¶106.)

One space *after* an abbreviation within a sentence. (See also ¶511.)

No space *after* a decimal point.

No space *after* when another mark of punctuation follows the period (for example, a closing quotation mark; a closing parenthesis; a closing dash, a comma, a semicolon, or a colon following an "abbreviation" period).

Question Mark (?) or Exclamation Point (!)

No space *before.*

One or two spaces *after* the end of a sentence. (See ¶102.)

One space *after* a question mark within a sentence. (See ¶¶116–117.)

No space *after* when another mark of punctuation follows (for example, a closing quotation mark, a closing parenthesis, or a closing dash).

Comma (,)

No space *before.*

One space *after* unless a closing quotation mark follows the comma.

No space *after* a comma within a number.

Semicolon (;)

No space *before;* one space *after.*

Colon (:)

No space *before.*

No space *before* or *after* in expressions of time *(8:20 p.m.)*, in proportions *(2:1)*, or in reference initials *(EJN:GPL)*.

One or two spaces *after* within a sentence. (See ¶187a, note.)

One or two spaces *after* reference notations, attention and subject lines, enclosure and copy notations, and postscripts. (See ¶194b.)

Two or more spaces *after* displayed guide words in memos *(TO:, FROM:, DATE:)* and in other business documents *(SHIP TO:, BILL TO:)*. (See ¶194c.)

Em Dash (—)

No space *before* or *after* an em dash. (See ¶216.)

No space *before, between,* or *after* hyphens used to represent an em dash.

One or two spaces *after* an em dash at the end of a statement that breaks off abruptly. (See ¶¶102, 207–208.)

Hyphen (-)

No space *before;* no space *after* except with a suspending hyphen or a line-ending hyphen. (See also ¶¶832, 833d.)

Opening Parenthesis (( ) or Bracket ([ )

One space *before* when parenthetical material is within a sentence.

One or two spaces *before* when parenthetical material follows a sentence. In this case the parenthetical material starts with a capital letter and closes with its own sentence punctuation. (See ¶¶226, 296.)

No space *after.*

Continued on page 84

¶299

Closing Parenthesis ( )) or Bracket ( ])

No space *before.*

One space *after* when parenthetical material is within a sentence.

One or two spaces *after* when parenthetical material is itself a complete sentence and another sentence follows. (See ¶¶102, 226, 296.)

No space *after* if another mark of punctuation immediately follows.

Opening Quotation Mark (")

One or two spaces *before* when quoted material starts a new sentence or follows a colon.

No space *before* when a dash or an opening parenthesis precedes.

One space *before* in all other cases.

No space *after.*

Closing Quotation Mark (")

No space *before.*

One or two spaces *after* when quoted material ends the sentence. (See ¶102.)

No space *after* when another mark of punctuation immediately follows (for example, a semicolon or colon).

One space *after* in all other cases.

Opening Single Quotation Mark (')

One space *before* when double quotation marks immediately precede.

One or two spaces *before* when the material within single quotation marks follows a colon *and* is not immediately preceded by double quotation marks.

One or two spaces *before* when the material within single quotation marks begins a new sentence and is not immediately preceded by double quotation marks.

No space *after.*

Closing Single Quotation Mark (')

No space *before.*

One space *after* when double quotation marks immediately follow.

No space *after* when some other mark of punctuation immediately follows. (See ¶¶245–246, 247b, 248b, 249d, 250b, 265b, 298a.)

One or two spaces *after* when the material within the single quotation marks ends a sentence and another sentence follows within the quotation. (See ¶102.)

One space *after* in all other cases.

Apostrophe (')

No space *before,* either within a word or at the end of a word.

One space *after* only if it is at the end of a word within a sentence.

No space *after* when another mark of punctuation immediately follows (for example, a comma or a period).

Ellipsis Marks (. . .)

One space *before* and *after* each of the three periods within a sentence. (See ¶¶274–275.)

No space *before* when an *opening* quotation mark precedes ellipsis marks.

No space *after* when a *closing* quotation mark follows ellipsis marks. (See last example in ¶275.)

One or two spaces *after* ellipsis marks that follow a period, a question mark, or an exclamation point at the end of a sentence. (See ¶102 and the example in ¶276.)

Asterisk (*)

No space *before* an asterisk following a word or punctuation mark within a sentence or at the end of a sentence.

One or two spaces *after* an asterisk at the end of a sentence. (See ¶102.)

One space *after* an asterisk following a word or punctuation mark within a sentence.

No space *after* an asterisk in a footnote. (See ¶292.)

Diagonal (/)

No space *before* or *after* a diagonal. (See ¶268 for an exception.)

SECTION **3**

Capitalization

> *For definitions of grammatical terms, see the appropriate entries in the Glossary of Grammatical Terms (Appendix A).*

The function of capitalization is to give distinction, importance, and emphasis to words. Thus the first word of a sentence is capitalized to indicate distinctively and emphatically that a new sentence has begun. Proper nouns like *George, Chicago, Dun & Bradstreet, the Parthenon, January,* and *Friday* are capitalized to signify the special importance of these words as the official names of particular persons, places, and things. A number of words, however, may function either as proper nouns or as common nouns—for example, terms like *the company* or *the board of directors.* For words like these, capitalization practices vary widely, but the variation merely reflects the relative importance each writer assigns to the word in question.

Despite disagreements among authorities on specific rules, there is a growing consensus against overusing capitalization in business writing. When too many words are emphasized, none stand out. The current trend, then, is to use capitalization more sparingly—to give importance, distinction, or emphasis only when and where it is warranted.

The following rules of capitalization are written with ordinary situations in mind. If you work or study in a specialized field, you may find it necessary to follow a different style.

Basic Rules

First Words

301 Capitalize the first word of:

a. Every sentence. (See ¶302 for exceptions.)

> Try to limit each of your e-mail messages to one screen.
> Will you be able to pull everything together by then?
> The deadline we have been given is absolutely impossible!

b. An expression used as a sentence. (See also ¶¶101b–c, 111, 119–120.)

> So much for that.   Really?   No!
> Enough said.   How come?   Congratulations!

c. A quoted sentence. (See also ¶¶272–273.)

> Mrs. Eckstein herself said, "We surely have not heard the complete story."

d. An independent question within a sentence. (See also ¶¶115–117.)

> The question is, Whose version of the argument shall we believe?
> **BUT:** Have you approved the divisional sales forecasts? the expense projections? the requests for staff expansion? (See ¶117.)

e. Each item displayed in a list or an outline. (See also ¶¶107, 1357c, 1424e, 1725d.)

> Here is a powerful problem-solving tool that will help you:
> • Become an effective leader.
> • Improve your relations with subordinates, peers, and superiors.
> • Cope with stressful situations on the job.

f. Each line in a poem. (Always follow the style of the poem, however.)

> From wrong to wrong the exasperated spirit
> Proceeds, unless restored by that refining fire
> Where you must move in measure, like a dancer.
> —T. S. Eliot

g. The salutation and the complimentary closing of a letter. (See also ¶¶1348, 1359.)

> Dear Mrs. Pancetta: Sincerely yours,

¶302

302 **a.** When a sentence is set off by *dashes* or *parentheses* within another sentence, do not capitalize the first word following the opening dash or parenthesis unless it is a proper noun, a proper adjective, the pronoun *I*, or the first word of a quoted sentence. (See ¶¶214, 224–225 for examples.)

b. Do not capitalize the first word of a sentence following a colon except under certain circumstances. (See ¶¶196–199.)

Proper Nouns

303 Capitalize every *proper noun*, that is, the official name of a particular person, place, or thing. Also capitalize the pronoun *I*.

William H. Gates III	Wednesday, February 8
Baton Rouge, Louisiana	the Great Depression
Sun Microsystems Inc.	the Civil Rights Act of 1964
the Red Cross	the Japanese
the Internet (**OR** the Net)	Jupiter and Uranus
the University of Chicago	French Literature 212
the World Trade Center	a Xerox copy
the Statue of Liberty	*Gone With the Wind*
the Center for Science in	the Smithsonian Institution
the Public Interest	United Farm Workers of America
a Pulitzer Prize	Flight 403
Microsoft Word	the House of Representatives

NOTE: Prepositions (like *of, for,* and *in*) are not capitalized unless they have four or more letters (like *with* and *from*). (See also ¶¶360–361.) The articles *a* and *an* are not capitalized; the article *the* is capitalized only under special circumstances. (See ¶324.) Conjunctions (like *and* and *or*) are also not capitalized. However, follow the capitalization style used by the owner of the name; for example, *3-In-One oil, One-A-Day vitamins, Microsoft At Work, Fruit of The Loom, Book-Of-The-Month Club, Diet Pepsi, diet Coke.*

304 Capitalize adjectives derived from proper nouns.

America (n.), American (adj.)	Machiavelli (n.), Machiavellian (adj.)
Norway (n.), Norwegian (adj.)	Hemingway (n.), Hemingwayesque (adj.)

EXCEPTIONS: Congress, congressional; the Senate, senatorial; the Constitution (U.S.), constitutional (see also ¶306)

305 Capitalize imaginative names and nicknames that designate particular persons, places, or things. (See ¶¶333–335 for imaginative place names; ¶344 for imaginative names of historical periods.)

the Founding Fathers	Smokey Bear
the First Lady	Whoopi Goldberg
the White House	the Gray Panthers
the Oval Office	a Big Mac
the Stars and Stripes	the Establishment
Air Force One	the Lower 48
the Black Caucus	Generation Xers
the Gopher State (Minnesota)	El Niño and La Niña
Mother Nature	the Information Superhighway

a Good Samaritan	the Middle Ages
every state in the Union	**BUT:** the space age
Fannie Mae (from the initials FNMA, referring to the Federal National Mortgage Association)	Big Brother (intrusive big government)
	BUT: my big brother

306 Some expressions that originally contained or consisted of proper nouns or adjectives are now considered common nouns and should not be capitalized. (See ¶309b.)

charley horse	napoleon	ampere	texas leaguer
plaster of paris	boycott	watt	arabic numbers
manila envelope	diesel	joule	roman numerals
bone china	macadam	kelvin	**BUT:** Roman laws

NOTE: Check an up-to-date dictionary to determine capitalization for words of this type.

Common Nouns

307 A *common noun* names a class of things (for example, *books*), or it may refer indefinitely to one or more things within that class *(a book, several books)*. Nouns used in this way are considered general terms of classification and are often modified by indefinite words such as *a, any, every,* or *some.* Do not capitalize nouns used as general terms of classification.

a company	every board of directors
any corporation	some senators

308 A common noun may also be used to name a *particular* person, place, or thing. Nouns used in this way are often modified (a) by *the, this, these, that,* or *those* or (b) by possessive words such as *my, your, his, her, our,* or *their.* Do not capitalize a general term of classification, even though it refers to a particular person, place, or thing.

COMMON NOUN:	our doctor	the hotel	the river
PROPER NOUN:	Dr. Tsai	Hotel Algonquin	the Colorado River

NOTE: Do not confuse a general term of classification with a formal name.

Logan Airport (serving Boston)	the U.S. Postal Service
BUT: the Boston airport	**BUT:** the post office

309 **a.** Capitalize a common noun when it is part of a proper name but not when it is used alone in place of the full name. (For exceptions, see ¶310.)

Professor Perry	**BUT:** the professor
the Goodall Corporation	the corporation
the Easton Municipal Court	the court
Sunset Boulevard	the boulevard
the Clayton Antitrust Act	the act

NOTE: Also capitalize the plural form of a common noun in expressions such as *the Republican and the Democratic Parties, Main and Tenth Streets, the Missouri and Ohio Rivers,* and *the Atlantic and Pacific Oceans.*

b. In a number of compound nouns, the first element is a proper noun or a proper adjective and the second element is a common noun. In such cases capitalize only the first element, since the compound as a whole is a common noun.

Continued on page 90

Capitalization

3

¶310

Brownie points	a Dutch oven	Danish pastry	a Labrador retriever
a Rhodes scholar	a Ferris wheel	French doors	Tex-Mex cooking
Botts dots (highway lane markers)		Wedgwood blue	
Canada geese (**NOT:** Canadian geese)		**BUT:** Deep Blue (IBM's chess-playing computer)	

NOTE: Check an up-to-date dictionary for words of this type. After extensive usage the proper noun or adjective may become a common noun and no longer require capitalization. (See ¶306.)

310 Some *short forms* (common-noun elements replacing the complete proper name) are capitalized when they are intended to carry the full significance of the complete proper name. It is in this area, however, that the danger of overcapitalizing most often occurs. Therefore, do not capitalize a short form unless it clearly warrants the importance, distinction, or emphasis that capitalization conveys. The following kinds of short forms are commonly capitalized:

PERSONAL TITLES: Capitalize titles replacing names of high-ranking national, state, and international officials (but not ordinarily local officials or company officers). (See ¶313.)

ORGANIZATIONAL NAMES: Do not capitalize short forms of company names except in formal or legal writing. (See ¶321.)

GOVERNMENTAL NAMES: Capitalize short forms of names of national and international bodies (but not ordinarily state or local bodies). (See ¶¶326–327, 334–335.)

PLACE NAMES: Capitalize only well-established short forms. (See ¶¶332, 335.)

NOTE: Do not use a short form to replace a full name unless the full name has been mentioned earlier or will be understood from the context.

Special Rules

Personal Names

311 **a.** Treat a person's name—in terms of capitalization, spelling, punctuation, and spacing—exactly as the person does.

Alice Mayer	Charles Burden Wilson
Alyce Meagher	L. Westcott Quinn
Steven J. Dougherty, Jr.	R. W. Ferrari
Stephen J. Dockerty Jr.	Peter B. J. Hallman

➤ *For the treatment of initials such as FDR, see ¶516b; for the use or omission of commas with terms such as Jr., see ¶156.*

b. Respect individual preferences in the spelling of personal names.

Ann Marie, Anne Marie, Anna Marie, Annemarie, Annamarie, Anne-Marie, AnneMarie

Macmillan, MacMillan, Mac Millan, Macmillen, MacMillen, MacMillin, McMillan, Mc Millan, McMillen, McMillin, McMillon

c. In names containing the prefix *O'*, always capitalize the *O* and the letter following the apostrophe; for example, *O'Brian* or *O'Brien*.

d. Watch for differences in capitalization and spacing in names containing prefixes like *d', da, de, del, della, di, du, l', la, le, van,* and *von*.

D'Amelio, d'Amelio, Damelio	deLaCruz, DeLacruz, Dela Cruz, DelaCruz
LaCoste, Lacoste, La Coste	VanDeVelde, Van DeVelde, vandeVelde

e. When a surname with an uncapitalized prefix stands alone (that is, without a first name, a title, or initials preceding it), capitalize the prefix to prevent a misreading.

> Paul de Luca   Mr. de Luca   P. de Luca   **BUT:** Is De Luca leaving?

f. When names that contain prefixes are to be typed in all-capital letters, follow these principles: If there is no space after the prefix, capitalize only the initial letter of the prefix. If space follows the prefix, capitalize the entire prefix.

> **NORMAL FORM:**   MacDonald   Mac Donald
>
> **ALL-CAPITAL FORM:** MacDONALD   MAC DONALD

g. When a nickname or a descriptive expression precedes or replaces a person's first name, simply capitalize it. However, if the nickname or descriptive expression falls between a person's first and last names, enclose it either in quotation marks or in parentheses.

> Ol' Blue Eyes   **BUT:** Frank "Ol' Blue Eyes" Sinatra   **OR:** Frank (Ol' Blue Eyes) Sinatra

➤ *For the plurals of personal names, see ¶¶615–616; for the possessives of personal names, see ¶¶630–633.*

Titles With Personal Names

312 **a.** Capitalize all official titles of honor and respect when they *precede* personal names.

> **PERSONAL TITLES:**
> Mrs. Norma Washburn (see ¶517)   Miss Popkin
> Ms. Terry Fiske   Mr. Benedict
>
> **EXECUTIVE TITLES:**
> President Julia McLeod   Vice President Saulnier
>
> **PROFESSIONAL TITLES:**
> Professor Henry Pelligrino   Dr. Khalil (see ¶517)
> Professor Emerita Ann Marx (see page 290)   Dean Aboud
>
> **CIVIC TITLES:**
> Governor Samuel O. Bolling   Ambassadors Ross and Perez
> Mayor-elect Louis K. Uhl (see ¶317)   ex-Senator Hausner (see ¶317)
>
> **MILITARY TITLES:**
> Colonel Perry L. Forrester   Commander Comerford
>
> **RELIGIOUS TITLES:**
> the Reverend William F. Dowd   Rabbi Gelfand

b. Do not capitalize such titles when the personal name that follows is in apposition and is set off by commas. (Some titles, like that of the President of the United States, are always capitalized. See ¶313 for examples of such exceptions.)

> Yesterday the *president,* Julia McLeod, revealed her plans to retire next June.
> **BUT:** Yesterday *President* Julia McLeod revealed her plans to retire next June.

c. Do not capitalize occupational titles (such as *author, surgeon, publisher,* and *lawyer*) preceding a name.

> The reviews of *drama critic* Simon Ritchey have lost their bite.
> (**NOT:** The reviews of *Drama Critic* Simon Ritchey have lost their bite.)

Continued on page 92

Capitalization

3

¶313

NOTE: Occupational titles can be distinguished from official titles in that only official titles can be used with a last name alone. Since one would not address a person as "Author Mailer" or "Publisher Johnson," these are not official titles and should not be capitalized.

d. Do not confuse a true title preceding a name (such as *Judge*) with a generic expression (such as *federal judge*).

> Judge Ann Bly **OR** federal judge Ann Bly (**BUT NOT:** federal Judge Ann Bly)

> President Julia McLeod **OR** company president Julia McLeod
> (**BUT NOT:** company President Julia McLeod)

313 **a.** In general, do not capitalize titles of honor and respect when they *follow* a personal name or are used *in place of* a personal name.

> Julia McLeod, *president* of McLeod Inc., has revealed her plans to retire next June. During her sixteen years as *president,* the company grew . . .

> Henry Fennel, *emeritus professor of English history,* will lead a tour of Great Britain this summer. (For a usage note on *emeritus,* see page 290.)

However, exceptions are made for important officials and dignitaries, as indicated in the following paragraphs.

b. Retain the capitalization in the titles of high-ranking national, state, and international officials when they *follow* or *replace* a specific personal name. Below are examples of titles that remain capitalized.

> **NATIONAL OFFICIALS:** the *President,* the *Vice President,* Cabinet members (such as the *Secretary of State* and the *Attorney General*), the heads of government agencies and bureaus (such as the *Director* or the *Commissioner*), the *Ambassador,* the *Speaker* (of the *House*), the *Representative,* the *Senator,* the *Chief Justice of the United States* (**NOT** of the Supreme Court)

> **STATE OFFICIALS:** the *Governor,* the *Lieutenant Governor* (**BUT:** the *attorney general,* the *senator*)

> **FOREIGN DIGNITARIES:** the *Queen of England,* the *King,* the *Prime Minister*

> **INTERNATIONAL FIGURES:** the *Pope,* the *Secretary General of the United Nations*

NOTE: Many authorities now recommend that even these titles not be capitalized when they follow or replace the names of high-ranking officials.

c. Titles of local governmental officials and those of lesser federal and state officials are not usually capitalized when they follow or replace a personal name. However, these titles are sometimes capitalized in writing intended for a limited readership (for example, in a local newspaper, in internal communications within an organization, or in correspondence coming from or directed to the official's office), when the intended reader would consider the official to be of high rank.

> The *Mayor* promised only last fall to hold the city sales tax at its present level. (Excerpt from an editorial in a local newspaper.)

> **BUT:** Francis Fahey, *mayor* of Coventry, Rhode Island, appeared before a House committee today. The *mayor* spoke forcefully about the need to maintain federal aid to . . . (Excerpt from a national news service release.)

> I would like to request an appointment with the *Attorney General.* (In a letter sent to the state attorney general's office.)

> **BUT:** I have written for an appointment with the *attorney general* and expect to hear from his office soon.

d. Titles of *company officials* (for example, the *president,* the *general manager*) should not be capitalized when they follow or replace a personal name. Exceptions are made in formal minutes of meetings (see page 508) and in rules and bylaws.

> The *president* will visit thirteen countries in a tour of company installations abroad. (Normal style.)
> The *Secretary's* minutes were read and approved. (In formal minutes.)

NOTE: Some companies choose to capitalize these titles in all their communications because of the great respect the officials command within the company. However, this practice confers excessive importance on people who are neither public officials nor eminent dignitaries, and it should be avoided.

e. In general, do not capitalize job titles when they stand alone. However, in procedures manuals and in company memos and announcements, job titles are sometimes capitalized for special emphasis.

> Marion Conroy has been promoted to the position of *senior accountant* (OR *Senior Accountant*).

f. Titles *following* a personal name or *standing alone* are often capitalized in formal citations and acknowledgments.

314 Do not capitalize titles used as general terms of classification. (See ¶307.)

> a United States senator   every king
> a state governor   any ambassador

EXCEPTION: Because of the special regard for the office of the President of the United States, this title is capitalized even when used as a general term of classification (for example, every *President, Presidential* campaigns).

315 Capitalize any title (even if not of high rank) when it is used in *direct address* (that is, quoted or unquoted speech made directly to another person).

> DIRECT ADDRESS: Please tell me, *Doctor,* what risks are involved in this treatment.
> INDIRECT ADDRESS: I asked the *doctor* what risks were involved in this treatment.

NOTE: In direct address, do not capitalize a term like *madam, miss,* or *sir* if it stands alone without a proper name following.

> Isn't it true, *sir,* that the defendant offered you money for trade secrets?

316 In the *inside address* of a letter, in the *writer's identification block,* and on an *envelope,* capitalize all titles whether they precede or follow the name. (See ¶¶1322–1325, 1362–1368, and the illustrations on page 389.)

317 Do not capitalize *former, late, ex-,* or *-elect* when used with titles. (See ¶363 for the style in headings.)

> the late President Truman   ex-President Bush   Mayor-elect Bawley

Family Titles

318 Capitalize words such as *mother, father, aunt,* and *uncle* when they stand alone or are followed by a personal name.

> Let me ask *Mother* and *Dad* whether that date is open for them.
> We'll be glad to put up *Aunt Peg* and *Uncle Fred* when they come to visit.
> I hear that *Brother Bobby* has gone off the deep end again.
> Do you think *Grandmother Harvey* will be pleased when she hears the news?

¶319

319 Do not capitalize family titles when they are preceded by possessives (such as *my, your, his, her, our,* and *their*) and simply describe a family relationship.

Let me ask my *mother* and *dad* whether that date is open for them.

Do you think your *brother* Bobby would like to meet my *sister* Fern?

NOTE: If the words *uncle, aunt,* or *cousin* form a unit when used together with a first name, capitalize these titles, even when they are preceded by a possessive.

Frank wants us to meet his *Uncle John.* (Here *Uncle John* is a unit.)

BUT: Frank wants us to meet his *uncle,* John Cunningham. (Here *uncle* simply describes a family relationship.)

I hope you can meet my *Cousin May.* (The writer thinks of her as *Cousin May.*)

BUT: I hope you can meet my *cousin* May. (Here the writer thinks of her as *May;* the word *cousin* merely indicates relationship.)

Names of Organizations

320 **a.** Capitalize the names of companies, unions, associations, societies, independent committees and boards, schools, political parties, conventions, foundations, fraternities, sororities, clubs, religious bodies, and teams.

DaimlerChrysler (see ¶366)	the Hopewell Chamber of Commerce
the Transport Workers Union of America	Johns (**NOT** John) Hopkins University
the American Society for Training and Development	the Democratic and Liberal Parties (see ¶309a, note)
the Committee for Economic Development	the Republican National Convention
the Financial Accounting Standards Board	the Andrew W. Mellon Foundation
the National Institutes of Health	Sigma Chi Fraternity
the B'nai B'rith	the Overseas Press Club of America
	St. Mark's United Methodist Church
	Parents Anonymous
	the Louisiana IceGators and the Macon Whoopee (hockey teams)

NOTE: Try to follow the style established by the organization itself, as shown in the letterhead or some other written communication from the organization.

Disney World   Kmart Corporation   **BUT:** Toys "R" Us, Inc. (don't try
BUT: Disneyland   U-Haul International   to replicate the backward *R*)
FULL NAME: E. I. du Pont de Nemours and Company   **SHORT FORM:** DuPont

➤ *See also ¶1328.*

b. Also capitalize imaginative names used to refer to specific organizations. (See also ¶333b.)

Big Blue (IBM)   the Big Board (the New York Stock Exchange)
Ma Bell (AT&T)   the Baby Bells (the U.S. regional phone companies)
After the last round of mergers, the large U.S. accounting firms—once known as the Big Eight—became the Big Four.

➤ *For the treatment of articles (like* the*), prepositions (like* of *or* for*), and conjunctions (like* and*), see ¶303, note; for the capitalization of abbreviations and acronyms used as organizational names, see ¶¶520, 522.*

321 When the common-noun element is used in place of the full name (for example, *the company* in place of *the Andersen Hardware Company*), do not capitalize the short form unless special emphasis or distinction is required (as in legal documents, minutes of meetings, bylaws, and other formal communications, where the short form is intended to invoke the full authority of the organization). In most cases, capitalization is unnecessary because the short form is used only as a general term of classification. (See ¶¶307–308.)

> The *company* has always made a conscientious effort to involve itself in community affairs. However, our *company* policy specifically prohibits our underwriting any activity in support of a candidate for public office. (As used here, *company* is a term of general classification.)
>
> **BUT:** On behalf of the *Company,* I am authorized to accept your bid. (Here the full authority of the company is implied; hence *Company* is spelled with a capital *C.*)
>
> Mr. Weinstock has just returned from a visit to Haverford College. He reports that the *college* is planning a new fund-raising campaign to finance the construction of the new media center.
>
> **BUT:** The *College* hopes to raise an additional $10,000,000 this year to finance the construction of the new media resource center. (Announcement in the alumni bulletin.)

NOTE: Do not capitalize the short form if it is modified by a word other than *the.* In constructions such as *our company, this company,* and *every company,* the noun is clearly a general term of classification. (See also ¶308.)

322 Common organizational terms such as *advertising department, manufacturing division, finance committee,* and *board of directors* are ordinarily capitalized when they are the actual names of units within the writer's own organization. These terms are not capitalized when they refer to some other organization unless the writer has reason to give these terms special importance or distinction.

> The *Board of Directors* will meet next Thursday at 2:30. (From a company memo.)
>
> **BUT:** Julia Perez, senior vice president of the Mulholland Bancorp, has been elected to the *board of directors* of the Kensington Trade Corporation. (From a news release intended for a general audience.)
>
> The *Finance Committee* will meet all week to review next year's budget. (Style used by insiders.)
>
> **BUT:** Gilligan says his company cannot discuss sponsorship of a new art center until its *finance committee* has reviewed our proposal. (Style normally used by outsiders.)
>
> The *Advertising Department* will unveil the fall campaign this Friday. (Style used by insiders.)
>
> **BUT:** The *advertising department* of Black & London will unveil its fall campaign this Friday. (Style used by outsiders.)

NOTE: Do not capitalize these organizational terms when they are modified by a word other than *the.* Constructions such as *this credit department, their credit department, every credit department, your credit department,* and *our credit department* are terms of general classification and should not be capitalized. (See also ¶321, note.)

> Black & London always seems to have a great deal of turnover in *its advertising department.*
>
> We don't have as much turnover in *our advertising department* as you may think. (Some insiders prefer to write *our Advertising Department* because of the special importance they attach to their own organizational structure.)
>
> I would like to apply for the position of copywriter that is currently open in *your advertising department.* (Some outsiders might write *your Advertising Department* if they wanted to flatter the reader by giving special importance to the reader's organizational structure.)

323 Capitalize such nouns as *marketing, advertising,* or *promotion* when they are used alone to designate a department within an organization.

> Paul Havlicek in *Corporate Communications* is the person to talk with.
>
> I want to get a reaction from our people in *Marketing* first.
>
> **BUT:** Talk to our *marketing* people first. (Here *marketing* is simply a descriptive adjective.)

¶324

324 **a.** Capitalize the word *the* preceding the name of an organization only when it is part of the legal name of the organization.

The Associated Press	The New York Times (see ¶289d)
The Vanguard Group	**BUT:** the Los Angeles Times

   b. Even when part of the organizational name, *the* is often not capitalized except in legal or formal contexts where it is important to give the full legal name.

   c. Do not capitalize *the* when the name is used as a modifier or is given in the form of an abbreviation.

   the Associated Press report   the AP   works for the Times

Names of Government Bodies

325 Capitalize the names of countries and international organizations as well as national, state, county, and city bodies and their subdivisions.

the United Nations	the Utah Bureau of Air Quality
the Clinton Administration	the Ohio Legislature
the Cabinet	the Court of Appeals of the State of
the Ninety-ninth Congress	Wisconsin (see ¶303, note)
(see ¶363)	the New York State Board of Education
the House of Representatives	the Coe County Shade Tree Commission
BUT: the federal government	the Boston City Council
(see ¶¶328–329)	the People's Republic of China

➤ *For city and state names, see ¶¶334–335.*

326 Capitalize short forms of names of national and international bodies and their major divisions.

   the House (referring to the House of Representatives)

   the Department (referring to the Department of Justice, the State Department, the Department of the Treasury, etc.)

   the Bureau (referring to the Bureau of the Budget, the Federal Bureau of Investigation, the Bureau of the Census, etc.)

   the Court (referring to the United States Supreme Court, the International Court of Justice, etc.)

   the Fed **OR** the Board (referring to the Federal Reserve Board)

   BUT: the feds (referring to federal regulators)

   Do not capitalize short forms of names of state or local governmental groups except when special circumstances warrant emphasis or distinction. (See ¶327.)

327 Common terms such as *police department, board of education,* and *county court* need not be capitalized (even when referring to a specific body), since they are terms of general classification. However, such terms should be capitalized when the writer intends to refer to the organization in all of its official dignity.

   We are awaiting the release of next year's budget from *City Hall.* (*City Hall* is capitalized here because the term refers to the seat of municipal power in its full authority.)

   You can't fight *City Hall.* (Here again, the term is intended to invoke the full authority of a particular city government.)

   BUT: The public school teachers will be staging a rally in front of *city hall.* (In this case a particular building is being referred to in general terms.)

The *Police Department* has announced the promotion of Robert Boyarsky to the rank of sergeant. (The short form is capitalized here because it is intended to have the full force of the complete name, the *Cranfield Police Department*.)

BUT: The Cranfield *police department* sponsors a youth athletic program that we could well copy. (No capitalization is used here because the writer is referring to the department in general terms and not by its official name.)

NOTE: Do not capitalize the short form if it is not actually derived from the complete name. For example, do not capitalize the short form *police department* if the full name is *Department of Public Safety.*

328 Capitalize *federal* only when it is part of the official name of a federal agency, a federal act, or some other proper noun.

the *Federal* Reserve Board   the *Federal* Insurance Contributions Act

BUT: . . . subject to *federal,* state, and local laws.

329 The terms *federal government* and *government* (referring specifically to the United States government) are now commonly written in small letters because they are considered terms of general classification. In government documents, however, and in other types of communications where these terms are intended to have the force of an official name, they are capitalized.

The *federal government* is still wrestling with the problem of corporate welfare—that is, *federal* subsidies to large corporations.

BUT: If you can't fight City Hall, what makes you think it's any easier to fight the *Federal Government?* (Here the writer wants to emphasize the full power of the national government as an adversary.)

330 **a.** Capitalize *union* only when it refers to a specific government.

Wilkins has lectured on the topic in almost every state in the *Union.*

b. Capitalize *commonwealth* only when it is part of an official name.

the Commonwealth of Independent States (formerly the U.S.S.R.)

the Commonwealth of Nations **OR** the Commonwealth (formerly the British Commonwealth)

➤ *See also ¶335c.*

Names of Places

331 Capitalize the names of places, such as streets, buildings, parks, monuments, rivers, oceans, and mountains. Do not capitalize short forms used in place of the full name. (See ¶332 for a few exceptions.)

Montgomery Street	**BUT:** the street
Empire State Building	the building
Stone Mountain Park	the park
Sacramento River	the river
Lake Pontchartrain	the lake
Colony Surf Hotel	the hotel
Rittenhouse Row	the row
Union Square	the square
Riverside Drive	the drive
Bighorn Mountain	the mountain
Shoshone Falls	the falls
the Washington Monument	the monument

Continued on page 98

Capitalization

3

¶332

Stapleton Airport	**BUT:** the airport
the Fogg Art Museum	the museum
Golden Gate Bridge	the bridge
Nicollet Mall	the mall

➤ *For plural expressions like* the Atlantic and Pacific Oceans, *see ¶309a, note; for the treatment of prepositions and conjunctions in proper names, see ¶303, note.*

332   A few short forms are capitalized because of clear association with one place.

the Coast (the West Coast)	the Hill (Capitol Hill)
the Continent (Europe)	the Street (Wall Street)
the Channel (English Channel)	the Village (Greenwich Village)

333 **a.** Capitalize imaginative names that designate specific places or areas.

the Bay Area (around San Francisco)	Down East (coastal Maine)
the Big D (Dallas)	the South Lawn of the White House
Back Bay (in Boston)	inside the Beltway (Washington, D.C.)
the Second City (Chicago)	La-La Land (Los Angeles)
the Magnificent Mile (in Chicago)	Tinseltown (Hollywood)
the Big Apple (New York)	the Big Muddy (the Missouri River)
SoHo (in New York)	the Beehive State (Utah)
Soho (in London)	the French Quarter (in New Orleans)
the Pacific Rim	Down Under (Australia and New Zealand)

NOTE: The terms *Sunbelt* and *Frostbelt* are now commonly spelled as one word; the terms *Farm Belt*, *Bible Belt*, and *Rust Belt* are still commonly spelled as two words. Within the same context treat these terms the same way—as two words; for example, *in the Farm Belt and the Frost Belt.*

b. Some place names are used imaginatively to refer to specific types of businesses or institutions.

Silicon Valley (the cluster of high-tech industries south of San Francisco)
Silicon Alley (the cluster of software development firms in Manhattan)
Siliwood (the collaboration between Silicon Valley and Hollywood)
Madison Avenue (the advertising industry)
Wall Street (the financial industry)
Off-Off-Broadway (experimental theater in New York City)
Foggy Bottom (the U.S. State Department)

334 Capitalize the word *city* only when it is part of the corporate name of the city or part of an imaginative name.

Kansas City   **BUT:** the city of Dallas   the Windy City (Chicago)

335 **a.** Capitalize *state* only when it follows the name of a state or is part of an imaginative name.

New York *State* is also called the Empire *State.*
The *state* of Alaska is the largest in the Union.
Washington *State* entered the Union in 1889, the forty-second *state* to do so.
Next year we plan to return to the *States.* (Meaning the *United States.*)

b. Do not capitalize *state* when used in place of the actual state name.

> He is an employee of the *state.* (People working for the state government, however, might write *State.*)

c. Kentucky, Massachusetts, Pennsylvania, and Virginia are actually commonwealths. In ordinary usage, however, they are referred to as states.

> the commonwealth of Kentucky   **OR**   the state of Kentucky

336 According to the U.S. Government Printing Office *Style Manual*, the terms used to refer to the residents of the fifty states are formed according to different patterns.

a. Sixteen states just add *n.*

Alaskan	Iowan	Nevadan	South Dakotan
Arizonan	Minnesotan	North Dakotan	Utahn
Californian	Montanan	Oklahoman	Virginian
Georgian	Nebraskan	Pennsylvanian	West Virginian

b. Eight states add *an.*

Delawarean	Idahoan	Massachusettsan	Missourian
Hawaiian	Illinoisan	Mississippian	Ohioan

c. Six states drop the final letter and add *n* or *an.*

Arkansan	Kansan	Tennessean
Coloradan	New Mexican	Texan

d. Two states add *ian.*

Oregonian	Washingtonian

e. Seven states drop the final letter and add *ian.*

Alabamian	Indianian	Louisianian	South Carolinian
Floridian	Kentuckian	North Carolinian	

f. Only one state adds *r.*

> Mainer   **OR:**   Mainiac (the term favored by some residents)

g. Five states add *er.*

Conncticuter	New Yorker	Vermonter
Marylander	Rhode Islander	

h. Four states add *ite.*

Michiganite	New Jerseyite	Wisconsinite	Wyomingite

i. One state drops the final letter and adds *ite.*

> New Hampshirite

337 **a.** Capitalize *the* only when it is part of the official name of a place.

The Dalles	**BUT:** the Bronx
The Hague	the Netherlands

b. Capitalize the words *upper* and *lower* only when they are part of an actual place name or a well-established imaginative name.

Upper Peninsula	Lower East Side
Upper West Side	Newton Lower Falls

¶338

Points of the Compass

338 **a.** Capitalize *north, south, east, west,* and derivative words when they designate definite regions or are an integral part of a proper name.

in the North	the Far North	the North Pole
down South	the Deep South	the South Side
out West	the Far West	the West Coast
back East	the Middle East	the Eastern Seaboard

b. Do not capitalize these words when they merely indicate direction or general location.

Many factories have relocated from the *Northeast* to the *South.* (Region.)

BUT: They maintain a villa in the *south* of France. (General location.)

OR: Go *west* on Route 517 and then *south* on I-95. (Direction.)

John is coming back *East* after three years on the *West Coast.* (Region.)

BUT: The *west coast* of the United States borders on the Pacific. (Referring only to the shoreline, not the region.)

Most of our customers live on the *East Side.* (Definite locality.)

BUT: Most of our customers live on the *east side* of town. (General location.)

339 Capitalize such words as *Northerner, Southerner,* and *Midwesterner.*

340 Capitalize such words as *northern, southern, eastern,* and *western* when they refer to the people in a region or to their political, social, or cultural activities. Do not capitalize these words when they merely indicate general location or refer to the geography or climate of the region.

Eastern bankers	**BUT:**	the eastern half of Pennsylvania
Southern hospitality		southern temperatures
Western civilization		westerly winds
the Northern vote		a northern winter

The *Northern* states did not vote as they were expected to. (Political activities.)

BUT: The drought is expected to continue in the *northern* states. (Climate.)

My sales territory takes in most of the *southeastern* states. (General location.)

NOTE: When terms like *western region* and *southern district* are used to name organizational units within a company, capitalize them.

The *Western Region* (referring to a part of the national sales staff) reports that sales are 12 percent over budget for the first six months this year.

341 When words like *northern, southern, eastern,* and *western* precede a place name, they are not ordinarily capitalized because they merely indicate general location within a region. However, when these words are actually part of the place name, they must be capitalized. (Check an atlas or the geographic listings in a dictionary when in doubt.)

Preceding a Place Name	**Part of a Place Name**
northern New Jersey	**BUT:** Northern Ireland
western Massachusetts	Western Australia

NOTE: Within certain regions it is not uncommon for many people who live there to capitalize the adjective because of the special importance they attach to the regional designation. Thus people who live in southern California may prefer to write *Southern California.*

Capitalization

3

¶**345**

Days of the Week, Months, Holidays, Seasons, Events, Periods

342 Capitalize names of days, months, holidays, and religious days.

Tuesday	Father's Day	St. Patrick's Day
February	Juneteenth (June 19)	Good Friday
New Year's Eve	the Fourth of July	All Saints' Day
Presidents' Day	Kwanza **OR** Kwanzaa	Rosh Hashanah
April Fools' Day	Martin Luther King Day	Yom Kippur
Veterans Day	Kamehameha Day	Ramadan

➤ *For the use of apostrophes in names of holidays, see ¶650.*

343 Do not capitalize the names of the seasons unless they are personified.

We hold our regional sales conferences during the *fall* and *winter,* but our national conference always takes place early in the *spring.*

We do not plan to announce our new line of software applications until our *fall* '00/*winter* '01 catalog.

> **BUT:** And this you can see is the bolt. The purpose of this
> Is to open the breech, as you see. We can slide it
> Rapidly backwards and forwards: we call this
> Easing the spring. And rapidly backwards and forwards
> The early bees are assaulting and fumbling the flowers:
> They call it easing the Spring.
>
> —Henry Reed

344 a. Capitalize the names of historical events and imaginative names given to historical periods.

the American Revolution	the Renaissance
World War II	the Counter-Reformation
the Holocaust	Prohibition
Fire Prevention Week	the Great Depression

b. References to cultural *ages* are usually capitalized. However, contemporary references are not usually capitalized unless they appear together with a capitalized reference.

the Bronze Age	**BUT:**	the space age
the Dark Ages		the atomic age
the Middle Ages		the digital age

The course spans the development of civilization from the *Stone Age* to the *Space Age.*

c. References to cultural *eras* are usually capitalized, but references to cultural *periods* are usually not.

the Christian Era	**BUT:**	the romantic period
the Victorian Era		the colonial period

d. Capitalize the names of sporting events.

the Super Bowl	the World Series **OR** the Series
the Masters	the Kentucky Derby **OR** the Derby
the U.S. Open	the Olympic Games **OR** the Games **OR** the Olympics

345 Do not capitalize the names of decades and centuries.

during the fifties	in the twenty-first century
in the nineteen-nineties	during the nineteen hundreds

Continued on page 102

¶346

NOTE: Decades are capitalized, however, in special expressions.

the Gay Nineties   the Roaring Twenties

➤ *For a discussion on how to label the first decade of the twenty-first century, see ¶439b.*

Acts, Laws, Bills, Treaties

346 **a.** Capitalize formal titles of acts, laws, bills, and treaties, but do not capitalize common-noun elements that stand alone in place of the full name.

the Americans With Disabilities Act	the act
Public Law 480	the law
the Treaty of Versailles	the treaty
the First Amendment	the amendment
the Constitution of the United States	**BUT:** the Constitution (see ¶304)

BUT: When Pelletier takes the stand next week, we think he is likely to take the *Fifth.* (Referring to the Fifth Amendment.)

b. Do not capitalize generic or informal references to existing or pending legislation except for proper nouns and adjectives.

environmental protection laws   the Brady gun control law

c. "Laws" that make humorous or satirical observations about human and organizational behavior are capitalized to suggest that they carry the same authority as an actual piece of legislation.

Parkinson's Law states that work expands to fill the time that has been allotted for its completion.

Parkinson's Law of Data states that data expands to fill the space available.

Murphy's Law holds that if something can go wrong, it will.

The *Peter Principle* maintains that people in an organization tend to be promoted until they reach their level of incompetence.

According to *Fudd's First Law of Opposition,* if you push something hard enough, it will fall over.

A relatively new proverb called *Hanlon's Razor* states, "Never attribute to malice that which can be adequately explained by stupidity."

d. In the names of authentic scientific laws, capitalize only proper nouns and adjectives.

Gresham's law	Newton's first law of motion
Mendel's law	the first law of thermodynamics

Programs, Movements, Concepts

347 **a.** Do not capitalize the names of programs, movements, or concepts when used as general terms.

social security benefits	the civil rights movement
BUT: the Social Security Administration	**BUT:** the Civil Rights Act
medicare payments	the big bang theory
BUT: the Medicare Act	existentialism and rationalism

b. Capitalize proper nouns and adjectives that are part of such terms.

the Socratic method	Newtonian physics
Keynesian economics	Marxist-Leninist theories

c. Capitalize imaginative names given to programs and movements.

the New Deal	the New Frontier
the Great Society	the War on Poverty

d. Capitalize terms like *democrat, socialist,* and *communist* when they signify formal membership in a political party but not when they merely signify belief in a certain philosophy.

a lifelong *Democrat* (refers to a person who consistently votes for candidates of the Democratic Party)

independent voters

the right wing

a lifelong *democrat* (refers to a person who believes in the principles of democracy)

leftists

fascist tendencies

Races, Peoples, Languages

348 **a.** Capitalize the names of races, peoples, tribes, and languages.

Caucasians	Americans	Native Americans	**BUT:** the blacks
the Japanese	Hispanics	Mandarin Chinese	the whites

NOTE: The people who live in the Philippines are called Filipinos, and the official language of the country is called Pilipino.

b. Do not hyphenate terms like *African Americans* or *French Canadians* when they are used as nouns, because the first word in each case modifies the second. However, hyphenate such terms when they are used as adjectives; for example, *African-American enterprises, French-Canadian voters.* Moreover, hyphenate such terms when the first element is a prefix; for example, *an Afro-American style, the Anglo-Saxons, the Indo-Chinese.*

➢ *For a usage note on ethnic references, see pages 292–293.*

Religious References

349 **a.** Capitalize all references to a supreme being.

God	the Supreme Being	Allah
the Lord	the Messiah	Yahweh
the Holy Spirit	the Almighty	Providence

NOTE: The word *God* is capitalized in such compound expressions as *God-fearing* and *Godspeed* but not in such terms as *godforsaken* and *god-awful.*

b. Capitalize personal pronouns referring to a supreme being when they stand alone, without an antecedent nearby.

Offer thanks unto *Him.*   **BUT:** Ask the Lord for *his* blessing.

NOTE: Some writers capitalize these personal pronouns under all circumstances.

c. Capitalize references to persons revered as holy.

the Prince of Peace	Buddha	John the Baptist
the Good Shepherd	the Prophet	Saint Peter (see ¶518e)
the Blessed Virgin	the Apostles	Luke the Evangelist

d. Capitalize the names of religions, their members, and their buildings.

Reform Judaism	Mormons	Saint Mark's Episcopal Church
Zen Buddhism	Methodists	Temple Beth Sholom

the Roman Catholic *Church* (meaning the institution as a whole)

BUT: the Roman Catholic *church* on Wyoming Avenue (referring to a specific building)

the Church of Jesus Christ of Latter-day Saints (see ¶363, note)

Continued on page 104

¶350

e. Capitalize references to religious events. (See also ¶342.)

the Creation	the Exodus	the Crucifixion
the Flood	the Second Coming	the Resurrection

f. In general, do not capitalize references to specific religious observances and services. However, if you are writing from the perspective of a particular religion, follow the capitalization style of that religion.

bar mitzvah	baptism	**BUT:** the Eucharist
seder	christening	the Mass

350 Capitalize (but do not quote, italicize, or underline) references to works regarded as sacred.

the King James Bible	the Koran	the Ten Commandments
BUT: biblical sources	the Talmud	the Sermon on the Mount
the Revised Standard	the Torah	Psalms 23 and 24
Version	the Our Father	Kaddish
the Old Testament	the Lord's Prayer	Hail Mary
the Book of Genesis	Hebrews 13:8	the Apostles' Creed

NOTE: Do not capitalize *bible* when the work it refers to is not sacred.

That reference manual has become my *bible.*

Celestial Bodies

351 Capitalize the names of planets *(Jupiter, Mars)*, stars *(Polaris, the North Star)*, and constellations *(the Big Dipper, the Milky Way)*. However, do not capitalize the words *sun, moon,* and *earth* unless they are used in connection with the capitalized names of other planets or stars.

With the weather we've been having, we haven't seen much of the *sun.*

We have gone to the ends of the *earth* to assemble this collection of jewelry.

Compare the orbits of *Mars, Venus,* and *Earth.*

Course Titles, Subjects, Academic Degrees

352 Capitalize the names of specific course titles. However, do not capitalize names of subjects or areas of study (except for any proper nouns or adjectives in such names).

American History 201 meets on Tuesdays and Thursdays. (Course title.)

Harriet got a bachelor's degree in *American history.* (Area of study.)

353 Do not capitalize academic degrees used as general terms of classification. However, capitalize a degree used after a person's name.

a bachelor of arts degree	received his bachelor's (see ¶644)
a master of science degree	working for a master's
a doctor of laws degree	will soon receive her doctorate
BUT: Claire Hurwitz, Doctor of Philosophy	

354 In references to academic years, do not capitalize the words *freshman, sophomore, junior,* and *senior.* In references to grade levels, capitalize the word *grade* when a number follows but not when a number precedes.

Harriet spent her *junior* year in Germany.

Our oldest child is in *Grade 6;* our second child is in the *third grade.*

NOTE: Some schools and colleges prefer to use *first-year students* in place of *freshmen*.

All incoming *freshmen* (**OR** *first-year students*) must register by September 4.

Commercial Products

355   Capitalize trademarks, brand names, proprietary names, names of commercial products, and market grades. The common noun following the name of a product should not ordinarily be capitalized; however, manufacturers and advertisers often capitalize such words in the names of their own products to give them special emphasis.

Elmer's glue   **BUT:** Krazy Glue

NOTE: Be alert to the correct spelling of proper nouns.

Macintosh computers   **BUT:** McIntosh apples

➤ *For the capitalization of short words in the names of products, see ¶303, note. For the use of intercaps, see ¶366.*

356   Capitalize all trademarks except those that have become clearly established as common nouns. To be safe, check an up-to-date dictionary or consult the International Trademark Association (1133 Avenue of the Americas, New York, NY 10036).

NOTE: You may contact the International Trademark Association either by e-mail <communications@inta.org> or on the Web <http://www.inta.org>.

Xerox, Photostat; **BUT:** photocopy

Telecopier; **BUT:** fax

DeskWriter, LaserJet; **BUT:** laser printer

Express Mail, Yellow Pages, Filofax;
   BUT: e-mail, voice mail, videotex

Scotch tape, Post-it notes, Rolodex

Jiffy bag, Carousel slide projector

Acrilan, Dacron, Lycra, Orlon,
   Ultrasuede; **BUT:** nylon, spandex

Naugahyde, Thinsulate, Perma-Prest

Levi's, Windbreaker, Snugli, L'eggs

Loafers, Air Jordan, 'Boks

Jeep, Dumpster, Hide-A-Bed

Airbus, Learjet, AAdvantage

Teflon, Velcro, Ziploc, Baggies, GLAD

AstroTurf, Styrofoam, Lucite, Mylar

Spackle, Plastic Wood, Sheetrock

Fiberglas; **BUT:** fiberglass

Jacuzzi, Disposall, Frigidaire, Sterno

Laundromat, Dustbuster, Drygas

Crock-Pot, Pyrex dish, Dixie cup

Off!, Oh Henry!, $H_2OH!$, Guess?

Band-Aid, Ace bandage, Q-Tips

Kleenex, Vaseline, Chap Stick

Tylenol, Novocain, Demerol,
   Valium; **BUT:** aspirin

Nicotrol, Nyquil, Motrin;
   BUT: penicillin, cortisone

Olean; **BUT:** olestra

Adrenalin; **BUT:** adrenaline

diet Coke, Diet Pepsi, Kool-Aid,
   Popsicle, Gatorade, Sanka

Kitty Litter, Seeing Eye dog

Day-Glo colors, Technicolor

Discman, Walkman, Polaroid;
   BUT: camcorder

StairMaster, Wiffle ball

Jazzercise, Ski-Doo, Tamagotchi

Frisbee, Ping-Pong, Rollerblades

Scrabble, Trivial Pursuit

Realtor; **BUT:** real estate agent

Neon (car); **BUT:** neon (gas)

NOTE: Trademark holders typically use a raised symbol (such as ™ or ®) after their trademarks in all of their correspondence, promotional material, and product packaging. When you make reference to trademarks that belong to others, you do not need to use these symbols. Capitalizing the trademarks is sufficient.

¶357

Advertising Material

357 Words ordinarily written in small letters may be capitalized in advertising copy for emphasis. (This style is inappropriate in all other kinds of communication.)

> Save money now during our *Year-End Clearance Sale.*
>
> It's the event *Luxury Lovers* have been waiting for . . . from Whitehall's!

Legal Documents

358 In legal documents, many words that ordinarily would be written in small letters are often written with initial capitals or all capitals—for example, references to parties, the name of the document, special provisions, and sometimes spelled-out amounts of money (see ¶420b).

> THIS AGREEMENT, made this 31st day of January 2002 . . .
>
> . . . hereinafter called the SELLER . . .
>
> WHEREAS the Seller has this day agreed . . .
>
> WITNESS the signatures . . .

NOTE: A number of lawyers no longer follow this style.

Nouns With Numbers or Letters

359 Capitalize a noun followed by a number or a letter that indicates sequence. **EXCEPTIONS:** Do not capitalize the nouns *line, note, page, paragraph, size, step,* and *verse.*

Account 66160	Class 4	Interstate 5 **OR** I-5	Policy 394857
Act 1	Column 1	Invoice 270487	Proposition 215
Appendix A	Day One	Item 9859D	Room 501
Article 2	Diagram 4	Lesson 20	Route 46
Book III	Exercise 8	line 4	Rule 3
Building 4	Exhibit A	Model B671-4	Section 1
Bulletin T-119	Extension 2174	note 1	size 10
Catch-22	Figure 9	page 158	step 3
Channel 55	Flight 626	paragraph 2a	Table 7
Chapter V	Form 1040	Part Three	Unit 2
Chart 3	(**BUT:** a W-2 form)	Plate XV	verse 3
Check 181	Illustration 19	Platform 3	Volume II

NOTE: It is often unnecessary to use *No.* before the number. (See ¶455a.)

> Purchase Order 4713 (**RATHER THAN:** Purchase Order *No.* 4713)
>
> **BUT:** Social Security No. 042-62-5340 (**NOT:** Social Security 042-62-5340)

Titles of Literary and Artistic Works; Headings

360 **a.** In titles of literary and artistic works and in displayed headings, capitalize all words with *four or more* letters. Also capitalize words with fewer than four letters except:

> **ARTICLES:** *the, a, an*
>
> **SHORT CONJUNCTIONS:** *and, as, but, if, or, nor*
>
> **SHORT PREPOSITIONS:** *at, by, for, in, of, off, on, out, to, up*

Capitalization

3

¶361

b. Be sure to capitalize short verb forms like *Is* and *Be.* However, do not capitalize *to* when it is part of an infinitive.

> *How to Succeed in Business Without Really Trying*
> "Redevelopment Proposal Is Not Expected to Be Approved"

NOTE: When citing titles in text, headings, source notes, or bibliographies, it is important to maintain a consistent style of capitalization. You may thus find it necessary to disregard the capitalization style used on the title page of a particular book or in the heading of a particular article or in the listings in a particular catalog. For reasons of typographic design or graphic appeal, titles may appear in such places in a variety of styles—in capital letters, small letters, small caps, or some combination of these styles. In some cases, only the first word of the title and subtitle is capitalized. In other cases, the first letter of *every* word is capitalized. In some books a different style of capitalization is used on the book jacket, the title page, and the copyright page. In light of all these variations in capitalization style that you are likely to encounter, impose a consistent style as described in ¶¶360–361. However, do not alter the all-cap style used for acronyms (for example, *AIDS*) and organizational names (for example, *IBM*).

361 Even articles, short conjunctions, and short prepositions should be capitalized under the following circumstances:

a. Capitalize the first and last word of a title.

> "*A* Home to Be Proud *Of* "
> "*The* New Economy: Signs and Signals to Watch *For*"

CAUTION: Do not capitalize *the* at the beginning of a title unless it is actually part of the title.

> For further details check *the Encyclopaedia Britannica.*
> This clipping is from *The New York Times.*

b. Capitalize the first word following a dash or colon in a title.

> *Abraham Lincoln—The Early Years*
> *The Treaty of Versailles: A Reexamination*

c. Capitalize short words like *in, out, off,* and *up* in titles when they serve as adverbs rather than as prepositions. (These words may occur as adverbs in verb phrases or in hyphenated compounds derived from verb phrases. See ¶¶803, 1070.)

> "Microsoft Chalks *Up* Record Earnings for the Year"
> "LeClaire Is Runner-*Up* in Election" (see also ¶363)
> **BUT:** "Sailing *up* the Mississippi"
>
> *The Spy Who Came In From the Cold*
> "Foxworth Is Considered a Shoo-*In* for Governor"
> **BUT:** "Pollsters Project an Easy Win for Foxworth *in* Heavy Voter Turnout"

d. Capitalize short prepositions like *in* and *up* when used together with prepositions having four or more letters.

> "Sailing *Up* and *Down* the Mississippi"
> "Happenings *In* and *Around* Town"
> "Mall Opening *On* or *About* May 1"
> "Voters *For* and *Against* the New Budget Clash at Hearing"

Continued on page 108

Capitalization

3

¶362

e. When a title or heading is displayed on more than one line, do not capitalize the first word of any turnover line unless it needs to be capitalized on the basis of the preceding guidelines.

Should You Invest for the Long Pull	Millions	Income
or Should You Trade Continually?	*of* Dollars	*per* Capita

➤ *For the capitalization of* Preface, Contents, Appendix, *and* Index, *see ¶242, note; for the use of all-capital letters with titles, see ¶289b.*

362   Do not capitalize a book title when it is incorporated into a sentence as a descriptive phrase.

In his book on *economics* Samuelson points out that . . .

BUT: In his book *Economics* Samuelson points out that . . .

Hyphenated Words

363 *Within a sentence,* capitalize only those elements of a hyphenated word that are proper nouns or proper adjectives. *At the beginning of a sentence,* capitalize the first element in the hyphenated word but not other elements unless they are proper nouns or proper adjectives. *In a heading or title,* capitalize all the elements except articles, short prepositions, and short conjunctions. (See ¶360.)

Within Sentences	Beginning Sentences	In Headings and Titles
e-mail (see ¶847)	E-mail	E-Mail
up-to-date	Up-to-date	Up-to-Date
Spanish-American	Spanish-American	Spanish-American
English-speaking	English-speaking	English-Speaking
mid-September	Mid-September	Mid-September
ex-President Bush	Ex-President Bush	Ex-President Bush
Senator-elect Murray	Senator-elect Murray	Senator-Elect Murray
self-confidence	Self-confidence	Self-Confidence
de-emphasize	De-emphasize	De-Emphasize
follow-up	Follow-up	Follow-Up (see ¶361c)
Ninety-ninth Congress	Ninety-ninth Congress	Ninety-Ninth Congress
post-World War II	Post-World War II	Post-World War II
one-sixth	One-sixth	One-Sixth
twenty-first	Twenty-first	Twenty-First

NOTE: In the hyphenated names of organizations and products, the word or letter following a hyphen may or may not be capitalized. Follow the organization's style in each case.

Snap-on tools	Post-it notepads	Etch-A-Sketch
Easy-Off oven cleaner	Book-Of-The-Month Club	La-Z-Boy

Awards and Medals

364   Capitalize the names of awards and medals.

Pulitzer Prize winners	the Congressional Medal of Honor
the Nobel Prize	the Distinguished Service Medal
Oscars and Emmys	the Purple Heart

Capitalization

3

Computer Terminology

365   **a.** Use all-capital letters for the names of many programming languages.

COBOL	FORTRAN	**BUT:** Java
BASIC	APL	Ada
BUT: QuickBASIC	LISP	Logo

b. Use all-capital letters for the names of many operating systems.

MS-DOS	UNIX	**BUT:** MacOS X
PC-DOS	OS/2	Linux

c. Capitalize the names of Internet search engines *(Excite, Yahoo!)*, Internet service providers *(UUNet)* and commercial online services *(America Online)*, Web sites *(HotWired)*, online communities *(Usenet)*, and online databases *(Lexis, Dialog)*. Some of these names (such as UUNet and HotWired) follow a special capitalization style known as *intercaps*. (See ¶366 for more examples.)

➤ *For the capitalization of words or phrases beginning with* Web, *see ¶847f.*

Intercaps

366 The names of many organizations and products are written with an unusual style known as *intercaps* or *BiCaps*. Follow the organization's style in each case.

a. The names of computer organizations and products commonly reflect an intercap style. For example:

AltaVista	SurfWatch	CorelDRAW
CyberPatrol	TrueType	iMac
HotWired	VirusScan	InterNIC
NetNanny	VisiCalc	NeXT
OmniPage	WebCrawler	QuarkXPress
PageMaker	WordPerfect	RealTIME Media
PowerPoint	ZipZapp	TK!Solver

b. The use of intercaps appears in other areas of business as well. For example:

AstroTurf	CreataCard greeting cards	PlaySkool toys
NordicTrack	DieHard batteries	ReaLemon juice
NutraSweet	DuraSoft contact lenses	TraveLodge motels
PowerBar	KitchenAid appliances	TripTik maps
SaladShooter	MasterCard purchases	VapoRub ointment

➤ *Capitalization of questions within sentences: see ¶¶115, 117.*
Capitalization after a colon: see ¶¶196–199.
Capitalization after an opening bracket: see ¶296.
Capitalization after an opening dash: see ¶214, note.
Capitalization after an opening parenthesis: see ¶¶224–226.
Capitalization after an opening quotation mark: see ¶¶272–273.
Capitalization of abbreviations: see ¶514.
Capitalization for special emphasis: see ¶285c.

Capitalization

3

SECTION 4

Numbers

➤ *For definitions of grammatical terms, see the appropriate entries in the Glossary of Grammatical Terms (Appendix A).*

There is a significant difference between using figures and using words to express numbers. Figures are big (like capital letters) and compact and informal (like abbreviations); when used in a sentence, they stand out clearly from the surrounding words. By contrast, numbers expressed in words are unemphatic and formal; they do not stand out in a sentence. It is this functional difference between figures and words that underlies all aspects of number style.

Basic Rules

The rules for expressing numbers would be quite simple if writers would all agree to express numbers entirely in figures or entirely in words. But in actual practice the exclusive use of figures is considered appropriate only in tables and statistical matter, whereas the exclusive use of words to express numbers is found only in ultraformal documents (such as proclamations and social invitations). In writing that is neither ultraformal nor ultratechnical, most style manuals call for the use of both figures and words in varying proportions. Although authorities do not agree on details, there are two sets of basic rules in wide use: the *figure style* (which uses figures for most numbers above 10) and the *word style* (which uses figures for most numbers above 100). Unless you deal with a very limited type of written communication, you should be prepared to use each style appropriately as the situation demands.

Figure Style

The figure style is most commonly used in ordinary business correspondence (dealing with sales, production, finance, advertising, and other routine commercial matters). It is also used in journalistic and technical material and in academic work of a technical or statistical nature. In writing of this kind, most numbers represent significant quantities or measurements that should stand out for emphasis or quick comprehension.

401 a. Spell out numbers from 1 through 10; use figures for numbers above 10. This rule applies to both exact and approximate numbers.

> I would like *ten* copies of this article, but I need only *two* or *three* right away.
>
> I sensed that the project was in trouble from *Day One*. (See ¶359.)
>
> At the convention we got more than *75* requests for a copy of your report.
>
> We expect about *30* to *35* employees to sign up for the graphic arts course.
>
> The advertising is deliberately pitched at the *40-plus* age group.
>
> My letter in last Sunday's paper provoked over *25* letters and some *60-odd* phone calls.
>
> There has been a *sixfold* increase in the number of reported incidents. (See ¶817b.)
>
> **BUT:** There has been a *20-fold* increase in the number of reported incidents.
>
> One bookstore chain has already ordered *2500* copies. (See ¶461, note, on the omission of commas in four-digit figures.)
>
> The exhibition drew more than *12,000* people in the first month.
>
> We send out about *200,000* catalogs almost every month, but our year-end holiday catalog is mailed to over *1,000,000* households. (See ¶403b.)

NOTE: In the statement of the rule above ("Spell out numbers from 1 through 10"), figures are used for 1 and 10 because these numbers are referred to as numbers. See ¶401b for a fuller explanation.

➤ *For a note on the use of* more than *and* over *with numbers, see Section 11, page 300.*

Continued on page 112

¶402

b. Use all figures—even for the numbers 1 through 10 (as in this sentence)—when they have technical significance or need to stand out for quick comprehension. This all-figure style is used in tables, in statistical material, and in expressions of dates *(May 3)*, money *($6)*, clock time *(4 p.m.)*, proportions and ratios *(a 5-to-1 shot)*, sports scores *(3 to 1)*, academic grades *(95)*, and percentages *(8 per-cent)*. This style is also used with abbreviations and symbols *(12 cm, 8°F)*, with numbers referred to as numbers *(think of a number from 1 to 10)*, with highway designations *(U.S. Route 1, I-80)*, and with technical or emphatic references to age *(a tristate clinical study of 5-year-olds)*, periods of time *(a 6-month loan)*, measurements *(parcels over 3 pounds)*, and page numbers *(page 1)*.

c. In isolated cases spell out a number above 10 in order to de-emphasize the number or make it seem indefinite.

> Jonathan could give you *a thousand and one* reasons for his inability to find a job that's right for him.
>
> I have *a hundred* things to do today. (In this context *100 things* would seem too precise, too exact.)
>
> Thanks *a million* for all your help on the Tennyson deposition.
>
> When I asked Fran to reconsider, all she said was, "*A thousand* times no!"

d. Also use words for numbers at the beginning of a sentence, for most ordinals *(our twenty-fifth anniversary)*, for fractions *(one-third of our sales)*, and for nontechnical or nonemphatic references to age *(my son just turned twelve)*, periods of time *(twenty years ago)*, and measurements *(I need to lose another thirty pounds)*.

➤ *For rules on how to express numbers in figures, see ¶¶461–464; for rules on how to express numbers in words, see ¶¶465–467.*

402 Use the same style to express *related* numbers above and below 10. If any of the numbers are above 10, put them all in figures.

> We used to have *two* dogs, *one* cat, and *one* rabbit.
>
> **BUT:** We now have *5* dogs, *11* cats, and *1* rabbit. (The rabbit is male.)
>
> When the museum guard was asked how he could be so sure that the dinosaur skeleton on display was precisely *80,000,009* years old, he explained that the dinosaur had been *80,000,000* years old when he started working at the museum *9* years earlier.
>
> Our *four* sons consumed a total of *18* hamburgers, *5* large bottles of diet Coke, *12* DoveBars, and about *2000* cookies—all at *one* sitting. (Figures are used for all the related items of food; the other numbers—*four* and *one*—are spelled out, since they are not related and are not over 10.)

NOTE: In the names of companies and products, follow the organization's style.

a 7-Eleven store	a can of 7UP	A.1. steak sauce
3-In-One oil	V8 juice	9-Lives cat food
Lotus 1-2-3 software	3M office products	One-A-Day vitamins

403 a. For fast comprehension, numbers in the *millions* or higher may be expressed as follows:

> 21 million (in place of 21,000,000)
>
> 3 billion (in place of 3,000,000,000)
>
> 14½ million (in place of 14,500,000)
>
> 2.4 billion (in place of 2,400,000,000)
>
> Bindel & Boggs is placing an order for *2.4 million* barrels of oil.
>
> **BUT:** Bindel & Boggs is placing a *2.4-million-barrel* order. (See ¶817a.)

Numbers

4

NOTE: This style may be used only when the amount consists of a whole number with nothing more than a simple fraction or decimal following. A number such as *4,832,067* must be written all in figures. However, if the situation permits numbers to be rounded, this number can be rewritten as *4.8 million.*

b. Treat related numbers alike.

> Last year we sold *21,557,000* items; this year, nearly *23,000,000.*
> (**NOT:** 21,557,000 . . . 23 million.)

➢ *For examples involving money, see ¶416.*

Word Style

The word style of numbers is used mainly in high-level executive correspondence (see ¶¶1394–1395) and in nontechnical material, where the writing is of a more formal or literary nature and the use of figures would give numbers an undesired emphasis and obtrusiveness. Here are the basic rules for the word style.

404 Spell out all numbers, whether exact or approximate, that can be expressed in one or two words. (A hyphenated compound number like *twenty-one* or *twenty-nine* counts as one word.) In effect, spell out all numbers from 1 through 100 and all round numbers above 100 that require no more than two words (such as *sixty-two thousand* or *forty-five million*).

> Mr. Ryan received *twenty-three* letters praising his talk last Wednesday at the Rotary Club.
> Last year more than *twelve million* people attended the art exhibition our company sponsored.
> Some *sixty-odd* people have called to volunteer their services.
> More than *two hundred* people attended the reception for Helen Russo.
> **BUT:** More than *250* people attended the reception. (Use figures when more than two words are required.)

NOTE: In writing of all ultraformal nature—proclamations, social invitations, and many legal documents—even a number that requires more than two words is spelled out. However, as a matter of practicality the word style ordinarily uses figures when more than two words are required.

➢ *For guidelines on how to express numbers in words, see ¶¶465–467.*

405 Express related numbers the same way, even though some are above 100 and some below. If any must be in figures, put all in figures.

> We sent out *three hundred* invitations and have already received over *one hundred* acceptances.
> **BUT:** We sent out *300* invitations and have already received *125* acceptances.
> (**NOT:** three hundred . . . 125.)

406 Numbers in the millions or higher *that require more than two words when spelled out* may be expressed as follows:

> 231 million (in place of 231,000,000)
> 9¾ billion (in place of 9,750,000,000)
> 671.4 million (in place of 671,400,000)

Even a two-word number such as *sixty-two million* should be expressed as *62 million* when it is related to a number such as *231 million* (which cannot be spelled in two words). Moreover, it should be expressed as *62,000,000* when it is related to a number such as *231,163,520.*

¶407

Special Rules

The preceding rules on figure style (¶¶401–403) and word style (¶¶404–406) are basic guidelines that govern in the absence of more specific principles. The following rules cover those situations that require special handling (for example, expressions of dates and money). In a number of cases where either figures or words are acceptable, your choice will depend on whether you are striving for emphasis or formality.

Dates

The following rules apply to dates in sentences. See ¶1314 for the treatment of date lines in business correspondence.

407   a. When the day *precedes* the month or *stands alone,* express it either in ordinal figures *(1st, 2d, 3d, 4th)* or in ordinal words *(the first, the twelfth, the twentieth).*

> **FOR EMPHASIS:** This year's international sales conference runs from Monday, the *2d* of August, through Thursday, the *5th.*

> **FOR FORMALITY:** We leave for Europe on the *third* of June and return on the *twenty-fifth.*

  b. When the day *follows* the month, use a cardinal figure *(1, 2, 3,* etc.) to express it.

> on March 6

  NOTE: Do not use the form *March 6th* or *March sixth,* even though those versions reflect the way the date would sound when spoken aloud.

408   a. Express complete dates in month-day-year sequence.

> March 6, 2003

  NOTE: In United States military correspondence and in letters from foreign countries, the complete date is expressed in *day*-month-year sequence.

> 6 March 2003

  b. The form *3/6/03* (representing a *month*-day-year sequence) is acceptable on business forms and in informal letters and memos. Avoid this form, however, if there is any chance your reader could misinterpret it as a *day*-month-year sequence.

  c. Avoid the following forms: *March 6th, 2003; Mar. 6, 2003; the 6th of March, 2003; the sixth of March, 2003.*

409   a. When you make a reference to a previous letter, memo, or document in the first sentence of a document you are composing, it is usually sufficient to cite only the month and the day.

> Thank you for your letter of May 22, in which . . . (A reader will assume that the current year—as shown in your date line—also applies to the letter of May 22.)

> ➤ *For the use of a comma between the date and the* in which *clause, see* ¶152.

  However, in cases where there can be no room for the slightest ambiguity (for example, in legal documents), it is safer to cite the full month-day-year date in the first sentence.

> Thank you for your letter of December 27, 2000, in which . . .

  NOTE: It is especially helpful to give the full date when the document you are citing was written in a prior year or when the document is part of a large file that spans two or more years. Some writers, as a matter of policy, cite the full date under all circumstances.

b. When you make reference to dates elsewhere in the document you are composing, the decision to include or omit the year in these dates will depend on the nature of the document. If the dates are significant from a legal perspective (for example, in schedules specifying deadlines for performance and incremental payments), include the year in all subsequent references to dates. In ordinary correspondence, however, when it is clear from the context that the subsequent dates all fall within the same year as the one shown in the date line or in the first sentence in your document, the use of month and day alone is sufficient.

410 Note the use of commas and other punctuation with expressions of dates.

On *August 13, 2001,* my husband and I received the bank loan that permitted us to start our own restaurant. (Two commas set off the year following the month and day.)

We set a formal opening date of *November 15, 2001;* we actually opened on *March 18, 2002* (because of the flash fire that virtually destroyed the restaurant and forced us to start from scratch). (Note that the second comma is omitted after *2001* and *2002* because in each case other punctuation—a semicolon or an opening parenthesis—is required at that point.)

Sales for *February 2002* hit an all-time low. (Omit commas around the year when it follows the month alone.)

BUT: Once we introduced our new product line in *September 2001,* it was clear that we were finally on the road to a strong recovery. (The comma following *2001* is needed to separate an introductory dependent clause from the rest of the sentence, not because of the date.)

The *May 2001* issue of *The Atlantic* carried an excerpt from Brenda's forthcoming book. (No commas are used when the month-year expression serves as an adjective.)

BUT: The *May 7, 2001,* issue of *Newsweek* broke the story. (Use two commas to set off the year when a complete date serves as an adjective. See ¶154.)

In *2001* we opened six branch offices in . . . (No comma follows the year in a short introductory phrase unless a nonessential element follows immediately.)

On *February 28* we will decide . . . (No comma follows the month and day in a short introductory phrase unless a nonessential element follows immediately.)

BUT: On *February 28,* the date of the next board meeting, we will decide . . . (Insert a comma when a nonessential element follows immediately.)

On *February 28,* 27 managers from the Iowa plant will . . . (Insert a comma when another figure follows immediately. See ¶456.)

Yesterday, *April 3,* I spoke to a group of exporters in Seattle. On Tuesday, *April 11,* I will be speaking at an international trade fair in Singapore. (Set off a month-day expression when it serves as an appositive. See ¶148.)

On *August 28,* when the malfunction was first reported, we notified all of our dealers by e-mail about an equipment recall. (The phrase *On August 28* establishes *when;* the *when* clause that follows is nonessential and is set off with commas.)

➢ *For the use or omission of a comma when a date is followed by a related phrase or clause, see ¶152.*

411 In formal legal documents, formal invitations, and proclamations, spell out the day and the year. A number of styles may be used:

May twenty-first	two thousand and two
the twenty-first of May	in the year of our Lord two thousand
this twenty-first day of May	and two

¶412

412 **a.** Well-known years in history may appear in abbreviated form.

the stock market crash in '29   the gold rush of '49 (1849)
the Olympic Winter Games of '96   **BUT:** the San Francisco 49ers

b. Years also appear in abbreviated form in certain business expressions. (See also ¶294.)

FY2001/02   **OR**   fiscal year 2001/02   the fall '02/'03 catalog

c. Class graduation years often appear in abbreviated form.

the class of '99   the class of '00   the class of '04

NOTE: There is still no consensus on how to refer *aloud* to academic classes in the first decade of the twenty-first century. On the basis of the style commonly used at the start of the twentieth century, the class of 2004 (or '04) could be referred to aloud as "the class of aught-four" or "the class of naught-four." The more challenging question is how to refer to the class of '00. One solution is simply to say "the class of two thousand." Other suggestions currently in circulation include "the class of aughty-aught," "the class of naughty-naught," "the double-ohs," "the oh-ohs," and even "the uh-ohs." In time, one expression will probably become established through usage as the dominant form. Until then feel free to choose (or devise) whatever form appeals to you.

➤ *For the expression of centuries and decades, see ¶¶438–439; for dates in a sequence, see ¶¶458–460.*

Money

413 **a.** Use figures to express exact or approximate amounts of money.

$7	over $1500	more than $5,000,000 a year	a $50 bill
$13.50	nearly $50,000	a $5,000,000-a-year account	$350 worth

➤ *For a note on the use of* more than *and* over *with numbers, see Section 11, page 300.*

b. When amounts of money from different countries are referred to in the same context, the unit of currency in each case usually appears as an abbreviation or symbol (or both) before the numerical amount.

US$10,000   (refers to 10,000 U.S. dollars)
Can$10,000   (refers to 10,000 Canadian dollars)
Mex$10,000   (refers to 10,000 Mexican pesos)
DM10,000   (refers to 10,000 German deutsche marks)
£10,000   (refers to 10,000 British pounds)
¥10,000   (refers to 10,000 Japanese yen)
€10,000   (refers to 10,000 euros)

NOTE: If your software provides special character sets, you can access the symbols for the British pound and the Japanese yen. The symbol for the euro—introduced early in 1999—is still so new that it may not be provided by your software. In that case use a small *e* to represent the euro: e10,000

c. An isolated, nonemphatic reference to money may be spelled out.

two hundred dollars	a half-dollar	five thousand dollars' worth
nearly a thousand dollars	half a million dollars	(note the apostrophe with
a twenty-dollar bill	a million-dollar house	*dollars*)

¶418

414   Spell out indefinite amounts of money.

>   a few million dollars   many thousands of dollars

415 It is not necessary to add a decimal point or zeros to a *whole* dollar amount that occurs in a sentence.

>   I am enclosing a check for *$125.*   This model costs $12.50; that one costs *$10.*

In a column, however, if any amount contains cents, add a decimal point and two zeros to all *whole* dollar amounts to maintain a uniform appearance. (See also ¶1629.)

$150.50
25.00
8.05
$183.55

416 **a.** Money in round amounts of a million or more may be expressed partly in words. (The style given in the first column is preferred.)

$12 million	**OR**	12 million dollars		
$10½ million	**OR**	10½ million dollars		
$10.5 million	**OR**	10.5 million dollars		
$6¼ billion	**OR**	6¼ billion dollars	**OR**	$6250 million
$6.25 billion	**OR**	6.25 billion dollars	**OR**	6250 million dollars

b. This style may be used only when the amount consists of a whole number with nothing more than a simple fraction or decimal following.

>   10.2 million dollars   **BUT:** $10,235,000

This style may also be used with the suffix *plus*. (See also ¶817b.)

>   a $10 million-plus deal

c. Express related amounts the same way.

>   from $500,000 to $1,000,000 (**NOT:** from $500,000 to $1 million)

d. Repeat the word *million* (*billion,* etc.) with each figure to avoid misunderstanding.

> $5 million to $10 million (**NOT:** $5 to $10 million)

417   Fractional expressions of large amounts of money should be either completely spelled out (see ¶427) or converted to an all-figure style.

>   one-quarter of a million dollars   **OR** $250,000
>   (**BUT NOT:** ¼ of a million dollars   **OR** $¼ million)
>   a half-billion dollars   **OR** $500,000,000
>   (**BUT NOT:** ½ billion dollars   **OR** $½ billion)

418 **a.** For amounts under a dollar, ordinarily use figures and the word *cents*.

>   I am sure that customers will not pay more than *50 cents* for this item.
>   This machine can be fixed with *80 cents'* worth of parts. (Note the apostrophe with *cents.*)
>   These *25-cent* tokens can be used at all tollbooths.

NOTE: An isolated, nonemphatic reference to cents may be spelled out.

>   I wouldn't give *two cents* for that car.

b. Do not use the style *$.75* in sentences except when related amounts require a dollar sign.

>   It will cost you *$5.47* a copy to do the company manual: *$.97* for the paper, *$1.74* for the printing, and *$2.76* for the special binder.

Continued on page 118

Numbers

4

¶419

c. The cent sign (¢) may be used in technical and statistical material.

> The price of aluminum, *78.6¢* a pound a year ago, now runs around *69.8¢* a pound; copper, then selling for *98.6¢* a pound, now costs *87.6¢* a pound.

419 When using the dollar sign or the cent sign with a price range or a series of amounts, use the sign with each amount.

> $5000 to $8000 $10 million to $20 million
>
> 10¢ to 20¢   (**BUT NOT:** $10 to $20 million)
>
> These three properties are valued at $832,900, $954,500, and $1,087,000, respectively.

If the term *dollars* or *cents* is to be spelled out, use the term only with the final amount.

420 **a.** In some legal documents, amounts of money are expressed first in words and then, within parentheses, in figures. (See also ¶¶465–467.)

> One Hundred Dollars ($100)   **OR**   One Hundred (100) Dollars
> **BUT NOT:** One Hundred ($100) Dollars
>
> Three Thousand One Hundred and 50/100 Dollars ($3100.50)

b. When spelling out amounts of money, omit the *and* between hundreds and tens of dollars if *and* is used before the fraction representing cents.

> Six Hundred Thirty-two and 75/100 Dollars
> (**NOT:** Six Hundred *and* Thirty-two and 75/100 Dollars)

NOTE: In whole dollar amounts, the use of *and* between hundreds and tens of dollars is optional.

> Six Hundred Thirty-two Dollars   **OR**   Six Hundred and Thirty-two Dollars

c. The capitalization of spelled-out amounts may vary. Sometimes the first letter of each main word is capitalized (as in the examples in ¶420a); sometimes only the first letter of the first word is capitalized (as on checks); sometimes the entire amount is in all-capital letters.

The following rules (¶¶421–428) cover situations in which numbers are usually spelled out: at the beginning of sentences and in expressions using indefinite numbers, ordinal numbers, and fractions.

At the Beginning of a Sentence

421 Spell out a number that begins a sentence, as well as any related numbers.

> *Thirty-four* former students of Dr. Helen VanVleck came from all parts of the country to honor their professor on the occasion of her retirement.
>
> *Eight hundred* people have already signed the recall petition.
>
> *Forty* to *fifty* percent of the people polled on different occasions expressed disapproval of the mayor's performance in office.
>
> (**NOT:** *Forty* to *50* percent . . .)

422 If the number requires more than two words when spelled out or if figures are preferable for emphasis or quick reference, reword the sentence.

> You ought to consider *550-MHz* Pentium III processors if you want to boost productivity.
> (**NOT:** *550-MHz* Pentium III processors are worth considering . . .)

¶**425**

The company sent out *298* copies of its consumer guidelines last month.
(**NOT:** *Two hundred and ninety-eight* copies of its consumer guidelines were sent out by the company last month.)

We had a good year in *2001*.
(**NOT:** *Two thousand one* [**OR** *2001*] was a good year for us.)

Our mining operations in Nevada provide *60* to *70* percent of our revenues.
(**NOT:** *Sixty* to *seventy* percent of our revenues come from our mining operations in Nevada.)

Indefinite Numbers and Amounts

423 Spell out indefinite numbers and amounts.

several hundred investors	hundreds of inquiries
a few thousand acres	thousands of readers
a multimillion-dollar sale	many millions of dollars
a man in his late forties	a roll of fifties and twenties

➤ *For approximate numbers, see ¶401 (figure style) and ¶404 (word style).*

Ordinal Numbers

424 In general, spell out all ordinal numbers (*first, second, third,* etc.) that can be expressed in one or two words. (A hyphenated number like *twenty-first* counts as one word.)

in the twenty-first century	the firm's one hundredth anniversary
twenty-first-century art	(**BUT:** the firm's 125th anniversary)
on the forty-eighth floor	the Ninety-ninth Congress (in text)
on my fifty-fifth birthday	the Ninety-Ninth Congress
the Fourteenth Ward	(in headings and titles; see ¶363)
the two millionth visitor	the 106th Congress
the Seventh-Day Adventist Church	the Eighteenth Amendment

NOTE: When a hyphenated term like *twenty-first* is the first element in a compound adjective (as in *twenty-first-century art*), the second hyphen may be changed to an en dash *(twenty-first–century art).*

➤ *For the rule on how to express ordinal numbers in words, see ¶465; for the distinction between ordinals and fractions, see ¶427d.*

425   **a.** Use figures for ordinals in certain expressions of dates (see ¶¶407–409), in numbered street names above 10 (see ¶1333b), and in situations calling for special emphasis.

In Advertising Copy
Come to our *25th* Anniversary Sale! (Figures for emphasis.)
Come to our *Twenty-fifth* Anniversary Sale! (Words for formality.)

In Ordinary Correspondence
Watkins & Glenn is having a *twenty-fifth* anniversary sale.

b. Ordinal figures are expressed as follows: *1st, 2d* or *2nd, 3d* or *3rd, 4th,* etc. Do not use an "abbreviation" period following an ordinal figure.

➤ *For the use of 2d in preference to 2nd, see ¶503.*

NOTE: Some word processing programs have a default feature that treats ordinal suffixes as superscripts. For example:

21st 32^d **OR** 32nd 43^d **OR** 43rd 54th

If you prefer the on-the-line style, you can undo the superscript feature.

¶426

426 Ordinals that follow a person's name may be expressed in arabic or roman numerals. As a rule, use arabic numerals unless you know that the person in question prefers roman numerals.

> James A. Wilson 3d **OR** James A. Wilson III
> C. Roy Post 4th **OR** C. Roy Post IV

➤ *For the use of commas with numerals after a person's name, see ¶156.*

Fractions

427 Fractions Standing Alone

a. Ordinarily, spell out a fraction that stands alone (without a whole number preceding); for example, *one-third.* Use figures, however, if the spelled-out form is long and awkward or if the fraction is used in a technical measurement or some type of computation.

> one-half the audience (see ¶427c)   three-fourths of the profits
> two-thirds of our employees   nine-tenths of a mile away
> multiply by 2/5   a quarter pound of butter
> 3/4-yard lengths (**BETTER THAN:** three-quarter-yard lengths)
> 5/32 inch (**BETTER THAN:** five thirty-seconds of an inch)
> He came back *a half hour* later (**OR** *half an hour* later).

NOTE: Hyphenate *half dozen* or *half a dozen* when this phrase is used as a compound modifier before a noun. (See also ¶817a.)

> I'll take a *half-dozen* eggs (**OR** *half-a-dozen* eggs).
> **BUT:** I'll take *a half dozen* (**OR** *half a dozen*).

b. When a fraction is spelled out, hyphenate the numerator and the denominator unless either element already contains a hyphen.

> five-eighths   thirteen thirty-seconds   twenty-seven sixty-fourths

NOTE: Some authorities hyphenate *simple fractions* (those that require only a single word for the numerator and the denominator) when they are used as adjectives but not as nouns.

> a *two-thirds* majority   **BUT:** *two thirds* of the voters

c. In constructions involving the balanced phrases *one half . . . the other half,* do not hyphenate *one half.*

> *One half* of the shipment was damaged beyond use; *the other half* was salvageable.

d. Distinguish between large spelled-out fractions (which are hyphenated) and large spelled-out ordinals (which are not).

> The difference is less than *one-hundredth* of 1 percent. (Hyphenated fraction meaning *1/100.*)
> **BUT:** This year the company will be celebrating the *one hundredth* anniversary of its founding. (Unhyphenated ordinal meaning *100th.*)

e. Fractions expressed in figures should not be followed by endings like *sts, ds, nds,* or *ths* or by an *of* phrase.

> 3/200 (**NOT:** 3/200ths)   9/64 inch (**NOT:** 9/64ths of an inch)

If a sentence requires the use of an *of* phrase following the fraction, spell the fraction out.

> three-quarters of an hour (**NOT:** 3/4 of an hour)

Numbers

4

f. Use a fractional expression to indicate that one thing is *smaller* than another.

> The old library was *one-third smaller* than the new one.
> (**NOT:** The old library was *three times smaller* than the new one.)
> **BUT:** The new library is *three times larger* than the old one.

428 Fractions in Mixed Numbers

a. Ordinarily use figures to express a mixed number (a whole number plus a fraction); for example, 3¼. Spell out a mixed number at the beginning of a sentence.

> Our sales are now 4½ times what they were in 1997.
>
> *Two and a quarter* (**OR** *Two and one-quarter*) inches of rain fell over the weekend. (Note the use of *and* between the whole number and the fraction.)

b. When constructing fractions that do not appear on the keyboard or in a special character set with word processing software, use the diagonal (/). Separate a whole number from a fraction by means of a space (not with a hyphen).

> Can you still get a fixed-rate mortgage for *7 3/8*? (**NOT:** 7-3/8.)

c. In the same sentence, do not mix ready-made fractions (½, ¼) with those that you construct yourself (7/8, 5/16).

> The rate on commercial paper has dropped from 5¾ percent a year ago to 5½ percent today. (**NOT:** 5 3/4 . . . 5½.)

NOTE: To simplify typing, convert constructed fractions (and simpler ones used in the same context) to a decimal form whenever feasible.

> The rate on commercial paper has dropped from *5.75* percent a year ago to *5.5* percent today.

d. When a mixed number is followed by a unit of measure, use the plural form of the unit of measure.

> 1½ inches   **OR**   1.5 inches   **BUT:** ¾ inch   1 inch

NOTE: If you are using an abbreviated form for a unit of measure, the abbreviation is usually the same for the singular and plural. (See ¶535a.)

The following rules (¶¶429–442) deal with measurements and with expressions of age and time (elements that often function as measurements). When these elements have technical or statistical significance, they are expressed in figures; otherwise, they are expressed in words.

Measurements

429 Most measurements have a technical significance and should be expressed in figures (even from 1 through 10) for emphasis or quick comprehension. However, spell out an isolated measurement that lacks technical significance.

> A higher rate is charged on parcels over *2 pounds*.
>
> **BUT:** I'm afraid I've gained another *two pounds* this week.
>
> Add *1 quart* of sugar for each *4 quarts* of strawberries.
>
> **BUT:** Last weekend we picked *four quarts* of strawberries from our own patch.
>
> There is no charge for delivery within a *30-mile* radius of Chicago.
>
> **BUT:** It's only a *thirty-mile* drive up to our summer place.

NOTE: Dimensions, sizes, and exact temperature readings are always expressed in figures.

Continued on page 122

Numbers

4

¶430

I'm looking for a *4- by 6-foot* rug for my reception room. (See also ¶432.)

Please send me a half-dozen blue oxford shirts, size *17½/33.*

The thermometer now stands at *32°F,* a drop of five degrees in the past hour.

BUT: The temperature has been in the low *thirties* (**OR** *30s*) all week. (An indefinite reference to the temperature may be spelled out or expressed in figures.)

430   When a measurement consists of several elements, do not use commas to separate the elements. The measurement is considered a single unit.

The package weighed *8 pounds 11 ounces.*

The punch bowl holds *4 quarts 1 pint.*

Hal is *6 feet 8 inches* tall in his stocking feet.

NOTE: If this type of measurement is used as a compound modifier before a noun, use hyphens to connect all the elements as a single unit. (See also ¶817.)

a *6-foot-8-inch* man

431   The unit of measurement may be abbreviated (for example, *12 ft*) or expressed as a symbol (for example, *12'*) in technical material or in tables. If either an abbreviation or a symbol is used, the number must be expressed as a figure.

➤ *For the style of abbreviations for units of measure, see ¶¶535–538; for the use of fig-ures with abbreviations and symbols, see ¶453.*

432   Dimensions may be expressed as follows:

GENERAL USAGE:	a room 15 by 30 feet	a 15- by 30-foot room
TECHNICAL USAGE:	{ a room 15 × 30 ft { a room 15' × 30'	a 15- × 30-ft room a 15' × 30' room
GENERAL USAGE:	a room 5 by 10 meters	a 5- by 10-meter room
TECHNICAL USAGE:	a room 5 × 10 m	a 5- × 10-m room
GENERAL USAGE:	15 feet 6 inches by 30 feet 9 inches	
TECHNICAL USAGE:	15 ft 6 in × 30 ft 9 in **OR** 15' 6" × 30' 9"	

➤ *For the use of suspending hyphens in dimensions, see ¶832a–b.*

NOTE: When using symbols to signify feet and inches, select either the *straight* style of quotation marks (' for feet and " for inches) or preferably the slanted style (´ and ˝), as shown in the examples above. (See ¶543.) If necessary, access an extended char-acter set to avoid the use of curly quotation marks (' and ") in expressions of feet and inches.

Ages and Anniversaries

433   Express ages in figures (including 1 through 10) when they are used as significant statistics or as technical measurements.

Ethel Kassarian, *38,* has been promoted to executive director of marketing services.

The attached printout projects the amount of the monthly retirement benefit payable *at the age of 65.* (See the entry for *Age–aged–at the age of* on page 283.)

A computer literacy program is being offered to all *8- and 9-year-olds.* (See ¶832.)

This insurance policy is specially tailored for people in the *50-plus* age group.

You cannot disregard the job application of a person *aged 58.* (**NOT:** age 58.)

Numbers

4

¶**439**

NOTE: When age is expressed in years, months, and days, do not use commas to separate the elements; they make up a single unit.

> On January 1 she will be *19 years 4 months and 17 days old.* (The *and* linking months and days may be omitted.)

434 Spell out ages in nontechnical references and in formal writing.

> My son is *three years old* and my daughter is *two.*
>
> Shirley is in her early *forties;* her husband is in his *mid-sixties.*
>
> Have you ever tried keeping a group of *five-year-olds* happy and under control at the same time?
>
> We've got a surprise party planned for Jack when he reaches the *Big Five-Oh.*

435 Spell out ordinals in references to birthdays and anniversaries except where special emphasis or more than two words are required. (See also ¶¶424–425.)

> on my thirtieth birthday   her forty-first class reunion
>
> our twenty-fifth anniversary   the company's 135th anniversary

Periods of Time

436 Use figures (even from 1 through 10) to express periods of time when they are used as technical measurements or significant statistics (as in discounts, interest rates, and credit terms).

> a 35-hour workweek   a 30-year mortgage   a note due in 6 months

NOTE: In legal documents, periods of time are often expressed twice: first in words and then in figures (enclosed in parentheses).

> payable in ninety (90) days   **NOT:** payable in ninety (90 days)

437 Spell out nontechnical references to periods of time unless the number requires more than two words.

> a twenty-minute wait   the next twelve days   forty-odd years ago
>
> eight hours later   a two-week cruise   three hundred years ago
>
> a half hour from now   in twenty-four months   **BUT:** 350 years ago
>
> **BUT:** 1½ hours from now (see ¶428a)   in the last thirty years   two thousand years ago

438 Centuries may be expressed as follows:

> the 1900s   **OR**   the nineteen hundreds   **OR**   the twentieth century
>
> the twenty-first century   twenty-first-century music

439 a. Decades may be expressed as follows:

> the 1990s   **OR**   the nineteen-nineties   **OR**   the nineties   **OR**   the '90s
>
> the mid-1960s   **OR**   the mid-sixties   **OR**   the mid-'60s
>
> in the 1980s and 1990s   **OR**   in the '80s and '90s
>
> (**BUT NOT:** in the 1980s and '90s   **OR**   in the 1980s and nineties)
>
> during the years 1993–2003   **OR**   from 1993 to 2003 (see ¶459)
>
> **OR**   between 1993 and 2003

b. There is still no consensus on how to refer to the first decade of the twenty-first century. One possibility is the *aughts* (the term used to refer to the first decade of the twentieth century). Among the other suggestions currently circulating are *the ohs, the zeros, the zips, the naughties,* and *the preteens.* Until one expression becomes established through usage as the dominant term, it may be safest to refer simply to *the first decade of the twenty-first century.*

Continued on page 124

Numbers

4

¶440

c. Decades are not capitalized except in expressions such as *the Gay Nineties* and *the Roaring Twenties.*

Clock Time

440 With *a.m., p.m., Noon,* and *Midnight*

a. Always use figures with *a.m.* or *p.m.*

> We take off at *8:45 a.m.*   The bus is due at *2 p.m.*

> By *8 p.m.,* CST, the first election returns should be in.

> **OR:** By *8 p.m.* (CST) the first election returns should be in.

➤ *For abbreviations of time zones such as* CST, *see ¶534.*

b. In books, journals, and similar publications, *a.m.* and *p.m.* usually appear in small capitals without internal space (A.M., P.M.). In other material, *a.m.* and *p.m.* typically appear in small letters without internal space; however, you can use small capitals if you have that option. Avoid the use of all-capital letters.

c. For time "on the hour," zeros are not needed to denote minutes unless you want to give special emphasis to the precise hour.

> Our store is open from *9:30 a.m.* to *6 p.m.* (**NOT:** 6:00 p.m.)

> **BUT:** Our store is always open until *6:00.* (See ¶442 for the use of zeros when *a.m.* or *p.m.* is omitted.)

> You may call me between *7:30 a.m.* and *4 p.m.,* Monday through Friday. You can reach me on the weekends between *2* and *5 p.m.*

> We always close from *12 noon* to *1:30 p.m.*

> From a church bulletin: The Low Self-Esteem Support Group will meet on Thursday between *9:30* and *11 a.m.* Please use the back door.

	Arr.	Dep.
	8:45	9:10
	9:00	9:25
	9:50	10:00

In tables, however, when some entries are given in hours and minutes, add a colon and two zeros to exact hours to maintain a uniform appearance. (For more complex illustrations showing the alignment of clock times in columns, see ¶1627b.)

d. Do not use *a.m.* or *p.m.* unless figures are used.

> this morning   tomorrow afternoon
> (**NOT:** this a.m.)   (**NOT:** tomorrow p.m.)

e. Do not use *a.m.* or *p.m.* with *o'clock.*

> 6 o'clock   **OR**   6 p.m.   ten o'clock   **OR**   10 a.m.
> (**NOT:** 6 p.m. o'clock)   (**NOT:** 10 a.m. o'clock)

NOTE: The expression *o'clock* is more formal than *a.m.* or *p.m.*

f. Do not use *a.m.* or *p.m.* with the expressions *in the morning, in the afternoon, in the evening,* and *at night.* The abbreviations themselves already convey one of these meanings.

> at 9 p.m.   **OR**   at nine in the evening (**NOT:** at 9 p.m. in the evening)

g. Use a colon (without space before or after) to separate hours from minutes (as in *3:22*).

h. The times *noon* and *midnight* may be expressed in words alone. However, use the forms *12 noon* and *12 midnight* when these times are given with other times expressed in figures.

> Dinner is served in the main dining room until *midnight.*
> **BUT:** Dinner is served from *6 p.m.* until *12 midnight.*

441 With *O'Clock*

a. With *o'clock*, use figures for emphasis or words for formality.

> 3 o'clock (for emphasis)   three o'clock (for formality)

b. To express hours and minutes with *o'clock*, use this style:

> half past four o'clock   **OR**   half after four o'clock
> (**BUT NOT:** four-thirty o'clock)

c. Expressions of time containing *o'clock* may be reinforced by such phrases as *in the morning* and *in the afternoon*.

> 10 o'clock at night   seven o'clock in the morning

For quick comprehension, use the forms *10 p.m.* and *7 a.m.*

442 Without *a.m., p.m.,* or *O'Clock*

When expressing time without *a.m., p.m.,* or *o'clock*, either spell the time out or—for quick comprehension—convert the expression to an all-figure style.

> arrive at eight   **OR**   arrive at 8:00 (**NOT:** at 8)
> five after six   **OR**   6:05
> a quarter past ten   **OR**   10:15
> twenty of four   **OR**   3:40
> a quarter to five   **OR**   a quarter of five   **OR**   4:45
> half past nine   **OR**   nine-thirty   **OR**   9:30
> nine forty-two   **OR**   9:42

NOTE: A hyphen is used between hours and minutes *(seven-thirty)* but not if the minutes must be hyphenated *(seven thirty-five)*.

The following rules (¶¶443–455) deal with situations in which numbers are always expressed in figures.

Decimals

443 Always write decimals in figures. Never insert commas in the decimal part of a number.

> 665.3184368 (no comma in decimal part of the number)
> 58,919.23785 (comma used in whole part of the number)

➤ *For the metric style of writing decimals, see ¶461b.*

444 When a decimal stands alone (without a whole number preceding the decimal point), insert a zero before the decimal point. (Reason: The zero keeps the reader from overlooking the decimal point.)

> 0.55 inch   0.08 gram   **EXCEPTIONS:** a Colt .45; a .36 caliber revolver

¶**445**

445   Ordinarily, drop the zero at the end of a decimal (for example, write *2.787* rather than *2.7870*). However, retain the zero (a) if you wish to emphasize that the decimal is an exact number or (b) if the decimal has been rounded off from a longer figure. In a column of figures add zeros to the end of a decimal in order to make the number as long as other numbers in the column. (For illustrations, see ¶¶1627, 1629, 1630, 1632.)

446   Do not begin a sentence with a decimal figure.

> The temperature was 63.7.   (**NOT**: 63.7 was the temperature.)

Percentages

447   Express percentages in figures, and spell out the word *percent.* (See ¶¶421–422 for percentages at the beginning of a sentence.)

> When your mortgage rate goes from *8 percent* to *8.8 percent,* it may have increased by less than 1 percentage point, but you'll pay *10 percent* more in interest.
>
> Yogi Berra once said, "Baseball is *90 percent* mental. The other half is physical."
>
> My client expected a *25 percent* discount. (**NOT**: a 25-percent discount.)
>
> Our terms are *2 percent* 10 days, net 30 days. (Abbreviate these credit terms as *2/10, n/30* on invoices and other business forms.)

NOTE: The % symbol may be used in tables, on business forms, and in statistical or technical material.

448   **a.** Fractional percentages *under 1 percent* may be expressed as follows:

> one half of 1 percent   **OR**   0.5 percent (see ¶444)

   b. Fractional percentages *over 1 percent* should be expressed in figures.

> 7½ percent   **OR**   7.5 percent   9¼ percent   **OR**   9.25 percent

449   In a range or series of percentages, the word *percent* follows the last figure only. If the symbol % is used (see ¶447, note), it must follow each figure.

> We give discounts of *10, 20, and 30 percent.* (**BUT**: 10%, 20%, and 30%.)

➤ *For the use of % in a column of figures, see ¶1630; for the use of* percent *and* percentage, *see page 302.*

Ratios and Proportions

450   As a rule, write ratios and proportions in figures.

> a proportion of 5 to 1   **OR**   a 5-to-1 ratio   **OR**   a 5:1 ratio
> the odds are 100 to 1   **OR**   a 100-to-1 shot

NOTE: A nontechnical reference may be spelled out.

> a *fifty-fifty* chance of success   **OR**   a *50-50* chance of success

Scores and Voting Results

451   Use figures (even for 1 through 10) to express scores and voting results.

> a score of 85 on the test   a vote of 17 to 6
> New York 8, Chicago 6   **BUT**: a 17-6 vote

Numbers Referred to as Numbers

452   Always use figures to express numbers referred to as numbers.

> pick a number from 1 to 10   divide by 16   multiply by ⅞

Figures With Abbreviations and Symbols

453   **a.** Always use figures with abbreviations and symbols.

$50	10:15 a.m.	43%	2 in **OR** 2″	FY2002 (see ¶1621c)
65¢	6 p.m.	No. 631	I-95	200 km (see ¶537)

    b. If a symbol is used in a range of numbers, it should be repeated with each number. A full word or an abbreviation used in place of the symbol is given only with the last number.

20°–30°C	**BUT:**	20 to 30 degrees Celsius (see ¶537, note)
5½″ × 8″		5½ by 8 inches **OR** 5½ × 8 in
9′ × 12′		9 by 12 feet **OR** 9 × 12 ft
30%–40%		30 to 40 percent
50¢–60¢		50 to 60 cents
$70–$80		seventy to eighty dollars

      NOTE: A symbol should be used with each number in a series.

        discounts of 5%, 10%, and 15%   **BUT:** discounts of 5, 10, and 15 percent

Telephone Numbers

454   **a.** Insert a hyphen after the first three digits of a telephone number; for example, 555-1789. If a company chooses to express its phone number partially or entirely in words, follow the company's style; for example, 345-GIFT, 4-ANGIES, JOB-HUNT, CASH-NOW, GOFEDEX, PICK-UPS.

    b. When providing a telephone extension along with the main number, use the following form: 555-4890, Ext. 6041. (In formal correspondence, spell out *Extension.*)

    c. When the area code precedes a phone number, there are several ways to treat the number. The style most commonly seen, especially in text material, uses a hyphen (with no space on either side) to connect the elements: 707-555-3998.

      The style that encloses the area code in parentheses—(707) 555-3998—is also frequently used, but it does not work well in text material when the phone number as a whole has to be enclosed in parentheses.

        You can reach me by phone (707-555-3998) during normal business hours.

        BUT NOT: . . . by phone ((707) 555-3998) during normal business hours.

      When telephone numbers are displayed (for example, in letterheads and on business cards), other styles are often seen. Some writers prefer to use a diagonal after the area code: 707/555-3998. Others simply leave spaces between the elements: 707 555 3998. And a relatively new style—707.555.3998—uses periods to separate the elements; because these periods resemble the dots in e-mail addresses, this style may well grow in popularity.

    ➤ *For the types of phone numbers used in business letterheads, see ¶¶1311–1312.*

    d. When an access code precedes the area code and the phone number, use a hyphen to connect all the elements.

        Please use our toll-free, 24-hour phone number: 1-800-555-6400.

        Now that there are no more 800 or 888 phone numbers available, our new toll-free, 24-hour phone number will be 1-877-555-8758.

Continued on page 128

Numbers

4

¶455

e. International phone numbers typically contain a series of special access codes. Use hyphens to connect all the elements.

011-64-9-555-1523
└ international access code from the United States
  └ country access code
    └ city access code

NOTE: The international access code 011 is valid only for international calls placed within the United States.

f. When you are providing a U.S. phone number in a printed or electronic document that may elicit calls from other countries, use a plus sign to represent the international access code and the numeral 1 to represent the country access code for the United States. For example:

+ 1-415-555-2998
└ a symbol representing another country's international access code
  └ the country access code for the United States
    └ a U.S. area code

Since each country has its own international access code—for example, 191 is the code for outgoing calls from France—use a plus sign rather than a specific international access code unless you are sure all international calls to your number will come from only one country.

NOTE: Telephone calls between the United States and Canada, Puerto Rico, and most places in the Caribbean/Atlantic calling region do not require the use of international access codes.

No. or # With Figures

455   a. If the term *number* precedes a figure, express it as an abbreviation (singular: *No.;* plural: *Nos.*). At the beginning of a sentence, however, spell out *Number* to prevent misreading.

Our check covers the following invoices: *Nos.* 8592, 8653, and 8654.
Number 82175 has been assigned to your new policy. (**NOT:** *No.* 82175 . . .)
Our manager says the Southern Region has to be No. 1 in sales—or else!

b. If an identifying noun precedes the figure (such as *Invoice, Check, Room,* or *Box*), the abbreviation *No.* is usually unnecessary.

Our check covers *Invoices* 8592, 8653, and 8654. (See ¶463 for other exceptions.)

c. The symbol # may be used on business forms and in technical material.

➤ *For the capitalization of nouns preceding figures, see ¶359.*

The following rules (¶¶456–470) deal with two technical aspects of style: (1) treating numbers that are adjacent or in a sequence and (2) expressing numbers in figures, words, or roman numerals.

Adjacent Numbers

456 When two numbers come together in a sentence and both are in figures or both are in words, separate them with a comma.

In *1995, 78* percent of our field representatives exceeded their sales goal.
Although the meeting was scheduled for *two, ten* people did not show up.
On page *192, 25* problems are provided for review purposes.
On Account *53512, $125.40* is the balance outstanding.
On May *8, 18* customers called to complain.

NOTE: No comma is needed when one number is in figures and the other is in words.

On May *9 seven* customers called to complain.

457 When two numbers come together and one is part of a compound modifier (see ¶817), express one of the numbers in figures and the other in words. As a rule, spell the first number unless the second number would make a significantly shorter word.

two 8-room houses   **BUT:**   500 four-page leatlets
sixty $5 bills   150 five-dollar bills

Numbers in a Sequence

458 Use commas to separate numbers that do not represent a continuous sequence.

on pages 18, 20, and 28   the years 1996, 2000, and 2004

459   **a.** Use an en dash (or a single hyphen if you do not have access to an en dash) to link two figures that represent a continuous sequence. The en dash means "up to and including" in the following expressions:

on pages 18–28   in Articles I–III
during the week of May 15–21   during the years 1999–2003

NOTE: Do not insert space before or after the en dash or the hyphen. (See also ¶299.)

➢ *For a full discussion of the use of the en dash and additional examples, see ¶217.*

b. Do not use the en dash (or hyphen) if the sequence is introduced by the word *from* or *between.*

from 1998 to 2001   between 2001 and 2002
(**NOT:** from 1998–2001)   (**NOT:** between 2001–2002)

460   **a.** In a continuous sequence of figures connected by an en dash or a hyphen, the second figure may be expressed in abbreviated form. This style is used for sequences of page numbers or years when they occur quite frequently. In isolated cases, do not abbreviate. (See ¶217.)

1997–98 (**OR** 1997–1998)   pages 110–12 (**OR** pages 110–112)
2001–2 (**OR** 2001–2002)   pages 101–2 (**OR** pages 101–102)

b. Do not abbreviate the second number when the first number ends in two zeros.

2000–2005 (**NOT:** 2000–05)   pages 100–101 (**NOT:** pages 100–1)

c. Do not abbreviate the second number when it starts with different digits.

1995–2003 (**NOT:** 1995–03)   pages 998–1004 (**NOT:** pages 998–04)

d. Do not abbreviate the second number when it is under 100.

46–48 A.D.   pages 46–48

➢ *For a usage note on A.D., see page 282.*

Numbers

4

¶461

Expressing Numbers in Figures

461 **a.** When numbers run to five or more figures, use commas to separate thousands, hundreds of thousands, millions, etc., in *whole* numbers. Do not use commas in the decimal part of a number. (See also ¶443.)

> 12,375   147,300 $11,275,478   4,300,000,000   **BUT:** 70,650.37248

NOTE: The comma is now commonly omitted in four-digit whole numbers except in columns with larger numbers that require commas.

> 3500   **OR**   3,500 $2000.50   **OR** $2,000.50

b. In metric quantities, use a space to separate digits into groups of three. Separate whole numbers and decimal fractions, counting from the decimal point.

> 12 945 181 (**RATHER THAN:** 12,945,181)   0.594 31 (**RATHER THAN:** 0.59431)

NOTE: When a four-digit number is used as a metric quantity, do not leave a space unless the number is used in a column that has larger numbers.

> 5181   **OR**   5 181   0.3725   **OR**   0.372 5

462 Do not use commas in year numbers, page numbers, house or building numbers, room numbers, ZIP Code numbers, telephone numbers, heat units, and decimal parts of numbers.

> 2003   8760 Sunset Drive   New York, NY 10021   1500°C
> page 1246   Room 1804   602-555-2174 (see ¶454)   13,664.9999

463 Serial numbers (for example, invoice, style, model, or lot numbers) are usually written without commas. However, some serial numbers are written with hyphens, spaces, or other devices. In all cases follow the style of the source.

> Invoice 38162   **BUT:** Social Security No. 152-22-8285   Patent No. 222,341

➢ *For the capitalization of nouns before numbers, see ¶359; for the use of* No., *see ¶455.*

464 To form the plurals of figures, add *s*. (See ¶624.)

> in the '90s (decades)   in the 90s (temperature)

Expressing Numbers in Words

465 **a.** When expressing numbers in words, hyphenate all compound numbers between *21* and *99* (or *21st* and *99th*), whether they stand alone or are part of a number over 100.

> twenty-one   twenty-one hundred
> twenty-first   twenty-one hundredth
>
> seven hundred and twenty-five (*and* may be omitted)
> five thousand seven hundred and twenty-five (no commas)

b. Do not hyphenate other words in a spelled-out number over 99.

> one hundred   nineteen hundred   six hundred million
> two thousand   three hundred thousand   fifty-eight trillion

c. When a spelled-out number appears in a place name, follow the style shown in an authoritative postal directory or atlas.

> Twentynine Palms, California   Ninety Six, South Carolina
> Eighty Four, Pennsylvania   Thousand Oaks, California

➢ *For the capitalization of hyphenated numbers, see ¶363.*

466 When there are two ways to express a number in words, choose the simpler form. For example, use the form *fifteen hundred* rather than *one thousand five hundred*. (The longer form is rarely used except in formal expressions of dates. See ¶411.)

467 To form the plurals of spelled-out numbers, add *s* or *es*. (For numbers ending in *y*, change the *y* to *i* before *es*.)

ones	twos	threes	sixes	twenty-fives
thirds	sixths	eighths	twenties	thirty-seconds

➤ *For spelled-out dates, see ¶411; for spelled-out amounts of money, see ¶¶413c, 414, 417, 418, 420; for spelled-out fractions, see ¶¶427–428.*

Expressing Numbers in Roman Numerals

468 Roman numerals are used chiefly for the important divisions of literary and legislative material, for main topics in outlines, for dates, and in proper names.

Chapter VI	Pentium III	MCMXCIX (1999)
Volume III	World War I	MMIV (2004)

NOTE: Pages in the front section of a book or a formal report (such as the preface and table of contents) are usually numbered in small roman numerals: *iii, iv, v,* etc. Other pages are numbered in arabic numerals: *1, 2, 3,* etc. (See ¶¶1420, 1427.)

469 To form roman numerals, consult the following table.

1	I	13	XIII	60	LX	1,100	MC
2	II	14	XIV	70	LXX	1,400	MCD
3	III	15	XV	80	LXXX	1,500	MD
4	IV	19	XIX	90	XC	1,600	MDC
5	V	20	XX	100	C	1,900	MCM
6	VI	21	XXI	200	CC	2,000	MM
7	VII	24	XXIV	400	CD	5,000	$\overline{V}$
8	VIII	25	XXV	500	D	10,000	$\overline{X}$
9	IX	29	XXIX	600	DC	50,000	$\overline{L}$
10	X	30	XXX	800	DCCC	100,000	$\overline{C}$
11	XI	40	XL	900	CM	500,000	$\overline{D}$
12	XII	50	L	1,000	M	1,000,000	$\overline{M}$

NOTE: A bar appearing over any roman numeral indicates that the original value of the numeral is to be multiplied by 1000.

Expressing Large Numbers in Abbreviated Form

470 In technical and informal contexts and in material where space is tight (such as tables and classified ads), large numbers may be abbreviated.

ROMAN STYLE:	48M (48,000); 6.3$\overline{M}$ (6,300,000)
METRIC STYLE:	31K (31,000); K stands for *kilo,* signifying thousands
	5.2M (5,200,000); M stands for *mega,* signifying millions
	8.76G (8,760,000,000); G stands for *giga,* signifying billions
	9.4T (9,400,000,000,000); T stands for *tera,* signifying trillions

➤ *Division of large numbers at the end of a line: see ¶915.*
House, street, and ZIP Code numbers: see ¶¶1332–1333, 1339, 1341c.

SECTION **5**

Abbreviations

➤ *For definitions of grammatical terms, see the appropriate entries in the Glossary of Grammatical Terms (Appendix A).*

¶**503**

Basic Rules

When to Use Abbreviations

501 **a.** An abbreviation is a shortened form of a word or phrase used primarily to save space. Abbreviations occur most frequently in technical writing, statistical material, tables, and notes.

b. Abbreviations that are pronounced letter by letter—for example, *IBM, Ph.D., p.m.*—may be referred to as *initialisms.* Abbreviations that are pronounced as words—for example, *ZIP* (Code), *AIDS, laser*—are called *acronyms* (see ¶522). Occasionally, an abbreviation may have two acceptable pronunciations—for example, *URL* (which stands for *uniform resource locator* and refers to a specific Web address for an individual or an organization). When URL is pronounced *yoo-arr-ell,* it is an initialism; when pronounced *erl,* it is an acronym.

NOTE: The use of *a* or *an* before an abbreviation will depend on whether the abbreviation is an initialism or an acronym. See the entry for *a–an* on pages 281–282.

c. When using an abbreviation, do not follow it with a word that is part of the abbreviation. Consider the following example, which uses the abbreviation for *compact disc (CD).*

Mary Jo has an enormous collection of *CDs* (**NOT:** CD discs).

➢ *See also ¶522f.*

502 **a.** In business writing, abbreviations are appropriate in expedient documents (such as business forms, catalogs, and routine memos and letters between business offices), where the emphasis is on communicating data in the briefest form. In other kinds of writing, where a more formal style is appropriate, use abbreviations sparingly. When in doubt, spell it out.

b. Some abbreviations are always acceptable, even in the most formal contexts: those that precede or follow personal names (such as *Mr., Ms., Mrs., Jr., Sr., Esq., Ph.D., S.J.*); those that are part of an organization's legal name (such as *Co., Inc., Ltd.*); those used in expressions of time (such as *a.m., p.m., CST, EDT*); and a few miscellaneous expressions (such as *A.D.* and *B.C.*).

c. Organizations with long names are now commonly identified by their initials in all but the most formal writing (for example, *NAACP, SEC*).

d. Days of the week, names of the months, geographic names, and units of measure should be abbreviated only on business forms, in expedient documents, and in tables, lists, and narrow columns of text (for example, in a newsletter or brochure where space is tight).

e. When an abbreviation is only one or two keystrokes shorter than the full word (for example, *Pt.* for *Part*), do not bother to abbreviate except to achieve consistency in a context where similar terms are being abbreviated. (See also ¶532 for abbreviations of months.)

503 Consult a dictionary or an authoritative reference work for the acceptable forms of abbreviations. When a term may be abbreviated in several ways, choose the form that is shortest without sacrifice of clarity.

Continued on page 134

¶504

continued:	Use *cont.* rather than *contd.*
2 pounds:	Use *2 lb* rather than *2 lbs* (see ¶620).
Enclosures 2:	Use *Enc. 2* rather than *Encs. 2* or *Encl. 2.*
second, third:	Use *2d, 3d* rather than *2nd, 3rd* (see also ¶425, note).
megabyte, kilobyte:	Use *MB, KB* for clarity rather than *M, K.*

NOTE: *Merriam-Webster's Collegiate Dictionary,* Tenth Edition, the basic authority for all spelling in this manual, shows virtually every abbreviation without any periods, even though in actual practice many abbreviations are still written with periods.* Thus, for example, unless your Latin is very good, you may not realize that in the expression *et al.,* the word *et* is a full word (meaning "and") and requires no period, whereas *al.* is short for *alii* (meaning "others") and does require a period. Under these circumstances, for specific abbreviations not shown in this manual, you will need to consult another up-to-date dictionary.

The forms shown here reflect the spellings found in Merriam-Webster, but the punctuation is based on observations of actual practice and is consistent with the style recommended by other authorities.

504 Be consistent within the same material: do not abbreviate a term in some sentences and spell it out in other sentences. Moreover, having selected one form of an abbreviation (say, *c.o.d.*), do not use a different style *(COD)* elsewhere in the same material. (See ¶542.)

NOTE: When using an abbreviation that may not be familiar to the reader, spell out the full term along with the abbreviation when it is first used.

> At the end of *fiscal year (FY) 2000,* we showed a profit of $1.2 million; at the end of *FY2001,* however, we showed a loss of $1.8 million.
>
> **OR:** At the end of *FY2000 (fiscal year 2000)* . . .

505 **a.** Given a choice between an abbreviation and a contraction, choose the abbreviation. It not only looks better but is easier to read.

cont. (**RATHER THAN:** cont'd)	govt. (**RATHER THAN:** gov't)
dept. (**RATHER THAN:** dep't)	mfg. (**RATHER THAN:** m'f'g)

b. When a word or phrase is shortened by contraction, an apostrophe is inserted at the exact point where letters are omitted and no period follows the contraction except at the end of a sentence.

you're	doesn't	could've	rock 'n' roll
let's	don't	o'clock	s'mores

EXCEPTIONS: c'mon (come on)   wannabes (want-to-bes)
li'l (little)   zine (magazine)

NOTE: Respect a company's preference when it uses a contraction in its corporate name or in the name of a product.

Wash'n Dri	Puss'N Boots	Dunkin' Donuts	Bran'nola
Sweet'n Low	Linens N' Things	Cap'n Crunch	Chock full o' Nuts
Shake 'n Bake	Light n' Lively	Ship 'n' Shore	Land O Lakes

---

*It is interesting to note that Merriam-Webster itself uses periods with certain abbreviations (for example, *masc., fem., trans., fr., prob., lit.,* and *ca.*) when they occur functionally within the main text of the dictionary, even though these same abbreviations are given *without* periods in the section on abbreviations at the back of the dictionary.

¶**508**

c. As a rule, contractions are used only in informal writing or in tables where space is limited. However, contractions of verb phrases (such as *can't* for *cannot*) are commonly used in business letters where the writer is striving for an easy, colloquial tone. In formal writing, contractions are not used (except for *o'clock*, which is considered a more formal way to express time than *a.m.* or *p.m.*).

d. Be sure to distinguish certain contractions from possessive pronouns that sound the same but do not use an apostrophe.

> Ron has been pushing the Kirschner proposal for all *it's* worth. (In other words, for all *it is* worth.)
>
> Let's get an outside consultant to analyze the Kirschner proposal and assess *its* worth. (Here *its* is a possessive pronoun; no apostrophe should be used.)

➤ *For further examples and a test on whether to use a contraction or a possessive pronoun, see ¶1056e.*

e. Note that certain contractions can have more than one meaning.

> What's her name? (What *is* her name?)
>
> What's he do for a living? (What *does* he do for a living?)
>
> What's been happening? (What *has* been happening?)
>
> When's the last time you saw her? (When *was* the last time you saw her?)
>
> Let's find out. (Let *us* find out.)

Punctuation and Spacing With Abbreviations

506 **a.** The abbreviation of a single word requires a period at the end.

Mrs.	Jr.	Corp.	pp.	Wed.
misc.	Esq.	Inc.	Nos.	Oct.

NOTE: When the abbreviations appear in the names of organizations and products, the period is occasionally omitted. Always follow the style of the organization.

> Dr. Denton's clothing   **BUT:** Dr Pepper soft drinks

b. Units of measurement are now commonly written without periods. (See ¶¶535a, 538a.)

507 Almost all small-letter abbreviations made up of single initials require a period after each initial but no space after each internal period.

a.m.	i.e.	f.o.b.	**BUT:** rpm	mpg
p.m.	e.g.	e.o.m.	cpi	mph

➤ *For the omission of periods with abbreviations of units of measure, see ¶535a; for the definition of business abbreviations like* f.o.b. *and* e.o.m., *see ¶541.*

508 All-capital abbreviations made up of single initials normally require no periods and no internal space.

AMA	IRS	CEO	PIN	WWW
UAW	UN	VIP	ATM	RAM
PBS	AICPA	PSAT	IRA	OCR
MIT	NFL	VCR	UFO	FTP

EXCEPTIONS: Retain the periods in abbreviations of geographic names (such as *U.S.A.*), academic degrees (such as *B.A., M.S.*), and a few expressions (such as *A.D.,*

Continued on page 136

¶509

B.C., and *P.O.*). Also retain the periods when they are used in the names of organizations and products (for example, *B.V.D. underwear, S.O.S. scouring pads*).

509 If an abbreviation of two or more words consists of more than single initials, insert a period and a space after each element in the abbreviation.

> N. Mex.   Lt. Col.   Rt. Rev.   loc. cit.   nol. pros.

EXCEPTIONS: Academic abbreviations, such as *Ph.D.* (doctor of philosophy), *LL.B.* (bachelor of law), and *Litt.D.* (doctor of letters), are written with periods but no spaces. Units of measurement such as *sq ft* and *cu cm* are written with spaces but no periods.

510 A number of shortened forms of words are not abbreviations and should not be followed by a period. (See ¶236c and ¶524, note.)

abs	deli	info	prefab	specs
app	demo	lab	prep	stereo
caps	exam	limo	promo	sync
cell phone	expo	logo	repro	temp
combo	fax	memo	req	typo
comp	glutes	micros	sales rep	zine
condo	high-tech	perks	sci-fi	before the 2d
co-op	hype	photo	sitcom	after the 5th

> A number of the *sales reps* have sent a *fax,* asking for some *info* on this year's incentive *comp* plans.
>
> When you check the *repros* for *typos,* please watch out for the problems we had with *caps* in our last *promo* piece, and make sure our *logo* is not left off this time.
>
> Also check everything against the original *specs,* and tell me what the total *prep* costs are.

511 *One space* should follow an abbreviation within a sentence unless another mark of punctuation follows immediately.

> You ought to talk to your CPA about that problem.
>
> Dr. Wilkins works in Washington, D.C., but his home is in Bethesda.
>
> Please call tomorrow (before 5:30 p.m.).
>
> When Jonas asked, "When do you expect to finish your Ph.D.?" Fred looked embarrassed. (See ¶261c regarding the omission of a comma after an introductory dependent clause.)
>
> I'm waiting for some word on Harrison, Inc.'s stock repurchase plan. (See ¶¶638–639 for possessive forms of abbreviations.)

512 *One or two spaces* should follow an abbreviation at the end of a sentence that makes a statement. (See ¶102.) If the abbreviation ends with a period, that period also serves to mark the end of the sentence. If the abbreviation ends without a period, insert one to mark the end of the sentence.

> Helen has just returned from a trip to Washington, D.C. Next year . . .

NOTE: Ordinarily, placing an abbreviation at the end of a sentence that makes a statement poses no problem. However, when the correct form of an abbreviation is the issue under discussion, place the abbreviation elsewhere in the statement. In that way the reader will not have to guess whether the period that marks the end of the statement also marks the end of the abbreviation.

¶516

The correct postal abbreviation for *Alaska* is *AK.* (Here the period applies only to the end of the sentence.)

CLEARER: AK is the correct postal abbreviation for *Alaska.*

The correct abbreviation for *numbers* is *Nos.* (Here the period applies to the end of the statement *and* the abbreviation.)

CLEARER: *Nos.* is the correct abbreviation for *numbers.*

If rewording the sentence is not feasible, then as a last resort use this solution:

The correct postal abbreviation for *Alaska* is *AK* (no period).

513 *No space* should follow an abbreviation at the end of a question or an exclamation. Insert a question mark or exclamation point directly after the abbreviation.

Did you see Jack Hainey being interviewed last night on CBS?

Because of bad weather our flight didn't get in until 4 a.m.!

Capitalization

514 Most abbreviations use the same capitalization as the full words for which they stand.

Mon.	Monday	e-mail	electronic mail
Btu	British thermal unit	D.C.	District of Columbia

> **EXCEPTIONS:** CST   Central standard time
> A.D.   anno Domini (see page 282)

➤ *For abbreviations with two forms (for example,* COD *or* c.o.d.*), see ¶542.*

The following rules (¶¶515–549) offer guidance on how to treat specific types of abbreviations.

Special Rules

Personal Names and Initials

515 Use periods with abbreviations of first or middle names but not with nicknames.

Thos.	Jos.	Robt.	Benj.	Jas.	Wm.	Saml.	Edw.
Tom	Joe	Bob	Ben	Jim	Bill	Sam	Ed

NOTE: Do not abbreviate first and middle names unless (a) you are preparing a list or table where space is tight or (b) a person uses such abbreviations in his or her legal name. (See also ¶1321a.)

516   **a.** Each initial in a person's name should be followed by a period and one space.

W. E. B. Du Bois	Mr. L. Bradford Anders
J. T. Noonan & Co.	L. B. Anders Inc. (see also ¶159)

NOTE: Respect the preference of individuals and of companies that use a person's initials in their company name.

Harry S Truman	BFGoodrich	FAO Schwarz
L.L. Bean	JCPenney	S.C. Johnson

b. When personal initials stand alone, type them preferably without periods or space. If periods are used, omit the internal space.

JTN   **OR**   J.T.N.

Continued on page 138

Abbreviations

5

c. For names with prefixes, initials are formed as follows:

> JDM (for John D. MacDonald)   FGO (for Frances G. O'Brien)

> **NOTE:** If you know that an individual prefers some other form (for example, *FGO'B* rather than *FGO*), respect that preference.

d. Do not use a period when the initial is only a letter used in place of a real name. (See also ¶109a.)

> I have selected three case studies involving a Ms. A, a Mr. B, and a Miss C. (Here the letters are used in place of real names, but they are not abbreviations of those names.)

> **BUT:** Call Mrs. *G.* when you get a chance. (Here *G.* is an initial representing an actual name like *Galanos.*)

e. The abbreviation *NMI* is sometimes used on forms and applications to indicate that an individual has n̲o m̲iddle i̲nitial.

Abbreviations With Personal Names

517 **a.** Always abbreviate the following titles when they are used with personal names:

> **SINGULAR:** { Mrs. (for Mistress)   Ms.   Mr.   Dr.
>   { Mme. (for Madame)

> **PLURAL:**   Mmes. **OR** Mesdames   Mses. **OR** Mss.   Messrs.   Drs.

> *Mr.* and *Mrs.* Pollo both speak highly of *Dr.* Fry.
> *Ms.* Harriet Porter will serve as a consultant to the Finance Committee.

> **NOTE:** The abbreviation *Ms.* is used (1) when a woman has indicated that she prefers this title, (2) when a woman's marital status is unknown, or (3) when a woman's marital status is considered not relevant to the situation. Always respect the individual woman's preference. If her preference is unknown, use the title *Ms.* or omit the title altogether. (See also ¶¶618, 1322b, 1366.)

> ➤ *For the proper use of the singular and plural forms of these titles, see ¶618; for the use of* Dr. *with degrees, see ¶519c.*

b. The titles *Miss* and *Misses* are not abbreviations and should not be followed by periods.

c. In general, spell out all other titles used with personal names.

> Vice President Howard Morse   Professor Harriman
> Mayor Wilma Washington   Father Hennelly
> Governor Warren R. Fishback   Dean Castaneda
> Senator Hazel Benner   Lieutenant Cowan

d. Long military, religious, and honorable titles are spelled out in formal situations but may be abbreviated in informal situations as long as the surname is accompanied by a first name or initials.

Formal	**Informal**
Brigadier General Percy J. Cobb	Brig. Gen. P. J. Cobb
Brigadier General Cobb (**NOT:** Brig. Gen. Cobb)	
Lieutenant Governor Nancy Pulaski	Lt. Gov. Nancy Pulaski
Lieutenant Governor Pulaski (**NOT:** Lt. Gov. Pulaski)	

NOTE: Do not abbreviate *Reverend* or *Honorable* when these words are preceded by *the*.

Formal	**Informal**
the Reverend William R. Bullock	Rev. W. R. Bullock
the Honorable Sarah T. McCormack	Hon. Sarah T. McCormack

➤ *For the treatment of titles in addresses, see ¶¶1322–1323; for the treatment of titles in salutations, see ¶¶1347–1350.*

518 **a.** Always abbreviate *Jr.*, *Sr.*, and *Esq.* when these terms follow personal names.

b. The forms *Jr.* and *Sr.* should be used only with a full name or initials. A title like *Mr.* or *Dr.* may precede the name.

Mr. Henry J. Boardman Jr. **OR** Mr. H. J. Boardman Jr.

Mr. and Mrs. Henry J. Boardman Jr. **OR** Henry J. Boardman Jr. and Sybil P. Boardman

(**BUT NOT:** Henry J. and Sybil P. Boardman Jr. **OR** Henry J. Jr. and Sybil P. Boardman)

NOTE: Ordinarily, do not use *Jr.* or *Sr.* with a surname alone. However, in an office where both father and son work, it may be necessary in internal communications to refer to *Mr. Boardman Sr.* and *Mr. Boardman Jr.* as the only practical way to tell them apart.

➤ *For the use or omission of commas with* Jr. *and* Sr., *see ¶156.*

c. The form *Esq.* should also be used only with a full name or initials, but no title should precede the name. (See ¶157.)

George W. LaBarr, *Esq.* (**NOT:** Mr. George W. LaBarr, *Esq.*)

NOTE: In the United States the form *Esq.* is used primarily by lawyers. Although by derivation the title applies strictly to males, it is now common practice for women who are lawyers to use the title as a professional designation.

d. The terms *2d* or *II* and *3d* or *III* following personal names are not abbreviations and should not be used with periods.

e. When the word *Saint* is part of a person's name, follow that person's preference for abbreviating or spelling out the word.

Yves Saint-Laurent   Camille Saint-Saëns   Ruth St. Denis   St. John Perse

NOTE: When used with the name of a person revered as holy, the word *Saint* is usually spelled out, but it may be abbreviated in informal contexts and in lists and tables where space is tight.

Saint Jude   Saint Peter Claver   Saint Thérèse   Saint Catherine

➤ *For the treatment of* Saint *in place names, see ¶529b.*

Academic Degrees, Religious Orders, and Professional Designations

519 **a.** Abbreviations of academic degrees and religious orders require a period after each element in the abbreviation but no internal space.

B.S.	LL.B.	B.Ch.E.	M.D.	S.J.
M.B.A.	Litt.D.	B.Arch.	D.D.S.	O.S.B.
Ph.D.	Ed.D.	M.Div.	R.N.	S.N.D.

Continued on page 140

¶520

NOTE: The term *ABD* (without periods) is often used to identify a graduate student who has completed all the requirements for a doctorate except the dissertation. (The initials stand for *all but dissertation.*)

> So far we have received résumés from two *Ph.D.s* and seven *ABDs*. (See ¶622a for guidelines on forming the plurals of these abbreviations.)

b. The term *M.B.A.* is now commonly written without periods when it is used to signify an executive with a certain type of training rather than the degree itself.

> We have just hired two Stanford *MBAs* and one from Harvard.
>
> **BUT:** After I get my *M.B.A.,* I plan to go on to law school.

c. When academic degrees follow a person's name, do not use such titles as *Dr., Mr., Ms., Miss,* or *Mrs.* before the name.

> Dr. Helen Garcia   **OR**   Helen Garcia, M.D.
>
> (**BUT NOT:** Dr. Helen Garcia, M.D.)

However, other titles may precede the name as long as they do not convey the same meaning as the degree that follows.

> Professor Rex Ford, Ph.D.   the Reverend John Day, D.D.
>
> President Jean Dill, L.H.D.   **OR** the Reverend Dr. John Day
>
> Dean May Ito, J.S.D.   (**BUT NOT:** the Reverend Dr. John Day, D.D.)

➤ *See also ¶¶1324c, 1324d, 1364a.*

d. Academic degrees standing alone may be abbreviated except in very formal writing.

> I am now completing my *Ph.D.*
>
> She received her *M.A.* last year.
>
> **OR** . . . her *master of arts* degree last year. (See also ¶353.)

e. Professional designations such as *CPA* (certified public accountant), *CPS* (certified professional secretary), *PLS* (certified professional legal secretary), *CFP* (certified financial planner), *CLU* (chartered life underwriter), and *FACS* (fellow of the American College of Surgeons) are commonly written *without* periods when they are used alone but *with* periods when they are used with academic degrees.

> Anthony Filippo, CPA   **BUT:** Anthony Filippo, B.S., M.B.A., *C.P.A.*
>
> Ruth L. Morris, CLU   Ruth L. Morris, B.A., *C.L.U.*

NOTE: List professional designations after a person's name (for example, in the signature line in a letter) only in situations where one's professional qualifications are relevant to the topic under discussion.

Names of Organizations

520 **a.** Names of well-known business organizations, labor unions, societies, associations (trade, professional, charitable, and fraternal), and government agencies are often abbreviated except in the most formal writing. When these abbreviations consist of all-capital initials, they are typed without periods or spaces.

> AFL-CIO   American Federation of Labor and Congress of Industrial Organizations
>
> ILGWU   International Ladies' Garment Workers' Union
>
> NAACP   National Association for the Advancement of Colored People
>
> NYSE   New York Stock Exchange

¶**522**

NAM	National Association of Manufacturers
NIMH	National Institute of Mental Health
YMCA	Young Men's Christian Association
IRS	Internal Revenue Service
SEC	Securities and Exchange Commission

b. The following terms are often abbreviated in the names of business organizations. However, follow the individual company's preference for abbreviating or spelling out.

Mfg.	Manufacturing	Co.	Company	Inc.	Incorporated
Mfrs.	Manufacturers	Corp.	Corporation	Ltd.	Limited

521 In ordinary correspondence, for the sake of brevity and simplicity, you may drop abbreviations and other elements in organizational names as long as your reader will know which company you are referring to. For example, *Charles Schwab & Co., Inc.,* may be referred to simply as *Schwab; America Online, Inc.,* may be referred to as *America Online* or *AOL.* In formal and legal documents, an organization's name should be given in full when it is first introduced; if appropriate, a shorter form may be used in subsequent references.

Acronyms

522 **a.** An acronym—for example, *NOW*—is a shortened form derived from the initial letters of the words that make up the complete form. Thus *NOW* is derived from *National Organization for Women.* Like all-capital abbreviations such as *IRS* and *NAM,* acronyms are usually written in all capitals and without periods; however, unlike those abbreviations, which are pronounced letter by letter, acronyms are pronounced as words. (See ¶501b.) Because they have been deliberately coined to replace the longer expressions they represent, acronyms are appropriate for use on all occasions.

C-SPAN	Cable Satellite Public Affairs Network
WATS	Wide-Area Telecommunications Service
POTS	plain old telephone service
ZIP (Code)	Zone Improvement Plan
PIN	personal identification number (see ¶522f)
SKU	stockkeeping unit (pronounced *SKEW*)
SOHO	small office, home office (as in *the SOHO market*)
BOGO	buy-one, get-one-free offer
AMEX	American Stock Exchange (see ¶522c for *AmEx*)
NASDAQ	National Association of Security Dealers Automated Quotations (see ¶522e)
DRIP	dividend reinvestment program
ESOP	employee stock ownership plan
OSHA	Occupational Safety and Health Administration
RICO	Racketeer Influenced and Corrupt Organization Act (pronounced *REE-koe*)
FOIA	Freedom of Information Act (pronounced *FOY-uh*)
EPIC	Electronic Privacy Information Center
AIDS	acquired immune deficiency syndrome
CARE	Cooperative for American Relief to Everywhere

Continued on page 142

¶522

NIMBY	not in my backyard (as in *a NIMBY protest*)
BANANA	build almost nothing anywhere near anything
SADD	Students Against Drunk Driving
FONZ	Friends of the National Zoo
EMILY's List	a political fund-raising group based on the concept that early money is like yeast (and makes the dough rise)
SPELL	Society for the Preservation of English Language and Literature
MEGO	my eyes glaze over
BOGSAT	bunch of guys sitting around a table (an ad hoc decision-making process)
SITCOMs	couples with a single income, two children, and an onerous mortgage
PONA	person of no account (someone not hooked up to the Internet; pronounced *POH-nuh*)
WOMBAT	waste of money, brains, and time
PEBCAK	problem exists between chair and keyboard (computer service technician's diagnosis in the absence of other problems)
YABA	yet another bloody acronym

b. In a few cases acronyms derived from initial letters are written entirely in small letters without periods.

scuba	self-contained underwater breathing apparatus
laser	light amplification by stimulated emission of radiation
yuppies	young urban professionals
gorp	good old raisins and peanuts (a high-energy snack)

c. Some coined names use more than the first letters of the words they represent. Such names are often written with only the first letter capitalized.

Ameslan	American Sign Language
Delmarva	an East Coast peninsula made up of Delaware and parts of Maryland and Virginia
Conrail	Consolidated Rail Corporation
Amtrak	American travel by track
Calpers	California Public Employees Retirement System
Echo	East Coast Hang Out (an online service)
The Well	The Whole Earth 'Lectronic Link (an online community)
radar	radio detecting and ranging
sonar	sound navigation ranging
modem	modulator and demodulator
canola (oil)	Canada, oil low acid
op-ed page	the page that is opposite the editorial page
pixel	picture element
domos	downwardly mobilc professionals
dinks	couple with double incomes and no kids
BUT: AmEx	American Express
FedEx	Federal Express
INTELPOST	International Electronic Postal Service

d. In a few cases all-capital abbreviations such as *MC* (for *master of ceremonies*) or *DJ* (for *disc jockey*) may also be spelled out in an uncapitalized form (*emcee* and *deejay*). The spelled-out forms are preferable when such abbreviations are used as verbs.

Fran Zangwill *emceed* (**RATHER THAN:** MC'd) the fund-raiser kickoff dinner.

Who has been *okaying* (**RATHER THAN:** OK'ing) these bills? (See ¶548.)

BUT: You'd find it easier to get up in the morning if you didn't *OD* on TV every night. (Here the choice is between *OD* and *overdose*, not *oh-dee*.)

e. Very long acronyms (with six or more letters) are sometimes written with only the initial letter capitalized to avoid the distracting appearance of too many capital letters.

UNESCO **OR** Unesco (the United Nations Educational, Scientific, and Cultural Organization)

UNICEF **OR** Unicef (the United Nations International Children's Emergency Fund; now simply called the United Nations Children's Fund)

f. When using an acronym, do not follow it with a word that is part of the acronym. Consider the following examples with *PIN* (personal identification number) and *ATM* (automated teller machine).

With all the PINs (**NOT** PIN numbers) I have to remember these days, I feel as if I were turning into a PINhead.

The ATM (**NOT** the ATM machine) at the State Street branch has swallowed my card again.

Names of Broadcasting Stations and Systems

523 The names of radio and television broadcasting stations and the abbreviated names of broadcasting systems are written in all-capital letters without periods and without spaces.

Portsmouth:	WRAP-AM	San Antonio:	KISS-FM	CNN (**BUT:** CNNfn)	
Houston:	KILT-FM	New Orleans:	WYES-TV	MSNBC	

According to *ABC* and *CBS,* the earthquake had a magnitude of 6.8.

Names of Government and International Agencies

524 The names of well-known government and international agencies are often abbreviated. They are written without periods or spaces.

FNMA   the Federal National Mortgage Association (often referred to as Fannie Mae, the result of trying to sound out the initials *FNMA*)

GNMA   Government National Mortgage Association (referred to as Ginnie Mae)

SLMA   Student Loan Marketing Association (referred to as Sallie Mae)

FHLMC   Federal Home Loan Mortgage Corporation (referred to as Freddie Mac)

FEMA   the Federal Emergency Management Agency

EEOC   the Equal Employment Opportunity Commission

NOTE: Expressions such as *the Fed* (for *the Federal Reserve Board*) and *the Ex-Im Bank* (for *the U.S. Export-Import Bank*) involve shortened forms rather than true abbreviations and thus are written without periods.

525 The name *United States* is usually abbreviated when it is part of the name of a government agency. When used as an adjective, the name is often abbreviated, though not in formal usage. When used as a noun, the name is spelled out.

U.S. Department of Agriculture	USDA
U.S. Air Force	USAF
the United States government	the U.S. government
United States foreign policy	U.S. foreign policy
throughout the United States (**NOT:** throughout the U.S.)	

¶526

Geographic Names

526 Do not abbreviate geographic names except in tables, business forms, and expedient documents (see ¶502) and in place names with *Saint.* (See ¶529b.)

NOTE: In informal writing, the city of Washington may be referred to as *D.C.* and Los Angeles as *L.A.* In general, however, spell these names out.

> **INFORMAL CONTEXT:** Did you know that Liz has been transferred from the *D.C.* office to the branch in *L.A.?*
>
> **OTHER CONTEXTS:** Did you know that Liz has been transferred from the *Washington, D.C.,* office to the branch in *Los Angeles?*

527 **a.** When abbreviating state names *in addresses,* use the two-letter abbreviations (without periods) shown in ¶1341 and on the inside back cover.

b. *In all situations other than addresses,* use the following abbreviations (with periods and spacing as shown).

Alabama	Ala.	North Dakota	N. Dak.
Arizona	Ariz.	Oklahoma	Okla.
Arkansas	Ark.	Oregon	Oreg.
California	Calif.	Pennsylvania	Pa.
Canal Zone	C.Z.	Puerto Rico	P.R.
Colorado	Colo.	Rhode Island	R.I.
Connecticut	Conn.	South Carolina	S.C.
Delaware	Del.	South Dakota	S. Dak.
District of Columbia	D.C.	Tennessee	Tenn.
Florida	Fla.	Texas	Tex.
Georgia	Ga.	Vermont	Vt.
Illinois	Ill.	Virgin Islands	V.I.
Indiana	Ind.	Virginia	Va.
Kansas	Kans.	Washington	Wash.
Kentucky	Ky.	West Virginia	W. Va.
Louisiana	La.	Wisconsin	Wis.
Maryland	Md.	Wyoming	Wyo.
Massachusetts	Mass.	Alberta	Alta.
Michigan	Mich.	British Columbia	B.C.
Minnesota	Minn.	Manitoba	Man.
Mississippi	Miss.	New Brunswick	N.B.
Missouri	Mo.	Newfoundland	Nfld.
Montana	Mont.	Northwest Territories	
Nebraska	Ncbr.	and Nunavut	N.W.T.
Nevada	Nev.	Nova Scotia	N.S.
New Hampshire	N.H.	Ontario	Ont.
New Jersey	N.J.	Prince Edward Island	P.E.I.
New Mexico	N. Mex.	Quebec	P.Q. or Que.
New York	N.Y.	Saskatchewan	Sask.
North Carolina	N.C.	Yukon	Y.T. or Yuk.

NOTE: Alaska, Guam, Hawaii, Idaho, Iowa, Maine, Ohio, and Utah are not abbreviated.

528 **a.** Geographic abbreviations made up of single initials require a period after each initial but *no* space after each internal period.

U.K.	United Kingdom	P.R.C.	People's Republic of China
N.A.	North America	C.I.S.	Commonwealth of Independent States
B.W.I.	British West Indies		(formerly the U.S.S.R.)

NOTE: When a company uses a geographic abbreviation in its corporate name or in the name of a product, respect the company's style.

U.S.A.	**BUT:** *USA Today*	U.S.	**BUT:** U S WEST Communications

b. If the geographic abbreviation contains more than single initials, space once after each internal period.

N. Mex.	N. Dak.	W. Va.	W. Aust.

529 **a.** In place names, do not abbreviate *Fort, Mount, Point,* or *Port* except in tables and lists where space is tight.

Fort Wayne	Mount Pleasant	Point Pleasant	Port Arthur
Fort Myers	Mount Rainier	Point Pelee	Port Ludlow

b. In U.S. place names, abbreviate *Saint.* For other place names involving *Saint,* follow the style shown in an authoritative dictionary or atlas.

St. Louis, Missouri	St. Lawrence River
St. Petersburg, Florida	St. Charles Avenue

➤ *For the abbreviation or the spelling out of names of streets, cities, states, and countries, see also ¶¶1334–1337, 1340–1341, 1343.*

Compass Points

530 **a.** Spell out compass points used as ordinary nouns and adjectives.

The company has large landholdings in the *Southwest.*

We purchased a lot at the *southwest* corner of Green and Union Streets.

➤ *For the capitalization of compass points, see ¶¶338–341.*

b. Spell out compass points included in street names except in lists and tables where space is tight. (See also ¶1334.)

143 South Mountain Avenue

1232 East Franklin Street

531 **a.** Abbreviate compass points without periods when they are used *following* a street name to indicate the section of the city. (See also ¶1335.)

1330 South Bay Boulevard, SW

NOTE: In some communities the predominant style is to use periods in such abbreviations; for example, *S.W., N.E.* (See ¶1335.)

b. In technical material (especially pertaining to real estate and legal or nautical matters), abbreviate compass points without periods.

N	north	NE	northeast	NNE	north-northeast
S	south	SW	southwest	SSW	south-southwest

Abbreviations

5

¶532

Days and Months

532 Do not abbreviate names of days of the week and months of the year except in tables or lists where space is limited. In such cases the following abbreviations may be used:

Sun.	Thurs., Thu.	Jan.	May	Sept., Sep.
Mon.	Fri.	Feb.	June, Jun.	Oct.
Tues., Tue.	Sat.	Mar.	July, Jul.	Nov.
Wed.		Apr.	Aug.	Dec.

NOTE: When space is extremely tight, as in the column heads of some computer reports, the following one- and two-letter abbreviations may be used.

Su   M   Tu   W   Th   F   Sa
Ja   F   Mr   Ap   My   Je   Jl   Au   S   O   N   D

Time and Time Zones

533 Use the abbreviations *a.m.* and *p.m.* in expressions of time. These abbreviations most commonly appear in small letters, but you may use small capitals (A.M., P.M.) if you have that option. (See ¶440.) For more formal expressions of time, use *o'clock* (see ¶441).

534   **a.** The standard time zones in the continental United States are abbreviated as follows:

EST (Eastern standard time)   MST (Mountain standard time)
CST (Central standard time)   PST (Pacific standard time)

➤ *For examples, see ¶440a.*

b. When daylight saving time is in effect, use DST (daylight saving time) or one of the following forms:

EDT (Eastern daylight time)   MDT (Mountain daylight time)
CDT (Central daylight time)   PDT (Pacific daylight time)

NOTE: When referring to daylight saving time, note that *saving* is singular. Do not say "daylight *savings* time."

c. An alternative style of time zone abbreviations eliminates all references to standard and daylight time.

ET (Eastern time)   MT (Mountain time)
CT (Central time)   PT (Pacific time)

These shorter abbreviations are especially useful in promotional materials that are to be distributed without change throughout the year.

To place an order, call our toll-free number between 7 a.m. and 6 p.m., PT.
OR . . . between 7 a.m. and 6 p.m. (PT).

d. Puerto Rico and the U.S. Virgin Islands are in the Atlantic standard time zone (AST). Hawaii is in the Hawaii-Aleutian time zone (abbreviated simply as HST with reference to Hawaii). Alaska falls in the Alaska time zone (which is commonly abbreviated as YST, referring to an earlier designation, the Yukon time zone). Within these areas only Alaska observes daylight saving time (YDT).

Customary Measurements

535 Abbreviate units of measure when they occur frequently, as in technical and scientific work, on invoices and other business forms, and in tables.

a. Units of measure are now commonly abbreviated without periods. The abbreviations are the same for the singular and the plural.

yd (yard, yards)	oz (ounce, ounces)	rpm (revolutions per minute)
ft (foot, feet)	gal (gallon, gallons)	cpi (characters per inch)
mi (mile, miles)	lb (pound, pounds)	mph (miles per hour)

NOTE: The abbreviation *in* (for *inch* or *inches*) may be written without a period if it is not likely to be confused with the preposition *in*.

8 in   **OR**   8 in.   **BUT:** 8 sq in   8 ft 2 in

b. In a set of simple dimensions or a range of numbers, use an abbreviation only with the last number. Repeat a symbol with each number.

a room 10 × 15 ft   **BUT:** a room 10′ × 15′ (see ¶543c)

35° to 45°F   **OR**   35°–45°F (see ¶¶538c, 543c)

NOTE: In a set of complex dimensions, where more than one unit of measure is involved, repeat the abbreviations with each number.

a room 10 ft 6 in × 19 ft 10 in   **OR**   a room 10′ 6″ × 19′ 10″ (see ¶432)

536 In nontechnical writing, spell out units of measure.

a 20-gallon container   8½ by 11 inches

a 150-acre estate   an 8½- by 11-inch book (see ¶817)

Metric Measurements

The following rules of style are based on the *Metric Editorial Guide,* published by the American National Metric Council (Washington, D.C.). For a full listing of metric terms, consult a dictionary.

537 The most common metric measurements are derived from three basic units and several prefixes indicating multiples or fractions of a unit, as shown below. The abbreviations for these terms appear in parentheses in the first column below.

Basic Units

meter (m)	One meter is 10 percent longer than a yard (39.37 inches).
gram (g)	A thousand grams (a *kilogram*) is 10 percent heavier than 2 pounds (2.2 pounds).
liter (L)*	A liter is about 5 percent bigger than a quart (1.057 quarts).

Prefixes Indicating Fractions

deci (d)	1/10	A *decimeter* (dm) equals 1/10 meter.
centi (c)	1/100	A *centigram* (cg) equals 1/100 gram.
milli (m)	1/1000	A *milliliter* (mL) equals 1/1000 liter.

Prefixes Indicating Multiples

deka (da)	10	A *dekameter* (dam) equals 10 meters (about 11 yards).
hecto (h)	100	A *hectogram* (hg) equals 100 grams (about 3½ ounces).
kilo (k)	1000	A *kilometer* (km) equals 1000 meters (about ⅝ mile).

Continued on page 148

*The abbreviation for *liter* is often shown as a lowercase *l.* However, because an *l* can easily be mistaken for the numeral *1,* the use of a capital *L* is recommended as the abbreviation for *liter.*

¶538

NOTE: Temperatures are expressed in terms of the Celsius scale (abbreviated *C*).

> Water freezes at 0°C (32°F) and boils at 100°C (212°F).
> With a temperature of 37°C (98.6°F), you can't be very sick.
> The temperature here on the island stays between 20° and 30°C (68° and 86°F).

➤ *For the use of spaces in figures expressing metric quantities, see ¶461b.*

538 Metric units of measurement, like the customary units of measurement described in ¶535, are abbreviated in technical and scientific work, on business forms, and in tables. In nontechnical writing, metric units are ordinarily spelled out, but some expressions typically appear in abbreviated form (for example, *35-mm film*).

a. Abbreviations of metric units of measurement are written without periods except at the end of a sentence.

> 100-mm cigarettes (10 centimeters or about 4 inches)
> a 30-cm width (about 12 inches or 1 foot)
> an office 5 × 3 m (about 5.5 by 3.3 yards)
> a 1000-km trip (620 miles)
> weighs 100 kg (about 220 pounds)
> 50 to 75 kg (about 110 to 165 pounds)
> feels like 10°C weather (50°F weather)

NOTE: In abbreviations of expressions like *kilometers per hour,* a diagonal is used to express *per.*

> an 80 km/h speed limit (50 miles per hour)

b. Metric abbreviations are the same for the singular and the plural.

> 1 kg (1 kilogram)   5 kg (5 kilograms)

c. When expressing temperatures, leave no space between the number and the degree symbol or between the degree symbol and the abbreviation for Celsius.

> 14°C (**NOT:** 14° C)

d. In printed material, metric measurements for area and volume are usually expressed with superscripts (raised numbers).

> m^2 square meter cm^3 cubic centimeter

If the equipment you are using makes it difficult or awkward to create raised numbers, use the following forms:

> sq m   square meter   cu cm   cubic centimeter

NOTE: In material that also uses superscripts for footnote references, use the forms *sq m* and *cu cm* to avoid the possibility of confusion.

Chemical and Mathematical Expressions

539 Do not use a period after the symbols that represent chemical elements and formulas.

> K (potassium)   NaCl (sodium chloride–table salt)
> The chemical notations H_2O and CO_2 stand for "dihydrogen oxide" (namely, water) and "carbon dioxide." They do not refer, as one student observed, to hot water and cold water.

540 Do not use a period after such mathematical abbreviations as *log* (for *logarithm*) and *tan* (for *tangent*).

Business Expressions

541 A number of terms are commonly abbreviated on business forms, in tables, and in routine business documents. In addition to the list of abbreviations shown below, several other lists are provided in the following paragraphs:

➤ *Computer abbreviations and acronyms: see ¶544.*
   Abbreviations in foreign expressions: see ¶545.
   Common abbreviations in general usage: see ¶546.

AA	administrative assistant, Alcoholics Anonymous, author's alteration(s)	CDC	community development corporation
A.A.	associate in arts (degree)	CEO	chief executive officer
acct.	account	CFO	chief financial officer
ack.	acknowledge	cg	centigram(s)
addl.	additional	chg.	charge
agt.	agent	c.i.f. **OR** CIF	cost, insurance, and freight (see ¶542)
AHS	automated highway systems	CIO	chief information officer
AI	artificial intelligence	CKO	chief knowledge officer
a.k.a.	also known as	cm	centimeter(s)
amt.	amount	Co.	Company
anon.	anonymous	c/o	care of
AP	accounts payable	c.o.d. **OR** COD	cash (or collect) on delivery (see ¶542)
APB	all points bulletin		
approx.	approximately	COLA	cost-of-living adjustment
APR	annual percentage rate	cont.	continued
AR	accounts receivable	COO	chief operating officer
ARM	adjustable-rate mortgage	Corp.	Corporation
ASAP	as soon as possible	CPA	certified public accountant (see ¶519e)
Assn.	Association		
assoc.	associate(s)	cpi	characters per inch (see ¶507)
asst.	assistant		
att.	attachment	CPI	consumer price index
Attn.	Attention	CPM	cost per thousand
avg.	average	CPS	certified professional secretary (see ¶519e)
bal.	balance		
bbl	barrel(s)	cr.	credit
bf	boldface type	ctn.	carton
bl	bale(s)	cwt.	hundredweight
BL **OR** B/L	bill of lading	d.b.a. **OR** DBA	doing business as (see ¶542)
bldg.	building	dept.	department
BO	back order	dis.	discount
BS **OR** B/S	bill of sale	dist.	district
B-school	graduate school of business	distr.	distributor, distribution, distributed
bu	bushel(s)	div.	division
c, cc	copy, copies (see ¶1376a)	DJIA	Dow Jones industrial average
C	100; Celsius (temperature)	doz.	dozen
CBD	central business district	dr.	debit

Continued on page 150

Abbreviations

5

¶541

dstn.	destination	IPO	initial public offering (of company shares)
dtd.	dated	ips	inches per second
DVD	digital videodisc	JIT	just in time
ea.	each	kg	kilogram(s)
EEO	equal employment opportunity	kHz	kilohertz
enc.	enclosed, enclosure	km	kilometer(s)
EOE	equal opportunity employer(s)	km/h	kilometers per hour
e.o.m. **OR** EOM	end of month (see ¶542)	l., ll.	line, lines
Esq.	Esquire	L	liter(s) (see ¶537)
ETA	estimated time of arrival	lb	pound(s)
ETD	estimated time of departure	LBO	leveraged buyout
exec.	executive	l.c.l. **OR** LCL	less-than-carload lot (see ¶542)
F	Fahrenheit (temperature)		
f.a.s. **OR** FAS	free alongside ship (see ¶542)	LIFO	last in, first out
f.b.o. **OR** FBO	for the benefit of (see ¶542)	LLP	limited licensed partners
FIFO	first in, first out	Ltd.	Limited
f.o.b. **OR** FOB	free on board (see ¶542)	m	meter(s) (see ¶537)
fps	feet per second	M	1000
ft	foot, feet	M&A	mergers and acquisitions
ft-tn	foot-ton(s)	max.	maximum
fwd.	forward	mdse.	merchandise
FY	fiscal year (see ¶504)	mfg.	manufacturing
FYI	for your information	mfr.	manufacturer
g	gram(s) (see ¶537)	mg	milligram(s)
GAAP	generally accepted accounting principles	mgr.	manager
gal	gallon(s)	mgt. **OR** mgmt.	management
GATT	General Agreement on Tariffs and Trade	MHz	megahertz
		mi	mile(s)
GM	general manager	min	minute(s)
gr.	gross	min.	minimum
gr. wt.	gross weight	misc.	miscellaneous
hdlg.	handling	mL	milliliter(s)
HMO	health maintenance organization	mm	millimeter(s)
		mo	month(s)
HOV	high-occupancy vehicle	MO	mail order, money order (see *M.O.* in ¶545)
HP **OR** hp	horsepower		
HQ	headquarters	mpg	miles per gallon
hr	hour(s)	mph	miles per hour
Hz	hertz (a unit of frequency)	msg.	message
in **OR** in.	inch(es) (see ¶535a, note)	mtg.	mortgage
Inc.	Incorporated	n/30	net in 30 days
incl.	including, inclusive	NA	not applicable, not available
ins.	insurance	n.d.	no date
intl.	international	NGO	nongovernmental organization
inv.	invoice	NIC	newly industrialized country

¶542

No., Nos.	number(s) (see ¶455)		recd.	received
nt. wt.	net weight		reg.	registered, regular
NV	no value		REIT	real estate investment trust
OAG	*Official Airline Guide*		ret.	retired
OJT	on-the-job training		rev.	revised
opt.	optional		RIF	reduction in force
OS	out of stock		ROA	return on assets
OTC	over the counter		ROE	return on equity
oz	ounce(s)		ROI	return on investment
p., pp.	page, pages		rpm	revolutions per minute
P&H	postage and handling		S&H	shipping and handling
P&L **OR** P/L	profit and loss (statement)		SASE	self-addressed stamped envelope
PC	personal computer, politically correct		sc **OR** SC	small caps (see ¶533)
P.C.	professional corporation		sec	second(s)
pd.	paid		sec.	secretary
PE	printer's error(s), Professional Engineer		shtg.	shortage
			SO	shipping order
P/E	price/earnings (ratio)		SSN	social security number
PERT	program evaluation and review technique		std.	standard
			stge.	storage
pkg.	package(s)		stmt.	statement
PO	purchase order		SUV	sport utility vehicle
P.O.	post office		t.b.a. **OR** TBA	to be announced (see ¶542)
p.o.e. **OR** POE	port of entry (see ¶542)			
pop.	population		t.b.d. **OR** TBD	to be determined (see ¶542)
POP	point of purchase			
POS	point of sale		™	trademark
POV	point of view		TO	table of organization
PP	parcel post		treas.	treasury, treasurer
ppd.	postpaid, prepaid (postage paid in advance)		UPC	Universal Product Code
			VAT	value-added tax
pr.	pair(s)		VP	vice president
PS, PS.	postscript		vs.	versus (v. in legal citations)
pt	pint(s)		w/	with
pt.	part, point(s), port		whsle	wholesale
QA	quality assurance		w/o	without, week of
Q&A	question and answer		wt.	weight
qt	quart(s)		yd	yard(s)
qtr.	quarter(ly)		YOB	year of birth
qty.	quantity		yr	year(s)
®	registered trademark		YTD	year to date

542 A few common business abbreviations listed in ¶541 are frequently typed in small letters (with periods) when they occur within sentences but are typed in all-capital letters (without periods) when they appear on business forms. For example:

c.i.f.	**OR**	CIF	e.o.m.	**OR**	EOM	l.c.l.	**OR**	LCL	t.b.a.	**OR**	TBA
c.o.d.	**OR**	COD	f.o.b.	**OR**	FOB	p.o.e.	**OR**	POE	t.b.d.	**OR**	TBD

¶543

Symbols

543 **a.** A number of symbols are often used on business forms, in tables and statistical material, and in informal business documents. If you are using software with special character sets, you can access these symbols.

@	at	°	degrees	#	number (before a figure)
&	and	=	equals	#	pounds (after a figure)
%	percent	´	feet	¶	paragraph
$	dollars	″	inches; ditto	×	by, multiplied by
¢	cents	§	section		

NOTE: When using symbols for feet and inches, use either the *slanted* version of the single and double quotation mark (´ and ″) or the *straight* version (' and "). Do not use the *curly* version (' and ").

b. Leave one space before and after the following symbols:

@	order 200 @ $49.95	=	if $a = 7$ and $b = 9$
&	Kaye & Elman Inc.	×	a room 12 × 18 ft

NOTE: As a rule, do not leave any space before and after an ampersand (&) in all-capital abbreviations.

AT&T pursues a wide range of R&D [research and development] activities.

At the next shareholders' meeting we need to anticipate some tough queries during the Q&A [question and answer] session about our M&A [merger and acquisition] activities.

c. Do not leave space between a figure and one of the following symbols:

%	a 65% sales increase	#	use 50# paper for the job
¢	about 30¢ a pound	´	a 9′ × 12′ Oriental carpet
°	reduce heat to 350°	″	an 8½″ × 11″ sheet of paper

d. Do not leave any space after these symbols when they are followed by a figure:

$	in the $250–$500 range	¶¶	as explained in ¶¶1218–1220
#	reorder #4659 and #4691	§	will be covered in §14.26

Computer Abbreviations

544 The following list presents some of the abbreviations commonly used in references to computers and the Internet.

ASCII	American Standard Code for Information Interchange (pronounced *as-kee*)
BASIC	Beginner's All-Purpose Symbolic Instruction Code
BBSs	bulletin board services (see ¶622a)
BCD	binary coded decimal
BIOS	basic input/output system
bit	binary digit
BLOB	binary large object
bps	bits per second
CAD	computer-aided design
CAI	computer-aided instruction
CAM	computer-aided manufacturing
CAR	computer-assisted retrieval
CD-ROM	compact disc–read-only memory

¶**544**

CGA	color graphics adapter
CPU	central processing unit
CRT	cathode-ray tube
DBMS	database management system
DOS	disk operating system
dpi	dots per inch
DTP	desktop publishing
e-mail	electronic mail
EOF	end of file
FAQ	frequently asked questions (pronounced *fak*)
FAT	file allocation table
FTP	file transfer protocol
GIGO	garbage in, garbage out
GUI	graphical user interface (pronounced *goo-ee*)
I-Way	Information Superhighway
IC	integrated circuit
I/O	input/output
ISP	Internet service provider
KB **OR** K	kilobyte (see ¶503)
LAN	local area network
LCD	liquid crystal display
LQ	letter quality
MB **OR** M	megabyte (see ¶503)
MICR	magnetic ink character reader
NC	network computer
NLQ	near letter quality
OCR	optical character recognition **OR** reader
OS	operating system
PC	personal computer
PIC	personal intelligent communicator
PPP	point-to-point protocol
RAM	random-access memory
RISC	reduced instruction set computer
ROM	read-only memory
SCSI	small computer system interface port (pronounced *scuzzy*)
SET	Secure Electronic Transactions
SLIP	serial line Internet protocol
TCP/IP	transmission control protocol/Internet protocol
UCE	unsolicited commercial e-mail (also called *spam*)
VDT	video display terminal
VM	voice mail
WAIS	wide area information server (pronounced *ways*)
WAN	wide area network
WORM	write once-read many times
WWW **OR** W3	the World Wide Web (sometimes pronounced *triple-dub* to avoid having to say *double-u, double-u, double-u*)
W3C	World Wide Web Consortium

Continued on page 154

Abbreviations

5

¶545

WYSIWYG	what you see is what you get (pronounced *wiz-ee-wig*)
XGA	extended graphics array
Y2K	the Year 2000 Problem; also known as the Millennium Bug (referring to the potential worldwide crash of computers not modified to recognize dates beginning with the year 2000)

NOTE: When using a computer abbreviation like those listed above, do not follow it with a word that is part of the abbreviation.

CD-ROM	(**NOT:** CD-ROM disc)	LCD	(**NOT:** LCD display)
DOS	(**NOT:** DOS operating system)	RAM	(**NOT:** RAM memory)
ISP	(**NOT:** ISP provider)	TCP/IP	(**NOT:** TCP/IP protocol)

➤ *For a glossary of computer terms, see Appendix B; for the capitalization of computer terms, see ¶¶365, 366a, 847f.*

Foreign Expressions

545 Many foreign expressions contain or consist of short words, some of which are abbreviations and some of which are not. Use periods only with abbreviations.

ad hoc	meaning "for a particular purpose"
ad val.	*ad valorem,* meaning "according to the value"
c. **OR** ca.	*circa,* meaning "approximately"
cf.	*confer,* meaning "compare"
Cie.	*Compagnie,* meaning "Company"
C.V.	*curriculum vitae,* meaning "course of one's life"; a résumé
e.g.	*exempli gratia,* meaning "for example"
et al.	*et alii,* meaning "and other people"
etc.	*et cetera,* meaning "and other things," "and so forth"
ibid.	*ibidem,* meaning "in the same place"
idem	meaning "the same"
i.e.	*id est,* meaning "that is"
infra	meaning "below"
inst.	*instans,* meaning "the current month"
loc. cit.	*loco citato,* meaning "in the place cited"
M.O.	*modus operandi,* meaning "the way in which something is done"
N.B.	*nota bene,* meaning "note well"
nol. pros.	*nolle prosequi,* meaning "to be unwilling to prosecute"
non seq.	*non sequitur,* meaning "it does not follow"
op. cit.	*opere citato,* meaning "in the work cited"
p.a. **OR** PA	*per annum,* meaning "for each year"
p.d. **OR** PD	*per diem,* meaning "for each day"
pro tem	*pro tempore,* meaning "for the time being"
prox.	*proximo,* meaning "in the next month"
Q.E.D.	*quod erat demonstrandum,* meaning "which was to be demonstrated"
q.v.	*quod vide,* meaning "which see"
re **OR** in re	meaning "in the matter of," "concerning"
R.S.V.P. **OR** R.s.v.p.	*Répondez s'il vous plaît,* meaning "please reply"
supra	meaning "above"
ult.	*ultimo,* meaning "in the last month"

Miscellaneous Expressions

546 The following list of expressions presents common abbreviations acceptable in general usage.

A-OK	very definitely OK	our morale is A-OK
ATM	automated teller machine	get $50 from the nearest ATM
AV	audiovisual	a list of AV materials
CB	citizens band	called in on her CB radio
CD	certificate of deposit,	investing in 6% CDs
	compact disc	the quality of a CD recording
CPR	cardiopulmonary resuscitation	a need for CPR training
ESP	extrasensory perception	their manager must have ESP
GDP	gross domestic product	the GDP for the fourth quarter
ID	identification data	show your user ID card
IOU	I owe you	holds my IOU for $500
IQ	intelligence quotient	take an IQ test
IRA	individual retirement account	make a tax-deductible deposit to your IRA
IV	intravenous	he's still hooked up to an IV (device)
PA	public address	a problem with our PA system
PAC	political action committee	limiting the role of PACs
PR	public relations	work on your PR campaign
R&D	research and development	need a bigger R&D budget
S&L	savings and loan association	a small S&L mortgage
SOP	standard operating procedure	find out the SOP for submitting expense reports
SRO	standing room only	an SRO audience at our show
TLC	tender, loving care	give this customer some TLC
TV	television	watch for it on TV
UFO	unidentified flying object	took off like a UFO
VCR	videocassette recorder	play this tape on your VCR
VIP	very important person	treat these VPs like VIPs

NOTE: Initialisms and acronyms are continually entering the language, and while they may not yet be widely used, in many cases they ought to be. For example:

IAD	Internet addictive disorder (a compulsive form of behavior in which the victim chooses cyberspace activities over real-world responsibilities and relationships)
QCD	quarterly charm deficiency (an emotional disorder that afflicts executives at the end of each fiscal quarter)

547 Do not use periods with letters that are not abbreviations. (See also ¶109a.)

Brand X	T-bill	f-stop	I-beam pointer	V-chip
X ray	T square	y-axis	U-turn	B picture

548 The abbreviation *OK* is written without periods. In sentences, the forms *okay*, *okayed*, and *okaying* look better than *OK, OK'd,* and *OK'ing,* but the latter forms may be used. (See also ¶522d.)

549 The dictionary recognizes *x* as a verb; however, *cross out, crossed out,* and *crossing out* look better than *x out, x-ed out,* and *x-ing out.*

➤ *Plurals of abbreviations: see ¶¶619–623.*
    Possessives of abbreviations: see ¶¶638–639.

Abbreviations

5

SECTION **6**

Plurals and Possessives

➤ *For definitions of grammatical terms, see the appropriate entries in the Glossary of Grammatical Terms (Appendix A).*

¶605

Forming Plurals

When you are uncertain about the plural form of a word, consult a dictionary. If no plural is shown, form the plural according to the rules in ¶¶601–626.

Basic Rule

601 Plurals are regularly formed by adding *s* to the singular form.

suburb	suburbs	rhythm	rhythms	league	leagues
fabric	fabrics	flight	flights	alibi	alibis
yield	yields	quota	quotas	ski	skis
egg	eggs	idea	ideas	taxi	taxis
length	lengths	committee	committees	menu	menus
check	checks	freebie	freebies	bayou	bayous

NOTE: A few words have the same form in the plural as in the singular. (See ¶¶603, 1014, 1016, 1017.)

Nouns Ending in *S, X, CH, SH,* or *Z*

602 When the singular form ends in *s, x, ch, sh,* or *z,* the plural is formed by adding *es* to the singular.

virus	viruses	sketch	sketches
summons	summonses	wish	wishes
business	businesses	quartz	quartzes
fax	faxes	**BUT:** quiz	quizzes

NOTE: When *ch* at the end of a singular word has the sound of *k,* form the plural by simply adding *s.*

epoch	epochs	monarch	monarchs
stomach	stomachs	**BUT:** arch	arches

➢ *For plural forms of proper names ending in* ch, *see ¶615b, 617.*

603 Singular nouns ending in silent *s* do not change their forms in the plural. (However, the *s* ending is pronounced when the plural form is used.)

one corps two corps	a rendezvous many rendezvous

Nouns Ending in *Y*

604 When a singular noun ends in *y* preceded by a *consonant,* the plural is formed by changing the *y* to *i* and adding *es* to the singular.

copy	copies	liability	liabilities
policy	policies	proxy	proxies

605 When a singular noun ends in *y* preceded by a *vowel,* the plural is formed by adding *s* to the singular.

delay	delays	guy	guys
attorney	attorneys	**BUT:** soliloquy	soliloquies
boy	boys	colloquy	colloquies

NOTE: The regular plural of *money* is *moneys.* The plural form *monies* does not follow the rule, but it often appears in legal documents nonetheless.

Plurals and Possessives

6

¶606

Nouns Ending in *O*

606 Singular nouns ending in *o* preceded by a *vowel* form their plurals by adding *s* to the singular.

stereo	stereos		shampoo	shampoos
ratio	ratios		boo	boos
portfolio	portfolios		tattoo	tattoos
scenario	scenarios		duo	duos

607 Singular nouns ending in *o* preceded by a *consonant* form their plurals in different ways.

a. Some nouns in this category simply add *s*.

ego	egos		memo	memos
photo	photos		placebo	placebos
macro	macros		two	twos
typo	typos		weirdo	weirdos
logo	logos		hairdo	hairdos

b. Some add *es*.

potato	potatoes		hero	heroes
tomato	tomatoes		embargo	embargoes
echo	echoes		fiasco	fiascoes

c. Some have two plural forms. (The preferred form is given first.)

cargo	cargoes, cargos		zero	zeros, zeroes
no	nos, noes		tuxedo	tuxedos, tuxedoes
motto	mottoes, mottos		innuendo	innuendos, innuendoes
proviso	provisos, provisoes		ghetto	ghettos, ghettoes

d. Singular musical terms ending in *o* form their plurals by adding *s*.

soprano	sopranos		piano	pianos
alto	altos		cello	cellos
basso	bassos		banjo	banjos

➢ *For foreign nouns ending in o, see ¶614.*

Nouns Ending in *F, FE,* or *FF*

608 **a.** Most singular nouns that end in *f, fe,* or *ff* form their plurals by adding *s* to the singular form.

belief	beliefs		safe	safes
proof	proofs		tariff	tariffs

b. Some commonly used nouns in this category form their plurals by changing the *f* or *fe* to *ve* and adding *s*.

half	halves		self	selves
wife	wives		shelf	shelves
leaf	leaves		knife	knives
thief	thieves		life	lives

c. A few of these nouns have two plural forms. (The preferred form is given first.)

scarf	scarves, scarfs		dwarf	dwarfs, dwarves

Plurals and Possessives

6

Nouns With Irregular Plurals

609 The plurals of some nouns are formed by a change of letters within.

wom*a*n	wom*e*n	f*oo*t	f*ee*t
m*ou*se	m*i*ce*	g*oo*se	g*ee*se

610 A few plurals end in *en* or *ren.*

ox	oxen	brother	brethren (*an alternative*
child	children		*plural to* brothers)

Compound Nouns

611 When a compound noun is a *solid* word, pluralize the final element in the compound as if it stood alone.

print*out*	print*outs*	birth*day*	birth*days*
flash*back*	flash*backs*	photo*copy*	photo*copies*
wine*glass*	wine*glasses*	grand*child*	grand*children*
hat*box*	hat*boxes*	foot*hold*	foot*holds*
eye*lash*	eye*lashes*	fore*foot*	fore*feet*
straw*berry*	straw*berries*	tooth*brush*	tooth*brushes*
book*shelf*	book*shelves*	mouse*trap*	mouse*traps*
stand*by*	stand*bys* (**NOT:** standbies)	work*man*	work*men*
BUT: *passer*by	*passers*by	**BUT:** talis*man*	talis*mans* (**NOT:** talismen)

612 **a.** The plurals of *hyphenated* or *spaced* compounds are formed by pluralizing the chief element of the compound.

father-in-law	*fathers*-in-law	couch *potato*	couch *potatoes*
senator-elect	*senators*-elect	*rule* of thumb	*rules* of thumb
looker-on	*lookers*-on	*letter* of credit	*letters* of credit
runner-up	*runners*-up	*account* payable	*accounts* payable
grant-in-aid	*grants*-in-aid	*attorney* at law	*attorneys* at law
bill of lading	*bills* of lading	deputy *chief* of staff	deputy *chiefs* of staff
editor in chief	*editors* in chief	lieutenant *general*	lieutenant *generals*
BUT: time-*out*	time-*outs*	**BUT:** chaise longue†	chaise *longues*

➢ *For the plurals of foreign compound words, see ¶614.*

b. When a hyphenated compound does not contain a noun as one of its elements, simply pluralize the final element.

go-*between*	go-*betweens*	come-*on*	come-*ons*
get-*together*	get-*togethers*	show-*off*	show-*offs*
hang-*up*	hang-*ups*	run-*through*	run-*throughs*
hand-me-*down*	hand-me-*downs*	two-by-*four*	two-by-*fours*
drive-*in*	drive-*ins*	no-*no*	no-*nos*
fade-*out*	fade-*outs*	has-*been*	has-*beens*

Continued on page 160

*Mice may refer to computer devices as well as to rodents. Some authorities prefer *mouse devices* when writing about computers.

†Note that the correct spelling of this word is *longue* (not *lounge*).

¶613

have-*not*	have-*nots* (see ¶625a)	do-it-*yourselfer*	do-it-*yourselfers*
know-it-*all*	know-it-*alls*	shoot-'em-*up*	shoot-'em-*ups*
so-and-*so*	so-and-*sos*	no-see-*um*	no-see-*ums*

c. Some of these compounds have two recognized plural forms. (The first plural form shown below is preferred because it adds the plural sign to the chief element of the compound.)

court-martial	*courts*-martial, court-*martials*
notary public	*notaries* public, notary *publics*
attorney general	*attorneys* general, attorney *generals*

d. When the first element of a compound is a *possessive,* simply pluralize the final element.

collector's item	collector's items
traveler's check	traveler's checks
rabbit's foot	rabbit's feet
proofreaders' mark	proofreaders' marks
seller's market	seller's markets
farmers' market	farmers' markets
women's college	women's colleges
witches' brew	witches' brews
finder's fee	finder's fees
visitor's permit	visitor's permits

NOTE: Do not convert a singular possessive form into a plural unless the context clearly requires it. (See also ¶652.)

The number of *driver's licenses* issued last year was 15 percent ahead of the number issued the year before.

BUT: As a result of the highway checkpoints set up by the state police, more than 200 *drivers' licenses* have been revoked in the past four weeks.

613 The plurals of compounds ending in *ful* are formed by adding *s.*

armful	armfuls	handful	handfuls
cupful	cupfuls	teaspoonful	teaspoonfuls
basketful	basketfuls	pocketful	pocketfuls

Compare the difference in meaning in these phrases:

six *cupfuls* of sugar (a quantity of sugar that would fill one cup six times)

six cups *full* of sugar (six separate cups, each filled with sugar)

Foreign Nouns

614 Many nouns of foreign origin retain their foreign plurals, others have been given English plurals, and still others have two plurals—an English and a foreign one. When two plural forms exist, one may be preferred to the other or there may be differences in meaning that govern the use of each. Consult your dictionary to be sure of the plural forms and the meanings attached to them.

➤ *For agreement of foreign-plural subjects with verbs, see ¶1018.*

¶614

WORDS ENDING IN *US*

Singular	English Plural	Foreign Plural
alumnus (m.)		alumni (see note below)
apparatus	apparatuses*	apparatus
cactus	cactuses	cacti*
census	censuses	
corpus		corpora
focus	focuses*	foci†
fungus	funguses	fungi*
genus		genera
locus		loci
nucleus	nucleuses	nuclei*
octopus	octopuses*	octopi
opus	opuses	opera*
prospectus	prospectuses	
radius	radiuses	radii*
status	statuses	
stimulus		stimuli
stylus	styluses	styli*
syllabus	syllabuses	syllabi*
terminus	terminuses	termini*
thesaurus	thesauruses	thesauri*

NOTE: The term *alumni* (the plural of *alumnus*) may be used to refer either to a group of male graduates or to a mixed group of male and female graduates. The term *alumnae* (the plural form of *alumna*, shown below) is used to refer only to a group of female graduates.

WORDS ENDING IN *A*

Singular	English Plural	Foreign Plural
agenda	agendas	
alga	algas	algae*
alumna (f.)		alumnae (see note above)
antenna	antennas (of radios)	antennae (of insects)
dogma	dogmas*	dogmata
formula	formulas*	formulae
lacuna	lacunas	lacunae*
larva	larvas	larvae*
minutia		minutiae
schema	schemas*	schemata†
stigma	stigmas	stigmata*
vertebra	vertebras	vertebrae*

Continued on page 162

---

*Preferred form.

†Merriam-Webster shows this form first.

Plurals and Possessives

6

¶614

WORDS ENDING IN *UM*

Singular	English Plural	Foreign Plural
addendum		addenda
auditorium	auditoriums*	auditoria
bacterium		bacteria
colloquium	colloquiums*	colloquia
consortium	consortiums*	consortia†
cranium	craniums*	crania
curriculum	curriculums*	curricula†
datum	datums	data* (see ¶1018)
erratum		errata
forum	forums*	fora
gymnasium	gymnasiums*	gymnasia
maximum	maximums*	maxima†
medium	mediums (spiritualists)	media (for advertising and communication)
memorandum	memorandums*	memoranda
millennium	millenniums*	millennia†
minimum	minimums*	minima†
momentum	momentums*	momenta†
optimum	optimums*	optima†
podium	podiums*	podia
referendum	referendums*	referenda†
sanitarium	sanitariums*	sanitaria
stadium	stadiums*	stadia†
stratum		strata
symposium	symposiums*	symposia†
ultimatum	ultimatums*	ultimata

WORDS ENDING IN *O*

Singular	English Plural	Foreign Plural
concerto	concertos	concerti*
graffito		graffiti
libretto	librettos*	libretti
paparazzo		paparazzi
tempo	tempos	tempi (in music)
virtuoso	virtuosos*	virtuosi

WORDS ENDING IN *ON*

Singular	English Plural	Foreign Plural
automaton	automatons*	automata
criterion	criterions	criteria*
phenomenon	phenomenons	phenomena*

*Preferred form.

†Merriam-Webster shows this form first.

¶**614**

WORDS ENDING IN *X*

Singular	English Plural	Foreign Plural
apex	apexes*	apices
appendix	appendixes*	appendices
codex		codices
crux	cruxes*	cruces
helix	helixes	helices*
index	indexes (of books)	indices (math symbols)
larynx	larynxes	larynges*
matrix	matrixes	matrices*
vertex	vertexes	vertices*
vortex	vortexes	vortices*

WORDS ENDING IN *IS*

Singular	English Plural	Foreign Plural
analysis		analyses
axis		axes
basis		bases
chassis		chassis
crisis		crises
diagnosis		diagnoses
ellipsis		ellipses
emphasis		emphases
hypothesis		hypotheses
oasis		oases
parenthesis		parentheses
prognosis		prognoses
synopsis		synopses
synthesis		syntheses
thesis		theses

WORDS ENDING IN *EU* OR *EAU*

Singular	English Plural	Foreign Plural
adieu	adieus*	adieux
beau	beaus	beaux*
bureau	bureaus*	bureaux
milieu	milieus*	milieux
plateau	plateaus*	plateaux
tableau	tableaus	tableaux*
trousseau	trousseaus	trousseaux*

NOTE: The *x* ending for the preceding foreign plurals is pronounced like *z*.

Continued on page 164

*Preferred form.

¶615

COMPOUND WORDS

Singular	English Plural	Foreign Plural
chaise longue	chaise longues*	chaises longues
coup d'état		coups d'état
éminence grise		éminences grises
fait accompli		faits accomplis
hors d'oeuvre	hors d'oeuvres*	hors d'oeuvre
idiot savant	idiot savants	idiots savants*
maître d'hôtel		maîtres d'hôtel
maître d'	maître d's	
nouveau riche		nouveaux riches
pas de deux		pas de deux

Proper Names

615 **a.** Most *surnames* are pluralized by the addition of *s*.

Mr. and Mrs. Brinton	the Brintons
Mr. and Mrs. Romano	the Romanos
Mr. and Mrs. Cobb	the Cobbs
Mr. and Mrs. Gray	the Grays

b. When a surname ends in *s, x, ch, sh,* or *z,* add *es* to form the plural.

Mr. and Mrs. Banks	the Bankses
Mr. and Mrs. Van Ness	the Van Nesses
Mr. and Mrs. Maddox	the Maddoxes
Mr. and Mrs. March	the Marches
Mr. and Mrs. Welsh	the Welshes
Mr. and Mrs. Katz	the Katzes
Mr. and Mrs. Jones	the Joneses
Mr. and Mrs. James	the Jameses
Mr. and Mrs. Barnes	the Barneses

NOTE: Omit the *es* ending if it makes the plural surname awkward to pronounce.

the Hodges (**NOT:** Hodgeses)   the Hastings (**NOT:** Hastingses)

c. Never change the original spelling of a surname when forming the plural. Simply add *s* or *es,* according to ¶615a and b.

Mr. and Mrs. McCarthy	the McCarthys (**NOT:** McCarthies)
Mr. and Mrs. Wolf	the Wolfs (**NOT:** Wolves)
Mr. and Mrs. Martino	the Martinos (**NOT:** Martinoes)
Mr. and Mrs. Goodman	the Goodmans (**NOT:** Goodmen)
Mr. and Mrs. Lightfoot	the Lightfoots (**NOT:** Lightfeet)
Mr. and Mrs. Fairchild	the Fairchilds (**NOT:** Fairchildren)

d. When a surname is followed by *Jr., Sr.,* or a number like *2d* or *II,* the plural can be formed two ways.

ORDINARY USAGE: the Roy Van Allen *Jrs.*   the Ellsworth Hadley *3ds*
FORMAL USAGE: the Roy Van *Allens* Jr.   the Ellsworth *Hadleys* 3d

---

*Preferred form.

Plurals and Possessives

6

616   To form the plurals of *first names,* add *s* or *es* but do not change the original spellings.

Marie	Maries	Douglas	Douglases	Timothy	Timothys
Ralph	Ralphs	Dolores	Doloreses	Beatrix	Beatrixes
Waldo	Waldos	Gladys	Gladyses	Fritz	Fritzes

617   To form the plural of other proper names, add *s* or *es* but do not change the original spelling.

three Texans	two Christmases ago
the Norwegians	checked our Rolodexes
the Dakotas	bought six Macintoshes
the Emmys and the Grammys	Marches (*es* after *ch* sound)
the two Kansas Citys (**NOT:** Cities)	Czechs (*s* after *k* sound)

EXCEPTIONS:

the Alleghenies (for Allegheny Mountains)
the Rockies (for Rocky Mountains)

Personal Titles

618   **a.** The plural of *Mr.* is *Messrs.* (not *Mrs.*); the plural of *Ms.* is *Mses.* or *Mss.;* the plural of *Mrs.* or *Mme.* is *Mmes.* (for *Mesdames*); the plural of *Miss* is *Misses* (with no period). However, the use of plural titles normally occurs only in formal situations. In ordinary usage, simply retain the singular form and repeat it with each name.

Formal Usage	**Ordinary Usage**
Messrs. Rae and Tate	Mr. Rae and Mr. Tate
Mmes. (**OR** Mesdames) Byrd and Clyde	Mrs. Byrd and Mrs. Clyde
Misses Russo and Dupree	Miss Russo and Miss Dupree
Mses. (**OR** Mss.) Lai and Cohen	Ms. Lai and Ms. Cohen

    b. When personal titles apply to two or more people with the same surname, the plural may be formed in two ways: (1) pluralize only the title (formal usage); (2) pluralize only the surname (ordinary usage).

Formal Usage	**Ordinary Usage**
the Messrs. Steele	the Mr. Steeles
the Mmes. (**OR** Mesdames) Bergeret	the Mrs. Bergerets
the Misses Conroy	the Miss Conroys
the Mses. (**OR** Mss.) Purdy	the Ms. Purdys

Abbreviations, Letters, Numbers, Words, and Symbols

619   Form the plurals of most abbreviations by adding *s* to the singular.

| apt. | apts. | vol. | vols. | No. | Nos. | Dr. | Drs. |
| bldg. | bldgs. | par. | pars. | Co. | Cos. | 401(k) | 401(k)s |

620   **a.** The abbreviations of many customary units of weight and measure, however, are the same in both the singular and the plural. (See also ¶535a.)

oz (ounce **OR** ounces)	ft (foot **OR** feet)
deg (degree **OR** degrees)	in (inch **OR** inches)
bbl (barrel **OR** barrels)	mi (mile **OR** miles)

Continued on page 166

¶621

NOTE: For a number of these abbreviations, two plural forms have been widely used: for example, *lb* or *lbs* (meaning "pounds"), *yd* or *yds* (meaning "yards"), *qt* or *qts* (meaning "quarts"). However, the trend is toward using *lb, yd,* and *qt* to signify the plural.

b. The abbreviations of metric units of weight and measure are the same in both the singular and the plural. (See also ¶¶537–538.)

km (kilometer **OR** kilometers)	cg (centigram **OR** centigrams)
mL (milliliter **OR** milliliters)	dam (dekameter **OR** dekameters)

➤ *For the omission of periods with abbreviations of measurements, see ¶¶535a, 538a.*

621 **a.** The plurals of a few single-letter abbreviations (such as *p.* for *page* and *f.* for *the following page*) consist of the same letter doubled.

p. 64 (page 64)	c. (copy)
pp. 64–72 (pages 64 through 72)	cc. (copies)
pp. 9 f. (page 9 and the following page)	n. 3 (note 3)
pp. 9 ff. (page 9 and the following pages)	nn. 3–4 (notes 3 and 4)
l. 23 (line 23)	
ll. 23–24 (lines 23 through 24)	

b. Plurals of certain symbols consist of the same symbol doubled.

¶ paragraph ¶¶ paragraphs	§ section §§ sections

622 **a.** Capital letters and abbreviations ending with capital letters are pluralized by adding *s* alone.

three Rs	HMOs	BBSs	R.N.s
four Cs	POs	IQs	M.D.s
five VIPs	S&Ls	PTAs	Ph.D.s

b. Some authorities still sanction the use of an apostrophe before the *s* (for example, *four C's, PTA's*). However, the apostrophe is functionally unnecessary except where confusion might otherwise result.

three A's	too many I's	two U's

BUT: His report card showed three As, two Bs, and one C. (When the context is clear, no apostrophes are necessary.)

623 For the sake of clarity, uncapitalized letters and uncapitalized abbreviations are pluralized by adding an apostrophe plus *s*. (See ¶285b.)

dotting the *i*'s	*p*'s and *q*'s	four c.o.d.'s	wearing pj's

NOTE: When initials are spelled out, the plurals are formed normally.

emcees	deejays	okays	Jaycees

624 **a.** Numbers expressed in figures are pluralized by the addition of *s* alone.

in the 1990s	in the '90s (decade)	in the 90s (temperature)	sort the W?s

b. Numbers expressed in words are pluralized by the addition of *s* or *es*.

ones	twos	threes	sixes	twenties	twenty-fives

625 **a.** When words taken from other parts of speech are used as nouns, they are usually pluralized by the addition of *s* or *es*.

ifs, ands, or buts	ins and outs	pros and cons	whereabouts
dos and don'ts	ups and downs	the haves and	whys and
yeses and nos	yeas and nays	the havenots	wherefores

b. If the pluralized form is unfamiliar or is likely to be misread, use an apostrophe plus *s* to form the plural.

> which's and that's   or's and nor's

c. If the singular form already contains an apostrophe, simply add *s* to form the plural.

> ain'ts   mustn'ts   don'ts   ma'ams

➤ *For the use of italics or underlining with words referred to as words, see ¶¶285, 290.*

Plural Endings in Parentheses

626 When referring to an item that could be either singular or plural, enclose the plural ending in parentheses.

> Please send the appropriate *form(s)* to the appropriate state *agency(ies)*.

Forming Possessives

Possession Versus Description

627 **a.** A noun ending in the sound of *s* is usually in the possessive form if it is followed immediately by another noun. In the following examples note that possessive forms may express a number of different relationships, only one of which refers literally to possession or ownership.

> my boss's approval (meaning the approval *of my boss*)
> Belknap's farm (meaning the farm *possessed* or *owned by Belknap*)
> IBM's product line (meaning the product line *made* or *sold by IBM*)
> Faulkner's novels (meaning the novels *written by Faulkner*)
> Matisse's paintings (meaning the paintings *created by Matisse*)
> Frank's nickname (meaning the nickname *given to* or *used by Frank*)
> a two weeks' vacation (meaning a vacation *for* or *lasting two weeks*)

NOTE: An apostrophe alone or an apostrophe plus *s* is the sign of the possessive. (See ¶¶630–640.)

b. To be sure that the possessive form should be used, try substituting an *of* phrase or making a similar substitution as in the examples above. If the substitution works, the possessive form is correct.

628 Do not mistake a descriptive form ending in *s* for a possessive form.

> sales effort (*sales* describes the kind of effort)
> savings account (*savings* describes the kind of account)
> news release (*news* describes the type of press release)
> earnings record (*earnings* describes the type of record)

NOTE: Some cases can be difficult to distinguish. Is it *the girls basketball team* or *the girls' basketball team?* Try substituting an irregular plural like *women*. You wouldn't say *the women basketball team;* you would say *the women's basketball team*. By analogy, *the girls' basketball team* is correct.

➤ *For descriptive and possessive forms in organizational names, see ¶640.*

¶629

629 In a number of cases only a slight difference in wording distinguishes a descriptive phrase from a possessive phrase.

Descriptive	**Possessive**
a six-month leave of absence	a six months' leave of absence
the California climate	California's climate
the Burgess account	Burgess's account
the Crosby children	the Crosbys' children
	OR: Mr. and Mrs. Crosby's children

Singular Nouns

630 **a.** To form the possessive of a singular noun *not* ending in an *s* sound, add an apostrophe plus *s* to the noun.

my lawyer's advice	Mr. and Mrs. Goodwin's party
a child's game	Alzheimer's disease
Gloria's career	Down's syndrome

b. When a singular noun ends in a silent *s,* add an apostrophe plus *s.*

Illinois's highways	the corps's leadership
Arkansas's mountains	Des Moines's mayor

631 To form the possessive of a singular noun that ends in an *s* sound, be guided by the way you pronounce the word.

a. If a new syllable is formed in the pronunciation of the possessive, add an apostrophe plus *s.*

your boss's approval	Mr. and Mrs. Morris's plane tickets
the witness's reply	Phoenix's suburbs
Congress's intention	Ms. Lopez's application
Dallas's business district	Mr. Marsh's office
St. Louis's airport	my coach's training regimen

b. If the addition of an extra syllable would make a word ending in an *s* hard to pronounce, add the apostrophe only.

Mrs. Phillips' request	Jesus' parables
Mr. Hastings' proposal	Moses' flight from Egypt
the Burroughs' condominium	for goodness' sake (see ¶646)
Los Angeles' freeways	Achilles' heel
New Orleans' restaurants	**BUT:** Achilles tendon

NOTE: Individual differences in pronunciation will affect the way some of these possessives are written. For example, if you pronounce the possessive form of *Perkins* as two syllables, you will write *Mr. Perkins' kindness;* if you pronounce the possessive of *Perkins* as three syllables, you will write *Mr. Perkins's kindness.* The important thing is to listen to your own pronunciation. When you hear yourself pronounce the possessive of *boss* as two syllables *(boss's)* and the possessive of *witness* as three *(witness's),* you will not be tempted to write *your boss' approval* or *the witness' reply.* Naturally, tradition should take precedence over your ear. For example, an ambassador to Great Britain is appointed to the *Court of St. James's* (not, as you might expect, *Court of St. James*).

Plurals and Possessives

6

c. When forming the possessive of any noun ending in *s* (for example, *Mr. Hodges*), always place the apostrophe at the end of the original word, never within it.

> Mr. Hodges' message (**NOT:** Mr. Hodge's message)

Plural Nouns

632 **a.** For a *regular* plural noun (one that ends in *s* or *es*), add only an apostrophe to form the plural possessive. (See ¶¶639–640 for the use of the apostrophe in organizational names.)

investors' objectives	the agencies' conflicting rules
the witnesses' contradictions	the Gaineses' legal residence
the United States' policy	an old boys' network
attorneys' fees	**BUT:** a teachers college (see ¶652)

b. Since the singular and plural possessives for the same word usually sound exactly alike, pay particularly close attention to the meaning in order to determine whether the noun in question is singular or plural.

> An *investor's* objectives should largely define investment strategy.
>
> **BUT:** *Investors'* objectives are often not clearly defined.
>
> We will need a ride to Mr. and Mrs. *Gaines's* party.
>
> **BUT:** We will need a ride to the *Gaineses'* party.
>
> I especially want to hear the last *witness's* testimony.
>
> **BUT:** I especially want to hear the last two *witnesses'* testimony.
>
> *Season's* greetings! (Referring to the holidays that occur in only one season—winter.)

NOTE: In some cases only a dictionary can help you determine whether the possessive form should be singular or plural. For example, a plural possessive is used in *Legionnaires' disease,* but a singular possessive is used in *Hodgkin's disease* since the discoverer's name was Dr. Hodgkin (and not, as you might have expected, the more common name Hodgkins). Unlike the term *deacon's bench* (which uses a singular possessive), the term *Parsons table* involves no possessive form at all.

633 For an *irregular* plural noun (one that does not end in *s*), add an apostrophe plus *s* to form the plural possessive.

women's blouses	men's shirts	the alumni's reunion
children's toys	**BUT:** menswear	the alumnae's contribution
	(originally, men's wear)	

IMPORTANT NOTE: To avoid mistakes in forming the possessive of plural nouns, form the plural first; then apply the rule in ¶632 or 633, whichever fits.

Singular	Plural	Plural Possessive
boy	boys (regular)	boys'
boss	bosses (regular)	bosses'
hero	heroes (regular)	heroes'
Mr. and Mrs. Fox	the Foxes (regular)	the Foxes'
child	children (irregular)	children's
alumnus	alumni (irregular)	alumni's
alumna	alumnae (irregular)	alumnae's

¶634

Compound Nouns

634 To form the *singular* possessive of a compound noun (whether solid, spaced, or hyphenated), add an apostrophe plus *s* to the last element of the compound.

my son-in-law's job prospects	my stockbroker's advice
the secretary-treasurer's report	the notary public's seal
the owner-manager's policies	an eyewitness's account
a do-it-yourselfer's obsession	the attorney general's decision

635 To form the *plural* possessive of a compound noun, first form the plural.

a. If the plural form ends in *s,* add only an apostrophe.

Singular	Plural	Plural Possessive
stockholder	stockholders	stockholders'
vice president	vice presidents	vice presidents'
wheeler-dealer	wheeler-dealers	wheeler-dealers'
salesclerk	salesclerks	salesclerks'

b. If the plural form does not end in *s,* add an apostrophe plus *s.*

Singular	Plural	Plural Possessive
editor in chief	editors in chief	editors in chief's
brother-in-law	brothers-in-law	brothers-in-law's

NOTE: To avoid the awkwardness of a plural possessive such as *editors in chief's* or *brothers-in-law's,* rephrase the sentence.

AWKWARD: We may have to invite my three *sisters-in-law's* parents too.

BETTER: We may have to invite the parents of my three *sisters-in-law* too.

AWKWARD: Mr. Ahmed's statement agrees with both *attorneys general's* views.

BETTER: Mr. Ahmed's statement agrees with the views of both *attorneys general.*

Pronouns

636 The possessive forms of *personal pronouns* and of the relative pronoun *who* do not require the apostrophe. These pronouns have their own possessive forms.

I: my, mine	he: his	we: our, ours
you: your, yours	she: her, hers	they: their, theirs
	it: its	who: whose

My copy of the letter arrived last week, so she should have received *hers* by now. (**NOT:** her's.)

Each unit comes carefully packed in *its* own carton. (**NOT:** it's.)

The two products look so much alike that it's [it is] hard to tell *ours* from *theirs.* (**NOT:** our's from their's.)

CAUTION: Do not confuse personal possessive pronouns with similarly spelled contractions. (See ¶1056e for examples.)

637 Some *indefinite pronouns* have regular possessive forms.

one's choice	the other's claim	anybody's guess
anyone else's job	the others' claim	no one's responsibility
one another's help	each other's claim	someone's chance

For those indefinite pronouns that do not have possessive forms, use an *of* phrase.

Although the children in this group seem very much alike, the needs *of each* are different. (**NOT:** each's needs.)

¶640

Abbreviations

638 To form the singular possessive of an abbreviation, add an apostrophe plus *s*. To form the plural possessive, add an *s* plus an apostrophe to the singular form. (See also ¶639.)

Singular	**Plural**
Mr. C.'s opinion	the M.D.s' diagnoses
PBS's programming	the Ph.D.s' dissertations
this HMO's doctors	the CPAs' meeting

Personal, Organizational, and Product Names

639 To form the possessive of a personal or an organizational name that ends with an abbreviation, a number, a prepositional phrase, or a mark of punctuation, add an apostrophe plus *s* at the end of the complete name.

the Winger Co.'s new plant	Hyde & Sikh Inc.'s dividends
the Knights of Columbus's drive	David Weild II's retirement
United Bank of Arizona's loan rates	Walter Frick Jr.'s campaign
Yahoo!'s Web site	**BUT:** Carl's Jr. restaurants

NOTE: If *no* extra *s* sound is created when you pronounce the possessive form, add only an apostrophe.

the Gerald Curry Jrs.' yacht

➤ *For the treatment of possessive forms when terms like* Jr. *and* Inc. *are set off by commas, see ¶¶156 and 159.*

640 The names of many organizations and products contain words that could be considered either possessive or descriptive terms.

a. As a rule, use an apostrophe if the term is a singular possessive noun or an irregular plural noun.

McCall's	*Harper's Bazaar*	*Women's Wear Daily*	*Barron's*
McDonald's	Levi's jeans	Macy's	Reese's Pieces

Children's Hospital (normal style)	St. Patrick's Cathedral
BUT: Childrens Hospital (in Los Angeles)	America's Cup (yachting)
St. Elizabeths Hospital (in D.C.)	**BUT:** Americas Cup (golf)

b. As a rule, do not use an apostrophe if the term is a regular plural.

Chemical Workers Union	American Bankers Association
Investors Trust Company	Government Employees Insurance Company
Underwriters Laboratories Inc.	U.S. Department of Veterans Affairs
Consumers Union	**BUT:** Reserve Officers' Training Corps

c. In all cases follow the organization's preference when known.

International Ladies' Garment Workers' Union	Mrs. Paul's frozen foods
Standard's & Poor's	Mrs. Fields cookies
Actors' Equity	Little Charlies pizza
Lloyd's of London	Thomas' English muffins
Lay's potato chips	Taster's Choice
Folgers coffee	Shoppers Choice
Diners Club membership	M&M's candy
Lands' End catalogs	Cliffs Notes

Continued on page 172

¶641

d. In titles of books, periodicals, and similar works, always follow the style as given.

> *Gulliver's Travels*   *Reader's Digest*
> **BUT:** *Finnegans Wake*   **BUT:** *Consumers Digest*

e. When adding the sign of the possessive to a phrase that must be italicized or underlined, do not italicize or underline the possessive ending. (See also ¶290d.)

> *The Wind in the Willows'* author   <u>Gone With the Wind</u>'s main characters

Nouns in Apposition

641 Sometimes a noun that normally would be in the possessive is followed by an *appositive,* a closely linked explanatory word or phrase. In such cases add the sign of the possessive to the appositive.

> Rockport, *Massachusetts'* beauty attracts many painters. (Note that the comma that normally follows an appositive is omitted after a possessive ending.)
>
> You will faint when you see Paul *the plumber's* bill. (If the noun and the appositive are closely linked as a unit, even the first comma is omitted. See also ¶150.)

NOTE: To avoid an awkward construction, use an *of* phrase instead.

> You will need to get the signature *of Mr. Bartel,* the executor.
>
> (**BETTER THAN:** You will need to get Mr. Bartel, *the executor's* signature.)

Separate and Joint Possession

642 a. To indicate separate possession, add the sign of the possessive to the name of each individual.

> the buyer's and the seller's signatures
> the Joneses' and the Browns' houses

NOTE: Repeating *the* with each name emphasizes that ownership is separate.

b. If one or both of the individuals' names are replaced by a possessive pronoun, watch out for awkwardness and reword if necessary.

> **AWKWARD:** my and the seller's signatures
> **BETTER:** the seller's and my signatures
> **OR:** the seller's signature and mine
>
> **AWKWARD:** their and our houses
> **BETTER:** their house and ours
>
> **AWKWARD:** your and your husband's passports
> **BETTER:** the passports for you and your husband

643 a. To indicate joint (or common) ownership, add the sign of the possessive to the *final* name alone.

> the Barneses and the Terrys' property line

NOTE: In organizational names, follow the company's preference.

> Ben & Jerry's ice cream
> Kroch's & Brentano's bookstores

b. If one of the owners is identified by a pronoun, make each name and pronoun possessive.

> Karen's and my ski lodge
> **BUT:** Karen and Brian's ski lodge

Possessives Standing Alone

644 Sometimes the noun that the possessive modifies is not expressed but merely understood.

Fred is getting a *master's* [degree] in international economics.
Ask for it at your *grocer's* [store].
Wear your oldest shirt and *Levi's* [jeans]. (The trademark *Levi's* is a singular possessive form.)

We have been invited to dinner at the *Furnesses'* [house].

BUT: We always enjoy an evening with the *Furnesses.* (The people themselves are referred to; hence no possessive.)

NOTE: The possessive form must be used in the following construction in order to keep the comparison parallel.

This year's product line is pulling better than *last year's* [product line].

NOT: This year's product line is pulling better than *last year*. (Incorrectly compares *product line* with *last year*.)

Inanimate Possessives

645 As a rule, nouns referring to inanimate things should not be in the possessive. Use an *of* phrase instead.

the bottom of the barrel (**NOT:** the barrel's bottom)
the wording of the agreement (**NOT:** the agreement's wording)
the lower level of the terminal (**NOT:** the terminal's lower level)

646 In many common expressions that refer to time and measurements, however, and in phrases implying personification, the possessive form has come to be accepted usage. (See also ¶817a.)

one day's notice	a dollar's worth	a stone's throw
a nine days' wonder	several dollars' worth	for heaven's sake
an hour's work	two cents' worth	for conscience' sake
two years' progress	at arm's length	(see ¶631b)
the company's assets	New Year's resolutions	the earth's atmosphere
the computer's memory	this morning's news	in today's world

NOTE: Be sure to distinguish possessive expressions like those above from similar wording where no possessive relation is involved.

two weeks' salary   **BUT:** two weeks ago, two weeks later, two weeks overdue

I bought *five dollars' worth* of chocolate truffles.

BUT: I found *five dollars lying* on the sidewalk.

Possessives Preceding Verbal Nouns

647 **a.** When a noun or a pronoun modifies a *gerund* (the *ing* form of a verb used as a noun), the noun or pronoun should be in the possessive.

What was the point of *our* asking any further questions? (**NOT:** of us asking.)

NOTE: The use of a possessive form before a gerund can produce a sentence that is grammatically correct but is awkward nonetheless. In such cases reword the sentence.

AWKWARD: He wanted to be reassured about his *children's* being given a ride home.

BETTER: He wanted to be reassured that his children would be given a ride home.

Continued on page 174

¶648

b. Not every noun or pronoun preceding the *ing* form of a verb should be in the possessive form. Compare the following pairs of examples:

> I heard *you* singing at the party. (Here the emphasis is on *you,* the object of *heard; singing* is a participle that modifies *you.*)
>
> I liked *your* singing at the party. (Here the emphasis is on *singing,* a gerund that is the object of *liked;* the pronoun *your* is in the possessive form because it modifies *singing.*)
>
> Our success in this venture depends on *Allen* acting as the coordinator. (This suggests that the success depends on Allen himself rather than on the role he is playing. Even if Allen's role should change, success seems likely as long as he is associated with the project in some way.)
>
> Our success in this venture depends on *Allen's* acting as the coordinator. (This puts the emphasis squarely on Allen's acting in a certain role. If he ceases to function as the coordinator, the venture may not succeed.)

Possessives in *Of* Phrases

648 **a.** The object of the preposition *of* should not ordinarily be in the possessive form, since the *of* phrase as a whole expresses possession. However, possessives are used in a few idiomatic expressions.

> Tony and Fiona are good friends of *ours* as well as our *children's.*
> Did you know that Polly and Fred are neighbors of the *Joneses'?*
> Bobby Busoni is a business associate of *Gordon's.*

b. Note the difference in meaning in the following phrases:

> a statue of Rodin (a statue showing the likeness of the sculptor Rodin)
> a statue of Rodin's (a statue created by Rodin)
>
> a controversial view of the President (a view held by someone else)
> a controversial view of the President's (a view held by the President)

c. Avoid adding the sign of the possessive to an *of* phrase.

> **AWKWARD:** *A friend of mine's house* burned down last night.
> **BETTER:** The *house of a friend of mine* burned down last night.
>
> **AWKWARD:** *One of my friends' son* has been named a Rhodes scholar. (**NOT:** One of my friend's son.)
> **BETTER:** The *son of one of my friends* has been named a Rhodes scholar.
>
> **AWKWARD:** I just found out that *the director of our training program's husband* is the chief information officer of your company.
> **BETTER:** I just found out that *the husband of the director of our training program* is the chief information officer of your company.

NOTE: Attaching the sign of the possessive to an *of* phrase can sometimes create humorous confusion in addition to awkwardness.

> **CONFUSING:** You must negotiate the purchase price with the owner of the horse's wife.
> **CLEAR:** You must negotiate the purchase price of the horse with the owner's wife.

Possessives Modifying Possessives

649 Avoid attaching a possessive form to another possessive. Change the wording if possible.

> **AWKWARD:** I have not yet seen the *utility company's lawyer's* petition.
> **BETTER:** I have not yet seen the petition of the *utility company's lawyer.*

¶**652**

Possessives in Holidays

650 Possessives in names of holidays are usually singular.

New Year's Eve	Valentine's Day	**BUT:** Presidents' Day
Lincoln's Birthday	Saint Patrick's Day	April Fools' Day
Mother's Day	Secretary's Day*	All Saints' Day

NOTE: Some holiday names contain a plural form rather than a plural possessive; for example: *Armed Forces Day, Veterans Day, United Nations Day.*

Possessives in Place Names

651 Place names that contain a possessive form typically do not use an apostrophe.

Bonners Ferry, Idaho	Grants Pass, Oregon	Pikes Peak, Colorado
Colts Neck, New Jersey	Howards Grove, Wisconsin	St. Marys, Georgia
Devils Lake, North Dakota	Kings Point, New York	Toms River, New Jersey
BUT: Devil's Island	Loves Park, Illinois	Travelers Rest, South Carolina
Farmers Branch, Texas	**BUT:** Martha's Vineyard	No Mans Land, Massachusetts

Miscellaneous Expressions

652 A number of common expressions contain possessive forms.

athlete's foot	proofreaders' mark
traveler's check	lovers' lane
collector's item	workers' compensation (see ¶809a)
visitor's permit	witches' brew
seller's market	women's room
BUT: farmers' market	**BUT:** woman's rights
finder's fee	states' rights
dog's life	**BUT:** state's evidence
cat's-paw	citizen's arrest
rabbit's foot	**BUT:** citizens band
bull's-eye	teacher's pet
lion's share	**BUT:** teachers college

NOTE: Although a number of states now issue *drivers licenses* (without an apostrophe), the preferred form remains *driver's licenses.*

➤ *For the plural forms of expressions like these, see ¶612d.*

*The International Association of Administrative Professionals, the association that awards the professional designation CPS (certified professional secretary) prefers a different style: *Professional Secretaries Day* (with no apostrophe).

SECTION 7

Spelling

Spelling Guides (¶¶701–718)

Words That Sound Alike or Look Alike (¶719)

Troublesome Words (¶720)

➢ *For definitions of grammatical terms, see the appropriate entries in the Glossary of Grammatical Terms (Appendix A).*

Section 7 offers three kinds of assistance: ¶¶701–718 present the basic guidelines for correct spelling; ¶719 provides a list of look-alike and sound-alike words for review and fast reference; ¶720 presents a list of troublesome words.

The authority for spelling in this manual is the 1997 printing of *Merriam-Webster's Collegiate Dictionary,* Tenth Edition, and *Webster's Third New International Dictionary.* Whenever two spellings are allowable, only the first form is usually given here.

NOTE: The dictionaries and spell checkers that are built into word processing software may not always agree with the dictionaries that serve as the authority for spelling in this manual. A spell checker will flag any word not listed in its own dictionary or in a supplemental dictionary you create, even if the word is spelled correctly. Reduce the number of "false alarms" by expanding your dictionary to include frequently used terms and names. In addition, always proofread carefully since no spell checker will flag words spelled correctly but used incorrectly. (See ¶1202b.) For example, if you write "Summer is our *peek* season for swimwear," the spell checker will not question *peek* because it is spelled correctly. You will have to find the error yourself or suffer the embarrassing consequences.

¶704

Spelling Guides

When a Final Consonant Is Doubled

701 When a word of one syllable ends in a single consonant (ba*g*) preceded by a single vowel (b*a*g), double the final consonant before a suffix beginning with a vowel (bag-*gage*) or before the suffix *y* (bagg*y*). (See ¶703.)

rub	rub*b*ed	swim	swim*m*er	stop	stop*p*ed
glad	glad*d*en	skin	skin*n*y	slip	slip*p*age
if	if*f*y	clan	clan*n*ish	star	star*r*ing
fog	fog*g*y	run	run*n*ing	bet	bet*t*or

EXCEPTIONS:

yes	yeses	dew	dewy	tax	taxing
bus	buses	bow	bowed	fix	fixed
gas	gases	sew	sewing	box	boxy

NOTE: When a one-syllable word ends in *y* preceded by a single vowel, do not double the *y* before a suffix beginning with a vowel. (See ¶711.)

pay	payee	joy	joyous	toy	toying
key	keyed	boy	boyish	buy	buyer

702 When a word of more than one syllable ends in a single consonant (ref*er*) preceded by a single vowel (ref*e*r) and the accent falls on the last syllable of the root word (ref*er*), double the final consonant before a suffix beginning with a vowel (referr*ed*). (See ¶704.)

forbid	forbid*d*en	begin	begin*n*ing	infer	infer*r*ed
unclog	unclog*g*ed	unzip	unzip*p*ed	occur	occur*r*ing
retag	retag*g*ing	concur	concur*r*ent	regret	regret*t*able
control	control*l*er	defer	defer*r*ing	admit	admit*t*ing

EXCEPTIONS (see ¶711):

display	displaying	obey	obeyed	enjoy	enjoyable

NOTE: When a suffix beginning with a vowel is added, do not double the final consonant if the accent *shifts* from the second syllable.

refer	refer*red*	prefer	prefer*red*	transfer	transfer*red*
BUT: ref*erence*		**BUT:** pref*erable*		**BUT:** transfer*ee*	

When a Final Consonant Is Not Doubled

703 When a word of one syllable ends in a single consonant (ba*d*) preceded by a single vowel (b*a*d), do not double the final consonant before a suffix beginning with a *consonant* (bad*ly*).

glad	glad*ness*	star	star*dom*	play	play*ful*
ten	ten*fold*	wit	wit*less*	joy	joy*fully*
ship	ship*ment*	flag	flag*ship*	boy	boy*hood*

704 When a word of more than one syllable ends in a single consonant (benefi*t*) preceded by a single vowel (benef*i*t) and the accent *does not* fall on the last syllable of the root word (*ben*efit), *do not* double the final consonant before a suffix beginning with a vowel (benefit*ed*).

Continued on page 178

¶705

catalog	cataloged, cataloging	differ	differed, different
total	totaled, totaling	credit	credited, creditor
cancel	canceled, canceling	profit	profited, profiting
	(**BUT:** cancellation)	benefit	benefited, benefiting
diagram	diagramed, diagraming	borrow	borrowed, borrowing
worship	worshiped, worshiper	index	indexed, indexing

EXCEPTIONS:

program	program*m*ed, program*m*ing	outfit	outfit*t*ed, outfit*t*ing
format	format*t*ed, format*t*ing	kidnap	kidnap*p*ed, kidnap*p*ing
overstep	overstep*p*ed, overstep*p*ing	handicap	handicap*p*ed, handicap*p*ing

705 When a word of one or more syllables ends in a single consonant (clou*d*, repea*t*) preceded by more than one vowel (cl*ou*d, rep*ea*t), *do not* double the final consonant before any suffix (cloud*less*, repeat*ing*).

gain	gain*ful*	bias	bias*ed*	wool	wool*en*
haul	haul*ing*	chief	chief*ly*		(**BUT:** wool*ly*)
dream	dream*y*	riot	riot*ous*	loud	loud*ness*
cheer	cheer*y*	broad	broad*ly*	equal	equal*ed*
deceit	deceit*ful*	poet	poet*ic*	duel	duel*ing*
feud	feud*al*	toil	toil*some*	buoy	buoy*ant*

EXCEPTIONS:

equip	equip*p*ed, equip*p*ing (**BUT:** equipment)	quit	quit*t*ing
quiz	quiz*z*ed, quiz*z*ing, quiz*z*ical	squat	squat*t*er

706 When a word of one or more syllables ends with more than one consonant (wor*k*, deta*ch*), do not double the final consonant before any suffix (workd*ay*, detach*ed*).

comb	comb*ing*	back	back*ward*	shirr	shirr*ing*
hand	hand*y*	curl	curl*y*	mass	mass*ive*
self	self*ish*	warm	warm*ly*	slant	slant*wise*
swing	swing*ing*	return	return*ed*	jinx	jinx*ed*
wish	wish*ful*	harp	harp*ing*	blitz	blitz*ing*

NOTE: Words ending in *ll* usually retain both consonants before a suffix. However, when adding the suffix *ly,* drop one *l* from the root word. When adding the suffix *less* or *like,* insert a hyphen between the root and the suffix to avoid three *l*'s in a row.

skill	skill*ful*	full	ful*ly*	hull	hull-*less*
install	install*ment*	dull	dul*ly*	shell	shell-*like*

Final Silent *E*

707 a. Words ending in silent *e* usually *drop* the e before a suffix beginning with a vowel.

sale	sal*able*	sense	sens*ible*	propose	propos*ition*
size	siz*able*	argue	argu*ing*	execute	execut*ive*
store	stor*age*	issue	issu*ing*	sincere	sincer*ity*
arrive	arriv*al*	blue	blu*ish*	desire	desir*ous*
accuse	accus*ation*	true	tru*ism*	use	us*ual*

EXCEPTIONS:

agree	agree*ing*	mile	mile*age*	dye	dye*ing*
see	see*ing*	acre	acre*age*	hoe	hoe*ing*

¶**710**

b. Words ending in silent *e* usually drop the *e* before the suffix *y*.

ease	eas*y*	ice	ic*y*	edge	edg*y*
chance	chanc*y*	bounce	bounc*y*	range	rang*y*

EXCEPTIONS:

cage	cage*y*	dice	dice*y*	price	price*y*

c. Words ending in *ce* or *ge* usually retain the *e* before a suffix beginning with *a* or *o* (so as to preserve the soft sound of the *c* or *g*).

enforce	enforce*able*	trace	trace*able*	change	change*able*
notice	notice*able*	advantage	advantage*ous*	knowledge	knowledge*able*
replace	replace*able*	courage	courage*ous*	manage	manage*able*
service	service*able*	outrage	outrage*ous*	marriage	marriage*able*

EXCEPTIONS:

pledge	pledg*or*	mortgage	mortgag*or*

NOTE: Before suffixes beginning with *i*, the *e* is usually dropped.

force	forc*ible*	college	colleg*ial*	age	ag*ing*
reduce	reduc*ible*	finance	financ*ial*	enforce	enforc*ing*

EXCEPTIONS:

singe	singe*ing*	tinge	tinge*ing*	age	age*ism*

708 Words ending in silent *e* usually *retain* the *e* before a suffix beginning with a consonant.

hope	hope*ful*	manage	manage*ment*	trouble	trouble*some*
care	care*less*	like	like*ness*	nine	nine*ty*
sincere	sincere*ly*	flame	flame*proof*	edge	edge*wise*

EXCEPTIONS:

wise	wis*dom*	true	tru*ly*	argue	argu*ment*
awe	aw*ful*	due	du*ly*	judge	judg*ment*
nine	nin*th*	gentle	gent*ly*	acknowledge	acknowledg*ment*
whole	whol*ly*	subtle	subt*ly*	abridge	abridg*ment*

709 Words ending in *ie* change the *ie* to *y* before adding *ing*.

die	dy*ing*	tie	ty*ing*	lie	ly*ing*

When Final *Y* Is Changed to *I*

710 Words ending in *y* preceded by a consonant change the *y* to *i* before any suffix except one beginning with *i*.

vary	vari*able*	fly	fli*er*	likely	likeli*hood*
custody	custodi*al*	easy	easi*er*	ordinary	ordinari*ly*
Italy	Itali*an*	heavy	heavi*est*	accompany	accompani*ment*
defy	defi*ant*	fifty	fifti*eth*	happy	happi*ness*
carry	carri*ed*	fancy	fanci*ful*	fallacy	fallaci*ous*

EXCEPTIONS:

dry	dry*ly*	shy	shy*ly*	country	country*wide*
try	try*ing*	thirty	thirty*ish*	lobby	lobby*ist*

EXCEPTIONS:

academy	academ*ic*	economy	econom*ic*	symphony	symphon*ic*

¶711

711 Words ending in *y* preceded by a vowel usually retain the *y* before any suffix.

okay	okay*ed*	convey	convey*ance*	employ	employ*able*
clay	clay*ey*	obey	obey*ing*	joy	joy*ful*
display	display*ing*	survey	survey*or*	buy	buy*er*

EXCEPTIONS:

pay	pa*id*	day	dai*ly*	gay	ga*ily*
lay	la*id*	say	sa*id*	slay	sla*in*

EI and *IE* Words

712 According to the old rhyme:

Put *i* before *e*
Except after *c*
Or when sounded like *a*
As in *neighbor* and *weigh.*

I Before E

believe	brief	field	niece	**BUT:** either	height
relieve	chief	wield	piece	neither	leisure
belief	thief	yield	anxiety	seize	foreign
relief	friend	view	variety	weird	caffeine

After C

deceive	receive	conceive	perceive	**BUT:** ancient	species
deceit	receipt	conceit	ceiling	science	financier

Sounded Like A

freight	their	eight	vein	beige	feign
weight	heir	sleigh	skein	deign	reign

Words Ending in *ABLE* and *IBLE*

713 **a.** The ending *able* is more commonly used.

admirable	knowledgeable	reasonable
advisable	likable	receivable
changeable	movable	salable
dependable	payable	transferable
doable	probable	valuable

➤ *For guidelines on dropping or retaining silent* e *before the ending, see ¶707.*

b. However, a number of frequently used words end in *ible.*

compatible	flexible	responsible
convertible	irrepressible	sensible
credible	irresistible	susceptible
eligible	legible	terrible
feasible	possible	visible

Words Ending in *ANT, ANCE, ENT,* and *ENCE*

714 Words ending in *ant, ance, ent,* and *ence* follow no clear-cut pattern. Therefore, consult a dictionary when in doubt.

exist*ent*	persist*ent*	defend*ant*	descend*ant*	occurr*ence*
insist*ent*	resist*ant*	depend*ent*	transcend*ent*	recurr*ence*
assist*ance*	mainten*ance*	relev*ance*	surveill*ance*	intellig*ence*

Words Ending in *IZE, ISE,* and *YZE*

715 **a.** Most words end in *ize.*

apologize	criticize	minimize	realize	summarize
authorize	economize	organize	recognize	vandalize
characterize	emphasize	prize	specialize	visualize

b. A number of common words end in *ise.*

advertise	compromise	enterprise	improvise	supervise
advise	devise	exercise	merchandise	surprise
arise	disguise	franchise	revise	televise

c. Only a few words end with *yze.*

analyze	paralyze	catalyze

Words Ending in *CEDE, CEED,* and *SEDE*

716 **a.** Only *one* word ends in *sede: supersede.*

b. Only *three* words end in *ceed: exceed, proceed, succeed.* (Note, however, that derivatives of these three words are spelled with only one *e: excess, procedure, success.*)

c. All other words ending with the sound of "seed" are spelled *cede: precede, secede, recede, concede, accede, intercede.*

Words Ending in *C*

717 Words ending in *c* usually take the letter *k* before a suffix so as to preserve the hard sound of the *c.*

mimic	mimicked, mimicking (**BUT:** mimicry)
panic	panicked, panicking, panicky
picnic	picnicked, picnicking, picnicker
shellac	shellacked, shellacking
traffic	trafficked, trafficking
BUT: arc	arced, arcing

Words With Diacritical Marks

718 Many French words are now considered part of the English language and no longer require italics or underlining (see ¶287). Some of these words still retain diacritical marks from the French form. If you are using software with special character sets, you can access these diacritical marks. Otherwise, you will have to insert them by hand.

Continued on page 182

¶719

a. Acute Accent. An acute accent (´) over the letter *e (é)* signifies that the letter is to be pronounced "ay" (as in *may*). Moreover, it signifies that at the end of a word the letter *é* is to be pronounced as a separate syllable.

attaché	crudités	fiancé (m.)	précis
blasé	détente	fiancée (f.)	risqué
café	éclat	habitué	touché
cliché	élan	née	**BUT:** matinee
communiqué	entrée	outré	melee
consommé	exposé	passé	puree

A few words call for two acute accents:

résumé	protégé	décolleté	déclassé

NOTE: The word *forte* does not have an acute accent over the *e*. It is pronounced *FOR-tay* only when it refers to a musical direction (meaning "loud"). When *forte* means "one's strong point," it should be pronounced as one syllable—*FORT.*

b. Grave Accent. A few French expressions retain a grave accent (`).

à la carte	vis-à-vis	déjà vu	pièce de résistance
à la mode	pied-à-terre	voilà	cause célèbre

c. The Circumflex. A few phrases derived from the French retain a circumflex (^).

maître d'hôtel	raison d'être	pâté	papier-mâché
table d'hôte	tête-à-tête	bête noire	**BUT:** fete

Words That Sound Alike or Look Alike

719 The following list contains two types of words: (a) words that are pronounced *exactly alike* though spelled differently, and (b) words that look and sound *somewhat alike*.

NOTE: For additional words that are frequently confused, see Section 11.

accede to comply with; to give consent
exceed to surpass

accent stress in speech or writing
ascent act of rising
assent consent

accept to take; to receive
except (v.) to exclude; (prep.) excluding (see page 293)

access admittance
excess surplus

ad short for *advertisement*
add to join

adapt to adjust
adept proficient
adopt to choose

addenda (see *agenda*)

addition something added
edition one version of a printed work

adherence attachment
adherents followers

adverse harmful; hostile; unfavorable (see page 283)
averse opposed (to)

advice (n.) information; recommendation
advise (v.) to recommend; to give counsel

affect to influence; to change; to assume (see page 283)
effect (n.) result; impression; (v.) to bring about

agenda list of things to be done
addenda additional items

aid (n.) a form of help; (v.) to help
aide an assistant

ail to be in ill health
ale a drink much like beer

air atmosphere
heir one who inherits
err to make a mistake

aisle (see *isle*)

allot to assign or distribute a share of something (see page 282)
a lot a great deal; **NOT:** alot

allowed permitted
aloud audibly

Spelling

7

allusion an indirect reference
illusion an unreal vision; misapprehension
delusion a false belief
elusion adroit escape

almost nearly (see page 284)
all most all very much

already previously (see page 284)
all ready all prepared

altar part of a church
alter to change

alternate (n.) substitute; (v.) to take turns
alternative (n.) one of several things from which to choose

altogether entirely (see page 284)
all together everyone in a group

always at all times (see page 284)
all ways all means or methods

annual yearly
annul to cancel

ante- a prefix meaning "before"
anti- a prefix meaning "against"

antecedence priority
antecedents preceding things; ancestors

anyone anybody (see ¶1010)
any one any one person in a group

anyway in any case (see page 285)
any way any method

apportion (see *portion*)

appraise to set a value on (see page 285)
apprise to inform

arc something arched or curved
ark a ship; a place of protection

are (see *hour*)

area surface; extent
aria a melody
arrears that which is due but unpaid

arrange to put in order
arraign to call into court

ascent (see *accent*)

assay to test, as an ore
essay (n.) a treatise; (v.) to attempt

assent (see *accent*)

assistance help
assistants those who help

assure (see *ensure*)

ate past tense of *eat*
eight a number

attain to gain; to achieve
attend to be present at

attendance presence
attendants escorts; followers; companions; associates

aught (see *ought*)

averse (see *adverse*)

awhile (adv.) for a short time (see page 286)
a whlle (phrase) a short period of time

bail (n.) security; the handle of a pail; (v.) to dip water
bale a bundle

baited past tense of *bait*
bated restrained (as in *bated breath*)

baloney nonsense
bologna smoked sausage

bare (adj.) naked; empty; (v.) to expose
bear (n.) an animal; (v.) to carry; to produce; to endure (as in *grin and bear it*)

base (n.) foundation; (adj.) mean
bass a fish (pronounced like *mass*); lower notes in music (pronounced like *base*)

bases plural of *base* and of *basis*
basis foundation

bated (see *baited*)

bazaar (see *bizarre*)

bear (see *bare*)

beat (n.) throb; tempo; (v.) to strike
beet a vegetable

berry a fruit
bury to submerge; to cover over

berth a bed
birth being born

beside by the side of, separate from (see page 287)
besides in addition to; also

better (adj.) greater than; more effective; (adv.) to a greater degree
bettor one who bets

bibliography list of writings pertaining to a given subject or author
biography written history of a person's life

billed charged
build to construct

birth (see *berth*)

bizarre fantastic; extravagantly odd
bazaar a place for selling goods

blew past tense of *blow*
blue a color

block (n.) a solid piece of material; (v.) to obstruct
bloc an interest group pursuing certain political or economic goals (as in *bloc voting*)

board a piece of wood; an organized group; meals
bored penetrated; wearied

boarder one who pays for meals and often for lodging as well
border edge

bolder more daring
boulder a large rock

bologna (see *baloney*)

born brought into life
borne carried; endured

bouillon (see *bullion*)

boy a male child
buoy a float

brake (n.) a retarding device; (v.) to retard
break (n.) an opening; a fracture; (v.) to shatter; to divide

Spelling

7

Continued on page 184

¶719

bread food
bred brought up

breath respiration
breathe to inhale and exhale
breadth width

bridal concerning the bride or the wedding
bridle (n.) means of controlling a horse; (v.) to take offense

broach to open; to introduce
brooch ornamental clasp

build (see *billed*)

bullion uncoined gold or silver
bouillon broth

buoy (see *boy*)

bury (see *berry*)

cache (see *cash*)

calendar a record of time
calender a machine used in finishing paper and cloth
colander a strainer

callous (adj.) hardened, unfeeling
callus (n.) a hardened surface

cannot usual form (meaning "to be unable")
can not two words in the phrase *can not only* (where *can* means "to be able")

canvas (n.) a coarse cloth
canvass (v.) to solicit

capital (n.) city serving as the seat of government; a principal sum of money; a large-sized letter; (adj.) chief; foremost; punishable by death
capitol the building in which a state legislative body meets
Capitol the building in which the U.S. Congress meets

caret a wedge-shaped mark (∧)
carat a unit of weight for precious stones
karat a unit of fineness for gold

carton a pasteboard box
cartoon a caricature

cash ready money
cache a hiding place

casual incidental
causal causing

cease to stop
seize to grasp

cede to grant; to give up
seed that from which anything is grown

ceiling top of a room; any overhanging area
sealing closing

cell (see *sell*)

cellar (see *seller*)

census statistics of population
senses mental faculties

cent (see *scent*)

cereal food made from grain
serial (adj.) arranged in a series; (n.) a work appearing in parts at intervals

cession a yielding
session the sitting of a court or other body

choose to select
chose did choose (past tense of *choose*)
chews masticates

chord combination of musical tones (as in *to strike a responsive chord*)
cord string or rope

chute (see *shoot*)

cite (v.) to quote; to summon
sight a view; vision
site a place

click a slight, sharp noise
clique an exclusive group
cliché a trite phrase

climatic referring to climate
climactic referring to a climax

clothes garments
cloths fabrics
close (n.) the end; (v.) to shut

coarse rough; common
course direction; action; a way; part of a meal

colander (see *calendar*)

collision a clashing
collusion a scheme to defraud

colonel military rank below general
kernel seed; germ; essential part

coma an unconscious state
comma a mark of punctuation

command (n.) an order; (v.) to order
commend to praise; to entrust

commence (v.) to begin
comments (n.) remarks

complement something that completes
compliment (n.) a flattering remark; (v.) to praise (see page 289)

comprehensible understandable
comprehensive extensive

comptroller term used for a financial officer in government
controller term used for a financial officer in business

concur to agree
conquer to overpower

confidant a friend; an adviser (feminine form: *confidante*)
confident sure; positive

confidently certainly; positively
confidentially privately

conquer (see *concur*)

conscience (n.) the sense of right and wrong
conscious (adj.) cognizant; sensible; aware

conservation preservation
conversation a talk

consul (see *council*)

consular (see *councillor*)

continual occurring steadily but with occasional breaks
continuous uninterrupted; unbroken

cooperation working together
corporation a form of business organization

cord (see *chord*)

core the central part; the heart
corps a group of persons with a
   common activity

corporation (see *cooperation*)

correspondence letters
correspondents those who write
   letters; journalists
corespondents certain parties in
   divorce suits

costume dress
custom habit

council an assembly
counsel (n.) an attorney; advice;
   (v.) to give advice
consul a foreign representative

councillor a member of a council
counselor one who advises
consular (adj.) of a consul

course (see *coarse*)

courtesy a favor; politeness
curtesy a husband's life interest
   in the lands of his deceased
   wife
curtsy a gesture of respect

credible believable
creditable meritorious; deserving
   of praise
credulous ready to believe

critic one who makes judgments
critique (n.) a critical assessment;
   (v.) to judge; to evaluate
criticize to judge negatively

cue a hint
queue a line of people

currant a berry
current (adj.) belonging to the
   present; (n.) a flow of water
   or electricity

curser one who curses
cursor a symbol used as a pointer
   on a computer screen

curtesy, curtsy (see *courtesy*)

custom (see *costume*)

dairy source of milk products
diary daily record

deceased dead
diseased sick

decent proper; right
descent going down
dissent disagreement

decree a law
degree a grade; a step

deduce to infer
deduct to subtract

defer to put off
differ to disagree

deference respect; regard for
   another's wishes
difference dissimilarity;
   controversy

definite distinct; certain;
   unquestionable
definitive authoritative; providing
   a final answer

defuse to make less harmful; to
   make less tense
diffuse wordy; badly organized

degree (sec *decree*)

delusion (see *allusion*)

deposition a formal written
   statement
disposition temper; disposal

depraved morally debased
deprived taken away from

deprecate to belittle
depreciate to lessen in value

descent (see *decent*)

desert (n.) barren land; (plural)
   a deserved reward; (v.) to
   abandon
dessert the last course of a meal

desolate lonely; sad
dissolute loose in morals

detract to take away from
distract to divert the attention of

device (n.) a contrivance
devise (v.) to plan; to convey real
   estate by will

dew (see *do*)

diary (see *dairy*)

die (n.) mold; (v.) to cease living
dye (n.) that which changes the
   color of; (v.) to change the
   color of

differ (see *defer*)

difference (see *deference*)

diffuse (see *defuse*)

disapprove to withhold approval
disprove to prove the falsity of

disassemble to take apart
dissemble to disguise; to feign

disburse to pay out
disperse to scatter

discreet prudent
discrete distinct; separate

diseased (see *deceased*)

disingenuous (see *ingenious*)

disinterested unbiased; impartial
uninterested bored;
   unconcerned

disperse (see *disburse*)

disposition (see *deposition*)

disprove (see *disapprove*)

dissemble (see *disassemble*)

dissent (see *decent*)

dissolute (see *desolate*)

distract (see *detract*)

divers (adj.) various or sundry;
   (n.) plural of *diver*
diverse different

do to perform
due owing
dew moisture

done finished
dun to demand payment

dose a measured quantity
doze to sleep lightly

dual double
duel a combat

duck (n.) a water bird; (v.) to
   avoid
ducked avoided
duct pipe or tube (as in *duct
   tape*)

due (see *do*)

dun (see *done*)

dye (see *die*)

Spelling

7

Continued on page 186

¶719

dying near death
dyeing changing the color of

edition (see *addition*)

effect (see *affect*)

eight (see *ate*)

elapse (see *lapse*)

elicit to draw forth
illicit unlawful

eligible qualified
illegible unreadable

elusion (see *allusion*)

elusive baffling; hard to catch
illusive misleading; unreal

emerge to rise out of
immerge to plunge into

emigrate to go away from a
   country
immigrate to come into a
   country

eminent well-known; prominent
imminent threatening; impending
immanent inherent; residing
   within
emanate to originate from; to
   come out of

en route (see *root*)

ensure to make certain (see
   page 291)
insure to protect against loss
assure to give confidence to
   someone

envelop (v.) to cover; to wrap
envelope (n.) a wrapper for a
   letter

equable even; tranquil
equitable just; right

erasable capable of being erased
irascible quick-tempered

err (see *air*)

especially to an exceptional
   degree
specially particularly, as opposed
   to generally

essay (see *assay*)

everyday ordinary (see
   page 293)
every day each day

everyone each one (see ¶1010)
every one each one in a group

ewe (see *you*)

exalt to glorify
exult to be joyful

exceed (see *accede*)

except (see *accept*)

excess (see *access*)

expand to increase in size
expend to spend

expansive capable of being
   expanded
expensive costly

expatiate to enlarge on
expiate to atone for

expend (see *expand*)

explicit clearly expressed
implicit implied

extant still existing
extent measure

exult (see *exalt*)

facet aspect
faucet a tap

facetious witty
factitious artificial
fictitious imaginary

facilitate to make easy
felicitate to congratulate

facility ease
felicity joy

faint (adj.) dim; weak; (v.) to pass
   out
feint a trick; a deceptive move

fair (adj.) favorable; just; (n.) an
   exhibit
fare (n.) cost of travel; food;
   (v.) to go forth

farther at a greater distance,
   referring to *actual* distance
   (see page 293)
further to a greater extent or
   degree, referring to *figurative*
   distance; moreover; in addition

faucet (see *facet*)

faze to disturb (as in *doesn't faze
   me a bit*)
phase a stage of development

feet plural of *foot*
feat an act of skill or strength

feint (see *faint*)

felicitate (see *facilitate*)

felicity (see *facility*)

fictitious (see *facetious*)

finale the end
finally at the end
finely in a fine manner

fineness delicacy
finesse tact

fir a tree
fur skin of an animal

fiscal (see *physical*)

flack (n.) one who provides publicity; (v.) to provide publicity
flak literally, debris from exploding
   antiaircraft shells; criticism (as
   in *to take a lot of flak*)

flair aptitude
flare a light; a signal

flaunt to display showily
flout to treat with contempt

flew did fly
flue a chimney
flu short for *influenza*

flounder to move clumsily
founder to collapse; to sink; one
   who establishes something

flour ground meal
flower blossom

flout (see *flaunt*)

flu, flue (see *flew*)

for a preposition
fore first; preceding; the front
four the numeral 4

forbear to bear with
forebear an ancestor

foreword (see *forward*)

forgo to relinquish; to let pass
forego to go before

formally in a formal manner
formerly before

fort a fortified place
forte (n.) area where one excels;
   (adv.) loud (musical direction;
   see ¶718a, note)

forth away; forward
fourth next after third

forward ahead
foreword preface

foul unfavorable; unclean
fowl a bird

founder (see *flounder*)

four (see *for*)

fourth (see *forth*)

fur (see *fir*)

further (see *farther*)

gaff hook, ordeal, rough treatment
gaffe blunder

gage pledge, token of defiance
gauge measuring device

genius talent
genus a classification in botany or zoology

gibe (n.) a sarcastic remark; (v.) to scoff at
jibe to agree

gourmet a connoisseur of food and drink
gourmand a person who eats and drinks to excess

grate (n.) a frame of bars (as in a fireplace); (v.) to scrape; to irritate
great large; magnificent

guarantee an assurance of some kind
guaranty a promise to answer for another's debt

guessed past tense of *guess*
guest visitor

hail (n.) a shower of icy pellets; (v.) to call out to (as in *to hail a cab*)
hale (adj.) healthy

hair a slender outgrowth from the skin (as in *a hair's breadth*)
hare a rabbit (as in *hare-brained*)

hall a corridor
haul to drag

hangar a building used for storing and repairing aircraft
hanger a device from which something (like clothing) can be hung

hare (see *hair*)

haul (see *hall*)

heal to cure
heel part of a foot or a shoe

healthful promoting health (e.g., a *healthful* food)
healthy being in good health (e.g., a *healthy* person)

hear to perceive by ear
here in this place

heard past tense of *hear*
herd a group of animals

heir (see *air*)

higher at a greater height
hire to employ; to use someone's services

hoard (n.) a hidden supply; (v.) to hide a supply
horde a crowd or throng

hoarse harsh or rough in sound
horse a large animal

holy sacred
holey full of holes
wholly entirely
holly a tree

hour sixty minutes
our belonging to us
are a form of *to be* (as in *we are, you are, they are*)

human pertaining to humanity
humane kindly

hypercritical overcritical
hypocritical pretending to be virtuous

ideal a standard of perfection
idle unoccupied; without worth
idol object of worship
idyll a description of rural life

illegible (see *eligible*)

illicit (see *elicit*)

illusion (see *allusion*)

illusive (see *elusive*)

imitate to resemble; to mimic
intimate (adj.) innermost; familiar; (v.) to hint; to make known

immanent (see *eminent*)

immerge (see *emerge*)

immigrate (see *emigrate*)

imminent (see *eminent*)

implicit (see *explicit*)

imply to suggest (see page 296)
infer to deduce; to guess; to conclude

inane senseless
insane of unsound mind

incidence range of occurrence
incidents occurrences; happenings

incinerate to burn
insinuate to imply

incite (v.) to arouse
insight (n.) understanding

indict to charge with a crime
indite to compose; to write

indifferent without interest (see page 296)
in different *in* (preposition) + *different* (adjective)

indigenous native
indigent needy
indignant angry

indirect not direct (see page 296)
in direct *in* (preposition) + *direct* (adjective)

inequity unfairness
iniquity wickedness; sin

infer (see *imply*)

ingenious clever
ingenuous naive
disingenuous pretending to be naive

insane (see *inane*)

insight (see *incite*)

insinuate (see *incinerate*)

insoluble incapable of being dissolved
insolvable not explainable
insolvent unable to pay debts

Spelling

7

Continued on page 188

¶719

instants short periods of time
instance an example

insure (see *ensure*)

intelligent possessed of understanding
intelligible understandable

intense acute; strong
intents aims

interstate between states
intrastate within one state
intestate dying without a will

intimate (see *imitate*)

into, in to (see page 296)

irascible (see *erasable*)

isle island
aisle passage between rows

its possessive form of *it*
it's contraction of *it is* or *it has* (see ¶1056e)

jibe (see *gibe*)

karat (see *caret*)

kernel (see *colonel*)

key a means of gaining entrance or understanding
quay a wharf (also pronounced *key*)

knew understood
new fresh; novel

know to understand
no not any

lapse to become void
elapse to pass
relapse to slip back into a former condition

last final (see page 297)
latest most recent

later more recent; after a time
latter second in a series of two (see page 298)

lath a strip of wood
lathe a wood-turning machine

lay to place (see page 298)
lie (n.) a falsehood; (v.) to recline; to tell an untruth
lye a strong alkaline solution

lead (n.) heavy metal (pronounced *led*); (v.) to guide (pronounced *leed*)
led guided (past tense of *to lead*)

lean (adj.) thin; (v.) to incline
lien a legal claim

leased rented
least smallest

legislator a lawmaker
legislature a body of lawmakers

lend to allow the use of temporarily
loan (n.) something lent; (v.) to lend
lone solitary

lessee a tenant
lesser of smaller size
lessor one who gives a lease

lessen (v.) to make smaller
lesson (n.) an exercise assigned for study

levee embankment of a river
levy (v.) to raise a collection of money; (n.) the amount that is thus collected

liable responsible
libel defamatory statement

lie (see *lay*)

lien (see *lean*)

lightening making lighter
lightning accompaniment of thunder
lighting illumination

load a burden to be carried
lode a mineral deposit; an abundant supply

loan, lone (see *lend*)

loath (adj.) reluctant
loathe (v.) to detest

local (adj.) pertaining to a particular place
locale (n.) a particular place

loose (adj.) not bound; (v.) to release

lose (v.) to suffer the loss of; to part with unintentionally
loss something lost

lye (see *lay*)

made constructed
maid a servant

magnificent having splendor
munificent unusually generous

mail correspondence
male masculine

main (adj.) chief; (n.) a conduit
mane long hair on the neck of certain animals

manner a way of acting (as in *to the manner born*)
manor an estate

marital pertaining to marriage
martial military (as in *martial law*)
marshal (n.) an official; (v.) to arrange (as in *to marshal the facts*)

maybe perhaps (see page 300)
may be a verb consisting of two words

mean (adj.) unpleasant; (n.) the midpoint; (v.) to intend
mien appearance

meat flesh of animals
meet (v.) to join; (adj.) proper
mete to measure

medal a badge of honor
meddle to interfere
metal a mineral
mettle courage; spirit (as in *to test one's mettle*)

mien (see *mean*)

miner a worker in a mine
minor (adj.) lesser, as in size, extent, or importance; (n.) a person who is under legal age

missal a book of prayers
missile a rocket; a projectile

mist haze
missed failed to do

mite a tiny particle
might (n.) force; (v.) past tense of *may*

mode fashion; method
mood disposition
mooed past tense of *moo*

¶719

monogram a set of initials
monograph a short book; a pamphlet

moot debatable; disputed (as in *a moot point*)
mute unable to speak

moral virtuous
morale spirit

morality virtue
mortality death rate

morning before noon
mourning grief

munificent (see *magnificent*)

naught (see *ought*)

new (see *knew*)

no (see *know*)

nobody no one (see page 301)
no body no group

noisome offensive, smelly
noisy clamorous

none not one (see ¶1013)
no one nobody (see ¶1010)

oculist an ophthalmologist or an optometrist
ophthalmologist a doctor who treats eyes
optician one who makes or sells eyeglasses
optometrist one who measures vision

official authorized
officious overbold in offering services

one a single thing
won did win

ordinance a local law
ordnance arms; munitions

ought should
aught anything; all; nothing; zero
naught nothing; zero

our (see *hour*)

overdo to do too much
overdue past due

packed crowded
pact an agreement

pail a bucket
pale (adj.) light-colored; (n.) an enclosure (as in *beyond the pale*)

pain suffering
pane window glass

pair two of a kind
pare to peel
pear a fruit

palate roof of the mouth; the sense of taste
pallet a bed; a mattress; a portable platform for stacking materials
palette a board holding a painter's pigments; a range of colors

parameter a quantity with an assigned value; a constant
perimeter the outer boundary

partition division
petition prayer; a formal written request

partly in part
partially to some degree

past (n.) time gone by; (adj., adv., or prep.) gone by
passed moved along; transferred (past tense of *pass*)

patience composure; endurance
patients sick persons

peace calmness
piece a portion

peak the top
peek to look slyly at
pique (n.) resentment; (v.) to offend; to arouse (as in *to pique one's interest*)
piqué cotton fabric

peal to ring out
peel (n.) the rind; (v.) to strip off

pear (see *pair*)

pedal (adj.) pertaining to the foot; (n.) a treadle
peddle to hawk; to sell

peek (see *peak*)

peel (see *peal*)

peer (n.) one of equal rank or age; (v.) to look steadily
pier a wharf

perfect (adj.) without fault; (v.) to make perfect
prefect (n.) an official

perimeter (see *parameter*)

perpetrate to carry out (a crime)
perpetuate to make perpetual

perquisite privilege
prerequisite a preliminary requirement

persecute to oppress
prosecute to sue

personal private
personnel the staff

perspective a view in correct proportion
prospective anticipated

peruse to read
pursue to chase

petition (see *partition*)

phase (see *faze*)

physic a medicine
physics science dealing with matter and energy
physique bodily structure
psychic (adj.) pertaining to the mind or spirit; (n.) a medium

physical relating to the body
fiscal pertaining to finance (see page 294)
psychical mental

piece (see *peace*)

pier (see *peer*)

pique, piqué (see *peak*)

plain (adj.) undecorated; (n.) prairie land
plane (n.) a level surface; an airplane; (v.) to make level or smooth

plaintiff party in a lawsuit
plaintive mournful

pleas plural of *plea*
please to be agreeable

Spelling

7

Continued on page 190

¶**719**

pole a long, slender piece of wood or metal
poll (n.) the casting of votes by a body of persons; (v.) to register the votes of

poor (adj.) inadequate; (n.) the needy
pore to study; to gaze intently
pour to flow

populace the common people; the masses
populous thickly settled

portend (see *pretend*)

portion a part
proportion a ratio of parts
apportion to allot

practicable workable; feasible
practical useful

pray to beseech
prey a captured victim

precede to go before
proceed to advance

precedence priority
precedents established rules

prefect (see *perfect*)

preposition a part of speech
proposition an offer

prerequisite (see *perquisite*)

prescribe to designate
proscribe to outlaw

presence bearing; being present
presents gifts

presentiment a foreboding
presentment a proposal

pretend to make-believe
portend to foreshadow

principal (adj.) chief; leading; (n.) a capital sum of money that draws interest; chief official of a school
principle a general truth; a rule; integrity

proceed (see *precede*)

profit gain
prophet one who forecasts

prophecy a prediction
prophesy to foretell

proportion (see *portion*)

propose to suggest
purpose intention

proposition (see *preposition*)

proscribe (see *prescribe*)

prosecute (see *persecute*)

prospective (see *perspective*)

psychic (see *physic*)

psychical (see *physical*)

purpose (see *propose*)

pursue (see *peruse*)

quay (see *key*)

queue (see *cue*)

quiet calm; not noisy
quite entirely; wholly
quit to stop

rain falling water
rein part of a bridle (as in *to give free rein to your imagination*)
reign (n.) the term of a ruler's power; (v.) to rule

raise (n.) an increase; (v.) to lift (see page 303)
raze to destroy
rays beams

rap to knock
wrap (n.) a garment; (v.) to enclose

rapt engrossed (as in *rapt attention*)
wrapped past tense of *wrap*

read to perform the act of reading
reed a plant; a type of musical instrument
red a color

real actual
reel (n.) a dance; (v.) to whirl

reality actuality
realty real estate

rebut to argue in opposition
refute to prove wrong

receipt an acknowledgment of a thing received
recipe a formula for mixing ingredients

recent (adj.) relating to a time not long past
resent (v.) to feel hurt by

red (see *read*)

reel (see *real*)

reference that which refers to something
reverence profound respect

refute (see *rebut*)

reign, rein (see *rain*)

relapse (see *lapse*)

resent (see *recent*)

residence a house
residents persons who reside in a place

respectably in a manner worthy of respect
respectfully in a courteous manner
respectively in the order indicated

reverence (see *reference*)

right (adj.) correct; (n.) a privilege
rite a ceremony (as in *a rite of passage*)
wright a worker; a maker (used as a combining form, as in *playwright*)
write to inscribe

role a part in a play
roll (n.) a list; a type of bread; (v.) to revolve

root (n.) underground part of a plant; (v.) to implant firmly
route (n.) an established course of travel; (v.) to send by a certain route
en route on or along the way
rout (n.) confused flight; (v.) to defeat

rote repetition
wrote did write

rye a grain used to make bread or whiskey
wry ironically humorous

sail (n.) part of a ship's rigging; (v.) to travel by water
sale the act of selling

scene a setting; an exhibition of strong feeling
seen past participle of *to see*

scent odor
sent did send
cent penny
sense (n.) meaning; (v.) to feel

sealing (see *ceiling*)

seam a line of junction
seem to appear

secd (see *cede*)

seen (see *scene*)

seize (see *cease*)

sell to transfer for a price
cell a small compartment

seller one who sells
cellar an underground room

sense, sent (see *scent*)

senses (see *census*)

serge a kind of cloth
surge (n.) a billow; (v.) to rise suddenly

serial (see *cereal*)

serve to help (see page 303)
service to keep in good repair

session (see *cession*)

sew (see *so*)

shear to cut; to trim
sheer transparent; utter

shoot to fire
chute a slide

shown displayed; revealed; past participle of *show*
shone gave off light; did shine

sight, site (see *cite*)

simple plain; uncomplicated
simplistic oversimplified; falsely simple

sleight dexterity (as in *sleight of hand*)
slight (adj.) slender; scanty; (v.) to make light of

so therefore
sew to stitch
sow to scatter seed

soar (see *sore*)

soared did fly
sword weapon

sole one and only
soul the immortal spirit

soluble having the ability to dissolve in a liquid
solvable capable of being solved or explained

some a part of
sum a total

someone somebody (see ¶1010)
some one some person in a group

sometime at some unspecified time (see page 305)
some time a period of time
sometimes now and then

son male child
sun the earth's source of light and heat

sore painful
soar to fly

soul (see *sole*)

sow (see *so*)

spacious having ample room
specious outwardly correct but inwardly false

specially (see *especially*)

staid grave; sedate
stayed past tense and past participle of *to stay*

stair a step
stare to look at

stake (n.) a pointed stick; a prize; (v.) to wager
steak a slice of meat or fish

stanch to stop the flow of something (such as blood or tears)
staunch faithful, steadfast

stationary fixed
stationery writing materials

statue a carved or molded figure
stature height
statute a law

stayed (see *staid*)

steak (see *stake*)

steal to take unlawfully
steel a form of iron

straight not crooked; directly
strait a water passageway; (plural) a distressing situation (as in *dire straits*)

succor (n.) something that provides relief; (v.) to relieve
sucker someone easily cheated

suit (n.) a legal action; clothing; (v.) to please
suite a group of things (such as rooms or furniture) forming a unit
sweet having an agreeable taste; pleasing

sum (see *some*)

sun (see *son*)

superintendence management
superintendents supervisors

surge (see *serge*)

sweet (see *suit*)

sword (see *soared*)

tack (n.) direction; (v.) to change direction (see page 306)
tact considerate way of behaving so as to avoid offending others

tail the end
tale a story

tare allowance for weight
tear (n.) a rent or rip (pronounced like *tare*); a secretion from the eye (pronounced like *tier*); (v.) to rip
tier a row or layer

taught did teach
taut tight; tense

team a group
teem to abound

tear (see *tare*)

tenant one who rents property
tenet a principle

than conjunction of comparison (see page 306)
then (adv.) at that time

Spelling

7

Continued on page 192

¶719

their belonging to them (see ¶1056e)
there in that place
they're contraction of *they are*

theirs possessive form of *they;* used when a noun does not follow
there's contraction of *there is* or *there has* (see ¶1056e)

therefor for that thing
therefore consequently

throes a painful struggle
throws hurls; flings

through by means of; from beginning to end; because of
threw did throw
thorough exhaustive

tier (see *tare*)

to (prep.) toward
too (adv.) more than enough; also
two one plus one

tortuous winding; twisty; devious
torturous cruelly painful

track a trail
tract a treatise; a piece of land

trial examination; experiment; hardship
trail a path

trustee a person to whom something is entrusted
trusty (n.) a convict who is considered trustworthy; (adj.) dependable

undo to open; to render ineffective
undue improper; excessive

uninterested (see *disinterested*)

urban pertaining to the city
urbane polished, suave

vain proud; conceited; futile
vane a weathercock
vein a blood vessel; a bed of mineral materials

vale a valley
veil a concealing cover or cloth

vendee purchaser
vendor seller

veracious truthful
voracious greedy

veracity truthfulness
voracity ravenousness; greediness

vial a small flask for liquids
vile disgusting, despicable

vice wickedness; a prefix used with nouns to designate titles of office (see ¶808c)
vise a clamp

voracity (see *veracity*)

waist part of the body
waste (n.) needless destruction; useless consumption; (v.) to expend uselessly

wait to stay
weight heaviness

waive (v.) to give up
wave (n.) a billow; a gesture; (v.) to swing back and forth

waiver the giving up of a claim
waver to hesitate

want (n.) a need; (v.) to lack; to desire
wont a custom (pronounced like *want*)
won't contraction of *will not*

ware goods
wear to have on; to diminish
were form of *to be*
where at the place in which

wave (see *waive*)

waver (see *waiver*)

way direction; distance; manner
weigh to find the weight

weak not strong
week seven days

weather (n.) state of the atmosphere; (v.) to come through safely
whether if (see page 308)

weigh (see *way*)
weight (see *wait*)

wet (v.) to moisten
whet (v.) to sharpen (as in *to whet one's appetite*)

where (see *ware*)

whoever anyone who
who ever two words (see page 308)

wholly (see *holy*)

whose possessive of *who*
who's contraction of *who is* or *who has* (see ¶1063)

willfully in a determined manner
willingly cheerfully; happily; with one's free will

won (see *one*)

wont, won't (see *want*)

wood lumber
would an auxiliary verb form (as in *they would like some*)

wrap (see *rap*)

wrapped (see *rapt*)

wright, write (see *right*)

wrote (see *rote*)

wry (see *rye*)

yoke a crosspiece that holds two things together; an oppressive constraint
yolk the yellow part of an egg

you second-person pronoun
yew an evergreen tree or bush
ewe a female sheep

your belonging to *you* (see ¶1056e)
you're contraction of *you are*

Troublesome Words

720 The following list presents a selection of words that business writers often misspell or stop and puzzle over. In some cases the difficulty results from the inability to apply an established rule; for such words, references to the rules are given. In many other instances, however, errors result from the peculiar spelling of the words themselves; in such cases the only remedy is to master the correct spelling of such words on an individual basis.

NOTE: For troublesome words that sound alike or look alike, see ¶719 and Section 11. For troublesome compound words, see Section 8.

abscess
absence
accessory
accidentally (see page 282)
accommodate
accompanying
acknowledgment (see ¶708)
acquaintance
acquiesce
acquire
acquisition
across
adjacent
advantageous (see ¶707c)
adviser
aegis
affidavit
aggressive
aging (see ¶707c, note)
Albuquerque
algorithm
alignment
all right (see page 284)
alleged
already (see page 284)
amateur
amortize (see ¶715a)
analogous
analysis
analyze (see ¶715c)
anomalous
answer
antecedent
appall
apparatus
apparent

architect
argument (see ¶708)
assistance (see ¶714)
asthma
attendance
attorney
autumn
auxiliary
bachelor
bankruptcy
bargain
basically
bellwether
beneficiary
benefited (see ¶704)
benign
Berkeley (California)
biased (see ¶705)
biscuit
bizarre
boundary
breakfast
brochure
buoyant
bureau
business
busy
calendar
caliber
calorie
campaign
canceled (see ¶704)
cancellation (see ¶704)
candor
Caribbean
carriage

catalog
category
ceiling
cemetery
census
chaise longue (see ¶612a)
changeable (see ¶707c)
chronological
Cincinnati
circuit
coincidence
collateral
colonel
colossal
column
comparison
condemn
Connecticut
connoisseur
conscience
conscientious
conscious
consensus
corduroy
correspondent
courtesy
debt
debtor
deductible
de-emphasize (see ¶835a)
defendant (see ¶714)
defense
deficit
definite
dependent (see ¶714)
Des Moines

Continued on page 194

¶720

descendant (see ¶714)

describe

desperately

detrimental

develop

dictionary

dilemma

disappear

disappoint

disastrous

dissatisfied

dissimilar

doctrinaire

dossier

double

ecstasy

eighth

either

eliminate

embarrass

emphasize

empty

entrepreneur

enumerate

environment

erroneous

escrow

exaggerate

exceed (see ¶716b)

excellent

exercise

exhaustible

exhibition

exhilarate

exonerate

exorbitant

extension

extraordinary

eyeing

facsimile

familiar

fantasy

fascinating

fatigue

February

fiery

financier

fluorescent

forbade

foreign (see ¶712)

foresee

forfeit

forty

fourteen

fourth

freight

fulfill

gauge

glamorous

glamour

goodwill

government

grammar

grateful

gray

grievous

gruesome (see ¶708)

guarantee

guardian

guesstimate

handkerchief

harass

harebrained

harken

hearten

height (see ¶712)

hemorrhage

heterogeneous

hindrance

homogeneous

hors d'oeuvre

hygiene

hypocrisy

idiosyncrasy

impasse

impostor

inasmuch as

incidentally

indict

indispensable

innocuous

innuendo

inoculate

interim

intern

irrelevant (see ¶714)

itinerary

jeopardy

judgment (see ¶708)

khaki

labeled (see ¶704)

laboratory

league

ledger

leisure

liable

liaison

library

license

lien

lieutenant

lightning

liquefy

literature

maintenance

maneuver

marriage

marshaled

martyr

medieval

mediocre

memento

mileage (see ¶707)

milieu

millennium

millionaire

miniature

minuscule

miscellaneous

mischievous

misspell

mnemonic

mortgage

motor

necessary

negotiate

neither (see ¶712)

nickel

niece (see ¶712)

ninety

ninth

¶**720**

noticeable (see ¶707c)
nuclear
obsolescent
offense
omelet
omission
ophthalmology
pamphlet
paradigm
parallel
parliament
part-time (see ¶816a)
pastime
patience
permissible (see ¶713b)
perseverance
persistent
persuade
phase
phenomenal
Philippines (see ¶348a, note)
phony
physician
Pittsburgh
plagiarism
poinsettia
potato, potatoes
practically
practice
preceding (see ¶716c)
preferable (see ¶702, note)
prerogative
presumptuous
pretense
privilege
procedure (see ¶716b)
proceed (see ¶716b)
programmed (see ¶704)
prohibition
pronunciation
protégé
psalm
pseudonym
psychiatric
psychological
publicly
pursue

quantity
questionnaire
queue
rarefy
recommend
reconnaissance
reconnoiter
recruit
reinforce
relevant (see ¶714)
renaissance
rendezvous
renowned
rescind
resistance (see ¶714)
restaurant
résumé (see ¶718)
rhapsody
rhetorical
rhyme
rhythm
sacrilegious
salable (see ¶707a)
San Francisco
sandwich
satellite
schedule
scissors
secretary
seize (see ¶712)
separate
sergeant
sieve
similar
simultaneous
sincerely (see ¶708)
siphon
skeptic
skiing
skillful
souvenir
specimen
sponsor
straitjacket
stratagem
strength
subpoena

subtlety
subtly
summary
superintendent
supersede (see ¶716a)
surgeon
surprise
surreptitious
surveillance (see ¶714)
synagogue
tariff
taxiing
technique
temperament
temperature
tempt
theater
their (see ¶712)
theory
thoroughly
threshold
through
totaled (see ¶704)
tragedy
traveler (see ¶704)
Tuesday
unctuous
unique
unmanageable (see ¶707c)
usage (see ¶707a)
vaccinate
vacillate
vacuum
vegetable
victim
vinyl
volume
warrant
Wednesday
weird (see ¶712)
whether
whiskey
wholly
withhold
woeful
woolly (see ¶705)
yield (see ¶712)

Spelling

7

SECTION 8

Compound Words

Compound Nouns (¶¶801–810)

Compound Verbs (¶¶811–812)

Compound Adjectives (¶¶813–832)
Basic Rules (¶¶813–815)
Adjective + Noun (*as in* short-term *note:* ¶816)
Compound With Number or Letter (*as in* 40-hour *week:* ¶817)
Compound Noun (*as in* high school *graduate:* ¶818)
Proper Name (*as in* Madison Avenue *agencies:* ¶819)
Noun + Adjective (*as in* tax-free *imports:* ¶820)
Noun + Participle (*as in* time-consuming *details:* ¶821)
Adjective + Participle (*as in* nice-looking *layout:* ¶822)
Adjective + Noun + *ED* (*as in* quick-witted *assistant:* ¶823)
Adverb + Participle (*as in* privately owned *stock* and
    as in well-known *facts:* ¶824)
Adverb + Adjective (*as in* very exciting *test results:* ¶825)
Participle + Adverb (*as in* warmed-over *ideas:* ¶826)
Adjective + Adjective (*as in* black leather *notebook:* ¶827)
Verb + Verb (*as in* stop-and-go *traffic:* ¶828)
Verb + Adverb (*as in* read-only *memory:* ¶829)
Verb + Noun (*as in* take-home *pay:* ¶830)
Phrasal Compound (*as in* up-to-date *accounts:* ¶831)
Suspending Hyphen (¶832)

Prefixes and Suffixes (¶¶833–846)

Compound Computer Terms (¶847)

Sometimes One Word, Sometimes Two Words (¶848)

➤ *For definitions of grammatical terms, see the appropriate entries in the Glossary of Grammatical Terms (Appendix A).*

¶801

Some compound words are written as solid words, some are written as separate words, and some are hyphenated. As in other areas of style, authorities do not agree on the rules. Moreover, style is continually changing: many words that used to be hyphenated are now written solid or as separate words. While the only complete guide is an up-to-date dictionary, a careful reading of the following rules will save you many a trip to the dictionary.

NOTE: The spellings in this section agree with those in the 1997 printing of *Merriam-Webster's Collegiate Dictionary,* Tenth Edition, and *Webster's Third New International Dictionary* unless otherwise indicated.

Compound Nouns

801 **a.** Compound nouns follow no regular pattern. Some are written solid, some are spaced, and some are hyphenated.

airfreight	air conditioner	air-conditioning (see ¶¶801b, 812b)
checklist	check mark	check-in
closeout	close shave	close-up
crossroad	cross section	cross-reference
daytime	day care	day-tripper
doubleheader	double take	double-dipper
eyewitness	eye shadow	eye-opener
freelance	free fall	free-marketer
goodwill	good sense	good-bye
halftime	half hour	half-truth
jobholder	job action	job-hopper
lifestyle	life span	life-form
lightbulb	light meter	light-year
moneylender	money market	money-grubber
placeholder	place mat	place-name
pocketbook	pocket money	pocket-handkerchief
showbiz	show business	show-off
sickroom	sick pay	sick-out
timetable	time deposit	time-saver
trademark	trade name	trade-off

bondholder	bond paper	paperwork	paper clip
bookstore	book review	payroll	pay dirt
bylaw	by-product	salespeople	sales tax
cashbook	cash flow	schoolteacher	school board
database	data processing	standby	stand-in
handbook	hand truck	voiceprint	voice-over
homeowner	home port	wageworker	wage earner
masterpiece	master plan	workstation	work stoppage

Continued on page 198

Compound Words

8

¶801

b. To be sure of the spelling of a compound noun, check an up-to-date dictionary. Since dictionaries pride themselves on being *descriptive* (simply showing how individual words are most commonly spelled) rather than *prescriptive* (imposing consistent spelling patterns on similar words), you will sometimes encounter troubling inconsistencies like these:

air conditioner (spaced)	layoff (solid)	copywriter (solid)
air-conditioning (hyphenated)	payoff (solid)	copyholder (solid)
makeup (solid)	play-off (hyphenated)	copyedit (solid)
shake-up (hyphenated)	skydiving (solid)	copy editor (spaced)
	skin diving (spaced)	

When such inconsistencies appear within the same context and are likely to distract the reader, you may treat the troubling words the same way:

• Choose the spaced form over the hyphenated form.

   air conditioner   air conditioning

• Choose the solid form over the hyphenated form.

   makeup   shakeup   layoff   payoff   playoff

• Choose the solid form over the spaced form.

   skydiving   skindiving   copywriter copyholder copyedit copyeditor

CAUTION: Do not convert a spaced or hyphenated compound noun to the solid form if the resulting word will be hard to grasp. For example, *co-op*—the short form of *cooperative*—is still written with a hyphen to avoid confusion with the word *coop* (even though the hyphen has now been dropped from *cooperative*). In short, do not pursue the goal of stylistic consistency if the result will confuse your reader.

Also keep in mind that adjusting dictionary spellings to avoid inconsistencies requires careful and experienced judgment. If you are not confident about your ability to make such judgments, follow the dictionary. Moreover, if you are working for an organization that strives for a consistent style in all of its written material, do not make any adjustments in spelling that could put you in conflict with the style of your organization.

c. When you cannot find a compound noun in the dictionary, the traditional guideline is to treat the noun in question as two words. As an alternative, you may treat the noun the same way that similar compounds appear in the dictionary.

   We now go *house hunting?/house-hunting?/househunting?* every weekend.

If you consult Merriam-Webster for similar words, you will find two patterns:

   SOLID: housebreaking, housecleaning, housekeeping, housewarming

   HYPHENATED: house-raising, house-sitting

According to the guidelines in *b* above, choose the solid form over the hyphenated form. On that basis you could safely write *househunting* as a solid word. Moreover, for the sake of consistency, you could also write *houseraising* and *housesitting* as solid words.

NOTE: The cautionary note in *b* above applies here as well. If you are not confident about the best way to treat compounds not in the dictionary, follow the traditional rule and treat the elements of the compound as separate words.

802 Some solid and hyphenated compound nouns closely resemble verb phrases. Be sure, however, to treat the elements in a verb phrase as separate words.

Nouns	Verb Phrases
a *breakdown* in communications	when communications *break down*
a thorough *follow-up* of the report	to *follow up* on your recommendation
operate a *drive-in*	*drive in* to your dealer's
a high school *dropout*	don't *drop out* of high school
at the time of *takeoff*	planes cannot *take off* or land
when they give us a *go-ahead*	we can *go ahead* with the plan
come to a *standstill*	we can't *stand still*
let's have a *run-through*	let's *run through* the presentation
plan a *get-together*	plan to *get together*
they have the *know-how*	they *know how* to handle it
expect a *turnaround* in sales	once our sales *turn around*
we have to make a *getaway*	we have to *get away*
to attempt a *takeover* of their firm	to attempt to *take over* their firm
I was a *standby* on Flight 968A	we can't *stand by* and do nothing
Paul's speech was merely a *put-on*	your requisition was *put on* hold
protect data with regular *backups*	always *back up* the data in the file
after you complete the *logon*	after you *log on* to the program
devise another plan as a *fallback*	we can always *fall back* on Plan B
need to reduce staff *turnover*	need to *turn over* a new leaf

803 **a.** ***Up* Words.** Compound nouns ending in *up* are solid or hyphenated. For example:

backup	linkup	call-up	mock-up
blowup	makeup	catch-up	runner-up
breakup	markup	close-up	send-up
brushup	pasteup	cover-up	shake-up
buildup	pileup	flare-up	sign-up
checkup	roundup	follow-up	start-up
cleanup	setup	frame-up	summing-up
cutup	slipup	grown-ups	tie-up
getup	smashup	hang-up	toss-up
holdup	speedup	higher-ups	touch-up
hookup	warmup*	jam-up	tune-up
letup	windup	lead-up	wrap-up
lineup	workup	mix-up	write-up

b. ***Down* Words.** Most compound nouns ending in *down* are solid. For example:

breakdown	lowdown	shakedown	**BUT:** dressing-down
closedown	markdown	showdown	put-down
comedown	meltdown	shutdown	sit-down
countdown	phasedown	slowdown	step-down
crackdown	rubdown	sundown	thumbs-down
letdown	rundown	turndown	write-down

Continued on page 200

Compound Words

8

---

*Merriam-Webster shows this as a hyphenated word, but it frequently appears as a solid word in business.

¶803

c. *In* Words. Compound nouns ending in *in* are typically hyphenated. For example:

break-in	fill-in	shoo-in	trade-in
cave-in	lead-in	shut-in	turn-in
check-in	log-in	sit-in	walk-in
drive-in	plug-in	stand-in	weigh-in
fade-in	run-in	tie-in	write-in

d. *Out* Words. Compound nouns ending in *out* are typically solid. For example:

bailout	foldout	readout	**BUT:** cop-out
blackout	handout	rollout	diner-out
blowout	hangout	sellout	fade-out
breakout	hideout	shakeout	falling-out
burnout	holdout	shutout	lights-out
buyout	layout	standout	log-out
carryout	lockout	tryout	pig-out
checkout	lookout	turnout	shoot-out
closeout	payout	walkout	sick-out
dropout	phaseout	washout	speak-out
fallout	printout	workout	time-out

e. *On* Words. Compound nouns ending in *on* are typically hyphenated. For example:

add-on	come-on	hangers-on	slip-on
carry-on	follow-on	lookers-on	turn-on
carryings-on	goings-on	run-on	**BUT:** logon (see ¶847b)

f. *Off* Words. Compound nouns ending in *off* are either solid or hyphenated. For example:

checkoff	liftoff	brush-off	send-off
cutoff	logoff (see ¶847b)	drop-off	show-off
falloff	payoff	play-off	sign-off
kickoff	shutoff	rake-off	spin-off
knockoff	standoff	rip-off	tip-off
layoff	takeoff	rub-off	trade-off
leadoff	turnoff	sell-off	write-off

g. *Over* Words. Compound nouns ending in *over* are typically solid. For example:

carryover	layover	slipover	turnover
changeover	leftover	spillover	walkover
crossover	pushover	stopover	**BUT:** going-over
hangover	rollover	switchover	once-over
holdover	runover	takeover	voice-over

h. *Back* Words. Compound nouns ending in *back* are typically solid. For example:

buyback	fallback	kickback	pullback
callback	feedback	leaseback	rollback
comeback	flashback	payback	setback
cutback	giveback	piggyback	snapback
drawback	hatchback	playback	throwback

¶**804**

i. *Away* **Words.** These compounds are typically solid. For example:

breakaway	giveaway	runaway	straightaway
getaway	hideaway	stowaway	throwaway

j. Compounds Ending in *About,* *Around,* **and** *By.* These compounds are typically solid. For example:

knockabout	turnabout	runaround	passersby
layabout	whereabouts	turnaround	standbys

k. Compounds Ending in *Between,* *Through,* **and** *Together.* These compounds are typically hyphenated. For example:

go-between	follow-through	walk-through	get-together
in-between	run-through	**BUT:** breakthrough	

804 **a.** Hyphenate a compound noun that lacks a noun as one of its elements.

the also-rans	know-it-alls	a set-to
a big to-do	hand-me-downs	a lean-to
a cure-all	the well-to-do	a talking-to
a go-ahead	a shoot-'em-up	give-and-take
a go-getter	do-it-yourselfers	a five-and-ten
a has-been	a good-for-nothing	half-and-half
the have-nots	a ne'er-do-well	my one-and-only
know-how	a merry-go-round	on the up-and-up
a look-alike	a free-for-all	show-and-tell
make-believe	the be-all and end-all	the old so-and-so
say-so	hide-and-seek	**BUT:** ups and downs
two-by-fours	no get-up-and-go	wear and tear
the old one-two	a sing-along	wannabes

b. Words coined from repeated syllables or rhyming syllables are typically hyphenated. Other coined words may be hyphenated or solid.

boo-boo	**BUT:** wingding
goody-goody	voodoo
no-no	mumbo jumbo
hocus-pocus	a no-brainer
razzle-dazzle	one-upmanship
yada-yada-yada	stick-to-itiveness
culture-vulture	comeuppance
hurly-burly	whodunit
nitty-gritty	twofers
walkie-talkie	a gofer

c. Many compound nouns that end with a prepositional phrase are hyphenated.

ambassador-at-large	stick-in-the-mud	**BUT:** bill of lading
attorney-at-law	man-about-town	editor in chief
brother-in-law	right-of-way	line of credit
grants-in-aid	stay-at-home	power of attorney
jack-of-all-trades	stock-in-trade	rule of thumb
Johnny-on-the-spot	theater-in-the-round	standard of living

¶805

805 **a.** As a general rule, treat a compound noun like *problem solving* as two words unless your dictionary specifically shows it as solid or hyphenated. (Many words of this pattern are not shown in a dictionary. However, the solid and hyphenated examples below have been taken from the 1997 printing of *Merriam-Webster's Collegiate Dictionary,* Tenth Edition.)

bean counting	brainstorming	consciousness-raising
data processing	downloading	fund-raising
decision making	downsizing	house-sitting
number crunching	housewarming	name-dropping
problem solving	letterspacing	price-cutting
profit sharing	logrolling	sight-seeing
saber rattling	safekeeping	soul-searching
skill building	tailgating	speed-reading
skin diving	trailblazing	whistle-blowing
BUT: skydiving	troubleshooting	witch-hunting

b. As an alternative to the approach described in *a* above, when you cannot find a word of this type in the dictionary, treat it like a similar compound that does appear in the dictionary. For example, if you know that *price-cutting* appears in Merriam-Webster (and in the list above) as a hyphenated word, then you may hyphenate *cost-cutting* (which does not appear in Merriam-Webster) for the sake of stylistic consistency. By the same token, when the dictionary treats similar compounds differently—for example, *skin diving* and *skydiving* or *housewarming* and *house-sitting* (as shown in the list above)—you may treat them the same way for stylistic consistency. See ¶801b–c for guidance on how to deal with these situations. Also see ¶812 for guidance on how to treat compound nouns derived from infinitives.

806 Hyphenate two nouns when they signify that one person or one thing has two functions. (See also ¶¶295b, 818b.)

actor-director	director-producer	secretary-treasurer
dinner-dance	owner-manager	wheeler-dealer
photocopier-printer	doctor-lawyer	editor-publisher

807 Compound nouns that have a single letter as their first element are either hyphenated or written as two words.

A-frame	H-bomb	U-turn
B-school	I beam	V neck
D-mark	I-280	X ray
f-stop	T-shirt	x-axis
G suit	T square	y-coordinate

NOTE: The term *X ray* (which is two words when used as a noun) is hyphenated when used as a verb or an adjective. (See also ¶815a.)

808 **a.** Do not hyphenate civil and military titles of two or more words.

Chief of Police Potenza	Attorney General Liebowitz
General Manager Werner	Rear Admiral Byrd
Vice President Vega	Lieutenant Colonel Payne

¶809

b. Hyphenate compound titles containing *ex* and *elect*.

> ex-President Clinton   Vice President-elect Jordan

NOTE: Also use a hyphen when *ex* is attached to a noun *(ex-wife, ex-convict)*, but omit the hyphen in Latin phrases *(ex officio, ex cathedra)*.

➤ *For the capitalization of titles with* ex *and* elect, *see ¶¶317, 363; for the correct usage of* ex, *see the entry for* Ex–former *on page 293.*

c. The hyphen is still customary in *vice-chancellor* and *vice-consul*, but it is gone from *vice president* and *vice admiral* (for example, *Vice President* Warren).

---

809 Compound nouns containing *man* or *men* as an element were traditionally used generically to refer to males and females alike. For example:

not for the average *layman*	the history of *mankind*
of concern to all *businessmen*	reduce the number of *man-hours*
write your *congressman*	a new source of *manpower*

a. The *generic* use of such terms is now considered unacceptable, because the masculine bias of these terms makes them unsuitable for reference to women. The following list suggests appropriate alternatives.

In Place of the Generic Term	Use
layman	layperson
businessmen	business owners, business executives, business managers, business people
congressmen	members of Congress, representatives
mankind	people, humanity, the human race, human beings
man-hours	worker-hours
manpower	work force, human resources, staff
salesmen	salespeople, sales representatives, salespersons, salesclerks, sales staff, sales force, sales associates
foremen	supervisors
policemen	police officers, the police
mailmen	mail carriers
workmen	workers

NOTE: *Workmen's compensation insurance* (or *workmen's comp*) is now referred to as *workers' compensation insurance* (or *workers' comp*).

➤ *For alternatives to words ending with feminine suffixes, see ¶840.*

b. Whenever possible, replace a word like *salesmanship* with an alternative expression (for example, *selling skills*). However, words such as *craftsmanship, workmanship, sportsmanship, brinkmanship, showmanship*, and *one-upmanship* are still widely used because of the difficulty in devising alternative expressions.

c. When naming a job or role, avoid the use of compound terms ending in *man* or *woman* unless the term refers to a specific person whose gender is known.

> There are ten candidates seeking election to the City *Council*. (**NOT:** . . . seeking election as city *councilmen.*)
>
> **BUT:** *Councilwoman* Walters and *Councilman* Holtz will study the proposal.

Continued on page 204

Compound Words

8

¶810

Write to your *representative in Congress.* (**NOT:** Write to your *congressman.*)
BUT: I was very much impressed by *Congresswoman* Nancy Pelosi of California.

Who will be appointed as *head* of the committee?   **OR**   Who will be appointed to *chair* the committee? (**NOT:** . . . appointed *chairman* of the committee?)
BUT: Robert Haas has been appointed *chairman* of the committee.

NOTE: Words like *chair, chairperson,* and *spokesperson* have been coined as a means of avoiding the generic use of masculine compound nouns. Personal taste or institutional policy will dictate whether to use these terms or not.

810 Terms like *doctor, lawyer,* and *nurse* are generic—that is, they apply equally to women and men. Therefore, do not use compound nouns like *woman lawyer* and *male nurse* unless there is a legitimate reason for making a distinction according to gender.

Next Wednesday there will be a seminar on the special problems facing *women lawyers* in the courtroom.

➢ *Capitalization of hyphenated compound nouns: see ¶363.*
  Plurals of compound nouns: see ¶¶611–613.
  Possessives of compound nouns: see ¶¶634–635.

Compound Verbs

811 **a.** Compound verbs are usually hyphenated or solid.

to air-condition	to jump-start	to backstop	to mastermind
to baby-sit	to nickel-and-dime	to bulldoze	to moonlight
to color-code	to pooh-pooh	to buttonhole	to pinpoint
to custom-tailor	to rubber-stamp	to downgrade	to proofread
to deep-six	to second-guess	to download	to sandbag
to double-click	to shrink-wrap	to downsize	to shortchange
to double-space	to soft-pedal	to ghostwrite	to sidetrack
to dry-clean	to spot-check	to hamstring	to troubleshoot
to field-test	to test-drive	to handpick	to waterproof
to fine-tune	to window-shop	to highlight	to whitewash

NOTE: If you try to check the spelling of a compound verb in a dictionary and do not find the verb listed, hyphenate the components.

b. Do not hyphenate verb phrases such as *make up, slow down, tie in.* (See ¶802 for other examples.)

812 **a.** If the infinitive form of a compound verb has a hyphen, retain the hyphen in other forms of the verb. (See the note on the following page for an exception.)

Would you like to *air-condition* your entire house?
The theater was not *air-conditioned.*
We need an *air-conditioning* expert to advise us.

You need to *double-space* all these reports.
Please *double-space* this letter.
This material should not be *double-spaced.*

BUT: Leave a *double space* between paragraphs. (No hyphen in *double space* as a compound noun.)

NOTE: The gerund derived from a hyphenated compound verb requires no hyphen unless it is followed by an object.

> *Air conditioning* * is no longer as expensive as it used to be.
> **BUT:** In *air-conditioning* an *office,* you must take more than space into account.
>
> *Double spacing* would make this table easier to read.
> **BUT:** *Double-spacing* this *table* would make it easier to read.
>
> *Spot checking* is all we have time for.
> **BUT:** In *spot-checking* the *data,* I found some disturbing errors.
>
> *Dry cleaning* is the best way to treat this garment.
> **BUT:** *Dry-cleaning* this *sweater* will not remove the spot.

b. If the infinitive form of a compound verb is solid, treat other forms of the verb solid as well.

> to copyedit a manuscript   finish the copyediting by Friday
> to handpick a candidate   handpicking the ripest tomatoes
> to proofread the galleys   proofreading the catalog copy

Compound Adjectives

No aspect of style causes greater difficulty than compound adjectives. When a compound adjective is shown hyphenated in the dictionary, you can assume only that the expression is hyphenated when it occurs directly *before* a noun. When the same combination of words falls elsewhere in the sentence, the use or omission of hyphens depends on how the words are used.

For the basic rules, see ¶¶813–815. For detailed comments, see the following paragraphs:

> ➢ *Adjective + noun (as in* short-term *note): see ¶816.*
> *Compound with number or letter (as in* 40-hour *week): see ¶817.*
> *Compound noun (as in* high school *graduate): see ¶818.*
> *Proper name (as in* Madison Avenue *agencies): see ¶819.*
> *Noun + adjective (as in* tax-free *imports): see ¶820.*
> *Noun + participle (as in* time-consuming *details): see ¶821.*
> *Adjective + participle (as in* nice-looking *layout): see ¶822.*
> *Adjective + noun + ed (as in* quick-witted *assistant): see ¶823.*
> *Adverb + participle (as in* privately owned *stock): see ¶824a.*
> *Adverb + participle (as in* well-known *facts): see ¶824b.*
> *Adverb + adjective (as in* very exciting *test results): see ¶825.*
> *Participle + adverb (as in* warmed-over *ideas): see ¶826.*
> *Adjective + adjective (as in* black leather *notebook): see ¶827.*
> *Verb + verb (as in* stop-and-go *traffic): see ¶828.*
> *Verb + adverb (as in* read-only *memory): see ¶829.*
> *Verb + noun (as in* take-home *pay): see ¶830.*
> *Phrasal compound (as in* up-to-date *accounts): see ¶831.*

NOTE: If you try to check the spelling of a compound adjective in a dictionary and do not find it listed, match up the components with one of the patterns shown above and follow the standard style for that pattern.

---

*Merriam-Webster treats this as a hyphenated word, even though it treats *air conditioner* as two words.

¶813

Basic Rules

813 A compound adjective consists of two or more words that function as a unit and express a single thought. These one-thought modifiers are derived from (and take the place of) adjective phrases and clauses. In the following examples the left column shows the original phrase or clause; the right column shows the compound adjective.

Adjective Phrase or Clause	Compound Adjective
terminals *installed at the point of sale*	*point-of-sale* terminals
a career *moving along a fast track*	a *fast-track* career
a guarantee *to give you your money back*	a *money-back* guarantee
a woman *who speaks quietly*	a *quiet-spoken* woman
an actor *who is well known*	a *well-known* actor
a conference *held at a high level*	a *high-level* conference
a building *ten stories high*	a *ten-story* building
a report *that is up to date*	an *up-to-date* report
an article *that is as long as a book*	a *book-length* article
an environment *where people work under high pressure*	a *high-pressure* environment
a PC *that delivers a high level of performance, carries a low cost, and is easy to use*	a *high-performance, low-cost, easy-to-use* PC
a stock split *that gives holders two shares for each one that they now own*	a *two-for-one* stock split

NOTE: In the process of becoming compound adjectives, the adjective phrases and clauses are usually reduced to a few essential words. In addition, these words frequently undergo a change in form (for example, *ten stories high* becomes *ten-story*); sometimes they are put in inverted order (for example, *who speaks quietly* becomes *quiet-spoken*); sometimes they are simply extracted from the phrase or clause without any change in form (for example, *well-known, high-level*).

814 Hyphenate the elements of a compound adjective that occurs *before* a noun. (**REASON:** The words that make up the compound adjective are not in their normal order or a normal form and require hyphens to hold them together.)

high-tech equipment (equipment *that reflects a high level of technology*)

a *worst-case* scenario (a scenario *based on the worst case that could occur*)

an *old-fashioned* dress (a dress *of an old fashion*)

a *$30,000-a-year* salary (a salary *of $30,000 a year*)

long-range plans (plans *projected over a long range of time*)

machine-readable copy (copy *readable by a machine*)

an *eye-catching* display (a display *that catches the eye*)

a *high-ranking* official (an official *who ranks high in the organization*)

same-day service (service *completed the same day you bring the item in*)

a *black-tie* affair (an affair *at which men must wear formal clothes with a black tie*)

the *rubber-chicken* circuit (a circuit or series *of banquets at which speeches are given and rubbery chicken or some equally bad food is served*)

revolving-door management (a management *with such rapid turnover that managers seem to be arriving and departing through a continuously revolving door*)

¶815

bottom-line results (the results that are *shown on the bottom line of a financial statement*)

open-collar workers (workers who dress casually, with *open collars;* in other words, those who work at home, telecommuters)

EXCEPTIONS: A number of compounds like *real estate* and *high school* do not need hyphens when used as adjectives before a noun. (See ¶818.)

815 **a.** When these expressions occur *elsewhere in the sentence*, drop the hyphen if the individual words occur in a normal order and in a normal form. (In such cases the expression no longer functions as a compound adjective.)

Before the Noun	Elsewhere in Sentence
an *X-ray* treatment	This condition can be treated by *X ray.* (Object of preposition.)
an *up-to-date* report	Please bring the report *up to date.* (Prepositional phrase.)
a *follow-up* letter	Let's *follow up* at once with a letter. (Verb + adverb.)
a *high-level* decision	The decision must be made at a *high level.* (Object of preposition.)
a *never-to-be-forgotten* book	Your latest book is *never to be forgotten.* (Adverb + infinitive phrase.)
an *off-the-record* comment	The next comment is *off the record.* (Prepositional phrase.)
a *no-nonsense* attitude	Marion will tolerate *no nonsense* from you. (Object of verb.)
a *low-key* sales approach	Christopher pitches his sales approach in a *low key.* (Object of preposition.)
a *cause-and-effect* relationship	Is there a relationship of *cause and effect* in this case? (Object of preposition.)
a *four-color* cover	Is this cover printed in *four colors?* (Object of preposition.)

b. When these expressions occur elsewhere in the sentence *but are in an inverted word order or an altered form,* retain the hyphen.

Before the Noun	Elsewhere in Sentence
a *tax-exempt* purchase	The purchase was *tax-exempt.*
	BUT: The purchase was exempt from taxes.
government-owned lands	These lands are *government-owned.*
	BUT: These lands are owned by the government.
a *friendly-looking* watchdog	That watchdog is *friendly-looking.*
	BUT: That watchdog *looks friendly.*
high-priced goods	These goods are *high-priced.*
	BUT: These goods carry a *high price.*

NOTE: The following kinds of compound adjectives almost always need to be hyphenated:

➤ *Noun + **adjective** (for example,* tax-exempt): *see ¶820.*
*Noun + **participle** (for example,* government-owned): *see ¶821.*
*Adjective + **participle** (for example,* friendly-looking): *see ¶822.*
*Adjective + **noun** + ed (for example,* high-priced): *see ¶823.*

Compound Words

8

¶816

Adjective + Noun (see also ¶¶817–819)

816 **a.** Hyphenate an adjective and a noun when these elements serve as a compound modifier *before* a noun. Do not hyphenate these elements when they play a normal role *elsewhere in the sentence* (for example, as the object of a preposition or of a verb). However, if the expression continues to function as a compound adjective, retain the hyphen.

Before the Noun	Elsewhere in Sentence
high-speed printers	These printers run at *high speed.* (Object of preposition.)
a *plain-paper* fax	Please be sure to order a fax that uses *plain paper.* (Object of verb.)
red-carpet treatment	They plan to roll out the *red carpet.* (Object of infinitive.)
a *closed-door* discussion	The discussion was held behind *closed doors.* (Object of preposition.)
an *all-day* seminar	The seminar will last *all day.* (Normal adverbial phrase.)
a *long-term* investment in bonds	This investment in bonds runs for a *long term.* (Object of preposition.)
	BUT: This investment in bonds is *long-term.* (Compound adjective.)
a *part-time* job	This job is *part-time.* (Compound adjective.)
	I work *part-time.* (Compound adverb.)
	I travel *part of the time.* (Normal adverbial phrase.)

NOTE: Combinations involving comparative or superlative adjectives plus nouns follow the same pattern.

Before the Noun	Elsewhere in Sentence
a *larger-size* shirt	He wears a *larger size.* (Object of verb.)
the *finest-quality* goods	These goods are of the *finest quality.* (Object of preposition.)

b. A few compound adjectives in this category are now written solid—for example, *a commonsense solution, a freshwater pond, a surefire success.*

Compound With Number or Letter

817 **a.** When a number and a noun form a one-thought modifier *before* a noun (as in *six-story* building), make the noun singular and hyphenate the expression. When the expression has a normal form and a normal function *elsewhere in the sentence,* do not hyphenate it.

Before the Noun	Elsewhere in Sentence
a *one-way* street	a street that runs only *one way*
a *first-person* account	a story written in the *first person*
a *first-rate* job	a job that deserves the *first* (or highest) *rating*
	BUT: a job that is *first-rate*
first-quarter profits	profits for the *first quarter* (see ¶1069b)
a *two-piece* suit	a suit consisting of *two pieces*
a *two-wage-earner* family	a family with *two wage earners*
a *three-ring* circus	a circus with *three rings*
a *four-point* program	a program containing *four points*
a *5-liter* container	a container that holds *5 liters*

an *8-foot* ceiling	a ceiling *8 feet* above the floor
a *20-year* mortgage	a mortgage running for *20 years*
twenty-first-century art (see ¶424, note)	art of the *twenty-first century*
a *50-cent* fee	a fee of *50 cents*
an *$85-a-month* charge	a charge of *$85 a month*
a *100-meter* sprint	a sprint of *100 meters*
an *8½-* by *11-inch* book (see ¶832)	a book *8½ by 11 inches*
a *55-mile-an-hour* speed limit	a speed limit of *55 miles an hour*
a *2-million-ton* shipment	a shipment of *2 million tons*
a *10-inch-thick* panel	a panel *10 inches thick*
a *7-foot-2-inch* basketball player	a basketball player *7 feet 2 inches* tall (see ¶430)
24-hour-a-day service	service *24 hours a day*
600-dpi graphics	graphics composed of *600 dpi* (dots per inch)

EXCEPTIONS: a *15 percent* decline, a *$4 million* profit, a *secondhand* car
(**BUT:** a *second-degree* burn)

➤ *For the hyphenation of fractional expressions serving as compound adjectives (like* half-dozen *or* 1/4-inch*), see* ¶427a.

NOTE: A hyphenated compound adjective and an unhyphenated possessive expression often provide *alternative* ways of expressing the same thought. Do not use both styles together.

a *one-year* delay	a *two-week* cruise
OR a one *year's* delay	**OR** a *two weeks'* cruise
(**BUT NOT:** a one-year's delay)	(**BUT NOT:** a two-weeks' cruise)

b. Hyphenate compound adjectives involving a number and *odd* or *plus*.

The embezzlement occurred some *twenty-odd* years ago.

I now give my age simply as *forty-plus.*

If the merger negotiations are successful, we could be looking at a *$25 million-plus* deal.

However, treat compound adjectives involving a number and *fold* as solid words.

Our profits have increased *fourfold* in the past year.

BUT: Our profits have increased *12-fold* in the past year. (Insert a hyphen when the number is expressed as a figure.)

c. Compound adjectives involving two numbers (as in ratios and scores) are expressed as follows:

a *50-50* (**OR** *fifty-fifty*) chance	an *18-7* victory	a *3-to-1* ratio **OR** a *3:1* ratio
20/20 (**OR** *twenty-twenty*) vision	a *1000-to-1* possibility	**BUT:** a ratio of *3 to 1*

➤ *See also* ¶¶450–451.

d. Other compound expressions involving a number or letter are expressed as follows:

our *number-one** (**OR** *No. 1*) goal	a *3-D* graphic	*Class A* materials
BUT: we will be *number one*	an *8-bit* machine	a grade of *A plus* (**OR** *A+*)
in *A1* condition	a *4-H* project	**BUT:** does *A-plus* (**OR** *A+*) work
BUT: *A.1.* steak sauce	a *G-7* member	a passing mark of *D minus* (**OR** *D−*)
Title IX provisions	an *NC-17* rating	**BUT:** a *D-minus* (**OR** *D−*) student

---

*Merriam-Webster does not hyphenate *number-one* before a noun.

¶818

Compound Noun

818 **a.** A number of adjective-noun combinations (such as *real estate* or *social security*) and noun-noun combinations (such as *life insurance* or *money market*) are actually well-established compound nouns serving as adjectives. Unlike *short-term, low-risk*, and the examples in ¶816, these expressions refer to well-known concepts or institutions. Because they are easily grasped as a unit, they do not require a hyphen.

accounts payable records	*life insurance* policy	*public relations* adviser
branch office reports	*mass production* techniques	*real estate* agent
high school diploma	*money market* funds	*social security* tax
income tax return	*nuclear energy* plant	*word processing* center

EXCEPTION: a *mail-order* business

NOTE: When dictionaries do not provide guidance on a specific adjective-noun combination, consider whether the expression is more like a well-known compound such as *social security* or more like *short-term*. Then space the combination or hyphenate it accordingly.

b. When a noun-noun combination involves two words of relatively equal rank, hyphenate the combination. (See also ¶¶295, 806.)

an *input-output* device	the *space-time* continuum	an *air-sea* search
cost-benefit analyses	*labor-management* relations	a *sand-gravel* mixture

EXCEPTION: the *price/earnings* ratio   **OR**   the *P/E* ratio

c. As a general rule, when a compound noun is used as a compound adjective, the decision to hyphenate or not will depend on how familiar you think your reader is with the term in question. Thus a term like *small business owner* would not be hyphenated if you feel your reader is familiar with the concept of *small business*. However, if your reader could misinterpret *small business owner* as a reference to the size of the person rather than to the size of the business, write *small-business owner.*

d. A compound noun like *African American* is hyphenated when used as an adjective. (See ¶348b.)

Proper Name

819 **a.** Do not hyphenate the elements in a proper name used as an adjective.

a *Supreme Court* decision	a *Rodeo Drive* location
a *Saks Fifth Avenue* store	*Mickey Mouse* procedures

b. When two or more distinct proper names are combined to form a one-thought modifier, use a hyphen to connect the elements.

a *German-American* restaurant	the cuisine is *German-American*

the *New York-Chicago-Los Angeles* flight (see also ¶821b, note)

BUT: the flight to *New York, Chicago, and Los Angeles*

NOTE: If one of the elements already contains a hyphen, use an en dash or two hyphens to connect the two proper names.

the *Winston-Salem–Atlanta* bus trip	the *Scranton–Wilkes-Barre* area

¶821

Noun + Adjective

820 **a.** When a compound adjective consists of a noun plus an adjective, hyphenate this combination whether it appears before or after the noun. (See ¶815b.)

accident-prone	ice-cold	tax-exempt
bone-dry	machine-readable	toll-free
brain-dead	paper-thin	tone-deaf
capital-intensive	pitch-dark	top-heavy
class-conscious	power-hungry	trigger-happy
color-blind	price-conscious	user-friendly
fork-tender	sky-high	water-repellent
fuel-efficient	street-smart	year-round

Your suggestion is ingenious but not *cost-effective*.
You are trying to solve an *age-old* problem.
She wants everything to be *letter-perfect*.
We import these *water-repellent* fabrics *duty-free*.
I want a computer that is *IBM-compatible*.

NOTE: Retain the hyphen in a noun plus an adjective combination when the expression functions as an adverb rather than as an adjective.

ADJECTIVE: Please call me on my *toll-free* number.

ADVERB: You can always call me *toll-free*.

ADJECTIVE: The information is encoded on *paper-thin* wafers.

ADVERB: The wafers have to be sliced *paper-thin*.

b. A few words in this category are now written solid. For example:

-wide: worldwide, nationwide, countrywide, statewide, countywide, citywide, communitywide, industrywide, companywide, storewide

-proof: waterproof, fireproof, shatterproof, weatherproof, childproof, bulletproof, foolproof, rustproof, soundproof, shockproof

-worthy: praiseworthy, newsworthy, trustworthy, creditworthy, noteworthy

-sick: homesick, airsick, carsick, heartsick, lovesick, seasick

-long: daylong, nightlong, yearlong, lifelong, agelong, headlong, hourlong*

Noun + Participle

821 **a.** When a compound adjective consists of a noun plus a participle, hyphenate this combination whether it appears before or after the noun. (See ¶815b.)

attention-getting	law-abiding	smoke-filled
awe-inspiring	market-tested	snow-covered
bell-shaped	mind-boggling	sugar-coated
decision-making	muscle-bound	tailor-made
hair-raising	nerve-racking	tax-sheltered
interest-bearing	panic-stricken	Windows-based

Continued on page 212

Compound Words

8

*Merriam-Webster shows this as a hyphenated word.

¶822

This *number-crunching* software uses *eye-popping* graphics.
Buying *custom-tailored* suits can easily become *habit-forming.*
The use of *computer-aided* design and *productivity-enhancing* equipment has boosted our profits enormously.
Thanks to an *SBA-guaranteed* loan, we expect to have a *record-breaking* year.
This *Republican-led* Congress will introduce additional *budget-cutting* measures.
Our company is now 40 percent *employee-owned.*

b. When an open compound noun is combined with a participle to form a one-thought modifier, insert a hyphen only before the participle.

U.S. government-owned lands	a *Pulitzer Prize-winning* play
a *Labor Department-sponsored* conference	*health care-related* expenditures
a *Dayton, Ohio-based* consortium	*solar energy-oriented* research

NOTE: For greater clarity use an en dash instead of a hyphen when combining an open compound with a participle. (See also ¶¶217, 819b.)

a *White House–backed* proposal	a *New Orleans–bound* traveler
a *Frank Lloyd Wright–designed* building	a *Windows NT–based* program

c. Combining an open compound noun with a participle to form a compound adjective can often lead to awkward constructions. Reword to eliminate this problem.

AWKWARD: This software is *Novell network-compatible.*
BETTER: This software can also be used on a Novell network.

d. A few words in this category are now written solid. For example:

hand-:	handheld, handmade, handpicked, handwoven, handwritten
heart-:	heartbreaking, heartbroken, heartfelt, heartrending, heartwarming
home-:	homebound, homegrown, homemade, homespun
time-:	timesaving, timeserving, timeworn
	BUT: time-consuming, time-honored, time-sharing, time-tested
pain-:	painkilling, painstaking

Adjective + Participle (see also ¶824b)

822 **a.** When a compound adjective consists of an adjective plus a participle, hyphenate this combination whether it appears before or after the noun. (See ¶815b.)

clean-cut	high-ranking	rough-hewn
friendly-looking (see ¶824a)	long-standing	smooth-talking
half-baked	odd-sounding	soft-spoken
hard-hitting	ready-made	sweet-smelling

EXCEPTIONS: easygoing, halfhearted

I'm *half-tempted* to apply for the Singapore opening myself.
He is a *smooth-talking* operator who never delivers what he promises.
Betty was anything but *soft-spoken* in arguing against the new procedures.

b. Retain the hyphen even when a comparative or superlative adjective is combined with a participle—for example, *nicer-looking, best-looking, oddest-sounding, better-tasting.*

As the *highest-ranking* official present, Mrs. Egan took charge of the meeting.
This year's brochure is *better-looking* than last year's.
Why can't we attract *better-qualified* people to our company?

¶823

Adjective + Noun + *ED*

823 a. When a compound adjective consists of an adjective plus a noun plus *ed*, hyphenate this combination whether it appears before or after the noun. (See ¶815b.)

broad-minded	light-fingered	closed-captioned
empty-headed	two-fisted	low-pitched
quick-witted	loose-jointed	high-priced
hot-tempered	double-breasted	middle-aged
good-humored	long-winded	old-fashioned
high-spirited	good-hearted	short-lived (pronounce the *i* as in *life*)
fair-haired	deep-seated	pint-sized (see ¶823d)
two-faced	flat-bottomed	fast-paced
clear-eyed	clean-limbed	broad-based
hard-nosed	weak-kneed	coarse-grained
tight-mouthed	long-legged	double-edged
thin-lipped	flat-footed	single-spaced (see ¶812a)
sharp-tongued	hot-blooded	deep-rooted
red-cheeked	thin-skinned	high-powered
round-shouldered	full-bodied	one-sided
empty-handed	open-ended	**BUT:** lopsided

Our success was *short-lived:* the business folded after six months. (*Short-lived* is derived from the phrase *of short life*. For that reason the *i* in *lived* is pronounced like the long *i* in *life*, not like the short *i* in *given*.)

These symptoms commonly occur in *middle-aged* executives.

I'm too *old-fashioned* to be that *broad-minded*.

b. Retain the hyphen in comparative or superlative forms—for example, *smaller-sized, highest-priced, best-natured*.

Our *higher-priced* articles sold well this year.

These goods are *higher-priced* than the samples you showed me.

Fred is the *longest-winded* speaker I ever heard.

Fred's speech was the *longest-winded* I ever heard.

c. Some words in this category are now written solid. For example:

-headed: bareheaded, bullheaded, chowderheaded, clearheaded, coolheaded, fatheaded, hardheaded, hotheaded, levelheaded, muddleheaded, pigheaded, redheaded, softheaded, soreheaded, thickheaded, woodenheaded, wrongheaded

   BUT: bald-headed, empty-headed, light-headed, pointy-headed

-hearted: bighearted, brokenhearted, coldhearted, halfhearted, heavyhearted, lighthearted, openhearted, softhearted, stouthearted, tenderhearted, warmhearted, wholehearted

   BUT: good-hearted, hard-hearted, single-hearted

-mouthed: closemouthed, openmouthed, widemouthed, bigmouthed, loudmouthed, mealymouthed

   BUT: tight-mouthed

-fisted: hardfisted, tightfisted, closefisted, ironfisted

   BUT: two-fisted, ham-fisted

Continued on page 214

Compound Words

8

¶824

-sighted:	nearsighted, shortsighted, farsighted, foresighted, longsighted
	BUT: clear-sighted, sharp-sighted
-brained:	birdbrained, featherbrained, harebrained (**NOT:** hairbrained), lamebrained, scatterbrained
-minded:	feebleminded, absentminded, simpleminded
	BUT: broad-minded, civic-minded, high-minded, like-minded, low-minded, narrow-minded, open-minded, serious-minded, single-minded, small-minded, strong-minded

d. Compound adjectives ending in *sized* (such as *pint-sized, pocket-sized, life-sized, full-sized, giant-sized, king-sized, queen-sized,* and *twin-sized*) may also be written without the final *d.*

Adverb + Participle (see also ¶825)

824 **a.** Do not hyphenate an adverb-participle combination if the adverb ends in *ly.*

a *poorly constructed* house	a *wholly owned* corporation
a *highly valued* employee	a *newly formed* division
a *clearly defined* set of terms	an *extremely tiring* trip

NOTE: Hyphenate adjectives ending in *ly* when they are used with participles. (See ¶822.)

a *friendly-sounding* voice	a *motherly-looking* woman

➤ *To distinguish between adjectives and adverbs ending in* ly, *see ¶¶1069a–b.*

b. Other adverb-participle compounds are hyphenated *before* the noun. When these same combinations occur in the predicate, drop the hyphen if the participle is part of the verb.

Before the Noun	Elsewhere in Sentence
a *well-known* consultant	This consultant *is* well *known.*
much-needed reforms	These reforms *were* much *needed.*
the *above-mentioned* facts	These facts *were mentioned* above.
the *ever-changing* tides	The tides *are* ever *changing.*
a *long-remembered* tribute	Today's tribute *will be* long *remembered.*
a *soon-forgotten* achievement	Her achievement *was* soon *forgotten.*

However, if the participle does not become part of the verb and continues to function with the adverb as a one-thought modifier in the predicate, retain the hyphen.

Before the Noun	Elsewhere in Sentence
a *well-behaved* child	The child is *well-behaved.*
a *clear-cut* position	Their position was *clear cut.*
a *well-intentioned* proposal	The proposal was *well-intentioned.*

NOTE: You couldn't say, "The child is behaved" or "Their position was cut" or "The proposal was intentioned." Since the participle is not part of the verb, it must be treated as part of a compound adjective. Compare the use of *fast-moving* in the following examples.

Before the Noun	Elsewhere in Sentence
a *fast-moving* narrative	The narrative is *fast-moving.*
	BUT: The narrative *is* fast *moving* toward a climax.

c. A hyphenated adverb-participle combination like those in ¶824b retains the hyphen even when the adverb is in the comparative or superlative.

a *better-known* brand	the *hardest-working* manager
the *best-behaved* child	a *faster-moving* stock clerk

d. A few words in this category are now written solid. For example:

-going:	ongoing, outgoing, thoroughgoing
far-:	farseeing, farsighted
	BUT: far-fetched, far-flung, far-reaching
free-:	freehanded, freehearted, freestanding, freethinking, freewheeling
	BUT: free-floating, free-spoken, free-swinging
wide-:	widespread
	BUT: wide-eyed, wide-ranging, wide-spreading

Adverb + Adjective

825 **a.** A number of adverb-adjective combinations resemble the adverb-participle combinations described in ¶824. However, since an adverb normally modifies an adjective, do not use a hyphen to connect these words.

a *not too interesting* report	a *very moving* experience
a *rather irritating* delay	a *quite trying* day

NOTE: In these examples you can omit the adverb and speak of an *interesting* report, an *irritating* delay, a *moving* experience, and a *trying* day; hence no hyphen is needed. However, as explained in the note at the bottom of page 214, you cannot speak of a *behaved* child, a *cut* position, or an *intentioned* proposal; for that reason, the adverb preceding *behaved*, *cut*, and *intentioned* must be linked by a hyphen.

b. Do not hyphenate a comparative or superlative form when the adverb *more, most, less,* or *least* is combined with an adjective.

a *more determined* person	a *less complicated* transaction
the *most exciting* event	the *least interesting* lecture

➤ *For a usage note on* more, *see page 300.*

Participle + Adverb

826 Hyphenate a participle-adverb combination *before* the noun but not when it occurs elsewhere in the sentence.

Before the Noun	Elsewhere in Sentence
filled-in forms	These forms should be *filled in.*
worn-out equipment	The equipment was *worn out.*
a *tuned-up* engine	The engine has been *tuned up.*
a *scaled-down* proposal	The proposal must be *scaled down.*
baked-on enamel	This enamel has been *baked on.*
a *cooling-off* period	Don't negotiate without *cooling off* first.
unheard-of bargains	These bargains were *unheard of.*
an *agreed-upon* date	We *agreed upon* a date.
warmed-over ideas	His ideas were *warmed over* for the occasion.

➤ *See also the examples in* ¶831.

¶827

Adjective + Adjective

827 **a.** Do not hyphenate independent adjectives preceding a noun.

> a *long* and *tiring* trip *(long* and *tiring* each modify *trip)*
>
> a *warm, enthusiastic* reception *(warm* and *enthusiastic* each modify *reception;* a comma marks the omission of *and)*
>
> a *distinguished public* orator *(public* modifies *orator; distinguished* modifies *public orator)*

➤ *For the use of commas with adjectives, see ¶¶168–171, especially the final examples in ¶169.*

b. In a few special cases two adjectives joined by *and* are hyphenated because they function as one-thought modifiers. These, however, are rare exceptions to the rule stated in *a.*

a *cut-and-dried* presentation	an *out-and-out* lie
a *hard-and-fast* rule	an *up-and-coming* lawyer
a *high-and-mighty* attitude	a *lean-and-mean* approach
a *tried-and-true* method	a *rough-and-tumble* environment
an *open-and-shut* case	a *spick-and-span* kitchen

> Henry views the matter in *black-and-white* terms. (A one-thought modifier.)
>
> **BUT:** Sue wore a *black and white* dress to the Mallory party. (Two independent adjectives.)

c. Hyphenate two adjectives that express the dual nature of the thing that they refer to. (See also ¶¶295b, 806.)

a *true-false* test	a *compound-complex* sentence

> **BUT:** a *bittersweet* ending

d. Hyphenate expressions such as *blue-black, green-gray, snow-white,* and *red-hot* before and after a noun. However, do not hyphenate expressions such as *bluish green, dark gray,* or *bright red* (where the first word clearly modifies the second).

> Sales have been *red-hot* this quarter.   Her dress was *bluish green.*
>
> *Blue-black* ink will show up best.   His moods range from black to *dark gray.*

Verb + Verb

828 **a.** Hyphenate a compound adjective consisting of two verbs (sometimes joined by *and* or *or*) when the adjective appears *before* the noun.

a *drag-and-drop* operation	a *plug-and-play* Web server
point-and-click navigating	a *wait-and-see* attitude
the *cut-and-paste* procedure	graded on a *pass-fail* basis
a *hit-or-miss* marketing strategy	a *can-do* spirit
a *make-or-break* financial decision	a *do-or-die* commitment
stop-and-go production lines	a *live-and-let-live* philosophy

> Our CEO's *ready-fire-aim* approach does not inspire confidence.
>
> Negotiations were conducted in a *give-and-take* atmosphere.

b. Do not hyphenate these elements when they play a normal function *elsewhere in the sentence.* However, retain the hyphen if these expressions continue to function as a compound adjective.

> They're never sure whether they'll *hit or miss* their marketing targets.
>
> **BUT:** Their marketing strategy can best be described as *hit-or-miss.*

Verb + Adverb

829 **a.** Hyphenate a compound adjective consisting of a verb plus an adverb when the adjective appears *before* the noun.

our *break-even* point	a *drop-dead* party dress
a *read-only* memory	*dress-down* Fridays
the *trickle-down* theory of financing	a *zip-out* lining
a *get-well* card	a *tow-away* zone
a *mail-in* rebate	*run-on* sentences
a *pop-up* menu	*carry-on* luggage
a *twist-off* cap	a *drive-through* window
their *die-hard* fans	a *set-aside* program

b. Do not hyphenate these elements when they play a normal function *elsewhere in the sentence.*

At what point will we *break even?*	Does this lining *zip out?*

Verb + Noun

830 **a.** Hyphenate a compound adjective consisting of a verb plus a noun (or pronoun) when the adjective appears *before* the noun.

take-home pay	a *show-me* kind of attitude
a *take-charge* kind of person	**BUT:** a *turnkey* computer system
a *thank-you* note	a *lackluster* approach

b. Do not hyphenate these elements when they play a normal function *elsewhere in the sentence.*

In terms of salary it's not so much what you gross as it is what you *take home.*
Betsy is inclined to *take charge* of any situation in which she finds herself.

Phrasal Compound

831 **a.** Hyphenate phrases used as compound adjectives *before* a noun. Do not hyphenate such phrases when they occur normally elsewhere in the sentence.

Before the Noun	Elsewhere in Sentence
up-to-date expense figures	The expense figures are *up to date.*
down-to-earth projections	These projections appear to be *down to earth.*
on-the-job training	I got my training *on the job.*
off-the-shelf software	You can buy that software *off the shelf.*
an *in-service* workshop	Modify only the equipment currently *in service.*
a *going-out-of-business* sale	Is Chelsea's Drugs *going out of business?*
an *out-of-the-way* location	Why is the shopping mall so far *out of the way?*
over-the-counter stocks	These stocks are sold only *over the counter.*
under-the-table payments	Don't make any payments *under the table.*
an *above-average* rating	Our unit's performance was rated *above average.*
below-the-line charges	These charges will show up *below the line.*
a *middle-of-the-road* position	His political position never strays far from the *middle of the road.*
before-tax earnings	What were our earnings *before taxes?*
after-dinner speeches	Speeches *after dinner* ought to be prohibited.

Continued on page 218

Compound Words

8

¶831

Before the Noun	Elsewhere in Sentence
around-the-clock service	We offer service *around the clock.*
across-the-board cuts	The CEO wants budget cuts *across the board.*
a *between-the-lines* reading	When you read *between the lines,* Jan's memo takes on a completely different meaning.
behind-the-scenes contract negotiations	Contract negotiations went on *behind the scenes.*
a *state-of-the-art* installation	This model reflects the current *state of the art.*
a *spur-of-the-moment* decision	Barra's decision was made on the *spur of the moment.*
a *change-of-address* form	Please show your *change of address.*
a *matter-of-fact* approach	Jan accepted the situation as a *matter of fact.*
a *dog-in-the-manger* attitude	Joe's attitude reminds me of the fable about the *dog in the manger.*
straight-from-the-shoulder talk	I gave it to him *straight from the shoulder.*
made-to-order wall units	These wall units were *made to order.*
a *pay-as-you-go* tax plan	The new tax plan requires you to *pay as you go.*
a *get-rich-quick* scheme	Don't trust any scheme that promises that you will *get rich quick.*
a *would-be* expert	Roy hoped he *would be* accepted as an expert.
coast-to-coast flights	I fly *coast to coast* about three times a month.
bumper-to-bumper traffic	The traffic stood *bumper to bumper.*
a *case-by-case* analysis	We must resolve these problems *case by case.*
a *by-invitation-only* seminar	Attendance at the seminar is *by invitation only.*
a *how-to* manual	This manual will show you *how to* get published.
a *soon-to-be-released* report	The consultant's report is *soon to be released.*
a *$150,000-a-year* fee	Our legal fees run about *$150,000 a year.*
a *well-thought-of* designer	Our former designer was *well thought of.*
a *well-thought-out* plan	The plan was *well thought out.*
a *much-talked-about* party	Your party was *much talked about.*
BUT: in the *not too distant* future (see ¶825a)	
a *nine-year-old* girl	Michelle is only *nine years old.*
BUT: a *9½-year-*old girl	Michelle is only *9½ years old.* (See ¶428a.)
(**NOT:** a nine-and-a-half-year-old girl)	

b. When two nouns joined by *and* are used as a compound adjective before a noun, hyphenate the phrase.

a *cock-and-bull* story	a *trial-and-error* approach
a *dog-and-pony* show	a *mom-and-pop* operation
a *chicken-and-egg* situation	a *carrot-and-stick* proposal
a *life-and-death* matter	a *meat-and-potatoes* kind of guy
a *David-and-Goliath* battle	a *cause-and-effect* hypothesis
bread-and-butter issues	a *cloak-and-dagger* operation

c. As a rule, do not hyphenate foreign phrases used as adjectives before a noun. (See also ¶287.)

an *ad hoc* committee	an *ex officio* member
an *à la carte* menu	a *pro rata* assessment
a *bona fide* transaction	a *per diem* fee
EXCEPTIONS: an *ad-lib* speech, a *laissez-faire* economic policy	

Compound Words

8

d. When a compound modifier consists of two or more hyphenated phrases, separate the phrases with a comma.

> a *penny-wise, pound-foolish* approach to handling money
> a *knock-down, drag-out** fight over ownership of the company
> an *all-out, no-holds-barred* strategy
> the *first-in, first-out** method of accounting
> a *first-come, first-served* policy of seating
> a *no-fee, no-load* IRA
> a *chin-up, back-straight, stomach-in* posture
> an *on-again, off-again* wedding
> **BUT:** a *go/no-go** decision (see also ¶295a)

e. Hyphenate repeated or rhyming words used before a noun.

> a *go-go* attitude
> a *rah-rah* spirit
> a *hush-hush* venture
> a *buddy-buddy* relationship
> a *teeny-weeny* salary increase
> a *palsy-walsy* deal

> a *razzle-dazzle* display
> a *fancy-schmancy* wedding
> a *rinky-dink* setup
> a *ticky-tacky* operation
> an *artsy-craftsy* boutique
> a *topsy-turvy* world

Suspending Hyphen

832 **a.** When a series of hyphenated adjectives has a common basic element and this element is shown only with the last term, insert a suspending hyphen after each of the incomplete adjectives to indicate a relationship with the last term.

> *long-* and *short-term* securities
> *private-* and *public-sector* partnerships
> *single-, double-,* or *triple-spaced* copy
> *ice-* and *snow-packed* roads
> *open-* and *closed-door* sessions

> *10-* and *20-year* bonds
> a *three-* or *four-color* cover
> *two-* and *four-wheel* drive
> *8½- by 11-inch* paper
> **BUT:** *8½" × 11"* paper (see ¶432)

b. Use one space after each suspending hyphen unless a comma is required at that point.

> a *six- to eight-week* delay
> a *10- to 12-hour* trip

> *3-, 5-,* and *8-gallon* buckets
> *6-, 12-,* and *24-month* CDs

c. When two or more solid compound adjectives with a common element are used together (for example, *lightweight* and *heavyweight*) and the common element is shown only with the last term, use a suspending hyphen with the incomplete forms to indicate a relationship with the common element.

> This product is available in *light-* and *heavyweight* versions.
> Please provide *day-* and *nighttime* phone numbers.

NOTE: Repeat the common element with each word if the use of the suspending hyphen looks odd or confusing; for example, *boyfriend or girlfriend* (rather than *boy- or girlfriend*).

➢ *For the use of a suspending hyphen with prefixes or suffixes, see ¶833d–e.*

*Merriam-Webster treats this expression differently.

¶833

Prefixes and Suffixes

833 **a.** In general, do not use a hyphen to set off a prefix at the beginning of a word or a suffix at the end of a word. (See ¶808b for two exceptions: *ex-* and *-elect.*)

*after*taste (see ¶842)	*mini*bike	change*able*
*ambi*dextrous	*mis*spell	patron*age*
*ante*date	*mono*syllable	free*dom*
*anti*trust (see ¶834)	*multi*tasking	six*fold*
*audio*visual	*non*essential	meaning*ful*
*bi*weekly	*off*beat (see ¶845)	sono*gram*
*by*line (**BUT:** by-product)	*out*sourcing	photo*graph*
*circum*locution	*over*confident	likeli*hood*
*co*author (see ¶835b)	*para*medical	convert*ible*
*counter*balance	*poly*syllabic	misspell*ing*
*de*centralize (see ¶835)	*post*test	fifty*ish*
*down*sizing	*pre*requisite (see ¶835)	thank*less* (see ¶846)
*extra*legal	*pro*active	book*let*
*fore*front	*pseudo*scientific	child*like* (see ¶846)
*hyper*sensitive	*re*organize (see ¶837)	induce*ment*
*hypo*critical	*retro*active	upper*most*
*il*legal	*semi*annual (see ¶834)	happi*ness*
*im*material	*sub*division	computer*nik*
*in*defensible (see ¶843)	*super*natural	fire*proof*
*infra*structure	*supra*natural	censor*ship*
*inter*office	*trans*continental	hand*some*
*intra*mural (see ¶834)	*tri*lateral	home*stead*
*intro*version	*ultra*conservative (see ¶834)	back*ward*
*macro*economics	*un*accustomed	nation*wide* (see ¶820b)
*micro*manage	*under*current	edge*wise* (see page 308)
*mid*winter (see ¶844)	*up*shot	trust*worthy*

NOTE: Be wary of spell checkers that may urge you to insert hyphens after these prefixes.

b. Whenever necessary, use a hyphen to prevent one word from being mistaken for another. (See ¶837.)

lock the *coop*	*multiply* by 12	a *unionized* factory
buy a *co-op*	a *multi-ply* fabric	an *un-ionized* substance

c. As a rule, when adding a prefix to a hyphenated or spaced compound word, use a hyphen after the prefix. (See ¶818.)

pre-high school texts	*non*-interest-bearing notes
post-bread-winning years	*non*-computer-litcrate adults
ex-attorney general	*non*-civil service position

EXCEPTIONS: coeditor in chief, unair-conditioned, unself-conscious

d. When two or more prefixes have a common element and this element is shown only with the final prefix, insert a suspending hyphen after each of the unattached prefixes to indicate a relationship with the common element. (See ¶832.)

pre- and *post*natal care	*maxi-*, *midi-*, and *mini*skirts
macro- and *micro*economics	*inter-* and *intra*office networks
pro- and *anti*union forces	*over-* and *under*qualified job applicants

¶836

e. When two or more suffixes have a common element, it is possible to leave one of the suffixes unattached and insert a suspending hyphen to indicate the relationship with the common element; for example, *servicemen* and *-women*. However, to avoid confusion or awkwardness, it is usually better to repeat the common element with each suffix.

> **AWKWARD:** I thought Nancy's reaction was more *thoughtless* than *-ful*.
>
> **BETTER:** I thought Nancy's reaction was more *thoughtless* than *thoughtful*.
>
> **AWKWARD:** I would characterize his behavior as *childlike* rather than *-ish*.
>
> **BETTER:** I would characterize his behavior as *childlike* rather than *childish*.

834 When the prefix ends with *a* or *i* and the base word begins with the same letter, use a hyphen after the prefix to prevent misreading.

ultra-active	anti-intellectual	semi-independent
intra-abdominal	anti-inflationary	semi-indirect

835 **a.** When the prefix ends with *e* or *o* and the base word begins with the same letter, the hyphen is almost always omitted.

reeducate	preeminent	**BUT:** de-emphasize
reelect	preemployment	de-escalate
reemphasize	preempt	
reemploy	preexisting	
reenforce	**BUT:** pre-engineered	

b. When the prefix is *co* and the base word begins with *o,* use a hyphen except in a few commonly used words.

co-occurrence	co-opt	**BUT:** coordinate
co-official	co-organizer	cooperate
co-op	co-owner	cooperative

However, when the base word following *co* begins with a letter other than *o*, omit the hyphen.

coauthor	coedition*	copromoter
cocaptain	coeditor	copublisher
cochair	cofounder	cosign*
coconspirator	copartner	cosigner
cocontributor	copayment*	cosponsor
codefendant	copilot	costar
codeveloper	coproducer	coworker

836 **a.** Use a hyphen after *self* when it serves as a prefix.

self-addressed	self-fulfilling	self-serving
self-confidence	self-help	self-study
self-destruct	self-important	self-supporting
self-evident	self-paced	self-worth

b. Omit the hyphen when *self* serves as the base word and is followed by a suffix.

selfdom	selfhood	selfness
selfish	selfless	selfsame

c. Avoid the expression *him- or herself.* Use *himself or herself.*

---

*Merriam-Webster hyphenates this word.

¶**837**

837 As a rule, the prefix *re* (meaning "again") should not be followed by a hyphen. A few words require the hyphen so that they can be distinguished from other words with the same spelling but a different meaning.

to *re-act* a part in a play	to *react* calmly to pressure
to *re-coil* the hose	to *recoil* from danger
to *re-collect* the slips	to *recollect* the mistake
to *re-cover* a chair	to *recover* from an illness
to *re-create* the crime scene	to *recreate* on a long vacation
to *re-dress* the mannequins	to *redress* a wrong
to *re-form* the rows	to *reform* a sinner
to *re-lay* the carpet	to *relay* a message
to *re-lease* the apartment	to *release* the hostage
she *re-marked* the ticket	as he *remarked* to me
to *re-press* the jacket	to *repress* one's emotions
to *re-prove* your point	to *reprove* an offender
to *re-search* the files for the missing contract	to *research* (investigate) a problem in depth
I *re-sent* the letter yesterday	I *resent* her criticisms
to *re-serve* your customers	to *reserve* the right to sue
to *re-side* my house	to *reside* in comfort and safety
to *re-solve* this riddle	to *resolve* the conflict
to *re-sort* the cards	to *resort* to violence
to *re-sign* the contracts	to *resign* the position
to *re-strain* one's wrist	to *restrain* one's impulses
to *re-treat* the cloth	to *retreat* to safer ground

838 When a prefix is added to a word that begins with a capital letter, use a hyphen after the prefix.

anti-Semitic	mid-January	non-Windows application
inter-African	trans-Canadian	pre-Revolutionary War days
un-American	pro-Republican	post-World War II period

BUT: transatlantic, transpacific, the Midwest

839 Always hyphenate family terms involving the prefix *great* or the suffix *in-law,* but treat terms involving *step* and *grand* solid.

my great-grandfather	your brother-in-law	my grandmother
their great-aunt	my stepdaughter	his grandchild

Note how the use or omission of a hyphen changes the meaning.

Martha Henderson is a *great-grandmother.* (At least one of her grandchildren has a child.)

Martha Henderson is a *great grandmother.* (She treats her grandchildren extremely well.)

840 Avoid feminine suffixes like *ess, ette,* and *trix.*

She has an established reputation as an *author* and a *poet.* (**NOT:** authoress and poetess.)

If you have any questions, ask your *flight attendant.* (**NOT:** stewardess.)

NOTE: A few terms with feminine suffixes are still widely used; for example, *actress, hostess, heroine, fiancée,* and *waitress.* In legal documents, the terms *executrix* and *testatrix* are increasingly being replaced by *executor* and *testator.*

841 Use a hyphen after *quasi* when an adjective follows.

quasi-judicial	quasi-public
quasi-legislative	**BUT:** quasi corporation

842 When *after* is used as a prefix, do not use a hyphen to set it off from the root word. When *after* is used as a preposition in a compound adjective, insert a hyphen.

aftereffect	aftershave	**BUT:** an after-dinner speech
afterlife	aftershock	an after-hours club
aftermath	afterthought	my after-tax income
afternoon	afterward	an after-theater snack

843 When *in* is used as a prefix meaning "not," do not use a hyphen to set it off from the root word. When *in* is used as a preposition in a compound adjective, insert a hyphen.

inactive	infallible	**BUT:** an in-depth analysis
inarticulate	insensitive	in-flight movies
incapable	insolvent	our in-house designers
indecisive	intolerable	an in-service program

844 Although a hyphen is not ordinarily used to set off the prefix *mid*, a hyphen normally follows *mid* in expressions involving numbers or capitalized words.

during the mid-sixties **OR** the mid-60s (see ¶¶434, 439a)
sailing in the mid-Atlantic in mid-June (see ¶838)

845 Many words beginning with the prefix *off* are written solid, but some are hyphenated.

offhand	offshore	**BUT:** off-color
offline	offspring	off-key
offset	offstage	off-season
offshoot	offtrack	off-white

846 If the addition of the suffix *less* or *like* causes three *l*'s to occur in succession, insert a hyphen before the suffix. (See also ¶706, note.)

lifelike	businesslike	**BUT:** bell-like
faultless	bottomless	shell-less

Compound Computer Terms

847 The free spirits who coin most computer terms typically feel no obligation to follow the standard rules for the treatment of compound words. Consider the term *World Wide Web*. According to ¶820b, *worldwide* should be a solid word, but actual usage—in this case, *World Wide*—must always take precedence over rules. Indeed, the rules merely represent an attempt to impose some order and consistency on a language that cheerfully persists in disorder and inconsistency.

The problem is especially severe in the treatment of compound words in computer terminology, where changes occur so rapidly that it is impossible to establish a style that one can confidently expect to last for several years. What's more, at any given time a particular word may be in a state of unsettled transition and appear in several ways—hyphenated, spaced, and solid. The general tendency is for hyphenated forms to give way to either spaced or solid forms and for the spaced forms to give way to solid forms.

Continued on page 224

Compound Words

8

¶847

Consider the word *e-mail.* Initially presented as *electronic mail,* the term evolved into *E-mail,* and conservative writers still write the word with a capital *E.* Writers on the cutting edge, who continually press for fewer hyphens and less capitalization, have already converted the term to *email.* Those currently occupying the middle ground treat the word as *e-mail,* but with the passage of time (two years? four years? six months?) *email* may become the standard form.

Dictionaries typically show the more conservative spellings, because they cannot keep pace with the changes rapidly taking place in the field. Where, then, do you turn for up-to-date guidance? The best places to look are (1) the magazines and dictionaries devoted to computer and Internet technology and (2) the manuals and style guides published by industry insiders. If you are writing for a knowledgeable audience of computer users, you can choose the emerging style for the treatment of compound words. If, on the other hand, you are writing for readers who are not immersed in the field, you may find it safer to stay with the more conservative treatment of these words, because such readers will more easily grasp, say, *file name* than *filename.*

The following paragraphs provide some guidelines on the current treatment of compound computer terms.

a. In the following list, the two-word forms (shown first) are still more common, but the one-word forms are starting to take hold.

file name	**OR**	filename	screen saver	**OR** screensaver
home page	**OR**	homepage	spell checker	**OR** spellchecker
menu bar	**OR**	menubar	voice mail	**OR** voicemail

b. In the following list, the one-word forms (shown first) are more common, but the spaced or hyphenated forms are still being used.

barcode	**OR**	bar code	offline	**OR** off-line
handheld	**OR**	hand-held	offscreen	**OR** off-screen
hardwired	**OR**	hard-wired	online	**OR** on-line
logoff (n.)	**OR**	log-off	onscreen	**OR** on-screen
BUT: log off (v.)			touchpad	**OR** touch pad
logon (n.)	**OR**	log-on	touchscreen	**OR** touch screen
BUT: log on (v.)			wordwrap	**OR** word wrap

c. In the following list, the two-word forms (shown first) are more common, but the hyphenated forms (which follow the standard rules) are also being used.

dot matrix printers	**OR**	dot-matrix printers
local area networks	**OR**	local-area networks
wide area networks	**OR**	wide-area networks

d. In the following list, the hyphenated forms (shown first) are more common, but the solid or spaced forms (if given) are now being used in materials aimed at industry insiders.

e-mail	**OR** email	drop-down menu	**OR**	dropdown menu
pop-up window		pull-down menu	**OR**	pulldown menu
read-only memory		ink-jet printer	**OR**	inkjet printer
write-only files		random-access memory	**OR**	random access memory

e. The following compound words are always solid except in a few special cases.

backup (n. & adj.)	lookup table	trackball
BUT: back up (v.)	**BUT:** look up (v.)	trackpad
desktop	newsgroup	uplink (v.)
downlink (v.)	newsreader	upload (v.)
download (v.)	**BUT:** news server	userid (derived from *user ID*)
keyword	palmtop	whois (derived from *who is*)
laptop	toolbar	workstation

f. Compound words beginning with *Web* are usually two words.

Web site	Web server	**BUT:** Webmaster
Web page	Web browser	Webcasting
Web surfer	Web directory	Webzine

NOTE: The term *Web site* is starting to appear as one word *(Website)*. Moreover, this word (as well as a few other *Web* compounds) is starting to lose the initial cap *(website)*. However, for the sake of consistency, it is better to retain the capital *W* until a majority of these terms (such as the *World Wide Web* and *the Web*) lose their initial cap as well.

Sometimes One Word, Sometimes Two Words

848 A number of common words may be written either as one solid word or as two separate words, depending on the meaning. See individual entries listed alphabetically in ¶1101 (unless otherwise indicated) for the following words:

Almost–all most	Indirect–in direct
Already–all ready	Into–in to (see *In*)
Altogether–all together	Maybe–may be
Always–all ways	Nobody–no body
Anymore–any more	None–no one (see ¶1013)
Anyone–any one (see ¶1010, note)	Onto–on to (see *On*)
Anytime–any time	Someday–some day
Anyway–any way	Someone–some one (see ¶1010, note)
Awhile–a while	Sometime–sometimes–some time
Everyday–every day	Upon–up on (see *On*)
Everyone–every one (see ¶1010, note)	Whatever–what ever
Indifferent–in different	Whoever–who ever

> *Hyphens in spelled-out numbers: see ¶¶427, 465.*
> *Hyphens in spelled-out dates: see ¶411.*
> *Hyphens in spelled-out amounts of money: see ¶420.*
> *Hyphens in spelled-out fractions: see ¶427.*
> *Hyphens in numbers representing a continuous sequence: see ¶¶459–460.*

SECTION 9

Word Division

Basic Rules (¶¶901–906)
Preferred Practices (¶¶907–918)
Breaks Within Word Groups (¶¶919–920)
Guides to Correct Syllabication (¶¶921–922)

➤ *For definitions of grammatical terms, see the appropriate entries in the Glossary of Grammatical Terms (Appendix A).*

Automatic hyphenation is a feature of many word processing programs. When the automatic hyphenation feature is turned on, the program consults its electronic dictionaries to determine where to insert a hyphen when dividing a word at the end of a line. The electronic dictionaries may not always agree with the authority for word divisions shown in this manual (the 1997 printing of *Merriam-Webster's Collegiate Dictionary,* Tenth Edition). Moreover, some of the electronic word divisions may break the "unbreakable" rules in ¶¶901–906. Therefore, always review all electronic word-division decisions and adjust them as necessary.

When the automatic hyphenation feature is turned on, the hyphen that divides a word at the end of a line is a *soft hyphen* (that is, a nonpermanent hyphen). If you subsequently change your text so that the divided word no longer falls at the end of a line, the soft hyphen will disappear. If you are typing an expression in which a hyphen must always appear, use a *regular hyphen*. If such an expression crosses the end of a line, it will be divided after the hyphen. If you are typing a hyphenated expression (such as a phone number) that should not be divided at the end of a line, use a *hard* (or *nonbreaking*) *hyphen.* In that way the complete expression will remain on the same line. (See ¶903b.)

Whenever possible, avoid dividing a word at the end of a line. Word divisions are unattractive and they may sometimes confuse a reader. However, an extremely ragged right margin is also very unattractive. When word division is unavoidable, try to divide at the point that is least likely to disrupt the reader's grasp of the word. The following word division rules include (1) those that must never be broken (¶¶901–906) and (2) those that should be followed whenever space permits a choice (¶¶907–920).

NOTE: Professional typesetters often take liberties with the rules of word division in order to fit copy within a limited amount of space. For that reason you may occasionally notice word divisions in this professionally typeset manual that do not follow the guidelines presented in Section 9.

➤ *For the division of URLs and e-mail addresses at the end of a line, see ¶¶1538–1539.*

Basic Rules

901 Divide words only between syllables. Whenever you are unsure of the syllabication of a word, consult a dictionary. (See also ¶¶921–922 for some guidelines on correct syllabication.)

> ex- traordinary **OR** extraor- dinary **OR** extraordi- nary **BUT NOT:** extra- ordinary

NOTE: Some syllable breaks shown in the dictionary are not acceptable as points of word division. (See ¶¶903–904.)

902 Do not divide one-syllable words. Even when *ed* is added to some words, they still remain one-syllable words and cannot be divided.

stressed	through	spring	hour
planned	thoughts	straight	rhythm

903 **a.** Do not set off a one-letter syllable at the beginning or the end of a word.

> amaze (**NOT:** a- maze)   ideal (**NOT:** i- deal)
> media (**NOT:** medi- a)   lucky (**NOT:** luck- y)

NOTE: So as to discourage word division at the beginning or end of a word, some dictionaries no longer mark one-letter syllables at these points.

b. When typing a word like *e-mail,* use a hard (or nonbreaking) hyphen so that the word will not be divided after the *e-*.

904 Do not divide a word unless you can leave a syllable of at least three characters (the last of which is the hyphen) on the upper line and you can carry a syllable of at least three characters (the last may be a punctuation mark) to the next line.

> *ad* -mit   *de*- ter   *un*- der   *in*- ert
> do- *ing*   re- *new*   set- *up,*   happi- *ly.*

NOTE: Whenever possible, avoid dividing any word with fewer than six letters.

905 Do not divide abbreviations.

ACTION	UNICEF	AMVETS	NASDAQ
irreg.	approx.	assoc.	introd.

NOTE: An abbreviation like *AFL-CIO* may be divided after the hyphen.

906 Do not divide contractions.

haven't	shouldn't	mustn't	o'clock

Preferred Practices

While it is acceptable to divide a word at almost any syllable break shown in the dictionary, it is often better to divide at some points than at others in order to obtain a more intelligible grouping of syllables. The following rules indicate preferred practices whenever you have sufficient space left in the line to permit a choice.

907 Divide a solid compound word between the elements of the compound.

> eye- witness   time- saving   photo- copy   socio- economic

908 Divide a hyphenated compound word at the point of the hyphen.

> self- confidence   father- in-law   cross- reference   senator- elect

Word Division

9

¶909

909 Divide a word *after* a prefix (rather than within the prefix).

Preferred		Acceptable	
....	intro-	....	in-
duce	inter-	troduce	in-
national	super-	ternational	su-
sonic	circum-	personic	cir-
stances	ambi-	cumstance	am-
dextrous		bidextrous	

However, avoid divisions like the following, which can easily confuse a reader.

Confusing		Better	
....	inter-	....	in-
rogate	super-	terrogate	su-
lative	circum-	perlative	cir-
ference	ambi-	cumference ...	am-
tious	hyper-	bitious	hy-
bole	extra-	perbole	ex-
neous	coin-	traneous........	co-
cide		incide	

910 Divide a word *before* a suffix (rather than within the suffix).

appli- cable (**RATHER THAN:** applica- ble)

comprehen- sible (**RATHER THAN:** comprehensi- ble)

911 When a word has both a prefix and a suffix, choose the division point that groups the syllables more intelligibly.

replace- ment (**RATHER THAN:** re- placement)

The same principle applies when a word contains a suffix added on to a suffix. Choose the division point that produces the better grouping.

helpless- ness (**RATHER THAN:** help- lessness)

912 Whenever you have a choice, divide after a prefix or before a suffix (rather than within the root word).

over- active (**RATHER THAN:** overac- tive)

success- ful (**RATHER THAN:** suc- cessful)

NOTE: Avoid divisions that could confuse a reader.

re- address (**NOT:** read- dress)	re- invest (**NOT:** rein- vest)
re- allocate (**NOT:** real- locate)	co- insure (**NOT:** coin- sure)
re- arrange (**NOT:** rear- range)	co- operate (**NOT:** coop- erate)

913 When a one-letter syllable occurs within the root of a word, divide *after* it (rather than before it).

impera- tive	pene- trate	simi- lar	congratu- late
nega- tive	reme- dies	apolo- gize	salu- tary

914 When two separately sounded vowels come together in a word, divide between them.

recre- ation	medi- ation	pro- active	situ- ated
pre- eminent	experi- ence	po- etic	influ- ential
spontane- ity	anti- intellectual	auto- immune	ingenu- ity
courte- ous	patri- otic	co- opting	continu- ous

¶**920**

NOTE: Do not divide between two vowels when they are used together to represent one sound.

main- tained	trea- surer	en- croaching	ac- quaint
extraor- dinary	es- teemed	ap- point	guess- ing
pa- tience	sur- geon	ty- coon	acquit- tal
por- tion	neu- tral	pro- nounce	mis- quoted

915 When necessary, an extremely long number can be divided after a comma; for example, *24,358,- 692,000.* Try to leave at least four digits on the line above and at least six digits on the line below, but always divide after a comma.

916 Try not to end more than two consecutive lines in hyphens.

917 Try not to divide at the end of the first line or at the end of the last full line in a paragraph.

918 Do not divide the last word on a page.

Breaks Within Word Groups

919 Try to keep together certain kinds of word groups that need to be read together—for example, page and number, month and day, month and year, title and surname, surname and abbreviation (or number), number and abbreviation, or number and unit of measure.

page 203	Mrs. Connolly	10:30 a.m.
April 29	Paula Schein, J.D.	465 miles
September 2002	Adam Hagerty Jr.	80 percent

NOTE: If you are using word processing software, insert a *hard space* (also known as a *nonbreaking space*) between the elements of a word group that should not be broken at the end of a line. The complete word group will remain on the same line.

920 When necessary, longer word groups may be broken as follows:

a. *Dates* may be broken between the day and year.

.... November 14,   **NOT:** .... November
2001, ...   14, 2001,..................................

b. *Street addresses* may be broken between the name of the street and *Street, Avenue,* or the like. If the street name consists of two or more words, the break may come between words in the street name.

.... 1024 Westervelt   **NOT:** 1024
Boulevard ....   Westervelt Boulevard ....
.... 617 North   **NOT:** 617
Fullerton Street ....   North Fullerton Street ....

c. *Names of places* may be broken between the city and the state or between the state and the ZIP Code. If the city or state name consists of two or more words, the break may come between these words.

.... Portland,   **OR:** .... Portland, Oregon
Oregon 97229, ...   97229, ...
.... Grand   **OR:** .... Grand Forks, North
Rapids, MI 49505, ...   Dakota, ...

Continued on page 230

¶921

d. *Names of persons* may be broken between the given name (including middle initial if given) and surname.

.... Mildred R. Palumbo ....

NOT: .... Mildred R. Palumbo ....

NOTE: If it is absolutely necessary, a person's name may be divided. Follow the same principles given for dividing ordinary words.

Eisen- hower   Spil- lane (see ¶922c)   **BUT:** Spell- man (see ¶922a)

e. *Names preceded by long titles* may be broken between the title and the name (preferably) or between words in the title.

.... Assistant Commissioner Roy N. Frawley ....

OR: .... Assistant Commissioner Roy N. Frawley ....

f. *Names of departments* may be broken between words.

.... Human Resources Department ....

.... Bureau of Public Safety ....

g. *A numbered or lettered enumeration* may be broken before (but not directly after) any number or letter.

.... these points: (1) All cards should ....

NOT: .... these points: (1) All cards should ....

h. *A sentence with a dash in it* may be broken after the dash.

.... Early next year— say, in March—let's ....

NOT: .... Early next year —say, in March—let's ....

i. *A sentence with ellipsis marks in it* may be broken after the ellipsis marks.

Tennis . . . health spa . . . golf . . . and more.

NOT: Tennis . . . health spa . . . golf . . . and more.

Guides to Correct Syllabication

921 Syllabication is generally based on pronunciation rather than on roots and derivations.

knowl- edge (**NOT:** know- ledge)   chil- dren (**NOT:** child- ren)   prod- uct (**NOT:** pro- duct)

Note how syllabication changes as pronunciation changes.

Verbs	Nouns
pre- sent (to make a gift)	pres- ent (a gift)
re- cord (to make an official copy)	rec- ord (an official copy)
pro- ject (to throw forward)	proj- ect (an undertaking)

922 **a.** If a word ends in double consonants *before* a suffix is added, you can safely divide *after* the double consonants (so long as the suffix creates an extra syllable).

sell- ers   staff- ing   bless- ing   buzz- ers   **BUT:** filled, distressed

b. If a final consonant of the base word is doubled *because* a suffix is added, you can safely divide *between* the double consonants if the suffix creates an extra syllable.

begin- ner   omit- ted   ship- ping   refer- ral   **BUT:** shipped, referred

c. When double consonants appear elsewhere *within* the base word (but not as the final consonants), you can safely divide between them.

| bub- bling | sup- pose | con- nect | dif- fer | bet- ter | neces- sary |
| suc- cess | recom- mend | mid- dle | strug- gle | cur- rent | mil- lion |

SECTION **10**

Grammar

Subjects and Verbs (¶¶1001–1029)

Verbs (¶¶1030–1048)

➤ *For definitions of grammatical terms, see the appropriate entries in the Glossary of Grammatical Terms (Appendix A).*

Subjects and Verbs

Basic Rule of Agreement

1001 **a.** A verb must agree with its subject in number and person.

I am eager to start work. (First person singular subject *I* with first person singular verb *am*.)

It seems odd that *Farmer has* not *followed up* on our last conversation. (Third person singular subjects *it* and *Farmer* with third person singular verbs *seems* and *has* not *followed up*.)

He is coming to stay with us for a week. (Third person singular subject *he* with third person singular verb *is coming*.)

She does intend to call you this week. (Third person singular subject *she* with third person singular verb *does intend*.)

We were delighted to read about your promotion. (First person plural subject *we* with first person plural verb *were*.)

They are convinced that the *Foys are* worth millions. (Third person plural subjects *they* and *Foys* with third person plural verbs *are convinced* and *are*.)

Your *order* for six laptop computers *was shipped* last Friday. (Third person singular subject *order* with third person singular verb *was shipped*.)

Our *efforts* to save the business *have been* unsuccessful. (Third person plural subject *efforts* with third person plural verb *have been*.)

NOTE: A plural verb is always required after *you,* even when *you* is singular, referring to only one person.

You alone *have understood* the full dimensions of the problem. (Second person singular subject *you* with second person plural verb *have understood*.)

You both *have been* a great help to us. (Second person plural subject *you* with second person plural verb *have been*.)

You do enjoy your work, don't you? (Second person singular subject *you* with second person plural verb *do enjoy*.)

b. Although *s* or *es* added to a *noun* indicates the plural form, *s* or *es* added to a *verb* indicates the third person singular. (See ¶1035.)

Singular	Plural
The price *seems* reasonable.	The prices *seem* reasonable.
The tax *applies* to everyone.	The taxes *apply* to everyone.

Subjects Joined by *And*

1002 **a.** If the subject consists of two or more words that are connected by *and* or by *both . . . and,* the subject is plural and requires a plural verb.

Ms. Rizzo and *Mr. Bruce have received* promotions.

Both the *collection* and the *delivery* of mail *are* to be curtailed as of July 1. (The repetition of *the* with the second subject emphasizes that two different items are meant.)

The *general managers* and the *controllers are attending* a three-day meeting in Chicago.

The *director of marketing* and the *product managers are* now *reviewing* the advertising budgets.

The *sales projections* and the *cost estimate do* not *have* to be revised.

b. Use a singular verb when two or more subjects connected by *and* refer to the same person or thing. (See also ¶1028a, fourth example.)

Our *secretary and treasurer is* Frances Eisenberg. (One person.)

Corned beef and cabbage was his favorite dish. (One dish.)

Wear and tear has to be expected when you're in the rental business. (One type of damage.)

Continued on page 234

¶1003

c. Use a singular verb when two or more subjects connected by *and* are preceded by *each, every, many a,* or *many an.* (See also ¶1009b.)

> *Every* computer, printer, and fax machine *is marked* for reduction.
>
> *Many a* woman and man *has responded* to our plea for contributions.

Subjects Joined by *Or* or Similar Connectives

1003 If the subject consists of two or more *singular* words that are connected by *or, either . . . or, neither . . . nor,* or *not only . . . but also,* the subject is singular and requires a singular verb.

> Either *July* or *August is* a good time for the sales conference.
>
> Neither the *Credit Department* nor the *Accounting Department has* the file.
>
> Not only a cost-profit *analysis* but also a marketing *plan needs* to be developed.

1004 If the subject consists of two or more *plural* words that are connected by *or, either . . . or, neither . . . nor,* or *not only . . . but also,* the subject is plural and requires a plural verb.

> Neither the *regional managers* nor the *salesclerks have* the data you want.
>
> Not only the *dealers* but also the *retailers are* unhappy about our new policy.

1005 If the subject is made up of both singular and plural words connected by *or, either . . . or, neither . . . nor,* or *not only . . . but also,* the verb agrees with the nearer part of the subject. Since sentences with singular and plural subjects usually sound better with plural verbs, try to locate the plural subject closer to the verb whenever this can be done without sacrificing the emphasis desired.

> Either *Miss Hertig* or her *assistants have* copies of the new catalog. (The verb *have* agrees with the nearer subject, *assistants.*)
>
> Neither the *buyers* nor the *sales manager is* in favor of the system. (The verb *is* agrees with the nearer subject, *sales manager.*)
>
> **BETTER:** Neither the *sales manager* nor the *buyers are* in favor of the system. (The sentence reads better with the plural verb *are.* The subjects *sales manager* and *buyers* have been rearranged without changing the emphasis.)
>
> Not only the *teachers* but also the *superintendent is* in favor of the plan. (The verb *is* agrees with the nearer subject, *superintendent.* With the use of *not only . . . but also,* the emphasis falls on the subject following *but also.*)
>
> Not only the *superintendent* but also the *teachers are* in favor of the plan. (When the sentence is rearranged, the nearer subject, *teachers,* requires the plural verb *are.* However, the emphasis has now changed.)
>
> Not only my *colleagues* but *I am* in favor of the plan. (The first person verb *am* agrees with the nearer subject, *I.* Rearranging this sentence will change the emphasis.)

NOTE: When the subjects reflect different grammatical persons (first, second, or third), the verb should agree in person as well as number with the nearer subject. If the result seems awkward, reword as necessary.

> **ACCEPTABLE:** Neither you nor *I am* in a position to pay Ben's legal fees.
>
> **BETTER:** Neither *one* of us *is* in a position to pay Ben's legal fees. (See ¶1009a.)
>
> **ACCEPTABLE:** Neither you nor *she has* the time to take on the Fuller case.
>
> **ACCEPTABLE:** Neither she nor *you have* the time to take on the Fuller case.
>
> **BETTER:** She and *you are* each too busy to take on the Fuller case. (See ¶1009c.)
>
> **AWKWARD:** If you or *Gary is coming* to the convention, please visit our booth.
>
> **BETTER:** If Gary or *you are coming* to the convention, please visit our booth.

¶1007

> ➤ *For* neither . . . nor *constructions following* there is, there are, there was, *or* there were, *see the last four examples in ¶1028a; for examples of subject-verb-pronoun agreement in these constructions, see ¶1049c.*

Intervening Phrases and Clauses

1006 **a.** When establishing agreement between subject and verb, disregard intervening phrases and clauses.

> The *purchase order* for new diskettes *has* not *been found.* (Disregard *for new diskettes.* The subject, *purchase order,* is singular and takes the singular verb *has* not *been found.*)
>
> The *prices* shown in our catalog *do* not *include* sales tax.
>
> Only *one* of the items that I ordered *has been delivered.* (See also ¶1008.)
>
> Her *experience* with banks and brokerage houses *gives* her excellent qualifications for the position.
>
> Several *phases* of our order processing system *are* out of sync.
>
> A key *factor,* the company's assets, *is* not *being given* sufficient weight in the analysis. (The subject *factor,* not the intervening appositive, determines that the verb should be singular in this case.)
>
> **BUT:** The company's *assets,* a key factor, *are* not *being given* sufficient weight in the analysis.

NOTE: When certain indefinite pronouns *(all, none, any, some, more, most)* and certain fractional expressions (for example, *one-half of, a part of, a percentage of*) are used as subjects, you may have to look at an intervening phrase or clause to determine whether the verb should be singular or plural. See ¶¶1013 and 1025 for examples.

b. When a sentence has both a positive and a negative subject, make the verb agree with the positive subject. Set off the negative subject with commas unless it is preceded by *and* or *but.*

> *Profit* and not sales *is* the thing to keep your eye on. (The verb *is* agrees with the positive subject *profit.*)
>
> The *design* of the container, not the contents, *determines* what the consumer's initial reaction to the product will be.
>
> The *members* of the Executive Committee and not the president *wield* the real power in the corporation.
>
> *It is* not the president but the *members* of the Executive Committee who *wield* the real power in the corporation. (In the main clause the verb *is* agrees with the subject *it;* the verb *wield* in the *who* clause is plural to agree with the antecedent of *who,* the positive subject *members.* See ¶1062c.)
>
> **BUT:** It is the *president* and not the members of the Executive Committee who *wields* the real power in the corporation. (In this sentence the positive subject is *president,* a singular noun; therefore, the verb *wields* in the *who* clause must also be singular.)

1007 The number of the verb is not affected by the insertion between subject and verb of phrases beginning with such expressions as:

along with	plus
together with	besides
and not (see ¶1006b)	including
as well as	except
in addition to	rather than
accompanied by	not even

Continued on page 236

Grammar

10

¶1008

If the subject is singular, use a singular verb; if the subject is plural, use a plural verb.

> This *study,* along with many earlier reports, *shows* that the disease can be arrested if detected in time.
>
> *Mr. and Mrs. Swenson,* together with their son and daughters, *are going* to New Mexico.
>
> *No one,* not even the executive vice presidents, *knows* whether the CEO plans to resign. (See ¶1010.)
>
> The *director* of finance, not the divisional controllers, *is authorized* to approve unbudgeted expenditures over $5000. (See ¶1006b.)

NOTE: When the construction of a sentence like those above requires a singular verb but a plural verb would sound more natural, reword the sentence to create a plural subject.

> **CORRECT:** The national sales *report,* along with the regional breakdowns you specifically requested plus the individual performance printouts, *was sent* to you last week.
>
> **BETTER:** The national sales *report,* the regional *breakdowns* you specifically requested, and the individual performance *printouts were sent* to you last week. (The three subjects joined by *and—report, breakdowns,* and *printouts—*call for a plural verb.)

One of . . .

1008 **a.** Use a singular verb after a phrase beginning with *one of* or *one of the;* the singular verb agrees with the subject *one.* (Disregard any plural that follows *of* or *of the.*)

> *One* of my backup disks *has been lost.*
>
> *One* of the reasons for so many absences *is* poor motivation.
>
> *One* of us *has* to take over the responsibility for in-service training.
>
> *One* of you *is* to be nominated for the office.
>
> *One* of the interviewers *is going* to call you early next week.

b. The phrases *one of those who* and *one of the things that* are followed by plural verbs because the verbs refer to *those* or *things* (rather than to *one*).

> She is one of *those* who *favor* increasing the staff. (In other words, of *those* who favor increasing the staff, she is one. *Favor* is plural to agree with *those.*)
>
> He is one of our *employees* who *are* never late. (Of our *employees* who *are* never late, he is one.)
>
> I ordered one of the new *copiers* that *were advertised* in Monday's paper. (Of the new *copiers* that *were advertised* in Monday's paper, I ordered one.)
>
> You are one of *those* rare individuals who *are* always honest with *themselves.* (Of those rare *individuals* who *are* always honest with *themselves,* you are one.)

EXCEPTION: When the words *the only* precede such phrases, the meaning is singular and a singular verb is required. Note that both words, *the* and *only,* are required to produce a singular meaning.

> John is *the only one* of the staff members who *is going* to be transferred. (Of the staff members, John is *the only one* who is going to be transferred. Here the singular verb *is going* is required to agree with *one.*)
>
> **BUT:** John is only one of the *staff members* who *are going* to be transferred. (Of the *staff members* who *are going* to be transferred, John is only one.)

Indefinite Pronouns Always Singular

1009 **a.** The words *each, every, either, neither, one, another,* and *much* are always singular. When they are used as subjects or as adjectives modifying subjects, a singular verb is required.

Each has a clear-cut set of responsibilities.

Each employee was informed of the new policy well in advance.

One shipment was sent yesterday; *another is* to leave the warehouse tomorrow morning.

Neither one of the applicants *is* eligible.

OR: *Neither applicant is* eligible.

Much remains to be done on the Belgravia project.

OR: *Much work remains* to be done on the Belgravia project.

➤ *For the use of* either . . . or *and* neither . . . nor, *see ¶¶1003–1005.*

b. When *each, every, many a,* or *many an* precedes two or more subjects joined by *and,* the verb should be singular.

Every customer and supplier has been notified.

Many a liberal and conservative has raised objections to that proposal.

➤ *See ¶1002c for other examples.*

c. When *each* follows a plural subject, keep the verb plural. In that position, *each* has no effect on the number of the verb. To test the correctness of such sentences, mentally omit *each.*

The *members* each *feel* their responsibility.

They each *have* high expectations.

Twelve each of these items *are required.*

1010 The following compound pronouns are always singular and require a singular verb:

anybody	everybody	somebody	nobody
anything	everything	something	nothing
anyone	everyone	someone	no one
OR any one	**OR** every one	**OR** some one	

Was anybody monitoring actual costs against the budget?

Everyone is required to register in order to vote.

Something tells me I'm wrong.

No one could explain why the project was so far behind schedule.

NOTE: Spell *anyone, everyone,* and *someone* as two words when these pronouns are followed by an *of* phrase or are used to mean "one of a number of things."

Every one of us (each person in the group) *likes* to be appreciated.

BUT: *Everyone* (everybody) *likes* to be appreciated.

1011 Use a singular verb when two compound pronouns joined by *and* are used as subjects.

Anyone and *everyone is entitled* to a fair hearing.

Nobody and *nothing is going* to stop me.

Indefinite Pronouns Always Plural

1012 The words *both, few, many, others,* and *several* are always plural. When they are used as subjects or as adjectives modifying subjects, a plural verb is required.

Several members were invited; the *others were overlooked.*

Both books are out of print.

Many were asked, but *few were* able to answer.

¶1013

Indefinite Pronouns Singular or Plural

1013 **a.** *All, none, any, some, more,* and *most* may be singular or plural, depending on the noun that they refer to. (The noun often occurs in an *of* phrase that follows.)

All of the manuscript *has been finished.*   *All* of the reports *have been handed in.*

Is there *any* (money) left?   *Are* there *any* (bills) to be paid?

Some of the software *seems* too high-priced.
Some of the videotapes *seem* too high-priced.

Some was acceptable. (Meaning some of the manuscript.)
Some were acceptable. (Meaning some of the reports.)

More of these computer stands *are* due.   *Most* of the stock *has been sold.*

More than one customer *has complained* about that item. (*More* refers to the singular noun *customer;* hence the singular verb *has complained.*)

More than five customers *have complained* . . . (*More* refers to the plural noun *customers;* hence the plural verb *have complained.*)

Do any of you *know* John Ferguson well? (*Any* is plural because it refers to the plural *you;* hence the plural verb *do know.*)

Does any one of you *know* John Ferguson well? (*Any* is singular because it refers to the singular *one;* hence the singular verb *does know.*)

b. In formal usage, *none* is still considered a singular pronoun. In general usage, however, *none* is considered singular or plural, depending on the number of the noun to which it refers. *No one* or *not one* is often used in place of *none* to stress the singular idea.

None of the merchandise *was stolen.*
None of the packages *were* properly *wrapped.*
None were injured. (Meaning none of the passengers.)
Not one of the associates *has* a good word to say about the managing partner.

NOTE: The relative pronouns *who, which,* and *that* (like the indefinite pronouns discussed in *a* above) may be singular or plural, depending on the noun they refer to. (See ¶1062c.)

Nouns Ending in *S*

1014 Some nouns appear to be plural but are actually singular. When used as subjects, these nouns require singular verbs.

news *(no plural)*   lens *(plural:* lenses)   measles *(no plural)*   summons *(plural:* summonses)
The *news* from overseas *is* very discouraging.   The *lens has* to be reground.

1015 A number of nouns are always considered plural, even though they each refer to a single thing. As subjects, they require plural verbs.

assets	dues	grounds	proceeds	savings
belongings	earnings	odds	quarters	thanks
credentials	goods	premises	riches	winnings

The *premises are* now available for inspection.   My *earnings* this year *have* not *gone* up.

NOTE: The following nouns are considered plural: *glasses, scissors, pliers, pants,* and *trousers.* However, when they are preceded by the phrase *pair of,* the entire expression is considered singular.

These *scissors need* sharpening.   **BUT:** This *pair of scissors needs* sharpening.

1016 A few nouns (not all of which end in *s*) have the same form in the plural as in the singular. When used as subjects, these nouns take singular or plural verbs according to the meaning.

series	means	chassis	headquarters	deer
species	gross	corps	sheep	moose

The *series* of concerts planned for the spring *looks* very exciting. (One series.)

Three *series* of tickets *are going* to be issued. (Three series.)

One *means* of breaking the impasse *is* to offer more money.

Other *means* of solving the problem *have* not *come* to mind.

Her *means* (referring to financial resources) *are* not sufficient to justify her current level of spending.

Headquarters is not pleased with the performance of the Northeastern Region. (Referring to top management or central authority.)

The Pesco Corporation *headquarters are located* at the intersection of Routes 80 and 287. (Referring to the offices of top management.)

Nouns Ending in *ICS*

1017 Many nouns ending in *ics* (such as *acoustics, economics, ethics, politics,* and *statistics*) take singular or plural verbs, depending on how they are used. When they refer to a body of knowledge or a course of study, they are *singular*. When they refer to qualities or activities, they are *plural*.

Economics (a course of study) *is* a prerequisite for advanced business courses.

The *economics* (the economic aspects) of his plan *are* not very sound.

Statistics is the one course I almost failed.

The *statistics indicate* that the market for this product line is shrinking.

Acoustics was not *listed* in last year's course offerings.

The *acoustics* in the new concert hall *are* remarkably good.

Ethics is a subject that ought to be part of the el-hi curriculum.

Frank's *ethics have* always *met* the highest standards.

Nouns With Foreign Plurals

1018 **a.** Watch for nouns with foreign-plural endings (see ¶614). Such plural nouns, when used as subjects, require plural verbs.

No *criteria have been established.*

BUT: No *criterion has been established.*

Parentheses are required around such references.

BUT: The closing *parenthesis was omitted.*

b. The noun *data,* which is plural in form, is commonly followed by a plural verb in technical and scientific usage. In general usage, *data* in the sense of "information" is followed by a singular verb; in the sense of "distinct bits of information," it is followed by a plural verb.

The *data* obtained after two months of experimentation *is* now *being analyzed.* (Here *data* means "information.")

BUT: The *data* assembled by six researchers *are* now *being compared.* (Here *data* refers to several distinct bits of information.)

Continued on page 240

¶1019

c. The noun *media* is the plural form of *medium* when that word refers to various forms of mass communication, such as the press, radio, and television.

> The *media* through which we reach our clients *are* quality magazines and radio broadcasts.
>
> **BUT:** The *medium* we find most effective *is* television.

NOTE: *Media* has acquired an acceptable singular meaning when it refers to reporters, journalists, and broadcasters acting in concert. However, treat *media* as a plural when these practitioners are not acting as a unified group.

> The *media has given* so much publicity to the claims against the defendant that a fair trial may not be possible.
>
> **BUT:** The *media have approached* the Bergamot case from a wide range of perspectives.

Collective Nouns

1019 The following rules govern the form of verb to be used when the subject is a collective noun. (A *collective noun* is a word that is singular in form but represents a group of persons, animals, or things; for example, *army, audience, board, cabinet, class, committee, company, corporation, council, department, faculty, firm, group, jury, majority, minority, public, school, society, staff.*)

a. If the group is acting as a unit, use the singular form of the verb.

> The *Board of Directors meets* Friday.   The *firm is* one of the oldest in the field.
>
> The *committee has agreed* to submit *its* report on Monday. (The pronoun *its* is also singular to agree with *committee.*)

b. If the members of the group are acting separately, use a plural verb.

> A *group* of researchers *are coming* from all over the world for the symposium next month. (The members of the group are acting separately in coming together from all over the world.)
>
> **BUT:** A *group* of researchers *is meeting* in Geneva next month. (The members of the group are acting as a unit in the process of meeting.)

NOTE: The use of a collective noun with a plural verb often produces an awkward sentence. Whenever possible, recast the sentence by inserting a phrase like *the members of* before the collective noun.

> **AWKWARD:** The *committee are* not in agreement on the action *they* should take. (The verb *are* and the pronoun *they* are plural to agree with the plural *committee.*)
>
> **BETTER:** The *members* of the committee *are* not in agreement . . .

c. In a number of constructions, the choice of a singular or plural verb often depends on whether you wish to emphasize the group as a unit or as a collection of individuals. However, once the choice has been made, treat the collective noun consistently within the same context. If the resulting sentence sounds awkward, recast it as necessary.

> I hope your *family is* well. (Emphasizes the family as a whole.)
>
> **OR:** I hope your *family are* all well. (Emphasizes the individuals in the family.)
>
> **SMOOTHER:** I hope all the *members* of your family *are* well.
>
> **OR:** I hope *everyone* in your family *is* well.
>
> The *couple was married* (**OR** *were married*) last Saturday.
>
> **OR:** *Bob and Pauline were married* last Saturday.
>
> The *couple have moved* into *their* new house. (More idiomatic than: The *couple has moved* into *its* new house.)
>
> **OR:** The *Goodwins have moved* into *their* new house.

NOTE: The expression *a couple of* is usually plural in meaning.

A couple of customers *have* already *reported* the error in our ad.

A couple of orders *have been shipped* to the wrong address.

BUT: *A couple of* days *is* all I need to complete the report. (When the phrase refers to a period of time, an amount of money, or a quantity that represents a total amount, treat the phrase as singular. See also ¶1024.)

Organizational Names

1020 Organizational names may be treated as either singular or plural. Ordinarily, treat the name as singular unless you wish to emphasize the individuals who make up the organization; in that case, use the plural. Once a choice has been made, use the singular or plural form consistently within the same context.

Brooks & Rice *has lost its* lease. *It is* now *looking* for a new location.

OR: Brooks & Rice *have lost their* lease. *They are* now *looking* for . . .

(**BUT NOT:** Brooks & Rice *has lost its* lease. *They are* now *looking* for . . .)

NOTE: If the organization is referred to as *they* or *who,* use a plural verb with the company name. If the organization is referred to as *it* or *which,* use a singular verb. (See ¶1049a.)

Geographic Names

1021 Geographic names that are plural in form are treated as *singular* if they refer to only one thing.

The *Netherlands is* the first stop on my itinerary.

The *Virgin Islands consists* of three large islands (St. John, St. Croix, and St. Thomas) and about fifty smaller islands.

The *United States has undertaken* a new foreign aid program.

BUT: These *United States are bound* together by a common heritage of political and religious liberty.

Names of Publications and Products

1022 The name of a publication or product is considered singular, even though it may be plural in form.

Physicians & Computers is one magazine you should consider if you want to market your software to doctors.

Consumer Reports is publishing an update on automobile insurance costs.

Changing Times is offering new subscribers a special rate for a limited time.

Miss Thistlebottom's Hobgoblins by Theodore M. Bernstein *deals* forcefully with the "taboos, bugbears, and outmoded rules of English usage."

The Number; a Number

1023 The expression *the number* has a singular meaning and therefore requires a singular verb; *a number* has a plural meaning and requires a plural verb.

The number of branch offices we have in the Southeast *has increased* in each of the last five years.

A number of our branch offices *are* now *located* in suburban malls rather than in the central business district.

¶1024

Expressions of Time, Money, and Quantity

1024 When subjects expressing periods of time, amounts of money, or quantities represent *a total amount,* use singular verbs. When these subjects represent *a number of individual units,* use plural verbs.

> *Three months is* too long a time to wait.
>
> **BUT:** *Three months have passed* since our last exchange of letters.
>
> That *$10,000 was* an inheritance from my uncle.
>
> **BUT:** *Thousands* of dollars *have* already *been spent* on the project.
>
> *Ten acres is considered* a small piece of property in this area.
>
> **BUT:** *Ten acres were plowed* last spring.
>
> A *total* of 52 *orders is* not a very good response rate to a full-page ad.
>
> **BUT:** A *total* of 52 *callers have placed* an order in response to our ad.
>
> A psychotic is convinced that *2 and 2 equals* 5, whereas a neurotic recognizes that *2 plus 2 is* 4 but can't stand it.
>
> *Less than $1 million was budgeted* for the restoration of City Hall. (For a usage note on *fewer–less,* see pages 293–294.)

Fractional Expressions

1025 When the subject is an expression such as *one-half of, two-thirds of, a part of, a majority of, a percentage of, a portion of,* or *the rest of:*

a. Use a *singular verb* if a *singular noun* follows *of* or is implied.

> *Three-fourths* of the *mailing list has been checked.*
>
> *Part* of our Norfolk *operation is being closed down.*
>
> *A majority* of *2000 signifies* a landslide in this town. (The noun *2000* is considered singular because it is a total amount; see ¶1024. For a usage note on *majority,* see page 299.)
>
> *A large percentage has* to be retyped. (Referring to a manuscript.)

b. Use a *plural verb* when a *plural noun* follows *of* or is implied.

> *Two-thirds* of our *customers live* in the suburbs.   *Part* of the *walls are* to be papered.
>
> *A majority* of our *employees have contributed* to the United Way fund drive.
>
> *A large percentage work* part-time. (Referring to the students at a college.)

NOTE: When used as a subject, the word *percentage* preceded by *the* requires a singular verb.

> *The percentage* of students who work part-time *is* quite large. (*The percentage* takes a singular verb, even though it is followed by a plural noun, *students.*)

c. Consider the word *half* as a condensed version of *one-half of.*

> Over *half* the *staff have signed up* for the additional benefits. (In this case *half the staff* is plural in meaning; the staff members are signing up as individuals and not as a group. See ¶1019b.)

Phrases and Clauses as Subjects

1026 When a phrase or clause serves as the subject, the verb should be singular.

> *Reading e-mail is* the first item on my morning agenda.
>
> *That they will accept the offer is* far from certain.
>
> *Whatever sales brochure they mail me goes* directly into the circular file.
>
> According to Bill Cosby, *whether the glass is half full or half empty depends* on whether you're pouring or drinking.

¶1028

EXCEPTION: Clauses beginning with *what* may be singular or plural, according to the meaning.

> *What we need is* a new *statement* of policy. (The *what* clause refers to *statement*; hence the verb is singular.)
>
> *What we need are* some *guidelines* on personal time off. (Here the *what* clause refers to *guidelines*; hence the verb is plural.)

Subjects in Inverted Sentences

1027 **a.** Whenever the verb precedes the subject, make sure they agree.

> *Attached is* a *swatch* of the fabric I'd like to order.
> *Attached are* two *copies* of the January mailing piece.
>
> *Enclosed is* a *copy* of the consultant's recommendations for boosting profits.
> Also *enclosed are* my *comments* on his suggested plan of action.
>
> Where *is* (**OR** Where's) this *strategy going* to take us?
> Where *are* the *reviews* of the Kelly book?
> **NOT:** Where *is* (**OR** Where's) the *reviews* of the Kelly book?
>
> What *is missing* from the report is the *rationale* for the decision.
> What *appear* to be problems *are* often *opportunities.*
> What *were* your *reasons* for resigning?
>
> *Should a position become* available, we will let you know. (In this case the helping verb *should* precedes the subject. If written in normal word order, this sentence would read: If *a position should become* available . . .)

b. When the verb is followed by two subjects joined by *and*, the verb should be plural. However, if the resulting sentence sounds awkward, reword as necessary.

> Where *are* the *address* and *phone number* for this customer?
> **BETTER:** Where can I find the address and phone number for this customer?
> **BUT NOT:** Where is (**OR** Where's) the address and phone number for this customer?
>
> **AWKWARD:** Why *are consumer spending* up and *retail sales* down?
> **BETTER:** Why are retail sales down and consumer spending up?
> **OR:** Why are retail sales down when consumer spending is up?

1028 **a.** In a sentence beginning with *there is, there are, here is, here are,* or a similar construction, the real subject follows the verb. Use *is* when the real subject is singular, *are* when it is plural.

> There *is* a vast *difference* between the two plans.
> There *are* a great many *angles* to this problem.
>
> Here *are* two *catalogs* and an *order blank.* (See ¶¶1002a, 1028b.)
> Here *is* an old *friend* and former *partner* of mine. (The subject, *friend and partner,* is singular because only one person is referred to. See ¶1002b.)
>
> There *is many an investor* who regrets not having bought our stock when it was only $5 a share. (See ¶1002c.)
> There *is* a *branch office* or an *agency* representing us in every major city in the country. (See ¶1003.)
> There *is* not only a 5 percent *state tax* but also a 2.5 percent *city tax.* (See ¶1003.)
> There *is* the *cost* of your own time in addition to the substantial outlay for materials that must be figured in. (See ¶1007.)

Continued on page 244

Grammar

10

¶1029

There's (There *is*) *more* than one *way* to solve the problem. (See ¶1013a.)

There're (There *are*) *more* than six *candidates* running for mayor. (See ¶1056e.)

(**NOT:** There's more than six candidates running for mayor.)

There *are a number* of problems to be resolved. (See also ¶1023.)

Here *is the number* of orders received since Monday.

Here *is ten dollars* as a contribution. (See also ¶1024.)

Here *are ten silver dollars* for your collection.

There *is* neither a *hospital* nor a *clinic* on the island. (See ¶1003 for two singular subjects joined by *neither . . . nor.*)

There *are* neither *motel rooms* nor *condominiums* available for rent this late in the season. (See ¶1004 for two plural subjects joined by *neither . . . nor.*)

There *were* neither *tennis courts* nor a *swimming pool* in the hotel where we finally found a room. (*Were* agrees with the nearer subject, *tennis courts.* See also ¶1005 for singular and plural subjects joined by *neither . . . nor.*)

There *was* neither central *air conditioning* nor *fans* for any of the rooms in the hotel. (*Was* agrees with the nearer subject, *air conditioning.* See also ¶1005.)

b. When the subject consists of two or more singular nouns—or several nouns, the first of which is singular—*there is* or *here is* usually sounds more idiomatic (despite the fact that the subject is plural) than *there are* or *here are.* If you do not feel comfortable with this idiomatic construction, change the wording as necessary.

In the higher-priced model there *is* a more powerful *processor,* a 13.3-inch *color display,* and a 6.4-GB *hard drive.* (In this construction, *there is* is understood to be repeated before the second and third subjects.)

OR: In the higher-priced model there *are* the following *features:* a more powerful *processor,* a 13.3-inch *color display,* and a 6.4-GB *hard drive.* (In this version *are* agrees with the plural subject *features;* the three subjects in the sentence above are now simply appositives modifying *features.*)

Within a mile of the airport there *is* a full-service *hotel* and three *motels.*

OR: Within a mile of the airport there *is* a full-service hotel *plus* (**OR** *in addition to* **OR** *as well as*) three motels. (By changing the connective from *and* to *plus* or something similar, you are left with a singular subject, *hotel,* that calls for the singular verb *is.*)

OR: Within a mile of the airport there *are* three *motels* and a full-service *hotel.* (When the first subject in the series is plural, the verb *are* not only is grammatically correct but also sounds natural.)

Subjects and Predicate Complements

1029 Sentences containing a linking verb (such as *become* or some form of *to be*) sometimes have a plural subject and a singular complement or a singular subject and a plural complement. In such cases make sure that the verb agrees with the *subject* (and not with the complement).

Bicycles are the only product we make.   The key *issue is* higher wages.

One of the things we have to keep track of *is* entertainment expenses. (Use *is* to agree with *one,* the subject.)

It is they who are at fault. (Use *is* to agree with *it,* the subject.)

NOTE: Do not confuse the last two examples with the *inverted* sentences shown in ¶1028. In a sentence beginning with *here is* or *there is,* the subject *follows* the linking verb. In a sentence beginning with *it is* or *one . . . is,* the subject *precedes* the linking verb.

¶**1030**

Verbs

This section deals with the correct use of verb tenses and other verb forms. For the rules on agreement of verbs with subjects, see ¶¶1001–1029.

Principal Parts

1030 The principal parts of a verb are the four simple forms upon which all tenses and other modifications of the verb are based.

a. For most verbs, form the past and the past participle simply by adding *d* or *ed* to the present; form the present participle by adding *ing* to the present. (Some verbs require a minor change in the ending of the present form before *ed* or *ing* is added.)

Present	Past	Past Participle	Present Participle	
taxi	taxied	taxied	taxiing	
drop	drop	dropped	dropping	(see ¶701)
occur	occurred	occurred	occurring	(see ¶702)
offer	offered	offered	offering	(see ¶704)
sneak	sneaked	sneaked	sneaking	(see ¶¶705, 1032b)
fill	filled	filled	filling	(see ¶706)
warm	warmed	warmed	warming	(see ¶706)
issue	issued	issued	issuing	(see ¶707)
die	died	died	dying	(see ¶709)
try	tried	tried	trying	(see ¶710)
obey	obeyed	obeyed	obeying	(see ¶711)
panic	panicked	panicked	panicking	(see ¶717)

b. Many verbs have principal parts that are irregularly formed. The following list presents the ones most commonly used, beginning with the most irregular of all—*to be.*

Present	Past	Past Participle	Present Participle	
am, is, are	was, were	been	being	
become	became	become	becoming	
begin	began	begun	beginning	(see ¶1032b)
break	broke	broken	breaking	(see ¶1033, note)
bring	brought	brought	bringing	(see ¶1032b)
buy	bought	bought	buying	
catch	caught	caught	catching	
choose	chose	chosen	choosing	
come	came	come	coming	
cost	cost	cost	costing	
do	did	done	doing	(see ¶1032b)
draw	drew	drawn	drawing	
drive	drove	driven	driving	
eat	ate	eaten	eating	
fall	fell	fallen	falling	
feel	felt	felt	feeling	
find	found	found	finding	

Continued on page 246

¶1030

Present	Past	Past Participle	Present Participle	
fly	flew	flown	flying	
forget	forgot	forgotten **OR** forgot	forgetting	
forgive	forgave	forgiven	forgiving	
get	got	gotten	getting	
give	gave	given	giving	
go	went	gone	going	
grow	grew	grown	growing	
hang (suspend)	hung	hung	hanging	
hang (execute)	hanged	hanged	hanging	
hold	held	held	holding	
keep	kept	kept	keeping	
know	knew	known	knowing	
lay (place)	laid	laid	laying	(see page 298)
lie (recline)	lay	lain	lying	(see page 298)
make	made	made	making	
mean	meant	meant	meaning	
pay	paid	paid	paying	
prove	proved	proved **OR** proven	proving	
ring	rang	rung	ringing	
rise	rose	risen	rising	(see ¶1033, note)
say	said	said	saying	
see	saw	seen	seeing	(see ¶1032b)
sell	sold	sold	selling	
send	sent	sent	sending	
set	set	set	setting	(see page 304)
shrink	shrank	shrunk	shrinking	(see ¶¶1032b, 1033, note)
sit	sat	sat	sitting	(see page 304)
speak	spoke	spoken	speaking	
swing	swung	swung	swinging	
take	took	taken	taking	
teach	taught	taught	teaching	
tell	told	told	telling	
think	thought	thought	thinking	
throw	threw	thrown	throwing	
understand	understood	understood	understanding	
wear	wore	worn	wearing	(see ¶1033, note)
write	wrote	written	writing	

NOTE: Dictionaries typically show the principal parts for all *irregular* verbs. If you are in doubt about any form, consult your dictionary. If the principal parts are not shown, the verb is regular. (See ¶1030a.)

c. The past participle and the present participle, if used as a part of a verb phrase, must *always* be used with one or more helping verbs, also known as auxiliary verbs. The most common helping verbs are:

is	was	can	do	has	have	might	shall	will
are	were	could	did	had	may	must	should	would

➤ *For a graphic view of how all the tenses are formed, see the chart on pages 248–249.*

Forming Verb Tenses

1031 The first principal part of the verb (the *present tense*) is used:

a. To express *present time.*

> We *fill* all orders promptly.   She *does* what is expected of her.

b. To make a statement that is *true at all times.*

> There *is* an exception to every rule (including this one).

c. With *shall* or *will* to express *future time.*

> We *will order* (**OR** *shall order*) new stock next week. (For the use of the helping verbs *shall* and *will* in the future tense, see page 304.)

> ➤ *For the third person singular form of the present tense, see ¶1035.*

1032 **a.** The second principal part of the verb (the *past tense*) is used to express *past time.* (No helping verb is used with this form.)

> We *filled* the order yesterday.   She *did* what was expected of her.

b. Do not use a past participle form to express the past tense.

> I *saw* it. (**NOT:** I *seen* it.)   He *drank* his coffee. (**NOT:** He *drunk* his coffee.)
> They *began* it together. (**NOT:** They *begun* it together.)
> He was the one who *did* it. (**NOT:** He was the one who *done* it.)
> I can't believe this sweater *shrank.* (**NOT:** . . . this sweater *shrunk.*)
> Jill *brought* me up to date on the Cox project. (**NOT:** Jill *brung* me . . .)
> Someone *sneaked* into my office last night. (**NOT:** Someone *snuck* . . .)

1033 The third principal part of the verb (the *past participle*) is used:

a. To form the *present perfect tense.* This tense indicates action that was started in the past and has recently been completed or is continuing up to the present time. It consists of the verb *have* or *has* plus the past participle.

> We *have filled* the orders. (**NOT:** We *have filled* the orders yesterday.)
> She *has* always *done* what we expect of her.
> Consumers *have become* an articulate force in today's business world.

b. To form the *past perfect tense.* This tense indicates action that was completed *before another past action.* It consists of the verb *had* plus the past participle.

> We *had filled* the orders before we saw your letter.
> She *had finished* the job before we arrived.

c. To form the *future perfect tense.* This tense indicates action that will be completed *before a certain time in the future.* It consists of the verb *shall have* or *will have* plus the past participle.

> We *will have filled* the orders by that time. (See page 304 for a usage note on *shall* and *will.*)
> She *will have finished* the job by next Friday.

NOTE: Be careful not to use a past tense form (the second principal part) in place of a past participle.

> I have *broken* the racket. (**NOT:** I have *broke* the racket.)
> The dress has *shrunk.* (**NOT:** The dress has *shrank.*)
> Prices have *risen* again. (**NOT:** Prices have *rose* again.)
> He has *worn* his shoes out. (**NOT:** He has *wore* his shoes out.)

Text continues on page 250

Grammar

10

¶1033 CONJUGATION OF THE VERB *TO SEE*

PRESENT, PAST, AND FUTURE TENSES (¶¶1031–1032)

INFINITIVE	TO SEE	TO BE	TO HAVE
PRESENT TENSE First Principal Part	I see you see he or she *sees*	I *am* you are he or she *is*	I have you have he or she *has*
	we see you see they see	we are you are they are	we have you have they have
PAST TENSE Second Principal Part	I saw you saw he or she saw	I *was* you were he or she *was*	I had you had he or she had
	we saw you saw they saw	we were you were they were	we had you had they had
FUTURE TENSE Helping Verb (*shall* OR *will*) + Main Verb (first principal part)	I *shall* see you will see he or she will see we *shall* see you will see they will see	I *shall* be you will be he or she will be we *shall* be you will be they will be	I *shall* have you will have he or she will have we *shall* have you will have they will have

PASSIVE TENSES (¶1036)

INFINITIVE	TO SEE
PRESENT PASSIVE TENSE Helping Verb (present tense of *be*) + Main Verb (past participle) +	I *am* seen you are seen he or she *is* seen we are seen you are seen they are seen
PAST PASSIVE TENSE Helping Verb (past tense of *be*) + Main Verb (past participle)	I *was* seen you were seen he or she *was* seen we were seen you were seen they were seen
FUTURE PASSIVE TENSE Helping Verb (future tense of *be*) + Main Verb (past participle)	I *shall* be seen you will be seen he or she will be seen we *shall* be seen you will be seen they will be seen

PROGRESSIVE TENSES (¶1034)

INFINITIVE	TO SEE
PRESENT PROGRESSIVE TENSE Helping Verb (present tense of *be*) + Main Verb (present participle)	I *am* seeing you are seeing he or she *is* seeing we are seeing you are seeing they are seeing
PAST PROGRESSIVE TENSE Helping Verb (past tense of *be*) + Main Verb (present participle)	I *was* seeing you were seeing he or she *was* seeing we were seeing you were seeing they were seeing
FUTURE PROGRESSIVE TENSE Helping Verb (future tense of *be*) + Main Verb (present participle)	I *shall* be seeing you will be seeing he or she will be seeing we *shall* be seeing you will be seeing they will be seeing

Grammar

10

PERFECT TENSES (¶1033)

INFINITIVE

PRESENT PERFECT TENSE
Helping Verb (present tense of *have*)

+

Main Verb (past participle)

PAST PERFECT TENSE
Helping Verb (past tense of *have*)

+

Main Verb (past participle)

FUTURE PERFECT TENSE
Helping Verb (future tense of *have*)

+

Main Verb (past participle)

	TO SEE		TO BE	
	I have	seen	I have	been
	you have	seen	you have	been
	he or she *has*	seen	he or she *has*	been
	we have	seen	we have	been
	you have	seen	you have	been
	they have	seen	they have	been
	I had	seen	I had	been
	you had	seen	you had	been
	he or she had	seen	he or she had	been
	we had	seen	we had	been
	you had	seen	you had	been
	they had	seen	they had	been
	I *shall* have	seen	I *shall* have	been
	you will have	seen	you will have	been
	he or she will have	seen	he or she will have	been
	we *shall* have	seen	we *shall* have	been
	you will have	seen	you will have	been
	they will have	seen	they will have	been

PERFECT PASSIVE TENSES (¶1036)

INFINITIVE

PRESENT PERFECT PASSIVE TENSE
Helping Verb (present perfect tense of *be*)

+

Main Verb (past participle)

PAST PERFECT PASSIVE TENSE
Helping Verb (past perfect tense of *be*)

+

Main Verb (past participle)

FUTURE PERFECT PASSIVE TENSE
Helping Verb (future perfect tense of *be*)

+

Main Verb (past participle)

TO SEE		
I have been	seen
you have been	seen
he or she *has* been	seen
we have been	seen
you have been	seen
they have been	seen
I had been	seen
you had been	seen
he or she had been	seen
we had been	seen
you had been	seen
they had been	seen
I *shall* have been	seen
you will have been	seen
he or she will have been	seen
we *shall* have been	seen
you will have been	seen
they will have been	seen

PERFECT PROGRESSIVE TENSES (¶1034)

INFINITIVE

PRESENT PERFECT PROGRESSIVE TENSE
Helping Verb (present perfect tense of *be*)

+

Main Verb (present participle)

PAST PERFECT PROGRESSIVE TENSE
Helping Verb (past perfect tense of *be*)

+

Main Verb (present participle)

FUTURE PERFECT PROGRESSIVE TENSE
Helping Verb (future perfect tense of *be*)

+

Main Verb (present participle)

TO SEE		
I have been	seeing
you have been	seeing
he or she *has* been	seeing
we have been	seeing
you have been	seeing
they have been	seeing
I had been	seeing
you had been	seeing
he or she had been	seeing
we had been	seeing
you had been	seeing
they had been	seeing
I *shall* have been	seeing
you will have been	seeing
he or she will have been	seeing
we *shall* have been	seeing
you will have been	seeing
they will have been	seeing

Grammar

10

¶1034

1034 The fourth principal part of the verb (the *present participle*) is used:

a. To form the *present progressive tense.* This tense indicates action still in progress. It consists of the verb *am, is,* or *are* plus the present participle.

> We *are filling* all orders as fast as we can.
> She *is doing* all that can be expected of her.

b. To form the *past progressive tense.* This tense indicates action in progress sometime in the past. It consists of the verb *was* or *were* plus the present participle.

> We *were waiting* for new stock at the time your order came in.
> She *was doing* a good job when I last checked her work.

c. To form the *future progressive tense.* This tense indicates action that will be in progress in the future. It consists of the verb *shall be* or *will be* plus the present participle.

> We *will be working* overtime for the next two weeks. (See page 304 for a usage note on *shall* and *will.*)
> They *will be receiving* additional stock throughout the next two weeks.

d. To form the *present perfect progressive*, the *past perfect progressive*, and the *future perfect progressive* tenses. These tenses convey the same meaning as the simple perfect tenses (see ¶1033) except that the progressive element adds the sense of continuous action. These tenses consist of the verbs *has been, have been, had been, shall have been,* and *will have been* plus the present participle. Compare the following examples with those in ¶1033.

> We *have been filling* these orders with Model 212A instead of Model 212. (Present perfect progressive.)
> We *had been filling* these orders with Model 212A until we saw your directive. (Past perfect progressive.)
> By next Friday *we will have been working* overtime for two straight weeks. (Future perfect progressive.)

1035 The first principal part of the verb undergoes a change in form to express the third person singular in the present tense.

a. Most verbs simply add *s* in the third person singular.

he feels	**BUT:** I feel, you feel, we feel, they feel
she thinks	I think, you think, we think, they think
it looks	I look, you look, we look, they look

b. Verbs ending in *s, x, z, sh, ch,* or *o* add *es.*

he misses	he wishes
she fixes	she watches
it buzzes	it does

c. Verbs ending in a vowel plus *y* add *s;* those ending in a consonant plus *y* change *y* to *i* and add *es.*

say: he says	buy: he buys
convey: she conveys	try: it tries
employ: she employs	apply: she applies

d. Verbs ending in *i* simply add *s.*

taxi: he taxis	ski: she skis

e. The verb *to be* is irregular since *be,* the first principal part, is not used in the present tense.

I am	we are
you are	you are
he, she, it is	they are

f. A few verbs remain unchanged in the third person singular.

PRESENT TENSE:	he may	she can	it will
PAST TENSE:	he might	she could	it would

➢ *See page 290 for a usage note on* don't.

Passive Forms

1036 The passive forms of a verb consist of some form of the helping verb *to be* plus the past participle of the main verb.

> it is intended (present passive of *intend*)
> we were expected (past passive of *expect*)
> they will be audited (future passive of *audit*)
> she has been notified (present perfect passive of *notify*)
> you had been told (past perfect passive of *tell*)
> he will have been given (future perfect passive of *give*)

1037 A *passive* verb directs the action toward the subject. An *active* verb directs the action toward an object.

> **ACTIVE:** Melanie *(subject)* will lead *(verb)* the discussion *(object)*.
> **PASSIVE:** The discussion *(subject)* will be led *(verb)* by Melanie.

➢ *For additional examples, see the entry for* voice *in Appendix A.*

a. The passive form of a verb is appropriate (1) when you want to emphasize the *receiver* of the action (by making it the subject) or (2) when the *doer* of the action is not important or is deliberately not mentioned.

> I was seriously injured as a result of your negligence. (Emphasizes *I,* the receiver of the action.) **RATHER THAN:** Your negligence seriously injured me.
>
> This proposal is based on a careful analysis of all available research studies. (Emphasizes the basis for the proposal; the name of the person who drafted the proposal is not important.)
>
> Unfortunately, the decision was made without consulting any of the board members. (Emphasizes how the decision was made and omits the name of the person responsible.)
>
> Mistakes were made. (A frequent comment made by politicians and corporate executives who have to acknowledge failure or wrongdoing but do not want to acknowledge personal responsibility or guilt.)
>
> Fred Allen once defined a conference as a gathering of important people who "singly can do nothing but together can decide that nothing can be done."

b. In all other cases use active verb forms to achieve a simpler and more vigorous style. Except in those circumstances cited in ¶1037a, passive verb forms typically produce awkward or stilted sentences.

> **WEAK PASSIVES:** It *has been decided* by the Human Resources Committee that full pay *should be given* to you for the period of your hospitalization.
>
> **STRONG ACTIVES:** The Human Resources Committee *has decided* that you *should receive* full pay for the period of your hospitalization.

Continued on page 252

¶**1038**

c. Watch out for passive constructions that unintentionally point to the wrong *doer* of the action.

CONFUSING: Two computers were reported stolen over the weekend by the head of corporate security.

CLEAR: The head of corporate security reported that two computers were stolen over the weekend.

CONFUSING: One of our second-shift workers was found injured by a Good Samaritan outside the parking lot entrance last night.

CLEAR: Last night one of our second-shift workers was injured outside the parking lot entrance and was found there by a Good Samaritan.

Verbs Following Clauses of Necessity, Demand, Etc.

1038 Sentences that express *necessity, demand, strong request, urging,* or *resolution* in the main clause require a *subjunctive* verb in the dependent clause that follows.

a. If the verb in the dependent clause requires the use of the verb *to be,* use the form *be* with all three persons (not *am, is,* or *are*).

NECESSITY: It is necessary (**OR** important **OR** essential) that these questions *be answered* at once. (**NOT:** are answered.)

DEMAND: I insist that I *be allowed* to present a minority report at the next board meeting. (**NOT:** am allowed.)

REQUEST: They have asked that you *be notified* at once if matters do not proceed according to plan. (**NOT:** are notified.)

URGING: We urged (**OR** suggested) that he *be given* a second chance to prove himself in the job. (**NOT:** is given.)

RESOLUTION: The committee has resolved (**OR** decided **OR** ruled) that the decision *be deferred* until the next meeting. (**NOT:** is deferred.)

b. If the verb in the dependent clause is a verb other than *be,* use the ordinary *present tense* form for all three persons. However, do not add *s* (or otherwise change the form) for the third person singular.

NECESSITY: It is essential that he *arrive* on time. (**NOT:** arrives.)

DEMAND: They insist that he *do* the work over. (**NOT:** does.)

REQUEST: They have asked that she *remain* on the committee until the end of the year. (**NOT:** remains.)

URGING: I suggested that she *type* the material triple-spaced to allow room for some very heavy editing. (**NOT:** types.)

RESOLUTION: They have resolved that Fred *represent* them. (**NOT:** represents.)

➤ *See the entry for* mood, subjunctive *in Appendix A.*

Verbs Following *Wish* Clauses

1039 Sentences that start with *I wish, she wishes,* and so on, require a subjunctive verb in the dependent clause that follows.

a. To express *present* time in the dependent clause, put the verb in the *past tense.*

I wish I *knew* how to proceed.

I wish I *could attend.*

NOTE: If the verb is *to be,* use *were* for all three persons.

I wish I *were going* to the reception. (**NOT:** was going.)

I wish he *were going* with me.

b. To express *past* time in the dependent clause, put the verb in the *past perfect tense.*

I wish she *had invited* me.   I wish I *had been* there.   I wish I *could have attended.*

c. To express *future* time in the dependent clause, use the helping verb *would* instead of *will.*

I wish he *would arrive* on time.   I wish she *would make* more of an effort.

Verbs in *If* Clauses

1040 When an *if* clause states a condition that is highly *improbable, doubtful,* or *contrary to fact,* the verb in the *if* clause requires special treatment, like that described in ¶1039. *To express present time, use the past tense; to express past time, use the past perfect tense.* (In the following examples note the relationship of tenses between the dependent clause and the main clause.)

If I *knew* the answer (but I don't), I *would* not *ask* you.

If I *had known* the answer (but I didn't), I *would* not *have asked* you.

If I *were* you (but I am not), I *would take* the job.

If I *had been* in your shoes (but I wasn't), I *would have taken* the job.

If he *were invited* (but he isn't), he *would be* glad to go.

If he *had been invited* (but he wasn't), he *would have been* glad to go.

NOTE: Do not use *would have* for *had* in an *if* clause. See page 308 for a usage note on *would have.*

1041 When an *if* clause states a condition that is *possible* or *likely,* the verb in the *if* clause requires no special treatment. *To express present time, use the present tense; to express past time, use the past tense.* Compare the following pairs of examples. Those labeled "Probable" reflect the verb forms described here in ¶1041. Those labeled "Improbable" reflect the verb forms described in ¶1040.

PROBABLE: If I *leave* this job (and I may do so), I *will take* a full-time teaching position.

IMPROBABLE: If I *left* this job (but I probably won't), I *would take* a full-time teaching position.

PROBABLE: If I *go* to Tokyo (and I may), I *will want* you to go too.

IMPROBABLE: If I *were going* to Tokyo (but I probably won't), I *would want* you to go too.

PROBABLE: If she *was* in yesterday (and she may have been), I *did* not *see* her.

IMPROBABLE: If she *had been* in yesterday (but she wasn't), I *would have seen* her.

Verbs in *As If* or *As Though* Clauses

1042 When an *as if* or *as though* clause expresses a condition *contrary to fact,* the verb in the clause requires special treatment, like that described in ¶1040.

She acts as if she *were* the only person who mattered. (But she isn't.)

He talks as if he *knew* the facts of the situation. (But he doesn't.)

You act as though you *hadn't* a care in the world. (But you have.)

1043 *As if* or *as though* clauses are now often used to express a condition that is *highly probable.* In such cases do not give the verb special treatment. *Use the present tense to express present time, the future tense to express future time, and the past tense to express past time.*

It looks as if it *will* rain. (**OR:** It looks as if it *is going* to rain.)

She acted as if she *planned* to look for another job.

¶1044

Infinitives

1044 An infinitive is the form of the verb preceded by *to* (for example, *to write, to do, to be*). When two or more infinitives are used in a parallel construction, the word *to* may be omitted after the first infinitive unless special emphasis is desired.

> Ask Ruth Gonzales *to sign* both copies of the contract, *return* the original to us, and *keep* the other copy. (*Return* and *keep* are infinitives without *to.*)

> I would like you *to explain* the job to Harry, *to give* him help if he needs it, and *to see* that the job is done properly. (For emphasis, *to* is used with all three infinitives—*explain, give,* and *see.*)

NOTE: The word *to* is usually dropped when the infinitive follows such verbs as *see, hear, feel, let, help,* and *need.*

> Will you please help me *prepare* the report? (**RATHER THAN:** help me *to prepare.*)

> You need not *return* the clipping. (**OR:** You do not need *to return* the clipping.)

1045 a. Infinitives have two main tense forms: present and perfect.

(1) The perfect infinitive is used to express action that has been completed before the time of the main verb.

> I *am sorry to have caused* you so much trouble last week. (The act of causing trouble was completed before the act of expressing regret; therefore, the perfect infinitive is used.)

(2) The present infinitive is used in all other cases.

> I planned *to leave* early. (**NOT:** *to have left.* The act of leaving could not have been completed before the act of planning, so the present infinitive is used.)

b. The passive form of the present infinitive consists of *to be* plus the past participle. Do not omit *to be* in such constructions.

> This office needs *to be repainted.* (**NOT:** This office needs *repainted.*)

1046 *Splitting an infinitive* (that is, inserting an adverb between *to* and the verb) is no longer considered incorrect. However, it should be avoided when it produces an awkward construction and the adverb functions more effectively in another location.

> **WEAK:** It was impossible to *even* see a foot ahead.
> **BETTER:** It was impossible to see *even* a foot ahead.

> **WEAK:** He always tries to *carefully* do the work.
> **BETTER:** He always tries to do the work *carefully.*

When alternative locations of the adverb produce an awkward or weakly constructed sentence, do not be afraid to split the infinitive.

a. Before splitting an infinitive, first try to place the adverb *after the object* of the infinitive. In many instances the adverb functions most effectively in that location.

> You ought *to review* these plans *thoroughly.* (**BETTER THAN:** You ought to thoroughly review these plans.)

> I need *to make* the decision *quickly.* (**BETTER THAN:** I need to quickly make the decision.)

b. If step *a* does not produce an effective sentence, try to locate the adverb directly *before* or directly *after* the infinitive. In some cases the adverb functions effectively in this position; in other cases the resulting sentence is awkward.

> **CONFUSING:** I want you *to supervise* the work that is to be done *personally.* (When the object of the infinitive is long, it is difficult to place the adverb after the object without creating confusion. Here *personally* seems to modify *to be done* when it should modify *to supervise.*)

> **AWKWARD:** I want you to supervise *personally* the work that is to be done.

> **GOOD:** I want you *personally* to supervise the work that is to be done.

Grammar

10

c. If steps *a* and *b* fail to produce an effective sentence, try splitting the infinitive. If a good sentence results, keep it; if not, try rewording the sentence.

> **CONFUSING:** I want you *to consider* Jenkins' proposal to handle all our deliveries *carefully.* (When *carefully* is located after the complete object, it no longer clearly refers to *to consider.*)
> **AWKWARD:** I want you *carefully* to consider Jenkins' proposal to handle all our deliveries.
> **AWKWARD:** I want you to consider *carefully* Jenkins' proposal to handle all our deliveries.
> **GOOD:** I want you to *carefully* consider Jenkins' proposal . . .

d. When an infinitive consists of *to be* plus a past or present participle of another verb, inserting an adverb before the participle is not considered splitting an infinitive. Nevertheless, in many such sentences it may be possible to locate the adverb to better advantage elsewhere in the sentence.

> These plans need to be *thoroughly* reviewed.
> Claude appears to be *continually* turning up with last-minute objections to any decision I make.

NOTE: By the same token, it is perfectly acceptable to position an adverb between a helping verb and a past or present participle. It is even acceptable to position an adverb *within* the elements of a helping verb.

> This new technology has *already* been *effectively* applied in many industries.
> I hear that Martha has been *seriously* considering early retirement.

Sequence of Tenses

1047 When the verb in the main clause is in the past tense, the verb in a dependent *that* clause should also express past time. Consider the following pairs of examples:

> She *says* (present) that she *is* now *working* (present) for CBS.
> She *said* (past) that she *was* now *working* (past) for CBS.

> He *says* (present) that he *has seen* (present perfect) your résumé.
> He *said* (past) that he *had seen* (past perfect) your résumé.

> I *think* (present) that he *will see* (future) you tomorrow.
> I *thought* (past) that he *would see* (past form of *will see*) you tomorrow.

EXCEPTION: The verb in the dependent clause should remain in the present tense if it expresses a general truth.

> Our lawyer *pointed out* (past) that all persons under 18 *are* (present) considered minors.

Omitting Parts of Verbs

1048 When compound verbs in the same sentence have a common element, that element does not need to be repeated.

> We *have received* your letter and *forwarded* it to our St. Louis office. (The helping verb *have* is shared by the two main verbs, *received* and *forwarded.*)
> We *can* and *will achieve* these goals. (The main verb *achieve* is shared by the two helping verbs, *can* and *will.*)

However, do not omit any element when different parts of the main verb are required.

> **WRONG:** I never *have* and I never *will forget* what you have done for me.
> **RIGHT:** I never *have forgotten* and I never *will forget* . . .

> **WRONG:** We *have* and still *are asking* for an accounting of the assets.
> **RIGHT:** We *have asked* and still *are asking* for . . .

¶1049

Troublesome Verbs

> See the individual entries listed alphabetically in Section 11 for the following verbs:

Affect–effect	Home–hone
Ain't	Imply–infer
Appraise–apprise	Lay–lie
Appreciate	Learn–teach
Being that	Leave–let
Bring–take	Look forward to
Cannot help but	May–can (might–could)
Come–go	Maybe–may be
Come and	Of–have
Complement–compliment	Rack–wrack
Comprise–compose	Raise–rise
Could not care less	Serve–service
Done	Set–sit
Don't	Shall–will
Ensure–insure–assure	Should–would
Enthused over	Supposed to
Graduated–was graduated	Try and
Grow	Type–key
Had better	Used to
Help	Would have

Pronouns

Agreement With Antecedents: Basic Rules

1049 **a.** A pronoun must agree with its *antecedent* (the word for which the pronoun stands) in number, gender, and person.

I must stand by *my* client, just as *you* must stand by *yours.*

Frank said that *he* could do the job alone.

Alice wants to know whether *her* proposal has been approved.

The *company* has not decided whether to change *its* policy on vacations. (See ¶¶1019–1020.)

We plan to explain *our* shift in corporate strategy at the next shareholders' meeting.

The company's *auditors* will issue *their* report tomorrow.

The *Vanderveers* are giving a party at *their* house.

The *grand jury* has completed *its* investigation. (See ¶1019 for collective nouns.)

Why not have *each witness* write *his* or *her* version of the accident? (See ¶1053 for indefinite pronouns as antecedents.)

It is *I* who *am* at fault. (*Who* agrees in person and number with the antecedent *I;* the verb *am* also agrees with *I.*)

It is *she* who *is* willing to compromise. It is *they* who *are* not.

It is *we,* the individual taxpayers, who *have* to make up for the loss of commercial ratables.

It is *you* who *are* to blame. (*Who* refers to *you;* hence the verb is *are* to agree with *you.* See ¶1001a, note.)

BUT: You are the *person* who *is* to blame. (Here *who* refers to *person;* hence the verb is *is* to agree with *person.*)

b. Use a plural pronoun when the antecedent consists of two nouns or pronouns joined by *and.*

> Can *Mary* and *you* give us *your* decision by Monday?
> *Sonia* and *Dave* say *they* will attend.
> The *Montaignes* and the *Reillys* have sent *their* regrets.
> Are *you* and *I* prepared to say that *we* can handle the assignment?

c. Use a singular pronoun when the antecedent consists of two *singular* nouns joined by *or* or *nor.* Use a plural pronoun when the antecedent consists of two *plural* nouns joined by *or* or *nor.* (See also ¶¶1003–1005.)

> Either *Will* or *Ed* will have to give up *his* office. (**NOT:** their.)
> Neither *Joan* nor *Helen* wants to do *her* share. (**NOT:** their.)
> Either the *Kopecks* or the *Henleys* will bring *their* videocassette recorder.

NOTE: When *or* or *nor* joins a singular noun and a plural noun, a pronoun that refers to this construction should agree in number with the nearer noun. However, a strict application of this rule can lead to problems in sentence structure and meaning. Therefore, always try to make this kind of construction plural by locating the plural subject nearer the verb.

> Neither Mr. Wing nor his *employees have* reached *their* goal. (The plural pronoun *their* is used to agree with the nearer noun, *employees;* the verb *have* is also in the plural.)
> **NOT:** Neither the employees nor *Mr. Wing has* reached *his* goal. (The sentence follows the rule— *his* agrees with *Mr. Wing,* the nearer noun, and the verb *has* is singular; however, the meaning of the sentence has been distorted.)

d. Make sure that the pronouns you use agree in gender with their antecedents.

> The entire *staff* of JTX wishes to express *its* gratitude. (Third person singular.)
> *We* (**OR** *All of us*) here at JTX wish to express *our* gratitude. (First person plural.)
> **BUT NOT:** The entire *staff* of JTX wishes to express *our* gratitude. (Do not use a first person pronoun to refer to a third person antecedent.)

➤ *See also ¶1053d.*

e. Make sure that the pronouns you use refer to the antecedents you intend. To avoid confusion, reword as necessary.

> **CONFUSING:** Unrealistic deadlines, excessive pressures, and unsafe working conditions can be very damaging to your employees. You must do everything you can to eliminate them. (The employees or the destructive conditions?)
> **CLEAR:** Unrealistic deadlines, excessive pressures, and unsafe working conditions can be very damaging to your employees. You must do everything you can to eliminate these destructive conditions.

Agreement With Common-Gender Antecedents

1050 Nouns that apply to both males and females have a *common* gender.

parent	manager	student	boss	writer
child	doctor	professor	supervisor	speaker
customer	lawyer	instructor	employee	listener

When a singular noun of common gender serves as a *definite* antecedent (one that names a specific person whose gender is known), use the pronoun *he* or *she.*

> My boss [previously identified as Robert Hecht] prefers to open *his* own mail.
> Ask your doctor [known to be a woman] to sign *her* name on this form.

¶1051

1051 When a singular noun of common gender serves as an *indefinite* antecedent *(a doctor, any doctor, every doctor)* or as a *generic* antecedent (*the doctor,* meaning "doctors in general"), the traditional practice has been to use *he* as a generic pronoun applying equally to males and females.

> The *writer* should include a table of contents with *his* manuscript.

When an indefinite or generic antecedent names an occupation or a role in which women predominate (for example, *the teacher, the secretary, the nurse*), the traditional practice has been to use *she* as a generic pronoun.

> A *secretary* needs to organize *her* work and set priorities each day.

This traditional use of *he* and *she* as generic pronouns (as described above) is offensive to many people, who feel that the masculine bias in the word *he* makes it unsuitable as a pronoun that applies equally to women and men. Moreover, they feel that the generic use of *she* serves to reinforce stereotyped notions about women's occupations or roles. The ideal solution would be a new generic pronoun without masculine or feminine connotations. However, until such a pronoun has been devised and accepted into common usage, consider various alternatives to the generic use of *he* or *she.* (See ¶1052.)

1052 **a.** Use *he or she, his or her,* or *him or her.* This solution works well in isolated cases but can be clumsy if repeated frequently in the same context. (In any case, avoid the use of *he/she, s/he,* and similar constructions.)

> An instructor should offer *his or her* students challenging projects.
> (**RATHER THAN:** An instructor should offer *his* students . . .)

b. Change the wording from singular to plural.

> *Parents* of teenage children often *wonder* where *they* went wrong.
> (**RATHER THAN:** The *parent* of a teenage child often *wonders* where *he or she* went wrong.)

c. Reword to avoid the generic pronoun.

> When a customer calls, be sure to ask for a phone number.
> (**RATHER THAN:** When a customer calls, ask *him or her* to leave *his or her* phone number.)
>
> An assistant tries to anticipate the needs of the boss.
> (**RATHER THAN:** An assistant tries to anticipate the needs of *his or her* boss.)

d. If the application of these various alternatives produces wordiness or an unacceptable shift in meaning or emphasis, then as a last resort use the generic *he* or the generic *she* as described in ¶1051. However, try to avoid doing so whenever possible.

Agreement With Indefinite-Pronoun Antecedents

1053 **a.** Use a singular pronoun when the antecedent is a singular indefinite pronoun. The following indefinite pronouns are always singular. They are typically used as nouns, but a few (such as *each* and *every*) are used as adjectives.

anyone	everyone	someone	no one
anybody	everybody	somebody	nobody
anything	everything	something	nothing
each	every	either	one
each one	many a	neither	another

> *Every company* has *its* own vacation policy. (**NOT:** their.)
> *Neither one* of the campaigns did as well as *it* was supposed to. (**NOT:** they were.)

NOTE: These singular indefinite forms often call for the generic use of *he* or *she* (see ¶¶1051–1052). The following sentences use alternative wording to show how the generic *he* or *she* can be avoided. The last sentence presents a situation for which no reasonable alternative exists.

> *Everyone* should submit *his* expense report by Friday.
>
> **BETTER:** All staff *members* should submit *their* expense reports by Friday.
>
> If *anyone* should ask for me, tell *him* that I won't return until Monday.
>
> **BETTER:** If anyone should ask for me, say that I won't return . . .
>
> Does *every assistant* know how *she* is to handle *her boss's* calls?
>
> **BETTER:** Do *all the assistants* know how *they* are to handle *their bosses'* calls?
>
> *Nobody* could have helped *himself* in a situation like that.

➤ *For agreement of these indefinite pronouns with verbs, see ¶¶1009–1011; for posses-sive forms of these pronouns, see ¶637.*

b. Use a plural pronoun when the antecedent is a plural indefinite form. The fol-lowing indefinite pronouns are always plural:

many	few	several	others	both

> *Many customers* prefer to help *themselves; others* usually like to have someone wait on *them.*
>
> *Several sales representatives* in the Southern Region made *their* annual goals in nine months.
>
> *Both managers* have said that *they* want to be considered for Mr. Hall's job when he retires.

➤ *For agreement of these indefinite pronouns with verbs, see ¶1012.*

c. The following indefinite forms may be singular or plural, depending on the noun to which they refer.

all	none	any	some	more	most

When these words are used as antecedents, determine whether they are singular or plural. Then make the pronouns that refer to them agree in number.

> *Some* of the *employees* have not yet had *their* annual physical checkup. (*Some* refers to *employ-ees* and is plural; *some* is the antecedent of *their.*)
>
> *Some* of the *manuscript* has been typed, but *it* has not been proofread. (*Some* refers to *manu-script* and is singular; *some* is the antecedent of *it* in the second clause.)

➤ *For agreement of these indefinite pronouns with verbs, see ¶1013.*

d. Since indefinite forms express the third person, pronouns referring to these antecedents should also be in the third person *(he, she, it, they).*

> If *anyone* wants a vacation pay advance, *he* or *she* should apply for it in writing.
>
> (**NOT:** If *anyone* wants a vacation pay advance, *you* should apply for it . . .)

If the indefinite form is modified so that it strongly expresses the first or second person, the personal pronoun must also agree in number.

> *Most parents* want *their* children to go to college. (Third person.)
>
> *Most* of *us* want *our* children to go to college. (First person.)
>
> A *few* have missed *their* deadlines. (Third person.)
>
> A *few* of *you* have missed *your* deadlines. (Second person.)
>
> *Each employee* knows how much *he* or *she* ought to contribute to the United Way fund drive. (Third person.)
>
> **BUT:** *Each* of us knows how much *he* or *she* ought to contribute to the United Way fund drive. (Third person. In this sentence, *of us* does not shift the meaning to the first person; the empha-sis is on what the individual contributes, not on what *we* contribute.)

Grammar

10

¶1054

IMPORTANT NOTE: Pronouns take different forms, not only to indicate a difference in person *(I, you, he)*, number *(he, they)*, and gender *(he, she)* but also to indicate a difference in case *(nominative, possessive, objective)*. Although a pronoun must agree with its antecedent in person, number, and gender, it does *not* necessarily agree with its antecedent in case. The case of a pronoun depends on its own relation to the other words in the sentence. The rules in ¶¶1054–1064 indicate how to choose the right case for pronouns.

Personal Pronouns

1054 Nominative Forms of Personal Pronouns

Use *I, we, you, he, she, it, they:*

a. When the pronoun is the subject of a verb.

> *I* wrote to Eileen McIntyre, but *she* hasn't answered.
> Debbie and *I* can handle the job ourselves.   (**NOT:** Debbie and me   **OR**   me and Debbie.)
> Either *he* or *I* can work late tonight. (**NOT:** him or me.)

NOTE: In sentences like the last two above, try each subject alone with the verb. You would not say "Me can handle the job" or "Him can work late tonight." Therefore, *I* and *he* must be used.

b. When the pronoun appears in the predicate after some form of the verb *to be (am, is, are, was, were)* or after a verb phrase containing some form of *to be* (see the list below). Pronouns that follow these verb forms should be in the nominative.

shall (**OR** will) be	have (**OR** has) been
should (**OR** would) be	had been
shall (**OR** will) have been	may (**OR** might) be
should (**OR** would) have been	may (**OR** might) have been
can (**OR** could) be	must (**OR** ought to) be
could have been	must have (**OR** ought to have) been
It could have been *they.*	Was it *he* or *she* who phoned?
It is *I.*	This is *she.*

NOTE: A sentence like *It could have been they*, while grammatically correct, would sound better if reworded in idiomatic English: *They could have been the ones.* Moreover, a sentence like *It's me* is acceptable in colloquial speech but not in writing. When you hear a telephone caller ask for you by name, do not respond by saying *This is him* or *This is her.* If you wish to respond correctly (and somewhat pompously), say *This is he* or *This is she.* If you wish to respond correctly and sound more natural, say *This is . . .* and then give your name.

> ➤ *For special rules governing pronouns with the infinitive* to be, *see ¶1064.*

1055 Objective Forms of Personal Pronouns

Use *me, us, you, him, her, it, them:*

a. When the pronoun is the direct or indirect object of a verb.

> Larry gave Maris and *us* tickets for the opening.
> They invited my husband and *me* for the weekend.

NOTE: When *my husband and* is mentally omitted, the objective form *me* is clearly the correct pronoun: "They invited *me* for the weekend."

¶**1056**

b. When the pronoun is the object of a preposition.

No one knows except *you* and *me*. (**NOT:** except you and I.)

Between *you* and *me,* that decision is unfair. (**NOT:** between you and I.)

EXCEPTION: He is a friend of *mine (yours, his, hers, ours, theirs).* (See ¶648.)

c. When the pronoun is the subject or object of an infinitive. (See ¶1064.)

The department head asked *him* to resign. *(Him is the subject of to resign.)*

Did you ask Janet to call *me*? *(Me is the object of to call.)*

1056 **Possessive Forms of Personal Pronouns**

a. Most personal pronouns have two possessive forms:

my	your	his	her	its	our	their
mine	yours	. . .	hers	. . .	ours	theirs

b. Use *my, your, his, her, its, our,* or *their* when the possessive pronoun immediately precedes the noun it modifies.

That is *my* book.   It was *their* choice.   George is *her* neighbor.

c. Use *mine, yours, his, hers, its, ours,* or *theirs* when the possessive pronoun stands apart from the noun it refers to.

That book is *mine.*   The choice was *theirs.*   George is a neighbor of *hers.*

NOTE: Do not insert an apostrophe before the final *s* in possessive pronouns.

yours (**NOT:** your's)   hers (**NOT:** her's)   ours (**NOT:** our's)   theirs (**NOT:** their's)

d. A pronoun that modifies a *gerund* (a verbal noun ending in *ing*) should be in the possessive. (See ¶647.)

I appreciated *your shipping* the order so promptly.

(**NOT:** I appreciated *you shipping* the order so promptly.)

e. Do not confuse certain possessive pronouns with contractions and other phrases that sound like the possessive pronouns.

its (possessive)	it's (it is **OR** it has)
their (possessive)	they're (they are) **OR** there're (there are)
theirs (possessive)	there's (there is **OR** there has)
your (possessive)	you're (you are)

As a test for the correct form, try to substitute *it is, it has, they are, there are, there is, there has,* or *you are,* whichever is appropriate. If the substitution does not make sense, use the corresponding possessive form.

The firm must protect *its* assets. ("Protect it is assets" makes no sense.)

BUT: *It's* time to take stock of our achievements.

Their investing in high-tech stocks was a shrewd idea.

BUT: *They're* investing in high-tech stocks.

Their complaints have proved to be unfounded.

BUT: *There are* complaints that have proved to be unfounded.

Theirs no longer works; that's why they borrow ours.

BUT: *There's* no use expecting him to change.

Your thinking is sound, but we lack the funds to underwrite your proposal.

BUT: *You're* thinking of applying for a transfer, I understand.

➤ *For other possessive pronouns, see also ¶¶636–637.*

Grammar

10

¶1057

1057 When a pronoun follows *than* or *as* in a comparison, determine the correct form of the pronoun by mentally supplying any missing words. To avoid correct but awkward sentences, actually supply the missing words.

> She writes better than *I*. (She writes better than *I do.*)
>
> Joe is not as talented as *she.* (Joe is not as talented as *she is.*)
>
> I like you better than *him.* (I like you better than *I like him.*)
>
> **BUT:** I like you better than *he.* (I like you better than *he does.*)

1058 When a pronoun is used to identify a noun or another pronoun, it is either nominative or objective, depending on how the antecedent is used.

> The committee has asked *us,* Ruth and me, to present the report. (Since *us* is objective, the identifying pronoun *me* is also objective.)
>
> The explanation was for the *newcomers,* Marie and *me.* (Was for *me.*)
>
> The exceptions were the *newcomers,* Marie and *I.* (Exception was *I.*)
>
> Let's *you* and *me* schedule a brown-bag lunch. (*Let's* is a contraction for *let us.* Since *us* is the objective form, the pronouns *you* and *me* are also objective.)

NOTE: In sentences like the following, mentally omit the noun *(employees)* to determine the correct form.

> The firm wants *us* employees to work on Saturdays. (The firm wants *us* to work on Saturdays.)
>
> *We* employees need to confer. (*We* need to confer.)

1059 Some writers consistently use *we* instead of *I* to avoid a seeming overemphasis on themselves. However, it is preferable to use *we* only when you are speaking on behalf of an organization you represent and to use *I* when speaking for yourself alone.

> We shall prepare the necessary forms as soon as you send *us* a signed release. (This writer is speaking on behalf of the firm.)
>
> It is *my* opinion that this patient may be discharged at once. (This writer is speaking only for himself. Under these circumstances it would sound pompous to say, "It is *our* opinion.")

Compound Personal Pronouns

1060 Compound personal pronouns end in *self* or *selves: myself, yourself, himself, herself, itself, ourselves, yourselves, themselves.*

a. They can direct the action expressed by the verb back to the subject.

> *She* found *herself* the only one in favor of the move.
>
> *We* have satisfied *ourselves* as to the wisdom of the action.

b. They can emphasize a noun or pronoun already expressed.

> *I* will write her *myself.*   The *trainees themselves* arranged the program.
>
> *I myself* am bewildered. (**BUT NOT:** *I myself* am *personally* bewildered. Using *myself* and *personally* in the same sentence creates redundancy rather than emphasis.)

c. Place a compound personal pronoun carefully to avoid confusion or misreading.

> **CONFUSING:** Now surgeons can have patients wheeled inside a new three-dimensional imaging machine; then they can step inside themselves to operate. (Are the surgeons stepping inside themselves or inside the machine?)
>
> **CLEAR:** . . . then they themselves can step inside the machine to operate.

If necessary, reword the sentence without using a compound personal pronoun.

> **CONFUSING:** Are you tired of cleaning yourself? Let us do it for you.
>
> **CLEAR:** Are you tired of doing your own cleaning? Let us do it for you.

¶1061

d. Do not use a compound personal pronoun unless the noun or pronoun to which it refers is expressed in the same sentence.

The tickets are for the Wrights and *me*. (**NOT:** myself.)

Henry and *I* can handle all the mail. (**NOT:** Henry and myself.)

The report will be prepared by Ray, Nessa, and *me*. (**NOT:** myself.)

Interrogative and Relative Pronouns

1061 *Who* and *Whom; Whoever* and *Whomever*

a. These pronouns are both *interrogative* pronouns (used in asking questions) and *relative* pronouns (used to refer to a noun or pronoun in the main clause).

Who is going? (Interrogative.)

Mr. Sears is the one *who* is going. (Relative, referring to *one*.)

To *whom* shall I deliver the message? (Interrogative.)

Ms. DeAngelis, *whom* I have never met, is in charge of the program. (Relative, referring to *Ms. DeAngelis*.)

b. These pronouns may be either singular or plural in meaning.

Who is talking? (Singular.)   *Whom* do you prefer for this job? (Singular.)

Who are going? (Plural.)   *Whom* do you prefer for these jobs? (Plural.)

c. *Who* (or *whoever*) is the nominative form. Use *who* whenever *he, she, they, I,* or *we* could be substituted in the *who* clause. (If in doubt, mentally rearrange the clause as is done in parentheses after each of the following examples.)

Who is arranging the teleconference? (*She* is arranging the teleconference.)

Who could it have been? (It could have been *he*. See ¶1054b.)

Who booked our sales conference in a honeymooners' hideaway? (*He* booked the sales conference.)

Who shall I say is calling? (I shall say *he* is calling.)

Who did they say was chosen? (They did say *she* was chosen.)

The matter of *who* should pay was not decided. (*He* should pay.)

Everybody wants to know *who you think should be appointed*. (You think *she* should be appointed.)

Whoever wins the primary will win the election. (*She* wins the primary.)

We will select *whoever meets our qualifications*. (*He* meets our qualifications.)

I will speak to *whoever answers the phone*. (*He* answers the phone.)

Please write at once to *whoever you think can supply the information desired*. (You think *she* can supply the information desired.)

Gloria is the one *who can best do the job*. (*She* can best do the job.)

James is the one *who we expect will win*. (We expect *he* will win.)

Please vote for the member *who you believe has done the most for the firm*. (You believe *he* has done the most for the firm.)

You are free to vote for *whoever appeals to you*. (*She* appeals to you.)

BUT: You are free to vote for *whomever you wish*. (You wish to vote for *him*.)

We have referred your claim to our attorney, *who we are sure will reply soon*. (We are sure *she* will reply soon.)

We have sent this order blank to all *who we have reason to believe are interested in our book*. (We have reason to believe *they* are interested . . .)

Continued on page 264

¶1062

d. *Whom* (or *whomever*) is the objective form. Use *whom* whenever *him, her, them, me,* or *us* could be substituted as the object of the verb or as the object of a preposition in the *whom* clause.

> *Whom* did you see today? (You did see *her* today.)
>
> To *whom* were you talking? (You were talking to *him*.)
>
> *Whom* were you talking about? (You were talking about *him*.)
>
> *Whom* did you say you wanted to see? (You did say you wanted to see *her*.)
>
> It depends on *whom* they mean. (They mean *him*.)
>
> The question of *whom* we should charge is at issue. (We should charge *her*.)
>
> *Whomever* you designate will get the promotion. (You designate *him*.)
>
> I will hire *whomever* I can find. (I can find *her*.)
>
> I will speak to *whomever* you suggest. (You suggest *her*.)
>
> I will give the job to *whomever* you think you can safely recommend. (You think you can safely recommend *him*.)
>
> **BUT:** I will give the job to *whoever* you think can be safely recommended. (You think *he* can be safely recommended.)
>
> I need a cashier *whom* I can trust. (I can trust *her*.)
>
> The man to *whom* I was referring is Ed Meissen. (I was referring to *him*.)
>
> The person *whom* I was thinking of doesn't have all those qualifications. (I was thinking of *her*.)
>
> The person *whom* we invited to address the committee cannot attend. (We invited *him* to address the committee.)
>
> Steve Koval is the person *whom* we all thought the committee would nominate. (We all thought the committee would nominate *him*.)
>
> Elaine Gerrity, *whom* I considered to be their most promising representative, resigned. (I considered *her* to be their most promising representative.)

1062 *Who, Which,* and *That*

a. *Who* and *that* are used when referring to persons. Select *who* when the individual person or the individuality of a group is meant and *that* when a class or type is meant.

> She is the only one of my managers *who* can speak Japanese fluently.
>
> He is the kind of student *that* should take advanced math.

b. *Which* and *that* are used when referring to places, objects, and animals. *Which* is always used to introduce nonessential clauses, and *that* is ordinarily used to introduce essential clauses.

> Laura's report on employee benefits, *which* I sent you last week, should be of some help. (*Which* introduces a nonessential clause.)
>
> The report *that* I sent you last week should be of some help. (*That* introduces an essential clause.)

NOTE: Many writers now use either *which* or *that* to introduce an essential clause. Indeed, *which* is to be preferred to *that* (1) when there are two or more parallel essential clauses in the same sentence, (2) when *that* has already been used in the sentence, or (3) when the essential clause is introduced by an expression such as *this . . . which, that . . . which, these . . . which,* or *those . . . which.*

> Vivian is taking courses *which* will earn her a higher salary rating in her current job and *which* will qualify her for a number of higher-level jobs.
>
> *That* is a movie *which* you must not miss.
>
> We need to reinforce *those* ideas *which* were presented in earlier chapters.

c. The verb in a relative clause introduced by *who, which,* or *that* should agree in number with the subject of the relative clause. In many cases the subject is clearly expressed.

> The laser printer that *you have ordered* will be delivered in two weeks. (The subject of the relative clause is *you,* which requires a plural verb, *have ordered.*)

However, when the relative pronoun *who, which,* or *that* is itself the subject of the relative clause, the verb in the relative clause must agree with the antecedent of the relative pronoun.

> The laser *printer* that *was ordered* on May 4 will be delivered in two weeks. (The relative pronoun *that* is the subject of the relative clause and refers to a singular antecedent, *printer.* Therefore, the verb in the relative clause—*was ordered*—must be singular.)
>
> **BUT:** The laser *printers* that *were ordered* . . .
>
> I am determined to succeed, not only for myself but for *you,* who *have* always *encouraged* me. (The relative pronoun *who* is the subject of the relative clause and refers to the antecedent *you,* which requires a plural verb—in this case *have encouraged.*)

Sometimes it is difficult to determine the antecedent of the relative pronoun. In such cases mentally rearrange the wording, as is done in the following example.

> Hyphenate the *elements* of a *compound adjective* that occur?/occurs? before a noun. (To determine whether the antecedent of *that* is the plural term *elements* or the singular term *compound adjective,* recast the sentence: "When a *compound adjective occurs* before a noun, hyphenate the elements." This makes it clear that in the original sentence *compound adjective* is the antecedent of *that;* thus the verb in the relative clause must be singular: *occurs.*)
>
> Hyphenate the elements of a *compound adjective* that *occurs* before a noun.

d. *Which, that,* and *who* may be used to refer to organizations. When you are referring to the organization as a single entity (in other words, as *it*), then use *which* or *that* as indicated in ¶1062b. However, when you are thinking of the organization in terms of the individuals who make up the organization (in other words, when you think of the organization as *they*), you may use *who* or *that* as indicated in ¶1062a. (See also ¶1020.)

> Whenever we run short of computer supplies, the Brown & Weiner Company is the one *that* gives us the best service and the best prices.
>
> We really like doing business with the people at the Brown & Weiner Company. They are a customer-oriented group *who* give us the best service and the best prices. (*That* may also be used in this sentence in place of *who.*)

e. Make sure that a relative clause is placed close to its antecedent to avoid unintended (and sometimes humorous) interpretations. (See also ¶1086.)

> **NOT:** Wanted: Nanny to take care of two-year-old who does not drink or smoke.
>
> **BUT:** Wanted: Nanny who does not drink or smoke; to take care of two-year-old.

1063 *Whose* and *Who's*

Do not confuse *whose* (the possessive form of *who*) with *who's* (a contraction meaning "who is" or "who has").

> *Whose* house is it? (It is *his.*)   *Who's* the owner of that house? (*She* is.)
>
> *Who's* had the most experience in that position? (*She* has had the most experience in that position.)
>
> *Who's* the most experienced person in that position? (*She* is the most experienced person in that position.)
>
> *Whose* experience is best suited to that position? (*Her* experience is.)

Grammar

10

¶1064

Pronouns With *To Be*

1064 a. If a pronoun is the subject of *to be,* use the *objective* form.

> I want *her* to be successful.   I expected *them* to be late.
>
> *Whom* do you consider to be the more expert driver? (You do consider *whom* to be the more expert driver?)

b. If *to be* has a subject and is followed by a pronoun, put that pronoun in the *objective* case.

> They mistook the *visitors* to be *us.* (*Visitors,* the subject of *to be,* is in the objective; therefore, the predicate pronoun following *to be* is objective—*us.*)
>
> They took *her* to be *me.*
>
> *Whom* did you take *him* to be? (You did take *him* to be *whom?*)

c. If *to be* has *no* subject and is followed by a pronoun, put that pronoun in the *nominative* case.

> The *caller* was thought to be *I.* (*I* agrees with the subject, *caller.*)
>
> The *Macauleys* were thought to be *we.*
>
> *Who* was *he* thought to be? (*He was* thought to be *who?*)

NOTE: The examples above are all grammatically correct, but they also sound quite awkward. Whenever possible, use more idiomatic wording. For example, the three sentences above could be recast as follows:

> They thought I was the one who called.
>
> The Macauleys were mistaken for us.
>
> Who did they think he was?

Troublesome Pronouns

➤ *See the individual entries in Section 11 for the following pronouns:*

All of (see ¶1101)	Each other-one another (see ¶1101)	Someone-some one (see ¶1010, note)
Anyone-any one (see ¶1010, note)	Everyone-every one (see ¶1010, note)	That-which-who (see ¶1062)
Between you and me (see ¶1055b)	Its-it's (see ¶1101)	These sort-these kind (see ¶1101)
Both-each (see ¶1101)	Most (see ¶1101)	Whatever-what ever (see ¶1101)
Both alike (see ¶1101)	Nobody-no body (see ¶1101)	Who-whom (see ¶1061)
Each-either-both (see ¶1101)	None-no one (see ¶¶1013b, 1101)	Whoever-who ever (see ¶1061)

Adjectives and Adverbs

➤ *For definitions of the terms* adjective *and* adverb, *see the appropriate entries in the Glossary of Grammatical Terms (Appendix A).*

1065 Only an adverb can modify an adjective.

> Packard's will give you a *really* good buy on printers.
>
> (**NOT:** Packard's will give you a *real* good buy on printers.)

1066 When a word in the predicate refers to the *action of the verb*, use an *adverb* (not an adjective).

> We guarantee *to ship* the portfolios *promptly*.
> They *were injured badly* in the accident.

TEST: If *in a . . . manner* can be substituted for the *ly*-ending word, choose the adverb.

> *Read* the directions *carefully* (in a careful manner).

1067 When a word in the predicate describes the *subject* of the sentence, use an *adjective* (not an adverb). Verbs of the *senses (feel, look, sound, taste, smell)* and *linking* verbs (the various forms of *be, seem, appear, become*) are followed in most cases by adjectives. A few other verbs (such as *grow, prove, get, keep, remain,* and *turn*) are sometimes followed by adjectives.

> I feel *bad* (**NOT** badly).   He has grown *tall*.
> She looked *happy*.   The work proved *hard*.
> Your voice sounded *strong*.   I got *lucky*.
> He seemed (**OR** appeared) *shy*.   Let's all keep (**OR** remain) *calm*.
> They became *famous*.   The weather has turned *cold*.

TEST: If *is, are, was, were,* or some other form of *be* can be substituted for the verb, choose the adjective.

> He *looks happy*.   He *is happy*.

NOTE: In the following group of cxamples, verbs of the senses and linking verbs are used as verbs of action (¶1066). Since the modifier refers to the action of the verb (and does not describe the subject), the modifier must be an adverb.

> She *looked suspiciously* at the visitor in the reception room.
> He *felt carefully* along the ledge for the key.
> Our market share *has grown quickly*.
> He *appeared quietly* in the doorway.

1068 Several of the most frequently used adverbs have two forms.

close, closely	fair, fairly	loud, loudly	short, shortly
deep, deeply	hard, hardly	quick, quickly	slow, slowly
direct, directly	late, lately	right, rightly	wide, widely

a. In a number of cases the two forms have different meanings.

> Ship the goods *direct*. (Meaning "straight," "without detour.")
> They were *directly* responsible. (Meaning "without any intervention.")

> They arrived *late*.   The truck stopped *short*.
> I haven't seen her *lately*.   You will hear from us *shortly*.

> You've been working too *hard*.   Turn *right* at the first traffic light.
> I could *hardly* hear him.   I don't *rightly* remember.

b. In some cases the choice is largely a matter of idiom. Some verbs take the *ly* form; others take the short form.

dig deep	go slow	open wide	come close	play fair
wound deeply	proceed slowly	travel widely	watch closely	treat fairly

c. In still other cases the choice is simply one of formality. The *ly* forms are more formal.

> sell cheap   **OR**   sell cheaply   talk loud   **OR**   talk loudly

¶1069

1069 **a.** Although the *ly* ending usually signifies an adverb, a few adjectives also end in *ly*—for example, *costly, orderly, timely, motherly, fatherly, friendly, neighborly, worldly, earthly, lively, lovely, lonely.*

> Let's look for a less *costly* solution.
> Her offer to help you was intended as a *friendly* gesture.

b. A few common *ly*-ending words are used both as adjectives and as adverbs—for example, *early, only, daily, weekly, monthly, quarterly, yearly.*

> I always try to leave for work at an *early* hour. (Adjective.)
> The surge in sales began *early* last month. (Adverb.)
>
> We issue our sales reports on a *quarterly* basis. (Adjective.)
> We issue our sales reports *quarterly*. (Adverb.)
>
> We are all waiting for the *first-quarter* sales report. (Compound adjective.)
> (**NOT:** We are all waiting for the *first-quarterly* sales report.)

c. The words *fast, long,* and *hard* are also used both as adjectives and as adverbs.

> **ADJECTIVES:** a *fast* talker   a *long, hard* winter
> **ADVERBS:** talks *fast*   thought *long* and *hard*

1070 Words such as *up, in, out, on,* and *off*—commonly recognized as prepositions—also function as adverbs, especially in verb phrases where these words are needed to complete the meaning of the verb. (See also ¶802.)

	Used as Adverbs	Used as Prepositions
up:	to look *up* the definition	to jog *up* the hill
down:	to take *down* your name	to walk *down* the street
in:	to trade *in* your old car	to see *in* the dark
out:	to phase *out* operations	to look *out* the window
on:	to put *on* a performance	to act *on* the stage
off:	to write *off* our losses	to drive *off* the road

NOTE: When used in headings and titles as *adverbs,* these short words are capitalized; when used as *prepositions,* they are not. (See ¶361c–d.)

1071 **Problems of Comparison**

a. Form the comparative degree of *one-syllable* adjectives and adverbs by adding *er* to the positive form. Form the superlative degree by adding *est*. (See ¶1071e for a few exceptions.)

> thin: thinner, thinnest   soon: sooner, soonest

b. Form the comparative degree of *two-syllable* adjectives and adverbs either by adding *er* to the positive form or by inserting either *more* or *less* before the positive form. Form the superlative degree by adding *est* in some cases or by inserting *most* or *least* before the positive form. In some cases the addition of *er* or *est* will create very awkward forms. Your ear will tell you when to avoid such forms.

> happy: happier, more (**OR** less) happy   more hopeful (**NOT:** hopefuller)
> likely: likeliest, most (**OR** least) likely   more hostile (**NOT:** hostiler)
> often: oftener, more (**OR** less) often   most complex (**NOT:** complexest)
> highly: highest, most (**OR** least) highly   most troubled (**NOT:** troubledest)

➤ *See ¶825b and page 300 for a usage note on* more.

¶**1071**

NOTE: If the positive form ends in a consonant plus *y* (for example, *happy, likely*), change the *y* to *i* before adding *er* or *est*. Some *ly*-ending words drop the *ly* in the comparative and superlative (for example, *highly, higher, highest; deeply, deeper, deepest*). (See also ¶710.)

c. Form the comparative degree of adjectives and adverbs containing *three or more syllables* by inserting *more* or *less* before the positive form. Form the superlative degree by inserting *most* or *least* before the positive form.

competent: more competent   adventurous: less adventurous
acceptable: most acceptable   carefully: least carefully

d. Avoid double comparisons.

cheaper (**NOT:** more cheaper)   unkindest (**NOT:** most unkindest)

e. A few adjectives and adverbs have irregular comparisons. For example:

Positive	Comparative	Superlative
good **OR** well (see page 294)	better	best
bad **OR** ill	worse	worst
far	farther, further (see ¶719)	farthest, furthest
late	later, latter (see ¶719)	latest, last
little	littler, less, lesser	littlest, least
many, much	more	most

f. Some adjectives and adverbs—for example, *square, round, unique, completely, universally, correct, perfect, always, never, dead*—do not logically permit comparison. A square cannot be any *squarer;* a circle cannot be the *roundest* of all circles. Nevertheless, a number of these words may be modified by *more, less, nearly, hardly, virtually,* and similar adverbs to suggest something less than absolute perfection in each case.

Next year we hope to do a *more complete* study.
He is looking for a *more universally* acceptable solution.
Handicraft of this caliber is *virtually unique* these days.
We *almost never* increase our prices more than once a year.

g. When referring to *two* persons, places, or things, use the comparative form; when referring to *more than two*, use the superlative form.

That is the *finer* piece of linen. (Only two pieces are involved.)
This is the *finest* piece of linen I could find. (Many pieces are involved.)

Of the two positions open, you have chosen the *more* promising.
Of the three positions open, you have chosen the *most* promising.

That is the *more* efficient of the two methods.
This is the *most* efficient method that could be devised.

I like Evelyn's plan *better* than Joe's or Betty's. (Although three things are involved, they are being compared two at a time; hence the comparative.)

NOTE: In a few idiomatic expressions (such as *Put your best foot forward* and *May the best man win*), the superlative form is used, even though only two things are referred to.

h. When comparing a person or a thing *within* the group to which it belongs, use the superlative. When comparing a person or a thing with individual members of the group, use the comparative and the words *other* or *else*.

Continued on page 270

Grammar

10

¶1072

Susan is the *most* conscientious employee on the staff.

Susan is *more* conscientious than any *other* employee on the staff. (Without the word *other,* the sentence would imply that Susan is not on the staff.)

Los Angeles is the *largest* city in California.

Los Angeles is *larger* than any *other* city in California. (Without *other,* the sentence would imply that Los Angeles is not in California.)

Bert's proposal was the *best* of all that were presented to the committee.

Bert's proposal was *better* than anyone *else's.* (**NOT:** anyone's.)

i. Be sure to compare like things. (See also ¶644, note.)

This year's output is lower than last year's. (In other words, "This year's *output* is lower than last year's *output.*")

NOT: This year's output is lower than last year. (Incorrectly compares *this year's output* with *last year.*)

1072 Adverbs such as *only, nearly, almost, ever, scarcely, merely, too,* and *also* should be placed as close as possible to the word modified—usually directly before it. Putting the adverb in the wrong position may change the entire meaning of the sentence. (See also ¶1087.)

Our list of depositors numbers *almost* 50,000. (**NOT:** almost numbers.)

Only the board can nominate the three new officers. (Cannot be nominated by anyone else.)

The board can *only* nominate the three officers. (They cannot elect.)

The board can nominate *only* the three officers. (They cannot nominate anyone else.)

Elvira and Frank Mancuso have been married for *not quite* two years.

(**NOT:** Elvira and Frank Mancuso have *not quite* been married for two years.)

1073 Do not use an adverb to express a meaning already contained in the verb.

assemble (**NOT:** assemble together)   finish (**NOT:** finish up or off)
begin (**NOT:** first begin)   follow (**NOT:** follow after)
cancel (**NOT:** cancel out)   refer (**NOT:** refer back)
continue (**NOT:** continue on)   repeat (**NOT:** repeat again)
convert (**NOT:** convert over)   return (**NOT:** return back)
cooperate (**NOT:** cooperate together)   revert (**NOT:** revert back)

Troublesome Adjectives and Adverbs

➢ *See the individual entries in Section 11 for the following adjectives and adverbs:*

A–an	Anymore–any more	Entitled-titled
Above	Anytime–any time	Equally–as good
Accidentally	Anyway–any way	Everyday–every day
Adverse–averse	Awhile–a while	Ex–former
Afterward–afterwards	Backward–backwards	Farther–further
All right	Bad–badly	Fewer–less
Almost–all most	Biannual–biennial–	First–firstly, etc.
Already–all ready	semiannual	Fiscal–financial
Altogether–all together	Biweekly–bimonthly	Flammable–inflammable
Always–all ways	Complementary–	Former–first
Another	complimentary	Fulsome
Anxious–eager	Different–differently	Good–well

Grammar

10

¶**1075**

Hardly	Maybe–may be	Someday–some day
Healthy–healthful	More	Sometime–
Historic–historical	More important–	sometimes–some time
Hopefully	more importantly	Sure–surely
Incidentally	More than–over	This here
Incredible–incredulous	Only	Unique
Indifferent–in different	Real–really	Up
Indirect–in direct	Reluctant–reticent	Verbal
Last–latest	Said	Very
Latter–last	Same	Wise
Literally	Scarcely	

Negatives

1074 To express a negative idea in a simple sentence, use only one negative expression in the sentence. (A *double negative*—two negative expressions in the same sentence—gives a *positive* meaning.)

> We can sit by and do *nothing.*
>
> We can*not* sit by and do *nothing.* (The *not* and *nothing* create a double negative; the sentence now has a positive meaning: "We ought to do something.")
>
> Jim is *un*aware of the facts. (Here the negative element is the prefix *un.*)
>
> Jim is *not un*aware of the facts. (With the double negative, the sentence means "Jim *is* aware of the facts.")

NOTE: A double negative is not wrong in itself. As the examples above indicate, a double negative may offer a more effective way of expressing a *positive thought* than a straightforward positive construction would. However, a double negative *is* wrong if the sentence is intended to have a negative meaning. Remember, two negatives make a positive.

1075 A negative expression gives a negative meaning to the *clause* in which it appears. In a simple sentence, where there is only one clause, the negative expression affects the entire sentence (see ¶1074). In a sentence where there are two or more clauses, a negative expression affects only the clause in which it appears. Therefore, each clause may safely contain one negative expression. A double negative results when there are two negative expressions within the *same* clause.

> If Mr. Bogosian can*not* lower his price, there is *no* point in continuing the negotiations. (The *if* clause contains the negative *not;* the main clause contains the negative *no.* Each clause has its own negative meaning.)
>
> I have *not* met Halliday, and I have *no* desire to meet him.
>
> **OR:** I have *not* met Halliday, *nor* do I have *any* desire to meet him. (When the negative conjunction *nor* replaces *and,* the adjective *no* changes to *any* so as to avoid a double negative in the second clause.)
>
> We have *never* permitted, *nor* will we permit, any lowering of our standards. (Here the second clause interrupts the first clause. If written out in full, the sentence would read, "We have *never* permitted any lowering of our standards, *nor* will we permit any lowering of our standards.")

NOTE: A second negative expression may be used in a clause to repeat or intensify the first negative expression. This construction is not a double negative.

> *No,* I did *not* say that. He would *never, never* do a thing like that. That's a *no-no.*

¶1076

1076 To preserve the *negative* meaning of a clause, follow these basic principles:

a. If the clause has a *negative verb* (a verb modified by *not* or *never*), do not use an additional negative expression, such as *nor, neither . . . nor, no, none, no one,* or *nothing.* Instead, use the corresponding positive expression, such as *or, either . . . or, any, anyone,* or *anything.*

> I have *not* invited *anyone.* (**WRONG:** I have *not* invited *no one.*)
>
> She does *not* want *any.* (**WRONG:** She does *not* want *none.*)
>
> Mary did *not* have *anything* to do. (**WRONG:** Mary did *not* have *nothing* to do.)
>
> I can*not* find *either* the letter *or* the envelope. (**WRONG:** I can*not* find *neither* the letter *nor* the envelope.)
>
> He did *not* say whether he would mail the money to us *or* whether he would bring it himself. (**WRONG:** He did *not* say whether he would mail the money to us *nor* whether he would bring it himself.)

b. If a clause contains any one of the following expressions—*no, no one, none, nothing,* or *neither . . . nor* (this counts as one expression)—make sure that the verb and all other words are *positive.*

> I see *nothing* wrong with *either* proposal. (**NOT:** neither proposal.)
>
> *Neither* Martha Gutowski *nor* Yvonne Christopher *can* attend the meeting. (**NOT:** cannot.)

c. The word *nor* may be used alone as a conjunction (see the second and third examples in ¶1075) or together with *neither.* Do not use *nor* in the same clause with any other negative; use *or* instead.

> There are *neither* diskettes *nor* printer cartridges in the stockroom.
>
> **BUT:** There are *no* diskettes *or* printer cartridges in the stockroom.
>
> (**NOT:** There are *no* diskettes *nor* printer cartridges.)
>
> There are *no* clear-cut rights *or* wrongs in the situation.
>
> (**NOT:** There are *no* clear-cut rights *nor* wrongs in the situation.)
>
> Francine has *not* called *or* written us for some time.
>
> (**NOT:** Francine has *not* called *nor* written us for some time.)
>
> Never try to argue *or* debate with Larry.
>
> (**NOT:** *Never* try to argue *nor* debate with Larry.)

➤ *For* hardly, only, *and* scarcely, *which have a negative meaning, see the appropriate entries in ¶1101.*

Prepositions

Words Requiring Certain Prepositions

1077 Usage requires that certain words be followed by certain prepositions. Some of the most frequently used combinations are given in the following list.

> **account for** something or someone: I find it hard to *account for* his behavior.
>
> **account to** someone: You will have to *account to* Anne for the loss of the key.
>
> **agree on** or **upon** (reach an understanding): We cannot *agree on* the price.
>
> **agree to** (accept another person's plan): Will you *agree to* their terms?
>
> **agree with** (concur with a person or an idea): I *agree with* your objectives.
>
> **angry at** or **about** something: He was *angry about* the total disorder in the office.
>
> **angry with** someone: You have every right to be *angry with* me.

¶**1078**

apply for a position: You ought to *apply for* Harry's job, now that he has left.

apply to someone or something: You must *apply* yourself *to* the job in order to master it. I am thinking of *applying to* the Field Engineering Company.

argue about something: We a*rgued about* the terms of the contract.

argue with a person: It doesn't pay to *argue with* Bremer.

compare to (assert a likeness): She *compared* my writing *to* E. B. White's. (She said I wrote like E. B. White.)

compare with (analyze for similarities and differences): When she *compared* my writing *with* E. B. White's, she said that I had a similar kind of humor but that my sentences lacked the clean and easy flow of White's material.

conform to (preferred to *with*): These copies do not *conform to* the originals.

consists in (exists in): Happiness largely *consists in* wanting what you have, not having what you want.

consists of (is made up of): Their new formula for a wage settlement *consists of* the same old terms expressed in different language.

convenient for (suitable): What time will be most *convenient for* you?

convenient to (near at hand): Our plant is *convenient to* all transportation facilities in the area.

correspond to (agree with): The shipment does not *correspond to* the sample.

correspond with (exchange letters with): It may be better to see him in person than to *correspond with* him.

differ about (something): We *differed about* means but not about objectives.

differ from (something else): This job *differs* very little *from* the one that I had.

differ with (someone): I *differ with* you over the consequences of our plan.

different from: This product is *different from* the one I normally use.

different than: I view the matter in a *different* way *than* you do. (Although *from* is normally preferred, *than* is acceptable in order to avoid sentences like "I view the matter in a different way from the way in which you do.")

identical with or **to:** This $180 suit is *identical with* (or *to*) one advertised for $235 at other stores.

independent of (not from): He wants to be *independent of* his family's money.

interested in: We are *interested in* discussing the matter further with you at the conference in July.

retroactive to (not from): This salary adjustment is *retroactive to* May 1.

speak to (tell something to): You must *speak to* them about their absences.

speak with (discuss with): It was good to *speak with* you yesterday.

Superfluous Prepositions

1078 Omit prepositions that add nothing to the meaning—as in the following examples. (See also page 283 for a usage note on *all of*.)

Where is she [at]?   Where did that paper go [to]?

She could not help [from] laughing.   His office is opposite [to] hers.

Your chair is too near [to] your terminal.   The carton apparently fell off [of] the truck.

Why don't we meet at about one o'clock? (Omit either *at* or *about*.)

The new applicant seems to be [of] about sixteen years of age.

The strike is now over [with].

We need to focus [in] on ways to boost sales.

I'm not [for] sure that I can go with you to Rome.

¶1079

Necessary Prepositions

1079 Conversely, do not omit essential prepositions.

I need to buy a couple *of* books.   (**NOT:** I need to buy a couple books.)
Of what use is this gadget?   (**NOT:** What use is this gadget?
We don't stock that type *of* filter.   (**NOT:** We don't stock that type filter.)
Jo will graduate *from* Yale next spring.   (**NOT:** Jo will graduate Yale next spring.)

What time will your plane arrive *at* Kennedy?
(**NOT:** What time will your plane arrive Kennedy?)

You have a great interest *in,* as well as a deep respect *for,* fine antiques.
(**NOT:** You have a great interest, as well as a deep respect *for,* fine antiques.)

She frequently appears in movies, *in* plays, and *on* television.
(**NOT:** She frequently appears in movies, plays, and on television.)

NOTE: The preposition *of* is understood in expressions such as *what color cloth* and *what size shoes.*

Prepositions at the End of Sentences

1080 **a.** Ending a sentence with a preposition is not incorrect. Whether you do so or not should depend on the emphasis and effect you want to achieve.

INFORMAL: I wish I knew which magazine her article appeared *in.*
FORMAL: I wish I knew *in which* magazine her article appeared.

b. Trying to avoid ending a sentence with a preposition may lead to very awkward results.

STILTED: It is difficult to know *about* what you are thinking.
NATURAL: It is difficult to know what you are thinking *about.*

c. Short questions and statements frequently end with prepositions.

How many can I count *on?*   What is this good *for?*
What is this made *of?*   We need tools to work *with.*
Where did he come *from?*   That's something we must look *into.*
He has nothing to worry *about.*   That's the car I want to look *at.*

d. Some sentences end with what seem like prepositions but are really adverbs.

I'm sure another job will soon turn *up.*
After Scott considers his alternatives, I'm sure he'll come *around.*

NOTE: Many people are familiar with Sir Winston Churchill's complaint to an editor who tried to discourage him from ending his sentences with prepositions:

This is the sort of English up with which I will not put.

At the other extreme is a sentence that probably takes the prize for piling the greatest number of prepositions at the end. It is the complaint of a small child who does not want to listen to a particular bedtime story:

What did you bring that book I don't want to be read to out of in for?

Both these examples reinforce the main point:

Use good sense in deciding whether or not to end a sentence with a preposition.

BETTER THAN: Use good sense in deciding whether or not to use a preposition to end a sentence with.

¶**1081**

Troublesome Prepositions

➤ *See the individual entries that are listed alphabetically in Section 11 for the following prepositions:*

At about	In–into–in to	Off
Beside–besides	In regards to	On–onto–on to
Between–among	Indifferent–in different	On–upon–up on
Due to–because of–on account of	Indirect–in direct	Opposite
Except	Like–as, as if	Per–a
From–off	Of–have	Toward–towards

➤ *For the treatment of words that can function as both prepositions and adverbs, see ¶¶802, 1070. For the capitalization of such words, see ¶361c–d.*

Sentence Structure

Parallel Structure

1081 Express parallel ideas in parallel form.

a. Adjectives should be paralleled by adjectives, nouns by nouns, dependent clauses by dependent clauses, and so on.

> **WRONG:** Your new sales training program was *stimulating* and a *challenge.* (Adjective and noun.)

> **RIGHT:** Your new sales training program was *stimulating* and *challenging.* (Two adjectives.)

> **WRONG:** The sales representatives have already started *using the new techniques* and *to produce higher sales.* (Participial phrase and infinitive phrase.)

> **RIGHT:** The sales representatives have already started *using the new techniques* and *producing higher sales.* (Two participial phrases.)

> **RIGHT:** The sales representatives have already started *to use the new techniques* and *produce higher sales.* (Two infinitive phrases.)

> **WRONG:** This scanner is *easy* to operate, *efficient,* and *it is relatively inexpensive.* (Two adjectives and a clause.)

> **RIGHT:** This scanner is *easy* to operate, *efficient,* and relatively *inexpensive.* (Three adjectives.)

> **NOTE:** Parallelism is especially important in displayed enumerations.

> **POOR:** This article will discuss:
> 1. How to deal with corporate politics.
> 2. Coping with stressful situations.
> 3. What the role of the manager should be in the community.

> **BETTER:** This article will discuss:
> 1. *Ways* to deal with corporate politics.
> 2. *Techniques* of coping with stressful situations.
> 3. The *role* of the manager in the community.

> **OR:** This article will tell managers how to:
> 1. *Deal* with corporate politics.
> 2. *Cope* with stressful situations.
> 3. *Function* in the community.

Continued on page 276

¶1082

b. Correlative conjunctions (*both . . . and, either . . . or, neither . . . nor, not only . . . but also, whether . . . or,* etc.) should be followed by elements in parallel form.

> **WRONG:** We are flying both to Chicago and San Francisco.
> **RIGHT:** We are flying to both *Chicago* and *San Francisco*.
> **RIGHT:** We are flying both *to Chicago* and *to San Francisco*.

> **WRONG:** He would neither apologize nor would he promise to reform.
> **RIGHT:** He would neither *apologize* nor *promise to reform*.
> **RIGHT:** *He would not apologize*, nor *would he promise to reform*.

> **WRONG:** Dwayne is not only gifted as a violinist but also as a music critic.
> **RIGHT:** Dwayne is gifted not only *as a violinist* but also *as a music critic*.

NOTE: When using the correlative conjunction *not only . . . but also,* you do not have to place *also* immediately after *but;* in fact, *also* may be omitted altogether.

> Dwayne is not only *a sensitive musician* but *a music critic* who is sensitive to the gifts of other musicians.

Dangling Constructions

1082 When a sentence begins with a participial phrase, an infinitive phrase, a gerund phrase, or an elliptical clause (one in which essential words are missing), make sure that the phrase or clause logically agrees with the subject of the sentence; otherwise, the construction will "dangle." To correct a dangling construction, make the subject of the sentence the doer of the action expressed by the opening phrase or clause. If that is not feasible, use an entirely different construction.

a. Participial Phrases

> **WRONG:** Stashed *away* in the attic for the past hundred years, the *owner* of the painting has decided to auction it off. (Who was stashed in the attic: the owner or the painting?)
> **RIGHT:** The owner of the painting that has been stashed away in the attic for the past hundred years has decided to auction it off.

> **WRONG:** After coming out of a coma, the *police officer* asked the driver what caused the accident. (As worded, this version suggests that the police officer had been in a coma.)
> **RIGHT:** After the driver came out of a coma, the police officer asked her what caused the accident.

> **WRONG:** Having studied your cost estimates, a few *questions* occur to me about your original assumptions. (As worded, this version implies that the *questions* have studied the cost estimates.)
> **RIGHT:** Having studied your cost estimates, I would like to ask you a few questions about your original assumptions. (In the correct version, the person who studied the cost estimates is now the subject of the sentence and is the one asking the questions.)

> **WRONG:** Putting the issue of costs aside, production delays need to be discussed.
> **RIGHT:** Putting the issue of costs aside, *we* need to discuss production delays.

NOTE: A few words ending in *ing* (such as *concerning, considering, pending,* and *regarding*) have now become established as prepositions. Therefore, when they introduce phrases at the start of a sentence, it is not essential that they refer to the subject of the sentence.

> *Considering* how long the lawsuit has dragged on, it might have been wiser not to sue.

¶**1084**

b. Infinitive Phrases

WRONG: To appreciate the full significance of Fox's latest letter, all the previous correspondence should be read.

RIGHT: To appreciate the full significance of Fox's latest letter, you should read all the previous correspondence.

WRONG: To obtain this free booklet, the enclosed coupon should be mailed at once.

RIGHT: To obtain this free booklet, mail the enclosed coupon at once.

c. Prepositional-Gerund Phrases

WRONG: By installing a computerized temperature control system, a substantial saving in fuel costs was achieved.

RIGHT: By installing a computerized temperature control system, we achieved a substantial saving in fuel costs.

WRONG: In analyzing these specifications, several errors have been found.

RIGHT: In analyzing these specifications, I have found several errors.

d. Elliptical Clauses

WRONG: If ordered before May 1, a 5 percent discount will be allowed on these goods.

RIGHT: If these goods are ordered before May 1, a 5 percent discount . . .

WRONG: When four years old, my family moved to Omaha.

RIGHT: When I was four years old, my family moved to Omaha.

e. Absolute Phrases

Absolute phrases (typically involving participles) are not considered to "dangle," even though they come at the beginning of a sentence and do not refer to the subject.

Strictly speaking, what you did was not illegal—but it wasn't right.

All things considered, Phyllis's plan may be the best way to proceed.

Weather permitting, the graduation ceremonies will be held in the quadrangle.

Speaking of weird performances, what did you think of George's presentation?

Judging by the response to our last ad campaign, our chances of meeting our sales goal this year are nil.

Avoid using absolute phrases when they produce awkward sentences.

AWKWARD: The speeches having been concluded, we proceeded to vote.

BETTER: After the speeches were concluded, we proceeded to vote.

1083 When verbal phrases and elliptical clauses fall elsewhere in the sentence, look out for illogical or confusing relationships. Adjust the wording as necessary.

WRONG: I saw two truck drivers get into a fistfight while jogging down the street.

RIGHT: While jogging down the street, I saw two truck drivers get into a fistfight.

1084 A prepositional phrase will dangle at the beginning of a sentence if it leads the reader to expect a certain word as the subject and then another word is used instead.

WRONG: As head of the program committee, we think you should make immediate arrangements for another speaker. (The head of the committee is *you,* not *we.*)

RIGHT: We think that as head of the program committee you should make immediate arrangements for another speaker.

Continued on page 278

¶1085

WRONG: As a young boy, the woman I was destined to marry did not appeal to me in any way. (That woman never was a "young boy.")

RIGHT: When I was a young boy, the woman I was destined to marry did not appeal to me in any way.

WRONG: You voted for change. As your next governor, you will get change. (The voters are not going to be the next governor.)

RIGHT: You voted for change. As your next governor, I will see to it that you get change!

1085 A verbal phrase will dangle at the end of a sentence if it refers to the meaning of the main clause as a whole rather than to the doer of the action.

WRONG: Our sales have been steadily declining for the past six months, thus creating a sharp drop in profits. (As worded, the sentence makes it appear that our sales, by themselves, have created the drop in profits. Actually, it is *the fact* that our sales have been declining which has created the drop in profits.)

RIGHT: The steady decline in our sales for the past six months has created a sharp drop in profits.

RIGHT: Our sales have been steadily declining for the past six months. As a result, we have experienced a sharp drop in profits.

Misplaced Modifiers

1086 Watch out for misplaced modifiers (either words or phrases) that provide the basis for unintended (and sometimes humorous) interpretations.

WRONG: I suspect that my assistant accidentally dropped the report I had been drafting in the wastebasket. (What an uncomfortable location in which to draft a report!)

RIGHT: The report I had been drafting has disappeared. I suspect that my assistant accidentally dropped it in the wastebasket.

WRONG: Here are some helpful suggestions for protecting your valuable possessions from our hotel security staff. (Can no one be trusted?)

RIGHT: Here are some helpful suggestions from our hotel security staff for protecting your valuable possessions.

WRONG: One of our assistant vice presidents has been referred to a personal finance counselor with serious credit problems. (Would you consult such a counselor?)

RIGHT: One of our assistant vice presidents has serious credit problems and has been referred to a personal finance counselor.

WRONG: Lincoln wrote the Gettysburg Address while traveling to Gettysburg on the back of an envelope.

RIGHT: Lincoln wrote the Gettysburg Address on the back of an envelope while traveling to Gettysburg.

1087 Squinting Modifiers

Watch out for *squinting modifiers*—modifiers placed in such a way that they can be interpreted as modifying either what precedes or what follows.

SQUINTING: Traveling abroad frequently can become exhausting. (Does *frequently* modify *Traveling abroad* or *can become exhausting*?)

CLEAR: *Frequently* traveling abroad (**OR** Making frequent trips abroad) can become exhausting.

CLEAR: Traveling abroad can *frequently* become exhausting.

➤ *See also ¶¶1062e, 1072.*

SECTION 11

Usage

A–An
A–Of
A Lot–Alot–Allot
Above
Accidentally
A.D.–B.C.
Additionally
Adverse–Averse
Affect–Effect
Afterward–Afterwards
Age–Aged–At the Age of
Ain't
All of
All Right
Almost–All Most
Already–All Ready
Altogether–All Together
Always–All Ways
Amount–Number
And
And Etc.
And/Or
Another
Anxious–Eager
Anymore–Any More
Anyone–Any One
Anytime–Any Time
Anyway–Any Way
Appraise–Apprise
Appreciate
As
As . . . as–Not so . . . as
As Far as
As Well as
At About
Awhile–A While
Backward—Backwards

Bad–Badly
Balance
Being That
Beside–Besides
Between–Among
Between You and Me
Biannual–Biennial–Semiannual
Biweekly–Bimonthly
Both–Each
Both Alike–Equal–Together
Bring–Take
But . . . However
But What
Cannot Help but
Come–Go
Come and
Compare to–Compare With
Complement–Compliment
Complementary–Complimentary
Comprise–Compose
Could Not Care Less
Data
Different–Differently
Different From–Different Than
Dilemma
Disc–Disk
Done
Don't (Do Not)
Doubt That–Doubt Whether
Due to–Because of–On Account of
Each–Either–Both
Each Other–One Another
Emeritus–Emerita
Ensure–Insure–Assure
Enthused Over
Entitled–Titled
Equally–As

Etc.

Ethnic References

Everyday–Every Day

Everyone–Every One

Ex–Former

Except

Farther–Further

Fewer–Less

First–Firstly, etc.

Fiscal–Financial

Flammable–Inflammable

Former–First

From–Off

Fulsome

Gender–Sex

Good–Well

Graduated–Was Graduated

Grow

Had Better

Hardly

Healthy–Healthful

Help

Historic–Historical

Home–Hone

Hopefully

However

If–Whether

Imply–Infer

In–Into–In to

In Regards to

Incidentally

Incredible–Incredulous

Indifferent–In Different

Indirect–In Direct

Individual–Party–Person–People

Irregardless

Is Where–Is When

Its–It's

Kind

Kind of–Sort of

Kind of a

Last–Latest

Latter–Last

Lay–Lie

Learn–Teach

Leave–Let

Like–As, As if

Literally

Look Forward to

Majority–Plurality

May–Can (Might–Could)

Maybe–May Be

Media

More

More Important–More Importantly

More Than–Over

Most

Nobody–No Body

None–No One

Of–Have

Off

On–Onto–On to

On–Upon–Up on

Only

Opposite

Per–A

Percent–Percentage

Period Ended–Period Ending

Plus

Principle–Principal

Rack–Wrack

Raise–Rise

Real–Really

Reason Is Because

Reluctant–Reticent

Retroactive to

Said

Same

Scarcely

Serve–Service

Set–Sit

Shall–Will

Should–Would

So–So That

Someday–Some Day

Someone–Some One

Sometime–Sometimes–Some Time

Supposed to

Sure–Surely

Sure and

Tack–Tact

Than–Then

That

That–Which–Who

These Sort–These Kind

Toward–Towards

Try and

Type–Key

Unique

Up

Used to

Verbal

Very

Vicious Circle

Ways

Whatever–What Ever

Where–That

Who–Which–That

Who–Whom

Whoever–Who Ever

Wise

Would Have

> ➤ *For a list of words that are frequently misused because they sound alike or look alike, see ¶719. For definitions of grammatical terms, see the appropriate entries in the Glossary of Grammatical Terms (Appendix A).*

1101 The following entries will help you avoid a number of common mistakes in usage.

A–an. In choosing *a* or *an*, consider the sound (not the spelling) of the word that follows. Use the article *a* before all *consonant* sounds, including sounded *h* (as in *hat*), long *u* (as in *use*), and *o* with the sound of *w* (as in *one*).

a day	a unit	a one-week delay
a week	a union	a 60-day note
a year	a uniform	a CPA
a home	a youthful spirit	a B.A. degree
a house	a euphoric feeling	a PSAT score
a hotel	a European trip	a UN resolution

Use *an* before all *vowel* sounds except long *u* and before words starting with silent *h*.

an asset	an heir	an AT&T product
an essay	an hour	an EPA ruling
an eyesore	an honor	an FTC ruling
an input	an honest man	an IRS audit
an outcome	an 8-hour day	an OPEC price cut
an umbrella	an 80-year-old man	an ROI objective
an upsurge	an 11 a.m. meeting	an X-ray reading

In speech, both *a historic occasion* and *an historic occasion* are correct, depending on whether the *h* is sounded or left silent. In writing, *a historic occasion* is the form more commonly used.

Continued on page 282

Usage

11

¶1101

NOTE: When you are dealing with an abbreviation, the choice of *a* or *an* will depend on whether you pronounce the expression letter by letter or as a word. Abbreviations pronounced letter by letter are called *initialisms;* abbreviations pronounced as words are called *acronyms.* (See also ¶501b.)

Pronounced Letter by Letter	Pronounced as a Word
an FBI agent	a FICA tax increase
an HMO physician	a HUD project
an L.A.-based firm	a LIFO method of inventory valuation
an M.B.A. degree	a MADD fund-raising drive
an NBC news report	a NATO strategy
an R.S.V.P.	a RICO investigation
an SRO performance	a SWAT team

A–of. Do not use *a* in place of *of.*

> What sort *of* turnout did you have at your seminar?
>
> (**NOT:** What sort *a* turnout did you have at your seminar?)
>
> The weather has been kind *of* cool for this time of year.
>
> (**NOT:** The weather has been *kinda* cool for this time of year.)

A lot–alot–allot. The phrase *a lot* (meaning "to a considerable quantity or extent") always consists of two words. Do not spell this phrase as one word *(alot).*

> Thanks *a lot* (**NOT** alot) for all your help on this year's budget.

Do not confuse this phrase with the verb *allot* (meaning "to distribute or assign a share of something").

> You will have to *allot* a portion of next year's budget to cover unforeseen expenses, even though you are not likely to have *a lot* of money left over after you cover your basic operations.

➤ *See* Kind of–sort of *and* Kind of a.

A–per. See *Per–a.*

Above. Avoid the use of *above* before a noun.

> in the paragraph *above* **OR** in the *preceding* paragraph
>
> (**RATHER THAN:** in the *above* paragraph)

Accidentally. Note that this word ends in *ally.* (The form *accidently* is incorrect.)

A.D.–B.C. *A.D.* (abbreviation of *anno Domini,* Latin for "in the year of our Lord") and *B.C.* ("before Christ") are usually written in all-capital letters, with a period following each letter and with no internal space. Do not use a comma to separate *B.C.* or *A.D.* from the year.

> 150 B.C.   465 A.D. (ordinary usage)
>
> in the first century B.C.   A.D. 465 (formal usage)

You may also type *A.D.* and *B.C.* in small caps (A.D., B.C.) if you have that option.

NOTE: In works of history and theology, the term *A.D.* is often replaced by the abbreviation *C.E.* (meaning "in the Common Era"); *B.C.* is replaced by *B.C.E.* (meaning "before the Common Era").

Additionally. Avoid the use of *additionally* as a transitional expression. Use *in addition, moreover, furthermore,* or *besides* instead. (See ¶138a.)

> **AWKWARD:** *Additionally,* the new packaging will reduce costs by 20 percent.
>
> **BETTER:** *Moreover,* the new packaging will reduce costs by 20 percent.

Adverse–averse. *Adverse* means "unfavorable, harmful, hostile." *Averse* means "opposed (to), having a feeling of distaste (for)."

> This research report will have an *adverse* (unfavorable) effect on our sales.
>
> The medication you are taking could have *adverse* (harmful) side effects.
>
> I am not *averse* (opposed) to working on weekends for the next month.
>
> I am *averse* (opposed) to exercise in any form.
>
> **BUT:** I have *adverse* (hostile) feelings about exercise in any form.

Affect–effect. *Affect* is normally used as a verb meaning "to influence, change, assume." *Effect* can be either a verb meaning "to bring about" or a noun meaning "result, impression."

> The court's decision in this case will not *affect* (change) the established legal precedent.
>
> She *affects* (assumes) an unsophisticated manner.
>
> It is essential that we *effect* (bring about) an immediate improvement in sales.
>
> It will be months before we can assess the full *effect* (result) of the new law.

NOTE: In psychology, *affect* is used as a noun meaning "feeling, emotion," and the related adjective *affective* means "emotional." Because of the limited context in which these terms are likely to be used with these meanings, it should be easy to distinguish them from *effect* as a noun and the related adjective *effective.*

> We need to analyze the *effects* (results) of this new marketing strategy.
>
> We need to analyze the *affects* (emotions) produced by this conflict.
>
> Which technique is *effective* (capable of producing the desired results)?
>
> Let's deal with the *affective* (emotional) factors first.

Afterward–afterwards. Both forms are correct, but *afterward* is more common in U.S. usage.

Age–aged–at the age of

> I interviewed a man *aged 52* for the job. (**NOT:** a man age 52.)
>
> I don't plan to retire *at the age of 65.* (**NOT:** at age 65.)

NOTE: Elliptical references to age—for example, *at age 65*—should not be used except in technical writing such as human resources manuals.

> See the chart on page 64 for the schedule of retirement benefits for employees who retire *at age 65.*

Ain't. *Ain't* has long been considered nonstandard usage, but it is acceptable in certain idiomatic expressions.

> Making that many mistakes in one document *ain't* easy.
>
> Two thousand dollars for a thirty-minute speech? That *ain't* hay!
>
> You *ain't* seen nothin' yet.
>
> If it *ain't* broke, don't fix it. (*If it isn't broken* is grammatically correct, but it lacks the punch of the original.)

All of. *Of* is not needed after *all* unless the following word is a pronoun serving as the object of the preposition *of.*

> *All* my plans have gone up in smoke.
>
> *All* the staff members belong to the softball team.
>
> (**ALSO:** *All of* the staff members belong to the softball team.)
>
> **BUT:** *All of* us belong to the softball team.

¶1101

All right. Like *all wrong*, the expression *all right* should be spelled as two words. (While some dictionaries list *alright* without comment, this spelling is not generally accepted as correct.)

Almost–all most. See also *Most.*

> The plane was *almost* (nearly) three hours late.
> We are *all most* pleased (all very much pleased) with the new schedule.

Already–all ready

> The order had *already* (previously) been shipped.
> The order is *all ready* (all prepared) to be shipped.

Altogether–all together

> He is *altogether* (entirely) too lazy to be a success.
> The papers are *all together* (all in a group) in the binder I sent you.

Always–all ways

> She has *always* (at all times) done good work.
> We have tried in *all ways* (by all methods) to keep our employees satisfied.

Among–between. See *Between–among.*

Amount–number. Use *amount* for things in bulk, as in "a large amount of lumber." Use *number* for individual items, as in "a large number of inquiries."

> Monday's ad generated a large *number* of *phone calls.* (**NOT:** a large amount.)
> Monday's ad generated a large *amount* of *interest.*

And. Retain *and* before the last item in a series, even when that last item consists of two words joined by *and.*

> We need to increase our expense budgets for advertising, staff training, *and* research and development.
>
> (**NOT:** We need to increase our expense budgets for advertising, staff training, research and development.)

Beginning a sentence with *and* or some other coordinating conjunction *(but, or,* or *nor)* can be an effective means—*if not overused*—of giving special attention to the thought that follows the conjunction. No comma should follow the conjunction at the start of a new sentence unless a parenthetical element occurs at that point.

> Last Friday George promised to submit the market analysis this Monday. *And* then he took off on a two-week vacation.
> Tell him to return to the office at once. *Or* else.
> **BUT:** George just called from Lake Tahoe to say that the report was undergoing some last-minute changes and would be on my desk by 11 a.m. *And,* to my delight, it was!

NOTE: Each of the sentences above illustrates how this device can be effectively used. However, these sentences also illustrate, when taken as a whole, how quickly the overuse of this device dissipates its effectiveness.

And etc. Never use *and* before *etc.* (See *Etc.*)

And/or. Avoid this legalistic term in ordinary writing.

Another. Although *another* is often used colloquially as a synonym for *additional*, avoid this usage in formal writing.

> **FORMAL:** I have four copies left, but I will need an *additional* ten copies.
> **INFORMAL:** . . . but I will need *another* ten copies.

Anxious–eager. Both *anxious* and *eager* mean "desirous," but *anxious* also implies fear or concern.

> I'm *anxious* to hear whether we won the bid or not.
>
> I'm *eager* (**NOT** anxious) to hear about your new house.

Anymore–any more

> We used to vacation in Bermuda, but we don't go there *anymore* (any longer).
>
> Please call me if you have *any more* (any additional) suggestions.

Anyone–any one. See ¶1010, note.

Anytime–any time

> Come see us *anytime* you are in town. (One word meaning "whenever.")
>
> Did you have dealings with Crosby at *any time* in the past? (Two words after a preposition such as *at*.)
>
> Can you spend *any time* (any amount of time) with Jill and me when you next come to Tulsa?

Anyway–any way

> *Anyway* (in any case), we can't spare him now.
>
> If we can help in *any way* (by any method), please phone.

Appraise–apprise

> We would like to *appraise* (set a value on) Mrs. Ellsworth's estate.
>
> I will *apprise* (inform) you of any new developments.
>
> I will keep you *apprised* of the reactions of the board members to your proposal.
>
> (**NOT:** I will keep you *appraised* of the reactions of the board members to your proposal.)

Appreciate. When used with the meaning "to be thankful for," the verb *appreciate* requires an object.

> **NOT:** We would appreciate if you could give us your decision by May 1.
>
> **BUT:** We would appreciate *it* if you could give us your decision by May 1. (Pronoun as object.)
>
> **OR:** We would appreciate *your* (**NOT** you) *giving us your decision by May 1.* (Noun clause as object. See ¶647b on the use of *your* before *giving*.)
>
> We will always appreciate the *help* you gave us. (Noun as object.)
>
> I will appreciate *whatever you can do for us.* (Noun clause as object.)

As. Do not use *as* for *that* or *whether.*

> I do not know *whether* (**NOT** as) I can go.

Use *because, since,* or *for* rather than *as* in clauses of reason.

> I cannot attend the meeting in Omaha, *because* (**NOT** as) I will be out on the West Coast that day.

As–as if–like. See *Like–as, as if.*

As . . . as–not so . . . as. The term *as . . . as* is now commonly used in both positive and negative comparisons. Some writers, however, prefer to use *not so . . . as* for negative comparisons.

> Bob is every bit *as* bright *as* his older sister. (Positive comparison.)
>
> It is *not as* important *as* you think. **OR:** . . . *not so* important *as* you think. (Negative comparison.)

NOTE: Do not replace the second *as* with *than.*

> In our family twice *as* much money is spent on entertainment *as* on food.
>
> (**NOT:** In our family twice *as* much money is spent on entertainment *than* on food.)

¶1101

As far as. *As far as* may be used as a preposition or as a subordinating conjunction.

> I can drive you *as far as* Spokane. (Used as a preposition.)
>
> I would recommend this template *as far as* format is concerned. (Used as a subordinating conjunction.)
>
> **BUT NOT:** I would recommend this template *as far as* format. (Either create a clause following *as far as,* as in the example above, or change *as far as* to *on the basis of* or a similar expression: *I would recommend this template on the basis of format.*)

As well as. When using *as well as,* be on guard against the possibility of misleading your reader.

> **CONFUSING:** Ms. Paglia plans to meet with Mr. Pierce and Mrs. Hamer as well as Ms. Fieno. (Is Ms. Paglia planning to meet with three people, or are Ms. Paglia and Ms. Fieno both planning to meet with two people?)
>
> **CLEAR:** Ms. Paglia plans to meet *with* Mr. Pierce and Mrs. Hamer as well as *with* Ms. Fieno. (Repeating the preposition *with* makes it clear that Ms. Paglia will meet with three people.)
>
> **CLEAR:** Ms. Paglia *as well as Ms. Fieno* plans to meet with Mr. Pierce and Mrs. Hamer. (Rearranging the word order makes it clear that both Ms. Paglia and Ms. Fieno will meet with two people. Note that an *as well as* phrase following the subject, *Ms. Paglia,* does not affect the number of the verb. See ¶1007.)

Assure. See *Ensure–insure–assure.*

At about. Use either *at* or *about* but not both words together. For example, "Plan to arrive *at* ten" **OR** "Plan to arrive *about* ten." (**BUT NOT:** Plan to arrive *at about* ten.)

Averse–adverse. See *Adverse–averse.*

Awhile–a while. The one-word form is an adverb; the two-word form is a noun.

> You may have to wait *awhile.* (Adverb.)
>
> You may have to wait for *a while.* (Noun; object of the preposition *for.*)
>
> I ran into him *a while* back.

Backward–backwards. Both forms are correct, but *backward* is more common in U.S. usage; for example, "to lean over *backward.*"

Bad–badly. Use the adjective *bad* (not the adverb *badly*) after the verb *feel* or *look.* (See ¶1067.)

> I feel *bad* (**NOT** badly) about the mistake.
>
> **BUT:** He was hurt *badly.*

NOTE: The only way you can "feel badly" is to have your fingertips removed first.

Balance. Do not use *balance* to mean "rest" or "remainder" except in a financial or accounting sense.

> I plan to use the *rest* of my vacation time next February.
> (**NOT:** I plan to use the *balance* of my vacation time next February.)
>
> **BUT:** The *balance* of the loan falls due at the end of this quarter.

B.C.–A.D. See *A.D.–B.C.*

Because. See *Reason is because.*

Because of. See *Due to–because of–on account of.*

Being that. Do not use *being that* for *since* or *because.*

> *Because* I arrived late, I could not get a seat.
> (**NOT:** *Being that* I arrived late, I could not get a seat.)

Beside–besides

> I sat *beside* (next to) Mr. Parrish's father at the meeting.
>
> *Besides* (in addition), we need your support of the measure.

Between–among. Ordinarily, use *between* when referring to *two* persons or things and *among* when referring to *more than* two persons or things.

> The territory is divided evenly *between* the two sales representatives.
>
> The profits are to be evenly divided *among* the three partners.

Use *between* with more than two persons or things when they are being considered in pairs as well as in a group.

> There are distinct differences *between* New York, Chicago, and Dallas.
>
> In packing china, be sure to place bubble sheets *between* the plates.
>
> The memo says something different when you read *between* the lines.
>
> *Between* you, me, and the gatepost, we don't stand a chance of making budget.

Between you and me (NOT I). See ¶1055b.

Biannual–biennial–semiannual. *Biannual* and *semiannual* both mean "occurring twice a year." *Biennial* means "occurring every two years." Because of the possible confusion between *biannual* and *biennial,* use *semiannual* when you want to describe something that occurs *twice* a year.

> **PREFERRED:** our *semiannual* sales conference
>
> **CLEARER THAN:** our *biannual* sales conference

If you think that your reader could misconstrue *biennial,* avoid the term and use *every two years* instead.

> Within our global organization each national company holds its own sales conference *on a semiannual basis* (**OR** *semiannually*); an international sales conference is scheduled *on a biennial basis* (**OR** *biennially* **OR** *every two years*).

Biweekly–bimonthly. These two words do not mean the same thing. Moreover, *bimonthly* has two quite different meanings, which could confuse your readers.

> If you are paid *biweekly* (every two weeks), you get 26 checks a year.
>
> If you are paid *bimonthly* (twice a month), you get only 24 checks a year.
>
> **OR:** If you are paid *bimonthly* (every two months), you get only 6 checks a year.

NOTE: To keep your meaning clear, avoid *bimonthly* and say "twice a month" or "every two months." You may also use *semimonthly* to mean "twice a month."

Both–each. *Both* means "the two considered together." *Each* refers to the individual members of a group considered separately.

> *Both* designs are acceptable.
>
> The designs are *each* acceptable.
>
> *Each* sister complained about the other.
> (**NOT:** *Both* sisters complained about the other.)

NOTE: Use *each* in cases where *both* leads to confusion or ambiguity.

> **CONFUSING:** There are two statues on *both* sides of the entrance hall. (Is there a total of two statues or four?)
>
> **CLEAR:** There are two statues on *each* side of the entrance hall.
>
> **OR:** There is a statue on *each* side of the entrance hall.

➤ *See* Each–either–both.

Usage

11

¶1101

Both alike–equal–together. *Both* is unnecessary when used with *alike, equal,* or *together.*

> These laser printers are *alike.* (**NOT:** both alike.)
>
> These tape systems are *equal* in cost. (**NOT:** both equal.)
>
> We will travel *together* to Japan. (**NOT:** both travel together.)

Bring–take. *Bring* indicates motion toward the speaker. *Take* indicates motion away from the speaker.

> Please *bring* the research data with you when you next come to the office.
>
> Please *take* the enclosed letter to Farley when you go to see him.
>
> You may *take* my copy with you if you will *bring* it back by Friday.

➤ *See note under* Come–go.

But . . . however. Use one or the other.

> We had hoped to see the show, *but* we couldn't get tickets.
>
> **OR:** We had hoped to see the show; *however,* we couldn't get tickets.
>
> (**BUT NOT:** . . . *but* we couldn't get tickets, *however.*)

But what. Use *that.*

> I do not doubt *that* (**NOT** but what) he will be elected.

Can–could. See *May–can (might–could).*

Cannot help but. This expression is a confusion of two others, namely, *can but* and *cannot help.*

> I *can but* try. (**BETTER:** I *can only* try.)
>
> I *cannot help* feeling sorry for her. (**NOT:** I cannot help but feel sorry for her.)

Class. See *Kind.*

Come–go. The choice between verbs depends on the location of the speaker. *Come* indicates motion *toward; go,* motion *away from.* (See also *Bring–take.*)

> When Bellotti *comes* back, I will *go* to the airport to meet him.
>
> *A manager speaking over the phone to an outsider:* Will it be convenient for you to *come* to our office tomorrow?

NOTE: When discussing your travel plans with a person at your destination, adopt that person's point of view and use *come.*

> *An outsider speaking over the phone to a manager:* Will it be convenient for me to *come* to your office tomorrow?
>
> *Midwesterner to Californian:* I am *coming* to California during the week of the 11th. I will *bring* the plans with me if they are ready.

However, if you are discussing your travel plans with someone who is *not* at your destination, observe the regular distinction between *come* and *go.*

> *An outsider speaking to an outsider:* I hope it will be convenient for me to *go* to their office tomorrow.
>
> *Midwesterner to Midwesterner:* I am *going* to California during the week of the 11th. I will *take* the plans with me if they are ready.

Come and. In formal writing, use *come to* instead of the colloquial *come and.*

> **FORMAL:** Come *to* see me.
>
> **INFORMAL:** Come *and* see me.

Compare to–compare with. See ¶1077.

Complement–compliment. *Complement* as a noun means "something that completes" or "one of two mutually completing parts"; as a verb it means "to complete, to be complementary to." *Compliment* as a noun means "an admiring or flattering remark"; as a verb it means "to praise, to pay a compliment to."

> A simple dessert of berries and sherbet makes a fine *complement* to an elaborate meal with several rich courses.
>
> The CEO was full of *compliments* for your sales presentation yesterday.

Complementary–complimentary. *Complementary* means "serving to complete" or "mutually supplying what each other lacks." *Complimentary* means "flattering" or "given free."

> Our top two executives work so well as a team because they bring *complementary* skills and expertise to their jobs.
>
> The CEO had many *complimentary* things to say about your sales presentation.
>
> May I get a *complimentary* copy of your new book?

Comprise–compose. *Comprise* means "to include, contain, consist of"; *compose* means "to make up." The parts *compose* (make up) the whole; the whole *comprises* (includes) the parts; the whole is *composed of* (**NOT** is comprised of) the parts.

> The parent corporation *comprises* (consists of) three major divisions.
>
> Three major divisions *compose* (make up) the parent corporation.

Do not use *comprise* in the passive.

> The parent corporation *is composed of* (is made up of) three major divisions.
>
> (**NOT:** The parent corporation *is comprised of* three major divisions.)

Could not care less. To say that you "could not care less" means that you do not care at all. To say that you "could care less" implies that your ability to care has not yet reached rock bottom. If the first meaning is the one you wish to communicate, do not omit *not*.

Couldn't–hardly. See *Hardly.*

Data. See ¶1018b.

Different–differently. When the meaning is "in a different manner," use the adverb *differently*.

> I wish we had done it *differently*.
>
> It came out *differently* than we expected. (See ¶1077.)

After linking verbs and verbs of the senses, the adjective *different* is correct. (See ¶1067.)

> That music sounds completely *different*.
>
> He seems (appears) *different* since his promotion.
>
> Don't believe anything *different*. (Meaning "anything that is different.")

Different from–different than. See ¶1077.

Dilemma. A *dilemma* is a situation in which one must make a choice between two or more unpleasant alternatives. Do not use *dilemma* as a synonym for *problem* or *predicament*.

> Many communities now face a common *dilemma:* raise taxes or cut services.
>
> Many communities now face a common *problem:* how to provide adequate shelter for the homeless.

¶1101

Disc–disk. *Disc* is the customary spelling in terms such as *compact disc, laser disc, optical disc,* videodisc,* and *disc jockey. Disk* is the customary spelling in terms such as *disk drive, disk space, disk directory, disk operating system, floppy disk, hard disk,* and *diskette.*

Done. Do not say "I *done* it." Say "I *did* it." (See also ¶1032b.)

Don't (do not). Do not use *don't* with *he, she,* or *it;* use *doesn't.*

> He *doesn't* talk easily.
> She needs help, *doesn't* she?
> It *doesn't* seem right to penalize them.
> **BUT:** I *don't* think so.
>> They *don't* want any help.
>> We *don't* understand.

Doubt that–doubt whether. Use *doubt that* in negative statements and in questions. Use *doubt whether* in all other cases. (See also *If–whether.*)

> We do not *doubt that* she is capable. (Negative statement.)
> Does anyone *doubt that* the check was mailed? (Question.)
> I *doubt whether* I can go.

Due to–because of–on account of. *Due to* introduces an adjective phrase and should modify nouns. It is normally used only after some form of the verb *to be* (*is, are, was, were,* etc.).

> Her success is *due to* talent and hard work. *(Due to* modifies *success.)*

Because of and *on account of* introduce adverbial phrases and should modify verbs.

> He resigned *because of* ill health. *(Because of* modifies *resigned.)*
> (**NOT:** He resigned *due to* ill health.)

Each–either–both. Use *each* in cases where *either* or *both* leads to confusion or ambiguity. (See also *Both–each.*)

> **CONFUSING:** The landscaper has planted two gingko trees on *either* side of the driveway. (A total of two trees or four trees?)
> **CONFUSING:** The landscaper has planted two gingko trees on *both* sides of the driveway. (Again, a total of two trees or four trees?)
> **CLEAR:** The landscaper has planted two gingko trees (**OR** one gingko tree) on *each* side of the driveway.

Each other–one another. Use *each other* to refer to two persons or things and *one another* for more than *two.*

> Al and Ed respected *each other's* abilities.   The four winners congratulated *one another.*

Eager–anxious. See *Anxious–eager.*

Effect–affect. See *Affect–effect.*

Either–each–both. See *Each–either–both.*

Emeritus–emerita. The terms *emeritus* (m.) and *emerita* (f.) are honorary designations used mainly with academic titles to signify that the holders of those titles are now retired from active service. These terms usually follow the title (for example,

---

*Merriam-Webster shows *optical disk,* but the form *optical disc* (which appears in other dictionaries) is more consistent with the spelling of *compact disc, laser disc,* and *videodisc.*

Paul Shea, professor emeritus; Jean Lovett, professor emerita). However, when a title is long, *emeritus* or *emerita* may precede the title for smoother reading (for example, *Denton Fox, emeritus professor of Asian studies* **OR** *Denton Fox, professor emeritus of Asian studies*). Capitalize these honorary titles when they appear before a person's name (for example, *Professor Emeritus Hugh Benz; Dean Emerita Ann Cory*).

Ensure–insure–assure. *Ensure* means "to make certain." *Insure* means "to protect against loss." *Assure* means "to give someone confidence"; the object of this verb should always refer to a person.

> I want to *ensure* (make certain) that nothing can go wrong tomorrow.
> I want to *insure* this necklace (protect it against loss) for $5000.
> I want to *assure* you (give you confidence) that nothing will go wrong.

Enthused over. Use *was* or *were enthusiastic about* instead.

> The sales staff *was enthusiastic about* next year's styles.
> (**NOT:** The sales staff *enthused over* next year's styles.)

Entitled–titled. The primary meaning of *entitled* is "having a right to."

> After a year you will be *entitled* to two weeks of vacation time.

It is now generally acceptable to say that a book or a similar item is *entitled* in a certain way.

> The book I plan to write about my attempts to survive marriage and five children will be *entitled* (**OR** *titled*) <u>Looking Out for Number Seven</u>.

Equal. See *Both alike–equal–together.*

Equally–as. Use either *equally* or *as* but not both words together.

> This printer is the latest model, but that one is *equally* good.
> **OR:** This printer is the latest model, but that one is just *as* good.
> (**BUT NOT:** This printer is the latest model, but that one is *equally as* good.)
> I would pick Pam for that job, but Joe is *equally* capable.
> **OR:** I would pick Pam for that job, but Joe is every bit *as* capable.
> (**BUT NOT:** I would pick Pam for that job, but Joe is *equally as* capable.)

Etc. This abbreviation stands for *et cetera* and means "and other things." Therefore, do not use *and* before *etc.* Use a comma before and after *etc.* (unless the expression falls at the end of a sentence or requires a stronger mark of punctuation, such as a semicolon). In formal writing, avoid the use of *etc.;* use a phrase such as *and the like* or *and so on* instead.

NOTE: Do not use *etc.* or an equivalent expression at the end of a series introduced by *such as, for example,* or *e.g.* Such terms imply that only a few selected examples will be given; therefore, it is unnecessary to add *etc.* or *and so on,* which suggests that further examples could be given.

> As part of its employee educational program, the company offers courses in report writing, business communication, grammar and style, *and so on.*
> **OR:** . . . the company offers courses *such as* report writing, business communication, and grammar and style.
> (**BUT NOT:** . . . the company offers courses *such as* report writing, business communication, grammar and style, *and so on.*)

➢ *For the use or omission of a comma before* such as, *see* ¶¶148–149.

¶1101

Ethnic references. When identifying U.S. citizens or residents as members of a certain ethnic group, use great care in choosing an appropriate term. There is often a good deal of disagreement within the group about which terms are acceptable and which are offensive, so always respect individual preferences if you know what they are. (See ¶348.)

a. Use *African Americans* or *Afro-Americans* to refer to black people of African ancestry. The terms *Negroes* and *colored people* are rarely used today except in the names of long-established organizations (for example, the United Negro College Fund and the National Association for the Advancement of Colored People). Use the term *blacks* only in a context where you might also refer to *whites*. Use a term like *African Americans* (which reflects ethnic ancestry rather than skin color) in a context where you are also referring to other ethnic groups such as Latinos.

> the votes of Latinos and *African Americans*
> (**RATHER THAN:** the votes of Latinos and *blacks*)

b. Use *Hispanics* to refer broadly to people who trace their roots to Latin America or Spain. Use *Latinos* to refer to people of Latin-American ancestry (that is, from Central or South America). The term *Chicanos* may be used to refer to people of Mexican ancestry; however, since some members of this group consider the term offensive, a safer alternative is *Mexican Americans.*

Within the groups designated *Hispanic, Latino,* or *Chicano,* some people are white and some black. Therefore, do not use these terms in the same context with *white* or *black.*

> the buying patterns of Hispanics and *African Americans*
> (**RATHER THAN:** the buying patterns of Hispanics and *blacks*)

NOTE: The terms *Latinos* and *Chicanos* refer either to groups of men or to mixed groups of men and women. When referring to groups of women, use *Latinas* or *Chicanas.*

c. The terms *Anglo-Americans* and *Anglos* are used in some parts of the United States to refer to white people who have an English-speaking background.

> Are there significant differences in the consumer preferences of Latinos, African Americans, and *Anglos?* (Note that all three groups are identified here by ethnic ancestry and not by color.)

Ideally, the term *whites* should be used only in a context where you might also refer to *blacks.* However, in the absence of a more widely accepted term than *Anglos* or *Anglo-Americans,* use *whites* even though other groups are identified by ethnic ancestry in the same context.

> Are there significant differences in the consumer preferences of Latinos, African Americans, and *whites?*

d. Use *Asian Americans* to refer to people of South and East Asian ancestry. When appropriate, use a more specific term—for example, *Japanese American* or *Korean American.* When referring to people who live in Asia, use *Asians* (rather than *Asiatics* or *Orientals,* which many now consider offensive).

e. The term *Native American* is now the preferred way to refer to American Indians. Although some members of this group still refer to themselves as *Indians,* use the term *Indians* to refer only to people who live in India.

f. The term *people of color* refers broadly to people who trace their roots to non-European countries—for example, African Americans, Native Americans, and Asian Americans.

g. Many ethnic references consist of two words, the second of which is *American.* Do not hyphenate terms like *an African American, a German American,* or *a Chinese American* when they are used as nouns, because the first element in each case modifies the second. Hyphenate such terms, however, when they are used as adjectives: *African-American entrepreneurs, a German-American social club, Chinese-American restaurants.* Also hyphenate such terms when the first element is a prefix; for example, *Afro-Americans, Anglo-Americans.*

> **NOTE:** The term *hyphenated American* refers to an earlier stylistic practice of hyphenating nouns like *Polish Americans* and *Swedish Americans.* This term has fallen into disfavor because of the implication that hyphenated Americans are not fully American.

Everyday–every day

> You'll soon master the *everyday* (ordinary) routine of the job.
>
> He has called *every day* (each day) this week.

Everyone–every one. See ¶1010, note.

Ex–former. Use *ex-* with a title to designate the person who *immediately* preceded the current titleholder in that position; use *former* with a title to designate an earlier titleholder.

> Charles Feldman is the *ex-president* of the Harrisburg Chamber of Commerce. (Held office immediately before the current president.)
>
> **BUT:** . . . is a *former* president of the Harrisburg Chamber of Commerce. (Held office sometime before the current president and that person's immediate predecessor.)

Except. When *except* is a preposition, be sure to use the objective form of a pronoun that follows. (See also ¶1055b.)

> Everyone has been notified *except* Jean and *me.* (**NOT:** except Jean and I.)

Farther–further. *Farther* refers to actual distance; *further* refers to figurative distance and means "to a greater degree" or "to a greater extent."

> The drive from the airport was *farther* (in actual distance) than we expected.
>
> Let's plan to discuss the proposal *further* (to a greater extent).

Fewer–less. *Fewer* refers to number and is used with *plural* nouns. *Less* refers to degree or amount and is used with *singular* nouns.

> *Fewer* accidents (a smaller number) were reported than we expected.
>
> *Less* effort (a smaller degree) was put forth by the organizers, and thus *fewer* people (a smaller number) attended.

The expression *less than* (rather than *fewer than*) precedes plural nouns referring to periods of time, distance, amounts of money, and quantities.

> less than ten years ago
>
> less than six miles away
>
> less than $1 million
>
> less than 20 pounds
>
> **FORMAL:** fewer than 60 people
>
> **COLLOQUIAL:** less than 60 people

Continued on page 294

Usage

11

¶1101

The expression *or less* (rather than *or fewer*) is used *after* a reference to a number of items.

in 100 words or less   in groups of six people or less

Note the difference in the meaning in the following pair of examples:

In the future our company may hire fewer skilled workers (a smaller number of workers who are skilled).

In the future our company may hire less skilled workers (workers with a lower level of skill).

➢ *See also the usage note on* more *on page 300.*

First–firstly, etc. In enumerations, use the forms *first, second, third* (**NOT** firstly, secondly, thirdly).

Fiscal–financial. The adjective *fiscal* (as in *fiscal year* or *FY*) can be used to refer to all types of financial matters—those of governments and private businesses. However, with the exception of *fiscal year*, it is better to use *fiscal* only in connection with government matters and to use *financial* in all other situations.

Flammable–inflammable. Both terms mean "easily ignitable, highly combustible." However, since some readers may misinterpret *inflammable* to mean "nonflammable," *flammable* is the clearer form.

Former–ex. See *Ex–former.*

Former–first. *Former* refers to the first of two persons or things. When more than two are mentioned, use *first.* (See also *Latter–last.*)

This item is available in wool and in Dacron, but I prefer the *former.*

This item is available in wool, in Dacron, and in Orlon, but I prefer the *first.*

From–off. Use *from* (**NOT** off) with persons.

I got the answer I needed *from* Margaret (**NOT** off Margaret).

Fulsome. Do not use *fulsome* to mean "lavish" or "profuse." As commonly used, *fulsome* has the negative sense of "excessive." For example, *fulsome praise* is praise so excessive as to be offensive.

Further–farther. See *Farther–further.*

Gender–sex. Use *gender* to refer to social or cultural characteristics of males and females; use *sex* to refer to biological characteristics.

The results of the lab tests have been broken down according to the age and *sex* of the participants in the study.

See Chart 2-5 for an analysis of Presidential voting patterns on the basis of *gender.*

Go–come. See *Come–go.*

Good–well. *Good* is an adjective. *Well* is typically used as an adverb but may be used as an adjective to refer to the state of someone's health.

Marie got *good* grades in school. (Adjective.)

I will do the job as *well* as I can. (Adverb.)

NOTE: *To feel well* means "to be in good health." *To feel good* means "to be in good spirits."

He admits he does not feel *well* today. (Adjective.)

The security guards feel *good* about their new contract. (Adjective.)

Graduated–was graduated. Both forms are acceptable. However, use *from* after either expression.

> My daughter *graduated from* (**OR** *was graduated from*) MIT last year.
> (**NOT:** My daughter *graduated* MIT last year.)

Grow. Avoid the use of *grow* as a transitive verb.

> make the economy *grow* **OR** improve economic *growth* (**RATHER THAN** *grow* the economy)

Had better. This idiomatic phrase means *ought to* or *must*. While *had* is often omitted in speech, be sure to retain it in written material.

> You *had better* (**OR** You'd better) be sure of your facts.
> (**NOT:** You *better* be sure of your facts.)

Hardly. *Hardly* is negative in meaning. To preserve the negative meaning, do not use another negative with it.

> You *could hardly* expect him to agree.
> (**NOT:** You *couldn't hardly* expect him to agree.)

Have–of. See *Of–have.*

Healthy–healthful. People are *healthy;* a climate or food is *healthful.*

> You need to move to a *healthful* (**NOT** healthy) climate.

Help. Do not use *from* after the verb *help.*

> I couldn't *help* (**NOT** help from) telling her she was wrong.

Historic–historical. *Historic* means "important" or "momentous." *Historical* means "relating to the past."

> The Fourth of July commemorates a *historic* event–the adoption of the Declaration of Independence in 1776.
> The following article provides a *historical* account of the events leading up to the adoption of the Declaration of Independence.

➤ *For a usage note on* a historic occasion *vs.* an historic occasion, *see* A–an.

Home–hone. One *homes in* (**NOT** hones in) on a target. *Hone* means "to sharpen something"—for example, an axe or one's professional skills.

Hopefully. Although the subject of much controversy, the use of *hopefully* at the beginning of a sentence is no different from the use of *obviously, certainly, fortunately, actually, apparently,* and similar words functioning as independent comments (see ¶138b). These adverbs express the writer's attitude toward what he or she is about to say; as such they modify the meaning of the sentence as a whole rather than a particular word.

> *Hopefully,* the worst is over and we will soon see a strong upturn in sales and profits.

However. Beginning a sentence with *however* is now considered perfectly acceptable. *However* (like other transitional expressions, such as *therefore* and *moreover*) helps readers relate the thought being introduced to the thoughts that went before. Many readers find it more helpful if they encounter the transitional expression at the beginning of the sentence. In that way they can tell from the start the direction in which the new sentence is proceeding. Compare these examples:

¶1101

When you are addressing a request to someone who reports to you, you expect that person to comply. A period can be properly used, *therefore,* to punctuate such requests. Since most people prefer to be asked to do something rather than be told to do it, *however,* a question mark establishes a nicer tone and often gets better results.

When you are addressing a request to someone who reports to you, you expect that person to comply. *Therefore,* a period can properly be used to punctuate such requests. *However,* since most people prefer to be asked to do something rather than be told to do it, a question mark establishes a nicer tone and often gets better results.

In any case, the location of a transitional expression in a sentence must be determined by the individual writer. (For a list of transitional expressions, see ¶138a.)

➤ *For the entry* But . . . however, *see page 288.*

If–whether. *If* is often used colloquially for *whether* in such sentences as "He doesn't know *whether* he will be able to leave tomorrow." In written material, use *whether,* particularly in such expressions as *see whether, learn whether, know whether,* and *doubt whether.* Also use *whether* when the expression *or not* follows or is implied.

Find out *whether* (**NOT** if) this format is acceptable *or not.*

Imply–infer. *Imply* means "to suggest"; you imply something by *your own* words or actions.

Verna *implied* (suggested) that we would not be invited.

Infer means "to assume, to deduce, to arrive at a conclusion"; you infer something from *another person's* words or actions.

I *inferred* (assumed) from Verna's remarks that we would not be invited.

In–into–in to

The correspondence is *in* the file. (*In* implies position within.)

He walked *into* the outer office. (*Into* implies entry or change of form.)

All sales reports are to be sent *in to* the sales manager. (*In* is an adverb in the verb phrase *are to be sent in; to* is a simple preposition.)

Mr. Boehme came *in to* see me. (*In* is part of the verb phrase *came in; to* is part of the infinitive *to see.*)

Failing to distinguish carefully between *into* and *in to* can create humorous confusion.

The fugitives turned themselves *in to* FBI agents.

(**NOT:** The fugitives turned themselves *into* FBI agents.)

In regards to. Substitute *in regard to, with regard to, regarding,* or *as regards.*

I am writing *in regard to* (**NOT** in regards to) your letter of May 1.

Incidentally. Note that this word ends in *ally.* Never spell it *incidently.*

Incredible–incredulous.

I thought their advertising claims were *incredible* (hard to believe).

I was *incredulous* (skeptical) when I read their advertising claims.

Indifferent–in different

She was *indifferent* (not caring one way or the other) to the offer.

He liked our idea, but he wanted it expressed *in different* (in other) words.

Indirect–in direct

Indirect (not direct) lighting will enhance the appearance of this room.

This order is *in direct* (the preposition *in* plus the adjective *direct*) conflict with the policy of this company.

¶1101

Individual–party–person–people. Use *individual* to refer to someone whom you wish to distinguish from a larger group of people.

> We wish to honor those *individuals* who had the courage to speak out at a time when popular opinion was defending the status quo.

Use *party* only to refer to someone involved in a legal proceeding.

> All the *parties* to the original agreement must sign the attached amendment.

Use *person* to refer to a human being in all other contexts.

> Please tell me the name of the *person* in charge of your credit department.

If reference is made to more than one person, the term *people* usually sounds more natural than the plural form *persons.* In any event, always use *people* when referring to a large group.

> If you like, I can send you a list of all the *people* in our corporation who will be attending this year's national convention.

Infer. See *Imply–infer.*

Inflammable–flammable. See *Flammable–inflammable.*

Insure. See *Ensure–insure–assure.*

Irregardless. Use *regardless.*

Is where–is when. Do not use these phrases to introduce definitions.

> A dilemma is a situation in which you have to choose between equally unsatisfactory alternatives.
>
> (**NOT:** A dilemma is *where* you have to choose between equally unsatisfactory alternatives.)

However, these phrases may be correctly used in other situations.

> The Ritz-Carlton *is where* the dinner-dance will be held this year.
>
> Two o'clock *is when* the meeting is scheduled to begin.

Its–it's. See ¶1056e.

Key–type. See *Type–key.*

Kind. *Kind* is singular; therefore, write *this kind, that kind, these kinds, those kinds* (**BUT NOT** *these kind, those kind*). The same distinctions hold for *class, type,* and *sort.*

Kind of–sort of. These phrases are sometimes followed by an *adjective* (for example, *kind of sorry, sort of baffled*). Use this kind of expression only in informal writing. In more formal situations, use *rather* or *somewhat (rather sorry, somewhat baffled).*

> I was *somewhat* (**NOT** kind of, sort of) surprised.
>
> She seemed *rather* (**NOT** kind of, sort of) tired.

NOTE: When *kind of* or *sort of* is followed by a *noun,* the expression is appropriate in all kinds of situations.

> What *sort of* business is Vern Forbes in?   What *kind of* expression is that?

➢ *See* A–of *and* Kind of a.

Kind of a. The *a* is unnecessary.

> That *kind of* (**NOT** kind of a) material is very expensive.

Last–latest. *Last* means "after all others"; *latest* means "most recent."

> Mr. Lin's *last* act before leaving was to recommend Ms. Roth's promotion.
>
> Attached is the *latest* report we have received from the Southern Region.

¶1101

Latter–last. *Latter* refers to the second of two persons or things mentioned. When more than two are mentioned, use *last*. (See also *Former–first*.)

> July and August are good vacation months, but the *latter* is more popular.
>
> June, July, and August are good vacation months, but the *last* is the most popular.

Lay–lie. *Lay* (principal parts: *lay, laid, laid, laying*) means "to put" or "to place." This verb requires an object to complete its meaning.

> Please *lay* the *boxes* on the pallets with extreme care.
>
> I *laid* the *message* right on your desk.
>
> I *had laid* two other *notes* there yesterday.
>
> He *is* always *laying* the *blame* on his assistants. (Putting the blame.)
>
> The dress *was laid* in the box. (A passive construction implying that someone *laid* the dress in the box.)

Lie (principal parts: *lie, lay, lain, lying*) means "to recline, rest, or stay" or "to take a position of rest." It refers to a person or thing as either assuming or being in a reclining position. This verb cannot take an object.

> Now he *lies* in bed most of the day.
>
> The mountains *lay* before us as we proceeded west.
>
> This letter *has lain* unanswered for two weeks.
>
> Today's mail *is lying* on the receptionist's desk.

TEST: In deciding whether to use *lie* or *lay* in a sentence, substitute the word *place, placed, or placing* (as appropriate) for the word in question. If the substitute fits, the corresponding form of *lay* is correct. If it doesn't, use the appropriate form of *lie*.

> I will *(lie or lay?)* down now. (You could not say, "I will *place* down now." Therefore, write "I will *lie* down now.")
>
> I *(laid or lay?)* the pad on his desk. ("I *placed* the pad on his desk" works. Therefore, write "I *laid* the pad on his desk.")
>
> I *(laid or lay?)* awake many nights. ("I *placed* awake" doesn't work. Write "I *lay* awake.")
>
> These files have *(laid or lain?)* untouched for some time. ("These files have *placed* untouched" does not work. Write "These files have *lain* untouched.")
>
> He has been *(laying or lying?)* down on the job. ("He has been *placing* down on the job" does not work. Write "He has been *lying* down.")

NOTE: When the verb *lie* means "to tell a falsehood," it has regularly formed principal parts *(lie, lied, lied, lying)* and is seldom confused with the verbs just described.

Learn–teach. *Learn* (principal parts: *learn, learned, learned, learning*) means "to acquire knowledge." *Teach* (principal parts: *teach, taught, taught, teaching*) means "to impart knowledge to others."

> I *learned* from a master teacher.   A first-rate instructor *taught* me how.
>
> (**NOT:** I *was learned* by a master teacher.)   I *was taught* by a first-rate instructor.

Leave–let. *Leave* (principal parts: *leave, left, left, leaving*) means "to move away, abandon, or depart." *Let* (principal parts: *let, let, let, letting*) means "to permit or allow." **TEST:** In deciding whether to use *let* or *leave*, substitute the appropriate form of *permit*. If *permit* fits, use *let*; if not, use *leave*.

> I now *leave* you to your own devices. (Abandon you.)
>
> Mr. Morales *left* on the morning train. (Departed.)
>
> *Let* me see the last page. (Permit me to see.)
>
> *Leave* me alone. **OR:** *Let* me alone. (Either is acceptable.)

Less–fewer. See *Fewer–less.*

Lie–lay. See *Lay-lie.*

Like–as, as if. *Like* is correctly used as a preposition. Although *like* is also widely used as a conjunction in colloquial speech, use *as, as if,* or a similar expression in written material.

> We need to hire another person *like* you.
> Kate, *like* her predecessor, will have to cope with the problem.
>
> *As* I told you earlier, we will not reorder for six months.
> (**NOT:** *Like* I told you earlier, we will not reorder for six months.)
>
> It looks *like* snow.
> It looks *as if* it will snow.
> (**NOT:** It looks *like* it will snow.)
>
> Mary looks *like* her mother.
> Mary looks *as* her mother did at the same age.
> **OR:** Mary looks the way her mother did at the same age.
> (**BUT NOT:** Mary looks *like* her mother did at the same age.)
>
> **COLLOQUIAL USAGE:** Ann Richards, former Governor of Texas, made this observation on the role of women in today's society: "Like we say in Texas, the roosters may crow but the hens deliver the goods."

Literally. This adverb means "actually, truly." Do not use it in the sense of "almost" to modify a reference to an exaggerated or unreal situation.

> **NOT:** When Jensen got the bill for all the "minor changes" made at the last minute, he *literally* hit the ceiling. (Omit the word *literally* or change it to *almost* unless Jensen actually exploded out of his chair and hit the ceiling headfirst.)

Look forward to. In this phrase *to* is a preposition and should be followed by a gerund (a verbal noun ending in *ing*) or some other type of noun. Do not mistake *to* in this phrase for the start of an infinitive to be followed by a verb.

> I look forward *to meeting* you next Friday. (*Meeting* is a gerund, serving as the object of the preposition *to.*)
> **OR:** I look forward *to* our *meeting* next Friday. (*Meeting* here is an ordinary noun, serving as the object of the preposition *to.*)
> **BUT NOT:** I look forward *to meet* you next Friday. (Do not use an infinitive after *look forward.*)

Majority–plurality. A *majority* means "more than half the total." A *plurality* means "more than the next highest number (but not more than half)."

> Edna Welling received a *majority* of the votes in her district. (She received more than 50 percent of the total votes cast.)
>
> Victor Soros won the election by a *plurality.* (He received 43 percent of the total votes cast; his two opponents received 31 percent and 26 percent respectively.)

May–can (might–could). *May* and *might* imply permission or possibility; *can* and *could,* ability or power.

> You *may* send them a dozen cans of paint on trial. (Permission.)
> The report *might* be true. (Possibility.)
> *Can* he present a workable plan? (Has he the ability?)
> The CEO *could* change this policy if he wanted to. (Power.)
> Please call me if you think I *can* be of any help. (Emphasizes the ability to help.)
> Please call me if you think I *may* be of any help. (Emphasizes the possibility of helping.)

Continued on page 300

Usage

11

¶1101

NOTE: When it is important to maintain sequence of tenses, use *may* to express the present and *might* to express the past. (See ¶1047.)

> I *think* (present) that I *may go* to Australia next winter.
>
> I *thought* (past) that I *might go* to Australia next winter.

Under certain circumstances *may* and *might* convey different meanings. Consider the following examples:

> The CFO's reorganization plan *may have saved* the company from bankruptcy. (Other factors may also have contributed to the outcome, but the company is still a going concern.)
>
> The CFO's reorganization plan *might have saved* the company from bankruptcy. (However, the CFO's plan was not implemented, and the company did fail.)

Maybe–may be. *Maybe* is an adverb; *may be* is a verb.

> If we don't receive a letter from them today, *maybe* (an adverb meaning "perhaps") we should give them a call.
>
> Mr. Boston *may be* (a verb) out of town next week.

Media. *Media,* referring to various channels of communication and advertising, is a plural noun. *Medium* is the singular.

NOTE: Under special circumstances *media* may be considered a singular noun. (See ¶1018c.)

More. In some sentences it may not be clear whether *more* is being used to form the comparative degree of an adjective (for example, *more experienced*) or is being used as an adjective meaning "a greater number of." In such cases reword to avoid confusion.

> **CONFUSING:** We need to hire more experienced workers. (A greater number of experienced workers? Or workers who are more experienced than those now on staff?)
>
> **CLEAR:** We need to hire a greater number of experienced workers.
>
> **CLEAR:** We need to hire workers who are more experienced.

➢ *See also a usage note on* fewer–less *on pages 293–294.*

More important–more importantly. *More important* is often used as a short form for "what is more important," especially at the beginning of a sentence. *More importantly* means "in a more important manner."

> *More important,* we need to establish a line of credit very quickly. (What is more important.)
>
> The incident was treated *more importantly* than it deserved. (In a more important manner.)

More than–over. Either *more than* or *over* may be used before numbers, but *more than* is preferable in formal writing.

> Our fall catalog brought in *more than* $400,000 in sales.
>
> How could you lose *over* $80,000 in the stock market when it was going up?

In some situations—especially involving age—*more than* is not appropriate.

> These provisions apply only to people *over* 50.

In all cases, choose the form that sounds more natural.

Most. Do not use *most* for *almost.*

> *Almost all* the money is gone.
>
> **OR:** *Most* of the money is gone.
>
> (**BUT NOT:** *Most all* of the money is gone.)

Nobody–no body

> There was *nobody* (no person) at the information desk when I arrived.
>
> *No body* (no group) of employees is more cooperative than yours. (Spell *no body* as two words when it is followed by *of.* See also ¶1010.)

None–no one. See ¶1013.

Not so . . . as. See *As . . . as–not so . . . as.*

Number. See *Amount–number.*

Of–a. See *A–of.*

Of–have. Do not use *of* instead of *have* in verb forms. The correct forms are *could have, would have, should have, might have, may have, must have, ought to have,* and so forth.

> What *could have* happened? (**NOT:** What *could of* happened?)

Off. Do not use *off of* or *off from* in place of *off.* (See also ¶1078.)

> The papers fell *off* the desk. (**NOT:** off of the desk.)

Off–from. See *From–off.*

On–onto–on to

> It's dangerous to drive *on* the shoulder. (*On* is a preposition that implies movement over.)
>
> He lost control of the car and drove *onto* the sidewalk. (*Onto* is a preposition that implies movement toward and then over.)
>
> She then went *on to* tell about her experiences in Asia. (*On* is part of the verb phrase *went on; to* is part of the infinitive *to tell.*)
>
> Let's go *on to* the next problem, which runs *on to* the next page. (*Go on* and *runs on* are verb phrases followed by the preposition *to.*)

On–upon–up on

> His statements were based *on* (**OR** *upon*) experimental data. (*On* and *upon* are interchangeable.)
>
> Please follow *up on* the case. (*Up* is part of the verb phrase *follow up; on* is a preposition.)

On account of. See *Due to–because of–on account of.*

One another–each other. See *Each other–one another.*

Only. The adverb *only* can be negative in meaning. Therefore, do not use another negative with it unless you want a positive meaning. (See ¶1072.)

> I use this letterhead *only* for formal matters. (I do not use this letterhead for anything else.)
>
> **BUT:** I do not use this letterhead *only* for formal matters. (I use it for other things too.)

Opposite. When used as a noun, *opposite* is followed by *of.*

> Her opinion is the *opposite of* mine.

In other uses, *opposite* is followed by *to* or *from* or by no preposition at all.

> Her opinion is *opposite to* (**OR** from) mine.   She lives *opposite* the school.

Over–more than. See *More than–over.*

Party. See *Individual–party–person–people.*

Per–a. *Per,* a Latin word, is often used to mean "by the," as in *28 miles per gallon (mpg)* or *55 miles per hour (mph).* Whenever possible, substitute *a* or *an;* for example, *at the rate of $8 an hour, 75 cents a liter. Per* must be retained, of course, in Latin phrases— for example, *per diem* (by the day) or *per capita* (for each person; literally, by the head).

NOTE: Do not use *per* in the sense of "according to" or "in accordance with."

> We are sending you samples *as you requested.* (**NOT:** per your request.)

¶1101

Percent–percentage. In ordinary usage, *percent* should always be accompanied by a number; for example, *20 percent, 0.5 percent, 150 percent.* In a table, a column of figures representing percentages may be headed *Percent of Total* or something comparable. In all other cases, use the term *percentage.*

> A large *percentage* of the calls we got yesterday came from customers who misread our ad. (**NOT:** A large *percent* of the calls . . .)
> What *percentage* of our subscribers are in the 30–49 age group? (See ¶1025.)

NOTE: In the percentage formula used in mathematics (base × rate = amount), the rate is called a *percent* and the amount is called a *percentage.* Thus you might be asked to calculate the *percentage* when a sales tax of 6 percent (the rate) is applied to a purchase of $50 (the base). By the same token, you might be asked to calculate the *percent* (the rate) if you know that a tax of $5 (the amount, or percentage) has been paid on an order of $200. Apart from this special context, *percent* and *percentage* should be used as noted above.

Period ended–period ending. When referring to a period of time that is already in the past, write *period ended.* When the period in question has not yet ended, write *period ending.*

> Enclosed are the sales figures for the *period ended* June 30. (It is now July.)
> Here are my sales projections for the *period ending* December 31. (It is only September.)

Person–people. See *Individual–party–person–people.*

Plurality–majority. See *Majority–plurality.*

Plus. *Plus* can be correctly used as a noun, an adjective, or a preposition. However, do not use it as a conjunction (with the sense of "and").

> Your presence at the hearing was a real *plus* for our cause. (*Plus* used correctly as a noun.)
> The decision to offer a 10 percent discount on all orders received by June 1 was a *plus* factor in the campaign. (*Plus* used correctly as an adjective.)
> Your willingness to innovate *plus* your patient perspective on profits has permitted this company to grow at an astonishing rate. (*Plus* used correctly as a preposition. Note that a *plus* phrase following the subject of a sentence does not affect the number of the verb. See ¶1007.)
> **BUT NOT:** You have always been willing to innovate, *plus* you have been patient about the profits to be derived from the innovations. (Do not use *plus* as a conjunction; use *and* instead.)

Principle–principal. The word *principle* can be used only as a noun. It can mean "a basic law or rule" *(a key principle of economics)* or "faithful adherence to a code of ethics" *(a person of principle).* The derivative adjective *principled* also refers to adherence to an ethical code *(a principled politician).*

The word *principal* can serve as a noun or an adjective. As a noun, it may refer to a business owner or a partner *(a principal in the firm),* the head of a school *(appointed principal of Edison Middle School),* or to a sum of invested money *(receiving an excellent return on my principal).* As an adjective, *principal* means "the most important" *(my principal reason for quitting, the principal parts of a verb).*

Rack–wrack. The words *rack* and *wrack* have been used interchangeably so often in certain contexts that some authorities now regard *wrack* as a spelling variant of *rack.* However, careful writers will want to respect the traditional distinction in usage.

to *rack* one's brains	a storm-*wracked* island
a nerve-*racking* encounter	a business *wracked* by heavy losses
to be *racked* with pain	let the property go to *wrack* and ruin

Raise–rise. *Raise* (principal parts: *raise, raised, raised, raising*) means "to cause to lift" or "to lift something." This verb requires an object to complete its meaning.

> Mr. Pinelli *raises* a good *question.*
> Most growers *have raised* the *price* of coffee.
> We *are raising money* for the United Fund.
> Our rent *has been raised.* (A passive construction implying that someone *has raised* the rent.)

Rise (principal parts: *rise, rose, risen, rising*) means "to ascend," "to move upward by itself," or "to get up." This verb cannot be used with an object.

> We will have to *rise* to the demands of the occasion.
> The sun *rose* at 6:25 this morning.
> The river *has risen* to flood level.
> The temperature *has been rising* all day.

TEST: Remember, you cannot "rise" anything.

Real–really. *Real* is an adjective; *really,* an adverb. Do not use *real* to modify another adjective; use *very* or *really.*

> One taste will tell you these cookies were made with *real* butter. (Adjective.)
> We were *really* expecting a lower price from you this year. (Adverb.)
> **BUT:** It was *very* **OR** *really* nice (**NOT** real nice) to see you and your family again.

Reason is because. Replace *because* with *that.*

> The *reason* for such low sales *is that* (**NOT** because) prices are too high.

Reluctant–reticent. *Reluctant* means "disinclined," "unwilling," or "hesitant." *Reticent* means "inclined to be silent." Although some dictionaries now show *reticent* as a synonym for *reluctant,* careful writers and speakers will avoid this usage.

> I am *reluctant* (**NOT** reticent) to agree to these changes in the contract.
> Phil is *reticent* when you ask what he thought of the CEO's speech.

Retroactive to. After *retroactive* use *to* (**NOT** from).

> These improvements in benefits under the company dental plan will be *retroactive to* July 1. (See also ¶1077.)

Rise–raise. See *Raise–rise.*

Said. The use of *said* in a phrase like "the *said* document" is appropriate only in legal writing. In normal usage write "the document referred to above." (In many cases the document being referred to will be clear to the reader without the additional explanation.)

Same. Do not use *same* to refer to a previously mentioned thing.

> We are now processing your order and will have *it* ready for you Monday.
> (**NOT:** We are now processing your order and will have *same* ready . . .)

Scarcely. The adverb *scarcely* is negative in meaning. To preserve the negative meaning, do not use another negative with it. (See ¶1072 for the placement of *scarcely.*)

> I *scarcely* recognized (**NOT** didn't scarcely recognize) you.

Semiannual. See *Biannual–biennial–semiannual.*

Serve–service. Things can be *serviced,* but people are *served.*

> We take great pride in the way we *serve* (**NOT** service) our clients.
> For a small additional charge we will *service* the equipment for a full year.

¶1101

Set–sit. *Set* (principal parts: *set, set, set, setting*) means "to place something somewhere." In this sense, *set* requires an object to complete its meaning. **REMEMBER:** You cannot "sit" anything.

> It's important to *set* down your *recollections* while they are still fresh.
> I must have dropped my wallet when I *set* my *suitcase* down.
> I *have set* my *alarm* for six in the morning.
> The crew *was setting* the *stage* for the evening performance.
> The date *was set* some time ago. (A passive construction implying that someone *set* the date.)

NOTE: *Set* has a few other meanings in which the verb does not require an object, but these meanings are seldom confused with *sit*.

> They *set* out on the trip in high spirits.
> The sun *set* at 5:34 p.m. Wednesday.
> Allow a full hour for the mixture to *set.*

Sit (principal parts: *sit, sat, sat, sitting*) means "to be in a position of rest" or "to be seated." This verb cannot be used with an object.

> So here we *sit,* waiting for a decision from top management.
> I *sat* next to Ebbetsen at the board meeting.

Sex–gender. See *Gender–sex.*

Shall–will. The helping verb *shall* has largely given way to the verb *will* in all but the most formal writing and speech. The following rules reflect both ordinary and formal usage.

a. To express simple future time:

(1) In *ordinary* circumstances use *will* with all three persons.

> *I* (**OR** *we*) *will* be glad to help you plan the program.
> *You will* want to study these recommendations before the meeting.
> *He* (**OR** *she, it, they*) *will* arrive tomorrow morning.

(2) In formal circumstances use *shall* with the first person *(I, we)* and *will* with the second and third persons *(you, he, she, it, they).*

> *I* (**OR** *we*) *shall* be glad to answer all inquiries promptly.
> *You will* meet the McGinnesses at the reception this evening.
> *They* (**OR** *he, she*) *will* not find the trip too tiring.

b. To indicate *determination, promise, desire, choice,* or *threat:*

(1) In *ordinary* circumstances use *will* with all three persons.

(2) In *formal* circumstances use *will* for the first person *(I, we)* and *shall* for the second and third persons *(you, he, she, it, they).*

> In spite of the risk, *I will* go where I please. (Determination.)
> *They shall* not interfere with my department. (Determination.)
> *I will* send my check by the end of the week. (Promise.)
> *We will* report you to the authorities if this is true. (Threat.)
> *You shall* regret your answer. (Threat.)
> *He shall* study or *he shall* leave college. (Threat.)

c. To indicate *willingness* (to be willing, to be agreeable to) in both *ordinary* and *formal* circumstances, use *will* with all persons.

> Yes, I *will* meet you at six o'clock.

¶1101

Should–would. *Should* and *would* follow the same rules as *shall* and *will* (see preceding entry) in expressions of future time, determination, and willingness. The distinctions concerning ordinary and formal usage also apply here.

> **ORDINARY:** I *would* like to hear from you.
> **FORMAL:** I *should* like to hear from you.
>
> **ORDINARY:** We *would* be glad to see her.
> **FORMAL:** We *should* be glad to see her.
>
> **ORDINARY:** I *would* be pleased to serve on that committee.
> **FORMAL:** I *should* be pleased to serve on that committee.

a. Always use *should* in all persons to indicate "ought to."

> I *should* study tonight.
> You *should* report his dishonesty to the manager.
> He *should* pay his debts.

b. Always use *would* in all persons to indicate customary action.

> Every day I *would* swim half a mile.
> Time and again they *would* only say, "No comment."
> She *would* practice day after day.

c. Use *should* in all three persons to express a condition in an *if* clause.

> If I *should* win the prize, I will share it with you.
> If you *should* miss the train, please call me collect.

d. Use *would* in all three persons to express willingness in an *if* clause.

> If he *would* apply himself, he could win top honors easily.
> If you *would* delay your decision, I could offer you more attractive terms.

Sit–set. See *Set–sit.*

So–so that. *So* as a conjunction means "therefore"; *so that* means "in order that."

> The work is now finished, *so* you can all go home. (See also ¶179.)
> Please finish what you are doing *so that* we can all go home.

Someday–some day

> Please set up a meeting with Al and Jerry *someday* (on an unspecified day) next week.
> **BUT:** Please set up a meeting with Al and Jerry *for some day* next week. (Two words when used as the object of a preposition such as *for.*)

Someone–some one. See ¶1010, note.

Sometime–sometimes–some time

> The order will be shipped *sometime* (at some unspecified time) next week.
> *Sometimes* (now and then) reports are misleading.
> It took me *some time* (a period of time) to complete the job.
> I saw him *some time* ago (a long time ago).

NOTE: Spell *some time* as two words when the term follows a preposition.

> We will be happy to reconsider your proposal *at some time* in the future.
> I've been thinking about retiring *for some time.*

Sort. See *Kind.*

Sort of–kind of. See *Kind of–sort of.*

Such as . . . etc. See *Etc.*

Usage

11

¶1101

Supposed to. Be sure to spell *supposed* with a *d*.

> Under the circumstances what was I *supposed to* think? (**NOT:** suppose to.)

Sure–surely. *Sure* is an adjective, *surely* an adverb.

> I am *sure* that I did not make that mistake. (Adjective.)
> You can *surely* count on our help. (Adverb.)

Do not use *sure* as an adverb; use *surely* or *very*.

> I was *very* glad to be of help. (**NOT:** sure glad.)

Sure and. In written material use *sure to* in place of the colloquial *sure and*.

> Be *sure to* give them my best regards. (**NOT:** Be *sure and* give them my best regards.)

Tack–tact. Use *tack* (**NOT** tact) in the expression *to take a different tack* (meaning "to move in a different direction"). *Tact* means "a considerate way of behaving so as to avoid offending others."

> We may have to take a different *tack* in our negotiations with Firebridge.
> Please use a great deal of *tact* when you reply to Korbman's letter.

Take–bring. See *Bring–take*.

Teach–learn. See *Learn–teach*.

Than–then. *Than* is a conjunction introducing a dependent clause of comparison. *Then* is an adverb meaning "at that time" or "next."

> The compulsory retirement age is higher now *than* it was *then*.
> They *then* asserted that they could handle the account better *than* we. (See ¶1057 for the case of pronouns following *than*.)

NOTE: Remember that *then* (like *when*) refers to time.

That. As a subordinating conjunction, *that* links the dependent clause it introduces with the main clause. *That* is often omitted (but understood).

> We realize *that* our bargaining position is not a strong one.
> **OR:** We realize our bargaining position is not a strong one.

However, under certain circumstances *that* should not be omitted:

a. When the word or phrase following *that* could be misread as the object of the verb in the main clause.

> **NOT:** I heard your speech next Wednesday had to be rescheduled.
> **BUT:** I heard *that* your speech next Wednesday had to be rescheduled.

b. When *that* introduces two or more parallel clauses.

> **NOT:** Hilary said she had narrowed the applicants for the job down to three people and *that* she would announce her choice by this Friday.
> **BUT:** Hilary said *that* she had narrowed the applicants for the job down to three people and *that* she would announce her choice by this Friday.

c. When an introductory or interrupting element comes between *that* and the subject of the dependent clause.

> **NOT:** I think whenever possible, you should consult everyone involved before making your decision.
> **BUT:** I think *that* whenever possible, you should consult everyone involved before making your decision. (See ¶130d.)

NOTE: If you are in doubt, do not omit *that*.

That–where. See *Where–that*.

That–which–who. See ¶1062.

These sort–these kind. Incorrect; the correct forms are *this sort, this kind, these sorts, these kinds.* (See also *Kind.*)

Titled–entitled. See *Entitled–titled.*

Together. See *Both alike–equal–together.*

Toward–towards. Both forms are correct but *toward* is more common in U.S. usage.

Try and. In written material use *try to* rather than the colloquial *try and.*

> Please *try to* be here on time. (**NOT:** Please try *and* be here on time.)

Type. See *Kind.*

Type–key. The verb *type* has traditionally been used to refer to actions performed on a typewriter keyboard. The verb *key* was introduced to refer to actions performed on a computer keyboard. However, *type* has supplanted *key* in many software manuals and even appears in screen displays.

Unique. Do not use *unique* in the sense of "unusual." A unique thing is one of a kind. (See ¶1071f.)

Up. Many verbs (for example, *end, rest, lift, connect, join, hurry, settle, burn, drink, eat*) contain the idea of "up"; therefore, the adverb *up* is unnecessary. In the following sentences, *up* should be omitted.

> You need to rest (up) for a bit.   Save $50 if you join (up) now.
> Let's divide (up) the workload.   I will call him (up) tomorrow.

Upon–up on. See *On–upon–up on.*

Used to. Be sure to spell *used* with a *d.*

> We *used* to use Forsgate as our main supplier. (**NOT:** We use to use . . .)

Verbal. The word *verbal* can often cause confusion because it means "expressed in words" as well as "oral, not written." Reword as necessary to make your meaning clear.

> **AMBIGUOUS:** How would you rate Sid's *verbal* skills?
> **CLEAR:** How would you rate Sid's ability to express himself in words?
> **CLEAR:** How would you rate Sid's ability to express himself orally?
> **CLEAR:** How would you rate Sid's ability to express himself in speech and writing?

Avoid expressions such as *verbal contracts* unless you are sure your audience knows that these are *oral agreements.*

Very. This adverb can be used to modify an adjective, another adverb, a present participle, or a "descriptive" past participle.

> We are *very happy* with the outcome. (Modifying an adjective.)
> This finish dries *very quickly.* (Modifying an adverb.)
> It was a *very disappointing* showing. (Modifying a present participle.)
> I was *very pleased* with the pictures. (Modifying a descriptive past participle.)

When the past participle expresses action rather than description, insert an adverb like *much* after *very.*

> They are *very much opposed* to your plan. (*Opposed* is part of the complete verb *are opposed* and expresses action rather than description.)
> (**NOT:** They are *very opposed* to your plan.)

¶1101

Vicious circle. The correct form is *vicious circle* (**NOT** vicious cycle).

Ways. Do not use *ways* for *way* in referring to distance. For example, "I live a short *way* (**NOT** *ways*) from here."

Well–good. See *Good–well.*

Whatever–what ever.

> You may write on *whatever* (any) topic you wish.
>
> *What ever* made you think that was true? (*Ever* is an adverb here.)

Where–that. Do not use *where* in place of *that.*

> I saw in yesterday's paper *that* Schuster's had decided to close its midtown store.
>
> (**NOT:** I saw in yesterday's paper *where* Schuster's had decided to close its midtown store.)

Whether–if. See *If–whether.*

Who–which–that. See ¶1062.

Who–whom. See ¶1061.

Whoever–who ever

> *Whoever* (anyone who) made such a statement should be fired.
>
> *Who ever* made such a statement? (*Ever* is an adverb here.)

Will–shall. See *Shall–will.*

Wise. Avoid the temptation to coin new words by attaching the suffix *wise* to various nouns. (Stylewise, it's considered bad form.)

> **NOT:** *Costwise,* we're already 20 percent over budget.
>
> **BUT:** We're already 20 percent over budget on costs.
>
> **NOT:** *Sizewise,* what comes after extralarge? Gross? (Even when used in a conscious attempt at humor, the approach leaves much to be desired. Once again, avoid the temptation.)
>
> **BUT:** *In terms of size,* what comes after extralarge? Gross?

NOTE: A number of words ending in *wise* are quite acceptable. For example:

clockwise	crosswise	lengthwise	otherwise
counterclockwise	edgewise	likewise	sidewise

In the examples above, *wise* is a suffix meaning "with regard to" or "in the manner of." *Wise* (in the sense of "knowledgeable about") is also used in compound adjectives like these:

penny-wise	weather-wise	worldly-wise	streetwise

Such words are also quite acceptable.

Would–should. See *Should–would.*

Would have. Note that the second word in this verb phrase is *have.* (The form *would of* is wrong.)

> I myself *would have* (**NOT** would of) taken a different tack.

In a clause beginning with *if,* do not use *would have* in place of *had.*

> If you *had* come early, you could have talked with Dr. Fernandez yourself.
>
> (**NOT:** If you *would have* come early, you could have talked with Dr. Fernandez yourself.)

Wrack–rack. See *Rack–wrack.*

PART 2

Techniques and Formats

SECTION **12**

Editing, Proofreading, and Filing

¶1201

Editing and Proofreading

In the traditional business world, *editing* and *proofreading* have been considered activities quite distinct from the act of *composing* (whether letters, reports, or some other documents). In this environment one person composes the document—either in the form of a written draft or in the form of dictated material on tape—and someone else assumes the responsibility for editing and proofreading the material and producing the final document. Although this separation of responsibilities still exists in many offices, only higher-level executives typically continue to enjoy this arrangement.

In the modern business world, the widespread use of computers has greatly affected the way in which documents are prepared and produced. Many people are now responsible both for composing and for producing the final document themselves. In this new environment editing and proofreading become fully integrated into the overall writing process.

Individuals approach the writing process in different ways. Some begin by planning what they want to say in the form of an outline (see ¶¶1722–1727). Then, on the basis of this outline, they compose a first draft of the document. Many other people find it difficult to plan and outline before they begin to write. For such people the first stage of writing is the means by which they discover what they are trying to say. They typically begin by jotting their thoughts down in random order, knowing that the result of this first effort may literally be a mess that needs to be cleaned up. People who are paralyzed by the sight of a blank screen or a blank sheet of paper find it comforting to begin the *serious* job of writing by looking at something already on the screen or on paper. (They may even find it helpful to pretend that someone else has created the mess that they are about to clean up.)

However writers arrive at a first draft—whether through careful planning and outlining or by means of a random outpouring of thoughts—they must now apply editing techniques to the writing process in order to determine (1) what material to add or leave out, (2) how to organize the material that remains, and (3) how to adjust the wording so as to achieve their objective. As they edit, they must also correct any problems they encounter in grammar, usage, and style. And as they go through one or more additional drafts, they must also apply proofreading techniques to confirm that each draft accurately presents the material in the form that was intended. When writers proceed in this way, editing and proofreading become totally integrated in the writing process almost from the very beginning.

Whether you are working on material composed by someone else or you are responsible for all phases of the writing process, the following guidelines on editing and proofreading should help you achieve a higher level of quality in the documents you produce.

1201 **The Editing and Proofreading Process**

a. *Proofreading* is the process by which you look at copy that you or someone else has written and confirm that this version faithfully reproduces the original material in the intended form. If the copy deviates in any way from the original, you have to mark it for correction. Once the corrections are made, you have to read the copy again to ensure that everything is now as it should be.

NOTE: Ordinarily, one person can handle the task of comparing the copy against the original and noting any necessary corrections. However, if the material is

¶1201

complex or involves many statistics or formulas, it is wise for two people to share the proofreading function: one (known as the *copyholder*) reads the original material aloud and also indicates the intended punctuation, capitalization, and paragraphing, as well as other significant details of style and format, while the other person (the *proofreader*) examines the copy closely to ensure that everything appears as it ought to.

b. *Editing* is the process by which you look at material that you or someone else has written and evaluate it on its own terms (either in original form or at a later stage). You question the material on the grounds of accuracy, clarity, coherence, consistency, and effectiveness. If you have drafted the material yourself, you may have to revise it several times in order to resolve all the problems you find. If you encounter problems while editing material that someone else has written, you resolve the ones you are equipped and authorized to handle. You refer the other problems (with suggestions for changes when possible) to the author of the original material, who will then decide how to resolve these problems.

c. If you encounter a set of figures as a proofreader, your responsibility—strictly speaking—is only to ensure that the figures on the copy agree with the corresponding figures in the original. However, as an editor, you may question whether the figures in the original are correct as given or even the best figures that might be supplied. By the same token, if you examine text material as a proofreader, your only responsibility is to confirm that the copy agrees with the original in wording, style, and format. However, as an editor, you might question—and change—the wording, the format, and the style in the interests of accuracy, clarity, coherence, consistency, and effectiveness.

d. Many people often function simultaneously as editors and proofreaders without realizing that they are operating at two levels—one essentially *mechanical* (checking for similarities and differences) and the other essentially *analytical* and *judgmental* (looking for problems and solving them). Ideally, editing should be done on the original material so that all problems of substance, grammar, style, and format are resolved before a copy is executed in final form. However, it would be a mistake to read the final copy merely as a mechanical proofreader, assuming that the original is perfect and that you only need to look for places where the copy deviates from the original. On the chance that problems may have gone undetected in the earlier editing, you need to read the final copy in that challenging, questioning way that distinguishes editing from simple proofreading. You may be able to edit and proofread at the same time, or you may need to make several readings, focusing each time on different things. The following paragraphs (¶¶1202–1203) will suggest the kinds of things you should be looking for when you proofread and edit. As you review these suggestions, keep in mind that a sharp eye and sound judgment are essential elements in this process.

The easy availability of spell checkers and grammar checkers has lulled many a computer user into a complacent (and false) sense of security. While these are extremely useful tools, they will not detect many types of errors. You will still have to read with a keen eye when you proofread, and you will always have to exercise sound judgment when you edit.

1202 What to Look For When Proofreading

When *proofreading* a document, be especially watchful for the following types of mistakes.

a. Repeated words (or parts of words), especially at the end of one line and the beginning of the next.

```
What are the chances of your      I have been awaiting some indi-
your coming to see us some-       indication of a willingness to
time this summer?                 compromise.

I can help you in the event       We are looking forward to the
in the event you have more        to the reception you are plan-
work than you can handle.         ning for the Lockwoods.
```

b. Substitutions and omissions, especially those that change the meaning.

Original Material	**Erroneous Copy**
The courts have clearly ruled that this kind of transaction is now legal.	The courts have clearly ruled that this kind of transaction is not legal.
In my opinion, there is no reason to suspect Fred.	In my opinion, there is reason to suspect Fred.
I hereby agree to pay you $87.50 in full settlement of your claim.	I hereby agree to pay you $8750 in full settlement of your claim.
Tom has probably reached the acme of his career.	Tom has probably reached the acne of his career.
When provoked, Gail has been known to turn violent.	When provoked, Gail has been known to turn violet.
All of Trent's actions reflect his strong, upright character.	All of Trent's actions reflect his strong, uptight character.
We want our managers to live in the communities where our plants are located.	We want our managers to lie in the communities where our plants are located.
He is quite proud of his flat stomach.	He is quite proud of his fat stomach.
The company needs a good turnaround strategy, but what that will be is still undetermined.	The company needs a good turnaround strategy, but what that will be is still undermined.
My son was ticketed yesterday for reckless driving.	My son was ticketed yesterday for wreckless driving.
I'll gladly give you the job if you'll do it in a week and if you'll reduce your price by $200.	I'll gladly give you the job if you'll reduce your price by $200.

Continued on page 314

¶1202

c. Errors in copying key data.

	Original Material	**Erroneous Copy**
NAMES:	Katharine Ann Jorgensen	Katherine Anne Jorgenson
	Johns Hopkins University	John Hopkins University
TITLES:	Ms. Margaret A. Kelley	Mrs. Margaret A. Kelly
ADDRESSES:	1640 Vauxhall Road Union, NJ 07083	140 Vauxhall Road Union, NH 07803
DATES:	October 13, 2002	October 31, 2020
PHONE NOS.:	419-555-1551	418-555-1515
AMOUNTS OF MONEY:	$83,454,000,000	$38,454,000
DECIMALS:	sales fell 5.2 percent	sales fell 52 percent
CLOCK TIME:	arrive at 4:15 p.m.	arrive at 4:51 p.m.
PERIODS OF TIME:	boil for 2 minutes	boil for 20 minutes

NOTE: Proofread addresses carefully, especially place names. An error in a single keystroke could create confusion, especially when cities with the same names are located in different states. (See also ¶1340a.)

Aberdeen, MD	Aberdeen, MS	Brunswick, MD	Brunswick, ME
Auburn, ME	Auburn, NE	Canton, MI	Canton, MO
Berlin, NH	Berlin, NJ	China, ME	China, MI

d. Transpositions in letters, numbers, and words as well as other typographical errors.

Original Material	**Erroneous Copy**
I'll buy two boats this May.	I'll buy tow boats this May.
a process of trial and error	a process of trail and error
Paul is a leader in today's world of public relations.	Paul is a leader in toady's world of public relations.
We'll need 82 binders for the seminar beginning July 12.	We'll need 28 binders for the seminar beginning July 21.
How can we thank you for all your thoughtfulness?	How can we thank you all for your thoughtfulness?
Capitalize the first letter of each word.	Capitalize the first word of each letter.

e. Errors in spacing and inconsistencies in format (for example, indenting some paragraphs but not others, leaving too little or too much space between words or after punctuation, improperly aligning lines).

Original Material	**Erroneous Copy**

Dear Mrs. Neilson:

    Thank you for your letter
of April 24. Let me try to
answer each of the questions
you raised.

    First, we do not sell the
components separately; they
only come packaged as a set.

Dear Mrs. Neilson:

    Thankyou for your letter
of April 24. Let me try to
answer each of the questions
you raised.

    First,we do not sell the com-
ponents separately; they only
come pack aged as a set.

NOTE: As a final step in proofreading, check the appearance of the document. Is the document printed clearly? Are there any smudges or marks that need to be cleaned up? Does each page as a whole look attractive? Apply standards that are appropriate for the occasion. Documents prepared for higher management and for clients or customers of your organization should meet the highest standards of appearance. On the other hand, manuscripts, drafts, and even rush memos to coworkers can be sent forward with minor corrections neatly inserted by hand. Naturally, if you are using a computer, you can make the corrections and quickly obtain a clean (and correct) page. (See ¶¶1203–1204.)

1203 What to Look For When Editing

When *editing* a document at any stage in the writing process, consider the material in light of the following factors.

➢ *For an explanation of the* proofreaders' marks *used to indicate the necessary corrections in the following examples, see ¶1205.*

a. Check for errors in *spelling* (see Section 7). Give special attention to compound words (see Section 8) and those that have plural or possessive endings (see Section 6). When the material is in its final form, confirm the correctness of all word divisions. (See Section 9.)

We had a similar break down in communications last May

when a high=level executive failed to inform us that the

corporations attornies had advised against it's proceed-

ing with merger negotions. However, that was only the

tip of the iceburg.

NOTE: Use a spell checker if you have one. However, since spell checkers are not infallible, keep an up-to-date dictionary at hand.

Continued on page 316

¶1203

b. Make sure that every necessary mark of *punctuation* is correctly inserted. (See Sections 1 and 2.)

> How do you account for the fact that, whenever we are
>
> about to launch a new product, the company cuts the mar-
>
> keting dollars we need to promote the product?

c. Inspect the material for possible errors in *capitalization, number,* and *abbreviation style.* (See Sections 3, 4, and 5.)

> Please be sure to attend the Managers' meeting scheduled
>
> for june 4th at three p. m. There will be 5 announcements
>
> of special interest.

d. Correct any errors in *grammar* and *usage.* (See Sections 10 and 11.)

> Everyone of the sales representatives have made less
>   has   fewer
>
> calls in the past six months then they did in the
>   a
>
> previous six-month period.

NOTE: Consult a grammar checker and an electronic thesaurus if your word processing software provides these features. The grammar checker will highlight many mistakes in grammar, and the thesaurus can help you find alternatives to a particular word that may not be appropriate in the document as it now stands. However, you will still have to exercise good judgment in identifying and correcting errors in grammar and usage.

e. Be on the lookout for *inconsistencies in the wording* of the document. If you are editing someone else's material, resolve any problems that you can and refer the rest to the author of the original material.

> When I met with you, Harry Mills, and Paula Fierro on
>
> May 8, we agreed that . . .   Ed: Wasn't Paula
>   at the 5/8 meeting?
>
> I think that you ought to fill Paula Fierro in on what
>
> happened at our May 8 meeting and get her thoughts about
>
> how we ought to proceed.

NOTE: Be especially alert to wording that conveys a meaning you did not intend.

> **BAD:** We take pride in offering excellent food and service every day except Sunday. (Does this mean that on Sundays the food and service are perfectly dreadful?)
>
> **BETTER:** We take pride in offering excellent food and service. We are open every day except Sunday.

BAD: To enjoy our specially priced pretheater menu, you must be seated by 6 p.m. Remember, the early bird gets the worm. (Does the menu offer anything more appetizing?)

BETTER: To enjoy our specially priced pretheater menu, you must be seated by 6 p.m. Please try to come earlier if you can.

f. Also look out for *inconsistencies in format.* Make sure that comparable elements in the document (for example, text, titles, headings, displayed extracts, and numbered or bulleted lists) have been treated the same way in terms of typeface, type size, placement, and so on.

g. Look for problems in *organization* and *writing style.* The material could be entirely correct in terms of grammar, style, and usage, and it could still contain unclear or repetitive wording, clumsy sentences, a weak organization, or a tone that is not appropriate for the occasion. Reference materials (for example, a thesaurus, a dictionary, or a style manual) can provide some real help as you try to improve the wording and structure of the document.

h. Look at the document as a whole, and consider whether it is likely to accomplish its *objective.* If the document is intended to persuade readers to accept a recommendation that they currently tend to oppose, has the writer (you or someone else) anticipated their objections and dealt with them? Or has the writer ignored the existence of such objections and thereby created the need for a follow-up document—or, what is worse, made it likely that the readers' negative leanings will harden into a flat rejection of the writer's recommendations?

NOTE: If you are editing material you yourself have written, consider all the points noted in ¶1203a–h. However, if you are editing material written by someone else, the extent of your editing will depend on your experience and your relationship with the writer. If you are working for a literate boss, determine whether your boss has any special preferences with regard to matters of style. (What may look like an error to you could be an acceptable practice that you are not familiar with.) On the other hand, a boss who does not pretend to grasp the technical points of style will no doubt welcome your editing for such things as spelling, punctuation, capitalization, grammar, usage, and inconsistencies (see ¶1203a–f).

How much your boss—or anyone else for that matter—will appreciate your comments about the organization, writing style, and effectiveness of the material (see ¶1203g–h) will depend not only on your relationship with the writer but also on the tact with which you make your comments. Do not assume that because you have a close relationship with the writer, you can speak bluntly. Indeed, the closer the relationship, the more tact you may need to exercise.

1204 Editing and Proofreading at the Computer

The computer provides some wonderful enhancements to the editing process. You can insert new copy, kill old copy, rearrange copy as many times as you like, and then print a clean version without any evidence of all the foregoing changes. Yet in the process of all this electronic "cutting and pasting," you may have failed to remove every bit of the old version you rejected; you may have changed the subject of a sentence from singular to plural without realizing the effect this change would have on the verb; you may even have inserted new copy in the wrong place and thus

¶1204

PROOFREADERS' MARK		DRAFT	FINAL COPY
ss⌷	Single-space	ss⌈ I have heard / he is leaving.	I have heard / he is leaving.
ds⌷	Double-space	ds⌈ When will you / have a decision?	When will you / have a decision?
+|ℓ#→	Insert 1 line space	+|ℓ#——→ **Percent of Change** 16.25	**Percent of Change** / 16.25
−|ℓ#→	Delete (remove) 1 line space	−|ℓ#→ Northeastern / regional sales	Northeastern / regional sales
◡	Delete space	to‿gether	together
#	Insert space	It# may be	It may not be
⌒	Move as shown	it is (not) true	it is true
∽	Transpose	belieivable	believable
		(is / it) so	it is so
◯	Spell out	②years ago	two years ago
		16 Elm (St.)	16 Elm Street
∧ or ⋏	Insert a word	How much ∧it? *is*	How much is it?
℘ or —	Delete a word or a punctuation mark	it may ~~not~~ be true.	it may be true
∧ or ⋏	Insert a letter	temperture *a*	temperature
ℱ or ℐ	Delete a letter and close up	commitzment to buy	commitment to buy
◡	Add on to a word	a real good day *lly*	a really good day
℘ or /	Change a letter	this superc*s*edes	this supersedes
℘ or —	Change a word	~~and~~ if you ~~won't~~ *but* *can't*	but if you can't

unintentionally produced pure gibberish. It is imperative, therefore, that copy that has been rewritten and edited on a computer be carefully proofread. Try to catch and correct as many errors as you can when reviewing copy on the screen. However, experienced users report that it is difficult to find every error when proofing on the screen. They stress the importance of giving the printout a very careful reading as well. In any case, whether you are dealing with material that you or someone else has written, edit it carefully in light of all the factors noted in ¶1203.

To maximize the benefits from a computer and minimize the drawbacks, follow these guidelines.

a. If you are composing at the computer, be especially careful when reviewing your work. Experienced writers recognize that when they read what they have written, they have a tendency to see what they intended to write rather than what is actually there. That's why even good writers always need good editors.

PROOFREADERS' MARK	DRAFT	FINAL COPY
Stet (don't delete)	I was ~~very~~ glad	I was very glad
Lowercase a letter (make it a small letter)	Federal Government	federal government
Capitalize	Janet L. greyston	Janet L. Greyston
Raise above the line	in her new book2	in her new book^2
Drop below the line	H2SO4	H_2SO_4
Insert a period	Mr Henry Grenada	Mr. Henry Grenada
Insert a comma	a large old house	a large, old house
Insert an apostrophe	my childrens car	my children's car
Insert quotation marks	he wants a loan	he wants a "loan"
Insert a hyphen	a first rate job	a first-rate job
	ask the coowner	ask the co-owner
Insert a one-em dash or change a hyphen to a one-em dash*	Success at last!	Success—at last!
	Here it is cash!	Here it is—cash!
Insert italics	Do it now, Bill!	Do it now, Bill!
Delete italics	Do it now! —no ital	Do it now!
Insert underline	an issue of Time	an issue of Time
Delete underline	a very long day	a very long day
Insert parentheses	left today May 3	left today (May 3)
Start a new paragraph	If that is so	If that is so
Indent 2 spaces	Net investment in tangible assets	Net investment in tangible assets
Move to the right	$38,367,000	$38,367,000
Move to the left	Anyone can win!	Anyone can win!
Align horizontally	Bob Muller TO:	TO: Bob Muller
Align vertically	Jon Peters Ellen March	Jon Peters Ellen March

*See ¶217c for special proofreaders' marks to signify the use of two-em, three-em, and one-en dashes. See ¶216 for the use of two hyphens in place of a one-em dash.

b. If someone else will be editing your material and preparing the final document, you may be tempted to deliver the material (whether on disk or in some other electronic format) in rough, first-draft form and expect the other person to resolve any problems that remain in your material. However, experience demonstrates that the most effective communication takes place when the writer takes full responsibility for the document, even though editorial assistance is provided.

NOTE: If you are delivering a rough draft along with specific instructions on how certain material should be handled, write the instructions in the margin and circle them so that they will not be confused with material to be inserted in the text.

Continued on page 320

¶1205

c. If you are typing material from hard copy, first edit it carefully. If someone else wrote the copy, then before you type it, get the writer's help in resolving any questions about content and style that you do not feel equipped or authorized to resolve yourself. By carefully editing this material prior to typing it, you greatly reduce the likelihood of undetected errors in the final document.

d. If you are transcribing from recorded input, you may have to consider the first version you print as a draft that must be shown to the dictator for alteration or approval.

e. By the same token, if you receive input in the form of a disk or via a modem, you may want to give the person who originated the document a chance to review and alter the document before you undertake the final editing and proofreading.

f. Before you print the material, run it through the spell checker and the grammar checker and make the necessary corrections. Also scan the material on the screen for any obvious mistakes (such as those noted in ¶¶1202 and 1203), and make the necessary changes. However, do not assume that no further editing or proofreading will be required. Spell checkers and grammar checkers are not infallible, and your earlier review of copy on the screen may not have detected every error. (See ¶1201d.)

NOTE: If you have transcribed from recorded dictation, you will have no original copy to proofread against. Moreover, in the act of transcribing, it is easy to misinterpret and mispunctuate words and phrases or to omit them altogether. Therefore, while you should try to identify and correct as many errors on the screen as you can, you need to recognize that the editing you have done at this stage is not likely to be sufficient.

g. After you print the material, examine it carefully for all types of errors as well as possible instances of inconsistency and incoherence. Make the necessary corrections, and then review the new material—first on the screen and then again on the final printout—to make sure that the corrections have been properly executed in the proper location. Also make sure that you have not introduced any new errors inadvertently.

1205 Proofreaders' Marks

Whether you are editing or proofreading, use the proofreaders' marks shown on pages 318 and 319 to indicate the corrections that need to be made. Minor variations in the way these marks are formed are unimportant as long as the marks clearly indicate what corrections have to be made.

Rules for Alphabetic Filing

There are three types of alphabetic filing: (1) letter by letter (in which spaces between words are disregarded); (2) word by word; and (3) unit by unit (in which every word, abbreviation, and initial is considered a separate unit). The Association of Records Managers and Administrators (ARMA) recommends the use of the unit-by-unit method.

The basic principles of the unit-by-unit method (see ¶¶1206–1208) and the more specific rules that follow (see ¶¶1209–1221) are consistent with the ARMA standards.[*] However, many acceptable alternative rules and variations are currently in use. The important thing to remember is that the goal of any set of filing standards and rules is to establish a consistent method of sorting and storing materials so that you and others you work with can retrieve these materials quickly and easily. Therefore, it makes sense to modify or change the following rules as necessary to accommodate the specific needs of your office or organization. Make sure, however, that everyone with access to your files knows what the modifications are so that a consistent set of standards can be maintained.

➤ *For guidelines on how to create a computerized file name, see ¶1371.*

IMPORTANT NOTE: Before names can be placed in alphabetic order, they must be *indexed;* that is, each name must be broken down into units, and the units must be arranged in a certain sequence. Once indexing is completed, the names can be compared unit by unit and alphabetic order can then be established.

Each of the following rules is accompanied by a chart that shows names in two ways: the first column (headed *Name*) shows the full name in a *standard* format, that is, as it would appear in an inside address of a letter; the remaining group of columns (headed *Unit 1, Unit 2,* and so on) shows the name in an *indexed* format, arranged unit by unit in a sequence appropriate for alphabetizing. Note that the "inside address" format presents the names in capital and small letters, with punctuation as necessary. The indexed format presents the names in all-capital letters because for purposes of alphabetizing, the differences between capital and small letters should be ignored. Moreover, the indexed format ignores punctuation; it even ignores a space or a hyphen between parts of a name.

If you want to use a computer (1) to print names in alphabetic order and (2) to insert names in inside addresses as well as ordinary text, you may have to create two name fields—one using the standard format, the other using the indexed format—as shown in the following charts.

Basic Principles

1206 Alphabetizing Unit by Unit

    a. Alphabetize names by comparing the first units letter by letter.

Name	Unit 1	Unit 2	Unit 3
AlphaNumerics	ALPHANUMERICS		
Butterfield	BUTTERFIELD		
Eagleton	EAGLETON		
Eaton	EATON		
Eberhardt	EBERHARDT		
Eberhart	EBERHART		
ERGOnomics	ERGONOMICS		
Office Space Designers	OFFICE	SPACE	DESIGNERS
Offices Incorporated	OFFICES	INCORPORATED	
Official Stationers	OFFICIAL	STATIONERS	

[*]*Alphabetic Filing Rules,* 2d ed., Association of Records Managers and Administrators, Inc., Prairie Village, Kansas, 1996.

Continued on page 322

b. Consider second units only when the first units are identical.

Name	Unit 1	Unit 2
Foley Associates	FOLEY	ASSOCIATES
Foley Enterprises	FOLEY	ENTERPRISES
Foley Industries	FOLEY	INDUSTRIES
Foley Mills	FOLEY	MILLS

c. Consider additional units only when the first two units are identical.

Name	Unit 1	Unit 2	Unit 3	Unit 4
Fox Hill Company	FOX	HILL	COMPANY	
Fox Hill Farm	FOX	HILL	FARM	
Fox Hill Farm Supplies	FOX	HILL	FARM	SUPPLIES
Fox Hill Incorporated	FOX	HILL	INCORPORATED	

NOTE: If two names are identical, they may be distinguished on the basis of geographical location. (See ¶1219.)

1207 Nothing Comes Before Something

a. A single letter comes before a name that begins with the same letter.

Name	Unit 1
O	O
Oasis	OASIS
Oberon	OBERON

b. A name consisting of one word comes before a name that consists of the same word plus one or more other words.

Name	Unit 1	Unit 2	Unit 3
Operations	OPERATIONS		
Operations Management Consultants	OPERATIONS	MANAGEMENT	CONSULTANTS
Operations Technologies	OPERATIONS	TECHNOLOGIES	

c. A name consisting of two or more words comes before a name that consists of the same two or more words plus another word, and so on.

Name	Unit 1	Unit 2	Unit 3	Unit 4
Oak Creek	OAK	CREEK		
Oak Creek Home Furnishings	OAK	CREEK	HOME	FURNISHINGS
Oak Creek Homes	OAK	CREEK	HOMES	

1208 **Deciding Which Name to Use**

ARMA advocates filing "under the most commonly used name or title." This helpful principle provides the basis for choosing which name you should use for a person or an organization when alternatives exist. Select the form most likely to be used and then provide cross-references for the alternatives. In that way anyone who is searching for material under an alternative name will be referred to the primary name being used for filing purposes. (See ¶¶1212c, 1214e, 1215a, note, and 1216a, note, for specific instances in which this principle can be applied.)

Personal Names

1209 **Rule 1: Names of Persons**

a. Treat each part of the name of a person as a separate unit, and consider the units in this order: last name, first name or initial, and any subsequent names or initials. Ignore any punctuation following or within an abbreviation.

Name	Unit 1	Unit 2	Unit 3	Unit 4
Jacobs	JACOBS			
L. Jacobs	JACOBS	L		
L. Mitchell Jacobs	JACOBS	L	MITCHELL	
Stephen Jacobson	JACOBSON	STEPHEN		
Stephen Brent Jacobson	JACOBSON	STEPHEN	BRENT	
Steven O'K. Jacobson	JACOBSON	STEVEN	OK	
B. Jacoby	JACOBY	B		
B. T. Jacoby	JACOBY	B	T	
Bruce Jacoby	JACOBY	BRUCE		

b. When you are dealing with a foreign personal name and cannot distinguish the last name from the first name, consider each part of the name in the order in which it is written. Naturally, whenever you can make the distinction, consider the last name first.

Name	Unit 1	Unit 2	Unit 3
Kwong Kow Ng	KWONG	KOW	NG
Ng Kwong Cheung	NG	KWONG	CHEUNG
Philip K. Ng	NG	PHILIP	K

c. In a name like *María López y Quintana,* the last name consists of three separate words. For purposes of alphabetizing, treat these separate words as a single unit (for example, *LOPEZYQUINTANA*).

NOTE: If you are using a computer, insert a hard (or nonbreaking) space between the parts of a name such as *López y Quintana.* Then the last name will be sorted as though it were typed without spaces, but it will appear *with spaces* in an alphabetized list of names.

➢ *For the treatment of hyphenated personal names, see ¶1211.*

¶1210

1210 Rule 2: Personal Names With Prefixes

a. Consider a prefix as part of the name, not as a separate unit. Ignore variations in spacing, punctuation, and capitalization in names that contain prefixes (for example, *d', D', Da, de, De, Del, De la, Des, Di, Du, El, Fitz, L', La, Las, Le, Les, Lo, Los, M', Mac, Mc, Saint, San, Santa, Santo, St., Ste., Ten, Ter, Van, Van de, Van der, Von,* and *Von Der*).

Name	Unit 1	Unit 2	Unit 3
A. Serafino Delacruz	DELACRUZ	A	SERAFINO
Anna C. deLaCruz	DELACRUZ	ANNA	C
Michael B. DeLacruz	DELACRUZ	MICHAEL	B
Victor P. De La Cruz	DELACRUZ	VICTOR	P
LaVerne F. Delano	DELANO	LAVERNE	F
Angela G. D'Elia	DELIA	ANGELA	G
Pierre Des Trempes	DESTREMPES	PIERRE	
Brian K. De Voto	DEVOTO	BRIAN	K

NOTE: If you are using a computer, insert a hard (or nonbreaking) space between the parts of a name such as *De La Cruz* (shown above) or *Mac Kay* (shown below). Then the last name will be sorted as though it were typed without spaces, but it will appear *with spaces* in an alphabetized list of names.

b. Consider the prefixes *M', Mac,* and *Mc* exactly as they are spelled, but ignore the apostrophe in *M'*. Consider a name such as *O'Keefe* as one word, and ignore the apostrophe.

Name	Unit 1	Unit 2	Unit 3
Marilyn R. Mack	MACK	MARILYN	R
Irene J. MacKay	MACKAY	IRENE	J
Roy F. Mackay	MACKAY	ROY	F
Walter G. Mac Kay	MACKAY	WALTER	G
F. Timothy Madison	MADISON	F	TIMOTHY
Agnes U. M'Cauley	MCAULEY	AGNES	U
Patrick J. McKay	MCKAY	PATRICK	J
Andrew W. O'Hare	OHARE	ANDREW	W

c. Treat the prefixes *Saint, San, Santa, Santo, St.,* and *Ste.* exactly as they are spelled.

Name	Unit 1	Unit 2	Unit 3
George V. Sahady	SAHADY	GEORGE	V
Kyle N. Saint Clair	SAINTCLAIR	KYLE	N
Jeffrey T. Sakowitz	SAKOWITZ	JEFFREY	T
Annette San Marco	SANMARCO	ANNETTE	
Felix Santacroce	SANTACROCE	FELIX	
Peter St. Clair	STCLAIR	PETER	
O. M. Ste. Marie	STEMARIE	O	M

¶1212

NOTE: If you are using a computer, insert a hard (or nonbreaking) space between the parts of a name such as *Saint Clair* or *San Marco.* Then the last name will be sorted as though it were typed without a space, but it will appear *with a space* in the alphabetized list of names.

1211 **Rule 3: Hyphenated Personal Names**

Consider the hyphenated elements of a name as a single unit. Ignore the hyphen.

Name	Unit 1	Unit 2	Unit 3
S. T. Laverty-Powell	LAVERTYPOWELL	S	T
Victor Puentes-Ruiz	PUENTESRUIZ	VICTOR	
Jean V. Vigneau	VIGNEAU	JEAN	V
Jean-Marie Vigneau	VIGNEAU	JEANMARIE	
Jean-Pierre Vigneau	VIGNEAU	JEANPIERRE	

1212 **Rule 4: Abbreviated Personal Names, Nicknames, and Pseudonyms**

a. Treat an abbreviated part of a name (such as *Wm.* for *William*) or a nickname (such as *Al* or *Kate*) exactly as it is written if that is how the person is known. Ignore any punctuation used with the abbreviation.

Name	Unit 1	Unit 2	Unit 3
Chas. E. Kassily	KASSILY	CHAS	E
Benjy Larson	LARSON	BENJY	
Bubbles Leaden	LEADEN	BUBBLES	
Moose Maguire	MAGUIRE	MOOSE	
Peggy Sue Marker	MARKER	PEGGY	SUE
Tommy Rae Marker	MARKER	TOMMY	RAE
B. J. Purcell	PURCELL	B	J
J. R. Purcell	PURCELL	J	R

b. If a person is known by a nickname alone (without a surname) or by a pseudonym, consider each word in the nickname or pseudonym as a separate unit. If the name begins with *The,* treat *The* as the last unit.

Name	Unit 1	Unit 2	Unit 3
Big Al	BIG	AL	
D. J. Clue	CLUE	D	J
The Fat Lady	FAT	LADY	THE
Handy Joe Bob	HANDY	JOE	BOB
Harry the Horse	HARRY	THE	HORSE
Heavy D	HEAVY	D	
Mad Man Marko	MAD	MAN	MARKO
Madonna	MADONNA		
Mr. Bill (see ¶1213b)	MR	BILL	
Tiny Tim	TINY	TIM	

Continued on page 326

Editing, Proofreading, and Filing

12

¶1213

c. When you have to decide whether to file material under a person's formal name or under a nickname, pseudonym, or some abbreviated form, choose the form that you and others you work with are most likely to think of when you want to find that person's name. (See also ¶1208.)

NOTE: You should also enter the person's alternative name in the appropriate alphabetic sequence and make a cross-reference to the primary name you have selected. For example, suppose that *Big Al* (the primary name you have selected) is formally named *Albert J. Degas.* In the appropriate alphabetic sequence you would provide this entry: *Degas, Albert J.: see Big Al.*

1213 **Rule 5: Personal Names With Titles and Suffixes**

a. A title (such as *Dr., Major, Mayor, Miss, Mr., Mrs.,* or *Ms.*) may be used as the *last* filing unit in order to distinguish two or more names that are otherwise identical. Treat any abbreviated titles as written, but ignore any punctuation.

Name	Unit 1	Unit 2	Unit 3	Unit 4
Dr. Leslie G. Mabry	MABRY	LESLIE	G	DR
Miss Leslie G. Mabry	MABRY	LESLIE	G	MISS
Mr. Leslie G. Mabry	MABRY	LESLIE	G	MR
Mrs. Leslie G. Mabry	MABRY	LESLIE	G	MRS
Ms. Leslie G. Mabry	MABRY	LESLIE	G	MS
Major Felix Novotny	NOVOTNY	FELIX	MAJOR	
Mayor Felix Novotny	NOVOTNY	FELIX	MAYOR	
Senator Felix Novotny	NOVOTNY	FELIX	SENATOR	
Sergeant Felix Novotny	NOVOTNY	FELIX	SERGEANT	
Bishop David Oliver	OLIVER	DAVID	BISHOP	
Brother David Oliver	OLIVER	DAVID	BROTHER	

b. When a title is used with only one part of a person's name, treat the title as the *first* unit. (See ¶1208.)

Name	Unit 1	Unit 2
Dr. Ruth	DR	RUTH
Grandma Moses	GRANDMA	MOSES
King Hussein	KING	HUSSEIN
Miss Manners	MISS	MANNERS
Mother Teresa	MOTHER	TERESA
Mr. Rogers	MR	ROGERS
Prince Andrew	PRINCE	ANDREW
Queen Elizabeth	QUEEN	ELIZABETH
Saint Elizabeth	SAINT*	ELIZABETH

*Note that *Saint* as a title is considered a separate unit, whereas *Saint* as a prefix in a personal name is considered only part of a unit. (See ¶1210c for examples of *Saint* as a prefix.)

c. Ordinarily, alphabetize a married woman's name on the basis of her own first name. However, consider the title *Mrs.* (as abbreviated) if a woman uses her husband's name and you do not know her first name.

Name	Unit 1	Unit 2	Unit 3	Unit 4
Mr. Fred Naylor	NAYLOR	FRED		
Mrs. Marie Naylor	NAYLOR	MARIE		
Mrs. June Y. Nearing	NEARING	JUNE	Y	
Mr. Peter J. Nearing	NEARING	PETER	J	
Mr. Harry L. Norton	NORTON	HARRY	L	MR
Mrs. Harry L. Norton *(whose own first name is unknown)*	NORTON	HARRY	L	MRS

d. Consider a seniority term (such as *Jr., Sr., 2d, 3d, II,* or *III*), a professional or academic degree (such as *CPA, M.D.,* or *Ph.D.*), or any other designation following a person's name in order to distinguish names that are otherwise identical. Numeric designations precede alphabetic designations. Moreover, arabic numerals precede roman numerals, and each set of numbers is sequenced in numeric order. When dealing with ordinal numbers such as *3d* or *4th,* ignore the endings.

Name	Unit 1	Unit 2	Unit 3	Unit 4
James R. Foster 2d	FOSTER	JAMES	R	2
James R. Foster 3d	FOSTER	JAMES	R	3
James R. Foster III	FOSTER	JAMES	R	III
James R. Foster IV	FOSTER	JAMES	R	IV
James R. Foster, CPA	FOSTER	JAMES	R	CPA
James R. Foster, D.D.	FOSTER	JAMES	R	DD
James R. Foster Jr.	FOSTER	JAMES	R	JR
James R. Foster, M.B.A.	FOSTER	JAMES	R	MBA
James R. Foster, M.D.	FOSTER	JAMES	R	MD
James R. Foster, Mr.	FOSTER	JAMES	R	MR
James R. Foster, Ph.D.	FOSTER	JAMES	R	PHD
James R. Foster, S.J.	FOSTER	JAMES	R	SJ
James R. Foster, Sr.	FOSTER	JAMES	R	SR

NOTE: If you are using a computer, all names in which the first significant unit consists of arabic numerals will be sequenced in numeric order and will precede all names with a comparable unit composed of letters of the alphabet (as shown in the chart above).

There is a problem, however, with roman numerals. Since roman numerals are written with letters of the alphabet, your software will consider them as letters (and not as numerals) and position them accordingly in an alphabetic sequence of names. Thus, if your software were sequencing the names shown in the preceding chart, the name ending with *D.D.* (for *Doctor of Divinity*) would be inserted before the name ending with *III.* To avoid this outcome, you will have to override the software and move the name ending with *D.D.* to the correct position (after *CPA,* as shown in the chart above).

¶1214

Organizational Names

1214 Rule 6: Names of Organizations

a. Treat each word in the name of an organization as a separate unit, and consider the units in the same order as they are written on the letterhead or some other authoritative document.

Name	Unit 1	Unit 2	Unit 3
American Data Control	AMERICAN	DATA	CONTROL
American Datacom	AMERICAN	DATACOM	
Computer Enterprises	COMPUTER	ENTERPRISES	
Computer Systems	COMPUTER	SYSTEMS	
I Deal Cards	I	DEAL	CARDS
Ideal Printers	IDEAL	PRINTERS	

b. When alphabetizing, ignore all punctuation—for example, periods, commas, hyphens, apostrophes, and diagonals. When words are joined by a hyphen or a diagonal, treat the phrase as a single unit.

Name	Unit 1	Unit 2	Unit 3
Baskins Advertising Agency	BASKINS	ADVERTISING	AGENCY
Baskins' Artworks	BASKINS	ARTWORKS	
Baskin's Basket Shop	BASKINS	BASKET	SHOP
Baskin-Shaw Films	BASKINSHAW	FILMS	
Baskin/Shaw Foods	BASKINSHAW	FOODS	
Curtis Imports	CURTIS	IMPORTS	
Curtis's China Gallery	CURTISS	CHINA	GALLERY
Curtiss Couriers	CURTISS	COURIERS	
Curtis's Marina	CURTISS	MARINA	
In-Service Trainers	INSERVICE	TRAINERS	
Oleander's Displays!	OLEANDERS	DISPLAYS	
O'Leary's Camera Shop	OLEARYS	CAMERA	SHOP
What's New?	WHATS	NEW	

c. Treat prepositions (such as *of* and *in*), conjunctions (such as *and* and *or*), and articles *(the, a,* and *an)* as separate units. When *the, a,* or *an* is the first word in a name, treat it as the last unit.

Name	Unit 1	Unit 2	Unit 3	Unit 4
In Touch With Life	IN	TOUCH	WITH	LIFE
In-Plant Catering	INPLANT	CATERING		
Over the Rainbow Gifts	OVER	THE	RAINBOW	GIFTS
The Pen and Pencil	PEN	AND	PENCIL	THE
Photos in a Flash	PHOTOS	IN	A	FLASH
A Touch of Glass	TOUCH	OF	GLASS	A

¶1215

d. When a compound expression is written as one word or hyphenated, treat it as a single unit. If the compound expression is written with spaces, treat each element as a separate unit.

Name	Unit 1	Unit 2	Unit 3
Aero Space Systems	AERO	SPACE	SYSTEMS
Aerospace Research	AEROSPACE	RESEARCH	
Aero-Space Unlimited	AEROSPACE	UNLIMITED	
Foy Brothers Associates	FOY	BROTHERS	ASSOCIATES
Foy North-South Properties	FOY	NORTHSOUTH	PROPERTIES
Foy-Brothers Financial Planners	FOYBROTHERS	FINANCIAL	PLANNERS
Pay Fone Systems	PAY	FONE	SYSTEMS
Paychex Incorporated	PAYCHEX	INCORPORATED	
Pay-O-Matic Company	PAYOMATIC	COMPANY	
South East Condos	SOUTH	EAST	CONDOS
Southeast Chemicals	SOUTHEAST	CHEMICALS	
South-East Medical Labs	SOUTHEAST	MEDICAL	LABS
Southeastern Medical Supplies	SOUTHEASTERN	MEDICAL	SUPPLIES

e. Although the words in an organizational name should normally be considered in the same order in which they are written, there are occasions when it makes good sense to allow exceptions to this rule. (See also ¶1208.) Suppose the name in question is *Hotel Plaza.* Strictly speaking, *Hotel* should be the first unit. However, if you and others are more likely to look for stored material in the P section of the files, choose *Plaza* as the first unit and *Hotel* as the second. On the other hand, suppose the name in question is *Motel 6.* Most people would look for material in the M section. Thus it would be best to treat this name exactly as written.

The formal name of a South Bend academic institution is the *University of Notre Dame.* Yet most people would not look for the name in the U section (as the formal rule suggests) but would turn instead to the Ns. However, for the *University of the South,* most people would turn to the U section rather than the S section.

CAUTION: When introducing exceptions to the basic rule for organizational names, be sure that these exceptions are supported by cross-references for the sake of those who may search the files for an alternative name. (See ¶1212c, note, for an example of a cross-reference.)

1215 Rule 7: Personal Names Within Organizational Names

a. When an organizational name includes a person's name, consider the parts of the personal name in the order in which they are written. Ignore any punctuation.

NOTE: A more traditional rule that is still widely followed requires that a person's name within an organizational name be considered in the same way as if the person's name stood alone—namely, last name first. (See ¶1209.) Regardless of

¶1215

which approach you are following, there are specific situations in which it would be wise to make exceptions, depending on the way you (and others with access to your files) are likely to look the name up.

Name	Unit 1	Unit 2	Unit 3	Unit 4
Frank Balcom Construc- tion Company	FRANK	BALCOM	CONSTRUCTION	COMPANY
Frank Balcom, Jr., Paving	FRANK	BALCOM	JR	PAVING
M. Clausen Optical Supplies	M	CLAUSEN	OPTICAL	SUPPLIES
M. G. Clausen Autos	M	G	CLAUSEN	AUTOS
Mark Clausen Interiors	MARK	CLAUSEN	INTERIORS	
Mark G. Clausen Homes	MARK	G	CLAUSEN	HOMES
Mark G. Clausen Hotel	MARK	G	CLAUSEN	HOTEL
Mark G. Clausen Roofing	MARK	G	CLAUSEN	ROOFING

For example, even if you follow the ARMA standard for personal names in organizational names (first name first), you might want to make an exception for the *John F. Kennedy Presidential Library,* since most people would look for the file under the Ks rather than the Js. Similarly, the file for the *Bernard J. Baruch College* might be more easily found if sequenced according to the surname, *Baruch,* rather than the first name, *Bernard.*

On the other hand, those who follow the last-name-first approach might be wiser to locate *Sarah Lawrence College* file in the S section rather than the L, to file materials on the *John Hancock Mutual Life Insurance Company* in the J section rather than the H, to store the *Fred Astaire Dance Studios* file under F rather than A, and to put the *Mary Kay Cosmetics* file under M rather than K.

The key here is to consider the way in which the name is most likely to be looked up (see ¶1208). Then provide cross-references between the alternative form and the primary form that has been selected. (See ¶1212c, note, for an example of a cross-reference.)

b. If a prefix is used in a personal name that is part of an organizational name, do not treat the prefix as a separate unit. (See ¶1210.)

Name	Unit 1	Unit 2	Unit 3	Unit 4
A. de La Cruz Securi- ties Company	A	DELACRUZ	SECURITIES	COMPANY
A. D'Elia Boat Sales	A	DELIA	BOAT	SALES
Peter Saint Clair Boatels	PETER	SAINTCLAIR	BOATELS	
Peter St. Clair Insurance Agency	PETER	STCLAIR	INSURANCE	AGENCY
R. San Marco Environ- mental Controls	R	SANMARCO	ENVIRONMENTAL	CONTROLS

¶1216

c. If a hyphenated personal name is part of an organizational name, treat the hyphenated elements as a single unit. (See ¶1211.)

Name	Unit 1	Unit 2	Unit 3	Unit 4
Mary Tom Packaging Consultants	MARY	TOM	PACKAGING	CONSULTANTS
Mary Tom-Katz Production Company	MARY	TOMKATZ	PRODUCTION	COMPANY

d. Consider a title in an organization's name as a separate unit in the order in which it occurs. Treat abbreviated titles as they are written and ignore punctuation.

Name	Unit 1	Unit 2	Unit 3	Unit 4
Capt. Jack Seafood	CAPT	JACK	SEAFOOD	
Captain Ahab Tours	CAPTAIN	AHAB	TOURS	
Dr. Popper Vision Services	DR	POPPER	VISION	SERVICES
Ma Blake Food Shops	MA	BLAKE	FOOD	SHOPS
Miss Celeste Sports-wear	MISS	CELESTE	SPORTSWEAR	
Mother Goose Nurseries	MOTHER	GOOSE	NURSERIES	
Mr. George Limousines	MR	GEORGE	LIMOUSINES	
Mrs. Ellis Bakeries	MRS	ELLIS	BAKERIES	
Princess Diana Gowns	PRINCESS	DIANA	GOWNS	
Saint Ann Thrift Shop	SAINT*	ANN	THRIFT	SHOP

*When Saint is used as a title rather than as a prefix in a personal name, treat it as a separate unit. (See ¶1213b.)

1216 Rule 8: Abbreviations, Acronyms, Symbols, and Letters in Organizational Names

a. Treat an abbreviation as a single unit. Consider it exactly as it is written, and ignore any punctuation.

Name	Unit 1	Unit 2	Unit 3	Unit 4
AFL-CIO	AFLCIO			
ILGWU	ILGWU			
NAACP	NAACP			
Smyly Grain Corp.	SMYLY	GRAIN	CORP	
Smyly Industries Inc.	SMYLY	INDUSTRIES	INC	
Smyth Data Systems Co.	SMYTH	DATA	SYSTEMS	CO
Smyth Datafax Ltd.	SMYTH	DATAFAX	LTD	
U. S. Data Sources*	U	S	DATA	SOURCES
U S Datalink	U	S	DATALINK	
U. S. Grant Foundation	U	S	GRANT	FOUNDATION
U.S. Data Files	US	DATA	FILES	
US Data Tracers	US	DATA	TRACERS	

*For the treatment of an abbreviation consisting of spaced letters (for example, *U. S.*), see ¶1216d.

Continued on page 332

¶1216

b. Treat acronyms and the call letters of radio and TV stations as single units.

Name	Unit 1	Unit 2	Unit 3
ASCAP	ASCAP		
CARE	CARE		
EPCOT	EPCOT		
MADD	MADD		
NASDAQ	NASDAQ		
NOW	NOW		
OPEC	OPEC		
OSHA	OSHA		
UNESCO	UNESCO		
VISTA	VISTA		
WBBM Radio Station	WBBM	RADIO	STATION

NOTE: When organizations are better known by their abbreviated names *(AFL-CIO* and *NAACP)* or acronyms *(NOW* and *UNESCO)* than by their formal names, use these short forms for filing purposes and provide cross-references as necessary. (See also ¶¶520, 522. For an example of a cross-reference, see ¶1212c, note.)

c. When the symbol & occurs in a name, consider it as if it were spelled out (that is, as *and*). If the symbol is freestanding (that is, with space on either side), treat it as a separate filing unit.

Name	Unit 1	Unit 2	Unit 3	Unit 4
A & L Fabrics	A	AND	L	FABRICS
A&B Publications	AANDB	PUBLICATIONS		
Allen & Korn	ALLEN	AND	KORN	
AT&T	ATANDT			

d. Treat single letters as separate units. If two or more letters in a sequence are written solid or are connected by a hyphen or a diagonal, treat the sequence as a single unit.

Name	Unit 1	Unit 2	Unit 3	Unit 4
A & D Terminals	A	AND	D	TERMINALS
A D S Graphics	A	D	S	GRAPHICS
AAA	AAA			
A&D Printers Inc.	AANDD	PRINTERS	INC	
ADS Reports	ADS	REPORTS		
A/V Resources	AV	RESOURCES		
A-Z Rental Corp.	AZ	RENTAL	CORP	
Triple A Realty Trust	TRIPLE	A	REALTY	TRUST
W Z Leasing Co.	W	Z	LEASING	CO
W. Y. Yee	YEE	W	Y	
(person's name)				

1217 **Rule 9: Geographic Names Within Organizational Names**

a. Treat each part of a geographic name as a separate unit. However, treat hyphenated parts of a geographic name as a single unit.

Name	Unit 1	Unit 2	Unit 3	Unit 4
Big Sur Tours	BIG	SUR	TOURS	
Lake of the Woods Camping Store*	LAKE	OF	THE	WOODS
New Jersey Shore Rentals	NEW	JERSEY	SHORE	RENTALS
Puerto Rico Sugar Traders	PUERTO	RICO	SUGAR	TRADERS
United States Telecom	UNITED	STATES	TELECOM	
West New York Bedding	WEST	NEW	YORK	BEDDING
Wilkes-Barre Mills	WILKESBARRE	MILLS		

*The words *Camping* and *Store* represent the fifth and sixth filing units in this name.

b. When a geographic name begins with a prefix followed by a space or hyphen, treat the prefix and the following word as a single unit. (See ¶1210a for a list of prefixes.)

Name	Unit 1	Unit 2	Unit 3
El Cajon Editorial Services	ELCAJON	EDITORIAL	SERVICES
La Crosse Graphics	LACROSSE	GRAPHICS	
Las Vegas Lenders	LASVEGAS	LENDERS	
Le Mans Auto Repairs	LEMANS	AUTO	REPAIRS
Los Angeles Film Distributors	LOSANGELES	FILM	DISTRIBUTORS
San Francisco Cable Systems	SANFRANCISCO	CABLE	SYSTEMS
Santa Fe Hotel Supplies	SANTAFE	HOTEL	SUPPLIES
Ste.-Julle Inn	STEJULIE	INN	
St. Louis Water Filters	STLOUIS	WATER	FILTERS

NOTE: A name like *De Kalb* or *Des Moines* is considered a single unit, whereas a name like *Fond du Lac* should be treated as three units (since the prefix *du* does not come at the beginning of the geographic name).

1218 **Rule 10: Numbers in Organizational Names**

a. Arabic numerals *(1, 3, 5)* and roman numerals *(IV, XIX)* are considered separate units. Treat ordinal numbers such as *1st, 3d,* and *5th* as if they were written *1, 3,* and *5.*

b. Units that contain arabic numerals precede units expressed as roman numerals and those consisting of letters of the alphabet (as shown in the chart at the top of page 334). Arrange the units containing arabic numerals in numeric order.

Continued on page 334

Editing, Proofreading, and Filing

12

¶**1218**

NOTE: For sequencing purposes most software programs will consider arabic numerals from the left. Given the arabic units in the chart below, a computer will place *1218* before *21* and *210*. To avoid this outcome, add zeros to the left of *21* and *210* to make them the same length as *1218: 0021, 0210, 1218.* Then the software will sequence these units in the correct order.

Name	Unit 1	Unit 2	Unit 3	Unit 4
21st Century Travel	21	CENTURY	TRAVEL	
210th St. Assn.	210	ST	ASSN	
1218 Corp.	1218	CORP		
III Brothers Outlets	III	BROTHERS	OUTLETS	
The VII Hills Lodge	VII	HILLS	LODGE	THE
The IX Muses Bookshop	IX	MUSES	BOOKSHOP	THE
AAA Leasing Company	AAA	LEASING	COMPANY	
ILGWU Local 134	ILGWU	LOCAL	134	
ILGWU Local 145	ILGWU	LOCAL	145	
Seventh Heaven Vacations	SEVENTH	HEAVEN	VACATIONS	
Sixth Street Fashions	SIXTH	STREET	FASHIONS	

c. Units that contain roman numerals follow those with arabic numerals but precede those consisting of letters of the alphabet (as shown above). Arrange units containing roman numerals in numeric order.

NOTE: For sequencing purposes, most software programs will consider roman numerals as letters of the alphabet and position them accordingly. If your software were sequencing the names shown above, the name beginning with *III* would fall between *AAA* and *ILGWU.* The name beginning with *VII* would come after *Sixth.* The name beginning with *IX* would fall between *ILGWU* and *Seventh.* To avoid having the roman numerals scattered in this way, you would have to override the program and move these names to the positions shown in the chart above.

d. Units containing numbers expressed in words are sequenced (along with other units containing words or letters) in alphabetic order.

e. When a number is written with a hyphen *(Seventy-Six),* ignore the hyphen and treat the number as a single unit *(SEVENTYSIX).*

Name	Unit 1	Unit 2	Unit 3	Unit 4
The Turtle Back Inn	TURTLE	BACK	INN	THE
Twelve Eighteen Realty Co.	TWELVE	EIGHTEEN	REALTY	CO
Twenty-Eight Benbow Street Studios	TWENTYEIGHT	BENBOW	STREET	STUDIOS
Twenty-Five Hundred Club	TWENTYFIVE	HUNDRED	CLUB	
The Warren 200 Colony	WARREN	200	COLONY	THE
The Warren House	WARREN	HOUSE	THE	
Warren Sixty-Fourth Street Salon	WARREN	SIXTYFOURTH	STREET	SALON

¶**1218**

f. When a phrase consists of a number (in figures or words) linked by a hyphen or a diagonal to a letter or word (for example, *1-A, A-1, 1-Hour, 4/Way, One-Stop*), ignore the punctuation and treat the phrase as a single unit.

g. When the phrase consists of a figure linked to another figure by means of a hyphen or a diagonal (for example, *80-20* or *50/50*), consider only the number that precedes the punctuation.

NOTE: Most software programs will consider the complete number as well as any punctuation.

h. When a phrase consists of a figure plus a letter or word (for example, *3M*) without any intervening space or punctuation, treat the phrase as a single unit.

Name	Unit 1	Unit 2	Unit 3	Unit 4
1-A Physical Trainers	1A	PHYSICAL	TRAINERS	
3 Pro Corp.	3	PRO	CORP	
3M	3M			
4X Investment Group	4X	INVESTMENT	GROUP	
5-10 Household Wares	5	HOUSEHOLD	WARES	
5 Star Video Arcade	5	STAR	VIDEO	ARCADE
5-Corners Pasta Dishes	5CORNERS	PASTA	DISHES	
7-Eleven Food Store	7ELEVEN	FOOD	STORE	
20/20 Eye Care	20	EYE	CARE	
The 30-45 Singles Club	30	SINGLES	CLUB	THE
A-1 Autos Inc.	A1	AUTOS	INC	
Adam's 10-Minute Pizza Service	ADAMS	10MINUTE	PIZZA	SERVICE
Adams' One-Hour Photos	ADAMS	ONEHOUR	PHOTOS	
Adam's One-Stop Shop	ADAMS	ONESTOP	SHOP	
The Fifty-Fifty Co-op	FIFTYFIFTY	COOP	THE	

i. When a symbol appears with a number, treat the two elements as a single unit only if there is no space between the symbol and the number. Consider the symbol as if it were spelled out; for example, & *(and)*, ¢ *(cent or cents)*, $ *(dollar or dollars)*, # *(number or pounds)*, % *(percent)* and + *(plus)*.

Name	Unit 1	Unit 2	Unit 3	Unit 4
The $50 Outerwear Shop	50DOLLAR*	OUTERWEAR	SHOP	THE
50% Off Clothing Outlet	50PERCENT	OFF	CLOTHING	OUTLET
The 50+ Retirement Community	50PLUS	RETIREMENT	COMMUNITY	THE
The #1 Pizza Parlor	NUMBER1	PIZZA	PARLOR	THE
The Original 5&10	ORIGINAL	5AND10	THE	
Plaza 5 & 10	PLAZA	5	AND	10

*When a $ sign precedes a number, consider the number and then the word *DOLLAR* (or *DOLLARS*) in that order.

Continued on page 336

12

¶1219

NOTE: Most software programs will consider these symbols on the basis of where they occur in the sequence of character sets. If you convert the symbol to a spelled-out form as shown in the chart on the bottom of page 335, it will be sequenced in the correct alphabetic order.

1219 Rule 11: Alphabetizing by Addresses

When two organizational names are otherwise identical, alphabetize them according to address.

a. First alphabetize by city.

b. If the city names are the same, consider the state. (For example, *Charleston, South Carolina,* comes before *Charleston, West Virginia.*)

Name	Unit 1	Unit 2	Unit 3	Unit 4
McDonald's Durango, Colorado	MCDONALDS	DURANGO	COLORADO	
McDonald's Springfield, Missouri	MCDONALDS	SPRINGFIELD	MISSOURI	
McDonald's Springfield, South Dakota	MCDONALDS	SPRINGFIELD	SOUTH	DAKOTA
McDonald's Torrington, Connecticut	MCDONALDS	TORRINGTON	CONNECTICUT	

c. If both the city and the state are identical, alphabetize according to the street name.

d. If the street name is a number, treat it exactly as written. Numbered street names expressed *in figures* precede street names (numbered or otherwise) expressed *in words.* Numbered street names expressed *in figures* are sequenced in numeric order. Numbered street names *in words* are sequenced (along with other street names in words) in alphabetic order.

Name	Unit 1	Unit 2	Unit 3	Unit 4
McDonald's 17th Street Tallahassee, Florida	MCDONALDS	TALLAHASSEE	17	STREET
McDonald's 41st Street Tallahassee, Florida	MCDONALDS	TALLAHASSEE	41	STREET
McDonald's Appleyard Drive Tallahassee, Florida	MCDONALDS	TALLAHASSEE	APPLEYARD	DRIVE
McDonald's Third Avenue Tallahassee, Florida	MCDONALDS	TALLAHASSEE	THIRD	AVENUE

e. If the street names are also the same, alphabetize by direction if it is part of the address (for example, *north, south, northeast, southwest*).

Name	Unit 1	Unit 2	Unit 3	Unit 4	Unit 5
McDonald's N. 16th Street Tallahassee, Florida	MCDONALDS	TALLAHASSEE	N	16	STREET
McDonald's S. 16th Street Tallahassee, Florida	MCDONALDS	TALLAHASSEE	S	16	STREET
McDonald's Swan Avenue East Tallahassee, Florida	MCDONALDS	TALLAHASSEE	SWAN	AVENUE	EAST
McDonald's Swan Avenue West Tallahassee, Florida	MCDONALDS	TALLAHASSEE	SWAN	AVENUE	WEST

f. If all the foregoing units are identical, consider the house or building numbers and sequence them in numeric order.

Name	Unit 1	Unit 2	Unit 3	Unit 4	Unit 5
McDonald's 110 Park Avenue Tallahassee, Florida	MCDONALDS	TALLAHASSEE	PARK	AVENUE	110
McDonald's 638 Park Avenue Tallahassee, Florida	MCDONALDS	TALLAHASSEE	PARK	AVENUE	638
McDonald's 23 Tier Street Tallahassee, Florida	MCDONALDS	TALLAHASSEE	TIER	STREET	23
McDonald's 870 Tier Street Tallahassee, Florida	MCDONALDS	TALLAHASSEE	TIER	STREET	870

Governmental Names

1220 Rule 12: Federal Government Names

a. For any organization that is part of the federal government, consider *United States Government* as the first three units.

b. If necessary, consider the name of the department, transposing *Department of* to the end. (For example, treat *Department of Labor* as three separate units: *LABOR DEPARTMENT OF.*)

c. Next consider the name of the office or bureau within the department. Transpose opening phrases such as *Office of* and *Bureau of* to the end. (For example, treat *Bureau of Labor Statistics* as four separate units: *LABOR STATISTICS BUREAU OF.*)

NOTE: It is permissible to omit the names of departments (as is done in the following examples) and move directly from *United States Government* to the name of the office or bureau.

Continued on page 338

Editing, Proofreading, and Filing

12

¶1221

Name	Unit 4*	Unit 5	Unit 6	Unit 7
Office of Con- sumer Affairs	CONSUMER	AFFAIRS	OFFICE	OF
Federal Bureau of Investigation	FEDERAL	BUREAU	OF	INVESTIGATION
Food and Drug Administration	FOOD	AND	DRUG	ADMINISTRATION
General Accounting Office	GENERAL	ACCOUNTING	OFFICE	
National Labor Relations Board	NATIONAL	LABOR	RELATIONS	BOARD
National Park Service	NATIONAL	PARK	SERVICE	

*The first three units are *United States Government.*

1221 **Rule 13: State and Local Government Names**

a. For any organization (except an educational institution) that is part of a state, county, city, or town government, first consider the distinctive place name (for example, *Idaho* or *Sandpoint*).

b. Then consider the name of the department, bureau, or other subdivision, trans- posing elements (if necessary) as was done with federal departments and bureaus in ¶1220.

NOTE: Do not add *state, city,* or a similar term after the distinctive place name unless it is necessary to distinguish such names as *New York State, New York County,* and *New York City.* Moreover, do not add *of, of the,* or a similar expression unless it is part of the official name.

Name	Unit 1	Unit 2	Unit 3	Unit 4	Unit 5
Illinois State Board of Education	ILLINOIS	STATE	EDUCATION	BOARD	OF
Iowa Division of Labor	IOWA	LABOR	DIVISION	OF	
Water Commission, City of Yuma	YUMA	CITY	OF	WATER	COMMISSION
Registry of Deeds, Yuma County	YUMA	COUNTY	DEEDS	REGISTRY	OF

SECTION **13**

Letters and Memos

Section 13 provides guidelines for formatting letters and memos. These guidelines are not intended as inflexible rules. They can—and should—be modified to fit specific occasions as good sense and good taste require.

Letters

Parts of Letters

1301 A business letter has four parts with a variety of features:

Parts	Standard Features	Optional Features
HEADING:	Letterhead or return address (¶¶1311–1313)	Personal or confidential notation (¶1315)
	Date line (¶1314)	Reference notations (¶1316)
OPENING:	Inside address (¶¶1317–1343)	Attention line (¶¶1344–1345)
	Salutation (¶¶1346–1351)	
BODY:	Message (¶¶1354–1357)	Subject line (¶¶1352–1353)
CLOSING:	Complimentary closing (¶¶1358–1360)	Company signature (¶1361)
	Writer's name and title (¶¶1362–1369)	File name notation (¶1371–1372)
		Enclosure notation (¶¶1373–1374)
	Reference initials (¶1370)	Delivery notation (¶1375)
		Copy notation (¶¶1376–1380)
		Postscript (¶1381)

➤ *Each of these features is illustrated in the model letters on pages 346–350.*

¶1301

IMPORTANT NOTE: Word processing programs typically provide templates that can greatly simplify your task of formatting letters as well as other documents. As you will see from the three illustrations of letter templates that follow, you simply insert the necessary copy in the appropriate places shown on the template. The program then completes the formatting and prints the final document.

If the existing templates do not fully satisfy your needs, you can modify these templates to some extent or you can create your own. In the process you can include macros in the templates so as to automate repetitive tasks, such as saving and backing up a file. You can also use autotext to store repetitive copy—for example, the name of a person or an organization to whom you frequently write, as well as phrases, sentences, paragraphs, or the closing that you frequently use in the letters you produce. Once you have typed the first few characters of such elements, the program will suggest replacement text. A simple command will then replace what you have partially typed with the complete text.

The following guidelines should prove helpful if you decide to modify the templates provided by your software or to design your own.

"Contemporary" letter template provided by Microsoft Word for Windows, using default specifications of 10-point Times New Roman, 1.25-inch side margins, and 1-inch top and bottom margins.

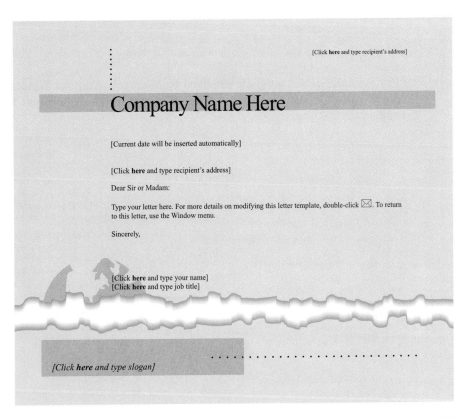

Continued on page 342

¶1301

"Elegant" letter template provided by Microsoft Word for Windows, using default specifications of 10-point Garamond, 1.25-inch side margins, and 1-inch top and bottom margins.

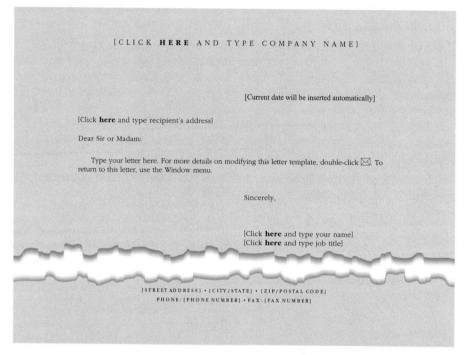

"Professional" letter template provided by Microsoft Word for Windows, using default specifications of 10-point Arial, 1.25-inch side margins, and 1-inch top and bottom margins.

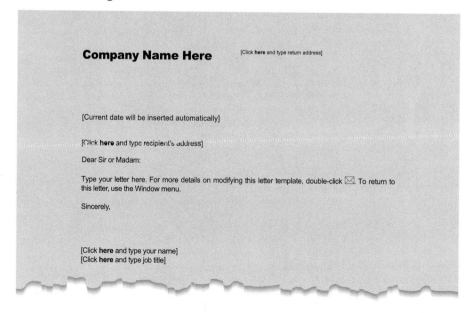

1302 A business letter is usually arranged in one of the following styles:

a. **Modified-Block Style—Standard Format.** The date line, the complimentary closing, the company signature, and the writer's identification all begin at center. All other lines begin at the left margin. This style is also referred to simply as the *modified-block style*. (See page 346 for an illustration.)

NOTE: This is still the style most commonly used.

b. **Modified-Block Style—With Indented Paragraphs.** This style is exactly the same as the standard format described in *a* above except for one additional feature: the first line of each paragraph is indented 0.5 inch. This style is also referred to as the *semiblock style*. (See page 348 for an illustration.)

c. **Block Style.** All lines typically begin at the left margin. Nothing is indented except for displayed quotations, tables, and similar material. This style is also referred to as the *full-block style*. (See page 349 for an illustration.)

d. **Simplified Style.** As in the block style, all lines begin at the left margin. However, the simplified style has these additional features: the salutation is replaced by a subject line in all-capital letters, the complimentary closing is omitted, the writer's identification is typed in all-capital letters on one line, and open punctuation (see ¶1309b) is always used. (See page 350 for an illustration.)

Stationery Sizes

1303 The three sizes of stationery most commonly used are *letter* (also called *standard*), *executive* (also called *monarch*), and *half letter* (also called *baronial*). For more information about stationery sizes, see ¶1305b.

Letter Placement

1304 Top Margin

a. **First Page.** As a general rule, leave a top margin of about 2 inches; this is the standard top margin for all business documents. To create a 2-inch top margin, space down 6 times from the default (preset) top margin of 1 inch. (See the illustration on page 346.)

If you are typing a one-page letter, you may center the letter vertically. (See the illustration on page 348.)

If you are using letterhead stationery, make sure there is at least a 0.5 inch space between the letterhead and the first element to be typed (ordinarily the date line). If the letterhead design is especially deep (as in the illustration on page 349), the use of vertical centering or a 2-inch top margin may not provide an adequate visual break between the letterhead and the date line.

b. **Continuation Pages.** Use a top margin of about 1 inch on each continuation page of a letter. These pages are always typed on unprinted stationery (even if the first page is prepared on a printed letterhead). (See also ¶¶1382–1387.)

¶1305

1305 Side Margins

a. Determine the default side margins of the word processing software you are using: 1.25 inch for Microsoft Word, 1 inch for WordPerfect. For letter and executive stationery, these default side margins are usually adequate.

b. Under certain circumstances, you may wish to use wider side margins—whether to lengthen a short letter or to make a letter more attractive or easier to read. The following table shows the extent to which you can widen side margins to produce a more open look.

Stationery	Default Side Margins	Longest Text Line	Adjusted Side Margins for Shorter Text Line	Shortest Text Line
Letter (Standard) 8 1/2" x 11"	MS Word: 1.25" WordPerfect: 1"	6" 6.5"	Up to 1.75"	5"
Executive (Monarch) MS Word: 7 1/2" x 10"	1.25"	5"	Up to 1.5"	4.5"
WordPerfect: 7 1/4" x 10 1/2"	1"	5.25"	Up to 1.5"	4.25"
Half Letter (Baronial) 5 1/2" x 8 1/2"	0.75"*	4"	Up to 1"	3.5"

*There are no default side margins for 5 1/2" x 8 1/2" stationery. The use of 0.75" side margins is recommended, however.

c. If you are using letterhead stationery with a column of printed copy running down the left side of the page, set the left margin 0.5 inch to the right of this copy. Set the right margin at a minimum of 1 inch, or simply use the default right margin.

d. Once you have established the side margins, the number of characters you can fit on a line of text will depend on the font (typeface) and the font size you select. The following chart displays some common fonts in different sizes so that you can see the variation in the number of characters that will fit in a given line.

Common Fonts and Sizes	Characters in 1 Inch	Sample Text (1.5 Inches)
12 point Times New Roman	abcdefghijklm	Now is the time for al
11 point Times New Roman	abcdefghijklmno	Now is the time for all g
10 point Times New Roman	abcdefghijklmnop	Now is the time for all gre
12 point Garamond	abcdefghijklmn	Now is the time for all
11 point Garamond	abcdefghijklmno	Now is the time for all gr
10 point Garamond	abcdefghijklmnop	Now is the time for all grea
12 point Arial	abcdefghijklm	Now is the time for
11 point Arial	abcdefghijklmn	Now is the time for all
10 point Arial	abcdefghijklmno	Now is the time for all gr

NOTE: If the default font of your word processing software is too small or too difficult to read, select a font in a size that best meets your needs.

Letters and Memos

13

1306 Bottom Margin

a. Leave a bottom margin of at least 1 inch. If you are typing a one-page letter and center it vertically, the bottom margin will be automatically established.

b. If the letter requires more than one page, you can increase the bottom margin on the first page up to 2 inches.

c. If you are using letterhead stationery with a band of printed copy running across the bottom of the page, leave a minimum margin of 0.5 inch between the last line of text and the band of printed copy.

➢ *For guidelines on carrying a letter over from one page to the next, see ¶¶1382–1387.*

1307 Lengthening a Short Letter

To *spread* a short letter (under 8 lines of text) over one page, use any combination of the following techniques:

a. Increase the side margins. (See the table in ¶1305b.)

b. Change the paper size from letter to executive or half letter.

c. Increase the font size or select a font that yields fewer characters to an inch.

d. Insert extra space above the inside address, the signature line, and the reference initials. (Do not use more than twice the recommended space in each case.)

1308 Shortening a Long Letter

To *condense* a long letter (over 23 lines of text), use any combination of the following techniques:

a. If you have been using wide side margins, reduce them to 1 inch on letter and executive stationery and to 0.75 inch on half letter stationery.

b. If you have been using executive or half letter stationery, change to letter stationery.

c. If a small amount of text carries over to a second page, you may be able to reduce the text to fit on a single page by using the make-it-fit or shrink-to-fit option in your word processing software. Another option is to use a slightly smaller font or font size that fits more characters on a line. Be sure, however, that after you make such adjustments, the type is still quite readable.

d. Reduce the space between the date and the inside address to 2 blank lines (instead of the customary 3).

e. Reduce the space for the signature from 3 blank lines to 2.

Text continues on page 351

Modified-Block Style—Standard Format

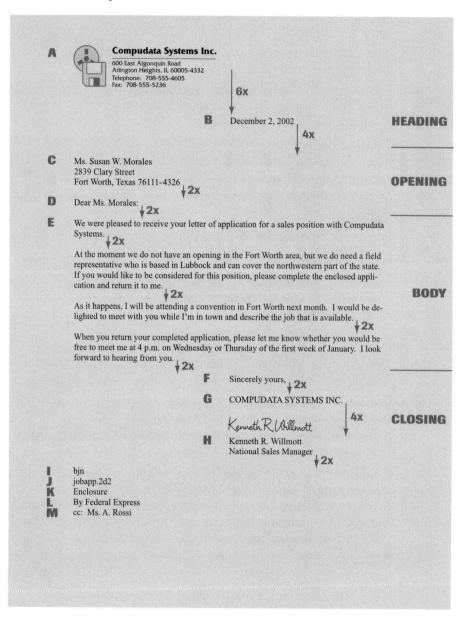

A

Compudata Systems Inc.
600 East Algonquin Road
Arlington Heights, IL 60005-4332
Telephone: 708-555-4605
Fax: 708-555-5236

↓6x

B   December 2, 2002

↓4x

HEADING

C   Ms. Susan W. Morales
2839 Clary Street
Fort Worth, Texas 76111-4326

↓2x

OPENING

D   Dear Ms. Morales:

↓2x

E   We were pleased to receive your letter of application for a sales position with Compudata
Systems.

↓2x

At the moment we do not have an opening in the Fort Worth area, but we do need a field
representative who is based in Lubbock and can cover the northwestern part of the state.
If you would like to be considered for this position, please complete the enclosed application and return it to me.

↓2x

BODY

As it happens, I will be attending a convention in Fort Worth next month. I would be delighted to meet with you while I'm in town and describe the job that is available.

↓2x

When you return your completed application, please let me know whether you would be
free to meet me at 4 p.m. on Wednesday or Thursday of the first week of January. I look
forward to hearing from you.

↓2x

F   Sincerely yours,

↓2x

G   COMPUDATA SYSTEMS INC.

↓4x

CLOSING

Kenneth R Willmott

H   Kenneth R. Willmott
National Sales Manager

↓2x

I   bjn
J   jobapp.2d2
K   Enclosure
L   By Federal Express
M   cc: Ms. A. Rossi

A **Letterhead.** The company's name and address, along with other information (such as a telephone number and a fax number). (See ¶¶1311–1312.)

B **Date Line.** The date (month, day, and year) on which the letter is typed. As a general rule, space down 6 times from the default margin of 1 inch before typing the date line (as in the illustration on page 346). One-page letters may be centered vertically (as in the illustration on page 348); in that case type the date on the first available line. On stationery with a deep letterhead (as in the illustration on page 349), type the date line about 0.5 inch below the letterhead. (For additional details, see ¶1314d–f.)

C **Inside Address.** The name and address of the person to whom you are writing. (See ¶¶1317–1343.)

D **Salutation.** An opening greeting like *Dear Ms. Morales*. (See ¶¶1346–1351.)

E **Message.** The text of the letter. All paragraphs are typed single-spaced with no indentions. Leave 1 blank line between paragraphs. (See ¶¶1354–1357.)

F **Complimentary Closing.** A parting phrase such as *Sincerely* or *Sincerely yours*. (See ¶¶1358–1360.)

G **Company Signature.** An indication that the writer is acting on behalf of the company. (See ¶1361.)

H **Writer's Identification.** The writer's name and title. (See ¶¶1362–1369.)

I **Reference Initials.** The initials of the typist and sometimes those of the writer as well. (See ¶1370.)

J **File Name Notation.** A coded notation that indicates where the document is stored in computer memory. (See ¶¶1371–1372.)

K **Enclosure Notation.** A reminder that the letter is accompanied by an enclosure. (See ¶¶1373–1374.)

L **Delivery Notation.** An indication that the letter has been sent a special way. (See ¶1375.)

M **Copy Notation.** The names of those who will receive copies of this letter. (See ¶¶1376–1380.)

Continued on page 348

Modified-Block Style—With Indented Paragraphs

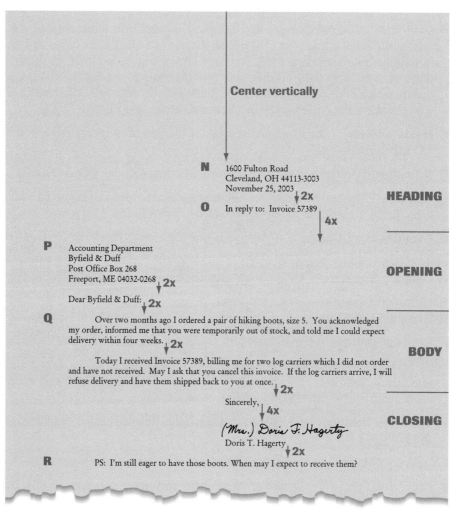

Center vertically

N 1600 Fulton Road
Cleveland, OH 44113-3003
November 25, 2003 ↓ **2x**

HEADING

O In reply to: Invoice 57389
↓ **4x**

P Accounting Department
Byfield & Duff
Post Office Box 268
Freeport, ME 04032-0268 ↓ **2x**

OPENING

Dear Byfield & Duff: ↓ **2x**

Q   Over two months ago I ordered a pair of hiking boots, size 5. You acknowledged
my order, informed me that you were temporarily out of stock, and told me I could expect
delivery within four weeks. ↓ **2x**

BODY

     Today I received Invoice 57389, billing me for two log carriers which I did not order
and have not received. May I ask that you cancel this invoice. If the log carriers arrive, I will
refuse delivery and have them shipped back to you at once. ↓ **2x**

Sincerely, ↓ **4x**

CLOSING

(Mrs.) Doris T. Hagerty

Doris T. Hagerty ↓ **2x**

R   PS: I'm still eager to have those boots. When may I expect to receive them?

N Return Address. The arrangement that is used in a personal-business letter when an individual writes on blank stationery from home. (For an alternative placement of the return address and other details, see ¶1313.) A person using word processing software can transform the return address into a professional-looking letterhead. (See ¶1312.)

O Reference Notation. A filing code used by the writer or the addressee. (See ¶1316.)

P Attention Line. A means of directing the letter to a particular person or a specific department, even though the letter is addressed to an organization as a whole. Traditionally positioned on a separate line below the inside address; now positioned as the first line of the inside address (without the word *Attention*) to reflect the recommended format for the mailing address. (See ¶¶1344–1345.)

Q Paragraph Indentions. Customarily 0.5 inch. (See ¶1356a.)

R Postscript. A device for presenting a final idea or an afterthought. (See ¶1381.)

Block Style

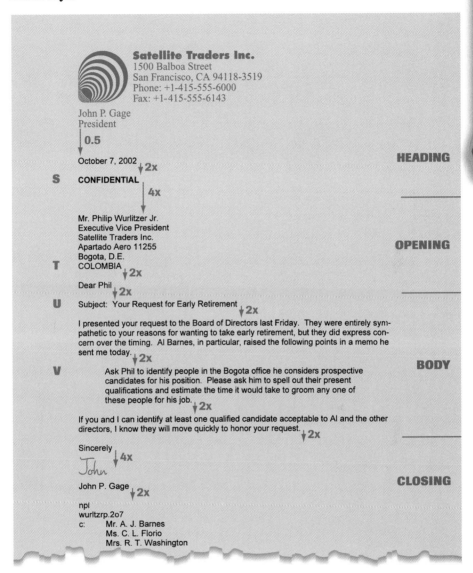

Satellite Traders Inc.
1500 Balboa Street
San Francisco, CA 94118-3519
Phone: +1-415-555-6000
Fax: +1-415-555-6143

John P. Gage
President

↓ **0.5**

October 7, 2002 ↓ **2x**   **HEADING**

S   **CONFIDENTIAL**

↓ **4x**

Mr. Philip Wurlitzer Jr.
Executive Vice President
Satellite Traders Inc.
Apartado Aero 11255
Bogota, D.E.   **OPENING**
T   COLOMBIA ↓ **2x**

Dear Phil ↓ **2x**

U   Subject: Your Request for Early Retirement ↓ **2x**

I presented your request to the Board of Directors last Friday. They were entirely sympathetic to your reasons for wanting to take early retirement, but they did express concern over the timing. Al Barnes, in particular, raised the following points in a memo he sent me today. ↓ **2x**

V   Ask Phil to identify people in the Bogota office he considers prospective   **BODY**
candidates for his position. Please ask him to spell out their present
qualifications and estimate the time it would take to groom any one of
these people for his job. ↓ **2x**

If you and I can identify at least one qualified candidate acceptable to Al and the other directors, I know they will move quickly to honor your request. ↓ **2x**

Sincerely ↓ **4x**

John

John P. Gage ↓ **2x**   **CLOSING**

npl
wurltzrp.2o7
c: Mr. A. J. Barnes
     Ms. C. L. Florio
     Mrs. R. T. Washington

➤ *For the use of +1 with telephone numbers (as in the letterhead above), see ¶454f.*

S **Confidential Notation.** A note indicating that the letter should be read only by the person addressed. (See ¶1315.)

T **International Address.** The name of the country typed in all-capital letters on a line by itself. (See ¶1343.)

U **Subject Line.** A means of stating what the letter is about. (See ¶¶1352–1353.)

V **Displayed Extract.** Copy set off from the rest of the letter for emphasis; indented 0.5 inch from the left and right margins. (See ¶1357a.)

Continued on page 350

Letters and Memos

13

Simplified Style

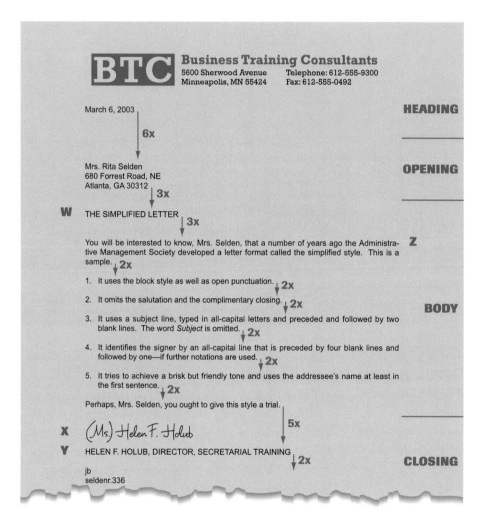

W Subject Line. Replaces the salutation; typed in all-capital letters on the third line below the inside address. (See also ¶1352.)

X Complimentary Closing. Omitted. (See also ¶¶1358–1360.)

Y Writer's Identification. Typed on one line in all-capital letters. (See also ¶1363.)

Z Justified Right Margin. Makes each line in the body of the letter end at the same point. This is an optional feature and may be used with any letter style. (See ¶1356b.)

NOTE: The numbered list in this illustration has been typed with a blank line between items to achieve a more open look. If you use the numbered list feature of your word processing program and accept all the defaults, the list will be typed single-spaced. (See ¶1357d for illustrations showing lists typed with and without space between items.)

Punctuation Patterns

1309 The message in a business letter is always punctuated with normal punctuation. The other parts may be punctuated according to one of the following patterns:

a. Standard (Mixed) Pattern. Use a colon after the salutation and a comma after the complimentary closing. (This is the style most commonly used.)

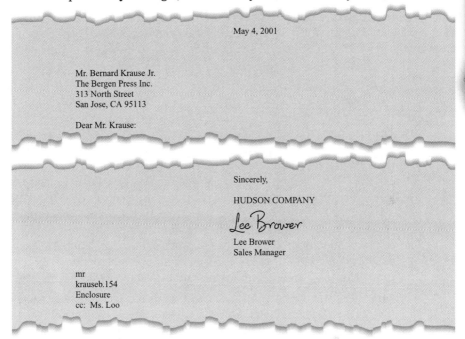

May 4, 2001

Mr. Bernard Krause Jr.
The Bergen Press Inc.
313 North Street
San Jose, CA 95113

Dear Mr. Krause:

Sincerely,

HUDSON COMPANY

Lee Brower

Lee Brower
Sales Manager

mr
krauseb.154
Enclosure
cc: Ms. Loo

b. Open Pattern. Use no punctuation at the end of any line outside the body of the letter unless that line ends with an abbreviation (for example, *Jr.*).

NOTE: For an additional illustration of the use of open punctuation, see page 349.

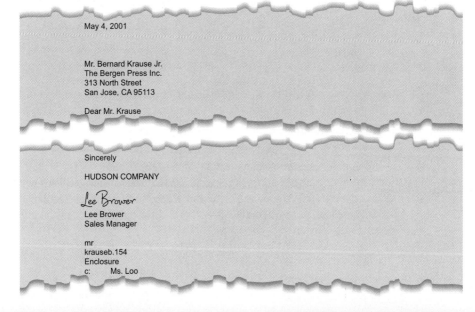

May 4, 2001

Mr. Bernard Krause Jr.
The Bergen Press Inc.
313 North Street
San Jose, CA 95113

Dear Mr. Krause

Sincerely

HUDSON COMPANY

Lee Brower

Lee Brower
Sales Manager

mr
krauseb.154
Enclosure
c: Ms. Loo

¶1310

Spacing

1310 Type all letters single-spaced. Leave 1 blank line between paragraphs. (See the illustrations on pages 346–350.)

The following rules (¶¶1311–1316) deal with the *heading* of a letter. The heading may include a letterhead or a return address (¶¶1311–1313), a date line (¶1314), a personal or confidential notation (¶1315), and a reference notation (¶1316). The model letters shown on pages 346–350 illustrate the position of these elements in the heading.

Letterhead or Return Address

1311 **Using a Printed Letterhead**

a. The first page of a standard business letter is customarily written on stationery with a *printed letterhead* containing at least these elements: the organization's name, the street address or post office box number (or both), and the city, state, and ZIP Code. The printed letterheads for most organizations also provide a telephone number and a logo or some other graphic element. They may also provide a fax number, an e-mail address, a Web site URL (¶1532), and a cable address. However, large organizations with a number of operating units widely dispersed at the same location often choose to provide a generic letterhead that contains only those elements that are common to all operating units. They rely on individual business cards to provide the variable details for each employee.

NOTE: Top executives may have special letterheads showing their name and title. (See page 349 for an illustration of a top executive's stationery.)

Cole, Steele & Backus

1800 Avenue of the Stars	**Los Angeles, CA 90067-4201**
Telephone: 310.555.4345	E-Mail: csb@aol.com
Fax: 310.555.4265	Cable: COSTEBA

b. Avoid using abbreviations in a letterhead except those that are part of the organization's name or that represent a state name.

NOTE: It is not essential to abbreviate a state name in a letterhead. In fact, if you want to achieve a more formal effect, spell out the state name. (See ¶1341a.)

c. Even if your organization uses a post office box number as its primary mailing address, show a street address as well. In that way others will know where to direct ordinary mail (the post office) and where to direct express mail (the organization's office). If the two addresses have different ZIP Codes, be sure to provide this information.

➤ *For guidelines on how to treat telephone numbers in letterheads and on business cards, see ¶454.*

1312 Creating a Letterhead

In place of printed stationery, you can use word processing templates and various fonts and font sizes to create a professional-looking letterhead on plain paper. The following illustrations show two computer-generated letterheads—one designed for a company and one designed for an individual working from home.

NOTE: Individuals who want to make themselves available to clients and customers at all hours may provide more than an address and a phone number. They may insert such elements as an e-mail address, a Web site URL, a home phone number, a mobile phone number, a pager number, and a voice mail number. All of these elements may appear as part of the letterhead at the top of the page, or some may be located at the foot of the page (to avoid a cluttered design at the top).

1313 Using a Return Address

If you are using plain paper for a *personal-business letter* (one you write as an individual from your home), you can supply the necessary address information in the form of a *return address*. There are two formats you can choose from.

a. Traditionally, the return address appears at the top of the page. Provide the following information on three or more single-spaced lines: (1) the street address; (2) the city, state, and ZIP Code; (3) the phone number (if you want the addressee to have it); and (4) the date (see ¶1314).

```
Apartment 2B              OR    212 West 22d Street, Apt. 2B
212 West 22d Street             New York, NY 10011-2706
New York, NY 10011-2706         212-555-9097
212-555-9097                    January 24, 2002
January 24, 2002
```

Continued on page 354

¶1314

NOTE: For the *modified-block* letter style, start each line of the return address at the center of the page. (See page 348.) For the *block* and *simplified* styles, start each line at the left margin. (See pages 349–350.)

b. An alternative style locates the return address in the *closing* section of the letter, starting on the line directly below the writer's typed name.

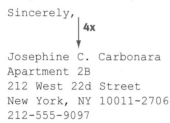

```
Sincerely,
                 4x

Josephine  C.  Carbonara
Apartment  2B
212  West  22d  Street
New  York,  NY  10011-2706
212-555-9097
```

NOTE: When the return address appears in the closing section, the first element to appear at the top of the letter is the date line. (See ¶1314.)

c. Each line of the return address should begin at the same point as the complimentary closing and the writer's typed name—at the center of the page for the *modified-block* style and at the left margin for the *block* and *simplified* styles.

d. Regardless of the format you use for a return address, establish a top margin in the same way. As a general guideline, space down 6 times from the default top margin of 1 inch to create a top margin of approximately 2 inches. One-page letters may be centered vertically; in this case simply type the start of the inside address (as in ¶1313a) or the date line (as indicated in ¶1313b, note, above) on the first available line.

Date Line

1314 **a.** The date line consists of the *name of the month* (written in full—never abbreviated or represented by figures), the *day* (written in figures and followed by a comma), and the *complete year*.

```
December 28, 2001 (NOT Dec. 28, 2001  OR  December 28th, 2001)
```

NOTE: Do not use the style *12/28/01* or *'01* in the date line of a business letter.

b. Some writers write the date in this order: day, month, year. This is the style typically used in military correspondence and letters from abroad.

```
28  December  2001
```

c. You can use the date insert feature of your word processing software to automatically insert the current date. You can also indicate (by selecting the appropriate option) whether or not you want the date to be automatically updated each time you open the document. Automatic updating is useful if the document is a form letter but should not be used if the document represents a permanent record.

d. For the *modified-block* letter style, start the date at the center. For the *block* and *simplified* letter styles, start the date at the left margin.

e. As a general rule, type the date about 2 inches from the top of the page. (See the illustration on page 346.) If you are typing a one-page letter and have decided to center it vertically, type the date on the first available line. (See the illustration on page 348.) If you are using stationery with a deep letterhead, type the date about 0.5 inch below the letterhead. (See the illustration on page 349.)

f. If you are using a return address at the top of a letter, type the date directly under the return address (as illustrated in ¶1313a). If you place the return address at the bottom of the page (as shown in ¶1313b), position the date as directed in ¶1314d and e.

Personal or Confidential Notation

1315 If a letter is of a personal or confidential nature, provide the appropriate notation on the second line below the date, at the *left* margin. Type the notation in bold all-cap letters. (See the illustration on page 349.)

     PERSONAL   **CONFIDENTIAL**

Reference Notation

1316 a. A reference notation—beginning with the guide words *When replying, refer to:* (or with something similar)—may be inserted on the second line below the date (or on the second line below any notation that follows the date). Start typing at the same point as the date.

```
When replying, refer to: watsonnd.363
```

NOTE: You may insert a file name notation here instead of at the bottom of the letter. (See ¶1372.)

b. When you are replying to a letter that contains a reference number or when you want to emphasize the fact that your letter concerns an insurance policy, an order, or a similar document, type a reference notation on the second line below the date (or on the second line below any notation that follows the date). Start typing at the same point as the date. (See the illustration on page 348.)

```
In reply to: G241 782 935    Refer to: Policy 234844
```

c. When there are two reference notations to be given, type your own reference notation first (as indicated in ¶1316a). Then type the addressee's reference notation on the second line below.

```
When replying, refer to: dingesc.524 ↓2x
Your reference: blockagc.747
```

d. Some writers prefer to give the addressee's reference notation in a subject line. (See ¶1353e.)

e. If you want the addressee of a given letter to send a response by fax or e-mail, you may make this request in the body of the letter or, for greater emphasis, in the form of a reference notation.

```
When replying, send fax to: 707-555-9985
When replying, send e-mail message to: mgallagher@aol.com
```

¶1317

The following rules (¶¶1317–1351) deal with the opening of a letter. The opening typically includes two elements: the inside address (¶¶1317–1343) and the salutation (¶¶1346–1351). It may also include an attention line (¶¶1344–1345).

Inside Address

1317 Letters to an Individual

a. The inside address for a letter to an individual's home should include the following information: (1) the name of the person to whom you are writing; (2) the street address, the box number (see ¶1338), or the rural route number (see ¶1317c); and (3) the city, state, and ZIP Code (see ¶1339).

```
Dr. Margaret P. Vanden Heuvel      Mrs. Bernell Williams
615 University Boulevard           5860 Spring-Cypress Road
Albuquerque, NM 87106-4553         Spring, Texas 77379
```

➤ *For the placement of the inside address, see ¶1319a; for the use of the nine-digit ZIP Code, see ¶1339, note.*

b. If the person lives in an apartment building, give the apartment number after the street address or, if it will not fit, on the line above.

```
Mr. William E. Slifka            Miss Susan H. Ellington
13 Cat Mousam Road, Apt. 1B      Apartment 2104
Kennebunk, Maine 04043           11740 Wilshire Boulevard
                                 Los Angeles, CA 90025
```

c. If you are writing to someone with a rural route address or a highway contract route address, do not use *rural route, highway contract route, number, No.,* or *#* in the address. Use the abbreviation *RR* or *HC* plus a box number. For example:

```
RR 2, Box 454      HC 67, Box 21A
```

Avoid using a street name in conjunction with an *RR* or *HC* address. If one is used, place it on the line above the *RR* or *HC* address.

NOTE: You may want to create an autotext entry containing the inside address and salutation for any individual or organization that you frequently write to.

1318 Letters to an Organization

a. The inside address for a letter to an organization should include the following information: (1) the name of the business or organization, (2) a street address or a post office box number, and (3) the city, state, and ZIP Code. Whenever possible, address the letter to a specific person in the organization and include that person's job title and department (if known). If you do not have the name of a specific person, use a title instead (for example, *Director of Marketing*).

```
Mr. Arthur L. Quintero           Director of Research
National Sales Manager           Stanton Chemical Company
Paragon Industries               Post Office Box 21431
211 North Ervay Street           Chattanooga, TN 37421-0431
Dallas, Texas 75201
```

➤ *For the placement of the inside address, see ¶1319a; for the use of the nine-digit ZIP Code, see ¶1339, note.*

b. When a room number or a suite number is included in the inside address, insert that number after the street address or, if it will not fit, on the line above.

```
Ms. Alice G. Alvarez              James W. Chiverton, M.D.
Werler Construction Company       Suite 1200
416 12th Street, Room 12          1111 West Mockingbird Lane
Columbus, Georgia 31901-2528      Dallas, TX 75247-3158
```

1319 **a.** Whether a letter is going to an individual's home or to an organization, start the inside address at the left margin, on the *fourth* line below the date or below any notation that falls between the date and the inside address (see ¶¶1315–1316).

➢ *See the illustrations on pages 346–350.*

NOTE: You may need to modify these guidelines if you are planning to use a window envelope (see ¶¶1389i, 1391d).

b. In social-business correspondence (see ¶¶1394–1395), type the inside address at the bottom of the letter, aligned at the left margin and starting on the *fourth* line below the writer's signature or title (whichever comes last). In a purely personal letter, no inside address is given at all.

c. Single-space the inside address and align each line at the left.

1320 **a.** If a letter is addressed to two or more people at different addresses, type the individual address blocks one under the other (with 1 blank line between) or position the address blocks side by side. If the address blocks take up too much space at the opening of the letter, type them at the end of the letter, starting at the left on the *fourth* line below the final notation or, if there are no notations, on the *fourth* line below the signature block.

b. If a letter is addressed to two or more people at the same address, list each name on a separate line. Do not show a position title for each person unless it is short and can go on the same line as the name. Moreover, omit the names of departments unless the persons are in the same department. In effect, type only those parts of the address that are common to the people named at the start. (On the respective envelopes for each individual, give the full address for that individual and omit all reference to others named in the inside address.)

```
Dr. Paul J. Rogers
Mr. James A. Dawes
Research Department
Sloan and Hewitt Advertising
700 North Harding Avenue
Chicago, Illinois 60624-1002
```

The following rules (¶¶1321–1343) provide additional details concerning the parts of inside addresses. See also the models in Section 18 for special forms of address used for individuals, couples, organizations, professional people, education officials, government officials, diplomats, military personnel, and religious dignitaries.

Letters and Memos

13

¶1321

Name of Person and Title

1321 When writing the name of a person in an inside address or elsewhere in a letter, be sure to follow that person's preferences in the spelling, capitalization, punctuation, and spacing of the name. (See ¶311.)

a. Do not abbreviate or use initials unless the person to whom you are writing prefers that style. For example, do not write *Wm. B. Sachs* or *W. B. Sachs* if the person to whom you are writing used *William B. Sachs* in his correspondence.

b. When writing to a married woman, follow her preference for first and last names if you know it. She may prefer to be addressed by her original name (for example, *Ms. Joan L. Conroy*). If you do know that she is using her husband's last name, continue to use her own first name and middle initial (for example, *Mrs. Joan L. Noonan*). The form that uses her husband's first name and middle initial as well (for example, *Mrs. James W. Noonan*) is acceptable only for social purposes. It should never be used when addressing a business letter to a married woman, and it should not be used when a married woman becomes a widow unless she indicates that this is her preference.

1322 In general, use a title before the name of a person in an inside address. (See ¶517 for appropriate abbreviations of such titles.)

a. If the person has no special title (such as *Dr.*, *Professor*, or *The Honorable*), use the courtesy title *Mr.*, *Ms.*, *Mrs.*, or *Miss*. (See also ¶1801.)

b. In selecting *Ms.*, *Mrs.*, or *Miss*, always respect the individual woman's preference. If her preference is unknown, use the title *Ms.* or omit the courtesy title altogether. (See also ¶1801b–c.)

NOTE: Follow the same procedure in the salutation. (See ¶1349.)

c. If you do not know whether the person addressed is a man or a woman, do not use any courtesy title. (See also ¶1801d.) Follow the same practice in the salutation. (See ¶1349.)

NOTE: People who use initials in place of their first and middle names or who have ambiguous names (like *Marion, Leslie, Hilary,* and *Lee*) should use a courtesy title when they sign their letters so that others may be spared the confusion over which title to use. If they choose not to provide a courtesy title, they will have to accept the likelihood that they will be inappropriately addressed. (See also ¶¶1365–1366.)

d. Address teenage girls as *Ms.* or *Miss* and respect the individual's preference if you know it. For girls younger than 13, *Ms.* or *Miss* may be used or omitted.

e. Address teenage boys as *Mr.* For boys younger than 13, omit the title. (*Master* is now rarely used except with the names of very young boys.)

1323 a. A letter to a husband and wife is traditionally addressed in this form:

```
Mr. and Mrs. Harold D. Bennisch Jr. (NOT: Mr. & Mrs.)
```

b. If the husband has a special title such as *Dr.* or *Professor,* the couple is addressed as follows:

```
Dr. and Mrs. Thomas P. Geiger
```

c. List the names of a married couple on separate lines when (1) the wife alone has a special title, (2) both spouses have special titles, or (3) each spouse has a different surname.

```
Dr. Eleanor V. Eberhardt-Ball        Ms. Eloise Baum
Mr. Joseph L. Eberhardt-Ball         Mr. Philip O'Connell

Dean Walter O. Goetz            OR   Mrs. Eloise Baum
Professor Helen F. Goetz             Mr. Philip O'Connell
```

d. Some married couples prefer a style of address which uses the first names of the spouses and omits *Mr.* and *Mrs.* Those who use this style typically do so because it treats both spouses as equals and does not imply that the wife can be identified only by her husband's name. Respect such preferences when you are aware of them.

```
Janet and Arnold Rogon     OR    Arnold and Janet Rogon
(RATHER THAN: Mr. and Mrs. Arnold Rogon)
```

NOTE: If *Jr.*, *Sr.*, or a roman numeral such as *III* accompanies the husband's name, choose one of the following forms:

```
Janet Rogon and Arnold Rogon Jr.
OR Arnold Rogon Jr. and Janet Rogon

BUT NOT: Janet and Arnold Rogon Jr.
OR Arnold Jr. and Janet Rogon
```

➤ *For other forms of address to use for couples in special circumstances, see ¶1802.*

1324 **a.** When *Jr.*, *Sr.*, or a roman numeral such as *III* is typed after a name, omit the comma before this element unless you know that the person being addressed prefers the use of a comma. (See also ¶156.)

b. Do not use a title before a name if the term *Esq.* follows the name. (See also ¶¶518c, 1804a.)

```
Rita A. Henry, Esq. (NOT: Ms. Rita A. Henry, Esq.)
```

NOTE: A comma separates the last name from the term *Esq.*

c. As a rule, do not use an academic degree with a person's name in an inside address. However, some doctors of medicine and divinity prefer the use of the degree after their names (rather than the title *Dr.* before). (See also ¶¶1804b, 1810d, 1811d.)

NOTE: If an academic degree follows the person's name, separate it from the last name with a comma. Moreover, omit the titles *Dr.*, *Miss*, *Mr.*, *Mrs.*, and *Ms.* before the name. Another title (for example, *Professor*, *The Reverend*, *Captain*, *Dean*) may be used before the name as long as it does not convey the same meaning as the degree that follows. (See ¶519c.)

```
Reva C. Calhoun, M.D.
The Reverend Ernest G. Wyzanski, D.D.
```

d. Abbreviations of religious orders, such as *S.J.* and *S.N.D.*, are typed after names and preceded by a comma. An appropriate title should precede the name, even though the abbreviation follows the name; for example, *The Reverend John DeMaio, O.P.* (See also ¶¶519a, 1809.)

¶1325

1325 a. A title of position, such as *Vice President* or *Sales Manager,* may be included in an inside address. If a title is to be used, place it on the line following the name; if the title requires a second line, you may either indent the turnover 2 or 3 spaces or align it at the left with the line above. Capitalize the first letter of every word in the title except (1) prepositions under four letters (like *of, for,* and *in*), (2) conjunctions under four letters (like *and*), and (3) the articles *the, a,* and *an* when they appear *within* the title.

```
Mrs. Martha Hansen              Mr. Harry F. Benjamin
Executive Vice President        Chairman of the Board

Mr. Ralph Nielsen               Ms. Evangeline S. Palmer
Vice President and (NOT &)       Director of In-Service
   General Manager                 Training
```

NOTE: In the last example above, *In* is capitalized because it is the first element in a compound adjective (rather than a pure preposition as in *Editor in Chief*). By the same token, in the title *Coordinator of On-the-Job Training, On* is capitalized as the first element in a compound adjective but *of* and *the* are not.

b. If the title is very short, it may be typed on the same line as the person's name or the person's department in order to balance the length of the lines in the address. However, do not type a title on the same line as the name of an organization. (See ¶1327.)

```
Mr. J. C. Lee, President             Mr. Armand F. Aristides
Merchants National Bank              Controller
                                     Dahl, Inc.

Mrs. Lucinda Hollingsworth     NOT:  Mr. Armand F. Aristides
Manager, Support Services            Controller, Dahl, Inc.
E. J. Haines & Company
```

In Care of . . .

1326 Sometimes a letter cannot be sent to the addressee's home or place of business; it must be directed instead to a third person who will see that the letter reaches the addressee. In such cases use an "in care of" notation. The following examples show two versions of this notation.

```
Professor Eleanor Marschak     OR   Professor Eleanor Marschak
In care of Henry Ward, Esq.         c/o Henry Ward, Esq.
```

Name of Organization

1327 Type the organization's name on a line by itself. If the name of a division or a department is needed in the address, it should precede the name of the organization on a line by itself.

```
Ms. Laura J. Kidd
Assistant Vice President
Department of Corporate Planning
Holstein, Brooks & Co.
```

1328 When writing the name of an organization in an inside address, always follow the organization's style for spelling, punctuation, capitalization, spacing, and abbreviations. The letterhead on incoming correspondence is the best source for this information. Note the variations in style in these names.

America Online, Inc.	Parker Pen USA Limited
Sierra On-Line, Inc.	Frye & Smith Ltd.
United Airlines	Fujitsu, Ltd.
Delta Air Lines	USLife Corp.
Time Inc.	U S WEST Communications
Newsweek, Inc.	Luce, Forward, Hamilton & Scripps
Prudential Securities Incorporated	Dean Witter Reynolds Inc.
Hewlett-Packard Company	Browning-Ferris Industries
Charles Schwab & Co., Inc.	Ply*Gem Industries
PepsiCo, Inc.	Ex-Cell-O Corporation
Xerox Corporation	La-Z-Boy Chair Co.
Engelhard Corp.	1 Potato 2 Inc.
BankAmerica Corp. (see ¶366)	Toys "R" Us, Inc. (see ¶320a, note)
Rogers Cablesystems of	!%@: Directory of Electronic Mail
America, Inc.	Addressing & Networks

NOTE: If the name is long and requires more than one line, you may either indent any turnover line 2 or 3 spaces or align it at the left with the line above. (See ¶1329e for examples.)

1329 If you do not have some way of determining the official form of a company name, follow these rules:

a. Spell out the word *and.* Do not use an ampersand (&).

Haber, Curtis, and Hall, Inc.

b. Write *Inc.* for *Incorporated* and *Ltd.* for *Limited.* Do not use a comma before the abbreviation.

c. As a rule, spell out *Company* or *Corporation.* If the name is extremely long, however, you may use the abbreviation *Co.* or *Corp.*

d. Do not use the word *the* at the beginning of a name unless you are sure it is part of the official name; for example, *The Wall Street Journal* (as illustrated at the top of page 362).

e. Capitalize the first letter of every word except (1) prepositions under four letters (like *of* and *for*), (2) conjunctions under four letters (like *and*), and (3) the articles *the, a,* and *an* when they appear within the organization's name.

```
American Society for the        Department of Health and
   Prevention of Cruelty        Human Services (see ¶1328, note)
   to Animals (see ¶1328, note) 200 Independence Ave, SW
424 East 92d Street             Washington, DC 20201-0001
New York, New York 10128
```

NOTE: In the following example note that the article *the* is capitalized because it comes at the start of the organization's official name. Note also that the name of

¶1330

the newspaper is not italicized or underlined because it refers to the organization rather than to the actual newspaper. (See also ¶289e.)

```
The Wall Street Journal
200 Liberty Street
New York, NY 10281-1099
```

➢ *For the use or omission of apostrophes in company names, see ¶640.*

Building Name

1330 If the name of a building is included in the inside address, type it on a line by itself immediately above the street address. A room number or a suite number should follow the street address, but if it will not fit on that line, insert it before the building name on the line above.

```
Park Square Building                Room 118, Acuff Building
31 St. James Avenue, Room 858       904 Bob Wallace Avenue, SW
Boston, MA 02116-4255               Huntsville, AL 35801
```

➢ *For additional examples, see ¶1318b.*

Street Address

1331 Always type the street address on a line by itself, immediately preceding the city, state, and ZIP Code. (See ¶¶1317–1318 for examples.)

1332 Use figures for house and building numbers. Do not include the abbreviation *No.* or the symbol # before such numbers. **EXCEPTION:** For clarity, use the word *One* instead of the figure *1* in a house or building number; for example, *One Park Avenue.*

NOTE: Some house numbers contain a fraction or a hyphen; for example, *234$\frac{1}{2}$ Elm Street, 220-03 46th Street.*

1333 Numbers used as street names are written as follows:

a. Spell out the numbers 1 through 10; for example, *177 Second Avenue.*

b. Use figures for numbers over 10; for example, *627 East 202d Street* or *144 65th Street.* (See ¶425b.)

c. Some grid-style addresses require a period in a numbered street name; for example, *26.2 Road.*

1334 When a compass point (for example, *East, West, Southeast, Northwest*) appears *before* a street name, do not abbreviate it except in a very long street address when space is tight.

```
330 West 42d Street          3210 Northwest Grand Avenue
```

1335 When a compass point appears *after* a street name, follow the style most commonly used in your area. In the absence of a local style, follow these guidelines:

a. Abbreviate compound directions *(NE, NW, SE, SW)* that represent a section of the city. Do not use a period with these abbreviations (see ¶531a). Insert a comma before them.

```
817 Peachtree Street, NE      120 112th Street, NW
```

b. Spell out *North, South, East,* and *West* following a street name, and omit the comma. (In such cases these compass points are typically an integral part of the street name rather than a designation of a section of the city.)

    10 Park Avenue South   2049 Century Park East

1336 Use the word *and*, not an ampersand (&), in a street address; for example, *Tenth and Market Streets.* However, avoid the use of such "intersection" addresses if a house or building number plus a single street name is available (such as *304 Tenth Street*).

1337 Avoid abbreviating such words as *Street* and *Avenue* in inside addresses. (It may be necessary to abbreviate in envelope addresses. See ¶1390a.)

➤ *For apartment and room numbers with street addresses, see ¶¶1317b, 1318b, 1330.*

Box Number

1338 a. A post office box number may be used in place of the street address. The following forms are acceptable:

    Post Office Box 1518 OR P.O. Box 1518

Do not use the form *Box 1518* except with a rural route (RR) address or a highway contract (HC) address. (See ¶1317c.)

NOTE: The U.S. Postal Service (USPS) prefers that a designation such as *Drawer L* be changed to *Post Office Box L.*

b. A station name, if used, should follow the post office box number (and a comma) on the same line. If very long, the station name may go on the line above.

    Box 76984, Sanford Station
    Los Angeles, CA 90076-0984

    Linda Vista Station
    P.O. Box 11215
    San Diego, CA 92111

NOTE: According to the USPS, station names are no longer needed.

c. Some organizations show both a street address and a post office box number in their mailing address. When you are writing to an organization with two addresses, use only one address: the post office box number for ordinary mail and the street address for express mail. If you provide both addresses on an envelope, the USPS will deliver the mail to the address that appears directly above the city-state-ZIP Code line.

d. If you are writing to someone who rents a mailbox from a private company, insert the *private mail box* number (formerly known as a *mailstop code*) on the line directly above the delivery address—that is, the street address of the private company where the mailbox is located. For example:

    Ms. Robin B. Kantor
    PMB 215
    621 Bloomfield Avenue
    Verona, NJ 07044

¶1339

City, State, and ZIP Code

1339 Always type the city, state, and ZIP Code on one line, immediately following the street address. Type the name of the city (followed by a comma and 1 space), the state (followed by 1 space but no comma), and the ZIP Code.

> Denver, Colorado 80217   **OR**   Denver, CO 80217-9999

NOTE: The USPS encourages the use of a nine-digit ZIP Code (consisting of the basic five digits followed immediately by a hyphen and another four digits); hence the designation ZIP + 4 Code. The use of the additional four digits is voluntary, but as an inducement the USPS offers discounts on postage fees. To qualify for a discount, mailers must submit a minimum of 500 *first-class* letters or postcards at one time, and the envelope addresses must be readable by electronic equipment known as optical character readers (OCRs). Moreover, the mailing list must be certified by USPS-approved software. Because of the number of criteria that must be satisfied, mailers who want to qualify for a discount should consult their local USPS business center for details. (See ¶¶1389–1390.)

1340 When writing the name of a city in an inside address:

a. Take special care in spelling city names. Do not go by sound alone.

Baldwin, LA	Baldwyn, MS	Hillsboro, OR	Hillsborough, NC
Center, PA	Centre, PA	Jessup, PA	Jesup, GA
Cortland, NY	Cortlandt, NY	Kenedy, TX	Kennedy, PA
Green, IN	Greene, IN	Lynnwood, WA	Lynwood, CA
Hamden, CT	Hampden, MA	Paterson, NJ	Patterson, NY

➤ *See also ¶1202c, note.*

b. Do not use an abbreviation (for example, *L.A.* for *Los Angeles*).

c. Do not abbreviate the words *Fort, Mount, Point,* or *Port.* Write the name of the city in full; for example, *Fort Worth, Mount Vernon, Point Pleasant, Port Huron.* (See also ¶529a.)

d. Abbreviate the word *Saint* in the names of American cities; for example, *St. Louis, St. Paul, St. Petersburg.* (See also ¶529b.)

NOTE: It may be necessary, for reasons of space, to abbreviate city names in envelope addresses. (See ¶1390a.)

1341 **a.** In an address, spell out the name of the state or use a two-letter abbreviation of the state name. Either form is correct for use with a ZIP Code, and either form can be read by OCRs.

NOTE: The two-letter abbreviations (for example, *AL* for *Alabama*) were created by the USPS and should be used only in mailing addresses. The more traditional abbreviations of state names (for example, *Ala.* for *Alabama*) should be used in other situations where abbreviations are appropriate. (See ¶527b for a list of the traditional abbreviations.)

b. When using two-letter state abbreviations, type them in capital letters, with no periods after the letters or space between them.

¶1342

Alabama	AL		Missouri	MO
Alaska	AK		Montana	MT
American Samoa	AS		Nebraska	NE
Arizona	AZ		Nevada	NV
Arkansas	AR		New Hampshire	NH
California	CA		New Jersey	NJ
Colorado	CO		New Mexico	NM
Connecticut	CT		New York	NY
Delaware	DE		North Carolina	NC
District of			North Dakota	ND
Columbia	DC		Northern Mariana	
Federated States			Islands	MP
of Micronesia	FM		Ohio	OH
Florida	FL		Oklahoma	OK
Georgia	GA		Oregon	OR
Guam	GU		Palau	PW
Hawaii	HI		Pennsylvania	PA
Idaho	ID		Puerto Rico	PR
Illinois	IL		Rhode Island	RI
Indiana	IN		South Carolina	SC
Iowa	IA		South Dakota	SD
Kansas	KS		Tennessee	TN
Kentucky	KY		Texas	TX
Louisiana	LA		Utah	UT
Maine	ME		Vermont	VT
Marshall Islands	MH		Virgin Islands	VI
Maryland	MD		Virginia	VA
Massachusetts	MA		Washington	WA
Michigan	MI		West Virginia	WV
Minnesota	MN		Wisconsin	WI
Mississippi	MS		Wyoming	WY

c. When giving an address in a sentence, insert a comma after the street address and after the city. Leave 1 space between the state and the ZIP Code. Insert a comma after the ZIP Code unless a stronger mark of punctuation is required at that point.

> In April my new address will be 501 South 71st Court, Miami, Florida 33144-2728.

1342 Omit the name of the county or area (such as *Long Island*) in an address. However, the name of a community, subdivision, or real estate development may be included as long as it comes before the lines containing the mail delivery address.

> Ms. Janet G. Arnold
> Muir Meadows
> 1039 Erica Road
> Mill Valley, CA 94941

NOT: Ms. Janet G. Arnold
1039 Erica Road
Muir Meadows
Mill Valley, CA 94941

¶1343

1343 **a.** In international addresses, type the name of the country on a separate line in all-capital letters. Do not abbreviate the name of the country.

```
Graf-Adolf Strasse 100      4-14-11 Ginza
Dusseldorf 4000             Chuo-Ku, Tokyo 104
GERMANY                     JAPAN
```

NOTE: If you are writing from another country to someone in the United States, type *UNITED STATES OF AMERICA* as the last line of the address.

b. In a Canadian address, the name of the province or territory may be spelled out or abbreviated. However, Canada Post has expressed a preference for the abbreviated form in order to keep the city, province, and postal code all on one line.

Alberta	AB	Nova Scotia	NS
British Columbia	BC	Ontario	ON
Manitoba	MB	Prince Edward	
New Brunswick	NB	Island	PE
Newfoundland	NF	Quebec	QC
Northwest Territories		Saskatchewan	SK
and Nunavut	NT	Yukon	YT

NOTE: In an inside address or an envelope address, insert a comma and 1 space between the city name and the two-letter abbreviation, followed by 2 spaces and the six-character postal code.

```
21 St. Clair Avenue
Toronto, ON   M4T 1L9
CANADA
```

When giving an address in a sentence, spell out the name of the province and leave only 1 space before the postal code. Then insert a comma, 1 space, and *Canada.*

```
Write to me at 21 St. Clair Avenue, Toronto, Ontario M4T 1L9, Canada.
```

Attention Line

1344 When a letter is addressed directly to an organization, an attention line may be used to route the letter to a particular person (by name or title) or to a particular department. Here is the format that has been used in the past.

```
Shelton & Warren Industries    Carrolton Labs
6710 Squibb Road               1970 Briarwood Court
Mission, KS 66202-3223         Atlanta, GA 30329


Attention:  Mr. John Ellery    ATTN:   SALES MANAGER
```

NOTE: This form of address is intended to emphasize the fact that the letter deals with a business matter (rather than a personal matter) and may be handled by someone other than the person named in the attention line. However, it is simpler to type the name of the person or department above the organization name and omit the attention line. When a letter without a personal or confidential notation is received by an organization, it will be presumed to deal with company business and may be handled by others in the absence of the person named in the address. For this reason an attention line is not really needed and in fact is no longer frequently used. Moreover, the arrangements shown on the preceding page—placing the attention line below the inside address—are not suitable if you are planning to use your computer to replicate the inside address on an envelope or mailing label.

1345 **a.** If you are using window envelopes or planning to generate the envelope address by repeating the inside address as typed, you should insert the attention line as the first line of the inside address—with or without the word *Attention.* (See also ¶¶1389n, 1390h.)

```
Mr. John Ellery                    Attention:  Sales Manager
Shelton & Warren Industries        Carrolton Labs
6710 Squibb Road                   1970 Briarwood Court
Mission, KS 66202-3223             Atlanta, GA 30329
```

b. Once the attention line is placed on the first line of the address block, the argument for omitting the word *Attention* is further strengthened. (See the note in ¶1344.) Indeed, when the USPS illustrates the use of an attention line, it typically omits the word *Attention.* In fact, the USPS uses the term *attention line* to refer to *any* information—whether a person's name *(Ms. Hilary Edwards)*, a person's title *(Marketing Director)*, or a departmental name *(Research Department)*—that appears on the line above the organizational name *(The E. J. Monagle Publishing Company).* If you read somewhere that the USPS wants the first line of a business address to be an "attention line," do not conclude that it is requiring the use of the word *Attention.* The USPS simply wants to have personal or departmental names or titles come above the name of the organization.

NOTE: The use or omission of the word *Attention* will affect the choice of salutation. See ¶1351.

➤ *For the treatment of an attention line on an envelope, see ¶¶1389n, 1390h.*

Salutation

1346 Type the salutation, beginning at the left margin, on the second line below the attention line (if used) or on the second line below the inside address. Follow the salutation with a colon unless you are using open punctuation (see ¶1309b) or are typing a social-business letter (see ¶1396b). Omit the salutation if you are using the simplified style, and replace it with a subject line. (See ¶1352.)

1347 Abbreviate only the titles *Mr., Ms., Mrs., Messrs.,* and *Dr.* Spell out all other titles, such as *Professor* and *Father.* (See Section 18 for titles used by officials, dignitaries, and military personnel.)

1348 Capitalize the first word as well as any nouns and titles in the salutation; for example, *Dear Mrs. Brand, Dear Sir.*

1349 **a.** A list of salutations appears on the next page. (See Section 18 for the salutations to be used with different forms of address.)

NOTE: The salutations identified as *more formal* are no longer frequently used.

Continued on page 368

¶1349

To One Person (Name, Gender, and Courtesy Title Preference Known)

Dear Mr. Smith: Dear Ms. Simpson:
Dear Mrs. Gray: Dear Miss Wells:

To One Person (Name Known, Gender Unknown)

Dear Marion Parker: Dear R. V. Moore:

To One Person (Name Unknown, Gender Known)

Dear Madam: **OR**   Madam: *(more formal)*
Dear Sir: **OR**   Sir: *(more formal)*

To One Person (Name and Gender Unknown)

Dear Sir or Madam: **OR**   Sir or Madam: *(more formal)*
OR Dear Madam or Sir: **OR**   Madam or Sir: *(more formal)*

To One Woman (Courtesy Title Preference Unknown)

Dear Ms. Malloy: **OR**   Dear Ruth Malloy: (see ¶1322b)

To Two or More Men

Dear Mr. Gelb and Mr. Harris: **OR**   Gentlemen:
OR Dear Messrs. Gelb and Harris: *(more formal)*

To Two or More Women

Dear Mrs. Allen, Ms. Ott, and Miss Day:

Dear Mrs. Jordan and Mrs. Kent: (see ¶618)
OR Dear Mesdames Jordan and Kent: *(more formal)*

Dear Ms. Scott and Ms. Gomez: (see ¶618)
OR Dear Mses. (**OR** Mss.) Scott and Gomez: *(more formal)*

Dear Miss Winger and Miss Rossi: (see ¶618)
OR Dear Misses Winger and Rossi: *(more formal)*

To a Woman and a Man

Dear Ms. Kent and Mr. Winston: Dear Mrs. Kay and Mr. Fox:
Dear Mr. Fong and Miss Landis: Dear Mr. and Mrs. Green:

To Several Persons

Dear Mr. Anderson, Mrs. Brodsky, Ms. Carmino, and Mr. Dellums:

Dear Friends (Colleagues, Members, *or some other suitable collective term*):

To an Organization Composed Entirely of Men

Gentlemen:

To an Organization Composed Entirely of Women

Ladies: **OR**   Mesdames: *(more formal)*

To an Organization Composed of Men and Women (see ¶1350)

b. Be sure that the spelling of the surname in the salutation matches the spelling in the inside address. If the person you are writing to has a hyphenated last name (for example, *Mrs. Hazel Gray-Sparks*), the salutation should include the entire last name *(Dear Mrs. Gray-Sparks)*.

c. When writing to someone you know well, use a first name or nickname in place of the more formal salutations shown on page 368. However, once you start using an informal salutation, be sure that anyone who prepares your letters for you maintains that form of address. Otherwise, a person who is used to getting *Dear Mike* letters from you may one day receive a *Dear Mr. Romano* letter and waste a good deal of time brooding over what could have caused the sudden chill in your warm relationship.

d. When you are preparing a letter that may be sent or shown to a number of as yet undetermined individuals, use *Dear Sir or Madam.* You may also use the simplified letter style and omit the salutation. (See page 350.)

e. In salutations involving two or more people, use *and,* not &.

1350 For an organization composed of both men and women, choose one of the following alternatives:

a. Use *Ladies and Gentlemen* or *Gentlemen and Ladies.* (Do not use *Gentlemen* alone.)

b. Address the letter, not to the organization as a whole, but to the head of the organization—by name and title if known, otherwise by title alone. Then the salutation would appear as shown in ¶1349a.

```
Mr. James V. Quillan              President
President                         (OR Chief Executive Officer)
United Services Corporation       United Services Corporation
100 Kendall Parkway               100 Kendall Parkway
Somerset, NJ 08873                Somerset, NJ 08873


Dear Mr. Quillan:                 Dear Sir or Madam:
```

c. Use the name of the organization in the salutation.

```
Dear United Services Corporation:
```

NOTE: This approach is acceptable in routine or informal letters but should not be used in formal communications. (See the illustration on page 348 and ¶1803a.)

d. Use the simplified letter style and omit the salutation. (See page 350.)

1351 a. If you have used an attention line beginning with the word *Attention* (see ¶¶1344–1345), the letter is considered to be addressed to the organization rather than to the person named in the attention line. Therefore, use one of the organizational salutations shown in ¶¶1349 and 1350.

b. If you drop the word *Attention* (as shown in ¶1345) and address the letter directly to an individual in the organization (either by name or by title), use one of the personal salutations shown in ¶1349.

The following rules (¶¶1352–1357) deal with the *body* of a letter. The body contains the text of the letter—in other words, the message (see ¶¶1354–1357). The body may also begin with a subject line (see ¶¶1352–1353), which briefly identifies the main idea in the message.

¶1352

Subject Line

1352 In the *simplified letter style:*

    a. Use a subject line in place of the salutation.

    b. Start the subject line on the third line below the inside address. Begin at the left margin and type the subject line in all-capital letters.

    c. Do not use a term like *Subject* to introduce the subject line. (See the illustration on page 350.)

1353 In *all other letter styles:*

    a. The subject line (if used) appears between the salutation and the text of the letter, with 1 blank line above and below. (See the illustration on page 349.)

    b. Ordinarily, the subject line starts at the left margin, but it may be centered for special emphasis. In a letter with indented paragraphs, the subject line may also be indented (typically, 0.5 inch).

    c. Type the subject line either in capital and small letters or in all-capital letters.

    d. The term *Subject* or *In re* or *Re* usually precedes the actual subject but may be omitted.

```
Subject:   Introductory Offer to
New Subscribers and Renewal Offer
to Present Subscribers

SUBJECT:   MORAN LEASE

In re:   Moran Lease
```

    NOTE: If the subject line is long, type it in two or more single-spaced lines of roughly equal length. (See the first example above as well as the illustrations on pages 415 and 506.)

    e. When replying to a letter that carries a "refer to" notation, you may put the desired reference number or filing code in a subject line or below the date line. (See ¶1316d.)

```
Subject:   Policy 668485   OR   Refer to:   Policy 668485
```

Message

1354 **a.** As a general rule, begin the text of the letter—the message—on the second line below the subject line, if used, or on the second line below the salutation. In the simplified letter style, begin the message on the third line below the subject line (which replaces the salutation).

    NOTE: With word processing software, you can use autotext to capture the keystrokes that represent frequently used names, phrases, sentences, or paragraphs. (See the note on page 341.)

    b. If you are writing in response to a letter or some other document, it is helpful to refer to that document by date in the first sentence of your letter.

```
Thank you for your letter of May 9 (OR   May 9, 2000).
```

NOTE: Whether you use the full date or the month and day alone to refer to the earlier document will depend on the nature of your letter. For a full discussion of this issue, see ¶409.

1355 Use single spacing and leave 1 blank line between paragraphs.

1356
  a. Align each line of the message at the left margin. However, if you are using the modified-block letter style with indented paragraphs, indent the first line of each paragraph 0.5 inch. (See the illustration on page 348.)

  b. You can use your word processing software to *justify* the right margin—that is, have each full line of text end at the same point. If you choose this format (known as *full justification*), your software will automatically insert extra space between words to make each line the same length. (See page 350 for an illustration of a letter with a justified right margin.)

  NOTE: While full justification (aligning the lines of text at both the left and the right margins) looks attractive, the insertion of extra space between words can sometimes produce unintended "rivers" of white space running vertically down through the text. Full justification can also produce significant variations in the space between sentences (as illustrated in ¶102e). More important, studies have demonstrated that text with a *ragged* (unjustified) right margin is easier to read. Moreover, some recipients of a fully justified letter tend to regard it as a form letter and not take it seriously.

  c. If you decide on a ragged right margin, try to avoid great variations in the length of adjacent lines. (See Section 9 for guidelines on dividing words in order to keep the lines of text roughly equal in length.)

  d. If a letter takes two or more pages, do not divide a short paragraph (with only two or three lines) at the bottom of a page. Always leave at least two lines of the paragraph at the foot of one page and carry over at least two lines to the top of the next page. (See ¶¶1382–1387.)

  NOTE: Use the widow/orphan control feature to prevent the creation of *orphans* (printing the first line of a new paragraph as the last line on a page) and *widows* (printing the last line of a paragraph as the first line of a new page).

1357
  a. Quoted Material. If a quotation will make four or more lines, type it as a single-spaced extract, indent it 0.5 inch from each side margin, and leave 1 blank line above and below the extract. (See the illustration on page 349.) With word processing software, you can change the indent settings, or you can use the *double indent* feature (if one is available), which will indent the extract equally from each side margin. If the quoted material represents the start of a paragraph in the original, indent the first word an additional 0.5 inch.

  ➤ *For different ways of handling a long quotation, see ¶265.*

  b. Tables. When a table occurs in the body of a letter, center it between the left and right margins. Try to indent the table at least 0.5 inch from each side margin. (If the table is very wide, reduce the space between columns to prevent the table from extending beyond the width of the text.) (See Section 16 for a full discussion on how to plan and execute tables.)

Continued on page 372

¶**1357**

c. **Items in a List.** Type the list with 1 blank line above and below the list as a whole. Either type the list on the full width of the letter, or indent the list 0.5 inch from each side margin. If each item in the list requires only one line, type the list single-spaced. If any item in the list requires more than one line, leave a blank line after each item in the list for a more open look. Align any turnovers with the first word in the line above.

1 inch When you are ready to distribute your analysis for the first round of comments, I **1 inch**
(min.) suggest you send it to the following people inside the company: ↓**2x**   **(min.)**

      Angela Lawless, director of information systems
      Thomas Podgorski, manager of corporate planning ↓**2x**

In addition, you may want to get reactions from two trustworthy consultants: ↓**2x**

0.5   Dr. Harriet E. Fenster, professor of computer science at Michigan   **0.5**
inch   State University ↓**2x**   **inch**
      Wilson G. Witherspoon, president of Witherspoon Associates in
      Princeton, New Jersey ↓**2x**

I can give you mailing addresses for these consultants if you decide to get in touch with them.

➤ *See ¶1424e, note, and the illustration on page 504.*

d. **Enumerated Items in a List.** If the items each begin with a number or a letter, you may use the numbered list feature of your word processing program. Each item will begin at the left margin, and no space will be left between items.

When I review the situation as you described it in your letter of June 24, it seems to me that you have only two alternatives: ↓**2x**

1. Agree to pay the additional amount that Henning now demands.
2. Drop Henning and start the search all over again for a new firm. ↓**2x**

Note the treatment of turnover lines when you use the numbered list feature.

When I review the situation as you described it in your letter of June 24, it seems to me that you have only two alternatives: ↓**2x**

1. Agree to pay the additional amount that Henning now demands before he will start construction.
2. Drop Henning and start the search all over again to find a firm qualified to handle a project of this size and this complexity. ↓**2x**

¶**1357**

13

For a more open look, leave one blank line after each item in the list if any item requires more than one line.

When I review the situation as you described it in your letter of June 24, it seems to me that you have only two alternatives: ↓**2x**

1. Agree to pay the additional amount that Henning now demands before he will start construction. ↓**2x**

2. Drop Henning and start the search all over again to find a firm qualified to handle a project of this size and this complexity. ↓**2x**

An enumerated list may be typed the full width of the letter, or it may be indented 0.5 inch from each side margin. However, if the first line of each text paragraph is indented, then for better appearance indent the enumerated list as well.

Default Style	Preferred Style
When I review the situation as yo seems to me that you have only two alter	When I review the situation as yo seems to me that you have only two alter
1. Agree to pay the additional amount th will start construction. 2. Drop Henning and start the search all handle a project of this size and this	1. Agree to pay the additional ai he will start construction. 2. Drop Henning and start the s to handle a project of this si
As painful as it may be, you may tor than to have to deal with new deman the way through the job.	As painful as it may be, you may tor than to have to deal with new demands the way through the job.

NOTE: The numbered list feature aligns numbers and letters at the left. If your list contains 10 or more items, you can make an adjustment so that the numbers will align at the right.

DEFAULT ALIGNMENT:	8.	STANDARD ALIGNMENT:	8.
	9.		9.
	10.		10.
	11.		11.
	12.		12.

The numbered list feature of some word processing programs (such as Microsoft Word) indents the first word that follows the number and any turnover lines 0.25 inch from the left margin (as shown in the illustration at the top of this page). The numbered list feature of other programs uses a default indent of 0.5 inch, but you can change this indent to 0.25 inch for a more attractive look.

Continued on page 374

¶1358

e. **Bulleted Items in a List.** Instead of numbers or letters, you can use *bullets* before the items in a list. With word processing software, you can choose from a variety of styles to create bullets. For example:

CIRCLES: ○ ●   TRIANGLES: ▷ ▶

SQUARES: □ ■   OTHER ASCII CHARACTERS: > → *

If you use the automatic bullet insert feature, the default position of the bullet is at the left margin and the text and any turnovers are automatically indented (as in the illustration below). If you prefer, you can position the bullets 0.5 inch from the left margin by pressing the tab before activating the bullet feature.

> When I review the situation as you described it in your letter of June 24, it seems to me that you have only two alternatives:
> ↓2x
>
> • Agree to pay the additional amount that Henning now demands before he will start construction.
>   ↓2x
>
> • Drop Henning and start the search all over again to find a firm qualified to handle a project of this size and this complexity.
>   ↓2x

The following rules (¶¶1358–1381) deal with the *closing* of a letter. The closing typically includes a complimentary-closing phrase (¶¶1358–1360), the writer's name and title (¶¶1362–1369), and reference initials (¶1370). The closing may also include a company signature line (¶1361), a file name notation (¶¶1371–1372), an enclosure notation (¶¶1373–1374), a delivery notation (¶1375), a copy notation (¶¶1376–1380), and a postscript (¶1381).

Complimentary Closing

1358 Type the complimentary closing on the second line below the last line of the body of the letter. In a modified-block-style letter, start the closing at center. In a block-style letter, start the closing at the left margin. In a simplified letter, omit the closing. (See the illustrations on pages 346–350.)

NOTE: Word processing software allows you to use autotext for the complimentary closing and other elements that are frequently used in the closing of a letter.

1359 a. Capitalize only the first word of a complimentary closing.

b. Place a comma at the end of the line (except when open punctuation is used).

1360 a. The following complimentary closings are commonly used:

```
Sincerely,              Sincerely yours,
Cordially,              Cordially yours,
```

NOTE: More formal closings—such as *Very truly yours* and *Respectfully yours*—are infrequently used these days.

b. An informal closing phrase may be inserted in place of one of the more conventional closings shown in *a*. If the wording is an adverbial phrase (one that tells *how* or *in what manner*—for example, *With all best wishes* or *With warmest regards*), follow the closing with a comma. If the wording is a complete sentence (for example, *See you in Boston*), follow the closing with a period. In each case the comma or the period may be replaced with stronger punctuation as appropriate—that is, a question mark, an exclamation point, or a dash.

NOTE: If you are using open punctuation, see ¶1309b.

c. If both a complimentary closing and an informal closing phrase are used, type the complimentary closing in its regular position, and (1) type the informal phrase at the end of the last paragraph or (2) treat the informal phrase as the final paragraph with the appropriate terminal punctuation.

d. Once a pattern of personal or informal closings is begun, it should not be discontinued without good reason. Otherwise, if a later letter returns to a more formal closing, the person who receives the letter may wonder what has happened to the established relationship. (See also ¶1349c.)

Company Signature

1361 A company signature may be used to emphasize the fact that a letter represents the views of the company as a whole (and not merely the individual who has written it). If included, the company signature should be typed in all-capital letters on the second line below the complimentary closing. Begin the company signature at the same point as the complimentary closing. (See the illustration on page 346.)

```
Very truly yours, ↓2x

HASKINS & COHEN Inc.
```

NOTE: When a letter is written on letterhead stationery, the recipient of the letter may reasonably assume that the individual who signs the letter does so on behalf of the organization named in the letterhead. For that reason a company signature (like an attention line) is not really needed. Nevertheless, follow the style of the organization you work for.

➤ *For the use of autotext and macros, see the note on page 341.*

Writer's Name and Title

1362 a. Ordinarily, type the writer's name in capital and small letters on the fourth line below the company signature, if used, or on the fourth line below the complimentary closing. In the simplified letter style, type the writer's name and title in all-capital letters on the *fifth* line below the body. (See the examples in ¶1363 and the illustrations on pages 346–350.)

NOTE: If the letter is running short, you can leave up to 6 blank lines for the signature. If the letter is running long, you can reduce the signature space to 2 blank lines. (See also ¶¶1307–1308.)

b. Ordinarily, start typing at the same point as the company signature or the complimentary closing. In the simplified letter style, start typing at the left margin.

Continued on page 376

¶1363

c. Although some writers prefer to give only their title and department name in the signature block, a typewritten signature should also be included so that the unsigned copies will clearly show who sent the letter. If the writer prefers to omit his or her name from the signature block, then it should be spelled out in the reference initials. (See ¶1370d.)

d. Top-level executives usually have special stationery with their name and title imprinted along with other elements of the letterhead. When using this type of stationery, supply a typewritten signature but omit the title. (For an illustration, see page 349.)

➢ *For the use of autotext and macros, see the note on page 341.)*

1363 a. Arrange the writer's name, title, and department on two or more lines to achieve good visual balance. If a title takes more than one line, align all turnovers at the left.

```
Janice Mahoney, Manager        Ernest L. Welhoelter
Data Processing Division       Chairman of the Board

Charles Saunders               Franklin Browning
Assistant Manager              Vice President and
Credit Department              General Manager
```

SIMPLIFIED STYLE: MARY WELLER, MANAGER, SALES DEPARTMENT

b. In signature blocks, capitalize the first letter of every word in the title and department except (1) prepositions under four letters (like *of, for,* and *in*), (2) conjunctions under four letters (like *and*), and (3) the articles *the, a,* and *an* when they appear within the title. (See also ¶1325a.)

1364 For the use of a special title in a signature block, observe the following guidelines:

a. A person who wants to be addressed as *Dr.* should use an appropriate academic degree after his or her name (not *Dr.* before it).

```
Jane Bishop, M.D.              Nancy Buckwalter, Ph.D.
Charles Burgos, D.D.S.         Morris Finley, D.D.
Lee Toniolo, D.O.              Henry Krawitz, D.H.L.
```

b. A person who wishes to be addressed by a title of academic or military rank *(Dean, Professor, Major)* should type this title *after* the name or on the next line, not before it.

```
Helene C. Powell               Joseph F. Corey
Dean of Students               Major, USAF
(NOT: Dean Helene C. Powell)    (NOT: Major Joseph F. Corey)
```

c. When a title cannot be placed after a surname or cannot be inferred from the initials of an academic degree, then it may precede the name.

```
Rev. Joseph W. Dowd            Mother Ellen Marie O'Brien
```

1365 Ordinarily, a man should not include *Mr.* in his signature. However, if he has a name that could also be a woman's name *(Kay, Adrian, Beverly, Lynn)* or if he uses initials in place of a first and middle name *(J. G. Eberle)*, he should use *Mr.* in either his hand-written or his typed signature when writing to people who do not know him. Otherwise, he will have to accept the fact that he may be addressed as a woman.

NOTE: If given in the handwritten signature, *Mr.* should be enclosed in parentheses. If given in the typed signature, *Mr.* should appear without parentheses.

Sincerely,

(Mr.) Lynn Treadway

Lynn Treadway

Sincerely,

Lynn Treadway

Mr. Lynn Treadway

1366 **a.** A woman may choose not to include any title along with her signature. In that case, someone writing to her may choose to address her as *Ms.* or give her full name without any title at all.

Sincerely,

Joan Beauregard

Joan Beauregard

Sincerely,

Leslie Ellis

Leslie Ellis

If she uses initials in place of a first name or if she has a first name that could also be a man's name (as in the case of Leslie Ellis shown above), she will have to accept the fact that by not indicating her gender, she may be addressed as a man.

➤ *For salutations to use when writing to someone whose gender is unknown to you, see*
¶1349.

b. A woman who wants to indicate her preference for *Ms.* should use this courtesy title in either her handwritten or her typed signature (but not both).

Sincerely yours,

(Ms.) Constance G. Booth

Constance G. Booth

Sincerely yours,

Constance G. Booth

Ms. Constance G. Booth

c. A single woman who wants to indicate her preference for *Miss* should include this title in her handwritten or her typed signature (but not both).

Cordially,

(Miss) Margaret L. Galloway

Margaret L. Galloway

Cordially,

Margaret L. Galloway

Miss Margaret L. Galloway

d. A married woman who retains her original name for career purposes or who does not change her surname at all may use either *Ms.* or *Miss,* as illustrated in ¶1366b–c.

Continued on page 378

¶1367

Letters and Memos

13

e. A married woman or a widow who prefers to be addressed as *Mrs.* has many variations to choose from. The following examples show the possible styles for a woman whose original name was Nancy O. Ross and whose husband's name is (or was) John A. Wells.

Sincerely,	Sincerely,
(Mrs.) Nancy O. Wells	*Nancy O. Wells*
Nancy O. Wells	Mrs. Nancy O. Wells
Sincerely,	Sincerely,
(Mrs.) Nancy R. Wells	*Nancy R. Wells*
Nancy R. Wells	Mrs. Nancy R. Wells
Sincerely,	Sincerely,
(Mrs.) Nancy Ross Wells	*Nancy Ross Wells*
Nancy Ross Wells	Mrs. Nancy Ross Wells
Sincerely,	Sincerely,
(Mrs.) Nancy O. Ross-Wells	*Nancy O. Ross-Wells*
Nancy O. Ross-Wells	Mrs. Nancy O. Ross-Wells

NOTE: Giving the husband's full name in the typed signature (as in the example below) is a style often used for social purposes. It should not be used in business, and it should not be used when a married woman becomes a widow unless she indicates that that is her preference.

Sincerely,

Nancy O. Wells

Mrs. John A. Wells

f. A divorced woman who has resumed her original surname may use *Ms.* or *Miss* in any of the styles shown in ¶1366b–c. If she retains her ex-husband's surname, she may use *Ms.* or *Mrs.* in any of the styles shown in ¶1366b and e. (**EXCEPTION:** The style that uses the husband's full name in the typed signature is not appropriate for a divorced woman.)

1367 An administrative assistant who signs a letter at the boss's request customarily signs the boss's name and adds his or her own initials. However, if the boss prefers, the administrative assistant may sign the letter in his or her own name.

¶**1370**

Sincerely yours,

Robert H. Benedict
        DK

Robert H. Benedict
Production Manager

Sincerely yours,

Dorothy Kozinski

Ms. Dorothy Kozinski
Administrative Assistant
to Mr. Benedict

1368 If the person who signs for another is not the administrative assistant, either of the following forms may be used:

Sincerely yours,

(Miss) Alice R. Brentano

For Robert H. Benedict
Production Manager

Sincerely yours,

Robert H. Benedict
        ARB

Robert H. Benedict
Production Manager

1369 When two people have to sign a letter, arrange the two signature blocks side by side or one beneath the other.

a. If they are placed side by side, start the first signature block at the left margin and the second block at center. If this arrangement is used, the complimentary closing should also begin at the left margin. (This arrangement is appropriate for all letter styles.)

b. If the signature blocks are positioned one beneath the other, start typing the second block on the fourth line below the end of the first block, aligned at the left. In a modified-block-style letter, begin typing at center; however, in a block-style or simplified letter, begin typing at the left margin.

Reference Initials

1370 **a.** When the writer's name is given in the signature block, the simplest and most unobtrusive way to provide the necessary information is to give the typist's initials alone in small letters. (See the illustrations on pages 346, 349, and 350.)

NOTE: Do not include reference initials in a personal-business letter (see the illustration on page 348) or a social-business letter (see ¶¶1394–1395 and the illustration on page 401). Moreover, omit reference initials on letters you type yourself unless you need to distinguish them from letters prepared for you by someone else.

b. Type the initials of the typist at the left margin, on the second line below the writer's name and title. If the writer wants his or her initials used, they should precede the initials of the typist.

c. Type the initials either in small letters or in capital letters. When giving two sets of initials, type them both the same way for speed and simplicity.

TYPIST ONLY:	gdl	**OR**	GDL
WRITER AND TYPIST:	dmd/mhs	**OR**	DMD/MHS

➤ *For the use of autotext, see ¶1354a, note; for initials based on names like* McFarland *and* O'Leary, *see ¶516c.*

Continued on page 380

¶**1371**

d. If the writer's name is not given in the signature block, type the writer's initials and surname before the initials of the typist; for example, *BSDixon/rp*.

e. When the letter is written by someone other than the person who signs it, this fact may be indicated by showing the writer's and the typist's initials (not the signer's and the typist's).

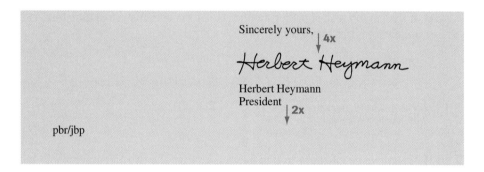

File Name Notation

1371 When you create documents using word processing software, each document needs a unique file name so that it can be readily retrieved from storage. Some organizations have specific guidelines for creating file names so that anyone in the organization can retrieve a document. If you are free to create your own file names, the following guidelines may be of some help.

a. A file name has three components: a name, a period (called a *dot*) used as a separator, and an extension typically consisting of 1 to 3 characters. Older programs allow a name preceding the dot of no more than 8 characters. Current Windows programs allow a name preceding the dot of up to 255 characters. Moreover, some current programs permit more than 3 characters after the dot and allow the use of more than one extension.

b. In creating a file name, try to make it as meaningful as possible. You can use the letters *a* to *z*, the figures *0* to *9*, and certain symbols. Do not use a period except to separate the name from the extension. Moreover, do not use any of the following characters: the forward slash (/), the back slash (\), the greater-than sign (>), the less-than sign (<), the asterisk (*), the question mark (?), the quotation mark ("), the colon (:), the semicolon (;), or the pipe symbol (|). Depending on the software that you are using, you may be able to use spaces in file names.

NOTE: Refer to your software help file or your user's manual to determine whether you can use spaces and to confirm which symbols may or may not be used.

c. If you are planning to file alphabetically, the first element in a file name may be the name of a person, an organization, or a subject. Try to limit the number of characters simply for the sake of efficiency. If you are dealing with a long name, abbreviate it in a way that suggests the full name. For example, a long name like *Yvonne Christopher* could be transformed into *chrstphr*—or better yet, *chrstphy* (to distinguish it from a file name created for *Henry Christopher*—*chrstphh*). An organizational name like *BankAmerica Corp.* could be abbreviated as *bankamer.* A subject name like *Direct Marketing Plans for 2003* could be shortened to *dmplns03.*

d. If you are planning to file numerically, the first element in a file name may be a date, a policy number, an order number, or something similar. If you are using dates, express months in a sequence that ranges from 01 to 12, days in a sequence that ranges from 01 to 31, and years in a sequence that ranges from 00 to 99. Express the date in year-month-day sequence; for example, the file name based on May 2, 2002, would be *020502.*

NOTE: If you create a lot of correspondence, you may want to include the first few letters of the recipient's surname following the date. For example, the file name for a letter sent to Alexander Grayson on June 4, 2003, might be *030604gry.* The file name for a letter sent to the American Automobile Association on the same day might be *030604aaa.*

e. If your software limits you to 8 characters before the dot, the 3-character extension that serves as the last component in a file name can be used to show (in abbreviated form) the date assigned to the document (in year-month-day order).

(1) To express the year, use the last digit of the year (for example, *0* for *2000*).

(2) To express the months from January to September, use the figures *1* to *9.* For October, November, and December, use the letters *o, n,* and *d.*

(3) To express days of the month, use the figures *1* to *31.* However, if you are planning to show the year as well, all figures over *9* will have to be expressed as a single character. Here is one possible code for the numbers 10 to 31:

10	11	12	13	14	15	16	17	18	19	20
a	b	c	d	e	f	g	h	i	j	k

21	22	23	24	25	26	27	28	29	30	31
l	m	n	o	p	q	r	s	t	u	v

NOTE: On the basis of the code shown above, an extension such as *28d* would signify *August 13, 2002; 4nn* would stand for *November 23, 2004.*

f. The 3-character extension may also be used:

(1) To show the initials of the writer.

(2) To indicate where a document falls in chronological order. (For example, *bonoj.12* would signify that a given document is the twelfth sent to J. Bono.)

(3) To identify a document in different stages of revision. (For example, *d1* could signify the first draft, *d3* the third draft, and *df* the final version.)

(4) To indicate the initials of the recipient of the letter if the primary component of the file name is the date.

NOTE: Some word processing programs will automatically insert an extension such as *.doc* or *.wpd* unless you provide one.

1372 It is not essential to provide a file name notation on your letters, but some organizations require it and some writers prefer to do so. If you want to insert a file name notation in a letter, type it on the line below the reference initials (see ¶1370). Some writers prefer to treat the file name notation as a reference notation and insert it after the phrase *When replying, refer to:.* (See ¶1316.)

¶1373

Enclosure Notation

1373 a. If one or more items are to be included in the envelope with the letter, indicate that fact by typing the word *Enclosure* (or an appropriate alternative) at the left margin, on the line below the reference initials or the file name notation, whichever comes last.

NOTE: Before sending the letter, make sure that the number of enclosures shown in the enclosure notation agrees with (1) the number cited in the body of the letter and (2) the number of items actually enclosed.

b. The following styles are commonly used:

```
Enclosure              2 Enclosures      Enclosures:
Enc. (See ¶503)        2 Enc.            1.   Check for $500
1 Enclosure            Enclosures 2      2.   Invoice A37512
Check enclosed         Enc. 2
```

c. Some writers use the term *Attachment* or *Att.* when the material is actually attached to the cover letter rather than simply enclosed.

➤ *For the use of autotext and macros, see the note on page 341; for the use of enclosure notations with copy notations, see ¶1379.*

1374 If material is to be sent separately instead of being enclosed with the letter, indicate this fact by typing *Separate cover* or *Under separate cover* on the line below the enclosure notation (if any) or on the line directly below the reference initials or the file name notation, whichever comes last. The following styles may be used:

```
Separate cover 1       Under separate cover:
                       1.   Annual report
                       2.   Product catalog
                       3.   Price list
```

Delivery Notation

1375 a. If a letter is to be delivered in a special way (other than ordinary first-class mail), type an appropriate notation on the line below the reference initials, the file name notation, or the enclosure notation, whichever comes last. Among the notations that could be used are *By certified mail, By Express Mail, By fax, By Federal Express* (**OR** *FedEx*), *By messenger, By registered mail,* and *By special delivery.*

```
crj                    HWM:FH                 tpg/wwc
Enc. 2                 By Federal Express     Enclosures 4
By certified mail      cc:  Mr. Fry           By fax
```

NOTE: If you send a letter by fax and want to record the fax number on your file copy, simply expand the delivery notation as follows:

```
By fax (203-555-4687)
```

b. When a letter is first faxed to the addressee and then sent through the mail as a confirmation copy, it is helpful to provide a "confirmation" notation on the letter being mailed so that the addressee will realize at once that the document now in hand is not a new letter but simply a duplicate of the fax. Type the confirmation notation on the second line below the date line (see ¶1314) or on the second line below any notation that follows the date (see ¶¶1315–1316). Starting at the left

¶1376

margin, type *Confirmation of fax sent on* and then supply the date on which the fax was transmitted.

NOTE: It is sometimes necessary to send a letter confirming a message already transmitted by e-mail. In such a case provide a confirmation notation like the example above, with a minor change in wording: *Confirmation of e-mail message sent on* [date on which message was transmitted].

➤ *For the use of autotext and macros, see the note on page 341.*

Copy Notation

1376 **a.** A copy notation lets the addressee know that one or more persons will also be sent a copy of the letter. The initials *cc* are still the most commonly used device for introducing this notation. Although the abbreviation originally referred to *carbon copies, cc* also means *copies* (in the same way that *pp.* means *pages* and *ll.* means *lines*). The initials *cc* may also stand for *courtesy copies;* indeed, that is how *cc* is defined in the Microsoft Word program.

Some writers object to using *cc,* now that the widespread use of photocopying has made the use of carbons obsolete when it comes to preparing duplicates of letters and memos. However, *cc* and its related form *bcc* (see ¶1378) continue to be widely used (regardless of how the copies are made), in much the same way that a *dial tone* continues to be heard on telephone instruments that use buttons rather than a rotary dial.

NOTE: The abbreviation *cc* is used in the heading of many memo templates and e-mail formats. (For illustrations see pages 394–395.)

b. Writers looking for an alternative to *cc* may use a single *c* or the phrase *Copies to* (or *Copy to*).

c. Start the copy notation on the line directly under any previous notation (such as reference initials or an enclosure notation). If there is no previous notation, type the copy notation on the second line below the writer's name and title.

d. Type *cc* or *c* or *Copies to* at the left margin, and follow it immediately with a colon.

e. If you are sending a copy to only one person, leave 1 or 2 spaces after the colon.

```
mfn                  Enclosure           pda/gfy
    cc:  Ms. Wu          c:  Mr. Case        Copy to:  Mrs. L. Bergamot
```

f. If you are sending copies to several people, start all names at the same point. To avoid alignment problems, either take advantage of a preset tab or set a tab 1 or 2 spaces after the colon. List the names in accordance with the rank of the persons or in alphabetic order. Type *cc* or *c* or *Copies to* only alongside the first name in the list.

```
    cc:  Ms. Aguirre      c:  Mr. Devoe
         Mr. Boulet           Ms. Eggleston
         Mrs. Corbin          Mrs. Franco
    Copies to:  Mrs. Gold
                Mr. Hunsicker
                Ms. Ismail
```

Letters and Memos

13

¶1377

1377 When first names or initials are given along with last names, omit personal titles *(Mr., Miss, Mrs., and Ms.)* except in formal letters. Moreover, do not use personal titles if nicknames are given with last names.

c: James Diaz	cc: J. Diaz	cc: Jim Diaz
Kenneth Eustis	K. Eustis	Ken Eustis
Margaret Foster	M. Foster	Peggy Foster
Katherine Gabor	K. Gabor	Kay Gabor

1378 If you do not want the addressee to know that one or more persons are also being sent a copy of the letter, use a *blind copy notation.*

a. Print the original letter plus any copies on which the regular copy notation is to appear.

b. Print the blind copies one at a time, with a blind copy notation showing the name of the designated recipient.

c. Under certain circumstances, you may wish to let all recipients of blind copies know who the others are.

d. Type the blind copy notation on the second line below the last item in the letter (whether reference initials, an enclosure notation, or any other notation).

e. The form of a blind copy notation should follow the form of the copy notation. If you have used *cc* or *c,* then use *bcc* or *bc* accordingly. If you have used *Copies to,* use *Blind copies to.*

f. The file copy should show all the blind copy notations, even though the individual copies do not. Whether the file copy is stored in computer memory or in hardcopy form, you may need to use the file copy later on to make additional copies for distribution. In such cases make sure that no prior blind copy notation appears on these new copies unless you want it to.

1379 When a letter carries both an enclosure notation and a copy notation, it is assumed that the enclosures accompany only the original letter. If a copy of the enclosures is also to accompany a copy of the letter, this fact may be indicated as follows:

cc: Mr. D. P. Wellak	(will receive only the letter)
Ms. N. A. Warren	(will receive only the letter)
cc/enc: Mr. J. Baldwin	(will receive the letter and the enclosures)
Mrs. G. Conger	(will receive the letter and the enclosures)

1380 A copy is not usually signed unless the letter is addressed to several people and the copy is intended for one of the people named in the salutation. However, a check mark is usually made on each copy next to the name of the person or department for whom that copy is intended. As an alternative, you may use a highlighting marker to identify the recipient of each copy.

c: Ms. M. Starr ✓	c: Ms. M. Starr	c: Ms. M. Starr
Mr. W. Fried	Mr. W. Fried ✓	Mr. W. Fried
Mrs. C. Bell	Mrs. C. Bell	Mrs. C. Bell ✓

NOTE: When an unsigned copy is likely to strike the recipient as cold and impersonal, it is appropriate for the writer to add a brief handwritten note at the bottom of the copy and sign or initial it.

➤ *For the use of autotext and macros, see the note on page 341.*

¶**1384**

Postscript

1381 **a.** A postscript can be effectively used to express an idea that has been deliberately withheld from the body of a letter; stating this idea at the very end gives it strong emphasis. A postscript may also be used to express an afterthought; however, if the afterthought contains something central to the meaning of the letter, the reader may conclude that the letter was badly organized.

b. When a postscript is used:

(1) Start the postscript on the second line below the copy notation (or whatever was typed last). If the paragraphs are indented, indent the first line of the postscript (see the illustration on page 348). Otherwise, begin it at the left margin.

(2) Type *PS:* or *PS.* before the first word of the postscript, or omit the abbreviation altogether. (If *PS* is used, leave 1 or 2 spaces between the colon or period and the first word.)

(3) Use *PPS:* or *PPS.* (or no abbreviation at all) at the beginning of an additional postscript, and treat this postscript as a separate paragraph.

```
PS:  Instead of dashing for the airport as soon as the meeting
is over, why don't you have dinner and spend the night with us
and then go back on Saturday morning?

PPS:  Better yet, why don't you bring Joyce with you and plan
to stay for the whole weekend?
```

Continuation Pages

1382 Use plain paper of the same quality as the letterhead (but never a letterhead) for all but the first page of a long letter.

1383 Use the same left and right margins that you used on the first page.

1384 If you use the header feature in your word processing program, type a continuation-page heading consisting of the following: the name of the addressee, the page number, and the date. Either of the following formats is acceptable in the modified-block letter style. The three-line format is preferred in the block and simplified letter styles.

Mrs. Laura R. Austin	2	September 30, 2002

↓2 or 3x

OR:

Mrs. Laura R. Austin
Page 2
September 30, 2002

↓2 or 3x

NOTE: If you are using a letter template provided by your word processing software, the program may automatically insert a continuation-page heading and correctly number each continuation page.

¶1385

1385 **a.** Leave 1 or 2 blank lines below the last line of the continuation-page heading and resume typing the letter. If you use the header feature of your word processing software to create a continuation-page heading, be sure there is at least 1 blank line between the header and the text of the letter.

> Ms. Jenny Applegate   2   February 23, 2001
> ↓ **2x**
> and comparison shopping on Web sites will help you research products and compare prices to find the best bargains.

OR:

> Ms. Jenny Applegate   2   February 23, 2001
> │ **3x**
> ▼
> and comparison shopping on Web sites will help you research products and compare prices to find the best bargains.

NOTE: If you use Microsoft Word's header feature for the one-line format, you will automatically get 2 blank lines below the continuation heading. If you use the same feature for the three-line format, you will need to insert 1 or 2 blank lines in the header box before resuming the text of the letter.

b. Do not divide a short paragraph (one that contains only two or three lines) at the bottom of a page. For a paragraph of four or more lines, always leave at least two lines of the paragraph at the bottom of the previous page. Carry over at least two lines to the continuation page. (See also ¶1356d.)

c. Never use a continuation page just for the closing section of a business letter. (The complimentary closing should be preceded by at least two lines of text.)

1386 Leave a bottom margin of at least 1 inch. The last page may run short. (See ¶1306.)

1387 Do not divide the last word on a page.

Envelopes

1388 **Addressing Envelopes**

a. The following chart indicates which envelopes may be used, depending on the size of the stationery and the way in which the stationery is folded (see ¶1391).

Stationery	Fold	Envelope
Letter ($8^1/2$" x 11")	In thirds In half, then in thirds	No. 10 ($9^1/2$" x $4^1/8$") No. $6^3/4$ ($6^1/2$" x $3^5/8$")

Executive
  (MS Word: $7^1/2$" x 10")
  (WordPerfect: $7^1/4$" x $10^1/2$")
	In thirds
	In thirds
		No. 9 ($8^7/8$" x $3^7/8$")
		Monarch ($7^1/2$" x $3^7/8$")

Half Letter ($5^1/2$" x $8^1/2$")	In thirds	No. $6^3/4$ ($6^1/2$" x $3^5/8$")

NOTE: If you are using stationery and envelopes other than those shown above, consult the standards established by the U.S. Postal Service (USPS) for envelope size and thickness in order to qualify for automated processing.

¶**1389**

b. Using the envelope feature of a word processing program, you can select the envelope size you plan to use from a preestablished menu. With regard to the placement of the return address and the mailing address, you can accept the default placement specifications provided for the envelope size you have selected, or you can modify them to suit your needs. You can also use a custom-size envelope (assuming your printer will support it) and establish appropriate placement specifications for that size.

➤ *For an illustration of an envelope prepared by Microsoft Word (using the envelope feature and all the default specifications), see page 388.*

1389 The Inside-Address Style for Addressing Envelopes

The traditional style for addressing envelopes—and the style most commonly seen on envelopes—uses capital and small letters plus punctuation as appropriate. This style may be thought of as the inside-address style, because it follows all aspects of the format for inside addresses, as discussed in ¶¶1317–1343. The advantage of using this style on envelopes is that you can use your computer to generate the same address information in both places. Moreover, the OCRs (optical character readers) used by the USPS are programmed to read this traditional style of address.

➤ *For the use of the all-cap style in addressing envelopes, see ¶1390.*

When using the inside-address style:

a. Always use single spacing and block each line at the left.

➤ *See the illustrations on pages 388–389. For specific details on the handling of elements within the address block, see ¶¶1317–1343.*

b. Capitalize the first letter of every word in an address except (1) prepositions under four letters (like *of* and *for*), (2) conjunctions under four letters (like *and*), and (3) the articles *the, a,* and *an* when they are used within a name or title. (Under certain circumstances even some of these short words are capitalized. See ¶¶1325a, 1329e.)

c. Type the city, state, and ZIP Code on the last line. If space limitations make it impossible for the ZIP Code to fit on the same line, the ZIP Code may be typed on the line directly below, blocked at the left.

d. Leave 1 space between the state name and the ZIP Code. (The USPS recommends either 1 or 2 spaces.)

e. The state name may be spelled out or given as a two-letter abbreviation. Either form is correct for use with a ZIP Code. (See ¶1341.)

f. The next-to-last line in the address block should contain a street address, a post office box number, a rural route address, or a highway contract address. (See ¶¶1317c, 1331–1338.)

```
Elvera Agresta, M.D.              Mr. Peter Schreiber
218 Oregon Pioneer's Building    Director of Research
320 Southwest Stark Street        Colby Electronics Inc.
Portland, Oregon 97204-2628       P.O. Box 6524
                                  Raleigh, NC 27628
```

Continued on page 388

¶1389

g. When using the envelope template of a word processing program to prepare an envelope, accept the default positions for the mailing address and the return address. Doing so will ensure that the mailing address falls within the OCR "read area" and that the return address does not.

   NOTE: The OCR read area starts $2^3/4$ inches above the bottom edge of the envelope, ends $5/8$ inch from the bottom edge, and extends horizontally so as to end $1/2$ inch in from the left and right edges. Do not allow any notations to fall alongside or below the OCR read area.

h. Your software may permit you to insert the USPS POSTNET bar code above or below the address block. (See ¶1390b.) Before you take advantage of this option, make sure that your complete database of mailing addresses has been certified by means of address-matching software approved by the USPS. For further information, contact your local Postal Service business center. (See also ¶1339, note.)

No. 10 envelope created by Microsoft Word for Windows, using all the default specifications.

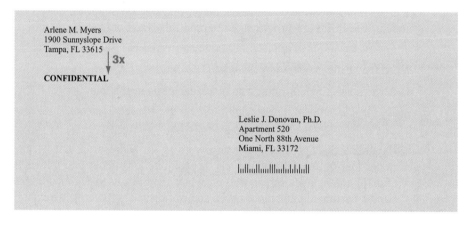

i. When using a window envelope, adjust the placement of the inside address on the material to be inserted so that there will be a minimum clearance of $1/8$ inch (and preferably $1/4$ inch) between the edges of the window and all four sides of the address block, no matter how much the inserted material shifts around inside the envelope. (See also ¶1391d.)

j. To facilitate OCR processing, make sure that the lines in the address block are parallel to the bottom edge of the envelope. Moreover, there should be good contrast between the typed address and the color of the envelope; black type on a white background is preferred. In addition, do not use a script or italic font, and avoid dot matrix print, especially if the dots that make up each character do not touch. The type should be clear and sharp, and adjacent characters should not touch or overlap.

k. When the envelope contains a printed return address for an organization, it is not possible to type the writer's name above the printed address. In such cases you may write the name in by hand above the printed address, or you may type the name on the second line below the printed return address.

No. 6³/4 envelope with mailing notation.

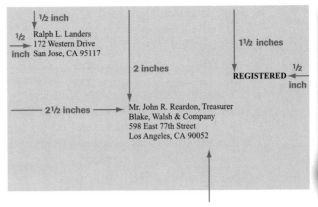

For OCR processing, start the mailing address no higher than 2³/4 inches from the bottom edge. Leave a minimum bottom margin of ⁵/8 inch and minimum side margins of ¹/2 inch. (See ¶1389j.)

No. 10 envelope with confidential notation.

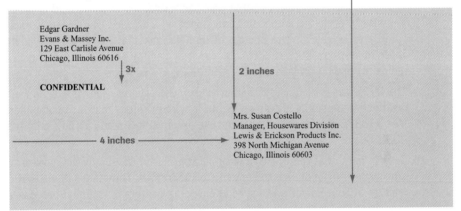

l. If you have to create a return address, it should contain the following information, arranged on single-spaced lines, aligned at the left: (1) the name of the writer, (2) the name of the company (if appropriate), (3) a street address or post office box number, and (4) the city, state, and ZIP Code. If you are using the envelope template of a word processing program, accept the default position for the return address.

m. If a notation such as *Confidential, Personal, Please Forward,* or *Hold for Arrival* is to be used, type it on the third line below the return address. Align the notation at the left with the return address. Begin each main word with a capital letter, and use boldface, italics, or underlining. For special emphasis type *Confidential* and *Personal* in all-capital letters.

NOTE: Do not allow any notations or graphics to fall alongside or below the area established for the mailing address (see ¶1389j). Copy placed in these locations will interfere with OCR processing.

Continued on page 390

¶1390

n. If an attention line was used within the letter itself, it should appear on the enve-lope as well. The attention line should be typed as the first line of the address block (see ¶1345).

➤ *See ¶¶1344–1345, note, on avoiding the use of attention lines.*

o. If a special mailing procedure is used, type the appropriate notation (such as *REGISTERED*) in all-capital letters in the upper right corner of the envelope. Type the notation 1½ inches from the top edge or on the third line below the bot-tom edge of the stamp, whichever is lower. Position the notation so that it ends ½ inch from the right margin.

➤ *See the illustration at the top of page 389.*

p. Make sure that the spelling of the name and address on the envelope agrees with the spelling shown in the inside address (and with the spelling shown on your records or the incoming document).

➤ *For letters being sent to two or more people at the same address, see ¶1320b.*

1390 The All-Cap Style for Addressing Envelopes

The all-cap style for addressing envelopes was devised by the U.S. Postal Service (USPS) primarily for the benefit of high-volume mailers who must contend with space limitations for the address blocks they generate by computer. The all-cap style typically appears on labels to be used in a mass mailing.

The USPS has issued many brochures urging everyone—individuals as well as orga-nizations—to use the all-cap style, but it acknowledges that the inside-address style (see ¶1389) is quite acceptable for use on envelopes and can be easily read by the USPS OCRs.

Keep in mind that the USPS now subjects *all* letter-sized mail and postcards to OCR processing—even mail with handwritten addresses. Only those items that cannot be read by OCR are diverted to special encoding centers for manual processing.

NOTE: If your organization maintains its mailing lists on tapes or disks and uses these to generate inside addresses in letters (as well as address blocks on envelopes), the all-cap (and no-punctuation) style designed for the envelope will look inappropriate inside the letter. Moreover, the heavy use of abbreviations in the all-cap style (see ¶1390a) often makes the address unintelligible to readers—another reason for not using this format for inside addresses. In such cases it makes sense to use the inside-address style described in ¶1389. You will then have a format that looks attractive as an inside address and that is also OCR-readable when used on an envelope.

When using the all-cap style:

a. Keep in mind the maximum number of keystrokes you can get in any one line. If necessary, use abbreviations freely and omit all punctuation except the hyphen in the ZIP+4 Code.

NOTE: To keep the line length down to 28 keystrokes, the USPS has provided three special sets of abbreviations: one for state names; another for long names of cities, towns, and places; a third for names of streets and roads and general terms like *University* or *Institute*. By means of these abbreviations (see the ZIP Code directory), it is possible to limit the last line of any domestic address to 28 keystrokes.

```
Pass-a-Grille Beach, Florida 33741-9999   (39 keystrokes)
12345678901234567890123456789012345678 9
PAS-A-GRL BCH FL 33741-9999               (27 keystrokes)
```

Abbreviations such as those shown above serve to facilitate OCR processing, but they also serve in some cases to make the address incomprehensible to all except devoted students of USPS manuals. (Read the copy in the illustration on page 446.)

b. Type the lines in all-capital letters, single-spaced and blocked at the left. Try to hold the address block to 5 lines. If possible, insert the USPS POSTNET bar code *above* or *below* the address block. (See the illustration below and the one on page 388.) In either position the top of the bar code should fall within 4 inches from the bottom and come no closer than 1/2 inch to the left or right edge of the envelope. (See ¶1389g, note.)

No. 10 envelope showing a mailing label and the all-cap address style.

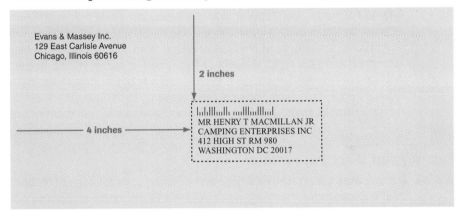

c. Type the city, state, and ZIP Code on the last line. If space limitations make it impossible for the ZIP Code to fit on the same line, the ZIP Code may be typed on the line directly below, blocked at the left.

d. Leave 1 space between the state name and the ZIP Code. (The USPS recommends either 1 or 2 spaces.)

e. Express the state name as a two-letter abbreviation.

f. The next-to-last line in the address block should contain a street address, a post office box number, a rural route address, or a highway contract address. (See ¶¶1317c, 1331–1338.)

g. If a room number, a suite number, or an apartment number is part of the address, insert it immediately after the street address on the same line. (See examples in ¶1390b and h.) When this information will not fit on the same line as the street address, place it on the line above but never on the line below. (See examples in ¶¶1317b, 1318b.)

Continued on page 392

¶1391

NOTE: Do not use the pound sign (#) if a term such as *Room, Suite,* or *Apartment* is available. If you do use the pound sign, the USPS asks that 1 space be left between the symbol and the number that follows; for example:

```
616 Ohio Avenue # 203
```

h. If an attention line is to be included in the address, insert it on the line directly above the organizational name or (in the absence of an organizational name) on the line directly above the street address or post office box number. If a serial number of some kind (for example, an account number or a file reference number) is required, insert it as the first line of the address block. (See ¶1345.)

```
H 048369 1078 AT5        OR    H 048369 1078 AT5
MRS M R TURKEVICH              ATTN MRS M R TURKEVICH
BROCK & WILSON CORP            BROCK & WILSON CORP
79 WALL ST STE 1212            79 WALL ST STE 1212
NEW YORK NY 10005-4101         NEW YORK NY 10005-4101
```

i. To facilitate OCR processing, make sure that the mailing address starts no higher than $2^3/4$ inches from the bottom edge, falls no lower than $5/8$ inch from the bottom edge, and comes no closer to either the left or the right edge than $1/2$ inch. Do not allow any notations or graphics to fall alongside or below the area established for the mailing address. Make sure that the lines in the address block are parallel to the bottom edge of the envelope. Moreover, there should be good contrast between the typed address and the color of the envelope; black type on a white background is preferred. Do not use a script or italic font, and avoid dot matrix print, especially if the dots that make up each character do not touch. The type should be clear and sharp. Adjacent characters should not touch or overlap.

Folding and Inserting Letters

1391 The following paragraphs describe several methods for folding letters and inserting them into envelopes. See the chart in ¶1388a to determine which method is appropriate for the stationery and envelope you are using.

a. To fold a letter in thirds:

 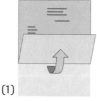 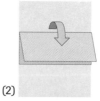 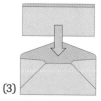

(1)   (2)   (3)

(1) Bring the bottom third of the letter up and make a crease.

(2) Fold the top of the letter down to within $3/8$ inch of the crease you made in step 1. Then make the second crease.

(3) The creased edge made in step 2 goes into the envelope first.

NOTE: Use this method for $8^1/2" \times 11"$ stationery with a No. 10 envelope; executive stationery with a No. 9 or a Monarch envelope; $5^1/2" \times 8^1/2"$ stationery with a No. $6^3/4$ envelope.

b. To fold a letter in half and then in thirds:

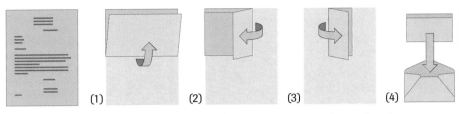

(1)   (2)   (3)   (4)

(1) Bring the bottom edge to within 3/8 inch of the top edge and make a crease.

(2) Fold from the right edge, making the fold a little less than one-third the width of the sheet before you crease it.

(3) Fold from the left edge, bringing it to within 3/8 inch of the crease you made in step 2 before you crease the sheet again.

(4) Insert the left creased edge into the envelope first. This will leave the crease you made in step 2 near the flap of the envelope.

NOTE: Use this method for $8^{1}/_{2}$" × 11" stationery with a No. $6^{3}/_{4}$ envelope.

c. To fold a letter in half:

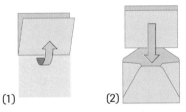

(1)   (2)

(1) Bring the bottom edge to within 3/8 inch of the top edge and make a crease.

(2) Insert the creased edge into the envelope first.

NOTE: Use this method for $5^{1}/_{2}$" × $8^{1}/_{2}$" stationery with a No. $5^{3}/_{8}$ envelope.

d. To fold a letter for insertion into a window envelope:

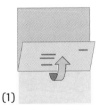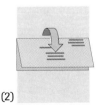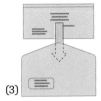

(1)   (2)   (3)

(1) Place the letter *face down* with the letterhead at the top, and fold the bottom third of the letter up.

(2) Fold the top third down so that the inside address shows.

(3) Insert the letter with the inside address toward the *front* of the envelope. The inside address should now be fully readable through the window of the envelope. Moreover, there should be at least 1/8 inch (and preferably 1/4 inch) between all four sides of the address and the edges of the window, no matter how much the letter slides around in the envelope.

Letters and Memos

13

¶1392

Memos

1392 An interoffice memo (or memorandum) is intended to expedite the flow of written communication within an organization. For that reason many organizations provide computerized formats (and less frequently, printed forms) in order to simplify and standardize the treatment of key information.

Depending on the circumstances, a memo may be as terse as a telegram, as impersonal as a formal announcement, or as warm and casual as a personal note. Those circumstances will help you determine whether a particular memo should contain or omit such features as a salutation or a signature line.

If your organization has not established a standard format, your word processing software may provide memo templates that you can use as is or modify to suit your preferences. Here are three sample templates provided by the Microsoft Word program.

**"Professional" memo template (using 10-point Arial),
provided by Microsoft Word for Windows.**

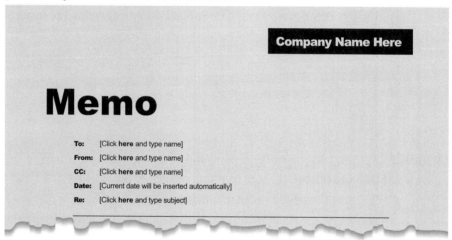

**"Contemporary" memo template (using 10-point Times New Roman),
provided by Microsoft Word for Windows.**

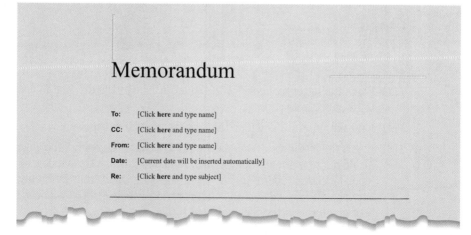

"Elegant" memo template (using 10-point Garamond), provided by Microsoft Word for Windows.

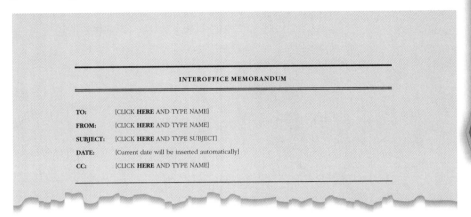

INTEROFFICE MEMORANDUM

TO: [CLICK **HERE** AND TYPE NAME]

FROM: [CLICK **HERE** AND TYPE NAME]

SUBJECT: [CLICK **HERE** AND TYPE SUBJECT]

DATE: [Current date will be inserted automatically]

CC: [CLICK **HERE** AND TYPE NAME]

You can always modify a memo template or create your own format. The following rule (¶1393) provides guidelines for formatting memos, and the illustrations on pages 396 and 397 show memos formatted according to these guidelines.

Please remember: There is no one correct format for a memo. Design the format to meet your needs and those of the organization you work for.

NOTE: Because many memos are now distributed as e-mail, see ¶¶1708–1711 for special guidelines on preparing e-mail messages.

1393 When preparing a memo on plain paper or letterhead stationery, observe the following guidelines. (Also see the illustrations on pages 396–397.)

a. For side margins, either choose the default settings (1.25 inches for Microsoft Word, 1 inch for WordPerfect) or, for better appearance and legibility, choose even wider side margins (as shown in the table in ¶1305b).

b. Leave a top margin of about 2 inches. (Space down 6 times from the default top margin of 1 inch.) If you are using stationery with a deep letterhead, begin typing about 0.5 inch below the letterhead.

NOTE: You can reduce the top margin to 1 inch if doing so will make a continuation page unnecessary.

c. If you are using plain paper, you can create a heading such as *INTEROFFICE MEMORANDUM* or simply *MEMORANDUM* (as shown in the illustrations at the bottom of page 396 and the top of page 397). In that case reduce the top margin to 1 inch to accommodate long messages and avoid the need for a continuation page.

d. The heading of the memo should include the following guide words—*TO, FROM, DATE,* and *SUBJECT.*

NOTE: If you do not use a heading such as *INTEROFFICE MEMORANDUM* or *MEMORANDUM,* change *TO* (the first guide word) to *MEMO TO* (as shown in the illustration at the top of page 396).

Continued on page 396

¶1393

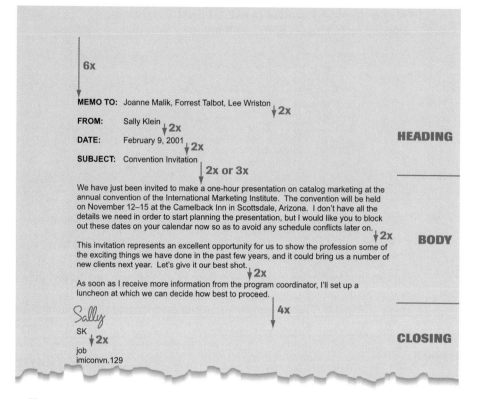

e. You may also wish to add a number of other guide words. For example, below the guide word *TO* you could insert *COPIES TO.* If you work in a large organization and are sending memos to people who do not know you, then below the guide word *FROM* you might want to insert such guide words as *DEPARTMENT, FLOOR, PHONE NO.,* or *FAX NO.* Start typing the guide words at the left margin and use double spacing. Type the guide words in bold all-capital letters, and follow each with a colon.

NOTE: If you plan to use a large number of guide words (beyond *TO, FROM, DATE,* and *SUBJECT*), you may want to arrange the guide words in two columns to prevent the heading from taking too much space. In that case, start the second column of guide words at center (as shown in the illustration below).

Interoffice Memorandum

To:	Bernard O'Kelly	From:	Janet R. Wiley
Dept.:	Special Sales	Dept.:	Software Products
Floor:	4	Floor and Ext.:	7/3825
Subject:	Test Marketing Arrangements	Date:	April 7, 2003

MEMORANDUM

TO: Bernard O'Kelly ↓**2x**

COPIES TO: Steve Kubat, Pat Rosario

FROM: Janet R. Wiley _JRW_

DATE: April 7, 2003

SUBJECT: Test Marketing Arrangements ↓**2 or 3x**

Dear Bernie: ↓**2x**

Let me try to summarize the outcome of our excellent meeting last Friday, in which we discussed how your group might sell our product lines to the markets you serve. ↓**2x**

1. Steve Kubat, chief product manager for my group, will provide you with product descriptions, catalog sheets, ad mats, and current price lists. If you need additional information, just call Steve (or me in his absence) and we'll be glad to help in any way that we can. ↓**2x**

2. We will pay you an 18 percent commission on all orders you generate for our products. Please forward a copy of these orders to Steve, who will arrange to have the commission credited to your account. ↓**2x**

3. We very much appreciate your offer to give us three hours at your weeklong sales meeting next month to present our products to your field staff. We'll be there. ↓**2x**

4. We have agreed to give this new arrangement a six-month test to determine (a) how much additional sales revenue you and your people can produce with our products and (b) what effect, if any, this special marketing effort will have on your sales of other products. At the end of the test period, we will analyze the results and decide whether to continue the arrangement, modify it in some way, or abandon it altogether. ↓**2x**

I don't think we'll be abandoning it, Bernie. In fact, I feel quite confident that this new arrangement is going to produce significant gains in sales and profits for both of us. I look forward to working with you to make it all happen. ↓**2x**

imm
okellyb.347

f. Set a tab or use a default tab so that the entries following the guide words will all block at the left and will clear the longest guide word by a minimum of 2 spaces.

g. After the guide words *TO* (or *MEMO TO*) and *FROM*, the names of the addressee and the writer are usually given without personal titles *(Mr., Miss, Mrs., Ms.)*. Indeed, when you are doing a memo to someone within your immediate unit, the use of initials or simply a first name may suffice. In short, the way you treat these names will depend on the relative formality or informality of the occasion.

    John A. Mancuso   **OR**   JAM   **OR**   Jack

h. If you want to provide additional information (such as a department name or title, a phone number, or a fax number), you can add the appropriate guide words to

¶1393

the heading of the memo, or you can insert the relevant information after the person's name. For example:

```
Cynthia Chen, Accounting Manager
OR Cynthia Chen (Ext. 4782)
```

i. If the memo is being addressed to two or three people, try to fit all the names on the same line.

MEMO TO: Hal Parker, Meryl Crawford, Mike Monagle

If there are too many names to fit on the same line, then list the names in one or more single-spaced columns alongside *TO* or *MEMO TO.* Leave 1 blank line before the next guide word and fill-in entry.

MEMO TO: Louise Landes
Fred Mendoza
Jim Norton
Ruth O'Hare

FROM: Neil Sundstrom

---

j. If listing all the addressees in the heading of a memo looks unattractive, then after the guide words *TO* or *MEMO TO,* type *See Distribution Below* or something similar (see the illustration on page 399). Then on the second line below the reference initials, the file name notation, or the enclosure notation (whichever comes last), type *Distribution.* Use capital and small letters, followed by a colon, and italicize or underline the word for emphasis. (If you use italics, italicize the colon as well. If you underline, do not underline the colon.) Leave 1 blank line and then list the names of the individuals who are to receive a copy of the memo. Arrange the names either by rank or in alphabetic order, and type them blocked at the left margin. (If space is tight, arrange the names in two or more columns.)

NOTE: For purposes of actual distribution, simply place a check mark next to one of the listed names to indicate who is to receive that particular copy. As an alternative, use a highlighting marker to identify the recipient of each copy.

k. If the fill-in after the guide word *SUBJECT* is long, type it in two or more single-spaced lines of roughly equal length. Align all turnover lines with the start of the first line of the fill-in. (For illustrations, see pages 415 and 506.)

l. Begin typing the body of the memo on the second or third line below the last line in the heading. (The illustration on page 399 shows the use of only 1 blank line between the heading and the body of the memo. The illustrations at the top of pages 396 and 397 show the use of 2 blank lines.)

NOTE: An interoffice memo ordinarily does not require a salutation, especially if the memo is an impersonal announcement being sent to a number of people or the staff at large. (See, for example, the illustration below.) However, when a memo is directed to one person (as in the illustration on page 397), many writers use a salutation—such as *Dear Andy* or *Andy* alone—to keep the memo from seeming cold or impersonal. (If a salutation is used, begin typing the body of the memo on the second line below the salutation.)

6x

MEMO TO: See Distribution Below   ↓ 2x

FROM: Stanley W. Venner (Ext. 3835)

DATE: May 10, 2002

SUBJECT: Car Rentals   ↓ 2 or 3x

We have just been informed that car rental rates will be increased by $1 to $2 a day, effective July 1.   ↓ 2x

This daily rate increase can be more than offset if you refill the gasoline tank before returning your rental car to the local agency. According to our latest information, the car rental companies are charging an average of 32 percent more per gallon than the gas stations in the same area. Therefore, you can help us achieve substantial savings and keep expenses down by remembering to fill up the gas tank before turning your rental car in.   ↓ 2x

SWV   ↓ 2x

jmb
venner.25a   ↓ 2x

Distribution: ↓ 2x

G. Bonardi
D. Catlin
S. Folger
✓ V. Jellinek
E. Kasendorf
P. Legrande
T. Pacheco
F. Sullivan
J. Trotter
W. Zysk

m. Use single spacing and either block the paragraphs or indent the first line of each paragraph 0.5 inch. Leave 1 blank line between paragraphs.

NOTE: If a numbered list appears within the body of a memo, the numbered items may be separated by 1 blank line for a more open look (as in the illustration on page 397). If you use the numbered list feature of your word processing program and accept all the defaults, the list will be typed single-spaced. (See ¶1357d for illustrations showing lists typed with and without space between items.)

n. Although memos do not require a signature line, some writers prefer to end their memos in this way. In that case type the writer's name or initials on the *second*

¶1393

line below the last line of the message (as shown in the illustration on page 399). If the writer plans to insert a handwritten signature or initials above the signature line, type the signature line on the *fourth* line below (as shown in the illustration at the top of page 396) to allow room for the handwriting. If the writer simply inserts handwritten initials next to the typed name in the heading (as in the illustration on page 397), omit the signature line altogether.

NOTE: The position of the signature line may vary. If all the lines in the memo heading begin at the left margin (see, for example, the illustration at the top of page 396), type the signature line at the left margin as well. If the memo uses a two-column heading format (as in the illustration at the bottom of page 396), start the signature line at the same point as the fill-ins for the second column in the heading.

o. Type the reference initials (see ¶1370) at the left margin, on the second line below the end of the message or the writer's typed name or initials, whichever comes last. (See the illustrations on pages 396, 397, and 399.)

p. Type a file name notation (if needed) on the line below the reference initials. (See ¶¶1371–1372 and the illustrations on 396, 397, and 399.)

q. Type an enclosure notation (if needed) on the line below the reference initials or the file name notation, whichever comes last. (See ¶1373.)

r. Type a copy notation (if needed) on the line below the reference initials, the file name notation, or the enclosure notation, whichever comes last. Use the same style for the copy notation as in a letter. (See ¶¶1376–1380.) If the addressee of the memo is not intended to know that a copy of the memo is being sent to one or more other persons, use a blind copy notation. (See ¶1378.)

NOTE: As an alternative, place the copy notation in the heading. (See the illustration on page 397.) On the second line below *TO* or *MEMO TO*, insert the guide words *COPIES TO* and then insert the appropriate names at the right, starting at the same point as the other fill-ins in the heading.

s. If the memo is of a confidential nature, type the word *CONFIDENTIAL* in bold all-capital letters. Center the confidential notation on the second line below the last line of the memo heading.

↓2x

CONFIDENTIAL ↓2 or 3x

Begin typing the body of the memo on the second or third line below this notation. (See ¶1393l.)

t. If the memo continues beyond the first page, use the software header feature to insert a continuation heading on a new sheet of paper. (Use the same style as shown in ¶1384 for a letter.) Leave 1 or 2 blank lines between the continuation-page heading and the message. (See ¶¶1385–1387 for additional details on continuing the message from one page to another.)

➤ *For the use of autotext and macros, see the note on page 341.*

Social-Business Correspondence

1394 The term *social-business correspondence* applies to the following types of letters:

a. Executive correspondence addressed to high-level executives, officials, and dignitaries. (Unlike ordinary business correspondence—which deals with sales, production, finance, advertising, and other routine commercial matters—these letters deal with such topics as corporate policy and issues of social responsibility, and they are written in a more formal style.)

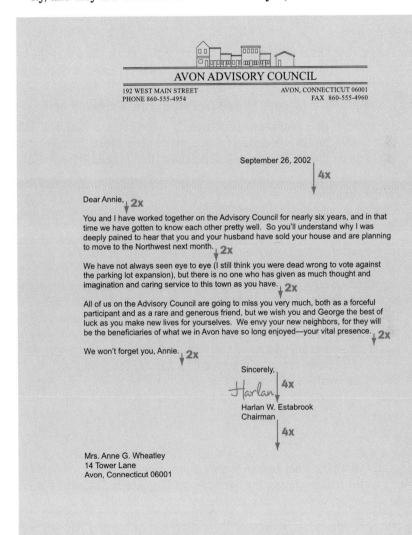

AVON ADVISORY COUNCIL

192 WEST MAIN STREET
PHONE 860-555-4954

AVON, CONNECTICUT 06001
FAX 860-555-4960

September 26, 2002
↓ 4x

Dear Annie, ↓ 2x

You and I have worked together on the Advisory Council for nearly six years, and in that time we have gotten to know each other pretty well. So you'll understand why I was deeply pained to hear that you and your husband have sold your house and are planning to move to the Northwest next month. ↓ 2x

We have not always seen eye to eye (I still think you were dead wrong to vote against the parking lot expansion), but there is no one who has given as much thought and imagination and caring service to this town as you have. ↓ 2x

All of us on the Advisory Council are going to miss you very much, both as a forceful participant and as a rare and generous friend, but we wish you and George the best of luck as you make new lives for yourselves. We envy your new neighbors, for they will be the beneficiaries of what we in Avon have so long enjoyed—your vital presence. ↓ 2x

We won't forget you, Annie. ↓ 2x

Sincerely,

Harlan ↓ 4x

Harlan W. Estabrook
Chairman
↓ 4x

Mrs. Anne G. Wheatley
14 Tower Lane
Avon, Connecticut 06001

Continued on page 402

Letters and Memos

13

¶1395

b. Letters expressing praise, concern, or condolence to someone within or outside the organization. (The occasion that prompts the letter could be exceptional performance on the job or in the community, an employment anniversary, the death or serious illness of a family member, or an upcoming retirement. Such letters may be formal or informal, depending on the relationship between the writer and the person addressed.)

c. Letters to business associates within or outside the company on purely social matters.

1395 Social-business correspondence differs from ordinary business correspondence in several ways:

a. The inside address is typed at the bottom of the letter, aligned at the left margin and starting on the fourth line below the writer's signature or title (whichever comes last).

b. The salutation is followed by a comma rather than a colon.

c. Reference initials and notations pertaining to file name, enclosures, delivery, and copies are typically omitted. (It would make good sense, however, to put such notations on the file copy in case this information is needed later on.)

d. If the letter requires a *Personal* or *Confidential* notation, place the notation only on the envelope, not on the letter itself. (For the appropriate placement of the notation on an envelope, see ¶1389m and the second illustration on page 389.)

NOTE: Include the *Personal* or *Confidential* notation on the file copy.

e. Social-business correspondence is also *more* formal or *less* formal than ordinary business correspondence. For example, correspondence to high-level officials and dignitaries is customarily more formal. In such cases use the word style for numbers (see ¶¶404–406) and one of the special salutations listed in Section 18. However, in letters to business associates who are also close friends, the salutation and the complimentary closing may be very informal, and the writer's typed signature and title—and even the inside address—may be omitted. Moreover, when such letters are purely personal in nature, the writer may use plain stationery and omit the return address.

Labels

1396 If you are using the label feature of a word processing program, you can quickly prepare a wide variety of labels (for example, mailing labels, file folder labels, and cassette labels) by following these guidelines:

a. Use commercially prepared labels (packaged in rolls and sheets) that have been specifically designed for the purpose you have in mind and that are compatible with your printer.

b. Many software programs provide a menu of label types and sizes. When you select the type and size you want to use, the program automatically sets up the label windows. All you need to do is type the necessary information in each window (as illustrated on page 403).

NOTE: You can also create your own specifications for a special type of label. See your software user's manual for the procedures to follow.

c. Before you begin to type text in each label window, consider the maximum number of characters you can fit on one line and the number of lines you can fit on one label. For example, if you are preparing mailing labels, you may very well find that some mailing addresses as you would style them in an inside address are too wide to fit on the labels you are planning to use. In such cases use the all-cap style designed by the U.S. Postal Service. The all-cap style, with its heavy reliance on abbreviations, was specifically created to take such limitations into account. (See ¶1390 and the illustration below.)

d. When applying a label to a No. 10 envelope or a smaller envelope, follow the placement guidelines provided in ¶1389h. (For an illustration showing the correct placement of a mailing label on a No. 10 envelope, see page 391.) On envelopes larger than No. 10, position the label so that it appears visually centered horizontally and vertically.

Screen dump showing label feature of Microsoft Word for Windows.

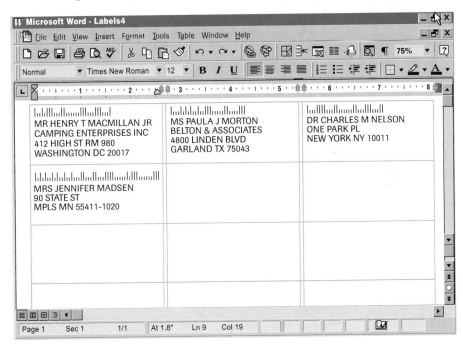

SECTION **14**

Reports and Manuscripts

Reports

Reports serve all kinds of purposes. Some simply communicate information—such as monthly sales figures or survey results—without any attempt to analyze or interpret the data. Others offer extensive analyses and make detailed recommendations for further action. As a result, reports come in all sizes and shapes. Some are done informally as memos or letters (depending on whether they are to be distributed inside or outside the organization). Some consist simply of fill-ins on printed or computer-generated forms. Many, however, are done in a more formal style. As you might expect, there is a wide variation to be found in what is considered acceptable—from one authority to another and from one organization to another. Regardless of which guidelines you follow, be prepared to modify them to fit a specific situation.

Word processing software typically provides templates that you can use as is or modify to suit your preferences. Three report templates provided by Microsoft Word are partially illustrated below and on page 406. Note in particular the differences in the way titles and headings are treated.

"Contemporary" report template provided by Microsoft Word for Windows.

FilmWatch Division Marketing Plan

Trey's Best Opportunity to Dominate Market Research for the Film Industry

How To Use This Report Template

Change the information on the cover page to contain the information you would like. For the body of your report, use Styles such as Heading 1-5, Body Text, Block Quotation, List Bullet, and List Number from the Style control on the Formatting toolbar.

This report template is complete with Styles for a Table of Contents and an Index. From the Insert menu, choose Index and Tables. Click on the tab you would like. Be sure to choose the Custom Format.

XE indicates an index entry field. The index field collects index entries specified by XE. To insert an index entry field, select the text to be indexed, and choose Index and Tables from the Insert menu. Click on the Index tab to receive the Index dialog box.

> *You can quickly open the Mark Index Entry dialog box by pressing ALT+SHIFT+X. The dialog box stays open so that you can mark index entries. For more information, see Indexes in Help.*

In addition to producing reports, this template can be used to create proposals and workbooks. To change the text or graphics, the following suggestions are provided.

- Select any paragraph and just start typing.

- To save time in the future, you can save the front cover of this report with your company name and address. For step-by-step instructions on how to perserve your changes with the template, please read the following section.

How To Modify This Report

Continued on page 406

"Elegant" report template provided by Microsoft Word for Windows.

> # PROPOSAL AND MARKETING PLAN
>
> BLUE SKY'S BEST OPPORTUNITY FOR EAST REGION EXPANSION
>
> ---
>
> ### HOW TO USE THIS REPORT TEMPLATE
>
> ---
>
> Change the information on the cover page to contain the information you would like. For the body of your report, use Styles such as Heading 1-5, Body Text, Block Quotation, List Bullet, and List Number from the Style control on the Formatting toolbar.
>
> ...ut .....ing .... steps above, your compa.... ....mation should appe... .. place. Now, type your report using Styles as needed.
>
> HOW TO CREATE BULLETS AND NUMBERED LISTS
>
> - To create a bulleted list like this, select one or more paragraphs and choose the List Bullet style from the Style drop-down list.
>
> - To create a numbered list like the numbered paragraphs above, select one or more paragraphs and choose the List Number style from the Style drop-down list — Word will automatically number the paragraphs for you.

"Professional" report template provided by Microsoft Word for Windows.

> **Chapter**
>
> # 1
>
> ---
>
> ## Blue Sky Marketing Plan
>
> Blue Sky's Best Opportunity for East Region Expansion
>
> **How to Modify This Report**
>
> To create your own version of this template, select File New and choose this template. Be sure to indicate "template" as the document type in the bottom right corner of the dialog. You can then:
>
> **How to Create a Report**
>
> To create a report from your newly saved template, select File New to re-open your template as a document. (Your company information should appear in place.) . For the body of your report, use Styles such as Heading 1-5, Body Text, Block Quotation, List Bullet, and List Number from the Style control on the Formatting toolbar.
>
> **How to Create Bullets and Numbered Lists**
>
> - To create a bulleted list like this, select one or more paragraphs and choose the List Bullet style from the Style drop-down list on the formatting toolbar. To create a numbered list like the numbered paragraphs above, select one or more paragraphs

If you do not wish to use one of the report templates provided by your software, you can always create your own format. This section provides format guidelines for formal and informal reports. The model below shows how the first page of an informal report would appear if executed according to these guidelines.

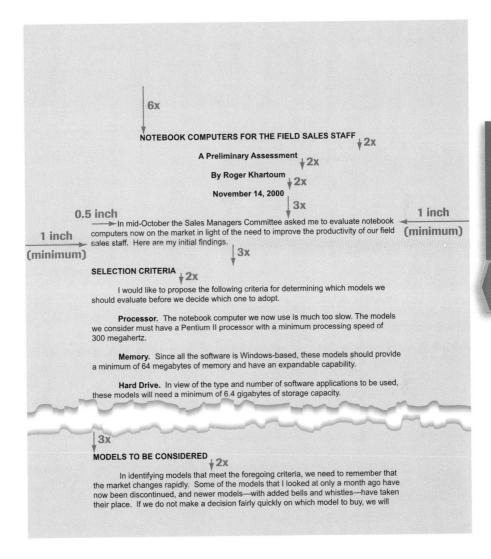

NOTE: In the model above, boldface is used for all four lines in the heading. To create a more open look, 2 blank lines have been inserted (a) between the heading and the text and (b) above the side heads.

As the illustration on page 408 shows, some writers prefer to use boldface only for the title and to insert only 1 blank line between elements in those places where the model above inserts 2.

➢ *For additional guidelines on spacing above heads, see ¶1426.*

Continued on page 408

¶1401

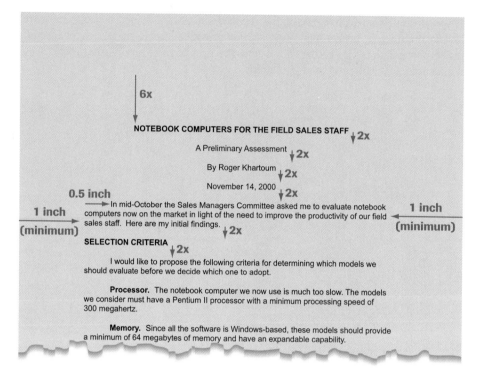

Choosing a Format

1401 If you are preparing a report at the request of someone else, always try to get some guidelines from that person on such matters as format, length, amount of detail desired, and distribution. Check the files for copies of similar reports done in the past. If guidelines or models are not provided or if you are preparing the report on your own initiative, consider the following factors in choosing a format.

a. *For whom are you writing the report?* If intended for your boss or a colleague on staff, the report could be done simply as a memo. If intended for top management or the board of directors, the report will often require a more formal approach. By the same token, an academic term paper will require a simpler format than a thesis for an advanced degree.

b. *What outcome do you hope to achieve?* If you are merely providing information without attempting to win someone over to your point of view, the simplest and clearest presentation of the information will suffice. If you are trying to persuade the reader to adopt your viewpoint and accept your recommendations, you may need to make a detailed argument and devise a more complex structure for your report. For example, you may need to develop a number of chapters, grouped by part. If you need to demonstrate that your argument is supported by much detailed research, you may have to quote from published sources and provide an elaborate set of data in the form of tables and charts. If you know that your intended reader already supports your argument or simply wants your judgment on a certain matter, a shorter and simpler document will usually suffice.

Parts of a Formal Report

1402 A *formal* report typically has three parts: front matter, body, and back matter. Each of these parts, in turn, typically contains some (if not all) of the following elements in the sequence indicated.

a. Front Matter

TITLE PAGE	*In a business report:* gives the full title, the subtitle (if any), the writer's name, title, and department, and the date of submission; may also indicate for whom the report was written. *In an academic report:* gives the name of the writer, the instructor, and the course, along with the date of submission. (See ¶1412.)
LETTER OR MEMO OF TRANSMITTAL	May be done as a letter (for distribution outside the company) or as a memo (for inside distribution); may be clipped to the front of the report (or the front of the binder in which the report is inserted); may be inserted in the report itself as the page preceding the title page. (See ¶1413.)
TABLE OF CONTENTS	A list of all chapters (by number and title), along with the opening page number of each chapter. If chapters are grouped by part, the titles of the parts also appear in the table of contents. Sometimes main headings within the chapters are also given under each chapter title. (See ¶¶1414–1415.)
LISTS OF TABLES AND ILLUSTRATIONS	Separate lists of tables and illustrations are included if they are numerous and likely to be frequently referred to by the reader. (See ¶¶1416–1417.)
FOREWORD	Written by someone other than the author of the report. May explain who commissioned the report, the reasons for doing so, and the qualifications of the writer to prepare the report. May also offer an evaluation of the report, and may ask those who receive copies of the report to give their assessment or take some other action after they have read the report. (See ¶1418.)
PREFACE	Written by the author of the report. Indicates for whom the report is written, the objectives and the scope of the report, and the methods used to assemble the material in the report. Acknowledgments of help received on the report are usually included here (placed at the end), but to give this material special emphasis, you can treat the acknowledgments as a separate element of the front matter, immediately following the preface. (See ¶1418.)
SUMMARY	Preferably limited to one page (two pages at most); designed to save the reader's time by presenting conclusions and recommendations right at the outset of the report. If a preface is not provided, the summary also includes some of the material that would have gone there. (See ¶1419.)

b. Body

INTRODUCTION	Sets forth (in greater detail than the preface) the objectives, the scope, and the methods, along with any other relevant background information. In a report with several chapters, the introduction may precede the first chapter of the text or it may be labeled as Chapter 1. (See ¶1421.)
MAIN DISCUSSION	Sets forth all the pertinent data, evidence, analyses, and interpretations needed to fulfill the purpose of the report. May consist of one long chapter that opens with an introduction and closes with conclusions and recommendations. May consist of several chapters; these may be grouped into *parts,* with a part-title page inserted to introduce

Reports and Manuscripts

14

Continued on page 410

	each sequence of chapters. May use different levels of headings throughout the text to indicate what the discussion covers and how it is organized. (See ¶¶1422–1426.)
CONCLUSION	Summarizes the key points and presents the recommendations that the writer hopes the reader will be persuaded to accept. In a report with several chapters, this material represents the final chapter or the final part.

c. Back Matter

APPENDIXES	A collection of tables, charts, or other data too specific or too lengthy to be included in the body of the report but provided here as supporting detail for the interested reader. (See ¶1429.)
ENDNOTES	A collection—all in one place at the end of the report—of what would otherwise appear as footnotes at the bottom of various pages in the report. (See ¶¶1501–1502, 1504–1505.)
BIBLIOGRAPHY	A list of all sources (1) that were consulted in the preparation of the report and (2) from which material was derived or directly quoted. (See ¶¶1547–1551.)
GLOSSARY	A list of terms (with definitions) that may not be readily understood when encountered in the body of the report. (See ¶1431.) May be treated as an appendix.

Parts of an Informal Report

1403 **a.** An *informal* report has no front matter. The information that would go on a separate title page appears at the top of the first page and is immediately followed by the body of the report. (See ¶¶1409–1411 for format guidelines.)

b. An informal report typically contains no back matter except possibly a list of *endnotes* (in place of separate footnotes throughout the body of the report) and a *bibliography*. (See ¶1505 for an illustration of endnotes and ¶1548 for an illustration of a bibliography.) Tables that cannot be easily incorporated in the body of the informal report may also be placed in an appendix in the back matter.

Margins

1404 **Side Margins**

a. Unbound Reports. If a report is to remain unbound or will simply be stapled in the upper left corner, use default side margins. However, you can reduce 1.25-inch default side margins to 1 inch if you are trying to limit the overall length of a report. By the same token, if length is not a problem, you can increase 1-inch default side margins to 1.25 inches to give the report a more open look.

b. Bound Reports. Use a 1.5-inch left margin. (The extra space at the left will provide space for the binding.) Ordinarily, accept the default right margin. However, reduce a 1.25-inch right margin to 1 inch if length is a problem, and increase a 1-inch right margin to 1.25 inches to achieve a more open look.

1405 **Top and Bottom Margins of Opening Pages**

The following guidelines apply to (a) the first page of each chapter, (b) the first page of each distinct element in the front matter and back matter, and (c) the first page of an informal report that consists of only one chapter (without any separate title page or other front matter).

a. On these opening pages, space down 6 times from the default top margin of 1 inch to create a top margin of about 2 inches. On the title page and on part-title pages, where the copy as a whole will be centered on the page, do not space down; simply begin typing on the first available line.

b. Use the page numbering feature of your word processing program, and select the format that automatically ends an opening page with a page number centered at the bottom. Some software programs insert the page number within the bottom margin area; others insert the page number on the last line above the bottom margin.

c. Ordinarily, nothing is typed in the space that represents the top margin. However, in informal academic reports, certain information is often typed in the upper right corner. (See ¶1411.)

➢ *For the numbering of opening pages, see ¶1420.*

1406 **Top and Bottom Margins of Other Pages**

a. Use the default top and bottom margins of 1 inch.

b. For pages in the *body* and *back matter* of a report, use the page numbering feature of your word processing program to position the page number in the upper right corner of the page. If you want to provide additional information along with the page number (for example, the title of the report or a chapter within the report), use the header feature of your word processing software.

c. For pages in the *front matter* of a report, use the page numbering feature of your word processing software to center the page number at the bottom of the report. If you want to provide additional information along with the page number, use the footer feature of your software.

1407 **Handling Page Breaks on a Computer**

Your word processing software can help you avoid most page-ending problems, as outlined in *a–e* below. There are, however, page-ending situations in which you must use your own judgment, as outlined in *f–j* on page 412.

a. Your software ensures that the bottom margin will always be 1 inch (or whatever margin you have selected). A *soft page break* is inserted when the bottom margin is reached, but because that break is "soft," you can easily adjust it if you do not like the page break created by the software.

NOTE: The *preview* feature permits you to see an entire page on the screen prior to printing so that you can tell whether adjustments will be necessary. See ¶1407f–j for page-ending situations that may require adjustments.

b. A *hard page break* permits you to end a page wherever you want and to ensure that any copy that follows will appear at the top of the next page.

c. The *keep lines together* feature ensures that a designated block of copy (such as a table, an enumerated list, or selected lines of text) will not be divided at the bottom of a page but will, if necessary, be carried over intact to the top of the next page.

Continued on page 412

¶1407

d. To prevent *widows* (a situation in which the last line of a paragraph appears as the first line of a page), the *widow/orphan control* feature ensures that at least two lines of that paragraph are carried over to the top of the next page. (As an illustration, see the four-line paragraph that begins at the bottom of page 410.)

e. To prevent *orphans* (a situation in which the first line of a paragraph appears as the last line of a page), the *widow/orphan control* feature ensures that at least two lines of that paragraph will appear at the bottom of a page or that the paragraph will begin at the top of the next page.

f. Do not type a *centered heading* or a *side heading* near the bottom of a page unless you can fit at least the first two lines of copy after the heading. Use the *keep lines together* feature. (For illustrations, see ¶1426a–c.)

NOTE: A *run-in heading* (in the first line of a paragraph) can fall near the bottom of a page if one additional line of the paragraph will also fit there. (For all illustrations, see ¶1426c.)

➤ *For a discussion of centered, side, and run-in headings, see ¶¶1425c, 1426.*

g. Do not divide a quoted extract (see ¶1424d) unless you can leave at least two lines at the bottom of one page and carry over at least two lines to the top of the next. Use the *widow/orphan control* feature.

h. If a list of items (see ¶1424e–g) has to be divided at the bottom of a page, try to divide *between* items (not within an item). Moreover, try to leave at least two items at the bottom of one page and carry over at least two items to the top of the next. Use the *widow/orphan control* feature or the *hard page break* feature.

NOTE: If you need to divide *within* an item, leave at least two lines at the bottom of one page and carry over at least two lines to the next.

i. If it is not possible to start typing a table at the desired point of reference and have it all fit on the same page, then insert a parenthetical note at the appropriate point in the text (referring the reader to the next page) and continue with the text to the bottom of the page. Then at the top of the next page, type the complete table and resume typing the text. (See Section 16 for guidelines on the typing of tables.) If you encounter a number of problems locating tables within the body of a particular report, you may want to consider placing all the tables in a separate appendix at the end of the report. (See ¶1402c.)

NOTE: If a table is so long that it will not fit on one page even when typed single-spaced, then look for a sensible division point in the body of the table and end the first page there. Your software will automatically carry the remaining lines in the table to the top of the next page. If you mark the table title and the column heads as "headings," the items marked in this way will be automatically inserted at the top of the next page. (See ¶1638.)

j. If a footnote cannot all fit on the page where the text reference occurs, continue it at the bottom of the following page. If you are using the *widow/orphan control* feature and the *footnote* feature, either the footnote will be automatically divided or the text containing the footnote reference and the footnote itself will be carried over to the next page. (See ¶1504d.)

1408 **Shortening a Long Report**

When the cost of photocopying and distributing a large number of copies of a long report becomes prohibitively expensive, consider the following devices for reducing the number of pages without having to cut the copy. (Note that these devices will also reduce the readability and the attractiveness of the report, so use them only in extreme circumstances.)

a. You can reduce the font size, or you can choose a different font that yields more characters to an inch. If absolutely necessary, you can also reduce the amount of space between words and letters.

b. Reduce the standard top margin for all opening pages from 2 inches to 1.5 inches. (See ¶1405.)

c. Reduce the top margin for all other pages from 1 inch to 0.5 inch. (See ¶1406.)

   NOTE: If you are using the header feature or the page numbering feature at the top and if the header or page number is placed in the margin area, you will not be able to reduce the top margin.

d. As an alternative to c, maintain the standard top margin and reduce the bottom margin from 1 inch to 0.5 inch. (See ¶1406.)

   NOTE: If you are using the footer feature or the page numbering feature at the bottom and if the footer or page number is placed in the margin area, you will not be able to reduce the bottom margin.

e. Single-space the report and leave 1 blank line between paragraphs. (See ¶1424a.)

f. If the report has only one level of heading, use run-in heads rather than side heads. (See ¶¶1425–1426.)

g. Wherever the guidelines allow for 2 blank lines between elements, reduce this space to 1 blank line. Wherever 1 blank line is called for, reduce this space to half a line (if your software offers this option).

Informal Business Reports

These guidelines apply to business reports that consist of only one chapter and have no separate title page or other front matter.

1409 If the first page is typed on a *blank sheet of paper* (as shown in the illustration on page 414):

a. Leave a top margin of approximately 2 inches.

b. Use single spacing while executing the title, the subtitle, the writer's name, and the date. (See c–f.)

c. On the first line below the top margin, type the title of the report centered in all-capital letters. If a subtitle is used, type it centered in capital and small letters on the second line below the main title. (If the title or subtitle is long, divide it into sensible phrases and arrange them on two or more single-spaced lines.)

   NOTE: Use boldface for the title and subtitle (and for the writer's name and the date as well). Some writers prefer to use boldface only for the title.

Continued on page 414

¶1409

d. Type *By* and the writer's name centered in capital and small letters on the second line below the title or subtitle.

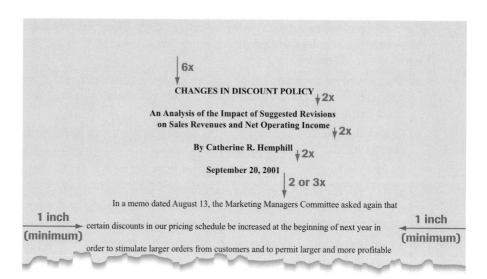

e. Type the date on which the report is to be submitted on the second line, centered, below the writer's name.

NOTE: Additional details that appear on a title page (such as the writer's title and affiliation or the name and affiliation of the person or group for whom the report has been prepared) are omitted when the title starts on the same page as the body. If these elements need to be provided, you will have to prepare a separate title page. (See ¶1412.)

f. On the second or third line below the date, start the body of the report. (See ¶¶1424–1426.) At this point switch to double spacing.

NOTE: On the first page of an informal business report, do not type a page number. However, count this page as page 1.

g. If the report requires more than one page, use the page numbering feature to automatically insert the page number at the top right margin. Leave 1 or 2 blank lines below the page number, and resume the text on the following line.

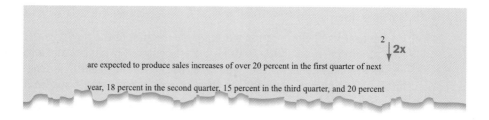

h. If the report requires one or more elements of back matter—for example, endnotes or a bibliography—follow the style established for a formal report. (See ¶¶1501–1502, 1504–1505, 1547–1551.)

1410 If the first page of a report is prepared in *memo form:*

a. Give the report title (and subtitle, if any) as the *subject* of the memo. Supply all the other elements called for in the heading of the memo in the usual way. (See ¶¶1392–1393.)

b. Then begin typing the body of the report on the second or third line below the last fill-in line in the heading. (See ¶¶1424–1426.)

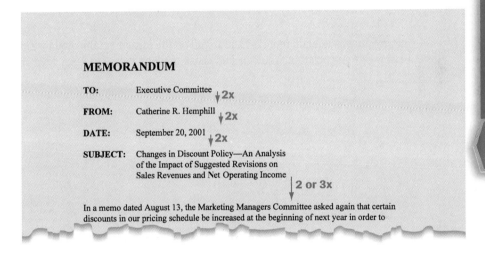

c. If the report requires more than one page, then type each continuation page on a blank sheet of paper. Use the header feature to insert the same kind of continuation heading called for in any long memo (see ¶1393t). Leave 1 or 2 blank lines and resume the text on the following line.

¶1411

Informal Academic Reports

1411 An academic report that consists of only one chapter and has no separate title page or other front matter is typed exactly like an informal business report (see ¶¶1409–1410) except for the opening of the first page.

  a. Leave a default top margin of 1 inch. Then type the following information on four separate lines, single-spaced, in the upper right corner of the first page: the writer's name, the instructor's name, the course title, and the date. Align these four lines at the left, with the longest line ending at the right margin.

  b. On the second or third line below the date, type the title just as in an informal business report. If a subtitle is used, type it on the second line below the title. (See ¶1409c.)

  c. Start typing the body of the report on the second or third line below the preceding copy (the title or subtitle). At this point switch to double spacing. (See ¶¶1424–1426.)

  NOTE: Many academic reports have to follow the format established by The Modern Language Association. You can find these guidelines in *The MLA Style Manual*.

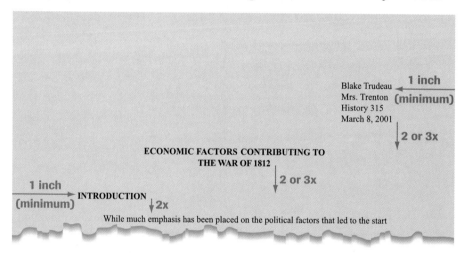

The Front Matter of Formal Reports

The following guidelines deal with the preparation of a title page, a letter or memo of transmittal, a table of contents, a list of tables, a list of illustrations, a preface or foreword, and a summary. For a formal report, only a separate title page is essential; all the other elements are optional.

1412 **Title Page**

There is no one correct arrangement for the elements on a title page. Here are two acceptable formats.

  a. **Three-Block Arrangement.** Group the material into three blocks of type, and leave equal space (1 to 2 inches) above and below the middle block. Then center the material as a whole horizontally and vertically on the page. (See the illustrations on page 417.)

b. Two-Block Arrangement. Group the material into two blocks of type, and leave 1 to 2 inches between blocks. Center the material as a whole horizontally and vertically on the page. (See the first illustration below on the right.)

NOTE: The two-block arrangement works well when the title page does not try to show the name of the person or group to whom the report is being submitted.

Three-Block Arrangement

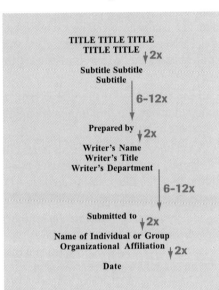

Two-Block Arrangement

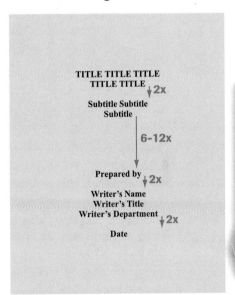

Business Report

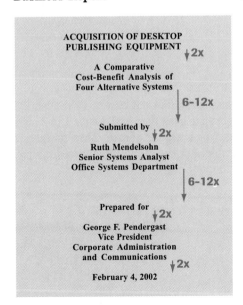

Academic Report

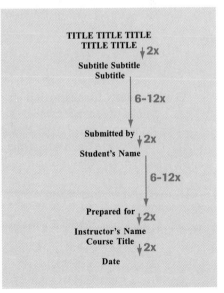

Continued on page 418

¶1412

c. **Margins.** Regardless of the arrangement you use, the side margins should be at least equal to those used for the body of the report (see ¶1404). The top and bottom margins should be a minimum of 1 inch, but make sure that they are at least equal to (and preferably slightly larger than) the space inserted between the blocks of text on the title page.

NOTE: When you set up the text for a title page, insert a 2-inch space between the blocks of text at the outset. Then center the material as a whole horizontally and vertically, and consider whether adjustments are necessary to achieve an attractively balanced page. At this point you can reduce the space between blocks if necessary to ensure that it does not exceed the space used for the top and bottom margins. You can also adjust line breaks in the text as necessary to preserve attractive side margins.

d. **Title.** Type the title in boldface all-capital letters. If the title is long, type it on two or more lines, single-spaced; try to divide the title into meaningful phrases. (See the illustration of a business report on page 417.)

e. **Subtitle.** Type the subtitle, if any, in boldface capital and small letters. If the subtitle requires more than one line, type it single-spaced. Leave 1 blank line between the main title and the subtitle. (See the illustrations on page 417.)

f. **Writer's Identification.** Leave 1 to 2 inches before typing the writer's identification block. The writer's name may be preceded by the word *By* on the same line or by a phrase such as *Prepared by* or *Submitted by* (or simply *By*) typed 2 lines above. If appropriate, the writer's name may be followed by a title on the next line and by an organizational affiliation on the following line.

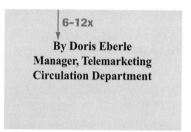

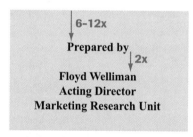

g. **Reader's Identification.** It is customary (but not essential) to identify the individual or group for whom the report has been prepared. Leave 1 to 2 inches before typing *Submitted to* or *Prepared for* or a similar phrase. Then on the second line below, type the name of the individual or the group. On succeeding lines, supply a title, an organizational affiliation, or both.

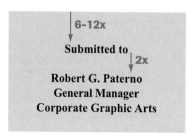

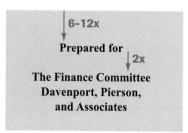

¶1413

h. **Date.** Supply the date (month, day, and year) on which the report is being submitted. Type it on the second line below the reader's identification block (or, if none is given, on the second line below the writer's identification). (See the illustrations on page 417.)

i. **Graphic Elements.** You can use special display type and add an organizational logo or some other graphic element to enhance the appearance of a title page.

NOTE: When word processing software provides a template for reports, it typically includes a recommended format for a title page.

1413 Letter or Memo of Transmittal

a. A formal report is often accompanied by a letter or memo of transmittal. If you are sending the report to people outside the company, use the letter format (see the illustration below); if you are sending the report only to people within the company, use a memo.

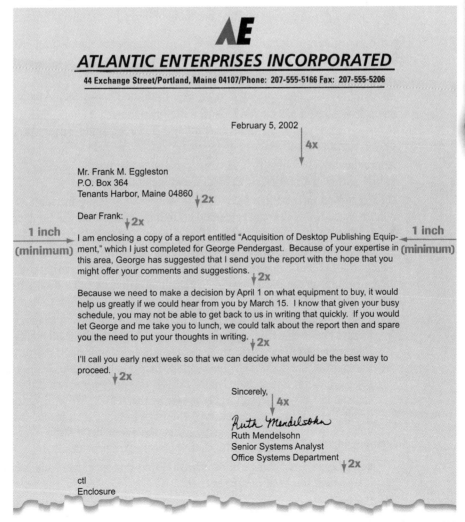

Continued on page 420

¶**1414**

   b. The message typically covers the following points: (1) a brief description of what is being transmitted; (2) a brief reference to the circumstances that prompted the report; (3) if necessary, a brief indication of why the report is being sent to the addressee; and (4) a statement about what action the addressee is expected to take. (See the illustration on page 419.)

   c. The letter or memo of transmittal is typically clipped to the front of the report. If the report is in a binder, the transmittal document may be clipped to the front of the binder or inserted in the binder preceding the title page.

Table of Contents

1414 If your word processing software has the appropriate feature, you can create a table of contents by scrolling through the text and coding (according to level of subordination) every part title, chapter title, main heading, and subheading that you wish to appear in the table of contents. If you subsequently add, delete, or change any titles or headings in the report, you can readily update your table of contents to reflect these changes.

1415 If you do not like the default style for a table of contents that is provided by your software, you may be able to modify that style or select a different style. If you prefer to create your own format, the following guidelines may be helpful.

   a. Type the table of contents on a new page. (See the illustration on page 421).

   NOTE: To achieve a more open look, the illustration uses 2 blank lines above each major element within the table of contents. However, some writers prefer to use only 1 blank line above these elements.

   b. Approximately 2 inches from the top of the page, center the heading *CONTENTS* (or *TABLE OF CONTENTS*) in boldface all-capital letters.

   c. On the second or third line below the heading, begin typing the table of contents double-spaced. Use the same side and bottom margins as for the text pages in the body of the report. (See ¶¶1404–1406.)

   d. In typing the body of the table of contents, list every separate element that *follows* the table of contents in sequence—whether in the front matter, the body of the report, or the back matter. In the illustration on page 421, note the following aspects of the format:

   (1) Type individual entries pertaining to *front matter* and *back matter* at the left margin, with the title in capital and small letters or in all-capital letters. Page numbers (roman for front matter and arabic for back matter) align on the right at the right margin. Leaders help guide the eye to the column of page numbers. Set a right leader tab for the page numbers. After you type each entry at the left margin, pressing the leader tab will automatically insert the leaders before you type the page number. The leader feature provides only solid leaders and establishes the space before and after each row of leaders. Accept the results that your software provides.

   NOTE: Leave 1 or 2 blank lines *after* the front matter entries and 1 or 2 blank lines *before* the back matter entries.

   (2) Center individual entries pertaining to *part titles* in all-capital letters. The part numbers that precede the titles may be in arabic or roman numerals or (for formality) may be spelled out. Leave 1 or 2 blank lines before each part title and 1 blank line after.

(3) Individual entries pertaining to *chapters* begin with a chapter number (roman or arabic), followed by a period, 1 or 2 spaces, and then the chapter title typed in capital and small letters or in all-capital letters. Align the chapter numbers at the right. If you are using roman numerals, set a decimal tab, with the longest number positioned as close to the left margin as possible. Press the tab key to insert a row of leaders before you type each page number.

(4) If any chapter title should require more than one line, type the turnover line single-spaced, aligned with the first letter of the chapter title in the line above.

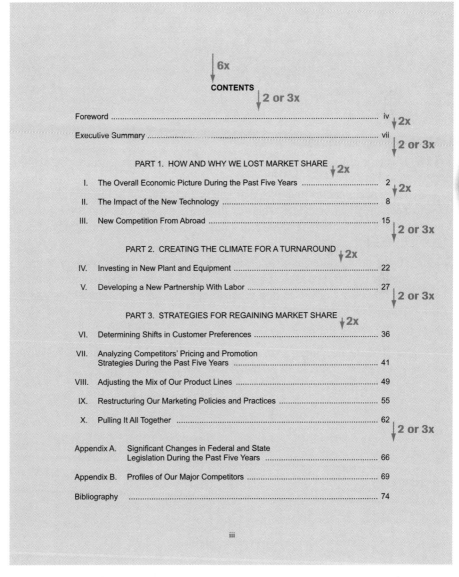

iii

Reports and
Manuscripts

14

Continued on page 422

¶1416

e. The *main headings* within each chapter may be included in the table of contents. One acceptable arrangement is to indent each heading from the start of the chapter title. Type the list of headings for each chapter in capital and small letters, and treat it as a single-spaced block, with 1 blank line above and below it. Page numbers may be provided with the headings if desired.

List of Tables or Illustrations

1416 If your word processing software has the appropriate feature, you can create separate lists of tables and illustrations by scrolling through the text and coding the titles of the tables and lists that you want to appear in the front matter. If you subsequently add or delete tables or illustrations, you will find it easy to update these lists. (The process is similar to using software to generate a table of contents. See ¶1414.)

1417 If you do not like the default style provided by your software, you may be able to modify that style or select a different style. If you prefer to create your own format for these lists of tables and illustrations, the following guidelines and the illustration below may be helpful.

a. Type each list on a new page.

b. Type the heading—*TABLES* (or *LIST OF TABLES*) or *ILLUSTRATIONS* (or *LIST OF ILLUSTRATIONS*)—in boldface all-capital letters.

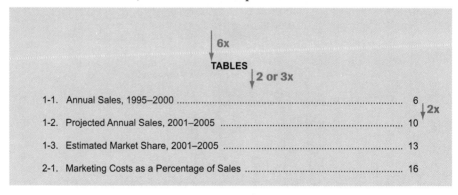

↓6x

TABLES ↓2 or 3x

1-1. Annual Sales, 1995–2000 .... 6 ↓2x

1-2. Projected Annual Sales, 2001–2005 10

1-3. Estimated Market Share, 2001–2005 13

2-1. Marketing Costs as a Percentage of Sales 16

c. On the second or third line below the heading, type the first entry in the list. Use the same format as for chapter titles in a table of contents. (See ¶1415.) The tables or the illustrations may be numbered consecutively throughout the report or consecutively within each chapter. The latter technique uses the chapter number as a prefix in the numbering scheme. (See the illustration on page 422.)

d. If your word processing software has the appropriate features, you can automatically number tables and illustrations throughout the report.

1418 Preface or Foreword

a. If a preface (written by the author) or a foreword (written by someone else) is to be provided, then on a new page type the appropriate title in boldface all-capital letters, and center the heading approximately 2 inches from the top of the page. Note that the correct spelling is *FOREWORD* (not *FORWARD*).

NOTE: If both a preface and a foreword are to appear in the front matter, the foreword should precede the preface.

b. On the second or third line below the heading, begin typing the actual text. Use the same side and bottom margins as for the text pages in the body of the report (see ¶¶1404–1407). Also follow the same guidelines for spacing, indentions, and headings as in the body of the report (see ¶¶1424–1426).

c. The preface should cover the following points: (1) for whom the report is written, (2) what prompted the writing of the report, (3) what the report aims to accomplish, (4) what the report covers and what it does not try to deal with, (5) how the data and the conclusions were arrived at, and (6) acknowledgments of those individuals and organizations who helped the writer of the report.

NOTE: The acknowledgments may be treated as a separate element in the front matter, following the foreword and the preface (if both are given) and using the same format.

d. The foreword typically deals with these topics: (1) who commissioned the report, (2) the reasons for doing so, (3) the writer's qualifications for undertaking the assignment, (4) an assessment of the job that the writer has done, and (5) a call for some follow-up action on the part of those who receive copies of the report.

1419 Summary

a. If a summary (frequently called an *executive summary*) is to be provided, follow the format guidelines provided for a preface in ¶1418a–b.

b. Since this element is intended to be a time-saver, keep it short—ideally one page, at most two pages. The summary may be handled as a series of ordinary text paragraphs or as a series of paragraphs typed as items in a list (see ¶1424e–g).

1420 Numbering Front Matter Pages

a. On all pages of front matter except the title page, use the page numbering feature or the footer feature to position the page number at the bottom of the page.

b. Type the page number in small roman numerals (*ii, iii, iv,* and so on).

Continued on page 424

¶1421

c. Consider the title page as *page i,* even though no number is typed on that page.

NOTE: You can direct the page numbering feature to (1) suppress the page number on the first page of the front matter and (2) insert a sequence of small roman numerals at the bottom of all the other pages in the front matter.

The Body of Formal Reports

1421 Introduction

a. If the body of a report contains several chapters and begins with a formal introduction, treat the introduction either as Chapter 1 or as a distinct element preceding Chapter 1.

(1) If you decide to treat it as Chapter 1, then consider *INTRODUCTION* to be the title of this chapter. You can then treat it as you would any other title on a chapter-opening page. (See ¶1423.)

(2) If you decide to have the introduction precede Chapter 1, then on a new page type *INTRODUCTION* in boldface all-capital letters, and center the heading approximately 2 inches from the top of the page. On the second or third line below, begin typing the text.

(3) In either case treat the first page of the introduction as page 1 of the report. (See ¶1427.)

➤ *For guidelines on margins, see ¶¶1404–1407; for guidelines on spacing, indentions, and headings, see ¶¶1424–1426.*

b. If a report contains only one chapter and begins with an introductory section, treat the title *INTRODUCTION* as a first-level head (see ¶¶1425–1426) and type it on the second or third line below the block of copy (title, etc.) at the top of the page.

1422 Part-Title Pages

a. If the report contains several chapters organized in parts, insert a separate part-title page directly in front of the chapter that begins each part. Either of the following formats is acceptable.

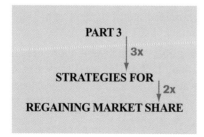
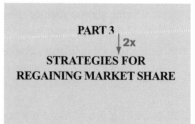

NOTE: If the body of the report begins with a formal introduction (see ¶1421a), then the part-title page for Part 1 should *follow* the introduction. (**REASON:** The introduction embraces the whole work and not simply Part 1.)

¶1424

b. Type the word *PART* and the part number on one line. Underneath type the part title on one or more lines as appropriate. Use boldface all-capital letters for emphasis, and arrange the copy for maximum display effect. Center the copy as a whole horizontally and vertically or, for a more attractive display, position the copy so that there is twice as much space below as there is above.

1423 Chapter-Opening Pages

a. On a new page, approximately 2 inches from the top, center the chapter number and title in boldface all-capital letters.

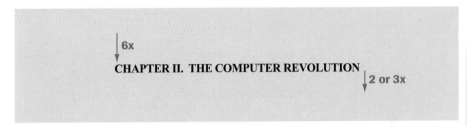

b. If the title is long, divide it into sensible phrases and arrange them on two or more single-spaced lines. Put the chapter number on a line by itself, and leave 1 blank line before starting the chapter title.

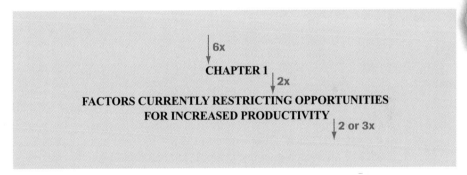

c. Begin typing the first line of copy (whether text matter or a heading) on the second or third line below the title.

1424 Text Spacing and Indentions

a. **Text.** Ordinarily, double-space all text matter. However, use single spacing or 1.5-line spacing in business reports when the costs of paper, photocopying, file space, and mailing are important considerations. (See ¶1408 for a number of ways to shorten a long report.)

➢ *For guidelines on dividing words and word groups at the ends of lines and between one page and the next, see ¶¶901–920; for guidelines on the use of footnotes, endnotes, or textnotes, see Section 15; for guidance on whether or not to justify the right margin, see ¶1356b–c.*

b. **Drafts.** Always double-space drafts that are to be submitted for editing or evaluation.

Continued on page 426

¶1424

c. Paragraphs. Indent the first line of text paragraphs 0.5 inch. Leave 1 blank line between paragraphs.

➤ *For guidelines on dividing short paragraphs at the bottom of a page, see ¶1407d–e.*

d. Quoted Material. If a quotation will make four or more lines, treat it as a single-spaced extract, indent it 0.5 inch from each side margin, and leave 1 blank line above and below the extract. With word processing software, you can change the indent settings or you can use the *double indent* feature (if one is available), which will indent the extract equally from each side margin. If the quoted matter represents the start of a paragraph in the original, indent the first word an additional 0.5 inch.

> 1 inch (min.) need to consider a new phenomenon in the software market. Here is an observation from Hal Pryor in a memo dated March 14: 1 inch (min.) ↓2x
>
> 0.5 inch →0.5 inch We're competing in an economy where the cost of raw technology is plummeting toward zero. This plunge will drive down prices on software products as well. The only way to survive in this economy is to establish a long-term relationship with a customer, even if that means giving the first generation of a product away. 0.5 inch ↓2x
>
> This is a startling idea and needs to be discussed at some length in our upcoming session on pricing strategy.

➤ *For another illustration, see page 349.*

e. Items in a List. Type the list single-spaced with 1 blank line above and below the list as a whole. Either type the list on the full width of the text (as illustrated on page 428), or indent the list equally from each side margin (as described in *d* above and illustrated below). If any item in the list requires more than one line, leave a blank line after each item in the list. If an item requires more than one line, align any turnover with the first word in the line above.

> 1 inch (min.) The market analysis conducted by Witherspoon Associates has yielded some surprising results. For example, over 50 percent of our sales are made in low-growth markets. On that basis we need to ask: 1 inch (min.) ↓2x
>
> 0.5 inch Will this heavy investment in low-growth markets permit us to meet our long-range profit goals? 0.5 inch ↓2x ↓2x
>
> How can we most effectively increase our sales in high-growth markets? ↓2x
>
> To what extent will domestic and international competition stymie our attempt to penetrate high-growth markets? ↓2x

¶1424

NOTE: Sometimes a list of one-line items (with no turnovers) is typed double-spaced to enhance readability.

➢ *For an example, see the illustration on page 504.*

f. **Enumerated Items in a List.** If each of the items begins with a number or a letter, you may use the numbered list feature of your word processing program. Each item will begin at the left margin, and turnovers will be indented to align with the first word in the line above. However, when the first line of each text paragraph is indented 0.5 inch (as is typically done in reports), an enumerated list that falls within the text looks best when indented 0.5 inch from each margin. (See the illustrations below.)

When you use the numbered list feature, the list will be typed single-spaced (as in the following illustration).

For a more open look, leave 1 blank line after each item in the list (as in the following illustration).

➢ *See ¶1357d, note, on the formatting of enumerated items in a list.*

Continued on page 428

¶1425

g. Bulleted Items in a List. Instead of numbers or letters, you can use *bullets* before the items in a list. The bullet feature of a word processing program permits you to choose from a variety of styles to create bullets. For example:

CIRCLES: ○ ●   TRIANGLES: ▷ ▶

SQUARES: □ ■   OTHER ASCII CHARACTERS: > → ∗

The default position of the bullet is at the left margin; the text and any turnovers are automatically indented (as shown in the illustration below). If you prefer, you can position the bullets 0.5 inch from the left margin by pressing the tab before activating the bullet feature.

h. Tables. Tables may be typed with single, double, or 1.5-line spacing. However, establish one style of spacing for all tables within a given report.

➤ *See Section 16 for a full discussion on how to plan and execute tables and for numerous illustrations.*

Text Headings

1425 Headings (or heads) are the key technique for letting readers see at a glance the scope of the writer's discussion and the way in which it is organized. Therefore, make sure that the heads used throughout the report properly reflect the coverage and the structure of the material. It is also essential that you type the heads in a way that clearly indicates different levels of importance or subordination.

Here are several techniques for achieving these objectives:

a. Try to limit yourself to three levels of text heads (not counting the chapter title). If you use more than three levels of text heads, it will be difficult for the reader to grasp the typographical distinction between one level and another. Moreover, the use of more than three levels of text heads suggests that you may be trying to cram too much into one chapter. Consider a different organization of the material to solve this problem.

NOTE: In order to clearly distinguish one level of text heading from another and the headings from the text, carefully choose fonts and font sizes, and make appropriate use of boldface, italics, and other devices.

b. Before preparing the final version of the report, make an outline of the heading structure as it then stands and analyze it for:

(1) *Comprehensiveness.* When the heads are viewed as a whole, do they cover all aspects of the discussion, or are some topics not properly represented?

(2) *Balance.* Is one part of a chapter loaded with heads while a comparable part has only one or two?

(3) *Parallel structure.* Are the heads all worded in a similar way, or are some complete sentences and others simply phrases? (See ¶1081.)

On the basis of this analysis, revise the heads as necessary.

NOTE: Using the outline feature of a word processing program will greatly simplify the process of reviewing and improving the wording of the heads. You can use the outline feature to generate a complete list of the heads as they currently appear in the report. Any changes in wording that you make on this list will automatically be reflected in the headings in the full text.

c. Headings come in three styles:

(1) A *centered head* is one centered on a line by itself. Type it in boldface all-capital letters. If the head is too long to fit on one line, center the turnover on the following line.

➤ *For spacing above and below heads, see ¶1426.*

(2) A *side head* starts flush with the left margin, on a line by itself. Type side heads in boldface, using all-capital letters or capital and small letters.

(3) A *run-in head* (also called a *paragraph heading*) is one that begins a paragraph and is immediately followed by text matter on the same line. Indent a run-in head 0.5 inch from the left margin. Type it in boldface capital and small letters. The run-in head should be followed by a period (unless some other mark of punctuation, such as a question mark, is required). The text then begins 1 or 2 spaces after the punctuation. (See the illustrations in ¶1426b–c.)

➤ *For capitalization in headings, see ¶¶360–361, 363.*

1426 The illustrations on pages 430 and 431 provide spacing guidelines for headings. You have two options. You can leave only 1 blank line above centered and side headings (as shown in the models in the right column). For a more open look, you can leave 2 blank lines above centered and side headings (as shown in the models in the left column).

Continued on page 430

Reports and Manuscripts

14

¶1426

a. In a report that calls for only *one* level of heading, choose a side heading and type it in one of the styles shown below.

Open Style

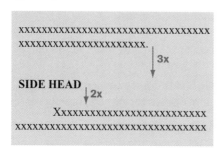

Condensed Style

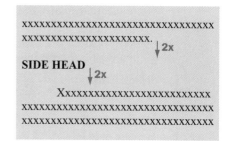

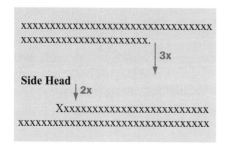

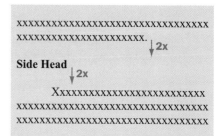

b. In a report that calls for *two* levels of headings, choose one of the styles shown below.

Open Style

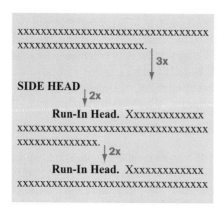

Condensed Style

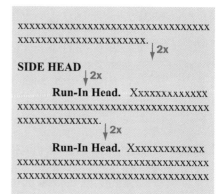

When a paragraph begins with a run-in head, leave 1 blank line above it. (Even paragraphs without run-in heads should be preceded by 1 blank line.)

NOTE: If you normally leave 2 blank lines above a side head, leave only 1 blank line when a side head comes directly below a centered head (without any intervening text).

Open Style   **Condensed Style**

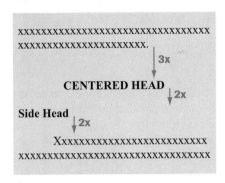
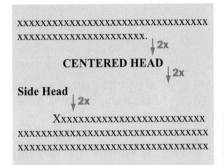

c. In a report with *three* levels of headings, choose one of the following styles.

Open Style   **Condensed Style**

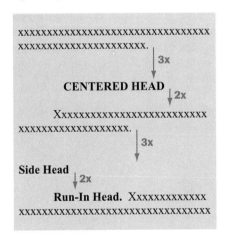
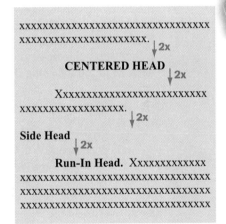

1427 Numbering Text Pages

a. When you use the page numbering feature of your word processing software, the appropriate page number will be properly positioned on each page in the correct sequence. If you later add or delete copy in a way that changes the overall length of the report, the page numbering will be automatically adjusted.

NOTE: The page numbering feature will insert space *below* a page number at the top of a page or *above* a page number at the bottom.

Continued on page 432

¶**1427**

b. When the first page contains the title of the report and the body starts on the same page, count this as page 1 but do not type the number on the page.

NOTE: With the page numbering feature you can easily hide or suppress a page number and still have the page counted in the overall numerical sequence.

c. When the report begins with a formal title page and one or more additional pages of front matter, give these pages a separate numbering sequence, using small *roman* numerals. (See ¶1420.)

d. In a formal report, consider the first page *following* the front matter as page 1 in the *arabic* numbering sequence.

e. If part-title pages are included in the report (see ¶1422), consider them in the numbering sequence for the body of the report but do not type a number on these pages. (Thus if the first page following the front matter is the part-title page for Part 1, it will count as page 1 but no number will appear.)

f. On the first page of each new element in the body or back matter of the report, use the page numbering feature to center the page number at the bottom of the page.

g. On all other pages in the body or back matter of the report, use the page numbering feature to position the page number in the upper right corner of the page.

h. If the final version of a report is to be printed on both sides of the paper (as in a book), the odd-numbered pages will appear on the front side of each sheet and the even-numbered pages on the back. If the report is bound, then on a spread of two facing pages, the even-numbered pages will appear on the left and the odd-numbered pages on the right. In such cases it is more convenient for the reader if the page numbers at the top or bottom of the page appear at the outside corners, as in the following illustration.

NOTE: You can direct the page numbering feature of a word processing program to alternate the placement of these page numbers in the outside corners, depending on whether the page has an odd or even number.

i. In a long report with several chapters written by different authors under a tight deadline, it may be necessary to prepare the final version of the chapters out of order. In such cases, you may use a separate sequence of page numbers for each chapter, with the chapter number serving as a prefix. Thus, for example, the pages in Chapter 1 would be numbered 1-1,1-2, 1-3, . . . ; those in Chapter 2 would be numbered 2-1, 2-2, 2-3, . . . ; and so on.

NOTE: If the authors submit their material on disk, it is easy to renumber the entire report at the last minute, using one continuous sequence of numbers throughout.

The Back Matter of Formal Reports

1428 Following the last page of the body of the report are those elements of back matter that may be needed: appendixes, endnotes, bibliography, and glossary. Begin each of these elements on a new page. Use the same margins as for other pages in the report (see ¶¶1404–1407), and treat the numbering of these pages as discussed in ¶1427f–i.

1429 Appendixes

a. If you plan to include more than one appendix, number or letter each one in sequence. (For an example of the treatment of two appendixes, see the illustration of the table of contents on page 421.)

b. On a new page, about 2 inches from the top, center *APPENDIX* (plus a number or letter if appropriate) and the appendix title in boldface all-capital letters.

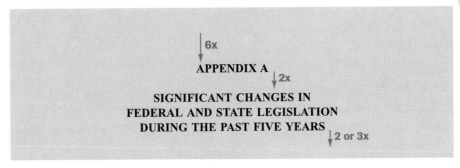

```
            │6x
            ▼

    APPENDIX B.  PROFILES OF OUR MAJOR COMPETITORS
                                                   │2 or 3x
                                                   ▼
```

NOTE: If the title is long, type it in two or more centered lines, single-spaced. Leave 1 blank line before starting the appendix title.

```
                    │6x
                    ▼

                APPENDIX A
                          │2x
                          ▼
            SIGNIFICANT CHANGES IN
        FEDERAL AND STATE LEGISLATION
          DURING THE PAST FIVE YEARS
                                    │2 or 3x
                                    ▼
```

c. Leave 1 or 2 blank lines before typing the body of the appendix. Since this material may be a table, a chart, a list, or regular text, choose the format that displays this copy to best effect.

1430 Endnotes and Bibliography

For detailed guidelines on endnotes and the bibliography, see ¶¶1501–1502, 1505–1506, 1547–1551.

1431 Glossary

If you plan to provide a glossary, then on a new page, approximately 2 inches from the top, center *GLOSSARY* or some other heading in boldface all-capital letters. Leave 1 or 2 blank lines before beginning the text.

Continued on page 434

¶1431

There are a number of ways to set up a glossary: in two columns, in one column with hanging indentions, and in paragraphs.

a. **Two Columns.** In the left column type the terms in alphabetic order, using boldface, italics, or underlining. In the right column put the corresponding definitions alongside. Begin the right column at least 2 spaces to the right of the longest term in the left column. Single-space each definition, and align turnover lines flush with the left margin of this column. Leave 1 blank line between entries.

> **Elliptical expression**   A condensed expression from which key words are omitted.
> ↓2x
>
> **Essential elements**   Words, phrases, or clauses that are necessary to the completeness of the structure or the meaning of a sentence.

b. **Hanging Indention.** Begin each term at the left margin, using boldface, italics, or underlining. Follow with a colon, a dash, or some other device and then the definition. Type the definition single-spaced and indent turnover lines 0.5 inch so that the term in the first line will stand out. Leave 1 blank line between entries.

> *elliptical expression:* a condensed expression from which key words are
> ⟶ omitted.
> **0.5 inch**   ↓2x
>
> *essential elements:* words, phrases, or clauses that are necessary to the completeness of the structure or the meaning of a sentence.

c. **Paragraph Style.** Indent each term 0.5 inch from the left margin, using boldface, italics, or underlining. Follow with a colon, a dash, or some other device and then the definition. Type the definition single-spaced, with turnover lines flush with the left margin. Leave 1 blank line between entries.

> **0.5 inch**
> ⟶ Elliptical expression—a condensed expression from which key words are omitted.
> ↓2x
>
> Essential elements—words, phrases, or clauses that are necessary to the completeness of the structure or the meaning of a sentence.

NOTE: Regardless of the format selected, the terms may be typed with initial caps or all in small letters (except for proper nouns and adjectives). The definitions may also be styled either way; however, if they are written in sentence form, it is best to use initial caps for both the term and the definition. The use of periods at the end of definitions is optional unless, of course, the definitions are written as complete sentences. (See the illustration in ¶1431a for an example of the use of initial caps for both the term and the definition.)

¶**1433**

Manuscripts

The preparation of manuscripts is subject to virtually the same considerations that apply to the preparation of reports (¶¶1401–1431). However, manuscripts differ from reports in one fundamental way: they are written with the idea of publication in mind—whether as a self-contained book, as an article in a magazine or some other printed periodical, or as an item to be included in a bulletin or newsletter. As a result, manuscripts require some special considerations concerning format.

NOTE: Some publishers now require authors to submit their manuscripts on disk as well as in the form of hard copy. Whenever possible, try to determine a publisher's manuscript submission requirements and preferences in advance.

Preparing Manuscript for an Article

1432 If you have been invited to write an article for a specific publication, ask the editor for concrete guidelines on matters of format—line length, spacing, paragraph indention, heading style, preferences in capitalization and punctuation, overall length of article, and so on. You may also want to ask for guidance on content.

1433 If you are writing an article only with the hope that it may be accepted by a certain publication, you will enhance your chances of favorable consideration by imitating all aspects of the publication's format and style.

  a. In particular, try to type your manuscript on a line length that equals an average line of copy in the finished publication. A manuscript prepared in this way will make it easy for the editor to determine how much space your article will fill in the publication. To determine the appropriate line length, copy 10 to 20 lines—on a line-for-line basis—from a representative article. Observe at what point most lines end, and set your margins accordingly.

  b. Even if the publication puts two or more columns on a page, type only one column on a manuscript page. The wider margins will provide space for editing.

  c. Type your manuscript double-spaced to allow room for editing.

  d. Be sure to keep the overall length of your manuscript within the range of the materials typically used by the intended publication. There is little point in submitting a 2000-line manuscript to a publication that carries articles of no more than 500 lines.

  NOTE: Your software very likely has a feature that will provide the following information you can share with your editor: the number of characters in your manuscript, the number of words, the number of lines, the number of paragraphs, and the number of pages.

  e. In trying to simulate the character count of a printed line on your computer, you may have to adjust some of the spacing and indentions you normally use. For example, if you usually use 2 spaces after periods, question marks, exclamation points, and colons, use only 1 space. If you indent paragraphs 0.5 inch, use a 0.25-inch indention instead.

¶1434

Preparing Manuscript for a Book

If you are writing a book or assisting someone who is, consider the following guidelines in the absence of specific guidance from a publisher.

1434 If the manuscript will consist essentially of regular text matter (with perhaps a few tables and illustrations), then in establishing a format for your manuscript, you can follow the standard guidelines for a formal report with respect to spacing, headings, page numbering, and other aspects involved in typing the front matter, the body, and the back matter. Use 1.5-inch side margins to provide extra space for editing.

> **NOTE:** A book manuscript should not be bound.

1435 If you think your manuscript, when set in type, will require a special format—for example, a larger-than-usual page size to accommodate extremely wide tables or to permit notes and small illustrations to run alongside the text or to allow for a two-column arrangement for the printed text—then the easiest way to establish a format for your manuscript page is to select a published work that has the kind of format and font size you have in mind. Then, on your computer, copy a full page of representative printed text—on a line-for-line basis, if possible—to determine the manuscript equivalent of a printed page. (If a printed line is too long to fit on one typed line and still leave side margins of 1.5 inches, choose some other format that you can readily execute.) The important thing is to determine how many pages of manuscript equal a page of printed text. Then, as you develop the manuscript, you can exercise some real control over the length of your material.

Precautions for All Manuscripts

1436 When sending material to a publisher, always retain a duplicate copy in case the material goes astray in the mail or the publisher calls to discuss the manuscript.

> **NOTE:** When you prepare your manuscript on a computer, be sure to save the file on disk. If you are subsequently asked to make changes in the manuscript, you can readily do so and then print a corrected manuscript.

1437 Your unpublished manuscript is automatically protected by the copyright law as soon as it is written, without your putting a copyright notice on it or registering it with the U.S. Copyright Office. If you are concerned that someone may copy your material without giving you appropriate credit or compensation, you may place a copyright notice on the first page *(Copyright © [current year] by [your name])* to call attention to your ownership of the material. Since the copyright law protects only the written expression of your ideas and not the ideas themselves, you should obtain the help of a lawyer if you have an original publishing idea that you are afraid may be misappropriated.

SECTION **15**

Notes and Bibliographies

Footnotes, Endnotes, and Textnotes

Functions of Notes

1501 **a.** In a report or manuscript, *notes* serve two functions: (1) they provide *comments* on the main text, conveying subordinate ideas that the writer feels might be distracting if incorporated within the main text; and (2) they serve as *source references,* identifying the origin of a statement quoted or cited in the text.

Comment

[1]The actual date on which Governor Galloway made this statement is uncertain, but there is no doubt that the statement is his.

Source Reference

[2]Michael Wolff, *Burn Rate: How I Survived the Gold Rush Years on the Internet,* Simon & Schuster, New York, 1998, p. 38.

b. When notes appear at the foot of a page, they are called *footnotes.* (See ¶¶1503–1504.)

---

an incredible range of bloopers to be found in classified ads. One anthology contains these gems: "Dog for sale: eats anything and is fond of children." "Illiterate? Write today for free help." "Auto Repair Service. . . . Try us once, you'll never go anywhere again."[1]

---

[1]Richard Lederer, *Anguished English,* Wyrick, Charleston, S.C., 1987, p. 38.

➤ *For a discussion of whether to type the note number as a superscript (as shown above) or on the line, see ¶1523b; for a discussion of default formats provided by word processing software, see ¶1503.*

c. When notes appear all together at the end of a complete report or manuscript (or sometimes at the end of each chapter), they are called *endnotes.* (See ¶¶1505–1506.)

NOTES

1. Richard Lederer, *Anguished English,* Wyrick, Charleston, S.C., 1987, p. 38.

2. Ibid., pp. 39-40.

➤ *For a discussion of default formats provided by word processing software, see ¶1505.*

d. When source references appear parenthetically within the main text, they are called *textnotes.* (See ¶1507.)

---

but the proper use of punctuation can sometimes have serious financial consequences. Consider the following predicament.

> We came upon a writer at his work . . . . Quite casually he mentioned that he was getting fifty cents a word. A moment or two later his face became contorted with signs of an internal distress. With his hand poised above the machine, he seemed to be fighting something out with himself. . . . "Listen," he said, grimly, "do you hyphenate 'willy-nilly'?" We nodded, and saw him wince as he inserted the little mark, at the cost of half a dollar. (E. B. White, "The Cost of Hyphens," *Writings From The New Yorker: 1927–1976,* HarperCollins, New York, 1991, p. 17.)

---

e. Footnotes or endnotes are ordinarily keyed by number to a word, phrase, or sentence in the text. Textnotes (which appear parenthetically at the desired point of reference right in the text itself) do not have to be keyed this way.

f. Endnotes are growing in popularity because they leave the text pages looking less cluttered and less complicated. They do present one drawback, however: the reader does not know in each instance whether the endnote will contain a comment of substance (which is typically worth reading) or simply a source reference (which is usually of interest only in special cases).

g. Textnotes are also growing in popularity for the same reason: lack of clutter. While it is possible to provide in a textnote all the information that a source reference typically contains, writers more often use the textnote to provide an abbreviated reference in the text, with the understanding that the reader who wants complete information will be able to consult a bibliography at the back of the report or manuscript. (See ¶1507 for examples of these abbreviated references.)

Continued on page 440

Notes and Bibliographies

15

¶1502

h. To take advantage of the benefits and avoid the drawbacks of these three types of notes, some writers use a hybrid system: they treat *comments* as footnotes and *source references* as endnotes or textnotes. In this way comments of substance are conveniently positioned at the bottom of the page, whereas all or most of the information about sources is tucked out of sight but accessible when needed. (See ¶1502g.)

Text References to Footnotes or Endnotes

1502 **a.** To indicate the presence of a comment or a source reference at the bottom of the page or in a special section at the end of the report or manuscript, insert a *superscript* (a raised figure) following the appropriate word, phrase, or sentence in the text.

NOTE: The footnote or endnote feature of your word processing software will insert superscripts in the text wherever you wish. (See *b* below for examples.)

b. There should not be any space between the superscript and the preceding word. If a punctuation mark follows the word, place the superscript immediately after the punctuation mark. (There is one exception: the superscript should precede, not follow, a dash.)

A research study published last month by a leading relocation consulting firm[2] provides the basis for the recommendations offered in Chapter 5.

The alternative approaches discussed in this report have been taken largely from an article entitled "Getting a Handle on Health Care Costs."[1]

An article entitled "Getting a Handle on Health Care Costs"[1]—written by an eminent authority in the field—was the source of the alternative approaches discussed in this report.

c. While the superscript should come as close as possible to the appropriate word or phrase, it is often better to place the superscript at the end of the sentence (if this will cause no misunderstanding) so as to avoid distracting the reader in the midst of the sentence.

ACCEPTABLE: Her latest article, "Automating the Small Legal Office,"[1] was published about three months ago. I urge you to read it.

PREFERABLE: Her latest article, "Automating the Small Legal Office," was published about three months ago.[1] I urge you to read it.

NOTE: Leave 1 or 2 spaces after a superscript that follows the punctuation at the end of a sentence. (See ¶102.)

d. When a paragraph calls for two or more footnotes or endnotes, try to combine all the necessary information within one note if this can be done without any risk of confusing the reader. This approach will reduce the sense of irritation that a large number of footnotes or endnotes tend to produce.

NOTE: When this approach is used, the superscript is typically placed after the last word in the sentence or paragraph, depending on how the text references are dispersed. (See the examples at the top of page 441.)

¶1503

AVOID: The following analysis draws heavily on recent studies undertaken by Andrew Bowen,[1] Frances Kaplan,[2] and Minetta Coleman.[3]

---

[1]Andrew Bowen, . . .
[2]Frances Kaplan, . . .
[3]Minetta Coleman, . . .

PREFERABLE: The following analysis draws heavily on recent studies undertaken by Andrew Bowen, Frances Kaplan, and Minetta Coleman.[1]

---

[1]Andrew Bowen, . . .; Frances Kaplan, . . .; and Minetta Coleman, ...

e. The numbering of footnotes or endnotes may run consecutively throughout or begin again with each new chapter.

f. Footnotes and endnotes are sometimes keyed by symbol rather than by number. This often occurs in tables with figures and in technical material with many formulas, where a raised figure—though intended to refer to a footnote or endnote—could be mistaken for part of the table text or the formula. When the use of symbols is appropriate, choose one of the following programmed sequences:

* † ‡ § ¶   **OR**   a b c d e

These tests confirmed that there was a reduction over time of the flexural strength of the marble unit from 1400 to 1200 lb/in^2.†

(**NOT:** These tests confirmed that there was a reduction over time of the flexural strength of the marble unit from 1400 to 1200 lb/in$^{2.2}$)

g. If you wish to treat *comments* as footnotes and *source references* as endnotes (as suggested in ¶1501h), use *symbols* for the notes containing comments (at the bottom of the page) and use *figures* for the notes containing source references (at the end of the report or manuscript).

Footnotes

1503 a. When you execute footnotes using the footnote feature of a word processing program, the software will automatically position your footnotes at the bottom of the page where the footnote reference appears in the text. The software will also (1) insert a horizontal line to separate the footnotes from the text above, (2) continue a footnote on the following page if it is too long to fit as a whole on the page where it started, and (3) automatically number your footnotes. If subsequent additions or deletions in the text cause the text reference to shift to another page, the related footnote will automatically shift as well. If a footnote is subsequently inserted or deleted, all the remaining footnotes (and their related text references) will be automatically renumbered from that point on.

b. The illustration at the top of page 442 shows you how your footnotes will look if you use the footnote feature of Microsoft Word for Windows and accept all the defaults. Note the following details: (1) the first line of each footnote begins at the left margin; (2) no extra space is inserted between footnotes; (3) no extra space is inserted between the horizontal rule and the first footnote; and (4) an ordinal abbreviation such as *th* (in the phrase *5th ed.*) appears as a superscript (*5th ed.*).

Continued on page 442

Notes and Bibliographies

15

¶1503

into the new century.[1] According to one source:

> The Internet—also known as the *Net*—is the world's largest computer network. . . . The Internet isn't really one network—it's a network of networks, all freely exchanging information. The networks range from the big and formal (such as the corporate networks at AT&T, Digital Equipment Corporation, and Hewlett-Packard) to the small and informal (such as the one in John's back bedroom, with a couple of old PCs bought through the *Want Advertiser*) and everything in between.[2]

---

[1] For a detailed analysis of these technological developments, see Chap. 2, pp. 29–38.
[2] John R. Levine et al., *The Internet for Dummies*, 5th ed., IDG Books, Foster City, Calif., 1998, p. 10.

c. In the standard format most commonly used, a horizontal rule 2 inches long appears 1 line below the text (as in the illustration below); the first line of each footnote is indented; a blank line is inserted between the horizontal rule and the first footnote as well as between all footnotes; and ordinal abbreviations are placed on the line (for example, *2d ed., 3d ed., 4th ed.*).

into the new century.[1] According to one source: ↓ **2x**

> **0.5** The Internet—also known as the *Net*—is the world's largest **0.5**
> computer network. . . . The Internet isn't really one network—
> → it's a network of networks, all freely exchanging information. ←
> **inch** The networks range from the big and formal (such as the **inch**
> corporate networks at AT&T, Digital Equipment Corporation,
> and Hewlett-Packard) to the small and informal (such as the
> one in John's back bedroom, with a couple of old PCs bought
> through the *Want Advertiser*) and everything in between.[2] ↓ **2x**

--- ↓ **2x**

[1]For a detailed analysis of these technological developments, see Chap. 2, pp. 29–38. ↓ **2x**

[2]John R. Levine et al., *The Internet for Dummies*, 5th ed., IDG Books, Foster City, Calif., 1998, p. 10.

NOTE: Whether you are writing business or academic reports or developing manuscript for a particular publisher, you will be expected in most cases to follow a prescribed style for footnotes (unless, of course, you are required to use endnotes or textnotes instead). In situations where no format is prescribed but professional editorial standards have to be met, follow the standard format illustrated above.

➤ *For guidelines on how to construct footnotes, see ¶¶1508–1531, 1540–1546.*

1504 When dealing with footnotes, consider the following guidelines.

a. If the text runs short on a page (say, the last page of a chapter), any footnotes related to that text should still be positioned at the *foot* of the page.

b. Ordinarily, single-space each footnote, but in material that is to be edited, use double spacing to allow room for the editing.

c. Type the footnote number as a superscript or on the line. (See ¶1523b for details on spacing and punctuation.)

d. Ideally, the *complete* footnote should appear on the same page as the superscript figure or symbol that refers to it. Occasionally, however, a footnote may be so long that it will not all fit on the page, even if it begins immediately following the line of text in which the superscript figure or symbol occurs. In such a case the footnote feature of your word processing software will automatically break the footnote and complete it at the bottom of the next page (as shown in the following illustrations).

Start of a Long Footnote

and computers should not be used to write thank-you notes.[2]

---

[2]Judith Martin (in *Miss Manners' Basic Training: Communications*, Crown, New York, 1998, p. 37) clearly supports this position: "Thank-you letters should be written by hand. Miss Manners . . . grants exemptions

Continuation of a Long Footnote

on which there still is a considerable difference of opinion.[3]

---

only to people with specific physical disabilities that prevent them from writing. Those who claim illegible handwriting should be home practicing their penmanship instead of bragging about it."

[3]Baldrige, p. 593.

NOTE: If you have a number of long notes that may not easily fit on the page where they are first referred to, you have an excellent reason for abandoning the footnote format and using endnotes instead. (See ¶¶1505–1506.)

➤ *For the treatment of footnotes that pertain to a table, see ¶¶1634–1636.*

¶1505

Endnotes

1505 a. The endnote feature of a word processing program will automatically position all endnotes at the end of the document. If you add or delete endnotes, all the remaining endnotes (and their related text references) will be automatically renumbered from that point on.

b. The endnote feature will also automatically format the endnotes for you. Here is how your endnotes will look if you accept all the defaults of the endnote feature of Microsoft Word for Windows. Note that the endnote section begins on the same page as the conclusion of the main text, separated by a short horizontal rule starting at the left margin but with no heading (such as *NOTES*) to introduce this section. Note also that each entry begins at the left margin with superscripts in small roman numerals and with no extra space between entries.

> Having now surveyed the ways in which innovation has traditionally been
>
> viewed, I would venture to say that the most striking definition has been
>
> provided by Bob Metcalfe, the inventor of the Ethernet. At a recent MIT
>
> panel discussion on innovation, he said, "Invention is a flower. Innova-
>
> tion is a weed."[ii]
>
> _____
>
> [i] Scott Kirsner, "The Legend of Bob Metcalfe," *Wired*, November 1998, p. 184.
> [ii] Ibid., p. 23.

1506 If you want to modify the default format shown above or if you prefer to create your own format for endnotes, consider the following guidelines. (The illustration at the top of page 445 reflects these guidelines.)

a. For better readability, use arabic rather than roman numerals in the text and the endnotes. The numbers in the endnotes sometimes appear as superscripts, but the on-the-line style is more commonly used.

b. Indent the first line of each endnote 0.5 inch. The turnovers should start at the left margin.

c. On a new page type the heading *NOTES*, centered in boldface capital letters, approximately 2 inches from the top of the page.

NOTE: If the document consists of only one chapter, the endnotes may begin on the same page where the main text ends. In that case leave about 3 blank lines before the heading and 1 or 2 blank lines after it.

d. Ordinarily, single-space each endnote, but in material that is to be edited, use double spacing to allow room for the editing. In either case leave 1 blank line between endnotes.

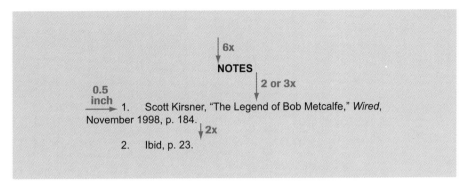

e. Use the same margins as for other pages in the body of the report or manuscript (see ¶¶1404–1407), and treat the numbering of these pages as described in ¶1427f–g.

➢ *For guidelines on how to construct source reference endnotes, see ¶¶1508–1531.*

f. If the numbering of endnotes starts again with each new chapter or with each new page, insert an appropriate heading—*Chapter 1, Chapter 2,* etc., or *Page 1, Page 2,* etc.—above each sequence of endnotes in this section. Type the heading at the left margin in capital and small letters (using boldface, italics, or underlining), and leave 2 blank lines above and 1 blank line below.

NOTE: If the numbering of endnotes is consecutive throughout, no headings are needed.

g. Insert this special section of endnotes in the back matter following any appendixes. If no appendix is given, the endnotes begin the back matter. (See also ¶1428.)

NOTE: When the individual chapters of a report or a manuscript are prepared by different writers, it may be advantageous to have the endnotes that each author prepares inserted at the end of the respective chapter instead of redoing all the endnotes as one continuous section in the back matter. If this approach is used, expand the heading *NOTES* in each case to read *NOTES TO CHAPTER 1, NOTES TO CHAPTER 2,* and so on. The disadvantage of this approach is that the reader will have a bit more difficulty locating the notes for each chapter than is true when all the endnotes are presented in one section at the very end.

Textnotes

1507 a. In a report or manuscript with only a few source references and no bibliography at the end, the complete source data may be inserted within the text in the form of parenthetical textnotes. (See the illustration at the top of page 446.)

➢ *For guidelines on how to construct source reference textnotes, see ¶¶1508–1531.*

Continued on page 446

¶1507

> recommended by the U.S. Postal Service. As for the abbreviations devised to hold down the length of place names in addresses, here is what one authority had to say:
>
> > And all you people with beautiful words in your addresses: Cut 'em down. There's a bright golden haze on the MDWS; a fairy dancing in your GDNS; and a safe HBR past the happy LNDG at the XING, where no hope SPGS. Environmentalists are now GRN, as in how GRN was my VLY. . . . Is the language not lessened when words like *meadow, gardens, harbor, landing, crossing, green, valley*—even *islands (ISS)*—are disemvoweled? (William Safire, *In Love With Norma Loquendi*, Random House, New York, 1994, p. 166.)

NOTE: If some of the data called for in a source reference is already provided in the main text, there is no need to repeat it in the textnote.

> recommended by the U.S. Postal Service. As for the abbreviations devised to hold down the length of place names in addresses, here is what William Safire had to say:
>
> > And all you people with beautiful words in your addresses: Cut 'em down. There's a bright golden haze on the MDWS; a fairy dancing in your GDNS; and a safe HBR past the happy LNDG at the XING, where no hope SPGS. Environmentalists are now GRN, as in how GRN was my VLY. . . . Is the language not lessened when words like *meadow, gardens, harbor, landing, crossing, green, valley*—even *islands (ISS)*—are disemvoweled? (*In Love With Norma Loquendi*, Random House, New York, 1994, p. 166.)

b. In a report or manuscript that contains a number of source references *and* a complete bibliography, textnotes may be used as follows:

(1) At the appropriate point in the main text, supply the author's last name and the appropriate page number in parentheses. The reader who wants more complete information can consult the full entry in the bibliography.

According to a fine book on time management (Bittel, p. 27), your ability to manage time depends in part on the way you experience the passage of time.

NOTE: Some authorities omit *p.* and *pp.* as well as the comma between the name and the page number. For example:

. . . book on time management (Bittel 27) . . .

(2) If the author's name already appears in the main text, give only the page number in parentheses.

Lester R. Bittel, in his fine book *Right on Time!* (p. 27), says that . . .

(3) If the bibliography lists more than one publication by the same author, then in the textnote use an abbreviated title or the year of publication to indicate which publication is being referred to.

According to a fine book on time management (Bittel, *Time,* p. 27), . . .

OR: . . . a fine book on time management (Bittel, 1991, p. 27), . . .

¶**1507**

(4) If the bibliography lists publications by two or more authors with the same surname, use each author's first name or initial along with the surname. For example:

According to a fine book on time management (L. Bittel, p. 27), . . .

(5) If the entries in the bibliography are numbered in sequence (see ¶1549c), then the textnote can simply list the appropriate "entry number" along with the page reference. Italicize or underline the entry number to distinguish it from the page number, especially if the abbreviation *p.* or *pp.* is omitted. For example:

According to a fine book . . . (*18*, p. 27), . . .   **OR**   (18, p. 27), . . .

Constructing Source Reference Notes

The following guidelines for constructing source reference notes deal with the situations that most commonly occur—whether in the form of footnotes, endnotes, or the type of textnote discussed in ¶1507. There is no clear-cut agreement among authorities on how these notes should be constructed; rather, there are several schools of thought on the subject, and within each school there are variations between one reference manual and another.

Of all the well-established conventions and variations, the style best suited for business use—and the one presented here—is a style that employs the simplest punctuation and the most straightforward presentation of the necessary data without any sacrifice in clarity or completeness. However, certain professional organizations—for example, the American Psychological Association (the APA)—have each established a distinctive style, the use of which sometimes shows up in other fields. Moreover, slightly different patterns are often used in academic materials, such as those featured in *The MLA [Modern Language Association] Style Manual* and *The Chicago Manual of Style*. If you are one of the many full-time business workers who are simultaneously taking one or more academic courses or one of the many full-time academic students who are concurrently holding down part- or full-time office jobs, you may need to familiarize yourself with more than one style. Note that along with the basic pattern for citing book titles (see ¶1508), you will find an "academic" variation that you may need to use from time to time. However, unless you are specifically directed to follow a particular style, the following "all-purpose" patterns—based on well-established conventions—should meet your needs in virtually every type of situation you encounter.

For detailed information about specific elements within these patterns, see the following paragraphs:

➤ *Note number: see ¶1523.*
Names of authors: see ¶1524.
Title of the work: see ¶1525.
Publisher's name: see ¶1526.
Place of publication: see ¶1527.
Date of publication: see ¶1528.
Page numbers: see ¶1529.
Subsequent references: see ¶¶1530–1531.

Notes and
Bibliographies

15

¶1508

1508 Book Title: Basic Pattern

a. Business Style

[1]Author, *book title,* publisher, place of publication, year of publication, page number [if reference is being made to a specific page].

[1]Ron Chernow, *Titan,* Random House, New York, 1998, p. 663.

OR

1. Ron Chernow, *Titan,* Random House, New York, 1998, p. 663.

NOTE: If any of these elements have already been identified in the text (for example, the author's name and the book title), they need not be repeated in the note. Moreover, if reference is made to the book as a whole rather than to a particular page, omit the page number. In the following illustration, observe that the quoted material requires more than three lines. For that reason, it is indented 0.5 inch from each side margin. (See ¶1424d.)

about the surprising frugality of immensely wealthy people. Ron Chernow, in *Titan*

(his award-winning biography of John D. Rockefeller, Sr.), offers this illustration:

> 0.5 inch
> The world's richest man never lost the thrifty boyhood habits that had made him the nonpareil of American business. One day at Ormond Beach, he was studying the blazing hearth when he turned to Michael, the butler, and asked, "How long are those sticks of wood?" Fourteen inches, Michael replied. "Do you think they would do just as well if they were cut twelve inches in length?" Michael conceded this was possible. "Then the next time the wood is being sawed have it made twelve inches in length." Since twelve inches gave sufficient light and heat at less expense, it became the new household standard.[1]

0.5 inch

0.5 inch

[1]Random House, New York, 1998, p. 663.

b. Academic Style

[1]Author, *book title* (place of publication: publisher, year of publication), page number [if reference is being made to a specific page].

[1]Ron Chernow, *Titan* (New York: Random House, 1998), p. 663.

NOTE: The key distinction between the business style and the academic style lies in a slightly different sequence of elements and a slightly different form of punctuation:

BUSINESS STYLE: . . . publisher, place of publication, year of publication . . .

ACADEMIC STYLE: . . . (place of publication: publisher, year of publication) . . .

The following patterns for books (in ¶¶1509–1516) show only the business style. However, you can readily convert them to the academic style by simply changing the treatment of these three elements.

➤ *For the academic style for entries in bibliographies, see ¶1551c.*

1509 Book Title: With Edition Number

> [1]Author, *book title*, edition number [if not the first edition], publisher, place, year, page number.

> [1]David Kairys, *The Politics of Law,* 3d ed., Basic Books, New York, 1998, p. 113.

NOTE: Use an edition number only when the book is not in the first edition. If included, the edition number follows the main title and any related elements, such as the subtitle or the volume number and title. (For an example, see ¶1511.) The following forms are commonly used: *2d ed., 3d ed., 4th ed.,* and *rev. ed.* (for "revised edition").

> [2]Jane Bryant Quinn, *Making the Most of Your Money,* rev. ed., Simon & Schuster, New York, 1997, p. 53.

1510 Book Title: With Subtitle

> [1]Author, *book title: subtitle,* edition number [if not the first edition], publisher, place, year, page number.

> [1]Pat Schroeder, *24 Years of House Work . . . and the Place Is Still a Mess: My Life in Politics,* Andrews McMeel, Kansas City, Mo., 1998, p. 97.

> [2]Ben Cohen and Jerry Greenfield, *Ben & Jerry's Double-Dip Capitalism: Lead With Your Values and Make Money Too,* Simon & Schuster, New York, 1997, p. 55.

NOTE: It is not necessary to supply the subtitle of a book unless it is significant in identifying the book or in explaining its basic nature. If a subtitle is to be shown, separate it from the main title with a colon (unless the title page shows some other mark such as a dash). Italicize the main title and the subtitle. Capitalize the first word of the subtitle, even if it is a short preposition like *for,* a short conjunction like *or,* or an article like *the* or *a.* (See ¶361.)

> [3]Joshua Quittner and Michelle Slatalla, *Speeding the Net: The Inside Story of Netscape and How It Challenged Microsoft,* Atlantic Monthly Press, New York, 1998, p. 124.

> [4]Joe S. Foote, *Live From the Trenches: The Changing Role of the Television News Correspondent,* Southern Illinois Univ. Press, Carbondale, Ill., 1998, p. 147.

1511 Book Title: With Volume Number and Volume Title

> [1]Author, *book title,* volume number, *volume title,* edition number [if not the first edition], publisher, place, year, page number.

> [1]E. Lipson, *The Economic History of England,* Vol. 1, *The Middle Ages,* 12th ed., Adam & Charles Black, London, 1959, pp. 511–594.

NOTE: As a rule, do not show the volume title in a note unless it is significant in identifying the book. When the volume title is included, both the volume number and the volume title follow the book title (and subtitle, if any) but precede the edition number. The volume number is usually preceded by the abbreviation *Vol.* or by the word *Book* or *Part* (depending on the actual designation). The volume number may be arabic or roman, depending on the style used in the actual book. Some writers prefer to use one style of volume number throughout the notes. (See also ¶1512.)

1512 Book Title: With Volume Number Alone

> [1]Author, *book title,* edition number [if not the first edition], publisher, place, year, volume number, page number.

> [1]Ruth Barnes Moynihan et al. (eds.), *Second to None: A Documentary History of American Women,* Univ. of Nebraska Press, Lincoln, 1994, Vol. II, p. 374.

> ➤ *For the use of* et al., *see* ¶*1524c; for the use of* eds., *see* ¶*1524e.*

Continued on page 450

¶1513

NOTE: When the volume number is shown without the volume title, it follows the date of publication. When the volume number and page number occur one after the other, they may be styled as follows:

Style for Roman Volume Number	**Style for Arabic Volume Number**
Vol. III, p. 197 **OR** III, 197	Vol. 5, pp. 681–684 **OR** 5:681–684

[1]Ruth Barnes Moynihan et al. (eds.), *Second to None: A Documentary History of American Women,* Univ. of Nebraska Press, Lincoln, 1994, II, 374.

Do not use the forms with figures alone if there is a chance your reader will not understand them.

1513 Book Title: With Chapter Reference

[1]Author, *book title,* publisher, place, year, chapter number, "chapter title" [if significant], page number.

[1]Will Durant and Ariel Durant, *The Age of Napoleon,* Simon & Schuster, New York, 1975, Chap. XII, "Napoleon and the Arts," pp. 278–285.

NOTE: When a note refers primarily to the title of a book, a chapter number and a chapter title are not usually included. If they are considered significant, however, these details can be inserted just before the page numbers. The word *chapter* is usually abbreviated as *Chap.,* the chapter number is arabic or roman (depending on the original), and the chapter title is enclosed in quotation marks. Some writers prefer to use one style of chapter number throughout the notes.

1514 Selection From Collected Works of One Author

[1]Author, "title of selection," *book title,* publisher, place, year, page number.

[1]Seamus Heaney, "A Basket of Chestnuts," *Seeing Things,* Farrar, Strauss and Giroux, New York, 1997, pp. 26–27.

1515 Selection in Anthology

[1]Author of selection, "title of selection," **in** editor of anthology **(ed.)**, *book title,* publisher, place, year, page number.

[1]Mary Corliss Pearl, "Ecology and the Environment," in Richard W. Bulliet (ed.), *The Columbia History of the 20th Century,* Columbia Univ. Press, New York, 1998, p. 173.

[2]Harris Breslow, "Civil Society, Political Economy, and the Internet," in Steven G. Jones (ed.), *Virtual Culture: Identity and Communication in Cybersociety,* Sage Publications, London, 1997, p. 253.

[3]E. B. White, "The Ring of Time," in Phillip Lopate (ed.), *The Art of the Personal Essay: An Anthology From the Classical Era to the Present,* Doubleday, New York, 1994, pp. 538–544.

[4]Lindsy Van Gelder, "The Great Person-Hole Cover Debate: A Modest Proposal for Anyone Who Thinks the Word 'He' Is Just Plain Easier," in *75 Readings: An Anthology,* 7th ed., McGraw-Hill, New York, 1999, pp. 347–349.

1516 Article in Reference Work

[1]Author [if known], "article title," *name of reference work,* edition number [if not the first edition], publisher [usually omitted], place [usually omitted], year, page number [may be omitted].

[1]Joel Cracraft, "Animal Systematics," *McGraw-Hill Encyclopedia of Science and Technology,* 8th ed., 1997.

[2]"Computers," *Encyclopedia Americana,* International Edition, 1995.

[3]Mary Jane Lupton, "Maya Angelou," *American Writers,* Scribner, New York, 1996, p. 18.

¶1518

NOTE: It is not necessary to give the name of the publisher or the place of publication unless there is some possibility of confusion or the reference is not well known.

[5]*Merriam-Webster's Collegiate Dictionary,* 10th ed., 1997, pp. 23a–30a.

[6]*The American Heritage Dictionary of the English Language,* 3d ed., 1997, pp. xxvi–xxx.

Moreover, if you are making reference to an article or an entry that appears in alphabetic order in the main portion of the work, even the page number may be omitted. If the reference work carries the name of an editor rather than an author, the editor's name is also usually omitted.

[7]"Data Processing," *The Columbia Encyclopedia,* 5th ed., 1993.

1517 Article in Newspaper

[1]Author [if known], "article title," *name of newspaper,* date, page number, column number.

[1]Albert B. Crenshaw, "Looking for a New Mortgage? A Car? There's a Site for It," *The Washington Post,* November 2, 1998, p. 7, cols. 1–3.

➤ *See ¶1518, note.*

NOTE: If a particular issue of a newspaper is published in several sections and the page numbering begins anew with each section, include the section letter or number before the page number.

[2]Donald M. Murray, "O Say Can We Find a Better National Anthem?" *The Boston Globe,* November 3, 1998, Sec. E, p. 1, col. 1.

OR: . . . November 3, 1998, p. E1, col. 1.

1518 Article in Magazine or Journal

a. Article in Magazine

[1]Author [if known], "article title," *name of magazine,* date, page number.

[1]"In Search of Quality Medical Care," *Consumer Reports,* October 1998, pp. 35–40.

[2]James A. Martin, "Work From Home, Get More Done," *PC World,* November 1998, pp. 45–48.

[3]Marcia Stepanek, "2000 Reasons to Celebrate," *Business Week,* November 9, 1998, p. 54.

[4]Wendy M. Beech, "Building a Successful Home-Based Business," *Black Enterprise,* September 1997, p. 92.

NOTE: Omit the comma between the article title and the name of the periodical if the article title ends with a question mark or an exclamation point.

[5]Margaret Mannix, "What's That Lurking on Your Phone Bill?" *U.S. News & World Report,* November 9, 1998, p. 74.

[6]Mark Frauenfelder, "Block That Site!" *Yahoo! Internet Life,* November 1998, pp. 92–98.

➤ *See also the second example in ¶1517 and the examples in* b *below.*

b. Article in Professional Journal

[1]Author, "article title," *title of journal* [frequently abbreviated], series number [if given], volume number, issue number [if given], date, page number.

[7]Suzy Wetlaufer, "After the Layoffs, What Next?" *Harvard Business Review,* Vol. 76, No. 5, September–October 1998, p. 24.

Continued on page 452

¶1519

NOTE: Titles of journals are often abbreviated in notes whenever these abbreviations are likely to be familiar to the intended readership or are clearly identified in a bibliography at the end.

[7]Suzy Wetlaufer, "After the Layoffs, What Next?" *HBR,* Vol. 76, No. 5, September–October 1998, p. 24.

1519 Quotation From a CD-ROM

[1]Author [if known], "article title" [if appropriate], *title of work* **(CD-ROM)**, publisher [may be omitted], place of publication [may be omitted], year of publication, reference to location of quotation [if available].

[1]"Jupiter," *McGraw-Hill Multimedia Encyclopedia of Science and Technology* (CD-ROM), 1994.

[2]*Guerilla Marketing: Winning Strategies for Greater Profits* (CD-ROM), Houghton Mifflin Interactive, Boston, 1998.

[3]*Inc.'s Customer Service Plan Pro* (CD-ROM), Inc., Boston, 1998.

NOTE: When citing material taken from a CD-ROM, try to provide some specific guidance on how to access the quoted passage on the disk. For example, if the material is organized in numbered paragraphs or pages, give the appropriate paragraph or page number. If the quoted passage is taken from a work organized like an encyclopedia or a dictionary (that is, in the form of brief articles or entries arranged in alphabetic sequence), provide the article title or key word used to identify the article or entry. Without such assistance, a person can usually input a key phrase (or character string) from the quoted material and use the search feature of a word processing program to locate the complete passage.

1520 Bulletin, Pamphlet, or Monograph

[1]Author [if given], "article title" [if appropriate], *title of bulletin,* series title and series number [if appropriate], volume number and issue number [if appropriate], sponsoring organization, place [may be omitted], date, page number.

[1]Lois Mai Chan and Diane Vizine-Goetz, "Toward a Computer-Generated Subject Validation File," *Library Resources & Technical Services,* Vol. 42, No. 1, American Library Association, Washington, January 1998.

NOTE: Because the data used to identify bulletins, pamphlets, and monographs may vary widely, adapt the pattern shown above as necessary to fit each particular situation. For example, the name of the sponsoring organization may be omitted if it is incorporated in the title of the bulletin.

1521 Unpublished Dissertation or Thesis

[1]Author, "title of thesis," **doctoral dissertation OR master's thesis** [identifying phrase to be inserted], name of academic institution, place, date, page number.

[1]David Clement Dvorak, "The Education Designed for Gainful Employment (EDGE) Program: An Analysis of Local Implementation," doctoral dissertation, Michigan State University, East Lansing, 1994, p. 169.

1522 Quotation From a Secondary Source

[1]Author, *book title,* publisher, place, date, page number, **quoted by OR cited by** author, *book title,* publisher, place, date, page number.

[1]Robert J. Dolan and Hermann Simon, *Power Pricing,* Free Press, New York, 1997, cited by Jack Trout with Steve Rivkin, *The Power of Simplicity,* McGraw-Hill, New York, 1999, p. 76.

NOTE: While it is always preferable to take the wording of a quotation from the original source, it is sometimes necessary to draw the wording from a secondary source.

¶**1524**

In such cases construct the note in two parts: in the first part, give as much information as possible about the *original* source (derived, of course, from the reference note in the secondary source); in the second part, give the necessary information about the *secondary* source (which is at hand). Bridge the two parts of the note with a phrase such as *quoted by* or *cited by.* The pattern shown at the bottom of page 452 assumes that the quotation originally appeared in a book and that the secondary source for the quoted material was also a book. Naturally, if the original source or the secondary source is a work other than a book, use the pattern appropriate for that work.

Elements of Source Reference Notes

1523 Note Number

a. Make sure that the number at the start of a footnote or an endnote corresponds to the appropriate reference number in the text.

b. Indent the note number 0.5 inch and type it (1) as a superscript (raised figure) without any space following it or (2) on the line (like an ordinary number), followed by a period and 1 or 2 spaces. The on-the-line style is more commonly used in endnotes. (See ¶¶1504–1505.)

> [1]Michael D. Woodard, *Black Entrepreneurs in America: Stories of Struggle and Success,* Rutgers Univ. Press, New Brunswick, N.J., 1997, p. 183.
>
> **OR**
>
> 1. Michael D. Woodard, *Black Entrepreneurs in America: Stories of Struggle and Success,* Rutgers Univ. Press, New Brunswick, N.J., 1997, p. 183.

➤ *For guidelines on numbering notes, see ¶1502e; for the use of symbols in place of figures, see ¶1502f–g.*

1524 Names of Authors

a. Type an author's name (first name first) exactly as it appears on the title page of a book or in the heading of an article. (See ¶1508a, note.)

> [1]William A. Henry III, *In Defense of Elitism,* Doubleday, New York, 1995, p. 23.
>
> [2]William Strunk Jr. and E. B. White, *The Elements of Style,* 3d ed., Macmillan, New York, 1979, pp. 32–33.
>
> [3]Michael Eisner with Tony Schwartz, *Work in Progress,* Random House, New York, 1998, p. 71.
>
> [4]John A. Byrne with a team of *Business Week* editors, *Business Week Guide to the Best Business Schools,* 6th ed., McGraw-Hill, New York, 1999, p. 67.

b. When two authors have the same surname, show the surname with each author's listing.

> [5]Nancy Baker Wise and Christy Wise, *A Mouthful of Rivets: Women at Work in World War II,* Jossey-Bass, San Francisco, 1994, p. 153.

c. When there are three or more authors, list only the first author's name followed by *et al.* (meaning "and others"). Do not italicize or underline *et al.*

> [6]Roger Fisher et al., *Getting to Yes,* Penguin, New York, 1998, p. 33.

NOTE: The names of all the authors may be given, but once this style is used in a source reference note, it should be used consistently.

> [7]Roger Fisher, William A. Ury, and Bruce Patton, *Getting to Yes,* Penguin, New York, 1998, p. 33.

Continued on page 454

¶1525

d. When an organization (rather than an individual) is the author of the material, show the organization's name in the author's position.

> [8]Society for Creative Anachronism, *Giants in the Earth,* Bennett & Kitchel, East Lansing, Mich., 1991, p. 54.

However, if the organization is both the author and the publisher, show the organization's name only once—as the publisher.

> [9]*Patterson's American Education,* rev. ed., Educational Directories, Mount Prospect, Ill., 1996.

e. When a work carries an editor's name rather than an author's name, list the editor's name in the author's position, followed by the abbreviation *ed.* in parentheses. (If the names of two or more editors are listed, use the abbreviation *eds.* in parentheses.)

> [10]Nan Stone (ed.), *Peter Drucker on the Profession of Management,* Harvard Business School Press, Cambridge, Mass., 1998.

> [11]Andrés Torres and José E. Velázquez (eds.), *The Puerto Rican Movement: Voices From the Diaspora,* Temple Univ. Press, Philadelphia, 1998.

NOTE: If a reference work (such as an encyclopedia, a dictionary, or a directory) carries the name of an editor rather than an author, the editor's name is usually omitted. (See ¶1516, note.)

> [12]*Dictionary of American Regional English,* Harvard Univ. Press, Cambridge, Mass., 1996, Vol. III, p. xxxii.

RATHER THAN:

> [12]Frederic G. Cassidy (ed.), *Dictionary of American Regional English,* Harvard Univ. Press, Cambridge, Mass., 1996, Vol. III, p. xxxii.

f. If the author of a work is unknown, begin the note with the title of the work. Do not use *Anonymous* in place of the author's name.

1525 Title of the Work

a. In giving the title of the work, follow the title page of a book or the main heading of an article for wording, spelling, and punctuation. However, adjust the capitalization as necessary so that all titles cited in the notes conform to a standard style. For example, a book entitled *Assertiveness,* with a subtitle *(the right to be you)* shown entirely in small letters on the title page for graphic effect, would appear in a note as follows: Claire Walmsley, *Assertiveness: The Right to Be You.*

> ➤ *For the capitalization of titles, see ¶¶360–363.*

b. If a title and a subtitle are shown on separate lines in the original work without any intervening punctuation, use a colon to separate them in the source reference note. (See ¶1510 for an example.)

c. As a general rule, use italics or underlining for titles of *complete* published works, and use quotation marks for titles that refer to *parts* of complete published works.

> ➤ *For the use of italics or underlining with titles, see ¶¶289, 1508a; for the use of quotation marks with titles, see ¶¶242–243.*

1526 Publisher's Name

a. List the publisher's name as it appears on the title page (for example, *John Wiley & Sons*) or in a shortened form that is clearly recognizable *(Wiley)*; use one form consistently throughout. If a division of the publishing company is also listed on the title page, it is not necessary to include this information in the footnote. Publishers, however, often do so in references to their own materials.

b. The following list of examples shows acceptable patterns for abbreviating publishers' names. If in doubt, do not abbreviate.

Full Name	Acceptable Short Form
Alfred A. Knopf	Knopf
John Wiley & Sons	Wiley
William Morrow and Company, Inc.	Morrow
Random House	———
The Brookings Institution	Brookings
The Free Press	Free Press
Houghton Mifflin Company	Houghton Mifflin
Addison-Wesley Publishing Co.	Addison-Wesley
HarperCollins Publisher	HarperCollins
The McGraw-Hill Companies, Inc.	McGraw-Hill
Simon & Schuster Inc.	Simon & Schuster
Merriam-Webster, Incorporated	Merriam
Little, Brown & Co.	Little, Brown
Farrar, Straus and Giroux	———
Yale University Press	Yale Univ. Press
University of California Press	Univ. of California Press

NOTE: The patterns of abbreviation typically depend on how the publishers are referred to in speech. Since one never hears Random House referred to as *Random*, the name is not abbreviated. By the same token, one hears Little, Brown & Co. referred to as *Little, Brown*, never simply as *Little*.

c. Omit the publisher's name from references to newspapers and other periodicals. The publisher's name is also usually omitted from references to dictionaries and similar works unless confusion might result or the work is not well known. (For examples, see ¶1516.)

1527 Place of Publication

a. As a rule, list only the city of publication (for example, *New York, Boston, Washington, Toronto*). If the city may not be well known to your intended audience (for example, readers from abroad) or the city is likely to be confused with another city of the same name, add the state or the country (for example, *Cambridge, Mass.; Cambridge, England*). If the title page lists several cities in which the publisher has offices, use only the first city named.

b. Omit the place of publication from references to periodicals and well-known reference works.

c. Incorporate the city name in the name of a newspaper that might otherwise be unrecognized. For example, *The Star-Ledger* (published in Newark, New Jersey) should be referred to in a note as *The Newark (N.J.) Star-Ledger.*

¶1528

1528 **Date of Publication**

    a. For books, show the year of publication. (Use the most recent year shown in the copyright notice.)

    b. For monthly periodicals, show both the month and the year. (See ¶1518 for examples.)

    c. For weekly or daily newspapers and other periodicals, show the month, day, and year. (See ¶¶1517–1518 for examples.)

1529 **Page Numbers**

    a. Page references in notes occur in the following forms:

        p. 3   p. v

        pp. 3–4   pp. v–vi

        pp. 301 f. (meaning "page 301 and the following page")

        pp. 301 ff. (meaning "page 301 and the following pages")

    NOTE: Whenever possible, avoid using the indefinite abbreviations *f.* and *ff.*, and supply a specific range of page numbers instead.

    b. In a range of page numbers the second number is sometimes abbreviated; for example, *pp. 981–983* may be expressed as *pp. 981–83.* (See ¶460.)

    c. There is a trend toward dropping *p.* and *pp.* when there is no risk of mistaking the numbers for anything but page numbers.

    ➤ *For the use of an en dash or a hyphen in a range of page numbers, see ¶459a.*

Subsequent References

1530   **a.** When a note refers to a work that was fully identified in the note *immediately preceding*, it may be shortened by the use of the abbreviation *ibid.* (meaning "in the same place"). *Ibid.* replaces all those elements that would otherwise be carried over intact from the previous note. Do not italicize or underline *ibid.*

        [1]Deborah Tannen, *For the Sake of Argument,* Random House, New York, 1998, pp. 61–62.

        [2]Ibid., p. 94. (*Ibid.* represents all the elements in the previous note except the page number.)

        [3]Ibid. (Here *ibid.* represents everything in the preceding note, including the same page number.)

    b. If you plan to use *ibid.* in a *footnote*, make sure that the footnote "immediately preceding" is no more than a few pages back. Otherwise, the interested reader will have to riffle back through the pages in order to find the "immediately preceding" footnote. To spare your reader this inconvenience, use the forms suggested in ¶1531.

    c. Do not use *ibid.* in a *textnote* unless the one "immediately preceding" is on the same page and easy to spot; otherwise, your reader will have to search through lines and lines of text to find it. To spare your reader, construct these "subsequent reference" textnotes along the same lines as "first reference" textnotes. (See ¶1507b.)

    NOTE: With *endnotes,* the use of *ibid.* will cause no inconvenience, since it refers to the note directly above.

1531 **a.** When a note refers to a work fully identified in an earlier note but *not the one immediately preceding*, it may be shortened as follows:

> [1]Author's surname, page number.

> [8]Tannen, p. 65. (Referring to the work fully identified in an earlier note; see the first example in ¶1530a.)

NOTE: When short forms are used for subsequent references, it is desirable to provide a complete bibliography as well, so that the interested reader can quickly find the complete reference for each work in an alphabetic listing.

b. When previous reference has been made to different authors with the same surname, the use of a surname alone in a subsequent reference would be confusing. Therefore, the basic pattern in ¶1531a must be modified in the following way:

> [1]Author's initial(s) plus surname, page number.

OR: > [1]Author's full name, page number.

> [1]David R. Johnson, *Illegal Tender,* Smithsonian, Washington, D.C., 1995, pp. 38–43.

> [2]Debbie Johnson, *Think Yourself Thin,* Hyperion, New York, 1997, p. 205.

> [3]D. R. Johnson, p. 48.

> [4]D. Johnson, p. 211.

c. If previous reference has been made to different works by the same author, any subsequent reference should contain the title of the specific work now being referred to. This title may be shortened to a key word or phrase; the word or phrase should be sufficiently clear, however, so that the full title can be readily identified in the bibliography or in an earlier note.

> [1]Author's surname, *book title* [shortened if feasible], page number.

> [1]Peter F. Drucker, *Managing for Results,* Harper Business, 1993, pp. 199–202.

> [2]Peter F. Drucker, *The Pension Fund Revolution,* Transaction Publishers, New Brunswick, N.J., 1995, p. 87.

> [3]Drucker, *Managing,* p. 144.

> [4]Drucker, *Pension,* p. 93.

If you are referring to an article in a periodical, use the periodical title rather than the article title.

> [2]Author's surname, *periodical title* [shortened if feasible], page number.

> [5]Stephen H. Wildstrom, "A New Chapter for E-Books," *Business Week,* November 2, 1998, p. 19.

> [6]Amy Borrus, . . .

> [7]Wildstrom, *Business Week,* p. 20. (Referring to the work identified in note 5 above.)

d. A more formal style in subsequent references uses the abbreviations *loc. cit.* ("in the place cited") and *op. cit.* ("in the work cited").

> [1]Author's surname, **loc. cit.** (This pattern is used when reference is made to the *very same page* in the work previously identified.)

> [2]Author's surname, **op. cit.,** page number. (This pattern is used when reference is made to a *different page* in the work previously identified.)

> [1]Helen Kennerley, *Overcoming Worries, Fears, and Anxieties,* New York Univ. Press, New York, 1997, p. 165.

> [2]Larry Hirschhorn, *Reworking Authority: Leading and Following in the Postmodern Organization,* MIT Press, Cambridge, Mass., 1997, p. 99.

Continued on page 458

Notes and
Bibliographies

15

¶1532

[3]Kennerley, op. cit., p. 169. (Referring to a different page in *Overcoming Worries, Fears, and Anxieties.*)

[4]Hirschhorn, loc. cit. (Referring to the same page in *Reworking Authority.*)

[5]Ibid. (Referring to exactly the same page as shown in note 4. *Ibid.* may be used only to refer to the note immediately preceding. See ¶1530.)

NOTE: Do not italicize or underline *loc. cit., op. cit.,* or *ibid.*

Notes Based on Online Sources

Business and academic writers increasingly rely on the Internet rather than on printed materials as the source of information to be quoted, paraphrased, or summarized in the reports and manuscripts they prepare. Hence the critical need for guidelines on how to construct *online citations*—that is, footnotes, endnotes, and bibliographic entries that are based on online sources.

Dealing With Online Addresses

The feature that distinguishes an online citation from one based on printed material is the inclusion of an *online address*—an element that takes the place of information about the name and location of the publisher. There are two major types of online addresses: a URL address (discussed in ¶1532) and an e-mail address (discussed in ¶1533).

1532 URL Addresses

Every unit of information on the Internet has its own unique address–a Uniform Resource Locator, commonly referred to as a URL and pronounced as individual letters *(you-are-el)* or as a word *(earl)*. (See ¶501b.) A URL represents not only the storage location of a particular document on the Internet but also the means by which a document can be retrieved. If a URL is not accurately presented in an online citation, it will be impossible to locate the material being cited.

A URL consists of at least two parts: (a) the *protocol* (the name of the system to be used in linking one computer with another on the Internet) and (b) the *host name* (the name of the host computer where the desired material is stored). Here, for example, is the URL for Yahoo!, a large directory of Web pages.

Protocol   Host Name
http://www.yahoo.com

a. **Protocol.** There are a number of protocols that you can use to locate material stored on another computer on the Internet.

- **HTTP (HyperText Transfer Protocol).** The most widely used of all the protocols, HTTP permits you to surf the World Wide Web—that part of the Internet that provides access not only to text material but also to photographs, drawings, animations, and video and sound clips.

- **FTP (File Transfer Protocol).** FTP permits you to transfer text material from an *ftp server* (the host computer where the desired material is stored) to your own computer.

- **Listserv.** Listserv (a short form for *mailing list server*) permits you to retrieve messages posted to a network of mailing lists and to post your own messages as well.

Notes and Bibliographies

15

- **Usenet.** Usenet is a network consisting of thousands of newsgroups (discussion groups each focused on a particular topic of interest). A message posted to a particular newsgroup can be read and commented on by any interested member of that newsgroup, and those comments may prompt additional rounds of comments. The original message (known as an *article*) and the subsequent series of comments create what is known as a *thread.* Users doing research on Usenet have the option of citing only the article, one or more of the comments, or the entire thread.

- **Gopher.** Gopher permits you to access text plus graphical and audio materials, but it first provides you with a series of menus that become progressively more specific until you locate the information you are looking for.

- **Telnet.** Telnet permits you to log onto another computer on the Internet and retrieve the desired information located there.

  NOTE: Now that HTTP has become the dominant protocol for locating information on the Internet, Gopher and Telnet are no longer widely used.

When these protocols appear as the first part of a URL, they are represented as follows:

HTTP:	http://	Listserv:	listserv://	Gopher:	gopher://
FTP:	ftp://	Usenet:	news://	Telnet:	telnet://

The first part of a URL always ends with a colon and two forward slashes (://).

b. Host Name. The second part of a URL——the host name—consists of several elements separated by *dots* (never referred to as *periods*). Here are some representative host names as they appear in Web-based URLs:

	Protocol	Host Name
eBay:	http://www.ebay.com
Gateway 2000:	http://www.gw2k.com
Intel:	http://www.intel.com/
PBS Online:	http://www.pbs.org
NASA:	http://www.nasa.gov.
PSINet:	http://www.psi.net/

In the host names shown above, the first element—*www*—refers to the World Wide Web. The second and third elements—for example, *.ebay.com* (referred to as *dot-ebay-dot-com*)—represent the domain name. The second element often reflects some form of the organization's name. The third element is usually a three-letter unit preceded by a dot; it is called a *top-level domain* (TLD) or a *zone,* and it indicates the type of organization that owns the host computer. For example:

.com	commercial organization	.mil	military site
.edu	educational institution	.net	network organization
.gov	government body or agency	.org	nonprofit or noncommercial
.int	international organization		organization

Seven new TLDs have been proposed and may soon be adopted:

.arts	an organization dealing with arts and entertainment activities
.firm	a business or firm
.info	a provider of information services

Continued on page 460

¶1533

.nom	an individual or personal terminology
.rec	an organization dealing with recreation and entertainment activities
.store	a business offering goods for sale
.web	an organization dealing with activities relating to the Web

Computers outside the United States usually have host names ending in a two-letter country code. For example:

ca	Canada	fr	France	jp	Japan
de	Germany	it	Italy	uk	United Kingdom

The following URL for the Bavarian Ministry for Economic Affairs reveals that the host computer is located in Germany:

http://www.bayern.de

c. File Name. A URL may also provide a file name as the final element. For example, the following URL directs a Web browser to retrieve a file named *iway.html* from a host computer named *www.cc.web.com* using the HyperText Transfer Protocol.

Protocol Host Name   File Name
http://www.cc.web.com/iway.html

NOTE: A *swung dash* (~)—also referred to as a *tilde*—is sometimes used to introduce a file name. For example:

http://www.netaxs.com/~harrington

d. Path. A URL may also include one or more elements between the host name and the file name. These elements indicate the electronic path to be taken (after the host computer is reached) in order to locate the desired file. For example:

Protocol Host Name   Path   File Name
http://www.yahoo.com/Computers/World_Wide_Web/HTML_Editors/

e. URLs are usually typed all in small letters, but when capital letters appear, follow the style of the particular URL exactly as shown (as in the example in *d* above). Also note that spaces between words in any part of a URL have to be signified by means of an underline (as in the example above) or some other mark of punctuation such as a hyphen (as in the example below).

http://www.cis.ohio-state.edu/hypertext/faq/usenet/FAQ-List.html

f. Note that some of the URLs shown in ¶1532b–e end with a forward slash and others do not. Always follow the style of a URL exactly as shown.

g. When Web-based URLs are given in documents and publications aimed at computer professionals, the protocol *http://* is often omitted; the fact that the host name begins with *www* makes it clear to knowledgeable readers which protocol is to be used. When constructing your own online citations, consider how much your readers will know. As a general rule, it is safer to insert the protocol at the start of a URL, even if it was omitted in your source.

1533 E-Mail Addresses

An e-mail address consists of two parts separated by an *at* sign (@). The part before the @ is called the *mailbox;* the part after the @ is called the *domain*.

¶**1537**

a. The mailbox typically consists of the user's name (the name used to sign on to an e-mail system). However, some commercial online services assign users a numerical mailbox.

Mailbox	Domain	Mailbox	Domain
apinkham@aol.com		73004,5077@compuserve.com	

b. The domain represents the system on which the e-mail message is delivered (for example, America Online and Compuserve in the examples above). The last part of the domain (for example, *.com*) is called the *zone.* (For a list of the most commonly used zones, see ¶1532b.)

➤ *For guidelines on the formatting of e-mail messages, see ¶¶1708–1711.*

General Guidelines for Online Citations

Making use of online sources can pose special problems. After you have quoted or made reference to certain online materials in your report or your manuscript, the person who originally posted the material may later decide to change it or transfer it to a new location (with a new URL or e-mail address) or remove it from the Internet altogether. If any of these things should happen, readers who try to confirm the accuracy of your citations may very well draw unfair conclusions about your competence as a researcher and as a writer. To protect yourself against these potential problems, take the following precautions.

1534 Every online document that you plan to cite should be saved in the form of hard copy and as part of your backup files. If the document is very long, save at least enough of the document to establish the full context from which the cited material was taken. In that way you can always demonstrate—if the need arises—that you have not taken the material out of context or otherwise distorted its intended meaning.

NOTE: Since much online material originally appeared in print (a much more stable medium), refer whenever possible to the printed source rather than the online source.

1535 In your citations of online material, include not only the date on which the material was posted on the Internet but also the date on which you accessed the material. Then if the material is subsequently changed or removed, you will still be able to prove the accuracy of your citation.

1536 When URLs or e-mail addresses appear in footnotes, endnotes, bibliographies, or even in the main text, enclose each address in angle brackets (< >). The use of angle brackets makes it possible to insert sentence punctuation before and after an online address and not have the punctuation mistaken for an integral part of the online address.

1537 Always present a URL or an e-mail address exactly as it is given. Never alter the capitalization, the internal spacing, or the symbols used. Failure to provide an accurate online address will usually make it impossible to locate the desired information. (See ¶1532g.)

¶1538

1538 Always try to fit a URL on one line. If it becomes necessary to divide a URL at the end of a line:

a. You may break after the double slash (//) that marks the end of a protocol (but not within the protocol itself).

Acceptable Line Ending	Next Line
<http://	www.nowonder.com>
NOT <http:	**NOT** //www.nowonder.com>

b. You may break *before* (but never after) a dot (.), a single slash (/), a hyphen (-), an underscore (_), or any other mark of punctuation.

Acceptable Line Ending	Next Line
<http://www	.pbs.org>
NOT <http://www.	**NOT** pbs.org>
<http://www.mcgraw	-hill.com/>
NOT <http://www.mcgraw-	**NOT** hill.com/>
<http://www.senate.gov	/~daschle>
NOT <http://www.senate.gov/	**NOT** ~daschle>

c. Never insert a hyphen within an online address to signify an end-of-line break.

1539 Always try to fit an e-mail address on one line. If it becomes necessary to divide it at the end of a line:

a. You may break before the *at* symbol (@) or before a dot.

Acceptable Line Ending	Next Line
<wryter6290	@aol.com>
NOT <wryter6290@	**NOT** aol.com>
<pbenner@lincoln	.midcoast.com>
NOT <pbenner@lincoln.	**NOT** midcoast.com>

b. Never insert a hyphen within an e-mail address to signify an end-of-line break.

Constructing Online Citations

The following guidelines provide a number of basic patterns for constructing online citations—source reference notes based on online sources. These patterns are much the same as those presented in ¶¶1508–1522 for printed works with one fundamental difference: the name and location of the publisher of a printed work are replaced in these patterns by URLs or e-mail addresses enclosed in angle brackets (< >).

The following patterns cannot cover every contingency that you may encounter when constructing online citations. Therefore, be prepared to adapt these patterns as necessary to fit each particular situation.

NOTE: These patterns are appropriate for use in constructing footnotes and endnotes in business and academic documents. For examples showing how these patterns should be adjusted for use in a bibliography, see ¶1551a, c.

¶**1546**

1540 **World Wide Web Sources**

[1]Author's name, "title of document," *title of complete work*, date of posting,[*] <URL beginning http://> (date of access).

[1]Nate Zelnick, "Wireless Net Access Gets Renewed Push," *Internet World,* November 16, 1998, <http://www.iw.com/print/current/news/19981116-wireless.html> (February 26, 1999).

1541 **E-Mail Sources**

[1]Author's name <author's e-mail address>, "subject line," date of posting,[*] type of e-mail[†] (date of access).

[1]Allie Goudy <Allie_Goudy@ccmail.wiu.edu>, "Continuing Education and Paraprofessionals," November 3, 1998, office communication (April 23, 1999).

1542 **Listserv Sources**

[1]Author's name <author's e-mail address>, "subject line," date of posting,[*] <URL beginning listserv://> (date of access).

[1]Bo Ekvall <bo@PARTENON.COM>, "NEW: FREE Business-Related E-Zine. FREE Ad!" November 23, 1998, <listserv://scout.cs.wisc.edu/> (March 3, 1999).

1543 **Usenet Sources**

[1]Author's name <author's e-mail address>, "subject line," date of posting,[*] <newsgroup's URL beginning news://> (date of access).

[1]Laura Beall <beall@azstarnet.com>, "Enterprises for Women," November 7, 1998, <news://alt.business> (May 27, 1999).

1544 **FTP Sources**

[1]Author's name, "title of document," date of posting,[*] <URL beginning ftp://> (date of access).

[1]L. R. E. Quin, "Summary of Meta Fonts Available," n.d., <ftp://sun.soe.clarkson.edu/pub/tex/texmag.4.06> (August 9, 1999).

1545 **Gopher Sources**

[1]Author's name, "title of document," date of posting,[*] <URL beginning gopher://> (date of access).

[1]American Association of University Professors, "Statement on Professional Ethics," n.d., <gopher://scsu.ctstateu.edu:70/> (December 14, 1999).

1546 **Telnet Sources**

[1]Author's name, "title of document," *title of complete work*, date of posting,[*] <URL beginning telnet://> (date of access).

[1]DeAnne Rosenberg, "Women in Business: Gender Differences in the Professional World—Are Male and Female Managers Like Oil and Water?" *Business Credit,* November 1, 1989, <telnet://132.162.37.16> (April 9, 1999).

Bibliographies

A bibliography at the end of a report or a manuscript typically lists all the works *consulted* in the preparation of the material as well as all the works that were actually *cited* in the notes. The format of a bibliography is also used for any list of titles, such as a list of recommended readings or a list of new publications.

---

[*]If the date of posting cannot be determined, insert the abbreviation *n.d.* (no date).

[†]Insert a phrase such as *personal e-mail* or *office communication.*

¶1547

1547 Word processing programs do not typically provide a template for bibliographies. Some special word processing applications, however, will format not only footnotes and endnotes but bibliographies as well. These programs ask you to create a database (also referred to as a *reference library*) in which you enter the necessary data for each title you plan to cite. Then you select (1) one of the standard formats built into the software or (2) a format that you have modified or created. In effect, once you have developed the reference library, you can extract the data in the form of footnotes, endnotes, or entries in a bibliography.

NOTE: ¶¶1548–1551 provide guidelines for formatting a bibliography.

1548 Consider the following guidelines for formatting a bibliography. (See the illustration on page 465.)

  a. On a new page type *BIBLIOGRAPHY* (or some other appropriate title) in boldface all-capital letters. Center this title on the first line after the top margin of approximately 2 inches, and begin the text on the second or third line below.

  b. Use the same margins as for other pages in the body of the report or manuscript (see ¶¶1404–1407), and treat the numbering of these pages as indicated in ¶1427f–g.

  c. Begin each entry at the left margin. Ordinarily, single-space the entries, but in material that is to be edited, use double spacing to allow room for editing.

  d. Indent turnover lines 0.5 inch so that the first word in each entry will stand out.

  e. Leave 1 blank line between entries (whether they are single- or double-spaced).

1549 a. List the entries alphabetically by author's last name.

  b. Entries lacking an author are alphabetized by title. Disregard the word *The* or *A* at the beginning of a title in determining alphabetic sequence. (For an example, see the second entry in the illustration on page 465. Note that this entry is alphabetized on the basis of *Critical,* following *Chandler.*)

  NOTE: When a publication lacks an author and the title begins with a figure (see the next-to-last entry in the illustration on page 465), alphabetize the title on the basis of how the figure would appear if spelled out. Thus, when *301* is converted to *Three Hundred and One,* the title is alphabetized on the basis of *Three,* following *Sitarz.*

  c. There is no need to number the alphabetized entries in a bibliography unless you plan to use the style of textnotes described in ¶1507b(5). In that case begin each entry of the bibliography with a number typed at the left margin, followed by a period and 1 or 2 spaces. Then type the rest of the entry in the customary way, but indent any turnover so that it begins under the first word in the line above. (In the parenthetical textnotes, you can then make reference to different works by their bibliographic "entry number" instead of by author.)

   9. Bamford, Janet, *Consumer Reports Money Book: How to Get It, Save It, and Spend It Wisely,* Consumers Union, Mount Vernon, N.Y., 1997.

   10. Farrell, Paul B., *Mutual Funds on the Net: Making Money Online,* Wiley, New York, 1997.

   11. Wilson, William Julius, *When Work Disappears: The World of the New Urban Poor,* Random House, New York, 1996.

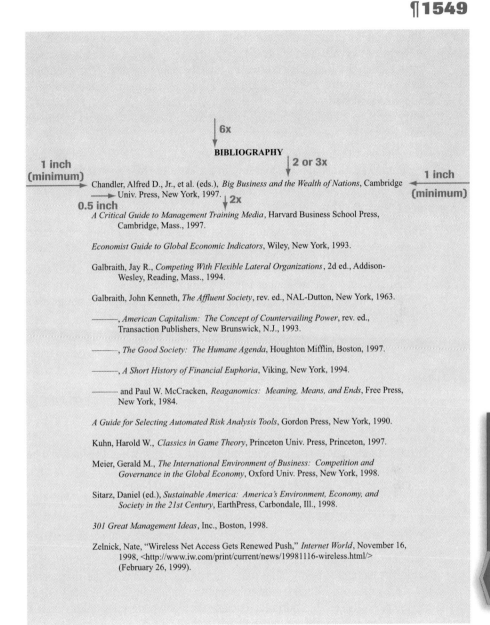

6x

BIBLIOGRAPHY

1 inch
(minimum)

2 or 3x

1 inch
(minimum)

Chandler, Alfred D., Jr., et al. (eds.), *Big Business and the Wealth of Nations*, Cambridge Univ. Press, New York, 1997.

0.5 inch

2x

A Critical Guide to Management Training Media, Harvard Business School Press, Cambridge, Mass., 1997.

Economist Guide to Global Economic Indicators, Wiley, New York, 1993.

Galbraith, Jay R., *Competing With Flexible Lateral Organizations*, 2d ed., Addison-Wesley, Reading, Mass., 1994.

Galbraith, John Kenneth, *The Affluent Society*, rev. ed., NAL-Dutton, New York, 1963.

———, *American Capitalism: The Concept of Countervailing Power*, rev. ed., Transaction Publishers, New Brunswick, N.J., 1993.

———, *The Good Society: The Humane Agenda*, Houghton Mifflin, Boston, 1997.

———, *A Short History of Financial Euphoria*, Viking, New York, 1994.

——— and Paul W. McCracken, *Reaganomics: Meaning, Means, and Ends*, Free Press, New York, 1984.

A Guide for Selecting Automated Risk Analysis Tools, Gordon Press, New York, 1990.

Kuhn, Harold W., *Classics in Game Theory*, Princeton Univ. Press, Princeton, 1997.

Meier, Gerald M., *The International Environment of Business: Competition and Governance in the Global Economy*, Oxford Univ. Press, New York, 1998.

Sitarz, Daniel (ed.), *Sustainable America: America's Environment, Economy, and Society in the 21st Century*, EarthPress, Carbondale, Ill., 1998.

301 Great Management Ideas, Inc., Boston, 1998.

Zelnick, Nate, "Wireless Net Access Gets Renewed Push," *Internet World*, November 16, 1998, <http://www.iw.com/print/current/news/19981116-wireless.html/> (February 26, 1999).

Notes and
Bibliographies

15

NOTE: If you use the numbered list feature of your word processing program, the turnover lines will automatically be indented. The list will also be typed single-spaced. For a more open look insert 1 blank line between entries (as shown in the illustration above). The numbered list feature also aligns single- and double-digit numbers on the left. However, you can make an adjustment so that the numbers align at the right (as in the examples in ¶1549c). For additional details and illustrations, see ¶1357d.

¶1550

1550 When a bibliography contains more than one work by the same author, replace the author's name with a long dash (using three-em dashes or six hyphens) in all the entries after the first. List the works alphabetically by title. (For examples, see the fifth, sixth, seventh, and eighth entries in the illustration on page 465. Note that these titles are alphabetized on the key words *Affluent, American, Good,* and *Short.* The ninth entry involves a coauthor and therefore follows the works written by the first author alone.)

NOTE: As an alternative, multiple entries pertaining to the same author may be listed in chronological sequence according to the date of each publication.

> ➤ *For guidelines on the typing of three-em dashes, see ¶216d; for guidelines on the marking of three-em dashes in manuscript, see ¶217c.*

1551 Entries in bibliographies contain the same elements and follow the same style as source reference notes except for two key differences.

a. Begin each entry with the name of the author listed in inverted order (last name first). When an entry includes two or more authors' names, invert only the first author's name. When an organization is listed as the author, do not invert the name.

> Ainley, Patrick, and Bill Bailey, *The Business of Learning,* Cassell, Herndon, Va., 1997.
>
> Apple Computer, *Multimedia Demystified?!* Random House, New York, 1995.
>
> Burchfield, R. W. (ed.), *The New Fowler's Modern English Usage,* 3d ed., Oxford Univ. Press, New York, 1996.
>
> Rosenberg, DeAnne, "Women in Business: Gender Differences in the Professional World—Are Male and Female Managers Like Oil and Water?" *Business Credit,* November 1, 1989, <telnet://132.162.37.16> (April 9, 1999).

> ➤ *For additional examples, see the illustration on page 465.*

b. Include page numbers in bibliographic entries only when the material being cited is part of a larger work. In such cases show the page number or numbers (for example, *pp. 215–232*) on which the material appears.

> Levy, Steven, "Beyond Silicon Valley: The Hot New Tech Cities," *Newsweek,* November 9, 1998, pp. 45–50.

> ➤ *For the use of an en dash or a hyphen in a range of page numbers, see ¶459a.*

c. In academic material, bibliographic entries typically follow a slightly different style. In the examples below, note that a period follows each of the three main parts of the entry (author's name, the title, and the publishing information). Also note that the parentheses that normally enclose the publishing information in an academic-style footnote or endnote are omitted in the bibliographic entry. (See ¶1508b.)

> Burchfield, R. W. (ed.). *The New Fowler's Modern English Usage,* 3d ed. New York: Oxford Univ. Press, 1996.
>
> Farrell, Paul B. *Mutual Funds on the Net: Making Money Online.* New York: Wiley, 1997.
>
> Levy, Steven. "Beyond Silicon Valley: The Hot New Tech Cities." *Newsweek,* November 9, 1998, pp. 45–50. (Note that the magazine title—in this case *Newsweek*—is considered part of the publishing information. Thus a period follows the article title to mark the end of the title information in the entry.)
>
> Rosenberg, DeAnne. "Women in Business: Gender Differences in the Professional World—Are Male and Female Managers Like Oil and Water?" *Business Credit,* November 1, 1989, <telnet://132.162.37.16> (April 9, 1999).

SECTION **16**

Tables

You can fit a good deal of material into a compact space when you present it in the form of a table—with items arranged in *rows* (to be read horizontally) and in *columns* (to be read vertically). However, in designing a table, you should aim for more than compactness. Your reader should be able to locate specific information faster—and detect significant patterns or trends in the data more quickly— than if the same information were presented in the regular text.

The following paragraphs provide detailed guidelines for creating a table. Modify these guidelines as necessary to achieve results that are easy to understand and attractive to look at.

Using the Software Table Feature

Before the introduction of word processing software, the execution of tables required a great deal of advance planning and careful typing. Now, thanks to the table feature of your word processing software, you can prepare tables with little or no advance planning and you can make corrections and adjustments with relative ease.

The table feature, however, does impose some limitations on the results you can achieve unless you are willing to invest additional time and effort. As a result, you may not always find it feasible or even possible to achieve the appearance of professionally typeset tables. Here, for example, is how a table might appear in a textbook or a magazine:

Table A-15

LIFE INSURANCE IN FORCE

($000,000 Omitted)

Year	Ordinary	Group
1940	79,346	14,938
1950	149,116	47,793
1960	341,881	175,903
1970	734,730	551,357
1975	1,083,421	904,695
1980	1,760,474	1,579,355
1985	3,247,289	2,561,595
1990	5,366,982	3,753,506
1996	8,337,188	5,158,538

Source: *The World Almanac and Book of Facts*, 1998, p. 970.

Note that within each column the head and the text are centered between vertical rules. Note also the use of extra space surrounding various elements of the table to give it an open look and make it easy to read.

Paragraphs 1601–1608 show you (1) the results you will achieve if you prepare this table with the Microsoft Word table feature, accepting all the default specifications, and (2) the steps you need to take in order to achieve the look of a professionally typeset table.

IMPORTANT NOTE: When you use the table feature to execute a table, how far you go in modifying the default specifications will depend on a number of factors. If the table is intended for your eyes alone (or those of your immediate associates) *and* speed rather than appearance is critical, you may not want to go very far (if at all) in modifying those default specifications. On the other hand, if the table will appear in a document to be presented to higher management or to people outside the organization, you will have to invest the extra time and effort needed to create a more professional-looking table.

¶**1602**

1601 The default format provided by the Microsoft Word table feature encloses the complete table (including any heading at the top and any notes at the bottom) in a grid of horizontal and vertical lines.

a. At the outset specify the number of columns the table should have (in this particular case, three). It is not necessary to specify the number of rows in advance since the act of tabbing at the end of a row will automatically add another row.

NOTE: If you are using an autoformat style (see ¶1608), you may need to specify the number of rows as well.

b. In the absence of other instructions, the table grid will have the same width as the regular text. You may find it simplest to accept this dimension at the outset and adjust the width of the table later on. (See ¶1603.)

1602 a. Begin by entering the column heads and the column text. Leave one blank row at the top for the heading and one blank row at the bottom for any notes. If you accept all the default specifications, the column heads and the text in each column will align at left.

Year	Ordinary	Group
1940	79,346	14,938
1950	149,116	47,793
1960	341,881	175,903
1970	734,730	551,357
1975	1,083,421	904,695
1980	1,760,474	1,579,355
1985	3,247,289	2,561,595
1990	5,366,982	3,753,506
1996	8,337,188	5,158,538

b. It is appropriate to use left alignment when the column text consists entirely of words or of figures representing years (as in the first column above). However, when the column text consists of figures that have to be added or compared in some way (as in the second and third columns above), the figures should align at the right.

Continued on page 470

Tables

16

¶1603

c. To save a step, select right alignment (or right justification) for the second and third columns before you enter any data in the grid. Moreover, to enhance the appearance of the table, select boldface for the column heads. If these modifications are made in advance, the first version of the table will look like this:

Year		Ordinary		Group
1940		79,346		14,938
1950		149,116		47,793
1960		341,881		175,903
1970		734,730		551,357
1975		1,083,421		904,695
1980		1,760,474		1,579,355
1985		3,247,289		2,561,595
1990		5,366,982		3,753,506
1996		8,337,188		5,158,538

1603 a. The table, as it now stands, has excessively wide columns. To remedy the situation, use the *autofit* feature to adjust the width of the columns to fit the column text.

Year	Ordinary	Group
1940	79,346	14,938
1950	149,116	47,793
1960	341,881	175,903
1970	734,730	551,357
1975	1,083,421	904,695
1980	1,760,474	1,579,355
1985	3,247,289	2,561,595
1990	5,366,982	3,753,506
1996	8,337,188	5,158,538

Note that now the text in each column is not perfectly centered between the vertical rules. Moreover, the use of the autofit feature creates a fairly tight appearance. You can widen a column by clicking on the appropriate vertical line and dragging it to the desired point. Then use the indent markers to visually center the column text as a block between vertical rules.

Year	Ordinary	Group
1940	79,346	14,938
1950	149,116	47,793
1960	341,881	175,903
1970	734,730	551,357
1975	1,083,421	904,695
1980	1,760,474	1,579,355
1985	3,247,289	2,561,595
1990	5,366,982	3,753,506
1996	8,337,188	5,158,538

¶1605

NOTE: If you try to widen a column simply by inserting extra space, all that extra space will appear on only one side of the column text (and not be evenly distributed on both sides). Thus in a column with left-justified text, all the extra space will appear on the right; in a column with right-justified text, all the extra space will appear on the left. To avoid this result, use the technique described in ¶1603a to visually center the column text.

b. When a table that initially extends from one side margin to the other is reduced in width (as in the illustrations in ¶1603a), the table as a whole will remain aligned at the left margin. Therefore, once you complete the table, center it horizontally on the page. Moreover, if the table occupies a page by itself, center the table vertically as well.

1604 Before you can enter the table heading at the top or any table notes at the bottom, you need to merge or join the cells in the lines reserved for these purposes.

Year	Ordinary	Group
1940	79,346	14,938
1950	149,116	47,793
1985	3,247,289	2,561595
1990	5,366,982	3,753,506
1996	8,337,188	5,158,538

1605 a. The heading of a table may consist simply of a table title. Or the title may be preceded by a table number and followed by a subtitle—all on the same line or on separate lines. (See ¶1620 for the various ways in which these elements may be positioned.) Whether the heading consists of only one line or several lines, enter the complete heading in one cell at the top of the grid.

b. If the table is accompanied by one or more footnotes, enter these elements in one cell at the bottom of the grid.

c. As the following illustration demonstrates, when you enter these elements in the grid, they are automatically aligned at the left.

Table A-15
LIFE INSURANCE IN FORCE
($000,000 Omitted)

Year	Ordinary	Group
1940	79,346	14,938
1950	149,116	47,793
1960	341,881	175,903
1970	734,730	551,357
1975	1,083,421	904,695
1980	1,760,474	1,579,355
1985	3,247,289	2,561,595
1990	5,366,982	3,753,506
1996	8,337,188	5,158,538

Source: *The World Almanac and Book of Facts*, 1998, p. 970.

Tables

16

¶1606

1606 To improve the appearance of the table, consider making these adjustments:

a. Use boldface for all the elements in the table heading. (Some writers prefer to use boldface only for the title.)

b. Select the centering option for the column heads and all the elements in the table heading.

c. Insert 1 blank line between the lines in the table heading and above and below the heading as a whole.

   NOTE: If the table title or subtitle will not fit all on one line, break it into sensible phrases and single-space the turnover. (See ¶1620 for illustrations of the ways in which the elements in the table heading may be arranged.)

d. Insert 1 blank line above and below the column heads.

e. Insert 1 blank line between the notes at the bottom of the table and above and below the notes as a whole.

f. If the footnotes each require no more than one full line, begin each note at the left margin of the table text. However, if any one of the notes turns over to a second line, indent the first line of each note. Ordinarily, the indention should be 0.5 inch, but if a table is relatively narrow (as in the illustration below), reduce the indention to 0.25 inch for better appearance. In any case, adjust the measure of the footnote so that the turnover aligns at the left margin of the table text and does not extend beyond the right margin of the table text.

g. Add shading to portions of the table as desired to give special emphasis to certain elements and make the table more attractive as a whole.

   NOTE: If all of these modifications are made, the table will then look like this:

Table A-15

LIFE INSURANCE IN FORCE

($000,000 Omitted)

Year	Ordinary	Group
1940	79,346	14,938
1950	149,116	47,793
1960	341,881	175,903
1970	734,730	551,357
1975	1,083,421	904,695
1980	1,760,474	1,579,355
1985	3,247,289	2,561,595
1990	5,366,982	3,753,506
1996	8,337,188	5,158,538

Source: *The World Almanac and Book of Facts*, 1998, p. 970.

Tables

16

1607 a. If you want to achieve a more open look, you can remove the grid and increase the space between rows, as in the illustration below.

Table A-15

LIFE INSURANCE IN FORCE

($000,000 Omitted)

Year	Ordinary	Group
1940	79,346	14,938
1950	149,116	47,793
1960	341,881	175,903
1970	734,730	551,357
1975	1,083,421	904,695
1980	1,760,474	1,579,355
1985	3,247,289	2,561,595
1990	5,366,982	3,753,506
1996	8,337,188	5,158,538

NOTE: Even if you ultimately intend to remove the grid from the table, be sure to enter all the elements in the table heading and the table notes within the grid at the outset. In that way, if you later decide to transfer the table to another location in the document, you can be sure that the table will be moved as a whole. If the table heading and the source note are not inserted in the grid, only the body of the table will be moved.

b. As an alternative, you can simply eliminate all the vertical rules in the grid.

Table A-15

LIFE INSURANCE IN FORCE

($000,000 Omitted)

Year	Ordinary	Group
1940	79,346	14,938
1950	149,116	47,793
1960	341,881	175,903
1970	734,730	551,357
1975	1,083,421	904,695
1980	1,760,474	1,579,355
1985	3,247,289	2,561,595
1990	5,366,982	3,753,506
1996	8,337,188	5,158,538

¶1608

1608 a. Some word processing programs provide a number of autoformats that can enhance the appearance of your tables. The following illustrations provide examples of three styles offered by Microsoft Word: Contemporary, Professional, and Elegant.

Contemporary

Table A-15

LIFE INSURANCE IN FORCE

($000,000 Omitted)

Year	Ordinary	Group
1940	79,346	14,938
1950	149,116	47,793
1960	341,881	175,903
1970	734,730	551,357
1975	1,083,421	904,695
1980	1,760,474	1,579,355
1985	3,247,289	2,561,595
1990	5,366,982	3,753,506
1996	8,337,188	5,158,538

Source: *The World Almanac and Book of Facts*, 1998, p. 970.

Professional

Table A-15

LIFE INSURANCE IN FORCE

($000,000 Omitted)

Year	Ordinary	Group
1940	79,346	14,938
1950	149,116	47,793
1960	341,881	175,903
1970	734,730	551,357
1975	1,083,421	904,695
1980	1,760,474	1,579,355
1985	3,247,289	2,561,595
1990	5,366,982	3,753,506
1996	8,337,188	5,158,538

Source: *The World Almanac and Book of Facts*, 1998, p. 970.

Elegant

	Table A-15	
	LIFE INSURANCE IN FORCE	
	($000,000 Omitted)	
Year	**Ordinary**	**Group**
1940	79,346	14,938
1950	149,116	47,793
1960	341,881	175,903
1970	734,730	551,357
1975	1,083,421	904,695
1980	1,760,474	1,579,355
1985	3,247,289	2,561,595
1990	5,366,982	3,753,506
1996	8,337,188	5,158,538

Source: *The World Almanac and Book of Facts*, 1998, p. 970.

b. If you make all of your modifications to the table before applying autoformat, you will lose the attributes of boldface and italic wherever you have added them. In the following illustration, note how the application of the Elegant autoformat causes the loss of boldface in the table heading and the column heads as well as the loss of italics in the table footnote. Moreover, the word *Table* (preceding the table number) and the word *Omitted* in the subtitle have been converted to all-capital letters. However, it is easy to restore these attributes so that the finished table looks like the illustration above.

	TABLE A-15	
	LIFE INSURANCE IN FORCE	
	($000,000 OMITTED)	
Year	Ordinary	Group
1940	79,346	14,938
1996	8,337,188	5,158,538

Source: The World Almanac and Book of Facts, 1998, p. 970.

c. If you select autoformat before making any modifications, those modifications will remain in place.

¶1609

Locating Tables Within the Text

1609 **a.** Tables should be easy to refer to. Therefore, try to locate each table on the same page where the subject of the table is introduced in the text. In this way the reader will have ready access to the table while reading the text commentary that may precede and follow.

b. Ideally, every table should fall immediately after the point in the text where it is first mentioned. However, if placing the table within a paragraph is likely to disrupt the reader's grasp of the material, then locate the table at the end of the paragraph or at the top or bottom of the page. (See ¶1611d.)

1610 **a.** Avoid breaking a table at the bottom of a page. If starting a table at the ideal point means that it will not all fit in the space remaining on the page, then place the complete table at the top of the next page. (At the point in the text where the table is first mentioned, insert an appropriate cross-reference. See ¶1615.)

NOTE: Many word processing programs have a feature called *keep lines together* which prevents tables from breaking across pages. (See ¶1639b.)

b. If you have to fit a number of relatively short tables (half a page or less) in a given document, single-space the table text to maximize your chances of locating each table in the ideal place. (See ¶1625.)

NOTE: Microsoft Word's table feature single-spaces the table text by default.

➤ *For other techniques to limit the length of a table to one page, see ¶1637; for guidelines on dealing with a table too long to fit on one page, see ¶¶1638–1639.*

1611 If a table is to appear on a page that also carries regular text:

a. Center the table horizontally within the established margins. (See ¶1609a.)

b. Try to indent the table at least 0.5 inch from each side margin. In any case, the width of the table should not exceed the width of the text. (See ¶¶1640–1641.)

c. Use blank lines to set off a table from the text above and below it as follows:

(1) Leave only 1 blank line above and below the table if horizontal rules or shading sets the table off from the text.

with prefixes indicating multiples or fractions of a unit. There are seven base units in the SI metric system: ↓**2x**

Quantity	Unit	Symbol
Length	meter	m
Mass	kilogram	kg
Time	second	s
Electric current	ampere	A
Thermodynamic temperature	kelvin	K
Amount of substance	mole	mol
Luminous intensity	candela	cd

↓**2x**

In addition, there are two supplementary units, the radian and the steradian.

Tables

16

¶1611

(2) Leave 1 blank line above and below an open table (one without horizontal rules) that has neither column heads nor a table title.

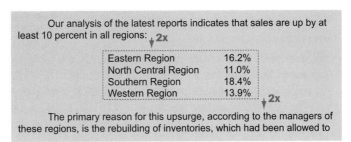

(3) Leave 2 blank lines above and below an open table that uses column heads as its first element.

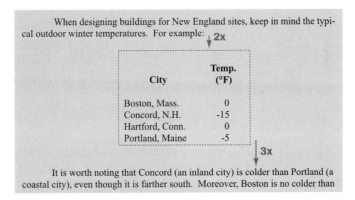

NOTE: If you have inserted a blank line above a column head or a title within the grid, you will automatically achieve the appearance of 2 blank lines above the table when you remove the grid.

(4) Leave 2 blank lines above and below an open table that begins with a table title. (See the note directly above.)

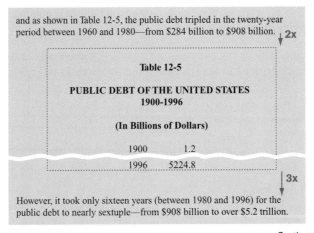

Continued on page 478

¶1612

d. If space is tight, place the table at the top or bottom of the page. In that way you can eliminate one set of blank lines and improve your chances of fitting the table on the desired page.

e. When using the table feature of a word processing program, simply insert the table copy at the desired location in the regular text. If you discover that the table will not all fit on the same page, you can move the table as a whole to the top or bottom of the page (as noted in *d* above), make other adjustments (as noted in ¶¶1637–1639), or place the table on a page by itself (see ¶¶1612–1615). If you use the *keep lines together* feature (see ¶1610a, note), the table will not be divided at the bottom of a page; instead the table as a whole will be moved to the top of the next page. (See ¶1639b.)

f. Be sure you can fit at least two full lines of regular text above or below the table. If the results look unattractive, devote the full page to the table and resume the text on the following page. (See ¶¶1612–1615.)

Locating Tables on Separate Pages

1612 When a table occupies more than two-thirds of a page, it can often be difficult to fit on the same page with regular text. In such cases type the table on a separate page and place it immediately after the text page on which the table is first referred to.

NOTE: Insert a hard page break before and after the table to ensure that the table will appear on a page by itself. (See ¶1639b.)

1613 If a given document contains a number of tables, most of which will each require a separate page, then all the tables (short as well as long) may be executed as an appendix or as an attachment. This arrangement—which permits the reader to keep the full set of tables alongside the regular text (except in the case of bound reports)—can be very convenient, especially if some tables are repeatedly cited throughout the regular text. (This arrangement also eliminates the problem of trying to fit tables within the text.)

1614 When a table is to appear on a page by itself, center the table horizontally and vertically within the established margins of the page.

NOTE: If no margins have been established, leave a minimum margin of 1 inch on all four sides of the table.

1615 When a table is not located on the same page on which it is referred to, provide a cross-reference in parentheses to the appropriate page.

(See Table 4 on page 18.)   **OR**   (See Table 2-2 on page 31.)

NOTE: These parenthetical cross-references may be treated as a separate sentence (as shown above) or as part of another sentence (see ¶220).

➢ *For the advisability of numbering tables to simplify cross-references, see ¶1618.*

Centering Tables

1616 a. The table feature of a word processing program extends the table to the full width of the regular text. If you decide to reduce the overall width of the table, first type

¶1620

the table. Then use autofit to adjust the width of the columns (see ¶1603), and choose *center alignment* to position the table horizontally.

b. If a table appears on a page by itself, center the table vertically as well. (Use the *center page* feature of your word processing software.)

Table Identification

1617 Identify tables by *title* unless they are not very numerous and the significance of the material in the table is clear without some descriptive label. (See ¶1620a.)

1618 Also identify tables by *number* unless they are quite short, not very numerous, and typically referred to only on the page on which they fall. The use of table numbers simplifies cross-references, an important consideration if you expect that a number of tables will not fit on the page where they are first mentioned or if you know that certain tables will be referred to repeatedly throughout the regular text.

NOTE: Tables may be numbered consecutively throughout a given document or consecutively within each chapter and each appendix. With the latter technique, the chapter number (or the appendix number or letter) is used as a prefix in the numbering scheme. For example, Table 3-2 would be the second table in Chapter 3, and Table A-5 would be the fifth table in Appendix A.

1619 The table title may be followed by a *subtitle,* which provides additional information about the significance of the table, the period of time it covers, or the manner in which the information is organized or presented. Since a subtitle should be held to one line if possible (two at the most), treat a lengthy comment on any of these points as a note to the table rather than as a subtitle. (See ¶¶1634–1636.)

1620 Type the elements of table identification as follows:

a. Table Title. Center the table title, using boldface all-capital letters.

➢ *For guidelines on spacing above the table title, see ¶¶1611c and 1614.*

b. Table Number. Type the word *Table* in capital and small letters, followed by the appropriate number. To give the table number special emphasis, center it on the second line above the table title and use boldface. To hold down the length of the table, type the table number on the same line with the table title; in this case insert a period after the table number and leave 1 or 2 spaces before typing the table title. (See the illustrations below.)

NOTE: Within a given document treat all table numbers the same way.

Table 2	**Table 1-5**
TITLE OF THE TABLE	**TITLE OF THE TABLE**

OR

Table 2. TITLE OF THE TABLE	**Table 1-5. TITLE OF THE TABLE**

Tables

Continued on page 480

16

¶1621

    c. Table Subtitle. Center the subtitle on the second line below the title, using bold-face capital and small letters. The subtitle is usually enclosed in parentheses when it simply comments on the listing of data in some special order (for example, *In Descending Order by Sales Revenue*) or on the omission of zeros from figures given in the table (for example, *In Millions* or *000 Omitted*).

➤ *For examples of subtitles enclosed in parentheses, see the tables illustrated on these pages: 468, 477, 481, 484, and 491.*

NOTE: If either the title or the subtitle requires more than one line, break it into sensible phrases; then single-space and center any turnover lines. If possible, try to hold the title and the subtitle to two lines each.

Table 5   **TITLE OF THE TABLE**   **WITH ONE TURNOVER LINE**   **Table Subtitle**

Table 3-4. TITLE OF THE TABLE   **WITH ONE TURNOVER LINE**   **Table Subtitle**   **With One Turnover Line**

➤ *For guidelines on how to enter the elements of the table heading in the grid provided by the table feature, see ¶¶1604–1605 and ¶1606a–d.*

Column Heads

1621   **a.** Unless a table is very simple and the significance of the material is clear without heads, provide a heading for each column. (A heading may be omitted over the first column, also known as the *stub*. See, for example, the table on page 491.)

    b. Whenever possible, use singular forms in the column heads. Thus, for example, over a column listing a number of cities, use the heading *City* rather than *Cities*. (See the illustration in the middle of page 477.)

    c. In order to hold down the length of column heads, use abbreviations and symbols as necessary. For example:

Acct. No.	Account number
% of Total	Percent of total
FY 2002 **OR** FY02	Fiscal Year 2002 (also used to indicate that a company's *fiscal* year does not coincide with the *calendar* year)
1Q/2003 **OR** 1Q/03	First Quarter of 2003 (also used with 2Q, 3Q, and 4Q to signify the other three quarters of the year)
Sales ($)	Sales results expressed as a dollar amount (in other words, sales revenues)
Sales (U)	Sales results expressed in terms of the number of units sold
Sales YTD ($)	Cumulative sales revenues so far this year (that is, year to date)
% O/(U) Last Year	Percentage by which this year's results are over (or under) last year's results
2001A	Actual results in 2001
2002B	Budgeted results in 2002
2002E	Estimated results in 2002
2003F	Forecast results in 2003

Tables

16

¶**1622**

If your reader may not understand some of the abbreviations and symbols you use, explain the unfamiliar ones in a footnote to the table. For example:

Note: A = actual; E = estimated; F = forecast.

NOTE: As an alternative to the use of abbreviations, select a smaller font size for the column heads.

d. Column heads should be single-spaced and may be broken into as many as five lines.

e. Capitalize the first letter of each word in a column head except articles *(a, an, the),* conjunctions under four letters (such as *and* and *or*), and prepositions under four letters (such as *of* and *in*). See ¶¶360–361, 363 for detailed guidance on capitalizing words in column headings.

f. Type all column heads in boldface.

g. If the column heads in a table do not all take the same number of lines, align the column heads at the bottom.

NOTE: When you use the table feature of a word processing program, choose the *bottom alignment* option to automatically align column heads that do not take the same number of lines.

h. Leave 1 blank line above and below the tallest column head.

Table 14-4

DISTRIBUTION OF PERSONAL INCOME: 1960 TO 1996

(In Billions of Dollars)

Year	Personal Income	Personal Taxes	Disposable Personal Income	Personal Savings
1960	411.7	48.7	362.9	23.3
1970	836.1	109.0	727.1	61.0
1980	2285.7	312.4	1973.3	161.8
1990	4791.6	624.8	4166.8	208.7
1996	6495.2	886.9	5608.3	239.6

1622 a. When you use the table feature of a word processing program, the default alignment for all column heads is at the left. (See the illustration in ¶1602a.)

b. If you change the alignment of the column text from left to right (for example, with a column of figures), align the column head at the right as well. (See the illustration in ¶1602c.)

Continued on page 482

Tables

16

¶1623

c. When a very narrow column head falls above a very wide column of text, the table will look more attractive if the column head is centered over the column text. It is easy to use center alignment in the table feature of word processing programs; therefore, as a general rule, plan to center all column heads.

Name	Name
A. Michael Ashworth	A. Michael Ashworth
Dwayne Gilpatrick Jr.	Dwayne Gilpatrick Jr.
Bradley M. Harrington	Bradley M. Harrington

Sales	Sales
95,517,833	95,517,833
1,039,875,742	1,039,875,742
874,320,199	874,320,199

d. When a very wide column head falls above a very narrow column of text, you may produce some very odd-looking tables. To avoid this problem, move the indent markers to visually center the column text as a block.

Applications Received	Applications Received
98	98
182	182
243	243
139	139
87	87
202	202

e. All column heads should be either blocked or centered. Do not mix styles within a table.

1623 Braced Column Heads

a. Some complex tables contain *braced* column heads (heads that "embrace" two or more columns). They are also called *straddle* heads because they straddle two or more columns. (See the illustration on page 483.)

b. There are two ways to create a table with braced headings. You can create the table body—5 columns in the illustration on page 483—and merge the cells that will be used for the braced headings. Or you can create a 3-column table, type the braced headings in the appropriate cells, and then split the cells below the braced headings to complete the table.

c. To achieve the best appearance, center each braced column head over the appropriate columns; center the other column heads and the related column text between the vertical rules in each case.

¶**1625**

	Table 12			
	CABLE DIVISION SALES AND NET OPERATING INCOME			
	From 1995 to 2002			
	Sales		**Net Operating Income**	
Year	**Thousands of Dollars**	**Percent of Increase**	**Thousands of Dollars**	**Percent of Increase**
1995A	1429	---	252	---

1624 Crossheads

a. Crossheads are used to separate the data in the body of a table into different categories. (See the illustration on page 484.)

b. The first crosshead falls immediately below the column heads across the top of the table; the other crossheads occur within the body of the table at appropriate intervals.

c. Type each crosshead in capital and small letters, centered on the full width of the table. Using the table feature of a word processing program, you can automatically center each crosshead after you join the cells in that row.

d. Each crosshead should be preceded and followed by a horizontal rule running the full width of the table. Leave 1 blank line between the rule and the crosshead.

Table Text

1625 Spacing

a. The table text may be typed with single or double spacing. However, you may find it simplest to accept the default spacing provided by your word processing program. (Microsoft Word uses single spacing.)

NOTE: Within the same document try to treat all tables alike.

b. Double-spaced tables are more readable. However, choose single spacing if the overall length of a document is a concern or you want to maximize your chances of locating each table on the page where it is first mentioned.

NOTE: You can make single-spaced tables more readable by retaining the horizontal rules between rows and by the use of shading. (See ¶1608 for illustrations of single-spaced tables that have been enhanced for better readability.) And even a slight increase in space between rows can make single-spaced tables more readable. (See the illustration in ¶1607a.)

Continued on page 484

Tables

16

¶1626

Table 8-4
SOCIAL SECURITY TAX RATE SCHEDULE
(Percent of Covered Earnings)

Year	Total	OASDI*	HI**
Employees and Employers Each			
1985	7.05	5.70	1.35
1986–1987	7.15	5.70	1.45
1988–1989	7.51	6.06	1.45
1990 and after	7.65	6.20	1.45
Self-Employed			
1985	14.10	11.40	2.70
1986–1987	14.30	11.40	2.90
1988–1989	15.02	12.12	2.90
1990 and after	15.30	12.40	2.90

Source: *The World Almanac and Book of Facts*, 1998, p. 715.

*Old-age, survivors, and disability insurance.

**Hospital insurance.

c. As a rule, type the table with the same spacing (or less) used for the regular text. Thus when the regular text is *single-spaced,* all the tables should also be single-spaced. When the regular text is *double-spaced,* then all the tables may be typed with double or single spacing.

1626 Items Consisting of Words

If the table text consists of items expressed entirely in words:

a. Capitalize only the first word of each item in the table text plus any proper nouns and proper adjectives.

NOTE: In special cases, where it may be important to show whether terms are capitalized or written with small letters, the first word in each item need not be consistently capitalized. (See, for example, the second and third columns of the table on page 476.)

¶1626

b. Use abbreviations and symbols as necessary to hold down the length of individual items. (See ¶1621c for examples.)

c. Align each item at the left margin of the column. If any item requires more than one line, set a tab to indent the turnover line 0.25 inch. However, if a column contains both main entries and subentries, begin the main entry at the left margin of the column text, set tabs to indent the first line of subentries 0.25 inch, and indent all turnover lines 0.5 inch.

Photographs, prints, 　　and illustrations Scientific or tech- 　　nical drawings Commercial prints Reproductions of 　　works of art

Total weekly 　　broadcast 　　hours General 　　programs Instructional 　　programs

NOTE: You can avoid the need to indent turnovers (but not subentries) if you use horizontal rules or extra space to separate the entries. The table feature will automatically align turnovers at the left, and the horizontal rules or extra space will help to make each entry visually distinct.

Photographs, prints, and illustrations
Scientific or tech- nical drawings
Commercial prints
Reproductions of works of art

Total weekly broadcast hours
General programs
Instructional programs

d. If an item in the first column requires more than one line and all the other items in the same row require only one line, align all the items in that row at the bottom.

Chemical and allied products	151	201
Petroleum refining and related products	69	73 ← Aligned at the bottom
Paper and allied products	391	364

Continued on page 486

Tables

16

¶1627

e. If two or more items in a row each require more than one line, align all entries in that row at the top.

		Aligned at the top
Employee Benefit Report	Prepared quarterly	Data based on administrative records

f. Do not use a period as terminal punctuation at the end of any item except in a column where all entries are in sentence form.

1627 Items Consisting of Figures

a. If a column of table text consists of items expressed entirely in figures:

(1) Align columns of whole numbers at the right.

(2) Align columns of decimal amounts on the decimal point.

(3) In a column that contains both whole numbers and decimals, add a decimal point and zeros to the whole numbers to maintain a consistent appearance.

(4) Omit commas in four-digit whole numbers unless they appear in the same column with larger numbers containing commas. (Some writers prefer to retain the comma in four-digit numbers under all circumstances.) In any case, never insert commas in the decimal part of a number. (See also ¶460.)

```
   325      465.2137
     1     1250.0004
152,657       1.0000
 1,489       37.9898
```

(5) Align the figures in a column by using right alignment or a decimal tab.

NOTE: If you want your software program to perform some calculations in the process of executing a table, you will need to select and follow one of the number formats presented by the software.

➤ For the way to handle a total line in a column of figures, see ¶1629d.

b. If a column of table text consists entirely of "clock" times (as in a program or schedule):

(1) Align the figures in "on the hour" expressions at the right.

```
11 a.m.
12 noon
 1 p.m.
 8 p.m.
12 midnight
```

(2) Align the figures in "hour and minute" expressions on the colon. (Add two zeros to exact times to maintain a uniform appearance.)

```
 8:15 a.m.
10:30 a.m.
12:00 noon
 1:45 p.m.
12:00 midnight
```

(3) When the items in a column each consist of a starting and an ending time, either align all the items at the left or align them on the en dash within the items. (See the illustration in ¶1627c and on page 505.)

8:30–9:30	**OR**	8:30–9:30
10:30–11:30		10:30–11:30
12:30–1:30		12:30–1:30
2:30–3:30		2:30–3:30
4:45–6:00		4:45–6:00

NOTE: When you use the table feature and want to align clock times at the right or on the colon or en dash, the hours 1 to 9 must be made equal in width with the hours 10 to 12. Since each figure occupies 2 spaces, simply type 2 spaces before the single-digit hours to make them the same width as the double-digit hours.

c. In the "24-hour" system of expressing clock time (in which midnight is 0000 and 11:59 p.m. is 2359), the alignment of clock times poses no problem since all times are expressed in four digits (with no colons and no need for reference to *a.m.* or *p.m.*).

0830–0930
1030–1130
1230–1330
1430–1530
1645–1800

1628 Items Consisting of Figures and Words

If a column consists of both figures and words (as in the second column below), align the items at the left. Note, however, that a column consisting only of words aligns at the left (as in the first column below) and a column consisting only of whole numbers aligns at the right (as in the third column below.)

Type of Food	Average Serving	Calorie Count
Bacon	2 strips	97
Beef, roast	4 oz	300
Broccoli	1 cup	44
Tomato, raw	Medium size	30

1629 Amounts of Money

a. In a column containing dollar amounts, insert a dollar sign only before the first amount at the head of the column and before the total amount.

$ 45.50	$ 165	$ 423.75
2406.05	3,450	584.45
783.25	98,932	1228.00
$3234.80	$102,547	$2236.20

Continued on page 488

¶1629

b. The dollar signs at the head and foot of the column should align in the first space to the left of the longest amount in the column. If the item at the head of the column is shorter than the one at the foot, aligning the dollar signs can be troublesome. Choose one of the following approaches to deal with the problem:

(1) Avoid the problem altogether by incorporating the dollar sign in the column head—for example *($000,000 Omitted)*. Then there is no need for dollar signs alongside the figures below.

(2) Insert the first dollar sign by hand. (This approach is not acceptable in documents that have to meet professional standards.)

(3) Type the dollar sign in the space before the first number. After the column is finished, insert spaces between the first dollar sign and the first digit to align the dollar signs (2 spaces for each digit, 1 space for each comma).

c. Do not insert commas to set off thousands in four-digit numbers unless they appear in the same column with larger numbers. (See the examples in ¶1627a and ¶1629a.) Moreover, if all the amounts in a column are whole dollar amounts, omit the decimal point and zeros (as in the second example in ¶1629a). However, if any amount in a column includes cents, use a decimal point with zeros with any whole dollar amount in the same column (as in the third example in ¶1629a).

NOTE: If you want your software program to perform some calculations in the process of executing a table, you will need to select and follow one of the number formats presented by the software.

d. If the table text ends with a *total* line, a horizontal rule should separate the body of the table from the total line.

(1) If the table displays the full default grid or only horizontal rules that set off key sections of the table, the necessary separation will be automatically provided. To give the total amount greater emphasis in a single-spaced table (as in the illustration below), adjust the spacing so that there is 1 blank line above and below the total line.

1998 SALES REVENUES			
Region	**1998B**	**1998A**	**Percent of Difference**
Eastern	$ 300,000	$ 345,108	15.0
Midwestern	450,000	467,380	3.9
Southern	260,000	291,849	12.2
Western	240,000	241,005	0.4
Totals	$1,250,000	$1,345,342	7.6

¶**1630**

(2) If the table has been executed in an *open* style (without horizontal and verti-cal rules), you must insert a horizontal rule that is as wide as the longest entry in the column (including the dollar sign at the left). Before typing the last amount before the total, choose the *underline appearance* option. You may have to insert spaces before the last amount above the total so that the hor-izontal line will be as wide as the longest entry (2 spaces for the dollar sign and each digit, 1 space for each comma).

$1115.59	$ 529,310	$21,348.75
803.61	1,114,310	
1027.64	_1,227.620_	2,294.35
_528.66_		
$3475.50	$2,871,240	_688.50_
		$24,331.60

NOTE: In a single-spaced table, type the total amount on the line directly below the underline (as in the first example above). To give the total amount greater empha-sis, type it on the second line below the underline (as in the second example above). In a double-spaced table, type the amount on the second line below the underline (as in the third example above).

e. If a *total* line is needed, type the word *Total* or *Totals* in the first column, depend-ing on the number of totals to be shown in this row. Use an initial cap only or (for emphasis) all-capital letters. Start the word at the left margin of the column or indent it 0.5 inch.

1630 Percentages

a. If all the figures in a column represent percentages, type a percent sign (%) directly after each figure unless the column heading clearly indicates that these are percentages.

b. Percentages involving decimals should align on the decimal point. If necessary, add zeros after the decimal part of the number so that each figure will align at the right. If any percentage is less than 1 percent, add one zero to the left of the decimal point.

Increase	Percent of Increase	Increase (%)
55.48%	11.63	24
0.80%	4.00	37
2.09%	24.60	120
13.00%	0.40	8
24.35%	71.08	55
66.67%	9.25	69
81.90%	0.08	103
0.25%	12.50	41

Tables

16

¶**1631**

1631 Special Treatment of Figures in Tables

    a. Columns of long figures can be reduced in width by omitting the digits representing thousands, millions, or billions and indicating this omission in parentheses. For example:

(In Thousands)	**OR**	(000 Omitted)
(In Millions)		(000,000 Omitted)
(In Billions)		(000,000,000 Omitted)

    NOTE: The word forms on the left are easier to grasp.

    b. If the parenthetical comment applies to all columns of figures in the table, insert it as a subtitle to the table. However, if the comment applies only to one column of figures, insert the parenthetical comment in the column head.

    NOTE: Sometimes because of space limitations a comment such as *(000 Omitted)* is reduced to *(000)*. The latter form is permissible if you are sure your reader will understand it.

    c. If the parenthetical comment applies to columns of dollar amounts, this fact can also be noted within parentheses, and the dollar sign can then be omitted from the columns of figures.

      ($000 Omitted) **OR** (In Thousands of Dollars) **OR** ($000)

    d. When omitting thousands, millions, or billions from a wide column of figures, you may use rounding or a shortened decimal (or both) to reflect the portion of the number that is being omitted.

Complete Version	**Shortened Versions**		
Sales Revenues	**Sales Revenues ($000 Omitted)**	**Sales Revenues (In Millions)**	**Revenues ($000,000)**
$ 5,878,044	5,878	$ 5.9	6
29,023,994	29,024	29.0	29
14,229,683	14,230	14.2	14
$49,131,721	49,132	$49.1	49

    e. A negative figure in a column may be designated by enclosing the figure in parentheses or by inserting a minus sign (represented by a hyphen or an en dash) directly to the left of the negative figure.

$1642.38	28.2%	Sales in 2000	$264,238
−82.41	-14.5%	Sales in 2001	262,305
$1559.97	6.1%	Gain/(loss)	$ (1,933)

    NOTE: When you use the table feature, you may not be able to easily achieve the alignment shown above for a negative figure in parentheses.

Tables

16

1632 **Leaders**

a. If the items in the first column vary greatly in length, you can use leaders (rows of periods) to lead the eye across to the adjacent item in the next column. Every line of leaders should have at least three periods.

Table 3. NATIONAL INCOME BY SELECTED INDUSTRIES			
(In Billions of Dollars)			
	1980	1990	1996
Agriculture, forestry, and fisheries	61.4	98.0	105.6
Construction	126.6	222.0	285.2
Finance, insurance, and real estate	279.5	684.2	1095.3
Government enterprises	321.8	661.1	855.3
Manufacturing	532.1	859.5	1110.1
Services	341.0	949.4	1410.1

b. To insert a row of leaders within a column, set a right leader tab as close to the right edge of the column as possible. After typing the text, use a hard tab to insert the leaders; then tab to the next column.

NOTE: In view of the extra steps involved in inserting leaders, you may find it more practical to retain the grid provided by the table feature. The horizontal rules that separate rows in the body of the table are sufficient to lead the eye across each row from one column to the next.

c. The *leader* feature in Microsoft Word offers the choice of solid periods, solid hyphens, or solid underscores. Other programs may allow you to specify the character to be used and the space to be left between characters.

1633 **Accounting for Omitted Items**

When there is no entry to be typed in a given row, you can simply leave a blank at that point. However, if doing so may raise a question in the mind of your reader, consider these alternatives:

a. Type the abbreviation *NA* (meaning "not available" or "not applicable") centered on the column width. (See the examples at the top of page 492.)

b. Type a row of periods or hyphens. Use as few as three (centered on the column width), or type the row to the full width of the column. (See the examples at the top of page 492.)

Continued on page 492

¶1634

23,804	23,804	23,804
16,345	16,345	16,345
……...	-----	NA
38,442	38,442	38,442

➤ *See page 483 for another illustration.*

NOTE: If any one of the columns in a table contains omitted items, you will not be able to use a formula to perform calculations.

Table Notes

1634 **a.** If a table requires any explanatory notes or an identification of the source from which the table text was derived, place such material at the foot of the table. (Do not treat it as part of a sequence of notes related to the main text.)

b. A horizontal rule should separate the body of the table from the table notes.

    (1) If the table displays the full default grid or only the horizontal rules that set off key sections of the table, the separation will be automatically provided.

1999	60,410,000,000	65%
2000	64,130,000,000*	68%

Source: *Business Week*, November 27, 2000, p. 167.

*Estimated for the full year.

    (2) If the table has been executed in an *open* style (without horizontal and vertical rules), leave 1 blank line below the last line of the table text and type a 1-inch line of underscores.

1999	60,410,000,000	65%
2000	64,130,000,000*	68%

Source: *Business Week*, November 27, 2000, p. 167.

*Estimated for the full year.

c. To give the table notes greater emphasis in a single-spaced table, insert 1 blank line above and below each note (as in the illustrations above).

d. If all the notes occupy no more than one full line each, begin each note at the left margin of the table text (for the sake of appearance). However, if any of the notes turn over onto a second line, indent the first line of each note. Ordinarily, use the standard indention of 0.5 inch (as in the open-style table above). If a relatively narrow table appears within a grid, reduce the indention to 0.25 inch for a more attractive look (as in the first illustration in *b* above). Also adjust the length of the notes so that the turnovers align with the left edge of the first column and do not extend beyond the right edge of the last column.

1635 If the material in the table has been derived from another source, indicate this fact as follows:

 a. Type the word *Source* with an initial cap or in all-capital letters, followed by a colon, 1 or 2 spaces, and the identifying data. (See ¶¶1508–1522 for models to follow in presenting the bibliographic data.)

 b. A source note should precede any other table note. (See the illustrations in ¶1634b.)

1636 a. If you use abbreviations or symbols that the reader may not understand, explain them in a note at the bottom of the table. This explanation should follow the source note (if any) and precede any other table note. If more than one abbreviation or symbol needs decoding, the explanation can be handled as a series of separate notes (each preceded by a superscript symbol or letter), or it may be done all in one note. (For an illustration, see page 484.)

 b. Except for source notes (like the one illustrated in ¶1634) and a single note explaining symbols and abbreviations, every table note should begin with a superscript symbol or letter that keys the note to the appropriate word or figure in the table text (or title or subtitle) above. Type the corresponding symbol or letter immediately after the appropriate word or figure above, without any intervening space. (See ¶1636d, note.)

 c. Use one of the following programmed sequences of symbols. (See also ¶1502f.)

 * † ‡ § ¶ **OR** a b c d e

 d. Use superscript lowercase letters ([a], [b], [c], etc.) in place of symbols when there are more than five footnotes for a given table.

 NOTE: Avoid the use of superscript *figures* to identify table notes. They could be confusing if used in conjunction with figures in the table text. Moreover, if superscript figures are already used for notes pertaining to the main text, it is wise to use letters or symbols so as to distinguish notes that pertain to a specific table.

 e. In assigning symbols or letters in sequence, go in order by row (horizontally), not by column (vertically).

Dealing With Long Tables

1637 To keep a table from extending beyond the page on which it starts, consider these techniques:

 a. Put the table number (if any) on the same line as the table title rather than on the second line above. (See also ¶1620b.)

 b. Use single spacing for the table text. (See also ¶1625.)

 c. Shorten the wording of the table title, subtitle, column heads, and items in the table text to reduce turnover lines. Use abbreviations and symbols toward this end. (See also ¶1621c.) If necessary, provide a brief explanation in the table notes of any abbreviations and symbols that your reader may not immediately understand. (See also ¶1636.)

Continued on page 494

¶1638

d. When the table text entails a long item that is out of proportion to all other items (or is to be entered in several places in the table text), try to convert the item into a table note, keyed by a symbol or letter appropriately placed in the table above.

e. If a table is narrow and long, you can save space by reformatting the table as shown below. Note that the table text is divided into two parts placed side by side and divided by a double vertical rule. The column heads are repeated over each part.

Table A-20					
DOW JONES INDUSTRIAL AVERAGE: 1989 –1998					
Year	**High**	**Low**	**Year**	**High**	**Low**
1989	2791.41	2144.64	1994	3978.36	3593.35
1990	2999.75	2365.10	1995	5216.47	3832.08
1991	3168.83	2470.30	1996	6560.91	5032.94
1992	3413.21	3136.58	1997	8340.14	6315.84
1993	3794.33	3241.95	1998	9380.20	7400.30

f. Select a smaller size of the font you are using for the other tables.

1638 If a table requires more than one page, follow this procedure:

a. At the bottom of the page where the table breaks, type a continuation line in parentheses—for example, *(Continued on page 14)*—unless it is quite obvious that the table continues on the next page. Merge the cells in the last row at the bottom of the page; then, using right alignment, type the continuation line.

Table 14		
TWENTIETH-CENTURY INVENTIONS		
Invention	**Date**	**Nation**
Airship, rigid dirigible	1900	Germany
Washer, electric	1901	United States
Pen, ballpoint	1938	Hungary
Teflon	1938	United States
Airplane jet engine	1939	Germany
		(Continued on page 14)

b. At the top of the next page, before continuing with the table text, insert the table number, title, and column heads by marking those rows as header rows. If your software will permit it, insert *Continued* in parentheses after the table number (if one is provided) or after the table title.

Table 14 (Continued)

TWENTIETH-CENTURY INVENTIONS

Invention	Date	Nation
CAT scan	1973	England
Microcomputer	1973	France
Disk player, compact	1979	Japan, Netherlands
Heart, artificial	1982	United States

If your software will not permit you to make insertions in the header rows, merge the cells in the first row beneath the column heads; then insert a continuation line in parentheses—for example, *(Continued from page 14)*—and align it at the left margin of the table text.

Table 14

TWENTIETH-CENTURY INVENTIONS

Invention	Date	Nation
(Continued from page 14)		
CAT scan	1973	England
Microcomputer	1973	France
Disk player, compact	1979	Japan, Netherlands
Heart, artificial	1982	United States

c. Ordinarily, all table notes should appear only on the page on which the table ends. However, if certain notes will help the reader interpret the data in the table (for example, notes explaining certain abbreviations or symbols), repeat these notes on each page on which the table appears. (A source note would appear only on the page where the table ends.)

1639 a. Do not start a table at the bottom of one page and continue it on the top of the next page if the entire table will fit on one page (either by itself or with regular text). In such a case start the table at the top of the next page and insert a cross-reference in the text. (See ¶1615.)

Continued on page 496

¶1640

b. Many word processing programs have a feature called *keep lines together,* which prevents a page break from occurring within a block of text. If you use this feature to keep a table from breaking at the bottom of a page, the table as a whole will appear at the top of the next page. However, the space previously occupied by the first part of the table will remain empty; the text that follows the table will not come forward to fill up this vacant space. If you want to avoid this result, do not use *keep lines together.* Use the following approach instead:

(1) Let the table break naturally and continue typing the rest of the document.

(2) When the document is completed in all other respects, select and cut the table; the text following the table will flow forward. Insert a hard page break at the bottom of the page where the table was removed, and paste the whole table at the top of the following page.

Dealing With Wide Tables

1640 To keep a wide table from extending beyond the margins established for the page, consider the following techniques:

a. Reduce the width of the columns by using the autofit feature.

b. Use abbreviations and symbols to hold down the length of lines in the column heads and the column text.

c. If only a few entries are disproportionately wide or are repeated in the table and make it difficult to fit the table in the space available, consider converting these items to table footnotes. (See also ¶1637d.)

d. Select a smaller font size in order to make the table fit within the space available.

1641 **Turning the Table Sideways**

a. Whenever possible, the page orientation of a table should be the same as that of the regular text. However, when other alternatives do not work or cannot be used, turn the table so that it prints in *landscape* (across the 11-inch dimension) on a page by itself. In such a case, the left margin of the table will fall toward the bottom of the page and the right margin toward the top.

NOTE: *Landscape printing* is the term that describes printing text on the 11-inch dimension of a standard page. *Portrait printing* is the term that describes the customary printing of text on the 8½-inch dimension of a standard page.

b. In planning the layout of a turned table, be sure that the overall dimensions of the table will fit within the established margins for the regular pages in the given document. If no margins have been established, leave a minimum of 1 inch on all sides of the turned table.

NOTE: If a turned table is to be part of a *bound* report, leave a minimum top margin of 1.5 inches. This top margin will represent the left margin when the turned table is bound into the report. (See also ¶1404b.)

Tables

16

Converting Tables Into Charts and Graphs

1642 Data presented in a table is easier to grasp and work with than when it is presented in running text. By the same token, a chart or a graph can often present data more effectively than a table, especially when you are trying to emphasize patterns of growth or want to contrast different levels of performance or achievement.

Most word processing programs provide a *chart* or *graph* feature that offers you a variety of formats to choose from. To create a chart or graph, first select the format you want; then insert the appropriate data in a *datasheet* (which looks like a spreadsheet). With some programs you can simply import the data from an existing table or some other source without having to reenter it in the datasheet. The following illustrations will show you some of the results you can achieve.

a. The following bar chart reflects the data presented in the table on page 468.

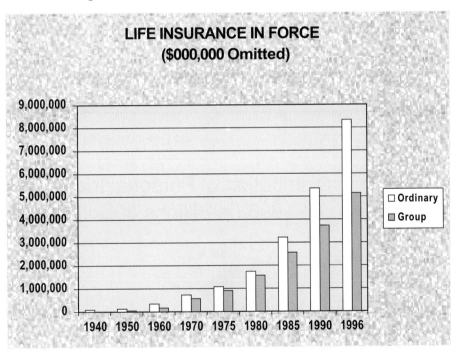

LIFE INSURANCE IN FORCE
($000,000 Omitted)

Legend: ☐ Ordinary   ▪ Group

x-axis: 1940 1950 1960 1970 1975 1980 1985 1990 1996

Continued on page 498

Tables

16

¶1642

b. The following graph reflects the data presented in the table at the top of page 494.

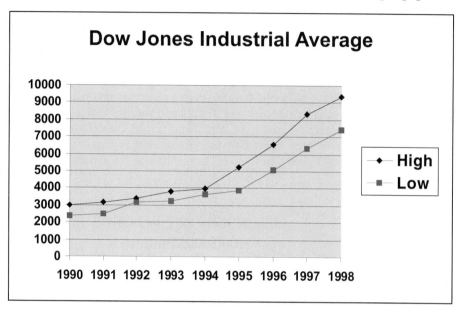

c. The following pie chart reflects the data presented in the table on page 481.

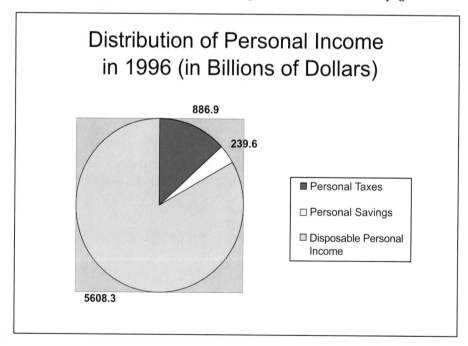

SECTION **17**

Other Business Documents

¶1701

Section 17 provides models for a number of common business documents. The models reflect formats widely used, but they are not to be regarded as rigid patterns that must be followed without deviation. Feel free to modify these formats to fit the needs of the situation at hand. As always, good sense and good taste (rather than an artificial notion of "absolute correctness") should prevail.

IMPORTANT NOTE: Your word processing software may provide templates for many of the documents discussed in Section 17. If you decide to use a template provided by your software, you may find it helpful to examine the corresponding model in this section to see whether there are certain features or details that are worth adding to the basic template.

General Format Considerations

Paragraphs 1701–1702 deal with the issues of establishing margins and the treatment of headings. These format considerations apply to all the specific types of documents discussed later in Section 17.

Margins

1701 **a.** **Top Margin.** If you are using plain 8½″ x 11″ stationery for the first page of a business document, use a top margin of about 2 inches. However, accept the default top margin of 1 inch in order to fit more copy on the page and avoid the need for a second page. If you are using letterhead stationery for the first page, leave at least 0.5 inch between the letterhead and the first element to be typed. If the document requires more than one page, use plain paper for the continuation pages and leave a top margin of 1 inch.

  b. **Side Margins.** If you are using 8½″ x 11″ stationery, the default side margins (1.25 inch for Microsoft Word, 1 inch for WordPerfect) should be adequate in most cases. However, you may increase the side margins if you want to achieve a more open look or a more balanced arrangement of copy on the page. (See, for example, the illustration on page 504.)

    NOTE: The table in ¶1305b offers guidelines on adjusting side margins.

  c. **Bottom Margin.** Leave a bottom margin of at least 1 inch.

Headings

1702 **a.** The main heading typically consists of the title of the document or the name of the organization. It ordinarily appears centered on the first line in all-capital letters. Additional details (such as a date or a location) appear in capital and small letters on separate lines, with 1 blank line between them.

    NOTE: If any item in the heading requires more than 1 line, type the turnover line single-spaced, centered on the line above.

  b. Use boldface for at least the first item in the heading. The remaining items in the heading may also be done in boldface (see the illustration on page 505) or in regular type (see the illustration on page 504).

  c. Leave 1 blank line—or, for a more open look, 2 blank lines—between the last line of the heading and the body of the document. The illustration on page 503 shows the use of 1 blank line; the illustrations on pages 504–506, 508, and 510 show the use of 2 blank lines.)

d. If a document requires more than one page, insert a continuation heading like the one used on the second page of a letter. Use the header feature to create and automatically position the continuation heading. (See ¶1384 for further details.)

NOTE: The second page of a résumé typically uses a slightly different continuation heading. (See pages 521, 523, and 525 for examples.)

Executive Documents

The following paragraphs (¶¶1703–1707) present commonly used formats for agendas, minutes, itineraries, fax cover sheets, and news releases.

Agendas

1703 An *agenda* is a list of items to be considered or acted upon. The format of an agenda varies with the circumstances. The agenda for an informal staff meeting may be done as a simple numbered list of topics in a memo addressed to the attendees. (See the illustration on page 503.) The agenda for a formal meeting (for example, of a corporate board of directors) will typically call for a more structured list of topics. (See the illustration on page 504.) The agenda for a formal program (for example, for a conference or a seminar) will be structured around a timetable, with specific time slots allotted to formal presentations by speakers and topical discussions in small groups. (See the illustration on page 505.)

There is no "correct" way to set up an agenda. The illustrations on pages 503–505 are intended only to suggest various ways in which an agenda can be formatted. The format you decide to use should be tailored to fit the needs of the meeting or program being planned.

Minutes

1704 *Minutes* provide a record of what was discussed and decided upon at a meeting. The minutes of small committee meetings within an organization are usually done in an informal style, in much the same way that the agendas for such meetings are also prepared. (Compare the informal agenda on page 503 with the informal minutes on page 506.) When the participants at a meeting come from a number of different organizations (as they would, for example, at meetings of professional associations and societies), the minutes tend to be somewhat more formal. And when the minutes may have to serve some legal use, they are typically done in a highly formal style. According to the American Society of Corporate Secretaries, increasing government regulation and stockholder lawsuits make it critically important that the minutes of a meeting of a corporation's board of directors be complete and accurate, since they may have to serve as legal evidence of what the corporation's directors did or intended to do. The *short form* of corporate minutes (illustrated on page 508) simply describes the decisions that were made, along with some brief indication of the key facts on which those decisions were made. By contrast, the *long form* describes in some detail the arguments for and against the decisions finally arrived at.

¶1705

Other Business Documents

17

Itineraries

1705 An itinerary should clearly set forth the travel arrangements and the appointment schedule of the person making the trip. If the itinerary is intended only for the use of the person traveling, it should be possible to eliminate certain items and abbreviate details that the person is quite familiar with. However, if the itinerary will be distributed to others (who may need to contact the person who is traveling), present the information as fully and as clearly as possible. (For example, see the illustration on page 510.)

Fax Cover Sheets

1706 Most messages sent by fax (facsimile) equipment are accompanied by a fax cover sheet that indicates (1) the name and the fax number of the person receiving the fax, (2) the name and fax number of the person sending the fax, (3) the number of pages being sent, and (4) the name and the telephone number of the person to be called in case the transmission is not satisfactorily completed. There are different ways to prepare a fax cover sheet. Your word processing software may provide a fax template that you can use as is or modify to suit your preferences. If you are designing a fax cover sheet as a form to be filled in by hand, you will need to add fill-in lines. (See the illustration on page 511.)

NOTE: The ready availability of small stick-on labels that accommodate all the essential information in a compact form is appealing to many people, who are pleased to save time and money as a result of not having to create or transmit a separate fax cover sheet. Therefore, do not feel compelled to use a fax cover sheet if a commercially prepared stick-on label will serve your purpose.

News Releases

1707 A news release (also referred to as a press release) is an announcement made by an organization about news that it considers important—for example, the acquisition of (or the merger with) another organization, the hiring or the promotion of key executives, the physical expansion or relocation of the organization, the achievement of better than expected financial goals, and the celebration of organizational anniversaries and other key events.

A news release is distributed to members of the media (representing newspapers, magazines, TV and radio stations, and Web sites) and to others who help shape public opinion (such as financial analysts and advertising agencies). This distribution is undertaken with the hope that these various people will bring this news to the attention of the audiences they serve. Because the recipients of news releases are typically inundated with these documents on a daily basis, it is important that your news release try to present its message in a manner that will make it seem truly newsworthy.

Your word processing software may provide one or more templates that you can use as is, or you may prefer to create your own template along the lines of the model illustrated on page 512.

Text continues on page 514

Agenda—Informal (Memo) Style

A   MEMO TO: Marketing Managers Committee ↓ **2x**

FROM: Dorothy Innie ↓ **2x** *Dl*

DATE: July 10, 2000 ↓ **2x**

SUBJECT: Agenda for July 20 Meeting ↓ **2 or 3x**

Our July 20 meeting will begin at 9:30 a.m. in the small conference room located on the second floor. (The large conference room, where we normally meet, has been reserved by Mrs. Harper for an all-day meeting.) ↓ **2x**

Please come prepared to discuss the following topics: ↓ **2x**

B   1. Sales through June for each product line. ↓ **2x**

2. Year-end sales forecast vs. budget for each product line.

3. Recommendations for changes in this year's marketing plans and requests for supplemental funding.

4. Proposed changes in next year's marketing strategies.

C   5. Preliminary marketing budgets for next year. (Please put these in writing for me so that I can share them with Bill Carr, our friendly bean counter in the Finance Department.) ↓ **2x**

ma ↓ **2x**

Distribution: ↓ **2x**

G. Albers
R. Fagan
K. Garcia-Lorca
S. Koechlin
F. Li
C. Mandel
T. Pavlick
P. Washington

A Memo Format. For the format of a memo done on plain paper (as shown here) or on letterhead stationery, see ¶1393.

B Numbered List. If you use the numbered list feature of your word processing program, each item will begin at the left margin, turnovers will be indented to align with the first word in the line above, and no space will be left between items. (See ¶1357d for an illustration of a single-spaced list created by the numbered list feature.) To make the list easier to read, leave 1 blank line after each item in the list, as in the illustration above. (For further details, see ¶1357d.)

C End Punctuation. The items in an agenda typically require no end punctuation. However, if any item involves the use of a complete sentence (as in item 5 in this illustration), place a period at the end of every item. For details on the use or omission of periods with items in a list, see ¶107.

Agenda—Formal Style

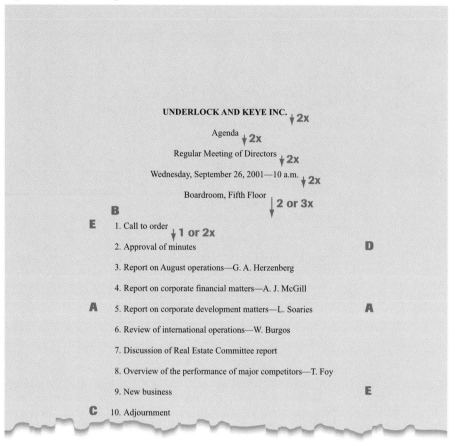

A **Margins.** This agenda has a number of very short items. If it were done using default side margins, it would have an unbalanced look, with a relatively small left margin and a very large right margin. Therefore, this agenda has been centered horizontally to achieve a balanced appearance.

B **Numbered List.** If you use the numbered list feature of your word processing program, each item will begin at the left margin and no space will be left between items. Ordinarily, when the items in a list contain no turnovers, single spacing is quite acceptable. However, in a document like an agenda, where each item will be the subject of discussion, the use of 1 blank line between items makes the list easier to read and work with. (For an illustration of a single-spaced list created by the numbered list feature, see ¶1357d.)

C When a numbered list contains 10 or more items, the numbered list feature of your word processing program will align the numbers at the left. (See the illustration in ¶1357d, note.) However, you can choose to align the numbers at the right (as in the illustration above).

D **End Punctuation.** Note that no periods are needed at the end of the items in this illustration. (See also ¶107.)

E **Formal Items.** In a formal agenda it is customary to include such items as *Call to order, Approval of minutes, New business,* and *Adjournment* (or similar types of expressions).

Agenda—Program for a Conference or Seminar

A

SOFTWARE APPLICATIONS SEMINAR ↓ 2x

Saddle Brook Marriott ↓ 2x

July 16–17, 2003

| 2 or 3x

B Wednesday, July 16 ↓ 2x

8:00–9:00	Registration and Continental Breakfast ↓ 2x	**C**	Lobby
9:00–9:40	Software Applications: A State-of-the-Art Overview Speaker: Joyce Stocker-Olsen		Salons A and B
9:50–10:30	Word Processing and Communications Applications Speakers: Louis Serrano and Roy Pfaltz	**E**	Salons A and B
10:30–10:50	Coffee Break		Lobby
10:50–11:30	Desktop Publishing and Graphics Applications Speakers: Sandra Scroggins and Ed Fox		Salons A and B
11:40–12:20	Spreadsheet and Database Management Applications Speaker: Esther W. Benoit	**E**	Salons A and B
12:30–1:45	Lunch		Ballroom
1:45–3:15	<u>Concurrent Sessions</u>		
D	Session 1: Microsoft Word 2000 Speaker: Irwin Manoogian		Red Oak Suite

A Headings. Include the location and date(s) of the conference or seminar in the main heading unless the program is part of a larger document that features this information prominently in some other way.

B If the program is scheduled to last more than one day, insert an appropriate side heading above each day's listing of events.

C Columnar Format. To create this three-column format, use the table feature.

D For the alignment of "clock" times in a column, see ¶1627d.

E Speaker Identification. The speakers listed on the program may be further identified by title, organization, and place of residence. Use commas to separate these elements of identification and, if you wish, use parentheses to enclose these elements as a whole. For example:

Roy Pfalz, software consultant,
Newton, Massachusetts

Esther W. Benoit (vice president,
Programmatic Associates,
Los Altos, California)

Other Business
Documents

17

Minutes—Informal (Memo) Style

A   MEMO TO: Marketing Managers Committee   ↓ **2x**

FROM: Paula Washington   ↓ **2x**

DATE: July 21, 2000   ↓ **2x**

B   SUBJECT: Minutes of the Marketing Managers
Committee Meeting of July 20, 2000
↓ **2 or 3x**

C   Present: Dorothy Innie (presiding), Georgia Albers, Ruth Fagan, Katherine
Garcia-Lorca, Sid Koechlin, Charles Mandel, Tim Pavlick   ↓ **2x**

Absent: Fay Li   ↓ **2x**

Guest: Bill Carr
↓ **2 or 3x**   **E**

D   1.   **Sales through June for each product line.** Each product line is behind budget for
the first six months of the year. Bill Carr of the Finance Department reported that the
company as a whole is running 11.2 percent behind budget and 6.3 percent behind
last year's sales for the first six months.   ↓ **2x**

F   2.   **Year-end sales forecast vs. budget for each product line.** Ruth Fagan and Sid
Koechlin each reported that on the basis of recent reports from the field, sales will

G   The next meeting of the Marketing Managers Committee will be held on August 24 in the
large conference room (as usual).   ↓ **2x**

Paula Washington   ↓ **2x**

nb   ↓ **2x**

Distribution: ↓ **2x**

D. Innie
G. Albers
R. Fagan
K. Garcia-Lorca
S. Koechlin
F. Li
C. Mandel
T. Pavlick

A **Memo Format.** For the format of a memo on plain paper (as shown on page 506) or on letterhead stationery, see ¶1393.

B **Subject Line.** For better appearance, the entry following *Subject* has been broken into two lines of roughly equal length. (See ¶1353d, note.)

C **Attendance Data.** This block of copy indicates who was present at the meeting (the person who presided is listed first), who was absent, and who attended as a guest.

D **Content Considerations.** List each topic in the order in which it was discussed at the meeting. (Compare these minutes with the agenda shown on page 503.)

E Treat each topic as a boldface run-in head, followed by a period and the comments that relate to that topic (as illustrated here). As an alternative, treat each topic as a boldface side head, with no period following. The related comments will then appear as a separate paragraph starting on the second line below. For example:

1. **Sales through June for each product line**

    Each product line is behind budget for the first six months of the year. Bill Carr of the Finance Department . . .

F When the items in a numbered list consist of paragraphs with two or more lines, leave a blank line between items for better readability and a more open look. (See ¶1357d.)

G Give the date and location of the next meeting in a concluding paragraph, starting at the left margin.

Other Business Documents

17

Minutes—Formal Style

A

UNDERLOCK AND KEYE INC. ↓ 2x

Minutes ↓ 2x

Regular Meeting of Directors ↓ 2x

September 26, 2001

↓ 2 or 3x

B
D
A regular meeting of the Board of Directors of Underlock and Keye Inc. was called to order at 4 Riverfront Plaza, Louisville, Kentucky, at 10 a.m. pursuant to the notice sent to all directors in accordance with the bylaws. ↓ 2x

E
The following directors were present, constituting all the directors: Jared G. Allison II, Kenneth L. Calderone, Deborah Dean Daniels, Gary Guyot, Henry Koyama, Anton Mika, Helen Roberts, Walter F. Tarshis, Samuel A. Tuleja, and D. J. Wikowski.

E
Also present by invitation were William Burgos, Thomas Foy, Gregory A. Herzenberg, Angela J. McGill, and Lester Soaries.

Jared G. Allison II, Chairman, presided and David K. Rust, Assistant Secretary, **J** recorded the proceedings of the meeting.

F
The minutes of the last meeting were approved.

Mr. Allison introduced Gregory A. Herzenberg, Executive Vice President of **J** Operations, who reported on August operations.

F
Henry Koyama reviewed the recommendations of the Real Estate Committee on the matter of building a new facility or renovating the existing facility to accommodate the Corporation's information processing needs over the next ten years. **I**

Minutes   2   September 26, 2001

B
After further discussion, upon motion duly made and seconded, the following resolutions were unanimously adopted: ↓ 2x

C
RESOLVED, that the Corporation is hereby authorized to undertake **I** construction and rehabilitation activities with respect to renovating the

G
The next meeting of the Board will be held on November 28 at 10 a.m. **I**

H
There being no further business before the meeting, it was, on motion duly made and seconded, adjourned at 1:05 p.m. ↓ 4x

_____
Assistant Secretary

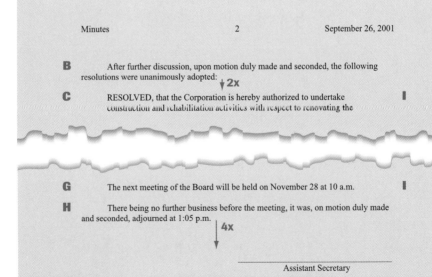

A Heading. Use all-capital letters for the name of the company in the first line. Use capital and small letters for the other lines. For the date line, use the date on which the meeting was held (not the date on which the minutes were prepared). Use boldface for the name of the company and, if desired, for all the elements in the heading.

B Format Considerations. Use default side margins. Indent the first line of each paragraph 0.5 inch.

C Treat resolutions as extracts, indented as a block 0.5 inch from each side margin. Type *RESOLVED* in all-capital letters, followed by a comma and *that* (as illustrated). As an alternative, type *RESOLVED* followed by a colon and *That.*

D Content Considerations. Use the opening paragraph to indicate the name of the company; the time and the place where the meeting was "called to order" (the first item on the agenda shown on page 504); and whether it was a regular or special meeting.

E Use the next paragraphs to indicate which directors were present (all were in this illustration); which were absent; which company officers and invited guests were present; who presided; and who recorded the proceedings and prepared the minutes.

F The body of the minutes should note in each paragraph what business was transacted and what actions were taken.

G Use the next-to-last paragraph to indicate the date and time of the next meeting.

H Use the final paragraph to indicate the time of adjournment.

I Capitalization Style. Minutes done in a formal style use a formal style of capitalization. Note that short forms such as *Corporation* and *Board* are capitalized.

J Also note that in formal minutes such titles as *Chairman, Assistant Secretary,* and *Executive Vice President of Operations* are capitalized when used after a person's name. (See ¶313d.)

Other Business
Documents

17

Itinerary

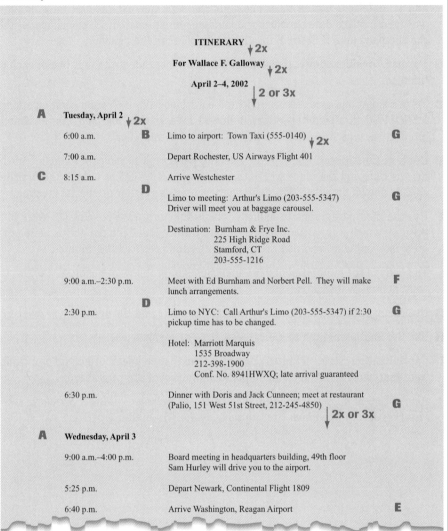

A **Headings.** If the itinerary is to cover more than one day, insert an appropriate side heading above each day's scheduled list of activities.

B **Columnar Format.** To create this two-column format, use the table feature.

C For the alignment of "clock" times in a column, see ¶1627b.

D **Spacing.** Leave 1 blank line between entries. Single-space any turnovers.

E **Content Considerations.** Provide the names of airports only when there is more than one airport serving the city (in this case, Washington, D.C.).

F Try to provide the first names (rather than simply titles or initials) for all the individuals whom the traveler is scheduled to meet.

G Provide phone numbers for all transportation services, hotels, and restaurants in case the plans have to be rescheduled or canceled.

Fax Cover Sheet

FAX... BURNHAM & FRYE INC.

225 High Ridge Road
Stamford, CT 06905

Date: **B** _____

To: _____

_____

Fax Number: _____

From: **A** _____

_____

Fax Number: A _____

Number of pages (including this cover sheet): _____

Message: **B** _____

If any part of this fax transmission is missing or not clearly received, please call:

Name: **B** _____

Phone number: _____

Other Business Documents

17

A **Format Considerations.** If you are using software to create a template for a fax cover sheet that only you will use, insert any information that will not change (such as your name and fax number) as a part of the template. However, if you are creating a form to be used by a number of people, provide blank fill-in lines for this variable information.

B **Fill-In Lines.** If the entries on the fax cover sheet are likely to be typed in, use consistent spacing between fill-in lines and try to arrange the fill-in lines so that all entries can start at a common point.

Confidentiality Statement. If you are faxing something that is confidential (and this may sometimes not be a wise thing to do), add an appropriate message to the cover sheet.

CONFIDENTIAL

The contents of this fax transmission are confidential. If this transmission has been directed to the wrong office, please destroy the contents of this fax immediately and notify [*sender's name*] at [*phone number*].

To further ensure the confidentiality of the transmission, call the appropriate person in the receiving office and (1) confirm the fax number to be used and (2) confirm that the person will be standing right by the receiving equipment while the fax is being transmitted.

Other Business Documents

17

News Release

News Release

BURNHAM & FRYE INC.

A

225 High Ridge Road
Stamford, CT 06905

B Contact: Norbert Pell

Phone: 203.555.1294

Fax: 203.555.1299

FOR IMMEDIATE RELEASE **C**

↓ **2 or 3x**

D **BURNHAM & FRYE ACQUIRES BRITISH TECHNOLOGY COMPANY** ↓ **2x**

Purchase Strengthens Burnham & Frye's Lifetime Learning Initiatives ↓ **2 or 3x**

E **Stamford, Connecticut, May 29, 2001:** Burnham & Frye today completed its

acquisition of Halsted Multimedia Solutions Ltd. of Maidenhead, Berkshire, England.

Halsted's multimedia management and employee training courses and its state-of-the-

art technology will expand Burnham & Frye's capabilities in delivering interactive training

programs for professionals over the Internet, corporate intranets, and other multimedia

platforms.

Halsted's product line includes 18 multimedia programs in CD-ROM format on

topics ranging from customer service to teamwork and marketing. All offer a rich mix of

video, audio, graphics, and text, and they also feature interactive exercises and easy

navigation. ↓ **2x**

F   # # #

A Heading. The heading should indicate the name and address of the organization sponsoring the news release.

B It should also show the name and phone numbers of the person to contact in case more information is needed.

C The heading should also indicate when the information contained in the news release may be distributed to the public. In many cases the phrase *For immediate release* is sufficient. If the information is to be kept confidential until a specific time and date, the heading should carry a notation like this:

For release 9 a.m. EST, May 7, 2001

D Headline. The text of the news release should begin with a descriptive title and, if desired, a subtitle.

E Content Considerations. The first paragraph should begin with a bold run-in head that indicates the city and state of origin and the date on which this material is to be released. This run-in head is usually followed by a colon or a dash (typical newspaper practice) rather than a period.

F At the end of the text, leave 1 blank line and type one of the following notations, centered: three spaced pound signs (# # #) or the phrase –30–. These notations, derived from long-standing newspaper practice, signify "the end."

Other Business Documents

17

¶1708

E-Mail

The volume of e-mail traffic continues to grow at an explosive rate. In 1994 U.S. computers carried an estimated 776 billion e-mail messages. By 1997 that number tripled to 2.6 trillion messages, and by 2000 that number was expected to nearly triple again—to 6.6 trillion messages. There is good reason for the speed with which this new technology has taken hold: the use of e-mail serves to overcome the problems associated with the delivery of regular mail (referred to as *snail mail* by some e-mail users) and the frustrations that result from playing telephone tag (leaving messages but never connecting). Do keep in mind that e-mail is not always the best means of communication, particularly when matters need to be treated confidentially. (See ¶1709d.)

The following guidelines (¶¶1708–1711) suggest how to compose and format e-mail messages so as to make the most of what this technology offers.

1708   Before composing an e-mail message, remember that the person you are addressing may receive more than 100 such messages a day. Many recipients report increasing frustration over the time it takes to read each day's e-mail messages, especially if many of those messages are the electronic equivalent of junk mail. To avoid frustrating the recipients of your e-mail:

a. Keep the distribution of your e-mail messages to a minimum. Given the ease of transmitting an e-mail message to everyone on an existing mailing list, you could be sending messages to people who don't need to see them and thus be adding to their e-mail overload.

b. Keep your messages short. Try to hold the overall length to the number of lines that will fit on one screen. Limit each line to a maximum of 80 characters.

c. Consider how much background your reader needs to have in order to understand your message. If you are responding to an issue raised in the earlier e-mail message, it is a great temptation to repeat the earlier message along with your response. Try to paraphrase the earlier message as briefly as possible so as to spare your reader unnecessary verbiage.

d. Provide a subject line for each message you compose. A subject line helps the recipient of a great many messages screen them quickly to determine which require the fastest action. (See ¶1711b.)

e. Restrict each message to one subject. It is better to send two separate messages than to cover several topics in one message.

f. Organize your sentences in short, single-spaced paragraphs to make your message easier to understand. Do not indent the opening line of each paragraph, but leave 1 blank line between paragraphs.

g. Edit and proofread each message carefully, and make the necessary corrections before sending the message. Because e-mail messages are usually composed on the computer, it is easy to make (and overlook) mistakes in grammar, usage, spelling, and style. (See ¶¶1202–1204.)

NOTE: Some e-mail systems provide spelling and grammar checkers, but these devices do not relieve you of the responsibility to check your own material with great care.

h. Do not use all-capital letters in your messages. (This practice is considered to be the equivalent of shouting.) Follow the standard rules of capitalization.

1709 When you are composing e-mail messages, keep these points in mind:

a. Watch your tone in composing the message. Before you send it, read the message from the recipient's point of view to make sure that your words and your tone are not likely to be misconstrued.

NOTE: Some e-mail users insert *smileys* [for example, :-)] in their messages to indicate their feelings about what they are writing. However, many people find the use of smileys overly cute and feel they are no more necessary in e-mail messages than in any other kind of written communication. (For further discussion of this issue, see the entry for *Smiley* in Appendix B.)

b. Do not send a message composed in anger (an act known as *flaming*). Moreover, if you receive *flames* (angry messages), it is wiser to ignore them than to respond in kind.

c. Do not use e-mail to send unsolicited ads or other material that the recipient is likely to regard as junk mail. People who receive such material often take revenge by responding with flames. Some recipients may go so far as to make use of special programs referred to as *bozo filters*. These programs automatically intercept and delete all future messages from such bozos.

d. Put nothing in an e-mail message that you would not want anyone other than the intended recipient to see. For example, do not provide confidential information that could wind up in the wrong hands. Moreover, do not use e-mail if you want to criticize or reprimand someone. In all such cases use another medium of communication. Remember: The privacy of the e-mail messages you send cannot be guaranteed.

e. Respect the privacy of the messages you receive. Do not pass such messages on to others unless you are sure the sender will not object.

1710 E-mail messages can be distributed through local and wide area networks, bulletin board systems, online services, and the Internet. Procedures for sending and receiving e-mail messages will therefore differ, depending on the system you use. Even the construction of mailing addresses will vary as a result.

a. An e-mail address has two parts separated by @ (the symbol for *at*).

NOTE: Because of its appearance, the @ symbol is sometimes referred to as a *strudel* (a type of rolled pastry).

b. The part that precedes @ is called the *mailbox*. It typically consists of your *username* (the name you use to sign on to an e-mail system); for example, *ritajbella*, *rjbella*, *rjb*, or *ritaj*. However, some systems may assign you an arbitrary mailbox.

c. The part that follows @ is called the *domain*. It represents the mail system on which you receive your mail. The domain consists of two or more elements separated by periods (referred to as *dots*). If you use America Online, the domain is *aol.com*; if you use CompuServe, the domain is *compuserve.com*. (Dots are used between the elements of the domain but not at the end.) If you are sending e-mail

Other Business Documents

17

to someone within your own domain, you can omit the domain from the e-mail address.

NOTE: The final element in the domain—called the *zone*—indicates what kind of system is being used. For example, *.com* signifies "commercial," *.gov* governmental," *.edu* "educational," and *.org* "organizational."

➤ *For a more detailed discussion of the zones now being used, see ¶1532.*

d. Here are a few sample e-mail addresses.

the President of the United States:	president@whitehouse.gov
The Internet Society:	isoc@isoc.org
Laboratory for Computer Science at MIT:	lcs@mit.edu
NewbieNewz (an electronic newsletter for newcomers to the Internet):	newbienewz-request@io.com

e. Never alter the spacing, the punctuation, the symbols, or the capitalization of an e-mail address.

➤ *For guidelines on how to divide a long e-mail address at the end of a line, see ¶1539.*

1711 The format of an e-mail message is very much like that of a simplified memo. The first illustration on page 517 shows how an e-mail message looks after the sender has written it. The second illustration on page 517 shows how the same message will appear to the person who receives it.

a. After the guide word *To* or *Mail To,* insert the recipient's name and e-mail address. If the message is addressed to more than one person, separate the entries showing each recipient's name and mailing address by means of a comma or a semicolon (depending on the system you use).

b. After *Subject* or *Re* insert an appropriate subject line. As noted in ¶1708e, try to deal with only one subject in each message. Since the recipient may look at only the subject line to decide how important your message is, be sure to choose wording that will get you the attention you want.

c. Your e-mail template may provide guide words such as *CC* or *cc* so that you can insert the name and e-mail address of anyone who is also intended to receive this message.

d. Your e-mail template may also provide a guide word such as *Reply to.* Make an entry here if you want the recipient to send a response to an address other than the one shown in the *From* entry.

e. You do not need to indicate whom the message is from. The software program will automatically insert your mailing address (as well as your full name) after *From.* It will also automatically display the date and time when the message was transmitted.

NOTE: The program will automatically display additional lines of information such as routing data. You may also have the option of displaying your conventional mailing address, your phone number, your fax number, and any other information you wish.

Other Business
Documents

17

E-Mail Message Sent

Filed Outgoing Message	Sub S Corporation	Page 1 of 1

```
Subject:    Sub S Corporation
Sent:       9/27/02 10:36 AM
To:         Jack Lynch, jlynch@lincoln.midcoast.com
CC:         Bev Funk, bevfunk@whidbey.net


Jack:

Bev and I have decided to take your advice and set up a Sub S corporation. I'll be in
town next Thursday and Friday. Can you spare me a little time either afternoon?
                                        Margaret
```

E-Mail Message Received

```
msabin, 10:42 AM 9/27/02     Sub S Corporation


    Return-Path: msabin@mail.viconet.com
    Date: Fri, 27 Sep 2002 10:42:39 -0400
    Subject: Sub S Corporation
    From: msabin <msabin@viconet.com>
    To:  Jack Lynch  <jlynch@lincoln.midcoast.com>
    cc:  Bev Funk  <bevfunk@whidbey.net>

    Jack:

    Bev and I have decided to take your advice and set up a Sub S corporation.
    I'll be in town next Thursday and Friday. Can you spare me a little time
    either afternoon?
                                        Margaret
```

f. In the interest of brevity, salutations and complimentary closings are often omitted. However, follow your personal preferences in such matters. (In the illustrations above note the use of *Jack* as a salutation and *Margaret* as a closing.)

➤ *For guidelines on message length, paragraphing, spacing, and capitalization, see ¶1708; for guidelines on sending a letter confirming an e-mail message already transmitted, see ¶1375b.*

g. Users of e-mail sometimes rely on special abbreviations to shorten their messages. For example:

BTW	by the way
IMHO	in my humble opinion
GMTA	great minds think alike
J/K	just kidding
BRB	be right back
BAK	I'm back at the keyboard
LOL	I'm laughing out loud at what I just read
ROTFL	I'm rolling on the floor laughing at what I just read

¶1712

Résumés

Preparing a Résumé

1712 When you prepare a résumé, keep the following things in mind:

a. The purpose of a résumé is not to get you a job but to get you a *job interview*.

b. The purpose of a résumé is not to tell a prospective employer about *your* long-term goals and aspirations but to indicate *what you can do for the employer* with the experience you have acquired and the skills you have developed.

c. Do not describe your past jobs in terms of duties and responsibilities. Emphasize things you have achieved, capabilities you have acquired, decision-making skills you have put to good use, activities you have initiated, and sales and profits that have increased (and expenses that have decreased) because of your efforts.

d. Describe your achievements and skills in a way that indicates they are readily applicable to other types of jobs and other fields.

e. Do not overstate your achievements by claiming to have accomplished certain things single-handedly when it will be clear to the prospective employer that your achievement had to be part of a team effort. In the attempt to come across as a self-starter, don't jeopardize your reputation for honesty.

f. While you want your résumé to stand out from all the others that are submitted at the same time, think of how an employer will view your résumé. If you're applying for a job in advertising, design, or some other creative field, an original format or even an off-the-wall approach may spark the interest you crave. But if you're after a job in management, finance, or marketing—where an image of maturity and dependability is important—you'll gain more ground by emphasizing how you can help the employer rather than by taking a far-out approach.

g. Weigh the advantages of preparing a custom-tailored résumé for each situation (in which you organize and focus your strengths in light of a specific employer's needs) over the savings in time and money that come from preparing a single résumé designed to fit a variety of job opportunities and a range of employers' needs. When you use a computer, preparing custom-tailored résumés is easy.

h. Keep the résumé as short as possible (no more than two pages). Some employers may ask for a one-page résumé. (See pages 526–527.)

i. Choose a format that yields a clean, uncluttered look. (See pages 520–531.)

j. Do not mention how much you earned in previous jobs or how much you expect to earn in the future.

k. Do not refer to your age, your marital status, your height and weight, your hobbies, or other personal details unless they enhance your suitability for the job.

l. Do not supply reasons for having left previous jobs or for gaps in your employment history. However, do prepare yourself for dealing with these issues if they come up in the interview.

m. Do not give references on the résumé. It is not even necessary to state that references are available upon request. Be prepared, however, to supply names, addresses, and phone numbers at the interview.

n. Use good-quality paper (of at least 20-pound weight and preferably 24), and consider having your résumé executed and reproduced professionally if you cannot create a crisp-looking document with the equipment you have at your disposal.

Choosing a Standard Format

1713 There is a wide range of formats you can choose from. Indeed, in a number of books dealing exclusively with the topic of résumés, you will find as many as a hundred models showing all kinds of variations in layout and approach. In addition, some word processing programs provide at least one résumé template and suggestions concerning the contents of each section of the document.

The illustrations on pages 520–525 show three different ways to format a standard résumé for Alison L. Bumbry, who majored in marketing in college, has had a number of secretarial and administrative positions in the marketing field, and is now attempting to move up to a managerial job in the same field.

The first two models illustrate the *chronological* approach, in which a person's employment history is sequenced by date, starting with the most current job and working backward. This is the approach most widely used.

In the first model (on pages 520–521) note that the dates for each job are highlighted in the left column; the corresponding job title, the name and location of the employer, and comments about the job are grouped together at the right. Also note that all the information about job *experience* typically comes before the information about *education*. If you are just out of school and have little job experience to cite, put the educational information first. (See the fourth model described below.)

The second model (on pages 522–523) also lists the jobs in reverse chronological order, but it highlights the job titles (rather than the dates) in the left column. This approach is especially effective when your employment history shows steady upward progress in a chosen field and you are applying for the next logical position in your career path.

The third model (on pages 524–525) illustrates the *functional* approach, which groups a person's achievements and skills in functional areas such as management, administration, marketing, and writing. The functional approach is the hardest to implement, but it does have the advantage of grouping your key strengths in meaningful categories (rather than leaving it to the employer to ferret out these patterns of strength from your chronological job descriptions). This approach is especially helpful (1) when you are trying to change to another field (since it emphasizes generic types of abilities that can be applied in various settings) and (2) when you are trying to play down gaps or frequent job changes in your employment history.

The fourth model (on pages 526–527) illustrates a one-page résumé for a person recently out of school (or soon to complete a college or high school program). This model is essentially an adaptation of the chronological approach, but because this person does not have a great deal of job experience to list, this résumé deals with the person's educational background first and goes into greater detail about the courses taken than would otherwise be appropriate.

➢ *For guidelines on formatting a scannable résumé, see ¶¶1714–1717.*

Résumé—Chronological Style (Emphasizing Dates)

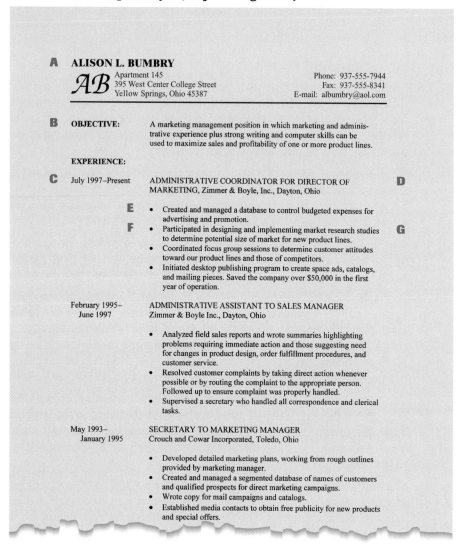

A **ALISON L. BUMBRY**

AB   Apartment 145   Phone: 937-555-7944
       395 West Center College Street   Fax: 937-555-8341
       Yellow Springs, Ohio 45387   E-mail: albumbry@aol.com

B **OBJECTIVE:**   A marketing management position in which marketing and adminis-
                         trative experience plus strong writing and computer skills can be
                         used to maximize sales and profitability of one or more product lines.

EXPERIENCE:

C July 1997–Present   ADMINISTRATIVE COORDINATOR FOR DIRECTOR OF   **D**
                            MARKETING, Zimmer & Boyle, Inc., Dayton, Ohio

E   • Created and managed a database to control budgeted expenses for
                              advertising and promotion.
F   • Participated in designing and implementing market research studies   **G**
                              to determine potential size of market for new product lines.
                            • Coordinated focus group sessions to determine customer attitudes
                              toward our product lines and those of competitors.
                            • Initiated desktop publishing program to create space ads, catalogs,
                              and mailing pieces. Saved the company over $50,000 in the first
                              year of operation.

       February 1995–   ADMINISTRATIVE ASSISTANT TO SALES MANAGER
       June 1997   Zimmer & Boyle Inc., Dayton, Ohio

                            • Analyzed field sales reports and wrote summaries highlighting
                              problems requiring immediate action and those suggesting need
                              for changes in product design, order fulfillment procedures, and
                              customer service.
                            • Resolved customer complaints by taking direct action whenever
                              possible or by routing the complaint to the appropriate person.
                              Followed up to ensure complaint was properly handled.
                            • Supervised a secretary who handled all correspondence and clerical
                              tasks.

       May 1993–   SECRETARY TO MARKETING MANAGER
       January 1995   Crouch and Cowar Incorporated, Toledo, Ohio

                            • Developed detailed marketing plans, working from rough outlines
                              provided by marketing manager.
                            • Created and managed a segmented database of names of customers
                              and qualified prospects for direct marketing campaigns.
                            • Wrote copy for mail campaigns and catalogs.
                            • Established media contacts to obtain free publicity for new products
                              and special offers.

A **Heading.** The heading should give all the key data an employer needs to get in touch with you. One possible arrangement is to present the data in two blocks: one aligned at the left margin, the other at the right.

B **Objective.** Use your "objective" statement to indicate the type of job you're looking for, the strengths you can bring to the job, and what you think you can accomplish for the employer's benefit.

C **Experience.** In this format the dates for each job are featured in the left column.

D At the right, each job history begins with the job title (in all-capital letters), followed by the employer's name and location (in capital and small letters) on the following line.

E The specific achievements in each job history are presented in a series of bulleted entries.

ALISON L. BUMBRY   Page 2

September 1991–   ASSISTANT TO DIRECTOR OF PUBLIC RELATIONS
April 1993   The Toledo Museum of Art, Toledo, Ohio

- Wrote news releases for new exhibits and special events.
- Wrote, designed, and laid out fund-raising brochures.
- Established and maintained effective media contacts with regional newspapers and TV and radio stations.

H EDUCATION: B.S. in marketing, 1991; minor in English
                     Arizona State University, Tempe, Arizona

- Wrote feature articles for *The Arizona Sundial* during sophomore and junior years.
G - Created (with two partners) an on-campus birthday celebration service. Managed the service during junior and senior years. Tested various direct marketing techniques to solicit orders from parents of students.

I CONTINUING   Courses in copywriting, telemarketing techniques, niche marketing,
   EDUCATION: and computer graphics, Wright State University, Dayton, Ohio,
                     1997–1999.

J COMPUTER   Microsoft Windows 98, Microsoft Word 2000, Microsoft
   SKILLS: PowerPoint 2000, Microsoft Money 99, Corel WordPerfect 8,
                     Corel Quattro Pro 8, Corel Presentations 8, Peachtree Office
                     Accounting, Adobe PageMaker 6.5 for Windows, Mac OS 8.1,
                     Adobe Illustrator 8.0, Adobe Photoshop 5.0, QuarkXPress 4.0.

K COMMUNITY   Wrote, designed, and laid out annual fund-raising brochures (since
   SERVICE: 1997) for the Dayton Homeless Shelter Coalition, using desktop
                     publishing and computer graphics software.

F Note that many entries begin with vigorous verbs (such as *created, initiated, resolved,* and *supervised*) to create the image of a dynamic, take-charge kind of person.

G Note also that to maintain credibility, the writer uses such terms as *participated in* and *created (with two partners)* to acknowledge the contribution of others whenever appropriate.

H **Education.** Provide information on college and any postgraduate degrees in that order. Provide information about your high school education only if that is the highest level so far attained. If you are currently enrolled in a degree program, note this fact along with an estimated date of completion. For example: *Pursuing a two-year program in business administration at Glendale Community College; will receive an A.A. degree in June 2001.*

I **Continuing Education.** Note any job-related courses you have taken. If you are changing careers or fields, note any other continuing education activity that shows you are a person committed to learning new things.

J **Special Skills.** Note any special skills that could be job-related; for example, mastery of software programs, experience with certain equipment or machinery, mastery of spoken or written foreign languages.

K **Community Service.** Note any activity that is job-related or that shows concern about the needs of others.

Optional Sections. Also provide job-related information under such labels as these: *Professional Affiliations* (memberships), *Professional Activities* (speeches and published articles and books), *Military Service,* and *Special Interests.*

Résumé—Chronological Style (Emphasizing Job Titles)

ALISON L. BUMBRY

AB Apartment 145
395 West Center College Street
Yellow Springs, Ohio 45387

Phone: 937-555-7944
Fax: 937-555-8341
E-mail: albumbry@aol.com

OBJECTIVE: A marketing management position in which marketing and administrative experience plus strong writing and computer skills can be used to maximize sales and profitability of one or more product lines.

EXPERIENCE:

A Administrative Coordinator for Director of Marketing

ZIMMER & BOYLE INC., Dayton, Ohio, July 1997–Present   **B**

C Created and managed a database to control budgeted expenses for advertising and promotion. Participated in designing and implementing market research studies to determine the potential size of market for new product lines. Coordinated focus group sessions to determine customer attitudes toward our product lines and those of competitors. Initiated desktop publishing program to create space ads, catalogs, and mailing pieces; saved the company over $50,000 in the first year of operation.

Administrative Assistant to Sales Manager

ZIMMER & BOYLE INC., Dayton, Ohio, February 1995–June 1997

Analyzed field sales reports and wrote summaries highlighting problems requiring immediate action and those suggesting need for changes in product design, order fulfillment procedures, and customer service. Resolved customer complaints by taking direct action whenever possible or by routing the complaint to the appropriate person; followed up to ensure the complaint was properly handled. Supervised a secretary who handled all correspondence and clerical tasks.

Secretary to Marketing Manager

CROUCH AND COWAR INCORPORATED, Toledo, Ohio, May 1993–January 1995

Developed detailed marketing plans, working from rough outlines provided by the marketing manager. Created and managed a segmented database of names of customers and qualified prospects for direct marketing campaigns. Wrote copy for mail campaigns and catalogs. Established media contacts to obtain free publicity for new products and special offers.

A **Experience.** In this format the job titles (rather than the dates) are featured in the left column.

B At the right the name and location of the organization plus the employment dates are given on one or two lines.

C Arranging the specific achievements for each job in one paragraph is a common format, but it is not as readable as the bulleted format used in the résumés on pages 520–521 and pages 524–525.

ALISON L. BUMBRY   **Page 2**

Assistant to Director of Public Relations	THE TOLEDO MUSEUM OF ART, Toledo, Ohio, September 1991–April 1993

Wrote news releases for new exhibits and special events.
Wrote, designed, and laid out fund-raising brochures.
Established and maintained effective media contacts with
regional newspapers and TV and radio stations.

EDUCATION: B.S. in marketing, 1991; minor in English
Arizona State University, Tempe, Arizona

Wrote feature articles for *The Arizona Sundial* during sophomore and junior years. Created (with two partners) an on-
campus birthday celebration service; managed the service
during junior and senior years. Tested various direct marketing
techniques to solicit orders from parents of students.

CONTINUING   Courses in copywriting, telemarketing techniques, niche
EDUCATION: marketing, and computer graphics, Wright State University,
Dayton, Ohio, 1997–1999.

COMPUTER SKILLS: Microsoft Windows 98, Microsoft Word 2000, Microsoft
PowerPoint 2000, Microsoft Money 99, Corel WordPerfect 8,
Corel Quattro Pro 8, Corel Presentations 8, Peachtree Office
Accounting, Adobe PageMaker 6.5 for Windows, Mac OS 8.1,
Adobe Illustrator 8.0, Adobe Photoshop 5.0, QuarkXPress 4.0.

COMMUNITY SERVICE: Wrote, designed, and laid out annual fund-raising brochures
(since 1997) for the Dayton Homeless Shelter Coalition, using
desktop publishing and computer graphics software.

Résumé—Functional Style

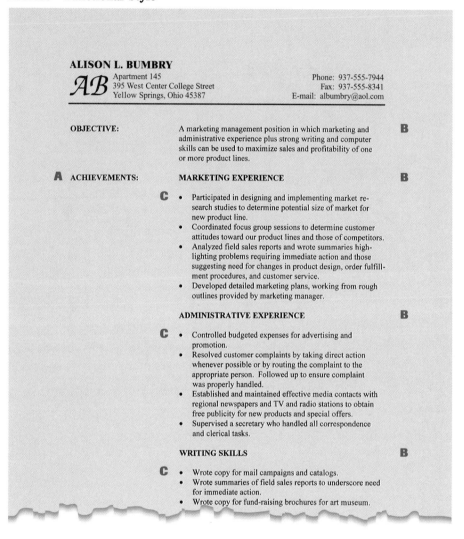

ALISON L. BUMBRY
AB Apartment 145
395 West Center College Street
Yellow Springs, Ohio 45387

Phone: 937-555-7944
Fax: 937-555-8341
E-mail: albumbry@aol.com

OBJECTIVE: A marketing management position in which marketing and   **B**
administrative experience plus strong writing and computer
skills can be used to maximize sales and profitability of one
or more product lines.

A ACHIEVEMENTS: **MARKETING EXPERIENCE**   **B**

C • Participated in designing and implementing market research studies to determine potential size of market for
new product line.
   • Coordinated focus group sessions to determine customer
attitudes toward our product lines and those of competitors.
   • Analyzed field sales reports and wrote summaries highlighting problems requiring immediate action and those
suggesting need for changes in product design, order fulfillment procedures, and customer service.
   • Developed detailed marketing plans, working from rough
outlines provided by marketing manager.

ADMINISTRATIVE EXPERIENCE   **B**

C • Controlled budgeted expenses for advertising and
promotion.
   • Resolved customer complaints by taking direct action
whenever possible or by routing the complaint to the
appropriate person. Followed up to ensure complaint
was properly handled.
   • Established and maintained effective media contacts with
regional newspapers and TV and radio stations to obtain
free publicity for new products and special offers.
   • Supervised a secretary who handled all correspondence
and clerical tasks.

WRITING SKILLS   **B**

C • Wrote copy for mail campaigns and catalogs.
   • Wrote summaries of field sales reports to underscore need
for immediate action.
   • Wrote copy for fund-raising brochures for art museum.

A Sideheads. In this illustration the customary sidehead *EXPERIENCE* in the left column
has been replaced by *ACHIEVEMENTS* because the term *experience* has been used in two
of the sideheads in the right column.

B Note how the wording of the "objective" statement *(in which marketing and administrative
experience plus strong writing and computer skills)* provides the springboard for the functional sideheads in the right column *(MARKETING EXPERIENCE, ADMINISTRATIVE
EXPERIENCE, WRITING SKILLS,* and *COMPUTER SKILLS).*

C Note how the entries under these sideheads in the right column have been reordered (and
in some cases reworded) so as to emphasize the applicant's strengths in each functional
area, independent of the job setting in which these strengths were developed.

ALISON L. BUMBRY Page 2

COMPUTER SKILLS **B**

C • Initiated an in-house desktop publishing program. Saved the company over $50,000 in the first year of operation.
• Designed and laid out space ads, catalogs, mailing pieces, and fund-raising brochures.
• Created and managed a database to control budgeted expenses for advertising and promotion.
• Created and managed a segmented database of names of customers and qualified prospects for direct marketing campaigns.
• Microsoft Windows 98, Microsoft Word 2000, Microsoft PowerPoint 2000, Microsoft Money 99, Corel WordPerfect 8, Corel Quattro Pro 8, Corel Presentations 8, Peachtree Office Accounting, Adobe PageMaker 6.5 for Windows, Mac OS 8.1, Adobe Illustrator 8.0, Adobe Photoshop 5.0, QuarkXPress 4.0.

D EMPLOYMENT
HISTORY:
• Administrative coordinator for director of marketing, Zimmer & Boyle Inc., Dayton, Ohio, July 1997–Present.
• Administrative assistant to sales manager, Zimmer & Boyle Inc., Dayton, Ohio, February 1995–June 1997.
• Secretary to marketing manager, Crouch and Cowar Incorporated, Toledo, Ohio, May 1993–January 1995.
• Assistant to director of public relations, the Toledo Museum of Art, Toledo, Ohio, September 1991–April 1993.

EDUCATION:
B.S. in marketing, 1991; minor in English
Arizona State University, Tempe, Arizona

• Wrote feature articles for *The Arizona Sundial* during sophomore and junior years.
• Created (with two partners) an on-campus birthday celebration service. Managed the service during junior and senior years. Tested various direct marketing techniques to solicit orders from parents of students.

CONTINUING
EDUCATION:
Courses in copywriting, telemarketing techniques, niche marketing, and computer graphics, Wright State University, Dayton, Ohio, 1997–1999.

COMMUNITY SERVICE:
Wrote, designed, and laid out annual fund-raising brochures (since 1997) for the Dayton Homeless Shelter Coalition, using desktop publishing and computer graphics software.

D **Employment History.** Although this section would not appear in a purely "functional" résumé, an employment history provides prospective employers with a brief chronological listing of previous job titles, the name and location of previous employers, and employment dates. Including this section in a functional résumé often serves to mollify employers who are more comfortable with résumés done completely in the chronological style.

Résumé—One-Page Style

RALPH A. PINKHAM
148 Biscay Road
Damariscotta, Maine 04543
207-555-3266

OBJECTIVE: To gain experience as a bank teller as a first step toward a career in banking.

A   **EDUCATION:**   *A.A. in business management, 1999*
University of Maine, Augusta, Maine

Courses in accounting, business communication, business management, finance, and office technology.   **E**

B   Academic scholarships, 1997–1999. Member of the intramural wrestling team, 1997–1998. Tutor in a university-sponsored community literacy program, 1998–1999.   **E**

C   **EXPERIENCE:**   *Sales associate, Reny's, Damariscotta, Maine, June 1999– Present*

Handled cash and credit card transactions, using electronic cash register. Helped customers with product selections and suggested tie-in purchases. Resolved customer problems. Assisted in taking inventory and restocking shelves. Suggested special promotions and helped design merchandise displays.   **E**

Cashier, Pinkham's Plantation, Damariscotta, Maine, May 1994– August 1997

Worked part-time in family-owned business. Handled cash and credit card transactions. Advised customers on planting and care of purchased items. Set up special seasonal displays and recommended special pricing arrangements to boost sales.   **E**

D   **SKILLS:**   Strong number sense and quick mastery of electronic cash register and calculators. Proven ability to handle large amounts of money accurately. Outgoing personality with the ability to grasp and to respond to customers' needs and concerns. Excellent communication skills in writing, over the phone, and face to face. Mastery of Microsoft Office and Lotus Notes software. Facility in the use of e-mail and accessing information on the Web.   **E**

A List your educational achievements in reverse order, starting with your most recent experience. If you have graduated from a college-level program, you do not need to cite your high school experience unless mentioning certain courses that you took or certain activities that you engaged in will enhance your qualifications. In that case, you could make the following kind of entry:

Lincoln Academy, Newcastle, Maine, graduated in May 1997

Then list any significant high school courses and activities in a paragraph underneath.

B Any special activities or honors connected with your education can be listed here, or they can be displayed at the end of the résumé in a special section labeled *Activities.* Creating a special Activities section makes sense if you also want to cite other significant items beyond those related to your education.

C In describing the tasks you performed in your limited job experience, give special emphasis to those activities that have direct relevance to the job you are now applying for. Ralph Pinkham's references to handling cash are directly related to the job of bank teller. Mentioning that he helped customers "with product selections and suggested tie-in purchases" or that he "suggested special promotions" and "special pricing arrangements to boost sales" indicates that he is the kind of person who takes the initiative in finding ways to do his job more effectively.

D The section labeled *Skills* gives you a real opportunity to demonstrate that despite your lack of previous experience in performing the job you are applying for, you already possess many of the desirable characteristics of an experienced employee. Ralph Pinkham's previous job experience, though relatively limited, has given him (1) the ability to handle a lot of cash competently, (2) the human relations skills needed to deal with customers, and (3) the ability to quickly master whatever equipment he is required to use on the job. Even a seemingly unrelated job like baby-sitting can be described in such a way as to demonstrate that one has acquired a variety of coping skills that carry over into the areas of management and human relations.

E In order to hold this résumé to one page, it is better to describe your educational activities, your job experience, and your skills in paragraph style rather than as bulleted items in a list.

NOTE: This illustration of a one-page résumé is specifically designed for someone who is recently out of school and does not have much work experience. However, individuals with a great deal of work experience can also make effective use of a one-page format. In that case, the section dealing with educational achievements should *follow* the sections dealing with work experience and skills.

¶1714

Formatting a Scannable Résumé

1714 Scannable résumés represent a significant innovation in the job-seeking process. They serve to match the best-qualified applicants with job openings that currently exist or that may soon be opening. Scannable résumés permit organizations to sift through large numbers of résumés by computer in order to identify a smaller (and much more manageable) number of suitable candidates for a particular job. In effect, the computer does the first round of screening. Then human beings enter the process of evaluating qualified individuals for a specific opening.

A scannable résumé is a hard-copy document designed to be scanned by an optical character reader (OCR) into a computerized database, where a computer will initially screen individual résumés for keywords that also show up in the description posted for a particular job opening. The more links between the keywords in a scannable résumé and those in the job description, the more likely that résumé (and the individual who wrote it) will be selected for further evaluation by real people.

a. In planning a scannable résumé, carefully read the ads and the postings for the kind of job you want. Try to incorporate in your résumé as many keywords from those job descriptions as you honestly can. Also make heavy use of industry jargon, acronyms, and abbreviations, as well as current industry buzzwords, even if these do not actually appear in the ads and the postings, since these are likely to be the kinds of keywords that the computer has been programmed to focus on. To increase the total number of keywords in your résumé, use synonyms whenever possible to avoid repeating the same keywords.

NOTE: If acronyms and abbreviations are used, some authorities recommend that they be accompanied by the spelled-out forms when they first appear.

b. It is important that a scannable résumé pose no difficulties for the OCRs currently in use. The very techniques and devices that serve to draw the attention of a human reader may in many cases interfere with the ability of certain OCRs to accurately transfer the contents of the résumé into the computerized database. Paragraphs 1715–1717 offer a number of guidelines to help you avoid such problems when you are formatting a scannable résumé.

1715 a. Do not use boldface, italics, underlining, script, bullets, logos, shading, horizontal or vertical lines, or any other graphic devices. If desired, asterisks may be used to introduce individual items in a list.

b. Do not arrange material in columns. Try to begin everything at the left margin, and do not justify the right margin (see ¶1356b).

c. To achieve the sharpest possible image for the sake of accurate scanning, use a laser printer, black ink, and good-quality paper (of 20- or 24-pound weight).

d. Do not fold or crease the résumé. If possible, insert the résumé in a plastic sleeve to keep it clean and wrinkle-free.

e. Try to limit the résumé to one page. If more than one page is required, use a paper clip (not a staple) to keep the pages together. Moreover, use a continuation heading (as illustrated on page 531).

1716 As you can tell from ¶1715 and from the illustrations on pages 530–531, the appearance of a scannable résumé tends to be quite bland—intentionally so because it has been designed with the needs of the OCR and not those of a human reader in mind. For that reason, consider submitting your résumé in two ways: (a) in a scannable format for the initial round of screening and (b) in a more visually attractive format (as illustrated on pages 520–527) for the benefit of the human readers who will subsequently evaluate you in light of the openings they have available.

Because of the differences between those two types of résumés, the illustrations on pages 530–531 show how a standard résumé for Alison Bumbry (featured in the illustrations on pages 520–525) might be reworked as a scannable résumé.

1717 In organizing the sections of a scannable résumé, keep these guidelines in mind:

a. Begin with a centered heading block that provides all the key data a prospective employer needs to get in touch with you. (See the illustration and the annotations on page 530 for additional details.)

b. Divide the rest of your résumé into sections identified by side headings like these: *Objective, Skills, Employment History, Education, Continuing Education.* Also consider optional headings such as *Community Service.* (See the illustration and annotations on pages 530–531 for additional details.)

c. Under the heading *Objective*, aim for a statement that matches as closely as possible the job description for the position you want. If a job description is not currently available for a specific opening, draw on your knowledge of the industry to describe your objective in language that uses attention-getting keywords.

d. You may list all your significant skills under the single heading *Skills*, or you may create a number of headings that group your skills appropriately—for example, *Marketing Skills, Administrative Skills, Writing Skills*, and *Computer Skills* (as is done in the illustration on page 530). No matter how you decide to label this section, the material you provide here should also be filled with attention-getting keywords. Indeed, some authorities recommend labeling this section of the résumé *Keyword Profile* or *Keyword Summary*, and some recommend placing this section at the end of the résumé instead of at the beginning.

NOTE: In the illustration on page 530, the material that appears under the various Skills headings has been derived from the functional-style résumé for Alison Bumbry on pages 524–525.

e. For the sections headed *Employment History, Education, Continuing Education,* and optional sections such as *Community Service*, see the illustration and the annotations on page 531 for details on how to format materials under these headings.

Continued on page 530

Other Business
Documents

17

Scannable Résumé

A   ALISON L. BUMBRY
Apartment 145
395 West Center College Street
Yellow Springs, Ohio 45387
Telephone: 937-555-7944
Fax: 937-555-8341
E-mail: albumbry@aol.com

B   OBJECTIVE

A position in marketing management in which marketing experience and administrative
expertise plus writing skills and computer skills can be used to promote sales growth and
exceed profit goals for one or more product lines.

B   MARKETING SKILLS

C   Design and implementation of market research studies. Assessment of potential market
size for new product lines. Coordination of focus group sessions. Assessment of customer attitudes toward product lines. Analysis of field sales reports. Pinpointing of
problems for immediate action. Pinpointing of need for changes in product design, order
fulfillment procedures, and customer service. Development of detailed marketing plans
based on input from marketing manager.

B   ADMINISTRATIVE SKILLS

C   Control of advertising and promotion expense budgets. Resolution of customer complaints. Contacts with newspapers, TV stations, and radio stations for free publicity.
Supervision of secretary.

B   WRITING SKILLS

C   Preparation of copy for mail campaigns, catalogs, and fund-raising brochures.
Summaries of field sales reports.

B   COMPUTER SKILLS

C   Start-up of in-house desktop publishing program, with first-year savings of $50,000.
Design and layout of space ads, catalogs, mailing pieces, and fund-raising brochures.
Creation and management of database for control of advertising and promotion expense
budgets. Creation and management of segmented database of customers and qualified
prospects for direct marketing campaigns. Mastery of Microsoft Windows 98, Microsoft
Word 2000, Microsoft PowerPoint 2000, Microsoft Money 99, Corel WordPerfect 8,

A **Heading.** On separate single-spaced lines centered in a block, provide your name, address, and phone number, plus a fax number and an e-mail address if these are available. Use all-capital letters only for your name. Do not use boldface or any other graphic device to highlight the information in this heading block.

B **Side Headings.** Identify each section of a scannable résumé with an all-capital side heading. Leave 1 blank line above and below each heading. Do not use boldface, italics, or any other graphic device to highlight these sideheads.

C **Skills.** Note how the copy in these sections (drawn from the functional-style résumé on pages 524–525) shifts the wording away from action verbs to keyword nouns. Also note that the copy under each side heading is organized as one paragraph consisting of phrases, each ending with a period. This arrangement, which takes less space, is not as readable as listing these items on separate lines, but remember that a scannable résumé is designed to be read by an OCR and not by a human pair of eyes.

H ALISON L. BUMBRY   Page 2

B EMPLOYMENT HISTORY

D * Administrative coordinator for director of marketing, Zimmer and Boyle Inc., Dayton, **I**
Ohio, July 1997–Present.
* Administrative assistant to sales manager, Zimmer and Boyle Inc., Dayton, Ohio, **I**
February 1995–June 1997.
* Secretary to marketing manager, Crouch and Cowar Incorporated, Toledo, Ohio,
May 1993–January 1995.
* Assistant to director of public relations, the Toledo Museum of Art, Toledo, Ohio,
September 1991–April 1993.

B EDUCATION

E B.S. in marketing, 1991, minor in English, Arizona State University, Tempe, Arizona.

Writer of feature articles for The Arizona Sundial during sophomore and junior years. **I**
Cofounder and manager of on-campus birthday service. Testing of various direct
marketing techniques to solicit orders.

B CONTINUING EDUCATION

F Courses in copywriting, telemarketing techniques, niche marketing, and computer
graphics, Wright State University, Dayton, Ohio, 1997–1999.

B COMMUNITY SERVICE

G Writing, design, and layout of annual fund-raising brochures for the Dayton Homeless
Shelter Coalition.

D Employment History. Note that the jobs are listed in reverse chronological order, starting with the most recent job. You may use an asterisk to introduce each job listing (as in the illustration above), but do not use bullets or any other graphic device for this purpose. Because the duties of each job have already been summarized in the Skills sections in the illustration on page 530, there is no reason to repeat them here.

E Education. List your educational experience in reverse order, starting with the most recent college or graduate program for which you have received (or expect to receive) a degree. List your secondary education only if you cannot cite enrollment in or completion of a college degree program.

F Continuing Education. Under this heading cite courses you have taken or are now taking but not as part of a formal degree program.

G Optional Sections. Use such headings as *Community Service, Professional Affiliations, Professional Activities* (including honors and awards), *Military Service,* and *Special Interests* to cover any activities that involve job-related skills or that show your involvement in addressing the needs of others.

H Continuation Heading. Provide a heading that gives your name and the page number.

I Elimination of Graphic Elements. Because some OCRs cannot properly scan ampersands, note that the ampersand in *Zimmer & Boyle* has been replaced by *and.* Moreover, because some OCRs cannot cope with italics or underlining, the title of the university newspaper—*The Arizona Sundial*—appears without any special display.

¶1718

Other Employment Documents

As part of the job-seeking process you will need to write three types of letters: letters of application, follow-up letters after an interview, and (hopefully) a letter of acceptance. Specific guidelines are provided in ¶¶1719–1721, but a few general guidelines (¶1718) apply to all employment communications.

General Guidelines

1718 **a.** Keep your letters short—less than one full page if possible.

b. Resist the temptation to copy sample letters word for word. Draw on these samples for ideas, but create your own letters—letters that communicate the distinctive flavor of your personality.

c. Edit and proofread your letters carefully. Simple typographical errors (not to mention more serious errors in grammar, style, and usage) will create a negative impression that damages your job-seeking campaign.

d. Always try to address your letters to a specific person, using that person's full name and title. If necessary, call the organization to obtain this information.

NOTE: The model letters on pages 534–537 are all written by Alison Bumbry, the fictitious person whose job qualifications are set forth in the résumés shown on pages 520–525 and 530–531. In these letters, Ms. Bumbry is trying to move up to a marketing management position.

Application Letters

1719 Letters you write to apply for a job will vary to some extent, depending on whether you are (a) following up on an ad, (b) taking the initiative to find out whether any openings exist for a person with your skills and experience, or (c) following up on the suggestion of a mutual friend or acquaintance to explore job opportunities with a specific person within an organization. Yet all application letters have the same three objectives: to indicate what you have to offer the organization, to transmit your résumé, and to obtain an interview. Consider the following guidelines and the illustration on page 534 when you write an application letter.

a. Before you draft your letter, try to get as much information as you can about the organization you have in mind. For example, what products or services does it offer? What special strategy or philosophy governs the way the organization operates? Such information can help you focus your letter more effectively and will let the recipient of the letter know that you have taken the initiative to learn something about the organization.

NOTE: If you are responding to a blind ad (one that provides no organizational name and only a box number address), you will not be able to undertake this research. However, the ad will spell out the qualifications desired, something not usually available when you are simply exploring the possibility of job openings.

b. Begin your letter by indicating whether you are responding to an ad, following up on the suggestion of a mutual friend or acquaintance, or simply exploring what job opportunities currently exist.

c. Indicate what you have to offer the organization. If you are responding to an ad that states the qualifications desired, clearly indicate how your skills and experience relate to each of the qualifications listed. If you are simply exploring job openings, do not focus on specific tasks that you have performed in the past. Instead, highlight the things you have accomplished as a result of the way you applied your skills and experience. This approach will make it easier for someone to gauge how well you might fit the job available, even if you have not performed those exact tasks in the past.

NOTE: The recipient of your letter will probably be receiving many other application letters at the same time. It is important, therefore, that your letter and your résumé make you stand out from the others. In your letter you should aim to achieve—in much shorter form—the same things you are trying to achieve in your résumé. (See ¶1712a–d for further details on this point.)

d. The primary short-term objective of this letter is to arrange for an interview. Rather than wait for the recipient of your letter to call you, indicate that you will call on a specific date to determine whether an interview can take place. In stating when you will call, allow enough time for your material to be delivered and looked at. Keep in mind that the recipient may be inundated with other matters or may be traveling and thus may not look at your letter and résumé as quickly as you would like.

NOTE: Keep a record of when you promised to call so that you follow through on time. Calling a day or two later could suggest that you are not a very good manager of your time.

Follow-Up Letters

1720 After an interview, follow up immediately with a letter that covers the following points. (Also see the illustration on page 535.)

a. Thank the interviewer for (1) taking the time to see you, (2) giving you better insight into the available job and the organization you would be working for, and (3) considering your qualifications in light of the available job.

b. Reinforce the positive impression you tried to make during the interview, and briefly restate why you think you would be an asset to the organization.

c. Offer additional information about your qualifications if they were not fully discussed during the interview. If you promised during the interview to supply additional information, do so now.

d. Address questions that arose during the interview that you were not fully prepared to answer at the time. If you know (or simply sense) that the interviewer had some doubts about your qualifications, use this opportunity to overcome such doubts if you can.

NOTE: If the interviewer made it clear at the time that you were not right for the current job opening, send a follow-up letter nonetheless. Offer thanks for having been considered for this job, and express hope that you will be considered for other jobs that may open in the future. On the other hand, if *you* decide the job is not right for you, send a follow-up letter in which you thank the interviewer and ask not to be a candidate.

Application Letter

A **ALISON L. BUMBRY**

AB   Apartment 145
       395 West Center College Street
       Yellow Springs, Ohio 45387

Phone: 937-555-7944
Fax: 937-555-8341
E-mail: albumbry@aol.com

March 3, 2001

Mr. Oliver Digby
Director of Human Resources
Hunt and Ketcham Inc.
1228 Euclid Avenue
Cleveland, Ohio 44115

Dear Mr. Digby:

B You advertised for a marketing manager in the March 2 *Plain Dealer*. I have used many Hunt and Ketcham texts in my computer courses, so I know that your company publishes books of consistently high quality. As the following comparison shows, my experience and background come close to satisfying all of the requirements stated in your ad.

C

Your Requirements	My Qualifications
College degree	B.S. in marketing plus continuing education courses in marketing and computer software applications
Knowledge of technical publishing market	Over six years' experience in sales and marketing divisions of two educational publishing companies
Field sales experience	Extensive contact with field sales reps and customers, resolving a wide range of sales support and customer service problems

The enclosed résumé will provide additional information about my marketing experience.

D I would appreciate the chance to meet with you and discuss the ways in which I can help Hunt and Ketcham achieve its marketing objectives and its profit goals. I will call your office on March 12 to determine whether there is a convenient time for you to see me.

Sincerely,

A Letterhead. The attractive letterhead design that Alison Bumbry has executed on her computer will help make her application letter stand out. It is the same letterhead she used on the first page of her résumé.

B First Paragraph. Alison uses her opening paragraph to indicate how she found out about the job, what she knows about the organization, and how her qualifications stack up against the job requirements stated in the ad.

C Displayed List of Qualifications. Alison does her best to play down her lack of specific knowledge about the technical publishing market and her lack of field sales experience. In this situation a résumé formatted in the functional style (see pages 524–525) will best highlight her strengths in the areas of marketing, administration, writing, and computers.

D Final Paragraph. Alison takes the initiative in saying she will call to see whether an interview can be arranged. At the same time, she stresses her willingness to focus the interview on how she can help the organization achieve *its* goals and objectives.

Follow-Up Letter

ALISON L. BUMBRY

AB Apartment 145
395 West Center College Street
Yellow Springs, Ohio 45387

Phone: 937-555-7944
Fax: 937-555-8341
E-mail: albumbry@aol.com

March 26, 2001

Mr. Oliver Digby
Director of Human Resources
Hunt and Ketcham Inc.
1228 Euclid Avenue
Cleveland, Ohio 44115

Dear Mr. Digby:

A Thank you for taking the time last Friday to explain why my lack of field sales experience in the technical publishing market would prevent me from being considered for the marketing manager's position at Hunt and Ketcham.

B Thank you, moreover, for arranging an interview that same day with your director of sales. Ms. Cantrell gave me a very detailed picture of a field rep's responsibilities. She also stated that in light of all my prior experience in educational publishing, I ought to make the transition to technical publishing very easily. I was also encouraged to learn that after a year or two of experience in the field, I would be a strong candidate for any marketing manager's position that might open at that time.

C Ms. Cantrell has promised to let me know within the next four weeks whether she is in a position to offer me a field rep's job. If she does, I very much look forward to seeing you again. In any event, thank you very much for all the help you have given me.

Sincerely,

Alison L. Bumbry

Alison L. Bumbry

A First Paragraph. Alison thanks the interviewer for clarifying the demands of the job and pointing out where her qualifications fell short.

B Second Paragraph. Alison thanks the interviewer for steering her to another opportunity in the organization and for setting up an interview that same day. (Alison should also send a follow-up letter to the second person who interviewed her.) Note that she reaffirms her hope for a marketing management job in a year or two.

C Third Paragraph. Alison ends on a warm note, thanking the first interviewer for all his help.

¶1721

Acceptance Letters

1721 Of all employment communications, this is the most pleasant letter to write. Use this occasion to:

   a. Formally accept the job.

   b. Confirm the key details of your working arrangements (including starting date) that have been previously discussed. If any of these details are not clear, ask the person who hired you to spell them out.

   c. Express your pleasure in coming to work for the organization and, more specifically, in working for the person who has offered you the job.

A First Paragraph. Alison accepts the job with pleasure, both for its immediate opportunities and for its long-term prospects.

B Second Paragraph. Alison uses this paragraph to deal with the technical details involved in starting a new job.

C Third Paragraph. Alison expresses her pleasure (perhaps a bit too effusively) at the prospect of working for the person who has offered her the job.

D Final Paragraph. Alison shows initiative in offering to undertake advance preparation for the job before she officially starts work.

Acceptance Letter

ALISON L. BUMBRY

AB Apartment 145
395 West Center College Street
Yellow Springs, Ohio 45387

Phone: 937-555-7944
Fax: 937-555-8341
E-mail: albumbry@aol.com

April 30, 2001

Ms. Jennifer Cantrell
Director of Sales
Hunt and Ketcham Inc.
1228 Euclid Avenue
Cleveland, Ohio 44115

Dear Jennifer:

A I am very pleased to accept the job of field sales representative, with the state of Ohio as my territory. What especially appeals to me is that this job not only represents an excellent opportunity in itself; it provides a springboard for higher-level marketing jobs with Hunt and Ketcham.

B The materials that Oliver Digby sent me answered all my questions about compensation arrangements and company policies. All the necessary paperwork has now been completed and returned. As I understand it, you want me to start work on June 4, spending the first month in Cleveland for orientation and training. I assume that someone in your department will provide me with information about my accommodations during the month of June.

C I am genuinely excited about the prospect of working with you and for you. From our conversations I can tell how supportive you are of the people who report to you. When I think of how much I will learn under your supervision, I realize just how lucky I am to be joining Hunt and Ketcham.

D If there is anything you think I should be reading or doing in the next month, please let me know. I would welcome the chance to get a head start on the job before I actually report for work on June 4.

Sincerely,

Alison L Bumbry

Alison L. Bumbry

¶1722

Outlines

1722 An outline can be used to *plan* the content and organization of a document. The outline identifies (a) the topics that are to be discussed and (b) the sequence in which they are to be introduced. In some cases, an outline may consist of a simple list of points to be covered. In other cases an outline may contain several levels of subtopics under each main topic (as in the illustrations on pages 539 and 541).

1723 After you have finished drafting a document, you can use an outline to *review* the document in terms of content and organization. An outline of this kind typically lists the key words or phrases used as headings throughout the document to identify topics and subtopics as they are each introduced. When you use an outline for reviewing purposes, you can more easily answer questions like these:

- Have all topics been included?
- Have all topics been fully developed?
- Does the heading structure—that is, the sequence of heads—provide a balanced representation of all aspects of the discussion, or are some parts of the text loaded with heads while other parts have very few?
- Are the heads all worded in a similar way, or are some complete sentences and others simply phrases?

1724 a. The outline feature of your word processing software will permit you to create an outline by scrolling through the text and coding (according to level of subordination) every heading in the text. If you later decide to revise the heading structure in the document, you can use the outline feature to generate a new outline to confirm that the document is now better organized.

NOTE: The illustration on page 539 shows an outline created by the outline feature (with all the default settings) of Microsoft Word for Windows. Note that the outline is single-spaced throughout. Moreover, note that the indentions established for each level of heading are based on preset tabs and do not permit the start of each new level of heading to align with the first word in the level above.

b. When you are creating an outline for your own use (say, for planning or reviewing purposes), an outline produced by the outline feature is quite acceptable. However, if the outline will be part of a formal document, you should consider using a more readable format with a more open look and a standard pattern of alignments. (See ¶1725 and the illustration on page 541.)

1725 If you want to devise your own format for an outline, consider these guidelines and the illustration on page 541.

a. **Margins.** Use default side and bottom margins. Space down 6 times from the default top margin of 1 inch to create a top margin of about 2 inches; leave a top margin of only 1 inch if doing so will prevent the outline from taking a second page. A one-page outline may also be centered vertically on the page.

b. **Heading.** Type the title in all-capital letters, and use capital and small letters for the other lines. Use boldface for the complete heading or, if you prefer, for the title alone. Leave 1 blank line between lines in the heading, and leave 2 blank lines below the last line of the heading.

Text continues on page 540

Outline Format Using the Outline Feature of Microsoft Word for Windows

EQUIPMENT AND SOFTWARE

Orientation for Department Staff

I. INTRODUCTION
II. EQUIPMENT AND SOFTWARE
    A. Equipment
        1. Computer
            a) Drives
                (1) Types
                    (a) Hard
                    (b) Floppy
                (2) Capacity
                    (a) Hard
                    (b) Floppy
            b) RAM
        2. Monitor
        3. Modem
        4. Mouse
        5. Printer
        6. Scanner
    B. Software
        1. System
            a) MS-DOS
            b) MS-Windows
            c) Other
        2. Applications
            a) Standalones
                (1) Database
                (2) Spreadsheet
                (3) Word Processing
                (4) Other
            b) Suites
        3. Registration procedure
            a) Fax
            b) Mail
            c) Online
III. OPERATION
    A. Startup
    B. Start/Quit a Program
    C. Get Help
    D. Modifications
        1. System Settings
        2. New Programs
    E. Shut Down

¶**1726**

   c. **Enumerations.** The numbers or letters that identify the items at different levels in an outline should all be followed by a period and 1 or 2 spaces. At the first four levels, align the numbers or letters on the period.

   d. **Capitalization.** Use all-capital letters for first-level items (those preceded by roman numerals). Use capital and small letters for items at all lower levels.

   e. **Indentions.** When using roman numerals to identify first-level items, start the widest numeral (III or VIII, for example) at the left margin. Align all the other roman numerals on the period. Align the second level of items (those beginning with A and B) on the first word after the roman I. Align the third level of items (those beginning with 1 and 2) on the first word after A in the second level. However, if the third level of items has more than nine entries, align the number 10 on the first word after A in the second level; then align all the single-digit numbers on the period following 10.

   f. **Spacing Between Items.** Leave 2 blank lines above and 1 blank line below each first-level item. For all other levels, use single spacing with no blank lines between items.

1726 The use of numbers and letters with the items in an outline indicates the relative importance of these items to one another. The illustration on page 541 shows six levels of heads, but many outlines do not require that many and a few may require more.

   a. In the illustration on page 541, the first level of items is identified by roman numerals, the second by capital letters, the third by arabic numerals, the fourth by small letters, the fifth by arabic numerals in parentheses, and the sixth by small letters in parentheses.

   b. At least two items are needed for each level used in an outline. If your outline shows a roman I at the first level, it must also show a roman II; if you use a capital A at the second level, you must also use a capital B; and so on.

1727 The outline feature of your word processing software may also be used to create a table of contents and a list of tables or illustrations. (See ¶¶1416–1417.)

Guidelines for Designing Forms

1728 When you are designing a form with fill-in lines:

   a. Lay out the fill-in lines so that most entries—and preferably all entries—can start at the same point. Reducing the number of tab stops required makes the task of filling out the form a great deal easier. See, for example, the design of the fax cover sheet on page 511, which permits all entries to begin at the same point.

   b. Use double spacing between the fill-in lines, and make the lines long enough to accommodate handwritten as well as typed entries.

   c. In any case, use equal vertical space between the fill-in lines. In that way no adjustment in line spacing will be required when the fill-in entries are inserted.

Standard Outline Format

EQUIPMENT AND SOFTWARE ↓ **2x**

Orientation for Department Staff ↓ **3x**

I.   INTRODUCTION ↓ **3x**

II. EQUIPMENT AND SOFTWARE ↓ **2x**

      A. Equipment
         1. Computer
           a. Drives
             (1) Types
               (a) Hard
               (b) Floppy
             (2) Capacity
               (a) Hard
               (b) Floppy
           b. RAM
         2. Monitor
         3. Modem
         4. Mouse
         5. Printer
         6. Scanner
      B. Software
         1. System
           a. MS-DOS
           b. MS-Windows
           c. Other
         2. Applications
           a. Standalones
             (1) Database
             (2) Spreadsheet
             (3) Word Processing
             (4) Other
           b. Suites
         3. Registration procedure
           a. Fax
           b. Mail
           c. Online ↓ **3x**

III. OPERATION ↓ **2x**

      A. Startup
      B. Start/Quit a Program

1729 When you are designing a multicolumn form, look for ways to reduce the number of tab stops required to fill in the form. For example, arrange the top of the form so that any entries to be inserted in the heading can start at the same point as entries in one of the columns below.

SECTION **18**

Forms of Address

Government Officials (¶1806)
- President of the United States (¶1806a)
- Vice President of the United States (¶1806b)
- Cabinet Member (¶1806c)
- United States Senator (¶1806d)
- United States Representative (¶1806e)
- Chief Justice of the United States (¶1806f)
- Associate Justice of the U.S. Supreme Court (¶1806g)
- Judge of Federal, State, or Local Court (¶1806h)
- Governor (¶1806i)
- State Senator (¶1806j)
- State Representative or Assembly Member (¶1806k)
- Mayor (¶1806l)

Diplomats (¶1807)
- Secretary General of the United Nations (¶1807a)
- Ambassador to the United States (¶1807b)
- Minister to the United States (¶1807c)
- American Ambassador (¶1807d)

Members of the Armed Services (¶1808)
- Army, Air Force, and Marine Corps Officers (¶1808a)
- Navy and Coast Guard Officers (¶1808b)
- Enlisted Personnel (¶1808c)

Roman Catholic Dignitaries (¶1809)
- Pope (¶1809a)
- Cardinal (¶1809b)
- Archbishop and Bishop (¶1809c)
- Monsignor (¶1809d)
- Priest (¶1809e)
- Mother Superior (¶1809f)
- Sister (¶1809g)
- Brother (¶1809h)

Protestant Dignitaries (¶1810)
- Protestant Episcopal Bishop (¶1810a)
- Protestant Episcopal Dean (¶1810b)
- Methodist Bishop (¶1810c)
- Minister With Doctor's Degree (¶1810d)
- Minister Without Doctor's Degree (¶1810e)

Jewish Dignitaries (¶1811)
- Rabbi With Doctor's Degree (¶1811a)
- Rabbi Without Doctor's Degree (¶1811b)

Forms of Address

18

¶1801

The following forms are correct for addressing letters to individuals, couples, organizations, professional people, education officials, government officials, diplomats, military personnel, and religious dignitaries. Some writers now omit courtesy titles with the names of individuals and married couples. For examples, see ¶¶1323d, 1349a, 1366a.

IMPORTANT NOTE: In the salutations that follow the forms of address, the most formal one is listed first. Unless otherwise indicated, the ellipsis marks in the salutation stand for the surname alone.

Because of space limitations, only the masculine forms of address have been given in some illustrations. When an office or a position is held by a woman, make the following substitutions:

For *Sir,* use *Madam.*

For *His,* use *Her.*

For *Mr.* followed by a name (for example, *Mr. Wyatt*), use *Miss, Mrs., or Ms.,* whichever is appropriate.

For *Mr.* followed by a title (for example, *Mr. President, Mr. Secretary, Mr. Mayor*), use *Madam.*

➤ *For a detailed discussion of how to construct inside addresses, see ¶¶1317–1343; for further information on salutations, see ¶¶1346–1351; for details on how to handle addresses on envelopes, see ¶¶1389–1390.*

1801 Individuals

a. Man With Courtesy Title

Mr. . . . *(full name)*
Address

Dear Mr. . . . :

b. Woman—Courtesy Title Preference Known

Ms. (**OR** Miss **OR** Mrs.) . . . *(full name)*
Address

Dear Ms. (**OR** Miss **OR** Mrs.) . . . :

NOTE: Always use the title that a woman prefers.

c. Woman—Courtesy Title Preference Unknown

Ms. . . . *(full name)*
Address

Dear Ms. . . . :

OR: . . . *(full name with no title)*
Address

Dear . . . *(first name and surname):*

d. Individual—Name Known, Gender Unknown

. . . *(full name with no title)*
Address

Dear . . . *(first name or initials plus surname):*

e. Individual—Name Unknown, Gender Known

. . . *(title of individual)*
. . . *(name of organization)*
Address

Madam:
Dear Madam:

OR: Sir:
Dear Sir:

f. Individual—Name and Gender Unknown

. . . *(title of individual)*
. . . *(name of organization)*
Address

Sir or Madam:
Dear Sir or Madam:

OR: Madam or Sir:
Dear Madam or Sir:

g. Two Men

Mr. . . . *(full name)*
Mr. . . . *(full name)*
Address

Gentlemen:
Dear Messrs. . . . and . . . : (see ¶1349)
Dear Mr. . . . and Mr. . . . :

h. Two Women

Ms. . . . *(full name)*
Ms. . . . *(full name)*
Address

Dear Mses. (**OR** Mss.) . . . and . . . :
Dear Ms. . . . and Ms. . . . :

OR: Mrs. . . . *(full name)*
Mrs. . . . *(full name)*
Address

Dear Mesdames . . . and . . . : (see ¶1349)
Dear Mrs. . . . and Mrs. . . . :

OR: Miss . . . *(full name)*
Miss . . . *(full name)*
Address

Dear Misses . . . and . . . :
Dear Miss . . . and Miss . . . :

OR: Ms. . . . *(full name)*
Mrs. . . . *(full name)*
Address

Dear Ms. . . , and Mrs. . . . :

OR: Miss . . . *(full name)*
Ms. . . . *(full name)*
Address

Dear Miss . . . and Ms. . . . :

OR: Mrs. . . . *(full name)*
Miss . . . *(full name)*
Address

Dear Mrs. . . . and Miss . . . :

i. Woman and Man—No Personal Relationship

Ms. (**OR** Mrs. **OR** Miss) . . . *(full name)*
Mr. . . . *(full name)*
Address

Dear Ms. (**OR** Mrs. **OR** Miss) . . .
  and Mr. . . . :

OR: Mr. . . . *(full name)*
Ms. (**OR** Mrs. **OR** Miss) . . . *(full name)*
Address

Dear Mr. . . . and Ms. (**OR** Mrs.
  OR Miss) . . . :

NOTE: When addressing a widow, choose the form for the inside address and the salutation that the widow uses in her signature line. (See ¶1366e for examples of the various styles that a widow has to choose from.)

1802 Couples

a. Married Couple With Same Surname—No Special Titles

Mr. and Mrs. . . . *(husband's full name)*
Address

Dear Mr. and Mrs. . . . *(husband's surname):*

OR: . . . *(wife's first name)* and
  . . . *(husband's first name and surname)* (see ¶1323d)
Address

Dear . . . *(wife's first name)* and
  . . . *(husband's first name and surname):*

OR: . . . *(husband's first name)* and . . .
  (wife's first name) . . .
  (husband's surname)
Address

Dear . . . *(husband's first name)*
  and . . . *(wife's first name)* . . .
  (husband's surname):

b. Married Couple With Same Surname—Husband Has Special Title

Dr. and Mrs. . . . *(husband's full name)*
Address

Dear Dr. and Mrs. . . . *(husband's surname):*

c. Married Couple With Same Surname—Wife Has Special Title

Senator . . . *(wife's full name)*
Mr. . . . *(husband's full name)*
Address

Dear Senator and Mr. . . . *(husband's surname):*

d. Married Couple With Same Surname—Both Have Special Titles

Dr. . . . *(wife's full name)*
Dr. . . . *(husband's full name)*
Address

Dear Drs. . . . *(husband's surname):*

OR: Captain . . . *(husband's full name)*
Professor . . . *(wife's full name)*
Address

Dear Captain and Professor . . .
  (husband's surname):

Forms of Address

18

➤ *For forms of address for teenagers and younger children, see ¶1322d–e.*

Continued on page 546

¶1803

e. Married Couple With Different Surnames

> Ms. (**OR** Miss) . . . *(wife's full name)*
> Mr. . . . *(husband's full name)*
> Address
>
> Dear Ms. (**OR** Miss) . . . *(wife's surname) and Mr. . . . (husband's surname):*

OR:
> Mr. . . . *(husband's full name)*
> Ms. (**OR** Miss) . . . *(wife's full name)*
> Address
>
> Dear Mr. . . . *(husband's surname)* and Ms. (**OR** Miss) . . . *(wife's surname):*

> **NOTE:** If either spouse has a special title (like those shown in ¶1802b–d), use that special title here as well.

f. Married Couple With Hyphenated Surname

> Mr. and Mrs. . . . *(husband's first name and middle initial, plus wife's original surname followed by hyphen and husband's surname)*
> Address
>
> Dear Mr. and Mrs. . . . *(wife's original surname followed by hyphen and husband's surname):*

g. Unmarried Couple Living Together

> Ms. (**OR** Miss) . . . *(full name)*
> Mr. . . . *(full name)*
> Address
>
> Dear Ms. (**OR** Miss) . . . and Mr. . . . :

OR:
> Mr. . . . *(full name)*
> Ms. (**OR** Miss) . . . *(full name)*
> Address
>
> Dear Mr. . . . and Ms. (**OR** Miss) . . . :

1803 Organizations

a. Organization of Women and Men

> . . . *(name of organization)*
> Address
>
> Ladies and Gentlemen:
> Gentlemen and Ladies:
> Dear . . . *(name of organization):*
>   (see ¶1350c)

OR:
> Mr. . . . *(name of organization head)**
> President *(or other appropriate title)*
> . . . *(name of organization)*
> Address
>
> Dear Mr. . . . :*

OR:
> Chief Executive Officer *(or other appropriate title)*
> . . . *(name of organization)*
> Address
>
> Sir or Madam:
> Madam or Sir:
> Dear Sir or Madam:
> Dear Madam or Sir:

b. Organization of Women

> . . . *(name of organization)*
> Address
>
> Mesdames: (see ¶1349)
> Ladies:

c. Organization of Men

> . . . *(name of organization)*
> Address
>
> Gentlemen:

1804 Professionals

a. Lawyers

> Mr. . . . *(full name)**
> Attorney-at-Law
> Address

OR:
> . . . *(full name),* Esq.†
> Address
>
> Dear Mr. . . . :*

b. Physicians and Others With Doctoral Degrees

> Dr. . . . *(full name)*
> Address

OR:
> . . . *(full name),* M.D.†
> Address
>
> Dear Dr. . . . :

1805 Education Officials

a. President of College or University

> . . . *(full name, followed by comma and highest degree)*
> President, . . . *(name of college)*
> Address

---

*See the note at the top of page 544.

†When an abbreviation such as *Esq., M.D.,* or *Ph.D.* follows a name, do not use a courtesy title such as *Mr., Ms.,* or *Dr.* before the name. (See also ¶¶518c, 519c.)

¶1806

OR: Dr. . . . *(full name)*
President, . . . *(name of college)*
Address

OR: President . . . *(full name)*
. . . *(name of college)*
Address

Dear President . . . :
Dear Dr. . . . :

b. Dean of College or University

. . . *(full name, followed by comma and
highest degree)*
Dean, . . . *(name of school or division)*
. . . *(name of college)*
Address

OR: Dr. . . . *(full name)*
Dean, . . . *(name of school or division)*
. . . *(name of college)*
Address

OR: Dean . . . *(full name)*
. . . *(name of school or division)*
. . . *(name of college)*
Address

Dear Dean . . . :
Dear Dr. . . . :

c. Professor

Professor . . . *(full name)*
Department of . . . *(subject)*
. . . *(name of college)*
Address

OR: . . . *(full name, followed by comma and
highest degree)*
Department of (**OR** Professor of) . . .
(subject)
. . . *(name of college)*
Address

OR: Dr. (**OR** Mr.) . . . *(full name)* *
Department of (**OR** Professor of) . . .
(subject)
. . . *(name of college)*
Address

Dear Professor . . . :
Dear Dr. (**OR** Mr.) . . . : *

d. Superintendent of Schools

Mr. (**OR** Dr.) . . . *(full name)* *
Superintendent of . . .
(name of city) Schools
Address

Dear Mr. (**OR** Dr.) . . . : *

e. Member of Board of Education

Mr. . . . *(full name)* *
Member, . . . *(name of city)* Board of
Education
Address

Dear Mr. . . . : *

f. Principal

Mr. (**OR** Dr.) . . . *(full name)* *
Principal, . . . *(name of school)*
Address

Dear Mr. . . . : *
Dear Dr. . . . :

g. Teacher

Mr. (**OR** Dr.) *(full name)* *
. . . *(name of school)*
Address

Dear Mr. . . . : *
Dear Dr. . . . :

1806 Government Officials

a. President of the United States

The President
The White House
Washington, DC 20500

Mr. President: *
Dear Mr. President: *

b. Vice President of the United States

The Vice President
United States Senate
Washington, DC 20510

OR: The Honorable . . . *(full name)*
Vice President of the United States
Washington, DC 20510

Dear Mr. Vice President: *

c. Cabinet Member

The Honorable . . . *(full name)*
Secretary of . . . *(department)*
Washington, DC ZIP Code

Dear Mr. Secretary: *

d. United States Senator

The Honorable . . . *(full name)*
United States Senate
Washington, DC 20510

---

*See the note at the top of page 544.

†When an abbreviation such as *Esq., M.D.,* or *Ph.D.* follows a name, do not use a courtesy title such as *Mr., Ms.,* or *Dr.* before the name. (See also ¶¶518c, 519c.)

Continued on page 548

¶1807

OR: The Honorable . . . *(full name)*
United States Senator
Local address

Dear Senator . . . :

e. United States Representative

The Honorable . . . *(full name)*
House of Representatives
Washington, DC 20515

OR: The Honorable . . . *(full name)*
Representative in Congress
Local address

Dear Representative . . . :
Dear Mr. . . . :*

f. Chief Justice of the United States

The Chief Justice of the United States
(see ¶313b)
Washington, DC 20543

OR: The Chief Justice
The Supreme Court
Washington, DC 20543

Dear Mr. Chief Justice:*

g. Associate Justice of the U.S. Supreme Court

Mr. Justice . . . *(last name only)*
The Supreme Court
Washington, DC 20543

Dear Mr. Justice:*
Dear Justice . . . :

h. Judge of Federal, State, or Local Court

The Honorable . . . *(full name)*
Judge of the . . . *(name of court)*
Address

Dear Judge . . . :

i. Governor

The Honorable . . . *(full name)*
Governor of . . . *(state)*
State Capital, State ZIP Code

Dear Governor . . . :

j. State Senator

The Honorable . . . *(full name)*
The State Senate
State Capital, State ZIP Code

Dear Senator . . . :

k. State Representative or Assembly Member

The Honorable . . . *(full name)*
House of Representatives
  (**OR** The State Assembly)
State Capital, State ZIP Code

Dear Mr. . . . :*

l. Mayor

The Honorable . . . *(full name)*
Mayor of . . . *(city)*
City, State ZIP Code

OR: The Mayor of the City of . . .
City, State ZIP Code

Dear Mr. Mayor:*
Dear Mayor . . . :

1807 Diplomats

a. Secretary General of the United Nations

His Excellency . . . *(full name)**
Secretary General of the United Nations
United Nations Plaza
New York, NY 10017

Excellency:
Dear Mr. Secretary General:*
Dear Mr. . . . :*

b. Ambassador to the United States

His Excellency . . . *(full name)**
Ambassador of . . . *(country)*
Address

Excellency:
Dear Mr. Ambassador:*

c. Minister to the United States

The Honorable . . . *(full name)*
Minister of . . . *(department)*
Address

Sir:*
Dear Mr. Minister:*

d. American Ambassador

The Honorable . . . *(full name)*
American Ambassador
  (**OR** The Ambassador of the United
  States of America)
Foreign address of U.S. Embassy

Sir:*
Dear Mr. Ambassador:*

---

*See the note at the top of page 544.

1808 Members of the Armed Services

The addresses of both officers and enlisted personnel in the armed services should include title or rank and full name followed by a comma and the initials USA, USN, USAF, USMC, or USCG. Below are some specific examples with appropriate salutations.

a. Army, Air Force, and Marine Corps Officers

> Lieutenant General ... *(full name),*
>   USA (**OR** USAF **OR** USMC)
> Address
>
> Dear General ... :†
> (**NOT:** Dear Lieutenant General ... :)

b. Navy and Coast Guard Officers

> Rear Admiral ... *(full name),* USN (**OR**
>   USCG)
> Address
>
> Dear Admiral ... :†

c. Enlisted Personnel

> Sergeant ... *(full name),* USA
> Address
>
> **OR:** Seaman ... *(full name),* USN
> Address
>
> Dear Sergeant (**OR** Seaman) ... :

1809 Roman Catholic Dignitaries

a. Pope

> His Holiness the Pope
>
> **OR:** His Holiness Pope ... *(given name)*
> Vatican City
> 00187 Rome
> ITALY
>
> Your Holiness:
> Most Holy Father:

---

*See the note at the top of page 544.

†Use the salutation *Dear General* ... whether the officer is a full general or only a lieutenant general, a major general, or a brigadier general. Similarly, use *Dear Colonel* ... for either a full colonel or a lieutenant colonel and *Dear Lieutenant* ... for a first or a second lieutenant. Use *Dear Admiral* ... for a full admiral, a vice admiral, or a rear admiral.

b. Cardinal

> His Eminence ... *(given name)*
>   Cardinal ... *(surname)*
> Archbishop of ... *(place)*
> Address
>
> Your Eminence:
> Dear Cardinal ... :

c. Archbishop and Bishop

> The Most Reverend ... *(full name)*
> Archbishop (**OR** Bishop) of ... *(place)*
> Address
>
> Your Excellency:
> Dear Archbishop (**OR** Bishop) ... :

d. Monsignor

> The Reverend Monsignor ... *(full name)*
> Address
>
> Reverend Monsignor:
> Dear Monsignor ... :

e. Priest

> The Reverend ... *(full name, followed
>   by comma and initials of order)*
> Address
>
> Reverend Father:
> Dear Father ... :
> Dear Father:

f. Mother Superior

> The Reverend Mother Superior
> Address
>
> **OR:** Reverend Mother ... *(name, followed
>   by comma and initials of order)*
> Address
>
> Reverend Mother:
> Dear Reverend Mother:
> Dear Mother ... :

g. Sister

> Sister ... *(name, followed by comma
>   and initials of order)*
> Address
>
> Dear Sister ... :
> Dear Sister:

h. Brother

> Brother ... *(name, followed by comma
>   and initials of order)*
> Address
>
> Dear Brother ... :
> Dear Brother:

Forms of Address

18

¶1810

1810 Protestant Dignitaries

a. Protestant Episcopal Bishop

> The Right Reverend . . . *(full name)*
> Bishop of . . . *(place)*
> Address
>
> Dear Bishop . . . :

b. Protestant Episcopal Dean

> The Very Reverend . . . *(full name)*
> Dean of . . . *(place)*
> Address
>
> Dear Dean . . . :

c. Methodist Bishop

> The Reverend . . . *(full name)*
> Bishop of . . . *(place)*
> Address

> **OR:**   Bishop . . . *(full name)*
> Address
>
> Dear Bishop . . . :

d. Minister With Doctor's Degree

> The Reverend Dr. . . . *(full name)*
> Address

> **OR:**   The Reverend . . . *(full name)*, D.D.
> Address
>
> Dear Dr. . . . :

e. Minister Without Doctor's Degree

> The Reverend . . . *(full name)*
> Address
>
> Dear Mr. . . . :*

1811 Jewish Dignitaries

a. Rabbi With Doctor's Degree

> Rabbi . . . *(full name)*, D.D.
> Address

> **OR:**   Dr. . . . *(full name)*
> Address
>
> Dear Rabbi (**OR** Dr.) . . . :

b. Rabbi Without Doctor's Degree

> Rabbi . . . *(full name)*
> Address
>
> Dear Rabbi . . . :

---

*See the note at the top of page 544.

PART 3

References

APPENDIX A

GLOSSARY OF GRAMMATICAL TERMS

Active verb. See *Voice, active.*

Adjective. A word that answers the question *what kind* (*excellent* results), *how many* (*four* laptops), or *which one* (the *latest*) data. An adjective may be a single word (a *wealthy* man), a phrase (a man *of great wealth*), or a clause (a man *who possesses great wealth*). An adjective modifies the meaning of a noun (*loose* cannon) or a pronoun (*unlucky* me, I was *wrong*).

Adjective, predicate. See *Complement.*

Adverb. A word that answers the question *when, where, why, in what manner,* or *to what extent.* An adverb may be a single word (speak *clearly*), a phrase (speak *in a clear voice*), or a clause (speak *as clearly as you can*). An adverb modifies the meaning of a verb, an adjective, or another adverb. (See also *Clause, adverbial.*)

> We closed the deal *quickly.* (Modifies the verb *closed.*)
> Caroline seemed *genuinely* pleased. (Modifies the adjective *pleased.*)
> My presentation went *surprisingly* well. (Modifies the adverb *well.*)

Adverbial conjunctive (or connective). An adverb that connects the main clauses of a compound sentence; for example, *however, therefore, nevertheless, hence, moreover, otherwise, consequently.* Also referred to as a *conjunctive adverb* or a *transitional expression.* (See also ¶¶138a, 178.)

Antecedent. A noun or a noun phrase to which a pronoun refers.

> She is the *person who* wrote the letter. *(Person* is the antecedent of *who.)*
> *Owning a home* has *its* advantages. *(Owning a home* is the antecedent of *its.)*

Appositive. A noun or a noun phrase that identifies another noun or pronoun that immediately precedes it. (See ¶¶148–150.)

> Mr. Mancuso, *our chief financial officer,* would like to meet you.

Article. Considered an adjective. The *definite* article is *the;* the *indefinite* articles are *a* and *an.* (For a usage note on *a–an,* see pages 281–282.)

Auxiliary verb. See *Verb, helping.*

Case. The form of a noun or of a pronoun that indicates its relation to other words in the sentence. There are three cases: nominative, possessive, and objective. *Nouns* have the same form in the nominative and objective cases but a special ending for the possessive. (See ¶¶627–652.) The forms for *pronouns* are:

Nominative	Possessive	Objective
I	my, mine	me
you	your, yours	you
he, she, it	his, hers, its	him, her, it
we	our, ours	us
they	their, theirs	them
who	whose	whom

Nominative case. Used for the subject or the complement of a verb.

> *She* publishes a newsletter. (Subject.)
> The person who called you was *I.* (Complement.)

Possessive case. Used to show ownership and other relationships. (See ¶¶627–652, especially the examples in ¶627.)

> *Your* copy of the report contains a statistical analysis. *Mine* doesn't.

Objective case. Used for (1) the object of a verb, (2) the object of a preposition, (3) the subject of an infinitive, (4) the object of an infinitive, and (5) the complement of the infinitive *to be*.

> Can you help *us* this weekend? (Object of the verb *help.*)
> Brenda has not written to *me.* (Object of the preposition *to.*)
> I encouraged *her* to enter the biathlon. (Subject of the infinitive *to enter.*)
> William promised to call *me* but he didn't. (Object of the infinitive *to call.*)
> They believed me to be *her.* (Complement of the infinitive *to be.*)

Clause. A group of related words containing a subject and a predicate. An *independent clause* (also known as a *main clause* or *principal clause*) expresses a complete thought and can stand alone as a sentence. A *dependent clause* (also known as a *subordinate clause*) does not express a complete thought and cannot stand alone as a sentence.

> I will go *(independent clause)* if I am invited *(dependent clause).*

Adjective clause. A dependent clause that modifies a noun or a pronoun in the main clause. Adjective clauses are joined to the main clause by relative pronouns *(which, that, who, whose, whom).*

> Their bill, *which includes servicing,* seems reasonable. (Modifies *bill.*)

Adverbial clause. A dependent clause that functions as an adverb in its relation to the main clause. Adverbial clauses indicate time, place, manner, cause, purpose, condition, result, reason, or contrast.

> These orders can be filled *as soon as stock is received.* (Time.)
> I was advised to live *where the climate is dry.* (Place.)
> She worked *as though her life depended on it.* (Manner.)
> Please write me at once *if you have any suggestions.* (Condition.)
> *Because our plant is closed in August,* we cannot fill your order now. (Reason.)

Coordinate clauses. Clauses of the same rank—independent or dependent.

> *Carl will oversee the day-to-day operations,* and *Sheila will be responsible for the finances.* (Coordinate independent clauses.)
> *When you have read the user's manual* and *you have mastered all the basic operations,* try to deal with these special applications. (Coordinate dependent clauses.)

Elliptical clause. A clause from which key words have been omitted (See ¶¶101b–c, 111, 119, 130b, and 1082d.)

> *Now, for the next topic.*   *Really?*   *If possible,* arrive at one.

Essential (restrictive) clause. A dependent clause that cannot be omitted without changing the meaning of the main (independent) clause. Essential clauses are *not* set off by commas.

> The magazine *that came yesterday* contains an evaluation of new software.

Nonessential (nonrestrictive) clause. A dependent clause that adds descriptive information but could be omitted without changing the meaning of the main (independent) clause. Such clauses are separated or set off from the main clause by commas.

> She has had a lot of success with her latest book, *which deals with corporate finance.*
> Her latest book, *which deals with corporate financial analysis,* has sold quite well.

Noun clause. A dependent clause that functions as a noun in the main clause.

> *Whether the proposal will be accepted* remains to be seen. (Noun clause as subject.)
> They thought *that the plan was a failure.* (Noun clause as object.)
> Then he said, *"Who gave you that information?"* (Noun clause as object.)

Comparison. The forms of an adjective or adverb that indicate degrees in quality, quantity, or manner. The degrees are positive, comparative, and superlative. (See ¶1071.)

Positive. The simple form; for example, *new, efficient* (adjectives); *soon, quietly* (adverbs).

Comparative. Indicates a higher or lower degree of quality or manner than is expressed by the positive degree. The comparative is used when two things are compared and is regularly formed by adding *er* to the positive degree *(newer, sooner)*. In longer words the comparative is formed by adding *more* or *less* to the positive *(more efficient, less efficient; more quietly, less quietly)*.

Superlative. Denotes the highest or lowest degree of quality or manner. The superlative is used when more than two things are compared and is regularly formed by adding *est* to the positive degree *(newest, soonest)*. In longer words the superlative is formed by adding *most* or *least* to the positive *(most efficient, least efficient; most quietly, least quietly)*.

Complement. A word or phrase that completes the sense of the verb. It may be an object, a predicate noun, a predicate pronoun, or a predicate adjective.

Object. Follows a transitive verb. (See *Verb*.)

I have already drafted the *contract.*

Predicate noun or pronoun. Follows a linking verb (such as *is, are, was, were, will be, has been, could be*). It explains the subject and is identical with it. (Also called a *predicate complement, subject complement,* and *predicate nominative.*)

Miss Kwong is our new *accountant. (Accountant* refers to *Miss Kwong.)*

The person responsible for the decision was *I.* (The pronoun *I* refers to *person.)*

Predicate adjective. Completes the sense of a linking verb. (Also called a *predicate complement.*)

These charges are *excessive.* (The adjective *excessive* refers to *charges.)*

NOTE: In this manual, the term *complement* is used to refer only to a predicate noun, pronoun, or adjective following a linking verb. The term *object* is used to denote the complement of a transitive verb.

Compound adjective. A phrase or clause that qualifies, limits, or restricts the meaning of a word. Also referred to as a *compound modifier.* (See also ¶¶813–832.)

Conjunction. A word or phrase that connects words, phrases, or clauses.

Coordinating conjunction. Connects words, phrases, or clauses of equal rank. The coordinating conjunctions are *and, but, or,* and *nor.*

Correlative conjunctions. Conjunctions consisting of two elements that are used in pairs; for example, *both . . . and, not only . . . but (also), either . . . or, neither . . . nor.*

Subordinating conjunction. Used to join a dependent clause to a main (independent) clause; for example, *when, where, after, before, if.* (See ¶132.)

Conjunctive adverb. See *Adverbial conjunctive.*

Connective. A word that joins words, phrases, or clauses. The chief types of connectives are conjunctions, adverbial conjunctives, prepositions, and relative pronouns.

Consonants. The letters *b, c, d, f, g, h, j, k, l, m, n, p, q, r, s, t, v, w, x, y, z.* The letters *w* and *y* sometimes serve as vowels (as in *saw* and *rhyme*). (See also *Vowels.*)

Contraction. A shortened form of a word or phrase in which an apostrophe indicates the omitted letters or words; for example, *don't* for *do not.* (See ¶505b–e.)

Dangling modifier. A modifier that is attached either to no word in a sentence or to the wrong word. (See *Modifier* and ¶¶1082–1086.)

Direct address. A construction in which a speaker or a writer addresses another person directly; for example, "What do you think, Sylvia?"

Elliptical expressions. Condensed expressions from which key words have been omitted; for example, *if necessary* (for *if it is necessary*). (See ¶¶101b–c, 111, 119a; see also *Clause; Sentence.*)

Essential elements. Words, phrases, or clauses needed to complete the structure or meaning of a sentence. (See also *Clause; Phrase.*)

Gender. The characteristic of nouns and pronouns that indicates whether the thing named is *masculine (man, boy, he), feminine (woman, girl, she),* or *neuter (book, concept, it).* Nouns that refer to either males or females have *common* gender *(person, child).*

Gerund. A verb form ending in *ing* and used as a *noun.*

> *Selling* requires special skills. (Subject.)
> I enjoy *selling.* (Direct object of *enjoy.*)
> She is experienced in *selling.* (Object of preposition *in.*)

Dangling gerund. A prepositional-gerund phrase that is attached either to no word in a sentence or to the wrong word. (See ¶1082c.)

Imperative. See *Mood.*

Indicative. See *Mood.*

Infinitive. The form of the verb usually introduced by *to* (see ¶¶1044–1046). An infinitive may be used as a noun, an adjective, or an adverb. (See *Phrase.*)

> **NOUN:** *To find affordable housing these days* is not easy. (Subject.)
> She is trying *to do a hatchet job on my proposal.* (Object.)
> **ADJECTIVE:** I still have two more contracts *to draft.* (Modifies *contracts.*)
> **ADVERB:** He resigned *to take another position.* (Modifies *resigned.*)

Interjection. A word that shows emotion; usually without grammatical connection to other parts of a sentence.

> *Wow!* What a weekend!   *Oh,* so that's what he meant.

Modifier. A word, phrase, or clause that qualifies, limits, or restricts the meaning of a word. (See *Adjective; Adverb; Compound adjective; Dangling modifier; Squinting modifier.*)

Mood (mode). The form of the verb that shows the manner of the action. There are three moods: indicative, imperative, and subjunctive.

Indicative. States a fact or asks a question.

> Our lease has expired.   When does our lease expire?

Imperative. Expresses a command or makes a request.

> Call me next week.   Please send me your latest catalog.

Subjunctive. Used in dependent clauses following main (independent) clauses expressing necessity, demand, or wishing (see ¶¶1038–1039); also used in *if, as if,* and *as though* clauses that state conditions which are improbable, doubtful, or contrary to fact (see ¶¶1040–1043).

> I demand that we *be* heard.   It is imperative that he *be* notified.
> We urge that she *be* elected.   If he *were* appointed, I would quit.
> I wish I *were* going.   If she *had* known, she would have written.

Nominative case. See *Case, nominative.*

Nonessential elements. Words, phrases, or clauses that are not needed to complete the structure or meaning of a sentence. (See also *Clause; Phrase.*)

Noun. The name of a person, place, object, idea, quality, or activity.

> **Abstract noun.** The name of a quality or a general idea; for example, *courage, freedom.*

> **Collective noun.** A noun that represents a group of persons, animals, or things; for example, *audience, company, flock.* (See ¶1019.)

> **Common noun.** The name of a class of persons, places, or things; for example, *child, house.* (See ¶¶307–310.)

> **Predicate noun.** See *Complement.*

> **Proper noun.** The official name of a particular person, place, or thing; for example, *Ellen, San Diego, Wednesday.* Proper nouns are capitalized. (See ¶¶303–306.)

Number. The characteristic of a noun, pronoun, or verb that indicates whether one person or thing (singular) or more than one (plural) is meant.

> **NOUN:** beeper, beepers   **PRONOUN:** she, they   **VERB:** (she) works, (they) work

Object. The person or thing that receives the action of a transitive verb. An object may be a word, a phrase, or a clause. (See *Case, objective.*)

> I need a new laptop *computer.* (Word.)
> She prefers *to work with hard copy.* (Infinitive phrase.)
> We did not realize *that your deadline was so tight.* (Clause.)

> **Direct object.** The person or thing that is directly affected by the action of the verb. (The object in each of the three sentences above is a *direct* object.)

> **Indirect object.** The person or thing indirectly affected by the action of the verb. The indirect object can be made the object of the preposition *to* or *for.*

> > Molly gave (to) *me* a hard time about my sales performance this quarter.

Ordinal number. The form of a number that indicates order or succession; for example, *first, second, twelfth* or *1st, 2d, 12th.* (See ¶¶424–426.)

Parenthetical elements. Words, phrases, or clauses that are not necessary to complete the structure or the meaning of a sentence.

> Gina Sala, *my wife's older sister,* is my accountant.

Participle. A word that may stand alone as an adjective or may be combined with helping (auxiliary) verbs to form different tenses (see ¶¶1033–1034). There are three forms: present, past, and perfect.

> **Present participle.** Ends in *ing;* for example, *making, advertising.*

> **Past participle.** Regularly ends in *ed* (as in *asked* or *filed*) but may be irregularly formed (as in *lost, seen,* and *written*). (See ¶1030a–b.)

> **Perfect participle.** Consists of *having* plus the past participle; for example, *having asked, having lost.*

When a participle functions as an *adjective,* it modifies a noun or a pronoun.

> The *coming* year poses some new challenges. (Modifies *year.*)
> *Having retired* last year, I now do volunteer work. (Modifies *I.*)

Because a participle has many of the characteristics of a verb, it may take an object and be modified by an adverb. The participle and its object and modifiers make up a *participial phrase.*

> *Seizing the opportunity,* Orzo offered to buy the business. *(Opportunity* is the object of *seizing.)*
>
> *Moving aggressively,* we can control the market. *(Aggressively* modifies *moving.)*

Dangling participle. A participial phrase attached either to no word in a sentence or to the wrong word. (See *Phrase* and ¶1082a.)

Parts of speech. The eight classes into which words are grouped according to their uses in a sentence: verb, noun, pronoun, adjective, adverb, conjunction, preposition, and interjection.

Passive verb. See *Voice, passive.*

Person. The characteristic of a word that indicates whether a person is speaking *(first person),* is spoken to *(second person),* or is spoken about *(third person).* Only personal pronouns and verbs change their forms to show person. All nouns are considered third person.

	Singular	Plural
FIRST PERSON:	*I* like this book.	*We* like this book.
SECOND PERSON:	*You* like this book.	*You* like this book.
THIRD PERSON:	*She* likes this book.	*They* like this book.

Phrase. A group of two or more words without a subject and a predicate; used as a noun, an adjective, or an adverb. (See *Predicate.*)

Noun phrase. A phrase that functions as a noun (such as a gerund phrase, an infinitive phrase, or a prepositional phrase).

> I like *running my own business.* (Gerund phrase as object.)
>
> *To provide the best possible service* is our goal. (Infinitive phrase as subject.)
>
> *Before 9 a.m.* is the best time to call me. (Prepositional phrase as subject.)

Adjective phrase. A phrase that functions as an adjective (such as an infinitive phrase, a participial phrase, or a prepositional phrase).

> The time *to act* is now! (Infinitive phrase indicating what kind of time.)

Adverbial phrase. A phrase that functions as an adverb (such as an infinitive phrase or a prepositional phrase).

> Let's plan to meet *after lunch.* (Prepositional phrase indicating when to meet.)

Gerund phrase. A gerund plus its object and modifiers; used as a noun.

> *Delaying payments to your suppliers* will prove costly. (Gerund phrase as subject.)

Infinitive phrase. An infinitive plus its object and modifiers; may be used as a noun, an adjective, or an adverb. An infinitive phrase that is attached to either no word in a sentence or to the wrong word is called a *dangling infinitive.* (See ¶1082b.)

> *To get TF's okay on this purchase order* took some doing. (As a noun; serves as subject of the verb *took.)*
>
> The decision *to close the Morrisville plant* was not made easily. (As an adjective; tells what kind of decision.)
>
> Janice resigned *to open her own business.* (As an adverb; tells why Janice resigned.)

NOTE: An infinitive phrase, unlike other phrases, may sometimes have a subject. This subject precedes the infinitive and is in the objective case.

> I have asked *her to review this draft for accuracy. (Her* is the subject of *to review.)*

Participial phrase. A participle and its object and modifiers; used as an adjective.

> The committee *considering your proposal* should come to a decision this week.
>
> I prefer the cover sample *printed in blue and yellow.*

Prepositional phrase. A preposition and its object and modifiers; may be used as a noun, an adjective, or an adverb.

> *From Boston to Tulsa* is about 1550 miles. (As a noun; serves as subject of *is.*)
>
> Profits *in the automobile industry* are up sharply this quarter. (As an adjective; indicates which type of profits.)
>
> You handled Dr. Waterman's objections *with great skill.* (As an adverb; indicates the manner in which the objections were handled.)

Prepositional-gerund phrase. A phrase that begins with a preposition and has a gerund as the object. (See *Gerund* and ¶1082c.)

> *By rechecking these figures before you release them,* you deal with any questions raised by higher management. *(By* is the preposition; *rechecking,* a gerund, is the object of *by.)*

Essential (restrictive) phrase. A phrase that limits, defines, or identifies; cannot be omitted without changing the meaning of the sentence.

> The study *analyzing our competitors' promotion activities* will be finished within the next two weeks.

Nonessential (nonrestrictive) phrase. A phrase that can be omitted without changing the meaning of the sentence.

> The Stanforth-Palmer Company, *one of the country's largest financial services organizations,* is expanding into satellite communications.

Verb phrase. This term is often used to indicate the individual words that make up the verb in a sentence. Sometimes the verb phrase includes an adverb. A verb phrase can function only as a verb.

> You *should work together* with Nora on the report. (The verb phrase consists of the verb form *should work* plus the adverb *together.)*

Positive degree. See *Comparison, positive.*

Possessive case. See *Case, possessive.*

Predicate. That part of a sentence which tells what the subject does or what is done to the subject or what state of being the subject is in. (See also *Verb.*)

Complete predicate. The complete predicate consists of a verb and its complement along with any modifiers.

> Barbara *has handled the job well.*

Simple predicate. The simple predicate is the verb alone, without regard for any complement or modifiers that may accompany it.

> Barbara *has handled* the job well.

Compound predicate. A predicate consisting of two or more predicates joined by conjunctions.

> Barbara *has handled the job well* and *deserves a good deal of praise.*

Predicate adjective. See *Complement.*

Predicate nominative. See *Complement.*

Prefix. A letter, syllable, or word added to the beginning of a word to change its meaning; for example, *a*float, *re*upholster, *under*nourished.

Preposition. A connective (such as *from, to, in, on, of, at, by, for, with*) that shows the relationship between a noun or pronoun and some other word in the sentence. The noun or pronoun following a preposition is in the objective case. (See ¶¶1077–1080.)

> Martin's work was reviewed *by Hedley and me.*

Principal parts. The forms of a verb from which all other forms are derived: the *present*, the *past*, the *past participle*, and the *present participle*. (See ¶¶1030–1035.)

Pronoun. A word used in place of a noun. (See ¶¶1049–1064.)

DEMONSTRATIVE:	*this, that, these, those*
INDEFINITE:	*each, either, any, anyone, someone, everyone, few, all,* etc.
INTENSIVE:	*myself, yourself, himself, herself, ourselves, themselves,* etc.
INTERROGATIVE:	*who, which, what,* etc.
PERSONAL:	*I, you, he, she, it, we, they,* etc.
RELATIVE:	*who, whose, whom, which, that,* and compounds such as *whoever*

Punctuation. Marks used to indicate relationships between words, phrases, and clauses.

Terminal (end) punctuation. The period, the question mark, and the exclamation point—the three marks that may indicate the end of a sentence.

NOTE: When a sentence breaks off abruptly, a dash may be used to mark the end of the sentence (see ¶207). When a sentence trails off without really ending, ellipsis marks (three spaced periods) are used to mark the end of the sentence (see ¶291a).

Internal punctuation. Commas, semicolons, colons, dashes, parentheses, quotation marks, apostrophes, ellipsis marks, asterisks, diagonals, and brackets are the most common marks of internal punctuation.

Question.

Direct question. A question in its original form, as spoken or written.

> He then asked me, "What is your opinion?"

Indirect question. A restatement of a question without the use of the exact words of the speaker.

> He then asked me what my opinion was.

Independent question. A question that represents a complete sentence but is incorporated in a larger sentence.

> The main question is, Who will translate this idea into a clear plan of action?

Quotation.

Direct quotation. A quotation of words exactly as spoken or written.

> I myself heard Ed say, "I will arrive in Santa Fe on Tuesday."

Indirect quotation. A restatement of a quotation without the use of the exact words of the speaker.

> I myself heard Ed say that he would arrive in Santa Fe on Tuesday.

Sentence. A group of words representing a complete thought and containing a subject and a predicate (a verb along with any complements and modifiers).

Simple sentence. A sentence consisting of one independent clause.

> I have no recollection of the meeting.

Compound sentence. A sentence consisting of two or more independent clauses.

> Our Boston office will be closed, and our Dallas office will be relocated.

Complex sentence. A sentence consisting of one independent clause (also called the *main clause*) and one or more dependent clauses.

> We will make an exception to the policy if circumstances warrant.

Compound-complex sentence. A sentence consisting of two independent clauses and one or more dependent clauses.

> I tried to handle the monthly report alone, but when I began to analyze the data, I realized that I needed your help.

Elliptical sentence. A word or phrase treated as a complete sentence, even though the subject and verb are understood but not expressed. (See ¶¶101b–c, 111, 119a.)

> Enough on that subject.   Why not?

Declarative sentence. A sentence that makes a statement.

> Our company is continually testing cutting-edge technologies.

Interrogative sentence. A sentence that asks a question.

> When will the conference begin?

Exclamatory sentence. A sentence that expresses strong feeling.

> Don't even think of smoking here!

Imperative sentence. A sentence that expresses a command or a request. (The subject *you* is understood if it is not expressed.)

> Send a check at once.   Please let us hear from you.

Sentence fragment. A phrase or clause that is incorrectly treated as a sentence. (See ¶101c.)

Squinting modifier. A modifier placed in such a way that it can be interpreted as modifying either what precedes or what follows. (See ¶1087.)

Statement. A sentence that asserts a fact. (See also *Sentence.*)

Subject. A word, phrase, or clause that names the person, place, or thing about which something is said. (See *Case, nominative.*)

> *The law firm with the best reputation in town* is Barringer and Doyle.
> *Whoever applies for the job from within the department* will get special consideration.

Compound subject. Two or more subjects joined by a conjunction.

> *My wife and my three sons* are off on a white-water rafting trip.

Subjunctive. See *Mood.*

Suffix. A letter, syllable, or word added to the end of a word to modify its meaning; for example, trend*y*, friend*ly*, count*less*, receiver*ship*, lone*some*. (See ¶833a.)

Superlative degree. See *Comparison, superlative.*

Syllable. One or more letters that represent one sound. (See ¶¶901–904.)

Tense. The property of a verb that expresses *time.* (See ¶¶1031–1035.) The three *primary* tenses correspond to the three time divisions:

PRESENT:	they think
PAST:	they thought
FUTURE:	they will think

There are three *perfect* tenses, corresponding to the primary tenses:

PRESENT PERFECT:	they have thought
PAST PERFECT:	they had thought
FUTURE PERFECT:	they will have thought

There are six *progressive* tenses, corresponding to each of the primary and perfect tenses:

PRESENT PROGRESSIVE:	they are thinking
PAST PROGRESSIVE:	they were thinking
FUTURE PROGRESSIVE:	they will be thinking
PRESENT PERFECT PROGRESSIVE:	they have been thinking
PAST PERFECT PROGRESSIVE:	they had been thinking
FUTURE PERFECT PROGRESSIVE:	they will have been thinking

There are two *emphatic* tenses:

PRESENT EMPHATIC:	they do think
PAST EMPHATIC:	they did think

➤ *For an illustration of how these tenses are formed, see pages 248–249.*

Transitional expressions. Expressions that link independent clauses or sentences; for example, *as a result, therefore, on the other hand, nevertheless.* (See also ¶138a; *Adverbial conjunctive.*)

Verb. A word or phrase used to express action or state of being. (See also *Mood.*)

> Enniston *has boosted* its sales goals for the year. (Action)
> My son-in-law *was* originally a lawyer, but he *has* now *become* a computer-game designer. (State of being.)

Helping (auxiliary) verb. A verb that helps in the formation of another verb. (See ¶¶1030c, 1033–1034.) The chief helping verbs are *be, can, could, do, have, may, might, must, ought, shall, should, will, would.*

Transitive verb. A verb that requires an object to complete its meaning.

> Fusilli *has rejected* all offers to purchase his business.

Intransitive verb. A verb that does not require an object to complete its meaning.

> As market growth *occurs* and customer interest *builds,* our sales expectations *are rising* and top management's excitement *has increased.*

Linking verb. A verb that connects a subject with a predicate adjective, noun, or pronoun. The various forms of *to be* are the most commonly used linking verbs. *Become, look, seem, appear,* and *grow* are also used as linking verbs. (See *Complement* and ¶1067.)

> Laura *seemed* willing to compromise, but Frank *became* obstinate in his demands.
> *Was* he afraid that any concession might make him *appear* a fool?

Principal parts of verbs. See *Principal parts.*

Verbal. A word that is derived from a verb but functions in some other way. (See *Gerund; Infinitive; Participle.*)

Voice. The property of a verb that indicates whether the subject acts or is acted upon.

Active voice. A verb is in the active voice when its subject is the doer of the act. (See ¶1037.)

> About a dozen people *reviewed* the report in draft form.

Passive voice. A verb is in the passive voice when its subject is acted upon. (See ¶¶1036–1037.)

> The report *was reviewed* in draft form by about a dozen people.

Vowels. The letters *a, e, i, o,* and *u.* The letters *w* and *y* sometimes act like vowels (as in *awl* or in *cry*). (See also *Consonants.*)

APPENDIX B

GLOSSARY OF COMPUTER TERMS

As the world of the office continues to undergo a series of rapid technological changes, a whole new vocabulary continues to evolve. The following glossary provides brief and simple definitions of the key terms and concepts that are part of this vocabulary.[*]

NOTE: When boldface type is used to highlight a word or phrase within a definition, it signifies that the highlighted word or phrase is defined elsewhere in this glossary.

➤ *See ¶544 for a list of common computer abbreviations and acronyms.*

Access. To call up information out of **storage.**

> **Random access.** A technique that permits stored information to be directly retrieved, regardless of its location on the storage medium.

> **Sequential access.** A technique for retrieving stored information that requires a sequential search through one item after another on the storage medium.

Access time. The amount of time it takes a **computer** to locate stored information.

Active matrix display. A type of **monitor** typically used on **laptop** or portable **computers;** provides a brighter, more readable display than older **LCD** equipment.

Adapter. A **circuit board** that plugs into a **computer** and gives it additional capabilities. (See *Circuit board.*)

AI. See *Artificial intelligence.*

Algorithm. A step-by-step procedure designed to solve a problem or achieve an objective.

Alphanumeric. Consisting of letters, numbers, and symbols.

Antivirus software. A **program** designed to look for and destroy a **virus** that may have infected a **computer's memory** or **files.**

Applet. A small **application,** that is, a **program** designed to perform a simple task. An applet is usually embedded within a larger program.

Application (also called *app*). A **program** designed to perform **information processing** tasks for a specific purpose or activity (for example, **desktop publishing** and **database management**). (See also *Applet; Killer app.*)

Archie. A tool for finding a **file** stored in a **file transfer protocol (FTP)** server.

Archive. A **file** compressed for more efficient use of storage space. The compression of files may be accomplished by means of such **programs** as StuffIt.

Artificial intelligence (AI). **Computer** systems that attempt to imitate human processes for analyzing and solving problems.

Ascending sort. Sorting records from A to Z or 0 to 9. (See *Descending sort.*)

---

[*]A number of works were consulted in the preparation of this glossary, but five were especially helpful: *Webster's New World Dictionary of Computer Terms,* 7th ed., Macmillan, New York, 1999; *Peter Norton's Introduction to Computers,* 3d ed., Glencoe, Westerville, Ohio, 1999; *Microsoft Press Computer Dictionary,* 3d ed., Redmond, Wash., 1997; *The New Hacker's Dictionary,* 3d ed., MIT Press, Cambridge, Mass., 1996; and *Wired Style: Principles of English Usage in the Digital Age,* Hardwired, San Francisco, 1996.

ASCII (pronounced *as-kee*). An acronym derived from <u>A</u>merican <u>S</u>tandard <u>C</u>ode for <u>I</u>nformation Interchange. ASCII is a standard 8-**bit** code that represents 256 **characters.** The use of this standard code permits **computers** made by different manufacturers to communicate with one another.

Background printing. The ability of a **computer** to print a **document** while other work is being done on the **keyboard** and the **display screen** at the same time.

Backup. Storage of duplicate **files** on **disks, diskettes,** or some other form of magnetic medium (such as tapes) as a safety measure in case the original medium is damaged or lost. (One word as a noun or an adjective: *backup* procedures; two words as a verb: *back up* your hard disk.)

Bandwidth. The volume of information that a network can handle (usually expressed in bits per second). The greater the bandwidth, the more quickly **data** can move from a **network** to a user's **computer.** The term *bandwidth* is now also used to refer to a person's attention span (as in "Burt is a low-bandwidth kind of guy") or a person's ability to handle an assignment (as in "Sally lacks the bandwidth to do this job").

Basic Input/Output System (BIOS). A set of **programs** stored in read-only **memory** (ROM) on IBM or IBM-compatible **computers.** These programs control the **disk drives,** the **keyboard,** and the **display screen,** and they handle start-up operations.

Baud rate. The rate of **data** transmission between two **computers** or other electronic equipment.

BBS. See *Bulletin board system.*

Binary numbering system. A numbering system in which all numbers are represented by various combinations of the digits 0 and 1.

BIOS. See *Basic Input/Output System.*

Bit. An acronym derived from <u>bi</u>nary digi<u>t</u>. The smallest unit of information that can be recognized by a **computer.** Bits are combined to represent **characters.** (See also *Byte.*)

Bitmap. A method of storing a graphic image as a set of **bits** in a computer's **memory.** To display the image on the screen, the **computer** converts the bits into **pixels.**

Bits per second (bps). A measurement that describes the speed of **data** transmission between two pieces of equipment. (See *Baud rate.*)

Bloatware. A **program** that uses an excessive amount of **disk** space and **memory.**

Block. A segment of **text** that is selected so that it can be moved to another location or processed in some other way. (See *Block delete; Block move; Cut and paste.*)

Block delete. A **command** to delete (or erase) a segment of **text.**

Block move. A **command** to reproduce a segment of **text** in another place and at the same time erase it from its original position. (See *Cut and paste.*)

Block protect. A **command** to prevent a **page break** from occurring within a block of **text** (for example, a table). (See also *Orphan protection; Widow protection.*)

Boilerplate. Standard wording (for example, sentences or paragraphs in form letters or clauses in legal documents) that is held in **storage.** When needed, it can be used as is, with minor modification, or in combination with new material to produce tailor-made **documents.**

Bookmark list. A customized list of a user's favorite **Web sites** (also referred to as a *hot list*). A bookmark list permits the user to access a particular Web site with a single **command.**

Boot (short for *bootstrap*). To start a **computer** and load the **operating system** to prepare the computer to **execute** an **application.**

Bozo filter. A **program** that screens out unwanted **e-mail** or other messages from individuals or organizations you no longer want to hear from.

bps. See *Bits per second.*

Brochureware. A product that is being actively marketed, even though the product is not yet (and may never be) ready for sale. (See also *Vaporware.*)

Browser. See *Web browser.*

Buffer. A holding area in **memory** that stores information temporarily. Also called *cache.*

Bug. A defect in the **software** that causes the **computer** to malfunction or cease to operate. Some writers now use *bug* to refer to **hardware** problems as well. (See also *Debugging; Glitch.*)

Bulletin board system (BBS). An **online** information system, usually set up by an individual (called a *system operator,* or **SYSOP**) on a nonprofit basis for the enjoyment of other individuals with similar interests. (See also *Internet.*)

Bundled software. Software that is sold along with a **computer** system; several software **programs** that are packaged together (also called *software suites*).

Bus. A pathway along which electronic signals travel between the components of a **computer** system.

Button bar. An on-screen element that offers instant **access** to commonly used **commands.** The commands are represented by **icons** on a row of buttons at the top of the screen. Also called a *tool bar.*

Byte. The sequence of **bits** that represents a **character.** Each byte has 8 bits.

Cache. See *Buffer.*

Cancelbot (from *cancel robot*). A **program** that detects **spamming** and automatically issues a cancel **command.**

Card. See *Circuit board; Adapter.*

Carpal tunnel syndrome. A wrist or hand injury caused by using a **keyboard** for long periods of time. A type of repetitive strain injury **(RSI)**. (See also *Mouse elbow.*)

Cathode-ray tube (CRT). See *Display screen.*

CD-ROM (pronounced *cee-dee-rom*). An acronym derived from compact disk–read-only memory. A form of optical **storage.** One compact **disk** can hold up to 250,000 text pages; it can also be used to store **graphics,** sound, and video. (See *DVD.*)

Cell. A box or rectangle within a table or **spreadsheet** where a **column** and a **row** intersect; an area in which information can be entered in the form of **text** or figures.

Central processing unit (CPU). The brains of an **information processing** system; the processing component that controls the interpretation and execution of instructions. (See *Motherboard.*)

Character. A single letter, figure, punctuation mark, or symbol produced by a **keystroke** on a **computer.** Each character is represented by a **byte.**

Character set. The complete set of **characters**—alphabetic, numeric, and symbolic—displayable on a **computer.** (See *ASCII.*)

Character string. A specified sequence of typed **characters,** usually representing a word or phrase. A character string is often used to locate a particular word or phrase wherever it appears in a **document** so that it can be automatically replaced with another word or phrase. If a person's name has been consistently misspelled or a date appears incorrectly in several places, the error can be easily corrected. (See also *Search and replace.*)

Characters per inch (cpi). The number of **characters** in a **font** that will fit within 1 inch.

Characters per second (cps). The number of **characters** printed in 1 second; a measurement frequently used to describe the speed of a **printer.**

Chat line. See *Newsgroup.*

Check box. A small box that appears on screen alongside each option displayed in a **dialog box.** When an option is selected, an X or a check mark appears inside the box.

Chip. An **integrated circuit** used in **computers.**

Chip jewelry. An obsolete **computer.**

Circuit board. A board or card that carries the necessary electronic components for a particular **computer** function (for example, **memory**). The circuit boards that come with the original equipment perform the standard functions identified with that type of equipment. Additional circuit boards expand the kinds of functions that the equipment can perform. (Also called a *board,* a *card,* or an *expansion board.*)

Clear. A **command** to erase information.

Click. To quickly press and release a **mouse** button *once* while the **cursor** (mouse pointer) is positioned over a specific item on the screen. (See also *Double-click.*)

Client/server computing. A **network** of **computers** that consists of a file server (a computer that runs a **database management system**) and individual clients (computers that request and process **data** obtained from the file server).

Clipboard. A holding area in **memory** where information that has been copied or **cut** (**text, graphics,** sound, or video) can be stored until the information is inserted elsewhere. (See *Copy; Cut; Cut and paste.*)

Column. A vertical block of **cells** in a table or **spreadsheet.** (See also *Row.*)

Command. An instruction that causes a **program** or **computer** to perform a function. A command may be given by means of a special **keystroke** (or series of keystrokes), or the command may be chosen from a **menu.**

Commercial online service. See *Internet service provider.*

Compatibility. The ability of one type of **computer** to share information or to communicate with another type of computer. (See also *ASCII.*)

Computer. An electronic device that is capable of (1) accepting, storing, and logically manipulating **data** or **text** that is **input** and (2) processing and producing **output** (results or decisions) on the basis of stored **programs** of instructions. Some computers are also capable of processing **graphics,** video, and voice input. Most computers include a **keyboard** for **text entry,** a **central processing unit,** one or more **disk drives,** a **display screen,** and a **printer**—components referred to as **hardware.**

Control menu. An on-screen Windows element that appears in a box in the upper left corner of a window. The control menu allows the user the option of adjusting the size of the window, closing or reopening the window, or switching to another window.

Cookie. A device that permits a **Web site** to identify and collect information about every user who visits that site.

Copy. To reproduce information elsewhere. The original information remains in place. (See *Cut.*)

cpi. See *Characters per inch.*

cps. See *Characters per second.*

CPU. See *Central processing unit.*

Cracker. The preferred term (rather than **hacker**) to refer to a **computer** criminal who penetrates a computer **program** to steal information or damage the program in some way.

Crash. A malfunction in **hardware** or **software** that keeps a **computer** from functioning. (See also *Bug; Glitch.*)

CRT. Cathode-ray tube. (See *Display screen.*)

Cursor. A special **character** (usually a blinking underline, dot, or vertical line) that indicates where the next typed **character** will appear on the **display screen.** Also refers to the **mouse** pointer (arrow) or **I-beam pointer.** Microsoft Word refers to the cursor as the *insertion point.* (See also *Prompt.*)

Cursor positioning. The movement of the **cursor** on the **display screen.** Most **computers** have four keys to control up, down, left, and right movement. Many computers also permit the use of a **mouse** to position the cursor.

Cut. To remove **text** from its original location and place it on a **clipboard.** (See *Copy; Paste.*)

Cut and paste. To move a **block** of **text** from one place to another.

Cyberspace. A realistic simulation of a three-dimensional world created by a **computer** system; also referred to as *virtual reality.* Now commonly used to refer to the world of the **Internet** as a whole.

Cybrarian. The electronic equivalent of a librarian. A person who makes a career of **online** research and data retrieval.

Data. Information consisting of letters, numbers, symbols, sound, or images—in a form that can be processed by a **computer.**

Data compression. A procedure for reducing the volume of **data** so as to shorten the time needed to transfer the data.

Database. A stored collection of information.

Database management system (DBMS). The **software** needed to establish and maintain a **database** and manage the stored information.

DDE. See *Dynamic data exchange.*

Dead-tree edition. The paper version of a publication available **online.**

Debugging. Locating and eliminating defects in a **program.** (See also *Bug.*)

Decimal tab. A type of tab that aligns **columns** of figures on the decimal point.

Default settings. The preestablished settings (for margins, **font,** type size, tab stops, and so on) that a **program** will follow unless the user changes them.

Delete. A **command** to erase information in **storage.**

Descending sort. Sorting records from Z to A or 9 to 0. (See also *Ascending sort.*)

Desktop. The electronic work area on a **display screen.**

Desktop computer. A **microcomputer** that is bigger than a **laptop.**

Desktop publishing (DTP). A system that processes the **text** and **graphics** and, by means of page layout **software** and a **laser printer,** produces high-quality pages suitable for printing or in-house reproduction.

Dialog box. A message box on the screen that supplies information to—or requests information from—the user.

Dictionary. A **program** used to check the spelling of each word entered in the **computer.**

Digerati. A term referring to the elite group of intellectuals in the computer world (in the same way that *literati* refers to the elite group of intellectuals in the literary world).

Directory. A list of the **files** stored on a **disk.**

Disk. A random-**access,** magnetically coated storage medium used to store and **retrieve** information. (See also *Diskette; CD-ROM.*)

Disk drive. The component of a **computer** into which a **disk** is inserted so that it can be read or written on.

Disk operating system. See *DOS.*

Diskette. A small, nonrigid **disk** with limited **storage** capacity (normally 30 to 200 pages). Also known as a *floppy disk.*

Display screen. A device similar to a television screen and used on a **computer** to display **text** and **graphics.** Also called a *cathode-ray tube (CRT)*, a *video display terminal (VDT)*, or a *monitor.*

Distributed processing system. A form of a **local area network** in which each user has a fully functional **computer** but all users can share **data** and **application software.** The data and software are distributed among the linked computers and not stored in one central computer.

Document. Any printed business communication—for example, a letter, memo, report, table, or form. (See *File.*)

Domain. Typically, a three-letter element in a Web address or an **e-mail** address. The domain—commonly referred to as the *zone*—indicates the type of organization that owns the **computer** being identified in the address. For example, *.com* signifies a commercial organization; *.edu* signifies an educational institution. (See ¶1532b for a list of the most common domains.)

Domain name. The second part of an **e-mail** address—what follows the @ symbol (for example, *aol.com*). The name of the **computer** intended to receive an e-mail message. (See ¶1533.) In Web addresses **(URLs)** this element is referred to as the **host** name. (See ¶1532b.)

DOS. An acronym derived from d̲isk o̲perating s̲ystem. A **program** that allows the **computer** to manage the **storage** of information on **disks** and controls other aspects of a computer's operation.

Dot. The period symbol used in **e-mail** addresses. Always referred to as a *dot* (never as a period). Thus the **domain name** *aol.com* would be pronounced *ay-oh-ell-dot-com.* **Internet** surfers who spend a lot of time in the *.com* domain are sometimes referred to as *dot communists.*

Dot matrix printer. A **printer** that uses pins to produce **characters** made up of small **dots.**

Double-click. To quickly press and release a **mouse** button *twice* while the **cursor** is positioned over a specific item on the **screen.** (See *Click.*)

Download. To transfer information to the user's **computer** from another computer.

Drag-and-drop editing. A **software** feature that allows the user to (1) highlight **text** to be moved and (2) use a **mouse** to drag the text to a new location.

DTP. See *Desktop publishing.*

Duplexing. A procedure that permits two **computers** to transmit **data** to each other simultaneously.

DVD. D̲igital v̲ideo d̲isc (predicted to replace the **CD-ROM**).

Dynamic data exchange (DDE). A technology that permits the user to transfer or **paste data** from one **application** (for example, a **spreadsheet**) to another (for example, a report). Because of the dynamic link created by this technology, any change in the data in the original application will be automatically reflected in the data copied in the second application. (See also *Object linking and embedding.*)

Easter egg. An unexpected image or message that pops up on the **display screen** when the user innocently enters a secret combination of **keystrokes.** Programmers playfully code Easter eggs into **software** and **operating systems** as a way of surprising and amusing users engaged in more serious tasks.

Editing. The process of changing information by inserting, deleting, replacing, rearranging, and reformatting. Also known as *changing* or *customizing.*

Ellipsis marks. Three dots (. . .) that appear as part of a **menu** option. Ellipsis marks indicate that a **dialog box** will appear if that option is selected.

E-mail. The term *e-mail* (short for *electronic mail*) refers to the transfer of messages or **documents** between users connected by an electronic **network.** (The original form—*E-mail*—is rarely seen anymore except at the beginning of a sentence, and a few cutting-edge publications have started to write the word without a hyphen—*email*.) One wit has suggested replacing the term *e-mail* with *e-pistle.*

Encryption. Coding confidential **data** so that only a user with the right **password** can read the data.

Enter. To **input data** into **memory.** (See *Type.*)

Escape key. A key that permits the user to leave one segment of a **program** and move to another.

Execute. To perform an action specified by the user or the **program.**

Expert system. See *Artificial intelligence.*

Export. To save information in a **format** that another **program** can read.

Extranet. A technology that permits users of one organization's **intranet** to enter portions of another organization's intranet in order to conduct business transactions or collaborate on joint projects.

E-zine. The term *e-zine* refers to a magazine published in an electronic format. Also called *Webzine.*

Face time. Time spent dealing with someone face to face (as opposed to time spent communicating electronically).

FAQ. F̲requently a̲sked q̲uestions. Pronounced as a word (to rhyme with *pack*) or as separate letters.

Fax (n.). A shortened form of the word *facsimile.* A copy of a **document** transmitted electronically from one machine to another.

Fax (v.). To transmit a copy of a **document** electronically.

Fax modem. A device built into or attached to a **computer** that serves as a facsimile machine and a **modem.**

Field. A group of related **characters** treated as a unit (such as a name); also the area reserved for the entry of a specified piece of information.

File. A collection of information stored electronically and treated as a unit by a **computer.** Every file must have its own distinctive name. (See *File name.*)

File name. The name assigned to a **file** stored on a **disk.**

File transfer protocol (FTP). A set of guidelines or standards that establish the **format** in which **files** can be transmitted from one **computer** to another.

Firewall. Software that prevents unauthorized persons from accessing certain parts of a **program, database,** or **network.**

Flame (n.). An inflammatory **e-mail** message; one deliberately designed to insult and provoke the recipient. (See also *Rave.*)

Flame (v.). To send an inflammatory message.

Floppy disk. See *Diskette.*

Folder. A **storage** area on a **disk** used to organize **files.**

Font. A typeface of a certain size and style. Includes all letters of the alphabet, figures, symbols, and punctuation marks. (See *Monospace font; Proportional font.*)

Footer. Repetitive information that appears at the bottom (the foot) of every page of a **document.** A page number is a common footer. (See also *Header.*)

Footnote feature. The ability of a **program** to automatically position footnotes on the same page as the **text** they refer to. If the text is moved to another page, any related footnotes will also be transferred to that page.

Footprint. The amount of space a **computer** occupies on a flat surface.

Forelash. Negative reactions to a technology not yet in existence but excessively promoted in advance.

Format. The physical specifications that affect the appearance and arrangement of a **document**—for example, margins, spacing, and **font.**

Forms mode. The ability of a **program** to store the **format** of a blank **document** or form so that it can later be viewed on the **display screen** and completed by the user. Once a fill-in has been entered, the **cursor** automatically advances to the beginning of the next area to be filled in. (See also *Style sheet; Template.*)

Forum. See *Newsgroup.*

Freenet. A local **network** that offers free (or low-cost) **access** to **host computers** located in libraries and to other public-interest groups in the community. A freenet may also offer limited access to the **Internet.**

Freeware. Copyrighted **software** that is available for use without charge. (See also *Shareware.*)

FTP. See *File transfer protocol.*

Function keys. Keys on a **keyboard** (for example, F1) that give special commands to the **computer**— for example, to set margins or tabs.

Gateway. A machine that links two **networks** using different **protocols.**

GIGO. Garbage in, garbage out. In other words, your **computer output** is only as good as your computer **input.**

Glitch. A **hardware** problem that causes a **computer** to malfunction or **crash.** (See *Bug.*)

Global. Describing any function that can be performed on an entire **document** without requiring individual **commands** for each use. For example, a global **search-and-replace** command will instruct the **computer** to locate a particular word or phrase and replace it with a different word or phrase wherever the original form occurs in the document.

Gopher. The term *gopher* refers to a **protocol** used for locating and transferring information on the **Internet.** The use of *gopher* is diminishing as the use of the Web's **hypertext transfer protocol (HTTP)** gains in popularity.

Graphical user interface (GUI). A **software** feature that permits the user to **click** on **icons** or select options from a **menu.**

Graphics. Pictures or images presented or stored using a **computer.**

Grok. To research and comprehend something in great detail and great depth.

GUI (pronounced *goo-ee***).** See *Graphical user interface.*

Hack. To work on an electronic project.

Hacker. A dedicated **computer** programmer. The term *hacker* is sometimes used erroneously to refer to a computer criminal who penetrates and damages a computer program. The preferred term for a computer criminal is **cracker.**

Handheld computer. A portable computer smaller than a **notebook computer.** Also called a **palmtop computer.**

Hard copy. **Text** or **graphics** printed on paper; also called a **printout.** (See also *Soft copy.*)

Hard disk. A rigid type of magnetic medium that can store large amounts of information.

Hard hyphen. A hyphen that is a permanent **character** in a word. A word that contains a hard hyphen will not be divided at this point if the word comes at the end of a line. (See also *Soft hyphen.*)

Hard page break. A page-ending code or **command** inserted by the user that cannot be changed by the **program.** A hard page break is often used (1) to prevent a table from being divided between two pages and (2) to signify that a particular section of a **document** has ended and the following **text** should start on a new page.

Hard return. A **command** used to end a paragraph, end a short line of **text,** or insert a blank line in the text. (See also *Soft return.*)

Hard space. A space inserted between words in a phrase that should remain together (for example, the word *page* and the number, month and day, number and unit of measure). The hard space ensures that the phrase will not be broken at the end of a line.

Hardware. The physical components of a **computer:** the **central processing unit,** the **display screen,** the **keyboard,** the **disk drive,** and the **printer.** (See also *Software.*)

Hardwired. Describing any **computer** function that cannot be easily modified.

Header. Repetitive information that appears at the top (the head) of every page of a **document.** A page number is a common header. (See also *Footer.*)

Hit. A single request for information made by a client **computer** from a Web server. The popularity of a given **Web site** is measured by the number of hits it receives.

Home. The upper left corner of the **display screen;** the starting position of a page or **document.**

Home page. The main page for a **Web site** established by an organization or an individual; it usually serves as the entrance for a series of related pages.

Host computer. A computer that provides information or a service to other computers on the **Internet.** Every host computer has its own unique host name.

Hot key. A **keyboard** shortcut that allows quick access to a **command** or **menu** option.

Hot list. See *Bookmark list.*

HTML. See *Hypertext markup language.*

HTTP. See *Hypertext transfer protocol.*

Hyperlink. A highlighted word or image on a Web page. When a user clicks on the word or image, the user is connected with another related Web page.

Hypermedia. An extension of **hypertext** that integrates audio, video, and **graphics** with **text.**

Hypertext. A technology that links **text** in one part of a **document** with related text in another part of the document or in other documents. A user can quickly find the related text by clicking on the appropriate keyword, key phrase, **icon,** or button.

Hypertext markup language (HTML). The formatting language used to establish the appearance of a Web page.

Hypertext transfer protocol (HTTP). The **protocol** used on the **World Wide Web** that permits Web clients **(Web browsers)** to communicate with Web servers. This protocol allows programmers to embed **hyperlinks** in Web documents, using **hypertext markup language.**

Hyphenation. The ability of a **program** to automatically hyphenate and divide words that do not fit at the end of a line. If the **text** is later revised so that the divided word no longer begins at the right margin, the hyphen is automatically removed and the word prints solid. (See also *Soft hyphen.*)

I-beam pointer. A **mouse**-controlled **cursor** that looks like a capital I.

Icon. A symbol (such as a picture of a trash can or a file folder) that represents a certain function. When the user **clicks** on the icon, the appropriate function is **executed.** (See *Graphical user interface.*)

Import. To **retrieve** any **text** or other information created by one **program** (for example, images created by a **graphics** program) and transfer it to another program (for example, a **spreadsheet** program).

Indexing. The ability of a **program** to accumulate a list of words or phrases that appear in a **document** (along with their corresponding page numbers) and to print or display the list in alphabetic order.

Information processing. The coordination of people, equipment, and procedures to handle information, including the **storage, retrieval,** distribution, and communication of information. The term *information processing* embraces the entire field of processing words, figures, **graphics,** video, and voice **input** by electronic means.

Information Superhighway (or I-way). The **Internet.** Also referred to as the *Infobahn* (based on the German term for its network of highways, the *Autobahn*).

Ink-jet printer. A nonimpact printer that forms **characters** by spraying tiny, electrically charged ink droplets on paper.

Input (n.). Information entered into the **computer** for processing.

Input (v.). To **enter** information into the **computer.** (See also *Type; Key.*)

Insert. To add information to a **file.**

Insertion point. See *Cursor.*

Integrated circuit. Multiple electronic components combined on a tiny silicon **chip.** (See *Microprocessor.*)

Integrated software. **Software** that combines in one **program** a number of functions normally performed by separate programs.

Interface. The electrical connection that links two pieces of equipment so that they can communicate with each other. Also, the **software** that controls the interaction between the **hardware** and the user.

Internet (or Net). A system that links existing **computer networks** into a worldwide network. The Internet may be accessed by means of commercial online services (such as America Online) and **Internet service providers.**

Internet community. A group of individuals with common interests, who frequently exchange ideas on the **Internet.**

Internet service provider (ISP). An organization that provides access to the **Internet** for a fee. Companies like America Online are more properly referred to as *commercial online services* because they offer many other services in addition to **Internet** access—for example, news, travel services, and financial and shopping information.

Intranet. A private **network** established by an organization for the exclusive use of its employees. **Firewalls** prevent outsiders from gaining access to an organization's intranet. (See also *Extranet.*)

I/O. An abbreviation for *input/output.*

ISP. See *Internet service provider.*

Justification. Aligning lines of **text** at the left margin, the right margin, both margins, or the center. Text aligned at both margins is considered *fully justified.* Text aligned only at the left margin is said to have a *ragged right margin.* (See ¶1356a–c.)

K or KB. See *Kilobyte.*

Kern. To make fine adjustments in the space between any two **characters.**

Key. To **enter characters** into the **memory** of a **computer.** (*Key* is being replaced by the word *type.* See *Type.*)

Keyboard. The device used to **enter** information into a **computer.**

Keystroke. The depression of one key on a **keyboard.**

Killer app (short for *application*). **Software** that is considered "so great it will blow you away." (Mosaic, a program that facilitates information retrieval for **Internet** users, was considered a killer app when it was introduced.)

Kilobyte. A measurement of the **storage** capacity of a **computer.** One kilobyte represents 1024 **bytes.** *Kilobyte* may be abbreviated *K* or *KB;* however, *KB* is the clearer abbreviation since *K* also stands for the metric prefix *kilo* (meaning 1000).

Kluge (pronounced *klooj*). An expedient (but often inelegant) way to solve a problem.

LAN. See *Network.*

Landscape orientation. The positioning of a page so that information is printed across the long dimension of the paper. (See *Portrait orientation.*)

Language. The **characters** and procedures used to write **programs** that a **computer** is designed to understand.

Laptop computer. A portable computer slightly larger than a **notebook computer.**

Laser printer. A nonimpact **printer** that produces sharper **text** and **graphics** than any other type of printer. (See also *Dot matrix printer; Ink-jet printer.*)

LCD. See *Liquid crystal display.*

Line or paragraph numbering. The ability of a **program** to automatically number each line or paragraph sequentially in a **document.** The line or paragraph numbers can be deleted before the preparation of the final **printout.**

Line spacing. The ability of a **program** to automatically change vertical line spacing (for example, from double to single to double again).

Liquid crystal display (LCD). A type of **monitor** typically used on **laptop computers** or portable **computers.** (See also *Active matrix display.*)

Listserv. Any **software** that manages a **mailing list.** The most widely used programs are LISTSERV (as distinct from *listserv,* a generic term), Listproc, and Majordomo.

Load. To transfer information or **program** instructions into a **computer's memory.**

Log off. To exit or leave a **computer** system. (See ¶803f.)

Log on. To **access** a **computer** system. (See ¶¶802, 803e.)

M or MB. See *Megabyte.*

Macro. A time-saving feature (like telephone speed dialing) that allows the user to store in **memory** a set of **keystrokes** or **commands** that will accomplish a certain task.

Mail merge. The process of taking information from a **database** and inserting it into a form letter or other **document** in order to customize the document for an individual recipient. For example, mail merge can be used to create the inside address and the salutation for a form letter. (See also *Forms mode.*)

Mailbomb. A deluge of **e-mail** messages from one or more sources, deliberately intended to overload the recipient's **computer** and make it **crash.** A mailbomb is typically sent to punish someone guilty of **spamming** or some other serious breach of **netiquette.**

Mailing list. An **e-mail** discussion group devoted to one or more specific topics.

Mainframe. A large **computer** system.

Megabyte. A measurement of the **storage** capacity of a **computer.** One megabyte represents more than 1 million **bytes.** *Megabyte* may be abbreviated *M* or *MB;* however, *MB* is clearer since *M* also stands for the metric prefix *mega* (meaning 1 million).

Megahertz. A measurement used to identify the speed of the **central processing unit.** One megahertz is equal to 1 million cycles per second.

Memory. The part of a **computer** that stores information. (See also *Storage.*)

> **Random-access memory (RAM).** The temporary memory that allows information to be stored randomly and accessed quickly and directly (without the need to go through intervening **data**).

> **Read-only memory (ROM).** The permanent **memory** of a **computer;** a set of instructions that has been built into the computer by the manufacturer and cannot be accessed or changed by the user.

Menu. A list of choices shown on the **display screen.** For example, a **format** menu would include such options as the type style and the type size to be selected. A menu is often referred to as a *pull-down menu* or a *pop-up menu* because it appears on screen after the user **clicks** on the **menu bar** or on some other item on the screen.

Menu bar. The bar across the top of the screen or window that displays the names of available **menus.**

Merge. A **command** to create one **file** by combining information that is stored in two different locations. For example, a **computer** can merge the **text** in a form letter with a mailing list to produce a batch of letters with a different name, address, and salutation on each letter. (See also *Mail merge.*)

Microcomputer. A small and relatively inexpensive **computer,** commonly consisting of a **display screen,** a **keyboard,** a **central processing unit,** one or more **disk drives,** and a **printer,** with limited **storage** based upon a **microprocessor.** (See also *Desktop computer; Laptop computer.*)

Microprocessor. An **integrated circuit** on a silicon **chip** that serves as the **central processing unit** of a **computer.**

MIPS. An acronym derived from m̲illions of i̲nstructions p̲er s̲econd. Used to measure the speed of a **computer.**

Modem. An acronym derived from m̲odulator/dem̲odulator. A device that (1) converts digital signals into tones for transmission over telephone lines and (2) converts the tones back into digital signals at the receiving end.

Monitor. The **display screen** of a **computer.**

Monospace font. A **typeface** such as Courier in which each **character** has exactly the same width `(like this)`.

Morph (from *metamorphosize*). To change one image into another by means of digital technology.

Motherboard. The **computer's** main **circuit board,** which contains the **central processing unit,** the **memory,** and expansion slots for additional circuit boards called *adapters* or *cards.* (See *Adapter.*)

Mouse. A hand-operated electronic device used to move a **cursor** or pointer on the **display screen.** Mostly used with **microcomputers.** (See *Word of mouse.*)

Mouse arrest. To be placed under mouse arrest is to be denied further access to an **Internet service provider** or a **commercial online service** as a result of violating the terms of service.

Mouse elbow. A repetitive strain injury (similar to tennis elbow) that is caused by repeatedly using a **mouse.** (See also *Carpal tunnel syndrome.*)

Mouse potato. A person who sits glued to a **computer** screen (in the same way that a couch potato sits glued to a TV screen).

MS-DOS (pronounced *em-ess-doss*). Derived from M̲icrosoft d̲isk o̲perating s̲ystem. An operating system used on IBM and IBM-compatible **microcomputers.**

Multimedia. The use of several types of media (such as **text, graphics,** animation, sound, and video) in a **document** or an **application.**

Multitasking. The ability of a **computer** to **execute** more than one **program** at a time.

Net. See *Internet.*

Netiquette. A set of guidelines for formatting and composing **e-mail** messages.

Netizen. A "citizen" of the Net; an active participant in the **Internet community.** Netizens in general are sometimes referred to as *netkind.*

Network. A system of interconnected **computers.** (See *Notwork; Sneakernet.*)

> **Local area networks (LANs)** use cable to connect a number of computers within the same location or at most a 2-mile radius.

> **Wide area networks (WANs)** use telephone lines or other **telecommunications** devices to link computers in widely separated locations.

> **Internet** is a system that links existing networks into a worldwide network.

Newbie. A newcomer to a **bulletin board system** or some other **network** facility.

Newsgroup (also called a *chat line* **or a** *forum***).** An electronic discussion group tied into a **bulletin board system.** Each newsgroup is typically organized around a specific interest or matter of concern.

Newsreader. A program that permits users to read and respond to messages posted on **Usenet.**

Notebook computer. A portable computer that is slightly smaller than a **laptop computer** and slightly larger than a **palmtop** (or **handheld**) **computer.**

Notwork. A **network** that does not live up to its advance billing. Also called a *nyetwork.*

Number crunching. Processing large amounts of numerical **data.**

Object linking and embedding (OLE). A process that permits the user to take material (referred to as an *object*) from one source and **insert** *(embed)* it in another **document.** If the user subsequently makes changes in the original material, those changes will be automatically transferred to the second document as a result of the OLE linking process. (See also *Dynamic data exchange.*)

OCR. See *Optical character reader.*

Offline. Referring to the state in which a **computer** is temporarily or permanently unable to communicate with another computer (even though it is turned on and capable of performing other functions). The term *offline* is also used humorously to refer to "real life."

Offscreen. Referring to any **computer** function that does not produce a display on the screen.

OLE (pronounced *oh-LAY***).** See *Object linking and embedding.*

Online. Referring to the state in which a **computer** is turned on and ready to communicate with other computers.

Onscreen. Referring to anything displayed on a **computer** screen.

Open. To transfer a **file** from a **disk** into a **computer's memory.**

Operating system (OS). **Software** that manages the internal functions and controls the operations of a **computer.**

Optical character reader (OCR). A device that can scan **text** from **hard copy** and **enter** it automatically into a **computer** for **storage** or **editing.** Also called an *optical scanner.*

Orphan protection. The ability of a **program** to prevent the first line of a paragraph from printing as the last line on a page. When the first line of a paragraph does appear as the last line on a page, it is referred to as an *orphan.* (See also *Widow protection.*)

OS. See *Operating system.*

Outlining. The ability of a **program** to automatically number and letter items typed in an indented **format.**

Output. The results of a **computer** operation.

Overwriting. Recording and storing information in a specific location on a storage medium that destroys whatever had been stored there previously.

Page break. A **command** that tells the **printer** where to end one page and begin the next. (See *Hard page break; Soft page break.*)

Page numbering. The ability of a **program** to automatically print page numbers on the pages that make up an entire **document.** If the document is revised and the total number of pages changes, the page numbering is automatically adjusted.

Glossary of
Computer Terms

Pagination. The ability of a **program** to take information and automatically divide it into pages with a specified number of lines per page. If the information is changed because of the addition, deletion, or rearrangement of copy, the material will be automatically repaged to maintain the proper page length. (See also *Soft page break.*)

Palmtop computer. A portable computer smaller than a **notebook computer.** Also called a **handheld computer.**

Papernet. Ordinary mail service. (See also *Voicenet.*)

Password. A user's secret identification code, required to **access** stored material. A procedure intended to prevent information from being accessed by unauthorized persons.

Paste. A **command** that transfers information from a **clipboard** and inserts it in another location. (See *Cut and paste.*)

Patch. A small program that improves an existing piece of **software** or corrects an error in it.

PC. See *Personal computer.*

PDA. See *Personal digital assistant.*

Peripheral. A device that extends the capabilities of a **computer** (for example, a **printer**).

Personal computer (PC). A **microcomputer** for personal and office use.

Personal digital assistant (PDA). A palm-sized, handheld **computer.**

Personal information manager (PIM). A **database management system** that permits a user to store and **retrieve** a wide range of personal information (for example, names, addresses, phone numbers, appointments, and lists of people to call and things to do).

Pica. A measurement used for a **font;** equal to 1/6 inch or 12 **points.**

Pitch. The number of **monospace characters** printed in a 1-inch line of **text.**

Pixel. An acronym derived from picture element. The smallest element (a dot) on a **display screen.** Pixels are used to construct images on the screen.

Plug-and-play. The ability to plug in a **peripheral** and have it work without difficulty. The term *plug-and-play* is now sometimes used to refer to a new employee who can immediately do the job without any preliminary training. Because of the problems some users have experienced with items so labeled, they refer instead to *plug-and-pray.*

Point. A measurement used to indicate the size of a **font;** 72 **points** equals 1 inch. (See also *Pica.*)

Pop-up menu. A menu that appears in a **dialog box.**

Port. A socket on a **computer** into which an external device (such as a printer cable) can be plugged.

Portrait orientation. Positioning paper so that information is printed across the short dimension of the paper. (See also *Landscape orientation.*)

Posting. An article sent to a **Usenet** newsgroup.

Print preview. A **software** feature that reduces the pages of a **document** so that a full page (or two facing pages) can be seen on the screen before being printed. This feature permits the user to spot and correct problems in **format** and **page breaks.**

Printers. Output devices of various types that produce copy on paper. (See *Dot matrix printer; Ink-jet printer; Laser printer.*)

Printout. The paper copy of information produced on a **printer.**

Program. An established sequence of instructions that tells a **computer** what to do. The term *program* means the same as **software.**

Prompt. An onscreen symbol (for example, a **cursor**) that indicates where to **type** a **command;** a message that indicates what action is to be taken.

Proportional font. A **typeface** in which the width of each **character** varies (as in this sentence), so that the letter I takes much less space than the letter M. (See *Font.*)

Protocol. A set of standards that permits **computers** to exchange information and communicate with each other.

Radio button. An onscreen element that allows a user to select one option from a group of items. An empty circle precedes each option not selected. A dot appears in a circle to signify that the user has selected that option.

RAM. See *Memory, random-access.*

Rave. To annoy someone by persistently talking about something. The act of raving is different from **flaming** in that flaming is deliberately provocative and even insulting, whereas raving is simply annoying because it goes on so long.

Read. To transfer information from an external storage medium into internal storage. (See also *Storage, external* and *internal.*)

Record (n.). A collection of all the information pertaining to a particular subject.

Redline. A **word processing** feature that shows deleted material by displaying it in a shaded panel, by printing a line through the **text,** or by using some other method. Redlining allows a user to see what has been deleted. Any redlined text may be easily removed from a **document** to produce the final copy.

> For example, this portion of text is shown using the redline feature.

Response time. The time a **computer** takes to **execute** a **command.**

Retrieve. To call up information from **memory** so that it can be processed in some way.

ROM. See *Memory, read-only.*

Row. A horizontal block of **cells** in a table or **spreadsheet.** (See also *Column.*)

RSI. Repetitive strain injury; sometimes referred to as *chiplash.* (See also *Carpal tunnel syndrome; Mouse elbow.*)

Ruler. A bar (displayed on the screen) that shows the width of the page, the margin settings, the paragraph indentions, and the tab stops.

Save. To store a **program** or **data** on a **storage** device such as a **disk.**

Scanner. An **input** device that can copy a printed page into a **computer's memory,** thus doing away with the need to **type** the copy. A scanner can also convert artwork and photographs into a digital format and store these in memory.

Screen. See *Display screen.*

Screen dump. A **printout** of what is displayed on the screen. (For an example, see the illustration in ¶1396.)

Screen saver. A **program** that changes the screen display while the user is away from the **computer.** Without the use of a screen saver, a screen image that remains on display for any length of time can damage the screen.

Scroll. To move information horizontally or vertically on a **display screen** so that one can see parts of a **document** that is too wide or too deep to fit entirely on one screen.

Scroll bar. An onscreen element that allows a user to **scroll** by using a **mouse.**

SCSI. See *Small computer system interface.*

Search and replace. A **command** that directs the **program** to locate a **character string** or information (**text,** numbers, or symbols) wherever it occurs in a **document** and replace this material with new information. (See *Global.*)

Search engine. A free program that helps Web users locate **data** by means of a key word or concept. Among the most popular search engines are Yahoo!, Excite, WebCrawler, and AltaVista.

Server. A **computer** that delivers **data** to other computers **(clients)** linked on the same **network.**

Shareware. Software that usually may be **downloaded** and used initially without charge; the author may subsequently ask for some payment. (Compare with *Freeware.*)

Shouting. The use of all-capital letters in **e-mail.** This practice is considered a violation of **netiquette** and is actively discouraged.

Shovelware. Mediocre material used to fill up space on a **CD-ROM** or a **Web site.**

Sig block. The signature block that automatically appears at the end of every outgoing **e-mail** message. Also referred to as a *.sig file.*

Small computer system interface (SCSI, pronounced *scuzzy*). A type of **hardware** and **software interface** for connecting **peripherals** such as a **disk drive** or a **CD-ROM.**

Smiley. In **e-mail** messages, a facial expression constructed sideways (for the "lateral-minded") with standard **characters.** Also referred to as *emoticons* (emotional icons). For example:

:-)	I'm smiling.	>:-(	I'm angry.	:-J	I'm being tongue-in-cheek.
:-D	I'm laughing.	:-@	I'm screaming.	:-+	I'm exhausted—my tongue
:-(	I'm sad.	:-&	I'm tongue-tied		is hanging out.
:-<	I'm very sad.	:-x	My lips are sealed.	%-)	I've been staring at the
:'-(	I'm crying.	#-)	I'm feeling no pain.		screen too long.
;-)	I'm winking.	:-O	I'm shocked.	8-|	What next?

Although some smileys are quite witty, many people find them excessively cute. Therefore, don't use smileys unless you are sure the recipient will appreciate them.

Snail mail. A term employed by **e-mail** users to refer to regular mail service.

Sneakernet. The procedure for transferring **files** from one **computer** to another when the computers are not connected by an electronic **network.** (Users remove **diskettes** from one computer and carry them on foot to another.)

Soft copy. Information shown on the **display screen.** (See also *Hard copy.*)

Soft hyphen. A hyphen that divides a word at the end of a line; considered soft (nonpermanent) because the hyphen will automatically be deleted if the word moves to another position as a result of a change in the **text.** (See *Hard hyphen; Hyphenation.*)

Soft page break. A line inserted by the **program** to show where a page will end. If copy is added or deleted, the original **page break** will be replaced with a new soft page break at the appropriate place. (By contrast, a **hard page break** will remain fixed, no matter what changes are made in the copy.) (See also *Pagination.*)

Soft return. A **software** feature that automatically breaks **text** between words at the right margin. The line ending is considered soft (nonpermanent) because the line ending will change if the user adds or deletes **text.** (See *Hard return; Word wrap.*)

Software. The instructions that a **computer** needs to perform various functions. The term *software* means the same as **program.** (See also *Hardware.*)

Sort. To arrange **fields, records,** or **files** in a predetermined sequence.

Spam (n.). The electronic equivalent of junk mail; also called <u>u</u>nsolicited <u>c</u>ommercial <u>e</u>-mail (UCE).

Spam (v.). To send an **e-mail** message to a great number of recipients without regard for their need to know. A user who spams sometimes receives a **mailbomb** in return as a form of retaliation.

Spider. A program that searches the Web for new **Web sites.**

Split screen. The ability of some **programs** to display information in two or more different areas on the screen at the same time.

Spreadsheet. A **program** that provides a worksheet with **rows** and **columns** to be used for calculations and the preparation of reports.

Storage. The **memory** of a **computer.**

    External storage. A magnetic medium such as a **disk, diskette,** or tape used to store information; can be removed from the **computer.**

    Internal storage. An integral component of a **computer;** cannot be removed.

Store. To place information in **memory** for later use.

Style sheet. A collection of the user's formatting decisions regarding **font,** type size, margins, **justification,** paragraph indentions, and the like.

Surfing the Net. Browsing through various **Web sites** on the **Internet** in search of interesting things.

SYSOP (pronounced *siss-op*). An acronym derived from <u>sys</u>tem <u>op</u>erator. A person who operates a **bulletin board system.**

Tab grid. A series of preset indentions (usually a half inch apart). If the tabs are reset by the user, the grid will change to show the new location of the tabs.

TCP/IP. See *Transmission Control Protocol/Internet Protocol.*

Telecommunications. The process of sending and receiving information by means of telephones, satellites, and other devices.

Telecommuter. An employee who works away from the office (usually at home) and uses a **computer** (1) to **access** needed information on the organization's **intranet** and the **Internet** and (2) to communicate with other employees, suppliers, and customers or clients.

Teleconferencing. Conducting a conference by using **computers,** video, and **telecommunications** to share sound and images with others at remote sites.

Telnet. A **protocol** that allows a **computer** to connect with a **host computer** on the **Internet.** The use of telnet is diminishing as the Web's **hypertext transfer protocol (HTTP)** gains in popularity.

Template. A preestablished **format** for a **document,** stored in a **computer.** The template determines the margins, the type style and size to be used for the **text,** placement instructions for various elements (such as the date line), and design specifications for certain items (such as a letterhead). A user can simply call up the appropriate template, **insert** text where needed, and then print a final document. The user can modify the original template or create a new template to satisfy personal preferences.

Terminal. Any device that can transmit or receive electronic information.

Text. The information displayed on a screen or printed on paper.

Text entry. The initial act of typing that places **text** in **storage.** (See *Type.*)

Thread. A series of posted messages that represents an ongoing discussion of a specific topic in a **bulletin board system,** a **newsgroup,** or a **Web site.**

Tool bar. See *Button bar.*

Touchpad. The device on a **laptop computer** that takes the place of a **mouse.**

Touchscreen technology. The technology that permits a user to perform a function simply by touching the screen in an appropriate spot.

Transmission Control Protocol/Internet Protocol. A collection of over 100 **protocols** that are used to connect **computers** and **networks.**

Treeware. Anything printed on paper.

Type. To enter **characters** into the **memory** of a **computer.** For a number of years the verb *type* began to be replaced by the verb *key* as a way of emphasizing the difference between a **computer** and a typewriter. However, the simpler verb *type* has made a comeback in computer terminology and is now the word commonly seen in users' manuals and on **display screens.**

Typeface. See *Font;* ¶1305d for samples.

Typeover. See *Overwriting.*

Uniform resource locator (URL). The specific Web address for an individual or an organization. (See *World Wide Web;* ¶1537.)

Upload. To transfer information from a **client computer** to a **host** computer. (See *World Wide Web;* ¶1537.)

URL (pronounced *you-are-el* or *erl*). See *Uniform resource locator.*

Usenet (from Users' Network). A **bulletin board system** that hosts thousands of **newsgroups.**

User-friendly. Describing **hardware** or **software** that is easy to use. A related phrase, *user-obsequious,* describes hardware or software that is so simplistic in design that it is virtually unusable.

Userid (pronounced *user-eye-dee*). The name a person must use, along with a **password,** to gain **access** to restricted areas on a **network.**

Vaporware. Software that is being widely advertised, even though it is still in the developmental stage and has serious problems which may doom its eventual release. The premature marketing of products like these is designed to deter prospective customers from buying competitive products already available for sale. (See *Brochureware.*)

Veronica. A tool for searching **gopher menus** to locate information on a particular topic.

Video display terminal (VDT). See *Display screen.*

Virtual reality. See *Cyberspace.*

Glossary of Computer Terms

Virus. A piece of **computer** code designed as a prank or malicious act to spread from one computer to another by attaching itself to other **programs.** Some viruses simply cause a humorous message to appear on the screen, some cause minor **glitches,** and some cause serious damage to a computer's **memory** or **disks.** (See *Antivirus software.*)

Voicenet. Ordinary telephone service.

WAIS (pronounced *ways*). See *Wide-area information service.*

WAN. See *Network, wide area.*

Web. See *World Wide Web.*

Web browser. Software that permits a user—with a click of a **mouse**—to locate, display, and download **text,** video, audio, and **graphics** stored in a **host computer** on the Web. The most common Web browsers now in use are HotJava, Netscape Navigator, and Microsoft Explorer.

Webcaster. An **application** that can be custom-tailored to satisfy an individual user's need for constantly updated information in specific areas. A Webcaster, when appropriately programmed, will automatically deliver the needed information to the user's **computer.**

Webmaster. The person who maintains a specific **Web site** and is responsible for what appears there.

Web site. One or more related pages created by an individual or an organization and posted on the **World Wide Web.** (See *Home page.*)

Wide-area information service. An **Internet** search system that will locate **documents** that contain key words specified by the user.

Widow protection. The ability of a **program** to avoid printing the last line of a paragraph as the first line on a page. When the last line of a paragraph does appear as the first line on a page, it is referred to as a *widow.* (See also *Orphan protection.*)

Windowing. The ability of a **program** to split its **display screen** into two or more segments so that the user can view several different **documents** or perform several different functions simultaneously. (See also *Split screen.*)

Wizard. A feature of Microsoft Word **software** that helps a user create a customized **document;** it asks the user questions about formatting and content options and uses the answers to create the document. (In WordPerfect this feature is called an *expert.*) The term *wizard* is also used to refer to the person in an organization who can quickly find and fix everyone else's **computer** problems.

Word of mouse. Gossip spread by **e-mail.**

Word processing. The electronic process of creating, formatting, **editing,** proofreading, and printing **documents.** (See *Information processing.*)

Word wrap. A **software** feature that detects when a word will extend beyond the right margin and automatically transfers it to the beginning of the next line.

Workstation. A **desktop computer** than runs **applications** and serves as an access point in a local area network. (See *Network.*)

World Wide Web. The component of the **Internet** that combines audio, video, and **graphics** with **text.** Also called the *Web* or *WWW.* Because of frequent delays in accessing the Web, some users prefer to translate WWW as *World Wide Wait.*

WWW. The World Wide Web. Sometimes pronounced *triple-dub* (to avoid pronouncing each *W* separately).

WYSIWYG (pronounced *wizzy-wig*). An acronym derived from <u>w</u>hat <u>y</u>ou <u>s</u>ee <u>i</u>s <u>w</u>hat <u>y</u>ou <u>g</u>et. A **computer** design standard that lets the user see on the screen how a page will look when it is printed.

APPENDIX C

Pronunciation Problems

The following list of terms represents common pronunciation problems that plague even highly educated people. A good part of the difficulty arises from the fact that the way a word is pronounced may have little relationship to the way it is spelled. (See, for example, the entry for *Natchitoches.*) Or the accent may fall on a syllable where you would not expect it to. (See the entry for *Willamette.*) Further complicating the problem is the existence of regional variations in pronunciation. (See the entries for *Louisville* and *New Orleans.*)

There is no national standard for pronunciation in the United States. Perhaps the nearest thing we have is the pronunciation used by the anchors of the evening news programs on the major TV networks. Thus it is not surprising that many dictionary entries show more than one way to pronounce a given word. In such cases, the first pronunciation shown is considered the preferred pronunciation, that is, the one most commonly heard or the one least likely to cause raised eyebrows. The entries in this appendix ordinarily show only the preferred pronunciation. A few entries will show two pronunciations when they appear to be equally in use.

The judgments reflected in the following entries may strike some readers as wrongheaded or totally at odds with local standards of pronunciation. If you feel confident about pronouncing a word differently from the way it is shown here, go right ahead and say it your way. When you feel less than confident, however, the following guidelines may be of some help.

A priori. Pronounce the *a* as in *hah* or in *hay.* Say *ah-pree-AW-ree* or *ay-pree-AW-ree.*

Abdomen. Put the accent on the first syllable. Say *AB-duh-mun* (**NOT** *ab-DOE-mun*).

Accessory. Say *ack-SESS-uh-ree* (**NOT** *ass-SESS-uh-ree*).

Across. Say *uh-KRAWSS* (**NOT** *uh-KRAWST*).

Ad hoc. Say *ADD-HOCK.*

Affluent, affluence. Put the accent on the first syllable, not the second. Say *AF-floo-ent* and *AF-floo-enss* (**NOT** *af-FLOO-ent* and *af-FLOO-enss*).

Albeit. Pronounce this word as three syllables. Say *awl-BEE-it.*

Alleged. Say *uh-LEJD* (**NOT** *uh-LEJ-ed*).

Alumnus, alumna. The male singular form *alumnus* is pronounced *uh-LUM-nus.* The female singular form *alumna* is pronounced *uh-LUM-nuh.* The male plural form *alumni* is pronounced *uh-LUM-neye.* The female plural form *alumnae* is pronounced *uh-LUM-nee.*

Amicable. Say *AM-ick-uh-bul* (**NOT** *uh-MICK-uh-bul*).

Analogy, analogous. The noun *analogy* is pronounced *uh-NAL-luh-jee.* The adjective *analogous* is pronounced *uh-NAL-luh-gus.*

Angina. Medical professionals typically pronounce this word as *ANN-jinn-uh.* Others typically say *an-JYE-nuh.*

Applicable. Pronounce the first *a* in *applicable* as in *apple.* Say *A-plih-kuh-bul* (**NOT** *uh-PLIH-kuh-bul*).

Apricot. Pronounce the *a* as in *apt* (**NOT** as in *ape*). Say *A-prih-kot.*

Arctic, Antarctic. Do not overlook the *c* in these words. Say *ARK-tick* and *ant-ARK-tick* (**NOT** *AR-tick* and *ant-AR-tick*).

Arkansas, Kansas. There's no sound of *Kansas* in *Arkansas*. Kansas is pronounced *KAN-zus*. Arkansas is pronounced *ARR-kin-saw*. However, when talking about the residents of these two states—Kansans and Arkansans—say *KAN-zuhnz* and *arr-KAN-zuhnz*.

Asterisk. Pronounce the last syllable exactly as it is spelled—*risk* (**NOT** *rick* or *rix*).

Athlete. This is a two-syllable word. Say *ATH-leet* (**NOT** *ATH-uh-leet*).

Aunt. Whether you say *ANT* (as in *can't*) or *ONT* (as in *font*) will depend on where you grew up. Either pronunciation is acceptable.

Awry. Say *uh-RYE* (**NOT** *AW-ree*).

Bass. Rhyme this word with *class* when it refers to fish. Rhyme it with *case* in all its other meanings.

Because. Say *bih-KAWZ* (**NOT** *bee-KUHZ* or *bee-KAWSS*).

Beijing. Say *bay-JEENG* (**NOT** *bay-ZHEENG*).

Beirut. Say *bay-ROOT* (**NOT** *by-ROOT*).

Beloit. This city in Wisconsin is pronounced *buh-LOYT*.

Berlin. The city in Germany is pronounced *buhr-LINN*. The cities in New Hampshire and Wisconsin are pronounced *BUHR-linn*.

Binghamton. See *-ham*.

Birmingham. See *-ham*.

Boise. This city in Idaho is pronounced *BOY-zee*.

Bow. Rhyme *bow* with *how* when it refers to the front part of a ship or the act of bending or yielding. Rhyme *bow* with *hoe* in all its other meanings.

Bowdoin. This college in Maine is pronounced *BOE-dun*.

Breech, breeches. The singular form, *breech*, is pronounced exactly as it is spelled—*BREECH*. The plural form, *breeches* (referring to a pair of pants), is pronounced *BRIH-chiz*.

Buffet. When referring to a sideboard or table covered with food, say *buh-FAY* (**NOT** *boo-FAY*). When using the word in all its other meanings, say *BUH-feht*.

Butte. This city in Montana is pronounced like *beaut* in *beautiful*.

Cairo. In Egypt this city is pronounced *KYE-roe*. In Illinois it is pronounced *KAY-roe*.

Calais. In France this city is pronounced *kal-LAY*. In Maine it is pronounced *KAL-lus*. The *cal* in Calais rhymes with *pal*.

Caribbean. There is no clear preference for *kuh-RIB-bee-yan* over *kar-rib-BEE-yan*, so take your pick.

Carmel. In California this city is pronounced *car-MEL*. In Indiana it's pronounced *CAR-mel*.

Caste. Rhyme *caste* with *past* (**NOT** with *paste*).

Cay, Cayman. The word *cay* is pronounced *KEY* and has the same meaning as *key* (an island or reef). However, *cay* is pronounced *KAY* when referring to the Cayman Islands.

Celtic. When referring to the people or their language, say *KELL-tick.* When referring to a Boston basketball player, say *SELL-tick.*

Chaise longue. This French term for a *long* reclining chair is pronounced *shayz LAWNG* (**NOT** *shayz LOWNJ*).

Chamois. This French term for a type of leather or fabric has a distinctly un-French pronunciation in the United States. Say *SHAM-mee* (**NOT** *sham-WAH*).

Chaos. Say *KAY-ahss* (**NOT** *CHAY-ahss*).

Chassis. This word has the same spelling in the singular and the plural but not the same pronunciation. Say *CHASS-see* for the singular and *CHASS-seez* for the plural.

Cheyenne. This city in Wyoming is pronounced *shy-ENN.*

Chimera. Say *kye-MEER-uh.*

Clapboard. This term for a type of house siding is pronounced *KLAB-bird* and not as the spelling might suggest.

Clique. Say *KLEEK* (**NOT** *KLICK*).

Coeur d'Alene. This city in Idaho is pronounced *CORE-duh-LANE.*

Comparable. Pronounce this word as three syllables. Say *COM-pruh-bul* (**NOT** *com-PAIR-uh-bul*).

Conch. Say *KONK* (**NOT** *KONCH*).

Connecticut. Ignore the *c* in the second syllable *(nect).* Say *kuh-NET-ih-kut.*

Consummate. When used as a verb, *consummate* is pronounced *KON-suh-MAYT.* When used as an adjective, this word is pronounced *KON-suh-muht.*

Copenhagen. Say *KOE-pen-HAY-gun* (**NOT** *KOE-pen-HOG-gun*).

Corps. When this word is singular (as in *the Marine Corps*), both the *p* and the *s* are silent. Say *KAWR.* When this word is plural, say *KAWRZ.*

Coupon. Say *KOO-pon* (**NOT** *KYOO-pon*).

Croat. Pronounce this word as two syllables. Say *KROH-aht.*

Croatian. Treat this word as three syllables, and pronounce the first *a* as in *day.* Say *kroh-AY-shun.*

Culinary. Say *KUH-lih-ner-ree* (**NOT** *KYOO-lih-ner-ree*).

Cupola. The final letter in this word is *a* (**NOT** *o*). Say *KYOO-puh-luh* (**NOT** *KYOO-puh-loe*).

Curaçao. This island in the Caribbean is pronounced *kyoo-rah-SOE.*

Dais. People sit or stand on the *DAY-iss* (**NOT** the *DYE-iss*).

Data. Pronounce the *da* in *data* as in *day* (**NOT** as in *dash*). Say *DAY-tuh.*

Defendant. Say *dif-FEN-dunt* (**NOT** *dih-FEN-DANT*).

Des Moines. This city in Iowa is pronounced *dih-MOIN.* (The *s* is silent in both parts of the name.)

Des Plaines. This city in Illinois is pronounced *dess-PLAINZ.* (Here the *s* is sounded in both parts of the name, but it is sounded differently in each case.)

Detroit. Say *dih-TROYT* (**NOT** *DEE-troyt*).

Dishevel. The *dis* in *dishevel* is not pronounced like the *dis* in *dishearten* or *dishonor.* Say *dih-SHEV-uhl.*

Dissociate. Say *dis-SOH-see-ate* (**NOT** *dis-uh-SOH-see-ate*).

Dour. Say *DEWR* (**NOT** *DOWR*).

Draw, drawer. Do not add an *r* sound at the end of *draw.* By the same token, do not omit the *r* sound at the end of *drawer.*

Dubuque. This city in Iowa is pronounced *duh-BYOOK.*

Duquesne. This city and university in Pennsylvania are both pronounced *doo-KANE.*

Durham. See *-ham.*

Eau Claire. This city in Wisconsin is pronounced *oh-CLAIR.*

Edinburgh. This city in Scotland is pronounced *EH-din-BURR-uh* (**NOT** *EH-din-BURG*).

Either, neither. These two words are more commonly pronounced *EE-thur* and *NEE-thur,* but *EYE-thur* and *NYE-thur* are also acceptable.

El Cajon. This city in California is pronounced *ell-kuh-HONE.*

Err. Pronounce *err* as in *berry.*

Espresso. There is no *x* in *espresso.* Say *ess-PRESS-oh* (**NOT** *ex-PRESS-oh*).

Et cetera. There is also no *x* in this phrase. Say *ett-SET-ter-uh* (**NOT** *ex-SET-ter-uh*).

Exquisite. Put the accent on the second syllable. Say *ex-KWIZ-zit.*

Extraordinary. Say *ex-STRAW-dih-ner-ree* (**NOT** *EX-truh-AWR-dih-ner-ree*).

February. Do not ignore the first *r* in *February.* Say *FEB-roo-err-ree* (**NOT** *FEB-yoo-err-ree*).

Forbade. The *bade* in *forbade* (the past tense of *forbid*) should rhyme with *glad* (**NOT** *glade*). Say *fur-BAD.*

Formidable. Put the accent on the first syllable. Say *FOR-muh-duh-bul* (**NOT** *for-MID-duh-bul*).

Forte. When *forte* means "strong point" (as in *Tact is not his forte*), pronounce it as one syllable—*FORT.* When *forte* means "loud" (as in a musical direction), pronounce it as two syllables—*FOR-tay.*

Framingham. See *-ham.*

Fraternize. Note that the second syllable is spelled *ter* (**NOT** *tra*). Say *FRAT-ter-nize* (**NOT** *FRAT-tra-nize*).

Gauge. The *gau* in *gauge* is pronounced *gay* (**NOT** *gaw* as in *gauze*). Say *GAYJ.*

Genuine. Say *JEN-yuh-win* (**NOT** *JEN-yoo-wine*).

Gloucester. This city in Massachusetts is pronounced *GLOSS-ter.*

Gorham. See *-ham.*

Government. Don't overlook the *n* in *vern.* Say *GUH-vern-ment* (**NOT** *GUH-ver-ment* or *GUH-vuh-mint*).

Greenwich. This name, whether it refers to the town in Connecticut or the borough in England or the village in Manhattan, is pronounced *GREN-nitch.* However, the town in Rhode Island—East Greenwich—is pronounced *eest-GREEN-witch.*

Grenada. This island in the Caribbean is pronounced *gruh-NAY-duh* (**NOT** *gruh-NAH-duh*).

Grievous. Do not make this a three-syllable word. Say *GREE-vus* (**NOT** *GREE-vee-yus*).

Groton. This name, whether it refers to the town in Connecticut or the private school in Massachusetts, is pronounced *GROTT-uhn.*

Grovel. Say *GRAH-vuhl* (**NOT** *GRUH-vuhl*).

-ham. The suffix *-ham* is usually pronounced *um* in short place names such as *Chatham, Dedham, Durham, Gorham, Hingham, Mendham,* and *Wareham.* In longer place names, such as *Birmingham* and *Framingham, ham* is fully sounded. When *ham* appears within a long place name, such as *Binghamton,* it is typically pronounced *um.*

Harass, harassment. Some authorities say that putting the accent on the second syllable—*huh-RASS, huh-RASS-ment*—is more common among U.S. speakers; others say that the practice of putting the accent on the first syllable is equally common—*HA-russ, HA-russ-ment* (where the *ha* is pronounced as in *hat*). In short, either set of pronunciations is acceptable.

Haverhill. This town in Massachusetts is pronounced as two syllables—*HAV-rill.*

Hawaii. Say *huh-WYE-yee* (**NOT** *huh-VYE-yee*).

Height. Although there is an *h* at the end of *width,* there is no *h* at the end of *height,* so pronounce this word *HITE* (to rhyme with *kite*) and not as *highth.*

Heinous. Say *HAY-nus.*

Helena. The capital of Montana is pronounced with the accent on the first syllable—*HEH-leh-nuh.*

Herb. The *h* is silent. Say *ERB.*

Heterogeneous. Say *heh-tuh-ruh-JEE-nyuhs.*

Hiatus. Say *high-ATE-us.*

Hilo. This city in Hawaii is pronounced *HEE-low.*

Hingham. See *-ham.*

Hiroshima. Both *HEER-uh-SHEE-muh* and *hih-ROE-shih-muh* are commonly used by U.S. speakers.

Hors d'oeuvre. This French term (meaning "appetizer") is pronounced *awr-DUHRV.* The plural form *hors d'oeuvres* is pronounced *awr-DUHRVZ.*

Houghton Mifflin. The first part of this publisher's name is pronounced *HOE-tun.*

Houston. The city in Texas is pronounced *HYOO-stun.* However, the street in New York City is pronounced *HOW-stun.*

Ian. The Gaelic form of the name *John* is pronounced *EE-yan.*

Illinois. The *s* is silent. Say *ill-lih-NOY* (**NOT** *ill-lih-NOYZ*).

Implacable. Say *im-PLACK-uh-bul* (**NOT** *im-PLAYK-uh-bul*).

Imprimatur. Say *im-pruh-MAH-tuhr.*

Incognito. Say *in-kog-NEE-toe* (**NOT** *in-KOG-nih-toe*).

Indefatigable. Put the accent on *fat.* Say *in-dih-FAT-ig-uh-bul.*

Indict, indictment. The spelling of these words is misleading. Say *in-DITE, in-DITE-ment* (**NOT** *in-DIKT, in-DIKT-ment*).

Indigenous. Say *in-DIH-jih-nus.*

Inexplicable. Say *in-ex-PLICK-uh-bul.*

Infamous. Put the accent on the first syllable. Say *IN-fuh-mus.*

Integral. Do not misplace the *r* when pronouncing this word. Say *IN-tih-grul* (**NOT** *IN-ter-gul* or *IN-trih-gul*). Be sure to accent the first syllable—*IN-tih-grul* (**NOT** *in-TEH-grul*).

International. Be sure to pronounce the first *t* in *international.* Say *in-ter-NASH-nul* (**NOT** *in-ner-NASH-nul*).

Introduce. Here again, be sure to pronounce the *t*. Say *in-truh-DOOSS* (**NOT** *in-ner-DOOSS*).

Irrelevant. Say *ir-REL-leh-vant* (**NOT** *ir-REV-veh-lent*).

Irreparable. Pronounce this five-syllable word as four syllables. Say *ir-REP-ruh-bul* (**NOT** *ir-reh-PAIR-uh-bul*).

Irrevocable. Say *ir-REV-vuh-kuh-bul* (**NOT** *ir-reh-VOE-kuh-bul*).

Itinerary. Say *eye-TIN-nuh-rer-ree* (**NOT** *eye-TIN-ner-ree*).

Jewelry. Say *JOO-well-ree* (**NOT** *JOO-luh-ree*).

Jodhpur, jodhpurs. The city in India, Jodhpur, is pronounced *JAHD-purr.* The plural form, *jodhpurs* (referring to riding breeches), is pronounced *JAHD-purz.* (Note that the word is spelled *hp,* not *ph.* Those who fail to recognize the correct spelling may be tempted to pronounce the word incorrectly as *JAHD-furz.*)

Junta. Pronounce the letter *j* like *h* and the letter *u* like *oo* in *wood.* Say *HOON-tuh.*

Kansas. See *Arkansas.*

Kilometer. Most U.S. speakers say *kuh-LOM-muh-ter,* even though *KILL-luh-MEE-ter* logically follows the way in which *centimeter* and *millimeter* are accented. Either pronunciation is acceptable.

La Jolla. This community is southern California is pronounced *luh-HOY-yuh.*

Laboratory. Do not pronounce the first *o.* Say *LAB-ruh-taw-ree.*

Lafayette. The city in California is pronounced *la-fee-ETT.* The county in Arkansas is pronounced *luh-FAY-ett.*

Lagniappe. This French word (used in places like Louisiana to signify a small gift or something extra that is given to a customer who makes a purchase) is pronounced *lan-YAP.*

Laredo. This city in Texas is pronounced *luh-RAY-doe.*

Leavenworth. The first part of this Kansas city name rhymes with *heaven.*

Length. Be sure to pronounce the *g.* Say *LENGTH* (**NOT** *LENTH*).

Liaison. Say *LEE-uh-zahn* (**NOT** *LAY-uh-zahn* or *lee-YAY-zahn*).

Library. Do not overlook the first *r.* Say *LIE-brer-ree* (**NOT** *LIE-ber-ree*).

Lilac. Say *LIE-lock* (**NOT** *LIE-lack*).

Lima. The city in Peru is pronounced *LEE-muh.* The city in Ohio is pronounced *LIE-muh* (as in *lima bean*).

Long-lived. Pronounce the *i* in *lived* as in *life* (**NOT** as in *liver*).

Los Angeles. Pronounce the *g* in *Angeles* as a *j* and the *es* as *us*. Say *lawss-ANN-juh-lus* (**NOT** *lawss-ANG-guh-leez*).

Louisiana. Residents of the state say *loo-zee-YAN-nuh*. Others usually say *loo-wee-zee-YAN-nuh*.

Louisville. Residents of Kentucky say *LOO-uh-vul*. Others usually say *LOO-wee-vill*.

Mackinac. The spelling for this island in Michigan does not reveal the correct pronunciation. Say *MACK-in-naw* (**NOT** *MACK-in-nack*).

Marseilles. The city in France is pronounced *mar-SAY*. The city in Illinois is pronounced *mar-SAILS*.

Memento. Note that this word begins with *me* (**NOT** *mo*). Say *meh-MEN-toe* (**NOT** *moe-MEN-toe*).

Mendham. See *-ham*.

Metairie. This suburb of New Orleans is pronounced *MET-uh-ree* (**NOT** *meh-TAIR-ree*).

Minuscule. Say *MIH-nus-kyool* (**NOT** *MINE-nus-kyool*).

Minute. When referring to a small period of time, say *MIN-nit*. When referring to something extremely small, say *my-NOOT*.

Mischievous. Do not insert an extra syllable when pronouncing this word. Say *MISS-chiv-vus* (**NOT** *miss-CHEE-vee-yus*).

Misled. Do not be misled by the spelling of this word. Say *miss-LED* (**NOT** *MYZ-zuhld*).

Mobile. The city in Alabama is pronounced *moe-BEEL*. The adjective (meaning "movable") is pronounced *MOE-bul*. The common noun referring to a type of sculpture that moves is pronounced *MOE-beel*.

Moscow. The city is Russia is pronounced *MAHSS-kow*. The city in Idaho is pronounced *MAHSS-koe*.

Mount Desert. This island in Maine is pronounced *mount-deh-ZERT* (**NOT** *mount-DEZ-zert*).

Nacogdoches. This city in Texas is pronounced *nack-kuh-DOE-chez*.

Natchitoches. You might think this city in Louisiana was pronounced much like *Nacogdoches*, but you'd be wrong. Ignore the spelling and say *NACK-kuh-tish*.

Neither. See *Either*.

Nevada. The state is pronounced *neh-VAH-duh*. The county in Arkansas is pronounced *nuh-VAY-duh*.

New Orleans. Residents of Louisiana typically say *noo-WAH-linz*; some even say *noo-wah-LEENZ*. Outsiders typically say *noo-ARR-linz*.

Newark. The city in New Jersey is pronounced *NOO-erk*. The city in Delaware is pronounced *NOO-ARK*.

Newfoundland. This Canadian province is pronounced with the accent on *New*. Say *NOO-finned-lund*.

Nuclear. Say *NOO-klee-ur* (**NOT** *NOO-kyoo-lur*).

Often. Ignore the *t*. Say *AWF-fen* (**NOT** *AWF-ten*).

Oregon. Many residents of this state pronounce the name as two syllables—*AWR-gun*. Others (including most outsiders) say *AWR-ruh-gun*. There seems to be substantial agreement that the *or* in Oregon should not be pronounced *ahr* and that *gon* should not be pronounced as in *Gone With the Wind*.

Paradigm, paradigmatic. The opening syllables *para* are pronounced as in *parachute*. The *g* is silent in the noun *paradigm*; say *PAR-uh-dime*. The *g* is pronounced in the adjective *paradigmatic*; say *par-uh-dig-MAT-tick*.

Parliament. Ignore the *i*. Say *PARR-luh-ment.*

Patronize. Pronounce the *pa* as in *pay* (**NOT** as in *pat*). Say *PAY-truh-nyze.*

Peabody. This town in Massachusetts is pronounced *PEA-buh-dee* (**NOT** *PEA-bah-dee*).

Pecan. Say *pih-KAN* (**NOT** *pih-KAHN*). However, pronounce the phrase *pecan pie* as *PEA-kan PIE.*

Pedagogue. Pronounce the *go* as in *got* (**NOT** as in *goat*). Say *PEH-duh-gahg.*

Pedagogy. Unlike the *go* in *pedagogue* (pronounced as in *got*), the *go* in *pedagogy* is pronounced as in *goat.* Moreover, the *gy* is pronounced *jee.* Say *PEH-duh-goe-jee.*

Perspiration. Say *PER-spuh-ray-shun* (**NOT** *PRESS-per-ray-shun*).

Phoenix. Pronounce this city in Arizona *FEE-nicks.*

Pianist. *Pee-ANN-ist* is the preferred pronunciation, but *PEE-uh-nist* is also acceptable.

Picture. Say *PIHK-chur* (**NOT** *PIT-chur*).

Pierre. This two-syllable French name (pronounced *pee-YAIR*) is pronounced as only one syllable—*PEER*—when it refers to the capital of South Dakota.

Poignant. Do not pronounce the *g*. Say *POY-nyent* (**NOT** *POYG-nant*).

Poinsettia. Ignore the second *i*. Say *poyn-SET-tuh.*

Posthumous. The *po* in *posthumous* is pronounced as in *pot* (**NOT** as in *post*). Say *POSS-chum-mus.*

Potpourri. This French word (meaning "mixture" or "medley") is pronounced *poe-puh-REE.*

Poughkeepsie. This city in the state of New York is pronounced *puh-KIPP-see.*

Precedent. Put the accent on the first syllable. Say *PRESS-uh-dent* (**NOT** *pruh-SEE-dent*).

Prerogative. Note that the first syllable is spelled *pre* (**NOT** *per*). Say *prih-ROGG-uh-tiv* (**NOT** *per-ROGG-uh-tiv*).

Preventive. Do not insert an extra syllable in this word. Say *prih-VEN-tiv* (**NOT** *prih-VEN-tuh-tiv*).

Primer. When referring to a very basic book, say *PRIM-mer.* For all other meanings of the word, say *PRYE-mer.*

Probably. Pronounce this word as three syllables. Say *PRAH-buh-blee* (**NOT** *PRAH-blee*).

Pronunciation. Unlike the *ounce* sound in the verb *pronounce,* there is no *ounce* sound in the noun *pronunciation.* Say *pruh-nun-see-YAY-shun* (**NOT** *pruh-noun-see-YAY-shun*).

Pseudo. The *p* is silent. Say *SOO-doe.*

Puerto Rico. *PWAIR-toe-REE-koe* is preferred, but *POR-toe-REE-koe* is also acceptable.

Pulitzer. The name of the prize is pronounced *PULL-uht-suhr* (**NOT** *PYOOL-uht-suhr*).

Puyallup. This city in Washington is pronounced *pyoo-AL-up* (**NOT** *poo-YAL-up*).

Quay. Say *KEE* (**NOT** *KAY* or *KWAY*).

Quincy. The city in Illinois is pronounced *KWIN-see.* The city in Massachusetts is pronounced *KWIN-zee.*

Re. The Latin preposition *re* (whether used alone or in the phrase *in re*) is usually pronounced *RAY,* but many lawyers say *REE.*

Reading. As an ordinary common noun, *reading* is pronounced *REE-ding.* However, as a proper noun referring to the city in Pennsylvania or the town in Massachusetts, *Reading* is pronounced *RED-ding.*

Realtor. This word is commonly mispronounced *REE-luh-ter,* as if the word were spelled *Relator.* Either pronounce the word correctly—*REE-uhl-ter*—or say *real estate agent* and avoid the problem altogether.

Recognize. Do not overlook the *g.* Say *REH-kug-nyze* (**NOT** *REH-kuh-nyze*).

Recur. Say *ree-KURR* (**NOT** *ree-uh-KURR*).

Reputable. Accent the first syllable. Say *REH-pyuh-tuh-bul.*

Respite. Say *RESS-pit* (**NOT** *re-SPITE*).

Row. This word rhymes with *how* when it means "uproar." *Row* rhymes with *hoe* in all its other meanings.

Sacrilege, sacrilegious. Pronounce the *sa* as in *sack.* Say *SA-kruh-lihj, sa-kruh-LIH-juhs.*

Sagacious. Say *suh-GAY-shus* (**NOT** *suh-GASH-us*).

Salisbury. When referring to the city in Maryland or North Carolina, say *SAWLZ-ber-ree.*

San Jacinto. The "proper" pronunciation of this town in California is *san-huh-SIN-toe.* Nevertheless, the pronunciation most commonly heard today is *san-juh-SIN-tuh.*

San Joaquin. When referring to the river or the county in California, say *san-wah-KEEN.*

San Jose. When referring to the city in California, say *san-uh-ZAY* or *san-hoe-ZAY.*

San Juan. The capital of Puerto Rico is pronounced *san-WAHN.*

San Rafael. This city in California is pronounced *san-ruh-FELL.*

Sandwich. Don't overlook the *d.* Say *SAND-witch* (**NOT** *SAN-witch* or *SAM-witch*).

Schedule. U.S. speakers say *SKED-jyool;* Canadian and British speakers say *SHED-jyool.*

Schism. Say *SIH-zum* (**NOT** *SKIH-zum*).

Sean. The Irish form of the name *John* is pronounced *SHAWN.*

Sieve. Say *SIV* (**NOT** *SEEV*).

Similar. Say *SIH-mill-er* (**NOT** *SIM-yoo-ler* or *sih-MILL-yer*).

Sioux City, Sioux Falls. Pronounce *Sioux* as *SOO.*

Solder, soldier. Pronounce *solder* as *SOD-der* and *soldier* as *SOUL-jer.*

Spokane. This city in Washington is pronounced *spoe-KAN* (**NOT** *spoe-KAIN*).

Spontaneity. Say *spon-tuh-NAY-uh-tee* (**NOT** *spon-tuh-NEE-uh-tee*).

St. Augustine. When referring to the city in Florida, pronounce *Augustine* as *AW-guh-steen.* When referring to the saint himself, say *uh-GUS-tin.*

St. Louis. When referring to the city in Missouri, pronounce *Louis* as *LOO-wiss* (**NOT** *LOO-wee*).

Status. The *sta* in *status* may be pronounced as in *stay* or in *stack.* In the expression *status quo, sta* is more commonly pronounced as in *stack.* Say *STA-tuhs KWOE.*

Strength. Do not overlook the *g* in this word. Say *STRENGTH* (**NOT** *STRENTH*).

Suave. Say *SWAHV* (**NOT** *SWAYV*).

Subpoena. Say *suh-PEE-nuh.*

Subtle, subtlety. Say *SUT-uhl* and *SUT-uhl-tee.*

Superfluous. Put the stress on the second syllable. Say *soo-PER-floo-us* (**NOT** *SOO-per-FLOO-us*).

Tempe. This city in Arizona is pronounced *tem-PEE* (**NOT** *TEM-pee*).

Temperament, temperature. Ignore the second *e* in these words. Say *TEM-pruh-ment* and *TEM-pruh-choor.*

Terre Haute. This city in Indiana is pronounced *ter-ruh-HOAT.* (*Haute* rhymes with *boat.*)

Tucson. This city in Arizona is pronounced *TOO-sahn.*

Tête-á-tête. Pronounce this French phrase *TET-uh-TET* (**NOT** *TATE-uh-TATE*).

Uranus. The planet Uranus is pronounced *YUR-uh-nus* (**NOT** *yuh-RAY-nus*).

Valparaiso. When referring to the city in Chile, say *val-puh-RYE-zoe.* When referring to the city in Indiana, say *val-puh-RAY-zoe.*

Vanilla. Say *vuh-NIL-luh* (**NOT** *vuh-NEL-luh*).

Vegan, vegetarian. Although a vegan is a vegetarian, the *g* is pronounced differently in these words. Say *VEE-gun* and *veh-juh-TAIR-ree-yan.*

Versailles. When referring to the palace in France, say *ver-SIGH.* When referring to the town in Ohio, say *ver-SAILS.*

Veterinarian. Say *veh-tuh-ruh-NAIR-ree-yun* (**NOT** *veh-tih-NAIR-ree-yan*).

Vichyssoise. Say *vih-shee-SWAHZ* (**NOT** *vih-shee-SWAH*).

Waco. This city in Texas is pronounced *WAY-koe* (**NOT** *WACK-koe*).

Wareham. See *-ham.*

Warwick. This city in Rhode Island is pronounced *WAR-rick.*

Waukegan. This city in Illinois is pronounced *waw-KEE-gun.*

Waukesha. This city in Wisconsin is pronounced *WAW-kuh-SHAW.*

Width. Don't overlook the *d.* Say *WIDTH* (**NOT** *WITH*).

Wilkes-Barre. This city in Pennsylvania is pronounced *WILKS-bar-ruh* (**NOT** *WILKS-bar-ree*). Pronounce the *a* in *Barre* as in *bat.*

Willamette. This river in Oregon is pronounced *will-LAM-met* (**NOT** *WILL-luh-met*).

Worcester, Worcestershire. The *Wor* in these words is pronounced *woo* as in *wood.* When referring to the city in Massachusetts, say *WOO-ster.* When referring to the sauce or the city in England, say *WOO-stuh-shirr.*

Ypsilanti. This city in Michigan is pronounced *ip-sil-LAN-tee.*

INDEX

This index contains many entries for individual words. If you are looking for a specific word that is not listed, refer to ¶719, which contains a 12-page guide to words that are frequently confused because they sound alike or look alike (for example, *capital—capitol—Capitol* or *stationary—stationery*).

NOTE: The **boldface** numbers in this index refer to paragraph numbers; the lightface numbers refer to page numbers.

INDEX

INDEX

INDEX

INDEX

INDEX

INDEX

INDEX

INDEX

INDEX

INDEX

INDEX

INDEX

INDEX

INDEX